# HANDBOOK OF THERAPEUTIC IMAGERY TECHNIQUES

*Editor*

## Anees A. Sheikh, Ph.D.

*Department of Psychology*
*Marquette University*
*and*
*Department of Psychiatry and Behavioral Medicine*
*Medical College of Wisconsin*

*Imagery and Human Development Series*
*Series Editor:  Anees A. Sheikh*

**Baywood Publishing Company, Inc.**
AMITYVILLE, NEW YORK

BS

Library of Congress Catalog Card Number 00-041422
ISBN: 0-89503-216-3 (Paper)
ISBN: 0-89503-207-4 (Cloth)


**Library of Congress Cataloging-in-Publication Data**


Handbook of therapeutic imagery techniques / editor, Anees A. Sheikh.
    p. cm.
   Includes bibliographical references and index.
   ISBN 0-89503-207-4 (cloth) - - ISBN 0-89503-216-3 (paper)
    1. Imagery(Psychology)- -Therapeutic use- -Handbooks, manuals, etc. 2.
Psychotherapy- -Handbooks, manuals, etc. I. Sheikh, Anees A.

RC489.F35 H36 2000
616.89'14- -dc21                                                  00-041422

3/28/04

# Contents

## PSYCHODYNAMIC/HUMANISTIC APPROACHES

## HUMANISTIC/TRANSPERSONAL APPROACHES

## MISCELLANEOUS APPROACHES

## IMAGERY ENHANCEMENT

# Preface

> However interesting, plausible, and appealing a theory may be, it is techniques, not theories, that are actually used on people. Study of the effects of psychotherapy, therefore, is always the study of the effectiveness of techniques.
>
> London, P. (1964). *The modes and morals of psychotherapy.* New York: Holt, p. 33.

During the last two decades, the use of imagery in health care has gained widespread acceptance, and an ever-growing number of health professionals are eager to add imagery techniques to their repertoire. Unfortunately, these have remained scattered and not easily accessible. This book, to my knowledge, constitutes the first comprehensive attempt to bring together a host of imagery techniques from a variety of sources.

Aside from the opening chapter, which is historical in nature, the *Handbook of Therapeutic Imagery Techniques* consists primarily of a description of a multitude of imagery techniques. These approaches have been loosely grouped into four major categories: hypnobehavioral, cognitive-behavioral, psychodynamic/humanistic, and humanistic/transpersonal, and therapists of varied persuasions can easily incorporate them into their practice.

Although imagery procedures have been used with quite remarkable success, it is nevertheless fitting to sound a note of caution. Since they are powerful tools, they should not be used indiscriminately. At times, they pierce resistances surprisingly quickly and uncover deeply disturbing emotional content with which the individual may be unprepared to cope.

In conclusion, I wish to cordially thank all those who contributed to this volume by their chapters, their support, and their good wishes. My gratitude also goes to the staff of Baywood Publishing Company, and particularly to Stuart Cohen, the President, and to Bobbi Olszewski and Julie Krempa who guided the project with sound advice and much patience. I am deeply grateful to Kim Sims for her cheerful and conscientious typing of several chapters.

Finally, and in particular, I would like to express my deep appreciation to my wife, Katharina, for her generous assistance and support throughout the preparation of this book. I hope that our combined efforts will be instrumental in rendering imagery techniques more accessible and thus more applied.

*Anees A. Sheikh*
*Milwaukee, Wisconsin*

## CHAPTER 1

# *Imagination in Disease and Healing Processes: A Historical Perspective*

*CAROL E. McMAHON
AND ANEES A. SHEIKH*

Aristotle' s understanding of human nature led him to regard imagination as causal in inducing physiological arousal. This theory was pervasive in premodern medical systems and contributed to a sophisticated conception of pathophysiology in the late European Renaissance.

In this chapter, first Aristotelian theory of the arousal function of imagination is presented. Second, the role of the image in pathogenesis from ancient through modern periods is reviewed. Next, the use of imagination in therapeutic procedures through the ages is examined.

The awareness that imagination was recognized as a contributor to health and disease already at the time of Aristotle inevitably leads to the question: Why is the concept so new to contemporaries? The explanation of this paradoxical state of affairs lies in the philosophical underpinnings of past and present theory. When Cartesian dualism became a determining philosophical basis of medical theory, the role of imagination lost its premodern status. The implications of dualism for modern formulations are of vital importance; thus, this philosophical issue is addressed throughout.

## PREMODERN THEORY: IMAGERY AND PHYSIOLOGICAL AROUSAL

Ancient and Renaissance medical approaches were "holistic" in the true sense of the word. In place of the Cartesian mind, an immaterial "thinking thing," a spirit or soul was assumed. This biological soul formed the substrate of psycho-physiologic events. Biological and psychological functions were governed and performed by the soul.

Imagination, along with sensation, digestion, and reason, were among the faculties of the soul. Sensation functioned by taking the object (minus its matter) from the external world into the heart where the soul was seated; and here the *sensus communis* (common or collective sense) working upon sensations to form images, dreams and illusions, or hallucinatory images.

1

Emotional arousal, conceived in terms of humoral imbalances, was stimulated by images thus formed in the heart. "Emotion" is close in meaning to its root, the Latin *emovere,* which means "to move out" or "to stir up." Such movements of the biological soul varied according to whether the image provoked states of desire or aversion. According to Aristotle, the emotional system did not function in the absence of an image.

The theory explained both the activation and direction aspects of motivation. An object of desire or aversion, represented in imagination, directed the physiological arousal which led to specific actions of pursuit or avoidance (McMahon, 1973).

According to Aristotle, images were "to the intellective soul as sense objects. But when it affirms or denies good or evil, it pursues or avoids" (Stark, 1861, p. 442). The image in the soul therefore was the prime motivating force in human action. It operated in two ways. The voluntary, where reason exerted control, was known as deliberative imagination. Irrational animals acted without deliberation and their behavior was controlled by sensitive appetite. An animal "is not capable of appetite without possessing imagination, and all imagination is either 1) calculative or 2) sensitive. In the latter all animals, and not only man, partake" (McKean, 1941, p. 559). In states of intoxication, fever, madness, and dreaming sleep, when persons functioned without the faculty of reason, imagination assumed absolute power.

Aristotle's interest was that of a natural philosopher rather than a physician, and he dealt only briefly with pathogenic effects. The theory, however, became central in medical and psychological concepts thereafter. Initially intended to explain human action, the theory soon became a powerful tool in understanding health and disease (McMahon, 1986).

## IMAGINATION AND PATHOGENESIS

It is not unusual to find post-Aristotelian thinkers defining images as "emotions," since images too were movements of the soul. Disturbing images enacted and indeed constituted the deviations from harmonious balance or proper proportioning of elements and humors which comprised health.

### The Stoic Preoccupation with Prevention

The Stoic philosophers provide interesting examples of the effects of imagination because the psychophysiology of emotion was of great interest to them. To the Stoics, all emotion was a moral violation and a pathological state of body and spirit. They regarded the ideal condition of human nature to be a harmoniously balanced and tranquil state. Health was associated with "the unruffled flow of life." Anyone who attained such perfection was "absolutely free of any form of emotion" (Gould, 1970, pp. 34-35).

The Middle Ages brought a change in localization of function: The faculty of imagination was placed in the cerebral ventricles. It resided here in its psychophysiologic form as "vital spirits." These spirits traveled between brain and heart; the latter remained the seat of emotion.

Imagination led to pathology by arousing emotions and the deleterious effects related to the emotion's intensity. If an image provoked fear, for instance, "we see the whole spirit throughout the members join in the feeling; sweat and pallor occur over the whole body, speech is broken, words fade away, eyes are darkened, ears ring, limbs give way, until we often see men collapse from terror" (Lucretius, 1965, p. 84). In the many Stoic treaties on the emotions, the characteristic formula for health is: "Wipe out imagination: check desire: extinguish appetite" (McMahon, 1974, p. 714).

## Pathogenesis in Renaissance Medicine

Renaissance physicians ascribed to imagination a predominant role in pathology. Little change occurred in underlying theory. When imagination conceived an object pleasing or repellent, spirits carried activation from the brain to the heart, via nerves, and induced arousal. Nemesium in 1636 put it thus:

> The Instruments of *Imagination,* are the former Panns of the braine; the Vitall Spirits, which are in them; The sinews proceeding from the braine; The nerves moistened by the Vitall Spirits, and the very frame of the places wherein the Senses are seated. (McMahon, 1976a, p. 180)

Humoral pathology entered at this point, because emotions tended to establish the internal milieu which favored their perpetuation. Spirits from the imagination created humoral imbalances, then the heart released spirits which ascended "into the imagination" and "moved diverse passions according to their nature." The ensuing circular pattern of disproportioning of humors instated illnesses or "distemperatures," such as melancholy which corresponded to a constitutional predominance of black bile. Such an imbalance corrupted the vital spirits which controlled all vital activities, including the higher mental processes. Madness, then, was as much a biological state as a psychological condition.

What we interpret today as the expressions of emotions, such as tears, sighs, respiratory changes, and redirection of blood flow, were understood during this period as functional processes. They operated as homeostatic mechanisms to restore balance or equilibrium.

In this context the heart was called the "domestic oracle." Its injunctions were to be followed, because they presaged action conducive to well-being. For instance: "If a man begins to imagine upon a minurie that hath been profered him, the arteries runs sodainly to the heart and stirs up the wrathful part, and gives the same heat and forces for revenge" (Huarte, 1575, p. 83).

In Shakespeare's *Macbeth,* imagining the future crime gives warning to Macbeth:

> Macbeth: Why do I yield to that suggestion
> Whose horid image doth unfix my hair,
> And makes my seated heart knock at my ribs,
> Against the use of nature?
> (Knight, 1876, Act 1, Scene 3)

Imagination prepared the organism for specific action: In Huarte's example of wrath, in response to an attack, blood and spirits perfused muscles used for striking.

Julius Caesar Scaliger, a French physician of the late fifteenth century, examined individual differences in temperament to emotional responses. If an insult were imagined, brave men felt the force of activation in the muscles used for striking, and cowardly individuals felt the force of the insult in the muscles used for speaking.

Lovesickness provides a good example of the entire pathogenic sequence in operation. Imagination of a love object is first stimulated by the sexual organs. This promotes the production of "seed." Increased quantity of seed (manufactured from a portion of the blood by a digestive process) in turn reinforced the passion and the image of the beloved, resulting in production of still more seed. Emotion thus tended to its own increase. The principle "they tread in a ring" described the images, spirits, and humors sequence, and is analogous to the feedback concept used today in psychophysiology.

If the passion of love was not abated by obtaining the object in imagination, by consummation and release of seed, the following pathogenic process commenced. Constitutional imbalances affected the brain, causing cognitive and imaginative faculties to retain the object constantly in memory. This obsession accelerated the progressive deterioration of temperament and established a chronic disturbance called "erotomania."

Lovesickness in advanced stages was believed to be a deadly disease. The abundant quantity of blood around the lover's heart degenerated over time due to the heat of passion. It became transformed into melancholy, the most pernicious of humors. In early stages of erotomania, physicians used bloodletting to arrest the production of seed. If the disease went untreated, however, death ultimately ensued from a "withered heart all burned." An autopsy performed on a victim of love-melancholy disclosed "instead of a heart . . . nothing but a drie shinne like to the leaues in Autumne" (Coeffeteau, 1621, p. 141).

Imagination was the "Medium deferens of passion by whose means they work and produce many times prodigious effects" (McMahon, 1976a, p. 180). The nature of the image determined the quality and quantity of the disturbance. An image leading to states of excitement, like joy or anger, propelled blood and spirits outward in all directions from the heart, reddening the face and perfusing the periphery. Depressing emotions, such as fear and dread, created the reverse effect: Blood and spirits, with their innate heat, retreated toward the heart.

Thomas Wright summarized the mechanism as follows:

> When we imagine any thing, presently the purer spirits, flocke from the brayne, by certaine secret channels to the heart, where they pitch at the dore, signifying what an object was presented, convenient or disconvenient for it. The heart immediately bendeth, either to prosecute it, or to eschew it: and the better to effect that affection, draweth other humors to help him, and so in pleasure concurre great store of pure spirits; in paine and sadness, much melancholy blood; in ire, blood and choller. . . . (Wright, 1604, p. 45)

The effects of any emotion, including joy, could be pathogenic. In Shakespeare's *King Lear* (Knight, 1876) the death of Gloucester followed an emotional shock:

> . . . his flaw'd heart
> Alack, too weak the conflict to support!
> 'Twixt two extremes of passion, joy and grief,
> Burst smilingly.
>
> (Act 5, Scene 3)

Similarly, in *King Henry IV, Part II* (Knight, 1876), the glad news of victory precipitated the monarch's death. Already weakened by prolonged emotional stress, the King did not survive the incident:

> King Henry: And wherefore should this good news make me sick? I should rejoice at this happy news;
> And how my sight fails, and my brain is giddy:
> Oh me! come near me, now I am much ill.
>
> (Act 4, Scene 4)

Because imagination sets the circular arousal sequence into operation, the image had greater powers of control than sensation or perception. Anticipation of a feared occurrence was presumed to be more damaging than the occurrence itself. The event given most consideration in this context was imaginary anticipation of death. Nymannus chose "horror of death" as the most pathogenic emotion, because its emotions inclined toward disease and morbidity. A strong imagination of a particular malady, such as fever, paralysis, or suffocation, was able to produce symptoms of that condition. Stigmata were explained by this theory:

> And thus did the contemplation of Christ nayled on the Crosse, imprint certain strakes, stampes, and markes upon the hands and feet of Saint Francis. (Lemnius, 1633, p. 150)

Images were the products of sensations, and thus imagery was a perceptual process. As such, an "imaginary pain" was a felt pain; "imaginary blindness" was an inability to see. Robert Burton, author of the oft cited *Anatomy of Melancholy* (Burton, 1621), believed disorders of imagination to be the only cause of melancholy. The sufferer's imagination was persistently engaged in conceiving states of ill-being:

> Imagination is eminent in al, so most especially it rageth in melancholy persons in keeping the species of objects so long, amplifying them by continuall and strong meditation, until at length it produceth reall effects, and causeth this and many other maladies. (Burton, 1621, p. 122)

Depending upon the strength of their powers of imagination, parents could influence the characteristics of their offspring at the time of conception. According to Charron (1601), imagination "marks and deforms, nay, sometimes kills Embryos in the womb, hastens Births, or causes Abortions." In 1657, Fienus attempted to explain how, despite parental efforts, imagination sometimes failed to "imprint its characteristics on the foetus" (McMahon, 1976a, p. 181).

## Imagination and Premodern Psychopathology

During this era of holism, prior to the modern definition of mind, all illness was regarded as psychosomatic. Given our present day concerns, however, the psychological aspects of illness merit separate consideration. Let us consider the formation of delusions and hallucinations.

As we have seen, lovesickness tended to its own increase: Images disturbed the internal milieu and the internal milieu reinforced the disturbed imagination. An extensive disturbance of imagination had a proportional effect upon sensation and perception. External events were perceived in specific ways depending upon the type and magnitude of humoral imbalances. All that is seen "passeth by the gates of imagination, and, a clowdie imagination interposeth a mist" between one's understanding and objective reality.

Imagined blindness, paralysis, and loss of sensation were distortions of reality. External events met with the same transfiguration when processed by the deranged system. Delusions, such as imagined pursuit by enemies and the belief of being a king, fit into this framework. The victim of erotomania saw the face of the beloved in the countenances of others and heard the beloved's voice in others' voices. A melancholic interpreted events in keeping with his state of misery and debilitation. The choleric individual who suffered from anxiety, saw threats and assaults where the unexcitable phlegmatic individual saw nothing. Reports of spectres and like apparitions were imputed to the passion of terror "which above all other passions, begets the strongest imaginations" (McMahon, 1976a, p. 182).

## Imagination and Pathogenesis after Descartes

The medical tradition of regarding this image as possibly pathogenic ended in the late seventeenth century. At this point Cartesian dualism of mind and body became a preeminent determining philosophical basis of medical and psychological theory. Before examining the impact of dualism on the traditional theory, it is necessary to understand the revolutionary nature of this philosophical redefinition of the biological soul.

In an effort to prove the immortality of the soul, Rene Descartes (1596-1650) defined the mind as an entity unto itself, an "immaterial substance" or "thinking thing," incapable of affecting matter in any way. According to Descartes, the mind's essence

> ... or nature consists entirely in thinking, and ... for its existence, has no need of place, and is not dependent on any material thing ... this soul is entirely distinct from the body ... and would not itself cease to all that it is, even should the body cease to exist. (Descartes, 1637, p. 119)

Descartes arrived at this definition in the following manner. His objective was absolute truth, knowledge beyond question. He sat in darkness doubting and systematically rejecting all which could be doubted. At length he arrived at the one notion which appeared indubitable: *Cogito ergo sum*; I think, therefore I am.

What then was this "I" he queried? It was not the biological soul, as he already had doubted and dismissed his body. Only one definition was possible—I am a thinking thing, a mind, a soul—and these three terms he used interchangeably.

It is important to note that the concept of mind (as mental functions of the soul) was traditionally assumed. What was revolutionary here was Descartes's use of the term "soul" as a synonym for "mind" or "thinking thing."

Two thousand years of meaning were thus expunged by a paragraph. The soul's faculties of imagination, passion, and reason were thenceforth regarded as "contents of the mind." Again, in a later work he wrote:

> I am a thinking thing. And although possibly I have a body with which I am very closely conjoined, ... in so far as I am only a thinking unextended thing, and ... in so far as it (my body) is only an extended unthinking thing, it is certain that I am truly distinct from my body and can exist without it. (Descartes, 1641, p. 237)

Several factors led to the acceptance of this unlikely view. Renaissance anatomists had tried with scant success to find the biological soul within the body. William Harvey's discovery of circulation of the blood conflicted with traditional concepts of the heart's functioning: "the pump" hardly seemed worthy to be the seat of the soul. Thus, Harvey's discovery strengthened mechanistic physiology.

When dualism converged with mechanistic physiology in the late 1600s, the weight of the proverbial last straw was added to the already weakened structure of soul theory. The dualistic metaphysic of Descartes gave philosophic justification to mechanistic interpretations of biologic functioning. In addition, the Church, which still exerted powerful influence, favored the Cartesian view. The topic of access to heaven by beasts had created considerable controversy within the Church. Descartes resolved this problem by defining animals as autonomously functioning mechanisms lacking an immaterial soul or mind.

A paradigmatic revolution brought a turmoil of protests. Thomas Hobbes wrote, "Had Descartes kept himself wholly to geometry . . . he had been the best geometer in the world, but his head did not lie for philosophy" (Durant & Durant, 1961, p. 643). Others were less generous: "I tell thee DesChartes is a whim and a wham without one why or wherefore" (Jones, 1950, p. 274). A notion thought to be pure nonsense by Descartes' contemporaries became axiomatic within half a century. The Cartesian view fit the Zeitgeist.

To explain the apparent existence of psychophysiologic events such as the influence of imagination, Descartes was at a loss. He suggested that we study mathematics and physics, as someday an explanation of "apparent unity" might be found therein.

The philosophic principle of parallelism emerged to replace the mysterious initial hypothesis of interaction, where divine intervention accounted for cause and effect across the dualistic barrier.

Descartes took the life out of the vital spirits, the mind and intelligence out of the body, and, as subsequent history teaches, the holism out of medicine. The body as subject matter was given to the physiologist and anatomist; the mind was assigned to the philosopher or psychologist, and their mutual influences to God. Consciousness, as an epiphenomenon of the body, was relegated to the domain of philosophy; and the body, as an automaton, was relegated to physiology or "animal mechanics." The ground plan for psychology and medicine now was designed as strictly prohibitive of the psychophysiological.

The meaning of the term "imagination" changed accordingly. In the predualistic era, when the diagnosis put the malady "in the imagination," specific therapeutic action followed. In the post-Cartesian era, the expression, "It's all in your imagination," implied that the patient was untreatable at best, or it carried an accusation of malingering. Let us examine the historic steps in this process of redefinition where the image lost its biological basis.

According to the received view, whatever was caused by a psychological variable could itself be none other than psychological. An "imaginary ailment" was not a genuine ailment. This factor left many somatic compliants beyond the reach of orthodox medicine. In response, huge numbers of suffers resorted to faith healing, mesmerism, and numerous forms of quackery. Cures purported to have derived from such practices were designed by orthodox physicians as cures of imaginary ailments.

Mesmerism, for instance, was directed at illness of a psychosomatic nature, including diarrhea, asthma, temporary blindness, depression, and transient attacks of paralysis. Mesmer (1734-1815) claimed success where standard procedures failed. A commission appointed by Louis XVI arrived at a negative decision regarding mesmerism. It was stated that in instances of apparent therapeutic success, "The imagination does everything, the magnetism nothing" (McMahon, 1980, p. 207).

Braid and Esdaile were the foremost nineteenth-century exponents of mesmerism. Braid's account of the phenomena was psychophysiologic. He proposed a role for imagination: "A strong direction of inward consciousness to any part of the body . . . is quite sufficient to change the physical action of the part" (Braid, 1846, p. 6). Esdaile, however, was vehemently opposed to such a view. Like most thinkers of his period, Esdaile employed a mentalistic definition of imagination:

> I am convinced that Mesmerism is a physical power and I should as soon adopt the diabolical theory as a satisfactory solution to the problem, as attempt to account for what I have seen and done by the action of imagination alone. (Podmore, 1963, p. 162)

Among other unconventional treatments, brass, iron, and zinc tractors were in common use in the late eighteenth century for treatment of disease by "galvanism." In 1800, John Haygarth argued that imagination, rather than galvanism, was the variable accounting for therapeutic success. Quite apart from being a vindication of the role of imagination, this statement meant that the symptoms and illnesses treated must have existed only in the patients' minds. Whatever was curable by imagination must have been imaginary.

By the middle of the eighteenth century, mechanism was instated where holism formerly had held sway. All bodily functions were accounted for by mechanical principles. To the influential Hermann Boerhaave (1668-1738), the greatest advance in the history of medicine was the demonstration of "the Human Being to be an Engine" (Boerhaave, 1715, p. 41). "Disease was caused by mobific matter," and the physician's task was identification of that matter and expulsion or eradication of the substance.

The status of temperament theory declined, and medical authors discontinued use of psychophysiologic concepts. Radical reductionism transformed emotions into mechanical phenomena. "Anguish or Anxiety," for instance, was defined by

Boerhaave as "the Blood being stopp'd in the very Heart; whence a cramp of the contracted Vessles, or an impossibility to the inflamed Matter of passing through them" (Boerhaave, 1715, p. 144). Imagination was understood as an involuntary function like respiration, and the causes of "absurd imaginations" in madness were "sundry material things" like bile and phlegm.

The former psychosomatic approach to therapy was not to be found among orthodox practitioners. The new mechanical treatments frequently were satirized in literary works of the period. Shakespeare had praised former medical practice, but Moliere denounced his medical contemporaries. In *Le Medcin malgre lui,* the patient's condition worsens after taking the remedy. "So much the better," Moliere's doctor replies, "that's a sign it operates" (Moliere, 1909, p. 284). John Cookley Lettsom, a prosperous physician of the early nineteenth century, was the butt of the following popular ridicule:

> When any sick to me apply
> I physics, bleeds, and sweats' em;
> If after that they choose to die,
> Why verily! I Lettsom.
>                     (Wolf, 1935, p. 420)

Descartes had initiated two independent intellectual movements, mentalism and materialism, and although one could adopt both without contradicting oneself, one could never hope for productive interchange between the two realms. Thus the date of psychophysiology became an embarrassing residue which was swept under the carpet until no room remained for more. The bulge became evident to the philosophers of the Age of Enlightenment, and those who brought it to the public attention suffered greviously for the indiscretion.

## Imagination and Pathogenesis in the Eighteenth and Nineteenth Centuries

The eighteenth-century thinkers criticized the implications of dualism for physiology and medicine. The Zeitgeist of Enlightenment was a revolutionary spirit: an esprit critique. Filled with revolutionary zeal, philosophers wielded weapons of satire, scientific demonstration, and empirical fact against the barren Cartesian conception of man as machine.

Ecclesiastic power declined, and science became an institution and a source of belief systems. The intellectual spirit of the age is captured in the words "reason and nature.".Human beings became the subject of observation, experimentation, and rational inquiry.

A bold few dared to liberate science from religion where human nature was concerned. La Mettrie (1709-1751) approached the subject as a psychophysiologist. He hoped to disentangle the soul from spiritualism and to reinstate the ancient naturalistic understanding. La Mettrie found dualism to be the central problem in philosophy and medicine and claimed that pathophysiology led him to see the failure of dualism. All illness was equally represented in the machine and in the mind. Imagination was a mover along with instinct and was seated in the brain. As a manifestation of the functioning of the soul, imagination demanded the physician's attention.

La Mettrie's naturalistic approach to the soul was his undoing. He was ostracized for depriving the soul of its immortality, and he died in Prussia three years after being exiled from France, improverished and friendless at the age of forty-two.

Enlightenment scholars had every intention of reinstating holism so that medicine "may be advanced and carried to the point where it was two thousand years ago" (Diderot, 1867, p. 183). The predicted return to holism did not occur. Dualism was by then axiomatic, and parallelism presented a less controversial alternative and was popularized widely by the British Empiricists.

The image was defined as a content of the mind and an end product of sensation. Aristotle's thinking on the subject was reproduced with one exception. Aristotle had linked imagination directly to arousal, but such causation was irreconcilable with dualism. As Hartley put it, an image may cause movement of the nerves "by no physical cause at all, but the immediate agency of God" (Hartley, 1749, p. ix).

Pierre Jean George Cabanis (1757-1808) shared La Mettrie's interest in psychophysiology and in imagination in particular. Cabanis, however, accepted parallelism and his ideas had great longevity. Mental events, he proposed, caused physiological disturbances and the latter likewise caused distressful images. "Cheerful or sombre ideas, kindly or harmful sentiments are due . . . to the manner in which certain abdominal viscera perform their functions" (Gardiner, 1937, p. 278). He also gives an instance of causation in the reverse direction: A meal in a healthy person is followed by active digestion but "let this man receive bad news, or let sad and troublesome emotions arise in his soul; at once his stomach and his intestines cease to act upon the food which they contain" (Gardiner, 1937, p. 279).

In his early work, Cabanis regarded the soul as a faculty of the body. It was this premodern influence on his thinking which encouraged holistic concepts. However, he was out of step with his contemporaries. As use of the soul concept declined, no theoretical framework existed to accommodate psychophysiologic concepts. Organic illness was explained by Virchow's cell theory and Pasteur's germ theory. Neither interpretation took into account the sufferer's ideational or emotional experience.

Illnesses which displayed no organic derangement were classified as "nervous." Nervous disorders were not organic diseases but merely functional, involving "no independent disease." Among these were all conditions related to "emotions of the mind." Because emotions did not qualify as natural causes of disease, nervous disorders were often interpreted as instances of malingering.

It was agreed that a disturbance caused by a psychological variable could itself be nothing but psychological. The conversion reaction, known in the nineteenth century as "physical hysteria," was among the nervous disorders. Physical hysteria was "a malady of the imagination." A survey of the literature on somatic symptoms, referred to as "hysterical," appeared in 1864. The consensus was that such symptoms were "merely the fanciful productions of idle women of inferior constitution" (McDougall, 1926, p. 34).

If the onset of such a disorder of imagination was associated with military training or active service, it was classified as "compensation hysteria." Not until 1913 were pensions granted for "nervous or hysterical disabilities," and these were granted only when "the nervousness intended is a real and not a ficitious nervous condition" (Boyd, 1913, p. 1038).

In 1859, Robert Macnish wrote, "When a physician pronounces a complaint to be nervous, it is a sure proof that he knows nothing about it" (Macnish, 1859). Illnesses related to imagination and psychosomatic disorders generally were without theoretical explanations. Those who attempted to explain such phenomena were defeated by dualism. John Newport Langley (1852-1925), for instance, made such an attempt. Langley was the Cambridge anatomist who gave us the nomenclature in use today for the autonomic nervous system and its subbranches. Langley introduced the term autonomic with one misgiving:

> The word "autonomic" does suggest a much greater degree of independence of the central nervous system than in fact exists. It is untrue that the "involuntary" actions are out of all control by the will . . . the will exercises more or less control over unstriated muscles and glands by recalling emotions and sensations. (Langley, 1921, pp. 6-7)

Langley ascribed a "mentalistic" role to imagination, and as such it found no place in the mechanistic physiology of the age.

However, to the early psychologists, mentalistic concepts were permissible. The "ideomotor-action" theory echoed the Aristotelian understanding of imagination and arousal. William James, the major exponent of this view, wrote as follows:

> Whether or not there be anything else in the mind at the moment when we consciously will a certain act, a mental conception made up of memory images of these sensations, defining which special act it is, must be there. (McMahon, 1973, p. 477)

The ideomotor theory was paralleled in psychopathology by the concept of the fixed idea or *idee fixe*. Alfred Fouillee was the principle exponent of this view. A fixed idea was morbid conception or delusion which dominated the reasoning processes and at times instated symptoms of organic diseases (Fouillee, 1893).

Ideomotor theory was almost universally accepted by early psychologists. It seemed to furnish the necessary theoretical basis for understanding the role of imagination in pathogenesis. However, at the very height of the theory's popularity, it was terminated by the behavioristic revolution. Images had been linked to arousal, but now "drives" were substituted. If psychology aspired to scientific status, the contents of the Cartesian mind could not comprise its subject matter.

## Twentieth-Century Thought

If a link does exist between imagination and pathology, imagery must be theoretically based in physiology. Several thinkers at the turn of the century undertook to demonstrate that this was so. Alexander Bain's *The Senses and the Intellect* demonstrates such an approach (Bain, 1872).

Bain used the physiology of his time to challenge the view that "the brain is a sort of receptacle of the impressions of sense, where they lie stored up in a chamber quite apart from the recipient apparatus" (Bain, 1872, p. 337). Bain found the "cerebral-closet" notion incompatible with nervous functioning. He proposed instead "completed circles" where imagery occupies "the same parts and in the same manner as the original sensory activation." Bain further argued that no matter how "enfeebled these neural and muscular activities appear upon introspection, they do not take refuge in any chambers of the brain" (Bain, 1872, p. 337).

In 1932, Edmund Jacobson confirmed Bain's view: he applied electrical measurements in an attempt to determine what takes place in the neuromuscular system during various forms of mental activity (Jacobson, 1932). Relaxed subjects were instructed to engage in particular mental activities when signaled to do so by clicks. When the polygraph registered minimal activity, subjects were signaled to imagine throwing a baseball, for instance. Significant activity was recorded in appropriate limbs and was observed to disappear when the signal to discontinue imagining was given. Jacobson's results led to numerous modern applications of imagery in the therapeutic context, most notably in the areas of biofeedback and self-regulation and desensitization (Wolpe, 1974).

Jacobson's research was conducted in an intellectual climate hostile to imagery. His work survived the attack on mentalism, because his results were not incompatible with behaviorism. The attack was directed at schools of thought, like Titchener's structuralism, which inspired an abundance of research on imagery that, however, in the long run, led to no consensus. The imageless-thought controversy was frequently cited as justification for banishing imagery as a subject of investigation along with the introspective method of study. According to John Watson (Watson, 1930, p. 3), "The behaviorist finds no evidence for 'mental existences' or 'mental processes' of any kind." What Jacobson measured, however, was considered "covert behavior" and thus was accepted as a suitable subject for research.

In subsequent decades, psychologists continued to prefer behavioristic variables to mentalistic constructs. The topic of imagery was neglected for nearly half a century, until verbal report, as an index of imagery, gained broad acceptance (Holt, 1972).

Today, an abundance of evidence links imagination and physiopathology. As noted in the concluding section, however, results, suggesting this relationship are largely derived from correlational data and Correlations fail to elucidate causal mechanisms (McMahon, 1976b).

## IMAGINATION IN THE CONTEXT OF THERAPY

We return now to the predualistic era to investigate uses of the image in diagnosis and therapy.

### Ancient and Renaissance Therapeutic Uses of Imagination

The tradition of dream imagery interpretation dates to the ancient period. The distinguished second-century physician, Claudius Galen, used dream imagery to assist in diagnosis. Galen presumed that dream content reflected the nature and severity of humoral imbalances. For instance, images of loss, disgrace, or grief indicated excessive melancholy; images of terror, fighting, and wounds signified predominance of choler (McMahon, 1976a).

Premodern image arousal theory led to clinical use in diagnosis, therapy, and prevention. By the same psychophysiologic means that imagination induced pathological changes, it could remove them and restore health. The image arousal function

> can thus take away or bring some disease of the mind or body. For the passions of the soul are the chiefest cause of the temperament of its proper body. So the soul, being strongly elevated, and inflamed with a strong imagination, sends forth health or sickness. (Cornelius Agrippa, 1510, as cited in McMahon, 1976a, p. 180)

Removal of a pathogenic image was necessary to cure an existing disorder and prevent its recurrence. William Vaughan (1612) outlined one therapeutic procedure:

> The physitian . . . must inuent and deuise some spirituall pageant to fortfie and help the imaginatiue faculty, which is corrupted and depraued; yea, hee must endeauour to deceiue and imprint another conceit, whether it be wise or foolish, in the patient's braine, thereby to put out all former phantisies. (McMahon, 1976a, p. 182)

However deranged the sufferer's imagination, it was still his/her reality. With sympathetic listening and attention to pulse, complexion, posture, and gait, the physician analyzed the disturbed imagination. It was necessary that the patient "open his heart" to the physician or, in some cases, to the physician's ally.

The ultimate objective of therapy was to restore equilibrium by rectifying internal imbalances. To this end, the ancient principle of opposites was applied. An image leading to excitation could arouse the phlegmatic personality; an image provoking joy or laughter could be of benefit to the melancholic. During this period, melancholy received the most attention. The following medical advice was common during that period:

> What is the principall naturall meanse to prolong life?
> Mirth.
> What are the effects of mirth?
> Mirth enlargeth the heart, and disperseth much naturall heat with the bloud, of which it sendeth a good portion to the face, especially if the mirth be so great, that it stirreth a man to laughter. Mirth I say, maketh the forehead smooth and cleere, causeth the eyes to glisten, and the cheeks to become ruddy. (Vaughan, 1612, p. 141)

Shakespeare, who evinced great respect for the medicine of his era, once remarked that the task of the physician was "To enforce the painted impotent to smile" (McMahon, 1976c, p. 279). In the Induction to *The Taming of the Shrew*, treatment for a case of melancholy was described:

> For so your doctors hold it very meet:
> Seeing too much sadness hath congeal'd you blood,
> And melancholy is the nurse to frenzy:
> Therefore, they thought it good you hear a play,
> And frame your mind to mirth and merriment,
> Which bars a thousand harms and lengthens life.
> (Knight, 1876, Act 1, Scene 17)

Suppression or repression of emotion was judged to be especially perilous, because the pathogenic imagination, left to its own mechanism, could do no other than worsen the condition. A victim of suppressed love is described in Shakespeare's *Twelfth Night:*

> She never told her love,
> But let concealment, like a worm i' the bud,
> Feed on her damask cheek: she pin'd in thought:
> And with a green and yellow melancholy,
> She sat, like patience on a monument
> Smiling at grief.
>
> (Knight, 1876, Act 2, Scene 5 )

As previously noted, the expressions of emotion were healthful releases; for instance, weeping expelled excess moisture through the eyes, and the increased respiratory rate of anger cooled the "boiling blood" of rage. In King Richard II (Knight, 1876), the king suffered from long repressed sorrow. In his looking glass he observed wrinkles:

> Bolingbroke: The shadow of your sorrow hath destroyed the shadow of your face.
> Richard: Say that again.
> The shadow of my sorrow? Ha!
> 'Tis very true, my grief lies all within;
> And these external manners of laments
> Are merely shadows to the unseen grief,
> That swells with silence in the tortur'd soul;
> There lies the substance.
>
> (Act 4, Scene 1)

If patients did not express their emotions, physicans would urge them to do so. They warned, however, not to go so far as to lose the controlling influence of reason. Balthasar Gracian discussed "the art of getting into a Rage."

> The first step in losing your temper is to realize that you are losing it, for you thus keep your emotions under control from the start, gauging the precise degree of rage that is necessary, and not going beyond it. (Gracian, 1953, p. 167)

### Imagination and the Historic Use of Placebos

What we know today as the "placebo effect" refers to reliable alterations in conditions of control group subjects in experimental tests of the effects of drugs, for example. Premodern theory of imagination-induced physiological changes predicted and explained this phenomenon, and it became a standard form of therapy.

Renaissance physicians sought naturalistic explanations for the mysterious faith cures of the Middle Ages. Cures were reported to follow ingesting relics, performing magic rituals, wearing charms, and so on. The explanation of these phenomena was found in the traditional theory. On the basis of that theory, highly respected medical thinkers, like Robert Burton and Jerome Cardan, wrote defenses of the use of spells, charms, chants, and like remedies.

"All the world knowes there is no vertue in such charmes" argued Burton, save their power to dominate imagination "which forceth a motion of the humors, spirits, and blood, which takes away the cause of the malady from the parts affected. The like we say of all our magical effects, superstitious cures, and such are done by Mountebanks and Wizards. An Empiricke many times, and a silly Chirugeon, doth more strange cures than a rationall Physition." (Burton, 1621, p. 124)

To be effective, the placebo-type remedy had to be accepted with unqualified confidence and the corresponding imagination had to be firmly implanted and capable of persistence. This occurred only when the patient had absolute belief in the physician's competence. H. Cornelius Agrippa advised that both physician and patient

> ... affect vehemently, imagine, hope and believe strongly for that will be a great help. And it is verified amongst physicians, that a strong belief, and an undoubted hope and love towards the physician and medicine conduce much to health; yea, more, sometimes, than the medicine itself. For the same [reason] that the efficacy and virtue of the medicine works, the same doth the strong imagination of the physician work, being able to change the qualities in the body of the sick, especially when the patient placeth much confidence in the physician, by that means disposing himself for receiving the virtue of the physician and physic. (Agrippa, 1898, p. 204)

Agrippa cited one extreme case of these principles in operation. He described a patient who

> ... at the sight of the medicine, was affected as much as he pleased; when, as neither the substance of the medicine, nor the odor, nor the taste, of it came to him, but only a kind of resemblance was apprehended by him. (Agrippa, 1898, p. 198)

If its power was imagined to be pathogenic, a placebo substance could likewise induce a malady. Witchcraft was surrounded by an aura of fear duing this period. Spells were cast and cures applied for the purpose of inflicting bodily harm. Burton described persons who are vulnerable to such suggestions (Burton, 1621):

> If they but see another man tremble, giddy, or sicke of some fearfull disease, their apprehension and feare is so strong in this kinde, that they will have the same disease. Or if by some South-sayer, Wiseman, Fortune-teller, or Physition, they be told they will have such a disease they will so seriously apprehend it, that they will instantly labour of it. A thing similar in China, saith Riccius the Jesuite, If it be told them they shall be sicke on such a day, when that day comes they will surely be sicke, and will be so terrible afflicted, that sometimes they will dye vpon it. (McMahon, 1976a, pp. 182-183)

According to patients' beliefs, physicians who gave placebos accompanied by explicit prediction and their effects, administered charms, chants, spells, talismans, and magic rituals. However, after the Cartesian revolution, when images became "contents of the mind," physicans who advocated such therapy were stepping outside the bounds of standard practice. Therapy now was based upon a mechanical model incompatible with the influence of any psychological process on physiologic functions.

## Imagination and the Placebo Effect in Post-Cartesian Medicine

While physicians no longer addressed the issue, philosophers regularly included treatments of imagination in their works on human nature. Not long after Descartes, the topic of imagination in the context of physiology appeared in the influential works of David Hartley (1705-1757). Hartley was a parallelist who felt that two sets of lawful principles could be devised, one for mental events and one for somatic processes, and that these two sets of principles would lead to medical applications (Hartley, 1966).

Dualism indeed did lead to two sets of laws but not to medical application, because causation could not logically enter the picture. Any causal influence across the dualistic barrier was logically impossible and causal principles, rather than correlations, were needed for medical application. As one early modern physician put it, with evident sarcasm: "How certain emotions of the mind should circulate through the arteries . . . or should for a time obstruct the ordinary return of blood by the veins, is a subject into which we shall not presume to enter" (Carson, 1815, as cited in McMahon, 1976b, p. 113).

Despite the implications of dualism,, it was evident to Hartley that imagination exerted control on involuntary functions, that is, on the functions of the autonomic nervous system. Hartley felt that cardiovascular activity could be increased or diminished in the following way:

> We seem to have a semivoluntary Power to alter the motion of the Heart immediately, by introducing strong Ideas, our power of introducing these being semivoluntary: Nay it may be possible for Persons . . . to acquire still greater Degrees of Power over the Motion of the Heart. (McMahon & Hastrup, 1980, p. 207)

Physicians who addressed questions of mental influences were ostracized as quacks. William Falconer, Benjamin Rush, and Daniel Hack Tuke were among the few who dared to propose a role for imagination. Their credibility had been established through earlier works well received. All three addressed the image in the context of placebo mechanisms. Falconer argued that numerous cures

> . . . have been performed by medicines of little, or even of no medical efficacy whatever in themselves, which effect could proceed only from the opinion the patient entertained of their powers; as a proof of which we find that the certainty of the cure has almost always depended on the degree of the patient's confidence in the success of the remedy. (Falconer, 1788, p. 23)

Falconer recommended a general therapeutic procedure of "redirecting the mind" of the patient in order to eliminate memory images of disorders and their symptoms. He urged that this approach be utilized especially with hypochondriacs due to their highly pathogenic images. Falconer advised that a sufferer's imagination be prevented from "dwelling on itself." The imagination should be thoroughly occupied with other things "leaving no room for the apprehension and recollection of the disorder to operate" (McMahon & Hastrup, 1980, p. 208).

D. H. Tuke (1827-1895) was the most prolific advocate of the role of imagination in the medical literature after Descartes. His confidence in the reality of the phenomenon derived not from familiarity with premodern literature but rather from a news report he had chanced upon. The article told of a bloody and dramatic railway accident from which one of the uninjured passengers emerged completely cured of a severe case of rheumatism. This aberration led Tuke to conduct a thorough search of the literature wherein he found the historic conception (Tuke, 1872).

He attempted to restate traditional theory for a modern audience in a major work titled "Illustrations of the Influence of the Mind upon the Body in Health and Disease, Designed to Elucidate the Action of Imagination." However, the numerous citations of imagination-related illnesses and cures were naught but medical curiosities to Tuke's contemporaries. Medical theory in no way could accommodate events that were by definition biologically and logically impossible.

Tuke strongly advocated the use of placebos, and he advised that physicians be present when such remedies were administered; for, at times, the dosage might be too potent and perhaps dangerous. He cited a French contemporary's "remarkable success" with two sets of pills composed of bread crumbs and covered with silver leaf. One set, the "pilules argentees antinerveuses," was used to treat disorders of unexplained origin and termed "nervous." Nervous disorders were the nineteenth-century analoa of what we now know as psychosomatic conditions (McMahon, 1976b). The remaining containers were marked "purgatives" and the dosage prescribed was five capsules every fifteen minutes for a period of several hours. Impressive results were claimed for this "most violent" purgative.

Benjamin Rush had an unorthodox liking for psychosomatic concepts and regarded imagination to be necessary in the workings of placebos. He frequently prescribed remedies of doubtful efficacy in the critical stages of acute diseases and claimed that "the success of this measure has much oftener answered than disappointed my expectations" (McMahon & Hastrup, 1980, p. 208).

With the emergence of psychology as a separate discipline in the late nineteenth century, came many treatments of imagery's role in arousal. Parallelism did not prevent William James from formulating a theory of "ideo-motor action" (James, 1950). In the psychology texts of the early twentieth century, we find James' theory accepted almost unanimously. It appeared that the time for a renaissance of Aristotelian theory had arrived. This was not to be the case however. The behaviorists were eminently successful in eliminating all mentalistic concepts from the arena of serious research. As Klinger notes, from 1920 to 1960 there was a moratorium in North American psychology on investigations of inner experience, including imagery; and not a single book on the topic of imagery appeared during this period (Klinger, 1971). However, this was not the case in Europe.

## EUROPEAN IMAGERY APPROACHES IN THE 1900s

European clinical psychologists and psychiatrists continued to demonstrate a deep sensitivity to an involvement in the realm of imagination. This attitude was relatively unperturbed by the growing influence of behavioristic psychology in America. reasons for the continuation of this largely subjective approach to imagery are many: 1) Many experimentalists fled Europe during the two World Wars; 2) The phenomenology of German and French origin permeated European clinical and scientific systems; 3) Jung's subjective approaches to the exploration of symbols in fantasies, dreams, and myths deeply influenced many European practitioners; 4) Europe had been affected by subjective Eastern psychology (Jordan, 1979; Sheikh & Jordon, 1983, p. 396).

The notable contributors to the therapeutic use of imagination, of the early 1900s, include Carl Happich, Eugene Caslant, Oscar Vogt, Johannes Schultz, Ludwig Frank, Marc Guillerey, Pierce Clark, Sigmund Freud, Anna Freud, and Carl Jung (see Sheikh & Jordan, 1983 for a review). More recently, Desoille and Fretigny and Virel in France, Leuner in Germany, and Assagioli in Italy have made significant contributions to the area and their influence has gradually infiltrated into North America (Sheikh & Panagiotou, 1975). It is worth noting, however, that although European clinicians managed to elude the stranglehold of Watsonian ideas, they could not escape the powerful influence of Cartesian dualistic formulations. Consequently, with a few exceptions, imaginative skills were utilized in the treatment of the so-called psychological problems and not applied to the physical ones.

## "Return of the Ostracized" in American Psychology

As Holt (1964) and Watkins (1976) point out, a renewed interest in imagery was initiated mainly by developments in areas peripheral to mainstream psychology, such as engineering psychology, sensory or perceptual deprivation research, biochemical and neuropsychological investigations, and studies of sleep and inactivity. However, gradually, psychologists realized that they could utilize the research techniques developed by the behaviorists, in investigations of topics that had been discarded but were critical to the understanding of human nature. And, ironically, behavior therapists themselves played a significant role in indirectly compelling clinicians to reexamine the relevance of imaginal variables. Experimental and clinical psychologists responded eagerly to Holt's invitation (Holt, 1964), "Come on in— the water is fine." The emergence of the "third force," the humanistic trend in psychology, lent the study and use of imagery further impetus and respectability. Recently, interest in widely varied image techniques has greatly expanded and intensified, and the therapeutic relevance of such techniques is being examined closely.

## Bases for the Clinical Efficacy of Images

The imaginal mode has numerous characteristics that make it an eminently suitable vehicle for clinical work. A number of these are listed below.

1. It appears that imagery represents the functioning of vital components of the same psychological apparatus which is exercised in all activities . . . imagery represents the core of perceptual response and retrieval mechanisms (Klinger, 1980). Therefore, several researchers (Klinger, 1980; Kosslyn, 1980; Neisser, 1976; Sheikh, 1983) propose that an experience in imagination can be regarded to be

psychologically equivalent in many important respects, to the actual experiences. Also, Perky (1910), Leuba (1940), Segal and Fusella (1910), and Richardson (1969), among others, have found that imagery and perception are experientially and neurophysiologically similar processes and share the same intrinsic qualities. Hebb and Pribram tend to support this view (Singer, 1974). Furthermore, Penfield (1963) showed that the locus of image excitation corresponds to the locus of sensory functions in the brain.

2. Aristotle proposed that images are the source of action and guide behavior by presenting the goal object (McMahon, 1973). A number of modern psychologists (Miller et al., 1960; Mowrer, 1977; and Sarbin & Coe, 1972), also believe that since images can represent situations and objects, they can act as motivators for future action. In fact, Shephard (1978) and Tower and Singer (1981) have found that people appear to act more according to imaginal consequences than to actual probabilities.

3. Apparently, meaning depends heavily on images; words elicit images which are accompanied by emotional responses, and these responses are the source of the words' meanings (Bugelski, 1970; Forisha, 1979). Arieta (1976) adds that images render it possible to retain an emotional attitude toward an absent object.

4. Mental images furnish the opportunity to examine "the integration of perception, motivation, subjective meaning, and realistic abstract thought" (Shorr, 1980, p. 99; Escalona, 1973).

5. Schachtel points out that as people are socialized, they generally rely increasingly on empty verbal cliches or abstractions and thus lose direct contact with experience (Schachtel, 1959). But, as Singer and Pope (1978) state, this contact is implicit in the "concrete modality-specific imagery system," which therefore is a source of extensive details about past occurrences (Singer, 1979).

6. Imagery may provide the main access to memories encoded during a developmental stage when language was not yet present or not yet predominant (Sheikh & Panagiotou, 1975).

7. Klinger maintains that the imaginal stream, present in image therapies, has a tendency to overrepresent the patient's problem area or "current concerns." "Unlike polite social discourse, imaginal techniques invite material that is likely to move selectively into the troubled areas of the client's life" (Klinger 1980, p. 12).

8. Also, Klinger (1980) observes that images are accompanied by emotional responses to internal and external cues contained in the situation. Singer, too, states that the "imagery system increases the likelihood that we will experience more fully a range of emotions" (Singer, 1979, p. 36). Numerous other researchers have noted that focusing on images may uncover intense affective changes or elicit emotional reactions (Sheikh & Jordan, 1983; p. 394). "Images may have a greater capacity than the linguistic mode for the attraction and focusing of emotionally loaded association in concentrated forms: Verbal logic is linear; whereas the image is a stimutaneous representation. The quality of simultaneity gives imagery greater isomorphism with the qualities of perception, and therefore greater capacity for descriptive accuracy" (Sheikh & Panagiotou, 1975, p. 577).

9. Numerous researchers have shown that imagery is capable of producing very diverse physiological changes. For example, Barber et al. reported that the directive to imagine that tap water was sour led to increase salivation (Barber, Chauncey, &

Winer, 1964). Simpson and Paivio (1966) observed alterations in pupillary size during imagery. May and Johnson (1973) found that arousing images caused increased heart rate. Yaremko and Butler (1975) noted that imagining a tone or shock and presentation of the actual stimuli led to comparable habituation. Several investigators have observed changes in electromyograms caused by images (Sheikh & Jordan, 1983, p. 294). Furthermore, Barber (1978) reported that images could lead to blood glucose increases, inhibition of gastrointestinal activity, increased gastric-acid secretion, blister formation, and changes in skin temperature. Several studies of meditation and biofeedback, which probably involved imagery, demonstrated reduction in blood pressure, heart rate, and oxygen consumption, and also alterations in gastrointestiinal activity and body temperature (Sheikh, Richardson, & Maleski, 1979). Neal Miller (1972) has proposed that the utilization of imagery may be the only practical means of developing a measure of control over autonomic processes.

10. Therapists have observed that at times, when individuals can no longer continue to express experiences verbally, spontaneous images may occur, filling in with perceptual, generally pictorial representations (Sheikh & Panagiotou, 1975). Also, when therapy seems to come to a dead end, imagery often uncovers new areas of exploration (Singer, 1974). Dave points out that if an impasse is reached on a certain problem, visualizing elements of the problem is more beneficial than utilizing a rational cognitive approach (Dave, 1976).

11. Researchers have shown that "free imagery," which is analogous to free associations, is highly effective in circumventing even stubborn defenses and bringing to light repressed material (Jordan, 1979; Klinger, 1980; Reyher, 1963). The resort to imagery may catch the patient by surprise and outwit his defenses (Singer, 1974, p. 251).

12. Horowitz (1970) remarks that the image mode is best suited to unconscious organization. It more readily allows for the spanning of the conscious-unconscious continuum than does overt or covert language; elements from the unconscious more easily enter imagoic cognition, and images more readily act as symbols. . . . Images are less likely to be filtered through the conscious critical apparatus than is linguistic expression. In most cases, words and phrases must be consciously understood before they are spoken; for in order to assume a grammatical order they must first pass through a rational censorship. Imagery, perhaps, is not subject to this filtering process, and therefore may have the opportunity to be a more direct expression of the unconscious (Sheikh & Panagiotou, 1975, p. 556).

## Imagery: Current American Approaches

From a position of near disgrace, imagery recently has risen to be one of the hottest issues in both clinical and experimental cognitive psychology. Cognitive psychologists have extensively debated the question whether images represent a direct encoding of perceptual experiences, an artifact of propositional structuring of reality, or a constructive and reconstructive process (Tower & Singer, 1981). But this issue has not been of any real concern to the majority of clincians. "They assume that everyone experiences mental representations of objects and events, and these representations constitute their subject matter" (Sheikh & Jordan, 1983, p. 395). A definition of imagery, such as the one provided by Richardson (1969), is implicit in most of these approaches:

> Mental imagery refers to all those quasi-sensory or quasi-perceptual experiences of which we are self-consciously aware, and which exist for us in the absence of those stimulus conditions that are known to produce their genuine sensory or perceptual counterparts. (p. 2)

Space limitations do not permit a detailed discussion of the various imagery approaches. Interested readers are referred to other sources (Sheikh & Jordan, 1983; Sheikh, Kunzendorf, & Sheikh, 1989).

But the multitude of existing imagery approaches can be classified perhaps into the following four broad categories.

1. The first group consists of a number of approaches that are based primarily on the Pavlovian and Skinnerian models. "They demonstrate the surface relationship between images and emotional reaction as well as the power of images to act as potent stimuli. . . . The method consist of several variations of counterconditioning and emotional flooding" (Sheikh & Jordan, 1983).

2. The second category includes the approaches of several clinicians who maintain that images very effectively provide individuals with a clear comprehension of their perceptual and affective distortions. Unlike the cognitive behavior therapists, they do not subscribe to the conditioning principles.

3. The third class basically deals with imagery rehearsal of physical and psychological health. The client may be asked to image a malfunctioning organ becoming normal or to practice in imagination a healthy interpersonal relationship. No complicated interpretation or theories are offered except the assumption that "sane" imagination will gradually lead to sane reality.

4. The fourth category includes the "depth" imagery techniques that place the healing of the psyche back into the "magical" model which emphasizes a transformation through "irrational" procedures as opposed to rational or reflexive therapies.

Extensive claims concerning the potential of imagery for therapeutic benefits are being made. However, the claims, with a few exceptions, are based largely on the reports of clinicians and are not sufficiently backed by well-controlled investigations. Further systematic research on the therapeutic outcome of imagery approaches is sorely needed.

## CONCLUDING REMARKS

In general, psychologists and physicians have explicitly or implicitly assumed dualism. Various attempts have been made to circumvent the problem, but never has dualism been rejected as inapplicable to, or irreconcilable with the phenomena of psychophysiology and psychosomatics. Recently, however, physicists have addressed the question of dualism's applicability to the life processes. Their consensus is that dualism must be replaced by a more reasonable conception.

Dualism is a form of reductionism, and because it simplified subject matter it led to great advances in the physical sciences. Only within the past few decades has its inadequacy been realized. Von Neumann (1966) and Polanyi (1958, 1966) expressed doubts concerning the possibility of explaining the phenomena of life on mechanistic grounds. Several eminent physicists, including Elsasser (1958, 1966), Wigner (1967), and Schrodinger (1944), founder of waver mechanics, have argued a need for a separate set of laws to account for organismic functioning. The consensus is that current knowledge in physics is neither adequate nor appropriate in application to living systems.

Elsasser's main thesis is "the time-honored dualism of the mutually exclusive system of thought, mechanistic biology on the one hand and vitalism on the other, express a pair of theoretical approaches which are both inadequate (1966, p. v). There are regularities in the organism, whose existence cannot be logico-mathematically derived from the laws of physics. To Elsasser, life is a "primary phenomenon, not deducible from physics or anything else" (1966, p. 52). Life is a "process," and he introduced the term "biotonic" to apply to the phenomena of living systems.

Wigner gave rigorous mathematical proof that mechanistic reductionism is inapplicable in biology (1967). Schrodinger used the stability of hereditary transmission to show the inapplicability of physical laws (1944). Physics fails "not on the grounds that there is any 'new force' or what not . . . but because the construction [of atoms within the living organism] is different from anything yet tested in the physical laboratory (1944, p. 81).

If the implications of dualism are prohibitive to physics, how much more so are they to psychologists and health professionals generally. A solution may reside in the concept of a "biotonic phase" of existence. Many distinguished writers, including the physicists just cited, have argued for the acceptance of a biotonic phase. Within psychology, Weimer has accepted the concept and has presented an analysis of causation (1976a, 1976b). If we accept the existence of three phases of existence, as distinguished from the Cartesian two, we are able to address causation without self-contradiction. These three dimensions of reality are 1) the psychic phase (where mnemic causality applies), 2) the material phase (as defined by classical and quantum physics, and 3) the biotonic phase, which is reducible neither to mental nor material phases.

The biotonic phase provides a substrate for psychophysiological functioning in the same manner that the biological soul of the pre-Cartesian era provided a substrate. It removes the burden of causation from mental events. It provides a rational basis for theory in psychophysiology and psychosomatics. With such a basis for theory we might easily restore the role of imagination to the position of prominence it once enjoyed.

## REFERENCES

Agrippa, H. C. (1898). In W. F. Whitehead (Ed.), *Three books of occult philosophy or magic.* Chicago: Hahn and Whitehead.

Arieti, S. (1976). *Creativity: The magic synthesis.* New York: Basic Books.

Bain, A. (1872). *The senses and the intellect.* New York: D. Appleton and Co.

Barber, T. X. (1978). Hypnosis, suggestions and psychosomatic phenomena, a new look from the standpoint of recent experimental studies. *The American Journal of Clinical Hypnosis, 21,* 13-27.

Barber, T. X., Chauncey, H. M., & Winer, R. A. (1964). The effect of hypnotic and non-hypnotic suggestions on parotid gland response to gustatory stimuli. *Psychosomatic Medicine, 26,* 374-380.

Boerhaave, H. (1715). *Aphorisms: Concerning the knowledge and cure of diseases.* F. Delacorste (Trans.). London: Cowse and Innys.

Boyd, J. H. (1913). *Workmen's compensation and industrial insurance* (Vol. III). Indianapolis: Bobbs-Merrill.

Braid, J. (1846). *The power of the mind over the body.* London: Churchill.

Bugelski, B. R. (1970). Words and things and images. *American Psychologist, 25,* 1002-1012.

Burton, R. (1621). *The anatomy of melancholy.* Oxford: John Lichfield and James Short.

Charron, P. (1601) *Of wisdom.* London: Bonwick.

Coeffeteau, F. (1621). *A fable of humane passions with their causes and effects.* E. Grimeston (Trans.). London.

Dave, R. P. (1976). *The effect of hypnotically induced dreams on creative problem solving.* Unpublished master's thesis, Michigan State University.

Descartes, R. (1958). Discours de la methode (1637). In N. K. Smith (Trans.). *Descartes' philosophical writing.* New York: Random House.

Descartes, R. (1958). Meditations de prima philosophia (1641). In N. K. Smith (Trans.). *Descartes' philosophical writings,* New York: Random House.

Diderot, D. (1967). *The encyclopedia,* S. J. Gendzier (Ed.). New York: Harper and Row.

Durant, W., & Durant, A. (1961). *The age of reason begins.* New York: Simon and Schuster.

Elsasser, W. M. (1958). *The physical foundations of biology.* New York: Pergamon Press.

Elsasser, W. M. (1966). *Atom and organism: A new approach to theoretical biology.* Princeton: Princeton University Press.

Escalona, S. K. (1973). Book review of mental imagery in children. *Journal of Nervous and Mental Diseases, 156,* 70-77.

Falconer, W. (1788). *A dissertation on the influence of passions upon disorders of the body.* London: Dilly.

Forisha, B. L. (1979). The outside and the inside: Compartmentalization of integration. In A. S. Sheikh & J. T. Shafer (Eds.). *The potential of fantasy and imagination.* New York: Brandon House.

Fouillee, A. (1893). La psychologie des idees fixes. *Philosphical Review, 36,* 515-535.

Gardiner, H. M. (1937). *Feeling and emotion.* New York: American Book Co.

Gould, J. B. (1970). *The philosophy of Chrysippus.* Leiden: E. J. Brill.

Gracian, B. (1953). *The oracle.* London: J. M. Dent and Sons, Ltd.

Hartley, D. (1966). *Observations of man (1749).* Gainesville: Scholars' Facsimiles and Reprints.

Holt, R. R. (1964). Imagery: The return of the ostracized. *American Psychologist, 19,* 254-264.

Holt, R. R. (1972). On the nature and generality of mental imagery. In P. W. Sheehan (Ed.), *The function and nature of imagery.* New York: Academic Press.

Horowitz, M. J. (1970). *Image formation and cognition.* New York: Appleton.

Huarte, J. (1575). *The examination of men's wits* (Carew, trans.), Gainesville: Scholars' Facsimiles & Reprints, 1959.

Jacobson, E. (1932). Electrophysiology of mental activities, *American Journal of Psychology, 44,* 677-694.

James, W. (1950). *Principles of psychology* (1890), Vol. II, New York: Dover.

Jones, H. W. (1950). Mid-seventeenth century science: Some polemics. *Asiris, 9,* 254-274.

Jordan, C. S. (1979). Mental imagery and psychotherapy: European approaches. In A. A. Sheikh & J. T. Shaffer (Eds.), *The potential of fantasy and imagination*. New York: Brandon House.

Klinger, E. (1971). *The structure and function of fantasy*. New York: Wiley.

Klinger, E. (1980). Therapy and the flow of thought. In J. E. Shorr, G. E. Sobel, P. Robin, and J. A. Connella (Eds.), *Imagery: Its many dimensions and applications*. New York: Plenum.

Knight, C. (Ed.) (1876). *Image formation and cognition*. New York: Appleton and Co.

Kosslyn, S. (1980). *Image and mind*. Cambridge, Massachusetts: Harvard University Press.

Langley, J. N. (1921). *The autonomic nervous system (Part I)*. Cambridge: W. Heffer and Sons.

Lemnius, L. (1633). *The touchstone of complexions*. London: E. A. for Michael Sparke.

Leuba, C. (1940). Images as conditioned sensations. *Journal of Experimental Psychology, 26,* 345-351.

Lucretius, C. T. (1965). *On nature*. R. M. Geer (Trans.). New York: Bobbs-Merrill Co.

Macnish, R. (1859). *Book of aphorisms*. London: W. R. McPhum.

May, J., & Johnson, H. (1973). Physiological activity to internally-elicited arousal and inhibitory thoughts. *Journal of Abnormal Psychology, 82,* 239-245.

McDougall, W. (1926). *Outline of abnormal psychology*. New York: Charles Scribner's Sons.

McKean, R. (Ed.) (1941). *The basic works of Aristotle*. New York: Random House.

McMahon, C. E. (1973). Images as motives and motivators: A historical perspective. *American Journal of Psychology, 86,* 465-490.

McMahon, C. E. (1974). Voluntary control of involuntary functions: The approach of the stoics. *Psychophysiology, 11,* 710-714.

McMahon, C. E. (1976a). The role of imagination in the disease process: Pre-cartesian history. *Psychological Medicine, 6,* 197-184.

McMahon, C. E. (1976b). Psychosomatic disease and the problem of causation. *Medical Hypotheses, 2,* 112-115.

McMahon, C. E. (1976c). Psychosomatic concepts in the works of Shakespeare. *Journal of the History of the Behavioral Sciences, 12,* 275-282.

McMahon, C. E., & Hastrup, J. L. (1980). The role of imagination in the disease process: Post-cartesian history. *Journal of Behavioral Medicine, 36*(2), 205-217.

McMahon, C. E. (1986). *Where medicine fails*. New York: Trade-Medic Books.

Miller, G. A., Galanter, E., & Pribram, K. H. (1960). *Plans and the structure of behavior*. New York: Holt.

Miller, N. E. (1972). Interactions between learned and physical factors in mental illness. In D. Shapiro et al. (Eds.), *Biofeedback and self-control,* Chicago: Aldine.

Moliere (1909). *The plays of Moliere* (Vol. 6). Boston: Little Brown and Company.

Mowrer, O. H. (1977). Mental imagery: An indispensible psychological concept. *Journal of Mental Imagery, 1,* 303-326.

Neisser, U. (1976). *Cognition and reality*. San Francisco: Freeman.

Neumann, J. V. (1966). *Theory of self-reproducing automats*. Urbana: University of Illinois Press.

Penfield, W. (1963). The brain's record of auditory and visual experience—final summary. *Brain, 86,* 595-696.

Perky, C. W. (1910). An experimental study of imagination. *American Journal of Psychology, 21,* 422-452.

Podmore, F. (1963). *Introduction of mesmerism to India*. New York: University Books.

Polanyi, M. (1958). *Personal knowledge*. New York: Harper.

Polanyi, M. (1966). *The tacit dimension*. Garden City, New York: Doubleday.

Reyher, J. (1963). Free imagery, an uncovering procedure. *Journal of Clinical Psychology, 19,* 454-459.

Richardson, A. (1969). *Mental imagery.* New York: Springer.

Sarbin, T. R., & Coe, W. C. (1972). *Hypnosis: A social psychological analysis of influence communication.* New York: Holt.

Schachtel, E. G. (1959). *Metamorphosis: On the development of affect, perception, attention, and memory.* New York: Basic Books.

Schrodinger, E. (1944). *What is life?* Cambridge: Cambridge University Press.

Segal, S. J., & Fusella, Y. (1910). Influence of imaged pictures and sounds on detection of visual and auditory signals. *Journal of Experimental Psychology, 26,* 458-464.

Sheikh, A. A. (Ed.) (1983). *Imagery: Current theory, research, and applications.* New York: Wiley.

Sheikh, A. A., & Jordan, C. S. (1983). Clinical uses of mental imagery. In A. A. Sheikh (Ed.), *Imagery: Current theory, research, and applications.* New York: Wiley.

Sheikh, A. A., Kunzendorf, R. G., & Sheikh, K. S. (1989). Healing images: From ancient wisdom to modern science. In A. A. Sheikh & K. S. Sheikh (Eds.), *Healing East and West: Ancient wisdom and modern psychology.* New York: Wiley.

Sheikh, A. A., & Panagiotou, N. C. (1975). Use of mental imagery in psychotherapy: A critical review. *Perceptual and Motor Skills, 41,* 555-585.

Sheikh, A. A., Richardson, P., & Moleski, L. M. (1979). Psychosomatics and mental imagery:z A brief review. In A. A. Sheikh & J. T. Shaffer (Eds.), *The potential of fantasy and imagination,* New York: Random House.

Shepard, R. N. (1978). The mental image. *American Psychologist, 33,* 125-137.

Shorr, J. E. (1980). Discoveries about the mind's ability to organize and find meaning in imagery. In E. Shorr et al. (Eds.), *Imagery: It's many dimensions and applications,* New York: Plenum.

Simpson, H. M., & Paivio, A. (1966). Changes in pupil size during an imagery task without motor involvement. *Psychonomic Science, 5,* 405-406.

Singer, J. L. (1974). *Imagery and daydream methods in psychotherapy and behavior modification.* New York: Academic Press.

Singer, J. L., & Pope, K. S. (1978). The use of imagery and fantasy techniques in psychotherapy. In S. L. Singer & K. S. Pope (Eds.), *The power of human imagination.* New York: Plenum.

Singer, J. L. (1979). Imagery and affect in psychotherapy: Elaborating private scripts and generating contexts. In A. A. Sheikh & J. T. Shaffer (Eds.), *The potential of fantasy and imagination,* New York: Random House.

Stark, D. W. (Ed.) (1861). *The De Anima of Aristotle.* London: W. Browne.

Tower, R. B., & Singer, J. L. (1981). The measurement of imagery: How can it be clinically useful? In P. C. Kendall & S. Holland (Eds.), *Cognitive behavioral interventions: Assessment methods.* New York: Academic Press.

Tuke, D. H. (1872). *Illustrations of the influence of the mind upon the body in health and disease, designed to elucidate the action of imagination.* London: J. A. Churchill.

Vaughan, W. (1612). *Approved directions for health.* London: T. S. for Roger Jackson.

Von Neumann, J. (1966). *Theory of self-reproducing automats.* Urbana: University of Illinois Press.

Watkins, M. M. (1976). *Waking dreams.* New York: Harper.

Watson, J. B. (1930). *Behaviorism.* New York: W. W. Norton.

Weimer, W. B. (1976a). Manifestations of mind: Some conceptual and empirical issues. In G. Globus (Ed.), *Consciousness and the brain,* New York: Plenum.

Weimer, W. B. (1976b). *Structural analysis and the future of psychology.* New York: Erlbaum.

Wigner, E. P. (1967). *Symmetries and reflections.* Bloomington, Indiana: Indiana University Press.

Wolf, A. A. (1935). *History of science, technology and philosophy in the sixteenth and seventeenth centuries.* London: Allen and Irwin.

Wolpe, J. (1974). *The practice of behavior therapy.* Elmsford, New York: Pergamon Press.

Wright, T. (1604) (1971). *The passions of the minde in general.* Urbana: University of Illinois Press.

Yaremko, R. M., & Butler, M. C. (1975). Imaginal experience and attenuation of the galvanic skin response to shock. *Bulletin of the Psychonomic Society, 5,* 317-318.

# CHAPTER 2
# Relaxing Images in Hypnobehavioral Therapy*

## W. S. KROGER
## AND W. D. FEZLER

The following is devoted to a description of some of the relaxing images used in hypnobehavioral therapy. These images are flexible and may be deleted or tailored to the individual needs of a patient. They do, however, provide a useful reference and core for the discussion of the hypnobehavioral model. The relaxing image is usually given after the initial standard induction and before any posthypnotic or autohypnotic suggestions are utilized. They are also given before any situations relating specifically to the presenting problems.

A primary purpose of the following standardized images is to produce relaxation and deepen the hypnosis so that conditioning will be stronger and more rapid. Since nearly all presenting problems are anxiety-mediated, anxiety reduction plays an important part in therapy for any condition. Anxiety manifests itself in different ways in different people: one individual may react to tension by smoking too much while another may develop an ulcer. In any event, the bulk of the problem behaviors to be discussed are the product of a person's faculty in coping with anxiety in his life.

The images are presented in order of increasing complexity. Each image serves to further deepen the hypnosis and associated relaxation. The reader should not be misled to believe that it is necessary to use all the images described herein to treat a patient. It is explained to the patient that the process of hypnotherapy is an infinite system. The hypnotic depth will be developed until sufficient anxiety reduction is achieved to alleviate the presenting problem. We have had patients who were successfully treated after only one image. On the other hand, we have had a few patients on whom we used as many as eighty different images in the course of their treatment. However, with 95 percent of our patients we have used less than twenty-five images. Also, a few would not accept this method. In those who refused, the reason was that the therapy was contrary to the patient's expectations. If, after an explanation of the rationale for the use of imagery, the patient was still unwilling to accept it as a treatment modality, we did not use imagery in the therapy. In these cases

*Reprinted with permission from Kroger, W., & Fezler, W. D. (1976). *Hypnosis and behavior modification: Imagery conditioning.* Philadelphia: J. B. Lippincott.

we relied solely on a standard hypnotic induction, posthypnotic suggestions related directly to the problem, and behavioral techniques (to be described).

While the images are usually given in sequence (1 each session or possibly 2, depending on how good a hypnotic subject the patient is), some of the standardized images are especially suited for the specific problems and are delineated in the appropriate clinical chapters. These may be given after Image I, before going on in the sequence. The patient should have some experience practicing pleasant hypnotic imagery of a more general nature to develop a facility for sensory recall before working on images. All imagery to be used in covert behavioral procedures will be stronger and more effective if the subject first practices Image I, or one of that nature. This develops his ability to vividly experience an image in all five sense modalities. The stronger the patient's hypnotic imagery, the greater will be the generalization to reality.

These images are to be used in conjunction with the behavioral and hypnotic techniques described in this book. We are not presenting imagery as a panacea but merely as an adjunctive method for decreasing anxiety, and developing self-control and hypnotic concentration.

## IMAGE I

The first image is usually given in the second session after the subject has had one week to practice self-hypnosis. Its focus is on the recall of five basic senses emphasizing tactile feelings of warmth and cold, visual colors, the basic taste and smell of salt, and rhythmic sound. The therapist paints the picture as follows:

### Beach Scene

You are walking along the beach; it is mid-July. It is very, very warm. It is five o'clock in the afternoon. The sun has not yet begun to set but it is getting low on the horizon. The sun is a golden blazing yellow, the sky a brilliant blue, the sand a dazzling glistening white in the sunlight. Feel the cold, wet, firm, hard-packed sand beneath your feet . . . . Taste and smell the salt in the air. There is a residue of salt deposited on your lips from the ocean spray. You can taste it if you lick your lips. Hear the beating of the waves, the rhythmic lapping to and fro, back and forth of the water against the shore. Hear the far-off cry of a distant gull as you continue to walk. . . .

Suddenly you come to a sand dune, a mound of pure white sand. . . . Covering the mound are bright yellow buttercups, deep pink moss roses. You sit down on its crest and look out to sea. The sea is like a mirror of silver reflecting the sun's rays, a mass of pure white light, and you are gazing intently into this light. As you continue to stare into the sun's reflection off the water, you begin to see flecks of violet, darting spots of purple intermingled with the silver. Everywhere there is silver and violet. There is a violet line along the horizon . . . a violet halo around the flowers. Now the sun is beginning to set. With each movement, with each motion of the sun into the sea you become deeper and deeper relaxed. [It is important to pair physical sensations such as breathing with elements in the image so that the imaginal elements will cue relaxation.] The sky is turning crimson, scarlet, pink, amber, gold, orange as the sun sets . . . you are engulfed in a deep purple twilight, a velvety blue haze . . . you look up to the night sky. It is a brilliant starry night. The beating of the waves, the smell and taste of the salt, the sea, the sky, . . . and you feel yourself carried upward and outward into space, one with the universe . . . I am now going to count to 3. At the count of 3, you will open your eyes, you will feel completely refreshed, totally relaxed. 1, 2, 3. [The subject is always brought out of hypnosis by reciting the above three lines.]

The last two lines in this image should produce a feeling of detachment and often dissociation.

## IMAGE II

Once again emphasis is on tactile feelings of warmth and cold. Patients usually experience the most difficulty with recall of taste and smell. Visual and auditory recall are easiest, and tactile recall intermediary.

### Mountain Cabin Scene

You are in a cabin in the mountains. It is midnight. It is the dead of winter. Outside the wind is howling. Inside you are sitting in front of a fireplace, gazing fixedly into the embers, staring intently into the coals. Feel the warmth of the flames against your body, feel the heat from the fire against your skin. There is a prickling almost itching sensation in your thighs; the heat on the front of your body is so intense. Hear the crackling of the logs as the sap hits the fire. Smell the smoke from the burning pine logs. See the flickering shadows on the wall. The only source of light comes from the fire. The rest of the cabin is in darkness.

Now you get up. You walk over to the window. There is a lace-like pattern of frost on the window pane. You put your warm fingertips to the cold, hard glass of the windowpane. Feel the heat from your fingers melt the frost. You look outside. The moon is full and silver, the snow a dazzling, sparkling white in the moonlight. There are tall, dark green fir trees casting deep purple shadows across the snowy whiteness. You are going to open the window. Feel it give way against the pressure of your hand. It opens. You take a big deep breath of cool, clean, crisp, fresh, pure mountain air. [The subject should actually take a deep breath at this point and the therapist takes a big breath while recounting it.] Your entire rib cage collapses in total, utter relaxation. It feels so good to breathe. Smell the pine!

Now you close the window. You walk to the fire. Feel its warmth. You lie down beside the fire on a bearskin rug. A drowsy feeling is coming over you. The howling of the wind, the warmth from the fire, the smell of the smoke, the crackling of the logs . . . all those sights and sounds and smells getting very, very far away . . . as you drift . . . and float and dream in that cabin that winter night. [The word "very" is often said in rhythm with the subject's inhalations and exhalations.]

## IMAGE III

The main emphasis in this scene is recall of taste and smell. Patients are told that if they are having difficulty recalling taste and smell they may use lemons, oranges, and roses as props. When in the scene they bite into the orange or lemon or smell the rose, they should do likewise in reality. Pairing the actual taste and smell of lemons and oranges or the smell of the rose with the imagery potentiates the entire scene.

### Garden Scene

You are in the middle of a vast garden. It is mid-summer. The air is warm and balmy. The garden stretches for miles and miles. You are walking down a path on either side of which are orange trees. The moon is full and yellow. The orange trees are deep green with brilliant orange oranges, phosphorescent in the moonlight. There are oranges on the ground. They are very ripe. The smell of orange is heavy in the air. You reach up. You pick an orange from the branch. Bite into the orange . . . the sweet orange juice squirts into your mouth, running down your throat and into your stomach. Taste the orange. Now you continue walking until you come to a place where two paths cross . . . you turn right, walking down a path on either side of which are lemon trees, bright yellow in the moonlight. You pick a lemon. Feel the rough outer texture of the lemon peel. You peel the lemon. Smell the lemony fragrance of the lemon rind. You sink your teeth into the lemon. The sour lemon juice squirts into your mouth. Taste the lemon. The saliva flows. Your mouth puckers as you swallow the sour lemon juice. You continue walking, the taste and smell of lemon lingering with you.

Suddenly before you is a long, descending, white marble staircase. Dazzling white in the moonlight. You begin to descend the stairs. With every step downward you become deeper and deeper relaxed. When you reach the base of the stairs you will be in a profound state of relaxation . . . you are now standing at the base of the stairs. In front of you is a huge marble swimming pool. All around the pool are red and white and yellow roses, velvety soft in the moonlight, covered with dew. The smell of roses is heavy in the air. You take off your clothes. You glide into the pool. The pool is filled with billions of rose petals. You float on your back in the rose water looking up at the stars, buoyant in the water.

Now you get out of the water. You stand up. The cool night air touches your wet body. It sends chills down your spine. You are shivering. Goose flesh appears. Suddenly you smell smoke. You look to the direction from which the smell is coming. There is a wooded area on the other side of the pool. You walk over toward the forest, the smell of smoke growing ever stronger in intensity as you approach the wooded area. You walk into the forest. There before you is a blazing bonfire of burning leaves. It smells like fall, it smells like autumn. You lie down beside the fire in a bed of dry leaves. The smell of wet earth beneath you, the smell of burning leaves beside you, the starry sky above you; you drift, you float, you dream of the mid-summer's night.

### IMAGE IV

In this image, the patient is taken back to the cabin scene with some deletions and embellishments in order to develop glove anesthesia, a sensory hallucination resulting in numbness of the hand from the fingers to the wrist. From the beginning of hypnotherapy the subject has been learning autonomic control of vasoconstriction.

A concentration of blood in a given area produces congestion and warmth, and its absence produces numbness and chill. Suggestions for the production of numbness were given in the first hypnotic session, and by now the subject should be fairly adept at creating a feeling of numbness at least in the extremities. Therefore it is good that the subject has already had some experience with this image as the procedure for glove anesthesia requires his undivided attention.

The ability to produce glove anesthesia has far-ranging therapeutic benefits and the patient should be given encouragement during the training states. It should be emphasized that he is not expected to master it in one week even though he will be given a new image the next time. The production of glove anesthesia in Image IV is to be worked on periodically throughout treatment. The other images are used only for the week they are given. An image can fade out, losing its vividness after repeated usage. Patients need a continual supply of new fantasy material. Glove anesthesia has been mentioned in the chapter on hypnotic techniques. It has no analogue in behavior modification techniques but lends itself admirably to behavior therapy. It is literally possible to transcend the pain threshold by using glove anesthesia. Any technique that permits this is certainly worthy of study.

Our world comprises two sets of stimuli, exteroceptive—those impinging on us from without in the external world—and interoceptive—those coming to us from inside our bodies. Glove anesthesia produces control over both exteroceptive and interoceptive tactile stimulation. We can receive inputs or we can choose not to receive them. Pain is a danger signal and should be responded to by seeing a physician. Once the reason for the discomfort is known and dealt with, however, the subject can decide whether or not he wants to continue to receive the signal. It is theoretically possible to control all sensory inputs, not only tactile ones.

Much research in perceptual defense shows that an individual will see what he wants to see. For example, when a list of words containing a taboo or "dirty" word is tachistoscopically presented for a fraction of a second many subjects do not recall this particular word. They just did not see it. Audio defense is also evident; many of us hear only what we want to. It is well known that when attention is directed to one thing, we become oblivious to sounds around us. For example, someone can speak to us while we are reading and we will not even hear them. We have shut out extraneous stimuli; since we are not attending to them, we are not receiving them. Such selective deafness is an everyday phenomenological response seen at both nonhypnotic and hypnotic levels of awareness.

Although we know of no research of olfactory defense or taste defense, such phenomena exist. We are reminded of a female patient who came with the presenting problem that her husband demanded she frequently perform fellatio on him. The taste made her ill. She was afraid that if she did not become more receptive and proficient in the act, he would leave her. Through sensory recall and appropriate pairing and conditioning, she was able to imagine the taste of a sloe gin fizz during fellatio. Hypnotic conditioning trials consisted of recalling the smell and taste of a sloe gin fizz in conjunction with the image of sexual intercourse with her husband. Not only was she able to shut out smells and tastes associated with fellatio, she was also able to revive any pleasant smell or taste she desired when engaging in this act. She had gone one step further from shutting out stimuli to actually creating her own gestalt.

She combined her current inputs on the visual, auditory, and tactile modalities (exteroceptive stimuli) with a recall of the desired olfactory and gustatory modalities (interoceptive stimuli). Once a sensation has been experienced, it is on tap forever. Human organisms can take these experiences and recall them in any combination and at any rate (time distortion) they wish; they can shut out or control the rate and degree of reception of all external stimuli. They can in fact make their own world.

## Mountain Cabin Scene with Glove Anesthesia

You are in a cabin in the mountains. It is midnight. Outside the wind is howling. Inside you are sitting in front of a fireplace, staring into the embers, gazing fixedly into the coals. Feel the heat from the fire. Feel the warmth from the flames against your skin. There is a prickling, almost itching sensation in your thighs; the heat on the front of your body is so intense. See the flickering shadows on the wall. Hear the crackling of the pine logs as the sap hits the fire. Smell the smoke from the burning pine logs. The only source of light comes from the fire; the rest of the cabin is in darkness.

Now you get up. You are going to go outside. You bundle up. You put on a coat, gloves, cap, boots. You go to the door. Feel the door give way against the pressure of your hand. You are outside in the cold winter air! Take a big deep breath of cool, fresh, pure, mountain air. Smell the pine. It feels so good to breathe! Your entire rib cage collapses in total, utter relaxation. The door closes behind you. The moon is full and silvery. It is 20 degrees below zero, bitter cold. You can see your breath in white puffs. You begin walking down a path on either side of which are tall deep green pine trees laden with snow. The snow is knee deep. Everything has a bluish tinge to it; even the snow looks blue. Ten minutes pass, twenty minutes, thirty minutes. You stop, take the glove off your right hand and thrust your warm hand into the snow making a fist compressing the snow into an ice ball in the palm of you hand . . . . You feel a numb, wooden, leathery-like sensation beginning in your right palm, spreading through your hand. When you feel this sensation I want you to place your right hand upon your right cheek. [The subject does as directed.] Good, now let all that numbness drain from your hand into your cheek. Your cheek is becoming numb, leathery, wooden, just as if Novacaine had been injected into it. Your hand is becoming warm, alive; the blood is rushing back into it. When all the numbness has drained from your hand into your cheek, place your hand once again at your side. [The subject does as directed.] Now once again place your hand on your cheek and let all the numbness in your cheek drain back into your hand. Your hand is becoming numb, leathery, woodenlike, just like a block of wood with nails. Your cheek is becoming hot, flushed, the blood is rushing to the surface of the skin in your cheek. When all that numbness has drained from your cheek back into your hand once again place your hand at your side. [The subject does so.]

Good! Now place the glove back on your right hand. You turn around and begin tracing your footsteps back to the cabin. Ten minutes pass, twenty minutes, thirty minutes. You are back to the cabin. You go inside. You take off your outer wraps and walk over to the fire. Hold your hands over the fire. Feel the warmth spreading throughout your body. [This suggestion eliminates the numbness and returns the hand to its normal condition.] You lie down beside the fire on a bearskin rug. The warmth of the fire, the smell of the pine smoke, the crackling of the logs, the howling outside of the wind, all these sights, and smells and sounds seem very, very far away as you drift further and further away.

## IMAGE V

The scene is the subject's first exposure to recall of external pressure. It should be noted that there are many sensations in each scene that enhance the potential for sensory recall. The authors remark only on things of special interest in each scene.

### Desert Scene

Everything is very, very dark. It is pitch black. It is warm. You are barefoot. Beneath your feet you can feel coarse, cracked clay. The ground is perfectly flat. Now it is beginning to get light. Every breath you take, the sky gets bluer and bluer. Every breath you take, it gets warmer and warmer. You now see that there is nothing but sunbaked clay as far as the eye can see. Everything is perfectly flat. There are no mountains, no hills, no vegetation . . . nothing but clay to the horizon line, to the vanishing point. It is like a surrealistic landscape. It is getting warmer and warmer, hotter and hotter, 80 degrees, 90 degrees, 100 degrees, 110 degrees. Beads of perspiration are running down your back, down your arm pits. Your hair is matted to your forehead. Clothes are clinging and sticking to your body. Eyes are stinging from the salt in your perspiration. You are wringing wet with sweat. Throat is getting parched . . . lips are dry . . . tongue is thickening. You are having difficulty swallowing.

Suddenly before you is a large, freshwater sea . . . a vast expanse of cool, fresh, pure water. You take off your clothes. You glide into the water. It is crystal clear. You drink, quenching your thirst. You float on your back in the water gazing up at the blue desert sky. Night falls. You get out of the water. The cool night air touches your wet body. It sends chills down your spine. You are shivering. Goose flesh appears. You wade to shore. Your feet touch the sand, which is still warm from the day, still retaining the heat from the sun. You lie down. A gentle breeze begins to cover you with a warm blanket of sand, inch by inch, layer by layer . . . feel the ever increasing pressure as the shifting sand covers you layer by layer. You are protected in a warm cocoon, safe, secure, at peace with the world, tranquil under the desert stars.

## IMAGE VI

Here is an example of how we produce time distortion. The specific post-hypnotic suggestion for time expansion is always given before the image. This scene also often produces a feeling of detachment and altered perspective. Kines-thetic sense is also greatly altered. The rationale for this particular image is that in five minutes of actual time (the approximate time it takes to describe this scene) an eternity of imaginal time elapses. If the scene is at all real to the subject, it will seem as if more than five minutes had lapsed. It is not uncommon to report a threefold expansion of time on the first session although the suggestion is usually that time will expand tenfold.

### Space Scene

One minute of actual time will seem like ten minutes to you. Time will go by very, very slowly. It will seem like an eternity. In less than ten minutes you can watch an entire motion picture again and actually see it better than when you first saw it.

You are lying on your back on a large round bed in a gigantic circular, black marble room. It is midnight. You are looking up at the ceiling, which is a glass dome, a clear, transparent bubble. The night is clear. The sky is filled with stars. You are gazing at the heavens.

Suddenly you notice that the room is beginning to turn. Ever so slightly at first, gradually picking up momentum. It is revolving like a turntable on a record player. Going round, and round, and round, and round, and round [the therapist continues saying this faster and faster] and the room is spinning. You are hurled upward and outward off the bed. The dome opens and you shoot out into space, traveling at an incredible rate of speed, going faster than the speed of light, a dizzy sensation in the pit of your stomach. Flashes of light streak into view as you pass other planets, other solar systems, other galaxies, hurling wildly through space.

Now you are beginning to fall. You are falling back to the point from which you came. Falling through space. You are now back to your source, but there is no bed, there is no room, there is no Earth. The Earth has long ceased to exist. You have gone billions of Earth years. You are suspended in space, in a vacuum. No sound, no touch, no smell . . . suspended animation.

### IMAGE VII

. In the second scene for time expansion, the amount of imaginal time passing is a morning. This is certainly less than an eternity and will probably be easier for the subject to identify with. Once again, if the scene is real for the subject, it will seem as if more than the actual five minutes taken to describe the scene had lapsed.

### Farm Scene

You are in a very warm, snug, comfortable bed. It is very early morning. The covers feel so good. You are in a farmhouse in Kansas. It is late August. You hear a rooster crow. It is 5:30 in the morning. You drift off back to sleep. Suddenly you are awakened by the shrill sound of an alarm clock.

It is 6:00 in the morning. You get out of bed and go to the window. The sun is just beginning to rise. The sky is turning scarlet, crimson, gold, orange, amber. Every breath you take the sky gets bluer and bluer. You go into the kitchen. There on a blue platter is a sizzling stack of smoked bacon, hot from the frying pan. Next to it on a white platter are piping hot squares of corn bread covered with rich melted butter. You sink your teeth into the bacon; feel it crunch between your teeth. Taste the smoky flavor. Now you eat the corn bread, feel the coarse texture of the bread and creamy taste of the butter. It is 6:30 in the morning.

You go out onto the porch. You sit down in a rocking chair and rock back and forth, to and fro, listening to the creaking of the porch boards beneath the weight of the rocker. You look out over the farm yard. You see the mud yard with ruts from the tractor, a white henhouse, a red barn, a garden with cucumbers, tomatoes, lettuce, squash, pumpkins, radishes, peas, and carrots, a ditch, a gravel road, bright green corn field, brilliant blue sky. Suddenly off to your left you hear the voices of children. You turn your head and see three boys, age eight, hurrying off to school. It is five minutes to nine and they are late. They rush down the gravel road, up the hill to your right, and disappear into a white schoolhouse. You continue rocking. You are getting hungry again. It is now 10 o'clock. You go back into the kitchen. There on the table is a blue platter with a piping hot stack of blueberry muffins fresh from the oven. You sink your teeth into a muffin. The ripe blueberries burst in your mouth. Taste the sweet blueberry juice. Taste the nutty flavor of the muffin.

You go back out onto the porch and continue to rock. Now you walk down the steps, across the farm yard, down the ditch, over the gravel road and into the corn field. Feel the dry corn rustle against your body. Now you come out into a field of sunflowers. Huge yellow flowers against the bright blue sky with large round brown centers. Next you find yourself in a field of clover. It smells like honey. Butterflies are darting back and forth among the clover blossoms. You lie down in the clover, the smell of wet earth beneath you, the smell of honey around you. You look at a wisp of a cloud in the blue sky. The sun is straight above you. It is high noon. A lazy, hazy August day. You drift, you float, you doze, in the summer sun, not a care in the world.

### IMAGE VIII

This scene is the subject's first real taste of dissociation. Many persons report that they can actually feel themselves shrinking during this image. There is a euphoric sense of timelessness akin to free floating. Time expansion has also been reported by patients from this scene. One patient exclaimed that the shrinking period seemed to last for an hour (actually 30 seconds); she felt herself getting large again during the therapist's counting to three to end the scene, and this time period seemed like another hour.

### Jungle Scene

It is very warm, very humid, very close. It is dark. You are in a sleeping bag. You can hear insects humming. Now it is beginning to get light. You sit up. All around you is dense tropical foliage. There are giant ferns and lilies. You are in the middle of a rain forest, a jungle. You hear monkeys chattering, birds cawing. There is steam rising off the jungle floor. It is early morning. Sunlight is filtering through the canopy of leaves above you, casting a lacelike pattern of light on the jungle floor. You get up. You begin making your way through the dense undergrowth cutting your way through with a machete. The ground is spongelike. It feels like steam heat, like a sauna bath. Perspiration is running down your armpits, the small of your back. Your clothing is clinging to your skin, soaked in sweat. Hair is matted to your forehead, blurring your vision. You continue cutting, making your way forward.

Suddenly you come to a clearing, to a grotto, a mineral hot spring. The grotto is composed of a white chalklike substance resembling coral, which crunches under the weight of your feet. The strong smell of sulfur is in the air. Interspersed in this white chalky substance are pools of brilliant aqua-blue mineral water. You walk over to one of these pools. You take off your clothes. You glide into the warm mineral water. It is like a whirlpool. Your muscles become soft and pliant. Now you notice a curious thing. The pool is getting larger. First the size of a pond, then a baseball field, then a small lake. You look up and see that the trees are miles high into the sky. You realize that the pool has not been getting larger, you have been getting smaller. You are shrinking. Getting smaller and smaller. A large orange Monarch butterfly lights beside you. You crawl onto his back. He soars high up into the blue sky, dipping and soaring like a roller coaster. Feel that sinking feeling in the pit of your stomach. And you continue to shrink, until finally there is nothing left at all.

This is a good technique for achieving hypnotic dissociation. The reader should not be perturbed by such verbalizations, as we have never seen the slightest danger from using this image.

## IMAGE IX

The purpose of this image is threefold. First of all, it is designed to enhance the intensification of recall of temperature. Second, it is the beginning of a series of images constructed to start the subject in recalling feeling components that concentrate on combinations of sensation. All experiences are comprised of combinations of given sensations. When all the sensations comprising a past experience can be recalled, the experience is totally revivified. For example, the sensation of the erection constitutes several feeling components. The two primary ones are warmth and congestion or pressure. By recalling the sensations of warmth and pressure in the genital area, an erection can be produced. Fortunately, most males suffering from impotence have experienced warmth and pressure in the genital area or an erection, and they work at merely recalling a given experience when they had an erection. Image IX concentrates on the combinations of the feeling components of cold-wet, hot-dry, hot-wet, and cold-dry, in that order.

Sometimes, however, the sensation we wish to produce has never occurred in the area we now wish to experience it in. We then have to recall the sensation in an area where we have felt it before and transfer it to the desired area. The transfer of numbness or glove anesthesia has already been described in relation to Image IV. We have all experienced anesthesia in some parts of our body. Legs and feet often "go to sleep" or become numb when we cut off the circulation, and numbness in the cheeks from the dentist's Novacaine is a common experience. Numbness in an area like the stomach, for example, is not as common and many people may never have experienced this sensation, or lack of sensation, in the stomach area. Anesthesia in the stomach has several uses including calming stomach contractions and quelling hunger pangs for weight control. If the subject has never experienced a numb stomach, he must first recall numbness in an area where he has experienced it, such as the hand, and then transfer it to the stomach area. It is important that the subject work on transferring all the sensations he is learning to recall so that he will be adept in this procedure when the time comes to utilize it.

This brings us then to the third function of Image IX, focus on the transfer of heat. The same procedure is used as was utilized in the transfer of numbness. Heat is first felt in the hand, then transferred to the cheek, and transferred back to the hand. Whenever a sensation is induced, it is always necessary to give a suggestion later that the affected area will return to its normal state. Sometimes this can be incorporated directly into the image, as in the mountain cabin scene when the subject is told at the end of the scene to hold his hands over the fire and feel the warmth running through them. The recall of warmth in the hands necessitates the alleviation of the numbness in that area without giving suggestion such as, "The numbness will now leave your hands and they will return to their normal state."

The ability to transfer heat has special import in cases of sexual inadequacy. While most impotent males have experienced an erection and can recall one, many females have never experienced a climax. Primary components of the orgasm are heat, congestion and sudden release of tension. The non-orgasmic female must recall these feeling components in areas of her body where she has experienced them and combine them by transferring them to the genital area. The male can produce an erection by transferring heat and pressure to the genital area. Sexually arousing imagery should be used in conjunction with this physical transfer. The sensory recall of given feeling components, their transfer and combination is the use of Skinner's method of successive approximations. It is truly shaping behavior. The orgasm and the erection thus can be shaped by the method of successive approximations. Any feeling or experience can be shaped by the right recall and combination of components.

### Pool Scene

You are sitting on a white ice-cream chair beside a table out of the center of which is a yellow and blue striped umbrella. It is mid-August. It is very, very hot—95 degrees. Next to you is a large swimming pool and sunken garden. All around the pool are brilliantly colored red hibiscus and coconut palms with monkeys chattering in them. You can also see multicolored parrots in the palms with orange, chartreuse, and purple plumage. On the far side of the pool are Arabian night-like cabanas of varicolored stripes. In front of you on the table is a cold glass of lemonade. Moisture has condensed in beads running down the cold slippery surface of the glass. You pick up the wet, cold glass in your warm right hand. You are wearing nothing but a white bathing suit. You stand up and walk toward the pool. Your bare feet touch the dry, hot cement of the pool area. You run to the edge of the pool where water has been splashed. The wet cement is still hot but not as hot as where it is dry. You stand there on the hot, wet cement in the blazing sun holding the lemonade. You put the glass to your lips. Hear the ice cubes clatter against the glass. Feel the ice cold liquid touch your lips, go down your throat and into your stomach. Feel the cold radiate out from the center of your body. Feel the contrast of the hot sun on the outside of your stomach against the cold on the inside of your stomach.

Now you go over and lie down on a chaise longue. You are getting hotter and hotter, thirstier and thirstier. You see a Coke machine on the other side of the pool. You get up and walk over to the machine. You press your warm, moist body against the cold, dry metal of the Coke machine. You press your cheeks, your stomach, your thighs against the machine. It takes your breath away. Now you put the money into the machine. The Coke is dispensed. Feel the carbonation, the bubbles against your nose as you drink the Coke. Taste it. You walk back over to the edge of the pool. You squat down. You place your right hand flat on the hot, wet cement. When you feel the heat in your hand, I want you to place your right hand against your right cheek. [The subject does as directed.] Good. Now let all that heat drain from your hand into your cheek. Your cheek is becoming warm, flushed, your hand is becoming cool. When all the heat has drained from your hand into your cheek, place your hand once again at your side. [The subject does so.] Now, once again place your right hand upon your right cheek. Let all the heat in your cheek drain back into your hand. Your hand is becoming warm, hot, your cheek is becoming cool, as if a gentle evening breeze were glowing over it. When all the heat has drained from your cheek back into your hand, once again place your hand at your side. [The subject does as directed.] Now, you stand up. You walk over to a grove of palms. You sit down in the shade. A cool breeze blows through the grove. Hear the wind rustling through the palm leaves. It lulls you into a dreamy, drowsy state. You feel limp all over as you drift away.

## IMAGE X

Extreme changes in temperature are experienced during this scene. This is the first scene in which combinations of feelings are transferred. The combinations of components to be transferred are hot-dry and hot-wet. No particular scenes for transfer of cold have been devised, as the sensation of cold is usually recalled in conjunction with the transfer of numbness in Image IV due to the nature of the scene (that is, thrusting one's hand in snow to produce numbness).

### Arctic Scene

It is very, very cold. It is 30 degrees below zero. All you can see is bright blue and stark white. There are masses of white snow and mountains of glistening ice. You are at the polar ice cap, you are at the North Pole. The sky is vivid blue, the sun a cold, pale yellow. You are making your way through the snow. You see the mouth of a cavern. All around the mouth are long, slender icicles sparkling in the sun light. You walk up to the cavern, you take the glove off your right hand, you grasp an icicle. The heat from your hand begins to melt the ice. You run your hand up and down the cold, wet surface of the icicle. Put your glove back on. Now you walk into the cave. In the center of the cave is a large pool of ice cold water, dark and deep. You take a tin cup from a knapsack on your back. You scoop up the water, holding the cup between your hands, you bring the cold, dry metal to your lips. The cold liquid pours down your throat and into your stomach. Feel the cold radiating from the center of your body.

Now you walk to the mouth of the cave. Your footsteps resound among the cavern walls. You stand looking at the white snow. Suddenly above, you hear a shrill mechanical sound. You look up and see a helicopter. A wind is created from the motion of the rotors. It lands. You walk over to the helicopter. You take off the glove from your right hand. You place your hand on the hot, dry metal of the copter where the engine is. When you feel that dry heat in your hand I want you to place your right hand upon your right cheek. [The subject does as instructed.] Now let the dry heat in your right hand drain into your cheek. Your cheek is becoming hot and flushed, the blood is running to the surface of the skin. It feels as if hot air is blowing against it. Your hand is becoming cold. When all the heat has drained from your hand into your cheek, once again place your hand at your side. [The subject does so.] Good. Now once again place your right hand upon your right cheek. Let the dry warmth in your cheek drain back into your hand. When all that warmth has drained back into your hand, once again place your hand at your side. Your hand is becoming hot and dry, your cheek is becoming cool. [The subject places his hand at his side.] Good.

You get into the helicopter. You fasten your seat belt. Feel the pressure around your midsection. The copter begins to ascend. You are surrounded by a silver mist as you continue to go higher and higher. You look at the altitude gauge. You are now 5,000 feet above sea level. When you go back down to 2,000 feet above sea level, you will land. In front of you on a tray is a sizzling T-bone steak and a bowl of crisp green salad. You begin eating the steak. It tastes delicious. Now you eat the salad. You keep eating and eating and your stomach begins to distend. Notice the contrast between the pressure on the inside of your stomach from the food and the pressure on the outside of your stomach from the seat belt.

Now the copter is beginning to descend. Feel that sinking feeling in the pit of your stomach . . . 5,000 feet, 4,000 feet, 3,000 feet, 2,000 feet, 1,000 feet. This is strange. You were to land at 2,000 feet above sea level, but the copter continues to descend. As the plane goes lower and lower it gets hotter and hotter inside the compartment . . . 1,000 feet, 80 degrees above zero, sea level, 90 degrees above zero, –1,000 feet, 100 degrees above zero, –2,000 feet, 110 degrees above zero. At 3,000 feet below sea level the copter lands. Beads of perspiration are running down your forehead and your armpits. Clothes are clinging to your body. The inside of the compartment is steamed up. Hair is matted to your forehead. It is very stuffy. You open the door. You get out. There before you is the world as it existed millions of years ago, a primeval forest. There are giant redwoods, colossal ferns—thick jungle with gigantic, gnarled trees. You walk over to a river of boiling water. You hold your hand above it. Feel the hot, wet steam collecting on the palm of your right hand. When you feel this wet heat on your right hand, place your right hand upon your right cheek and let that wet heat drain into your cheek. [The subject does as directed.] The cheek is getting wet and hot and sweaty, the hand is cool as if being held in front of a fan. When all the wet heat has drained from your hand into your cheek, once again place your hand at your side. [The subject does so.] Now once again place your right hand upon your right cheek and let the wet heat in your cheek drain back into your hand. When all the wet heat in your cheek has drained back into your hand, once again place your hand at your side. Your cheek is becoming cool and dry, your hand is moist and hot as if being held over a pressure cooker. [The subject places his hand again at his side.] Good. Now you lie down beside the river. The smell of wet earth beneath you, you drift in a world as it existed millions of years ago . . . drifting and floating . . . and dreaming. . . .

*     *     *

*Editor's Note:* Drs. W. S. Kroger and W. D. Fezler have developed numerous other imagery exercises for which the reader is referred to their book (*Hypnosis and Behavior Modification: Imagery Conditioning*), Philadelphia: J. B. Lippincott, 1976). The preceding exercises have been reproduced here with the permission of the publisher.

# CHAPTER 3
# Visualization Techniques and Altered States of Consciousness

## ERROL R. KORN

Imagery has played a significant role in the development of the human species, both ontogenetically and phylogenetically. It has been implied that human beings thought in images long before the development of languages. Thoughts and ideas are encoded in images and language was developed in response to the human need to make those thoughts and ideas known to others. Words are merely symbols and do not have intrinsic meaning, whereas imagery itself or its more abstract manifestations, patterns, are the basis of brain function.

Although imagery has many functions, activities that take place whether or not people are aware of them, imagery also has uses, needs which are actively directed on a conscious level.

Imagery is successful in effecting changes even in our waking state. However, for it to be maximally successful requires a change in state of consciousness. I have called these states altered states of consciousness (ASC). ASC are elicited by numerous methods (Korn & Johnson, 1983). Techniques as varied as hypnotic induction, progressive relaxation, autogenic training, meditation, and others are all capable of eliciting a group of subjective and physiological experiences which characterize these ASC. The basic characteristics of ASC are mental and physical relaxation. These states are self-induced, inherently safe, and produce the physiologic changes of relaxation response, changes that are nature's own way of modulating the detrimental effects of the stress response.

For simplicity's sake, we have divided the useful types of imagery into three parameters. Images are either: 1) spontaneous or induced, 2) concrete or abstract, and 3) general or specific. The uses of these types of imagery will be explained later.

For personal and professional uses I suggest the participant first learn a method of inducing ASC (see below) and then fortify it with induced, concrete, general images. Once this has been practiced, learned, and perfected, end result imagery (the image of the result the individual wishes to obtain) and process imagery (the image of the process, or method, by which this end result can be obtained) can be added to the experiential session.

Basic guidelines for using imagery:

1. Practice and perfect ASC.
2. Use end result imagery first because it is usually more powerful and long lasting. Because it may take longer for end result imagery to be effective, for more urgent needs introduce process images.
3. Have confidence in the imaging process because the initial changes may be subtle and difficult to recognize.
4. Make a commitment to the process if you want the maximum benefits of the imagery techniques. This commitment means daily practice.
5. The creation of an image in all five senses is more successful than images in only one sense.
6. It is more important for you to be able to control the image than for the image to be vivid and life-like. The image is a sensory method by which we "program" the brain to affect the multiple changes required to bring the image or idea to fruition. The image should be dynamic rather than static.

## GENERAL RELAXATION

This is a visualization used to induce altered states of consciousness and should be modified according to the needs of the individual.

Move into as comfortable a position as you possibly can. The position can be a seated position with legs uncrossed and arms resting comfortably . . . or it can be lying down with feet uncrossed and toes pointed slightly to the sides . . . arms down comfortably by the sides. . . . Remove eyeglasses and loosen all constrictive clothing. . . . Now simply close your eyes. . . . This in itself is enough to produce a quietness . . . and rest . . . and relaxation. . . . Now to experience even further comfort and relaxation, begin to breathe deeply . . . and as you do pay particular attention to the sensations you experience as the air leaves the body. . . . Let yourself feel that with every breath you take out . . . you are breathing out tension . . . discomfort . . . stress and strain. . . . When you do that you can feel the muscles in the body relax . . . most prominently in the chest, but also in other muscles that are particularly tense . . . such as the shoulders . . . and neck . . . and back. . . . It is just as though as you exhale the air . . . you are exhaling with it all your troubles . . . all of your discomforts . . . and all of your anxieties. . . . You may hear noises and sounds in your environment . . . but you can use those to even deepen your state of relaxation. . . . In reality, when you breathe out you really are eliminating tension . . . discomfort . . . and stress. . . . Experience then what really does take place. . . . With the breath, we eliminate toxins and waste products. . . . The lungs are one of the most efficient eliminators of waste we have in the body. . . . So just let yourself feel that with every breath out you are becoming more comfortable. . . . With this process alone . . . you may be surprised . . . to find that you can eliminate almost all of the tension and discomfort . . . that you have accumulated. . . . However, if there are still residual areas of discomfort or tension . . . you can eliminate them in a progressive fashion. . . .

I'm going to ask you now to put your consciousness into your toes. . . . Now that may sound difficult to do, but realize that your consciousness doesn't have to be where most of us think it is, that is the head. . . . We only perceive our consciousness to be in our head because the brain, the most concentrated organ of consciousness, resides in the head. . . . You can place your consciousness anywhere in the body . . . you want to. . . . In fact, if you were to stub your toe . . . your consciousness would travel there instantly. . . . At this time, just place your awareness there . . . not because you have to . . . but because you want to. . . . With your consciousness in your toes, simply let yourself experience whatever it is you experience when you think of the word . . . relax. . . . It may be a heaviness . . . or a lightness . . . or a tingling . . . or numbness . . . or warmth . . . or coolness . . . or maybe something else . . . but even if you feel there has been no change, rest assured that at some level of your being there is a change . . . a lessening of tension in that toe. It may be that its change is too subtle for you to perceive at this time . . . but no matter whether you perceive it . . . or not, it still takes place.

Now, let the relaxation spread to the toes of the other foot . . . and whatever it is you feel, just let it spread upward through the feet . . . through the lower portions of the legs . . . and in the knees . . . as though you were standing knee-deep in a swirling . . . warm . . . relaxing Jacuzzi . . . . Allow the comfort and relaxation to spread upward into the thighs . . . and into the groin area. . . . Let it spread through the pelvis and buttocks . . . into the abdomen and back all the way to the waist . . . as though you are now standing waist-deep in that warm . . . comfortable Jacuzzi . . . allowing the entire body from waist down to feel relaxed . . . comfortable . . . loose . . . and limp . . . . In fact . . . you may be surprised . . . to find parts of your body feeling so relaxed . . . that you lose awareness for those parts. . . . That's perfectly all right, those parts are still there and functioning just as your lungs and heart functions when you are not aware of them. . . . You can regain the awareness whenever you wish to . . . but for now . . . let the comfort and relaxation spread upward into the upper abdomen and midback . . . and in the chest . . . both front and back, so that the breathing which has been . . . relaxed . . . to this point . . . becomes even more comfortable and relaxed. Now . . . let the soothing wave of relaxation go into the shoulders . . . an area in which we hold much of our tension. . . . Just let the shoulders . . . drop. . . . If you are sitting . . . feel them being pulled down by gravity and . . . if you are lying down . . . just feel your shoulders melting into the floor. . . . Let this looseness and warmth and comfort travel from the shoulders . . . all the way down the arms . . . past the elbows . . . into the wrists . . . hands . . . and fingers . . . feeling the arms just dangling without substance . . . loose and limp . . . like a rag doll. . . . Now allow the comfort to spread into another area in which we hold much tension . . . the . . . neck. . . . Feel the neck become loose . . . and limp . . . comfortable . . . and feel that comfort spread into another area in which we hold much tension . . . and rarely realize it . . . and feel how good it will feel to let the tension go from this area . . . so good you'll not only feel it in the local area . . . but also in the rest of the face . . . head . . . and neck. . . . The area I am referring to is the . . . jaw. . . . And feel how good it feels to just let . . . the jaw drop. . . . And now let the comfort spread into the face . . . around the eyes . . . letting the eyes become relaxed . . . the area of the temples . . . the forehead . . . and the top of the head . . . letting the entire head and face become very comfortable and relaxed. . . . At this point, the entire body should be loose . . . and limp . . . and relaxed. . . .

If there is any residual discomfort present . . . take a few more deep breaths . . . and concentrating on that area of discomfort . . . feel each breath remove more . . . and more of that discomfort until that part of the body is as comfortable and relaxed . . . as the remainder of the body. . . .

Remember that in this relaxed state, you are still totally . . . in control . . . of the situation. . . . If any emergency were to arise, you would be able to come out of the state . . . and respond to it . . . rapidly and efficiently. . . . If at any time you feel apprehensive . . . it is only necessary to open your eyes and you can emerge from this relaxed state . . . feeling calm and comfortable . . . alert and relaxed. . . . Remember, in this relaxed state you are still . . . fully in control. . . . At some level, your mind will perceive everything . . . but your mind is discriminating . . . and will choose only those things that are appropriate to your growth and development . . . only the things that you are able to tolerate . . . at the present time. . . .

Now begin to take a few deep breaths again . . . and become aware of what it feels like when you inhale. . . . Remember the importance of the substances that you take in with the breath. . . . We take in water . . . but we can survive several days without water. . . . However, we can only survive . . . a few minutes . . . without that which we take in through the breath. . . . So feel the energy coming back into the body . . . entering a body that is fully relaxed . . . and feel it not just in the lungs . . . but feel it spread from the lungs into . . . every single cell . . . of the body. . . . Feel the energy, and remember that you can feel energetic and vigorous . . . at the same time that you remain . . . comfortable and relaxed. . . . And as you feel the energy coming in, become more aware of the room that you are in . . . the time and place you are experiencing . . . and become more aware of your body . . . and especially any body parts that you may have lost awareness of . . . and whenever you are fully ready . . . you can open your eyes . . . feeling the benefits of all that you have just experienced.

## SAFE PLACE

The safe place is a general image used to attain the benefits of ASC in overcoming the detrimental effects of the stress response, realizing one's full potential, enhancing the creative process and promoting health and well being.

Think of the words peace . . . safety . . . comfort . . . and happiness . . . peace . . . comfort . . . and happiness. . . . Now . . . let your mind spontaneously take you to a place . . . that means as many of those things as possible to you. . . . It may be a place that you go to frequently . . . or one that you have visited only in the distant past . . . or maybe one that's totally imaginary. . . . But stay with the first place that comes to your mind. . . . If you find yourself going from place to place . . . those are tricks being played on you by the conscious part of your mind . . . the part of your mind that says that you can't do something or put judgments on things . . . or that leads you to an external rather than an internal experience. . . . The first place, . . . the one that appeared spontaneously . . . is the place to stay with because that place appeared spontaneously . . . is the place to stay with because that place appeared to you from deep down . . . inside . . . and is associated at some level of your being . . . with comfort . . . with relaxation . . . with peace . . . and with safety. . . .

Appreciate this scene with all of your senses. . . . See it or imagine it . . . as vividly as you can. . . . Hear the sounds . . . appreciate the aromas . . . touch and feel the environment . . . and objects therein . . . and appreciate the tastes. . . . Perceive above you . . . beneath you . . . and all around you . . . exploring in fine detail all of the ingredients of this scene . . . whether it be outside . . . or inside. . . .

As you practice this image . . . this place becomes associated in the important . . . deep . . . parts . . . of your mind . . . with the concepts of peace . . . safety . . . comfort . . . happiness . . . and relaxation. . . . Over time, the associations will strengthen . . . to the point where you could go to this place mentally . . . and dissociate completely from what was happening to you in waking consciousness. . . . You could feel relaxed . . . when you normally would be unrelaxed. . . . You could feel comfort . . . when usually you would feel pain, and later . . . as your practice increases . . . even in your waking state . . . simply thinking about this place . . . could institute all of the feelings of comfort . . . peace . . . safety . . . relaxation . . . and quietness . . . that you experience now. . . . In addition, you could practice this image by just thinking . . . of it . . . several times . . . a day in your usual waking state. . . . Remember, every time you practice . . . going to this safe place . . . it becomes imprinted in your mind . . . so that as time goes by it will become . . . easier . . . to achieve the benefits of this image. . . . Even more important is that each time the concepts and images become . . . more permanently fixed . . . in your mind, and when they are there, they become . . . active . . . creating changes in your life that are . . . beneficial . . . to you and leading toward a . . . realization of those changes. . . .

## PICTURE GALLERY

This is a three part image that allows the user to obtain a true perspective of his/her self-perception. The parts can be used together or separately. The third part of the image elicits an end result image that can be used for such varied goals as weight control, health maintenance, sports performance, and business performance. In fact, its use is virtually unlimited.

Imagine now that you are in a very large, private . . . comfortable . . . room of an art gallery. . . . All of the walls are empty except for one . . . and on that wall there are three empty frames of identical size and structure . . . placed side . . . by side . . . by side. . . . Approach the first frame . . . and as your attention focuses on that blank space . . . let there appear an image, an image of you . . . as you perceive yourself to be. . . . As you have previously learned . . . allow whatever image appears spontaneously . . . to be the one that you study. . . . And even if it is indistinct . . . just appreciate whatever of its essence that you are able to perceive. . . . And appreciate not only the visual image . . . but the feeling . . . that you get as you study it . . . and any other sensations that pervade your consciousness. . . . Study the image intensively and if you can, even . . . allow the image to move . . . so that you can see it from various sides and so that you can . . . appreciate . . . not just the static qualities but the . . . movement qualities as well. . . . All of these will add to the sense . . . of what this image really conveys. . . . And spend a few moments studying the image . . . in all its fine detail. . . .

Move your attention now to the second frame . . . and allow an image spontaneously to appear there . . . of you . . . as you really are. . . . Take a few moments now . . .

to fully perceive . . . this image . . . in the manner that you perceived image number 1. . . . And now compare . . . and contrast . . . images 1 and 2. . . . In most people there are differences . . . and these differences . . . represent the fact that our own . . . perceptions of ourselves . . . are very rarely the same . . . as we really are. . . . From time to time . . . by going back to these two images . . . you may be able to judge . . . progress . . . become more aware of yourself . . . as you really are.

Now become aware of the third frame . . . and allow spontaneously to appear there . . . an image of . . . how you wish yourself to be. . . . And as you previously have done with numbers 1 and 2 . . . allow yourself to . . . fully study and appreciate . . . the image of how you . . . wish to be. . . . Then compare and contrast the second and third images . . . how you really are with . . . how you wish yourself to be . . . and become keenly aware of the similarities . . . and differences. . . . By periodically . . . reevaluating . . . these images . . . you will be able to perceive . . . changes . . . that have been made. . . . You will be able . . . to appreciate . . . the progress. . . . The method of instituting these changes is by . . . identifying clearly . . . with the third image . . . not just by looking at it but by . . . feeling it . . . merging with it . . . actually feeling your consciousness . . . become that image. . . . Remember, the language of the brain is pictures . . . and by using this particular picture . . . the one in the third frame . . . you send the message to the brain . . . of what you desire. . . . The brain controls . . . all bodily functions . . . and has the ability to translate these desires . . . into the changes in habits . . . life style . . . activity . . . and so on . . . that will lead to the attainment . . . of your goal.

## PAIN OR ANXIETY AS OBJECT

This image is used to give a more concrete representation to abstract sensations such as pain, anxiety, discomfort, or disease. We can then work with the image to change the subjective feelings of discomfort represented by the symbol to positive sensations.

Most of us at one time or another . . . experience . . . sensations . . . that we would regard as unpleasant . . . such as pain, discomfort, tension, stress, and strain. . . . Just by relaxing and concentrating on the . . . exhalation phase . . . of respiration, we have already learned one method . . . of alleviating . . . these uncomfortable sensations. . . . These sensations are all subjective phenomena. . . . We feel them . . . but as we know only too well . . . it is very difficult to . . . consciously . . . modify these . . . feelings. . . . We usually find it easier to modify concrete objects . . . so the purpose of this image is to . . . change our unpleasant sensation . . . into an object . . . which is a . . . symbol . . . of the sensation. . . . If you now have a pain . . . discomfort . . . tension . . . or disease . . . or even if you don't . . . going through the procedure anyway at this time will enable you to use it later . . . when these problems do develop. . . . Take the pain . . . tension . . . stress . . . strain . . . anxiety . . . or disease . . . and . . . give it a shape . . . by imagining or visualizing the first shape . . . that comes to mind. . . . The shape may be . . . abstract . . . or concrete. . . . It can be an object . . . inanimate form . . . a geometric design . . . or it can be amorphous. . . . The first shape that comes to you mind is the . . . appropriate one . . . to work with. . . . Anything else tends to be conscious . . . judgmental efforts. . . . Next . . . give the shape a color. . . . Now . . . give it a size. . . . You can establish a size just by knowing it . . . or by picturing next to it . . . an object of known size. . . . Realize that the shape is a symbol . . . of your tension or discomfort . . . and the larger it is . . . the more vibrantly and vividly colored it is . . . the more intense the discomfort it represents will be . . . and conversely . . . the smaller . . . and less vividly colored it is . . . the less severe . . . and less significant . . . the discomfort will be. . . . So practice . . . by changing the size of the object. . . . Because we usually are able to increase the discomfort much more easily than decrease it . . . make the object larger. . . . Make it as large as you need to make it . . . to feel somewhat more uncomfortable . . . and when it is as large as it needs to be . . . make it smaller. . . . If you have any difficulty in making it smaller by just wishing it . . . to be smaller . . . then . . . you can attempt to kick it away . . . or throw it away . . . place it on a boat . . . or on a truck . . . or tie it to an airplane . . . and let it fly away. . . . Or if it is a balloon . . . you can put a needle into it . . . and deflate it. . . . Realize that as the symbol becomes smaller . . . the feelings associated with it become . . . less intense . . . You can make it as small as it is comfortable for you to do so. . . . Practice making it larger and smaller, because these are skills and, as with any skill . . . the more you practice . . . the more . . . powerful . . . the skill becomes.

## INTERNAL PROGRESSIVE RELAXATION

This is a relaxation image to directly stabilize and comfort the internal organs. The image is particularly useful for controlling visceral disorders such as gastrointestinal disease.

Now . . . with the body and mind relaxed . . . we can begin to focus our attention inward . . . enabling the internal organs . . . to become as relaxed . . . as we feel externally. . . . We can allow the internal organs of the body to become more relaxed . . . by thinking of the organs . . . and by feeling . . . the relaxation . . . deepen . . . every time . . . you exhale. . . .

You can allow that glow . . . that wave . . . of comfort and relaxation . . . to travel down the food pipe . . . or esophagus . . . as though you just swallowed a potent . . . magic . . . elixir . . . containing all the ingredients necessary . . . to alleviate all the distress . . . of any tissue . . . with which it comes into contact. . . . And as it travels . . . down . . . the food pipe . . . it can also lead to relaxation . . . and healing . . . of the adjacent organs . . . the trachea and bronchial tubes . . . the heart and major arteries . . . and the lungs . . . enabling all of them to function more leisurely . . . and more effectively. . . . It is not even necessary for you to know . . . consciously . . . what these organs look like. . . . Deep in the mind . . . you have a precise . . . unconscious . . . knowledge . . . of the functioning and structure . . . of all the organs. . . .

And feel the relaxation . . . travel into the stomach . . . relaxing it . . . and the nearby organs of the spleen . . . and the upper left of the abdomen . . . the liver . . . and the upper right of the abdomen . . . and the pancreas . . . lying deep . . . in the upper abdomen. . . . And enable the relaxation wave . . . to travel through the small intestine . . . all twenty-four feet of it . . . coiled up in the midportion of the abdomen. . . . And it now . . . can travel through the large intestine . . . six feet of structure . . . in the right . . . upper . . . and left portions of the abdomen. . . . Then the relaxation can extend . . . to the kidneys . . . the ureters . . . connecting the kidneys to the bladder . . . the bladder . . . and the genital organs. . . . At this point . . . the internal organs and structures of the body . . . can be as relaxed . . . comfortable . . . and healthy . . . as the muscles . . . blood vessels . . . bones . . . and joints . . . already are.

## WHITE LIGHT HEALING IMAGE

The following image allows the user to consciously direct and channel the forces of the body that lead to health and healing. By translating desires into images, people can begin to direct the forces of the central nervous system that are usually beyond their conscious control.

Allow yourself to concentrate . . . on the area in the midportion of your forehead . . . so that you may even begin to feel . . . a tingling sensation. . . . As you do so . . . you are bringing all your attention . . . all your consciousness . . . to this area. . . . By centering your consciousness . . . you can bring the . . . full power . . . of it to . . . enhance . . . the establishment of . . . wellness . . . in the body-mind axis. . . . Now allow the spot of attention . . . to become as small as you possibly can . . . so that all your consciousness is . . . concentrated . . . in a very small area. . . . Now project this point . . . to an area about a foot above your head . . . and let it expand . . . to the size of a baseball. . . . Let this sphere obtain the appearance of . . . a glowing sphere . . . of radiant . . . fiery . . . white . . . light. . . . Perceive the glowing and fiery nature . . . feel the warmth . . . and maybe even hear . . . the vibratory qualities of this object. . . . Now let it begin to slowly . . . expand . . . until it achieves the size of a moderately sized melon . . . still radiant . . . fiery . . . glowing . . . white. . . . Allow the bottom to open . . . as though the top were hinged . . . and as it does . . . begin to see the downpour of fiery . . . white . . . radiant . . . light energy. . . . Feel and see the energy entering the body through the top of the head . . . and flowing downward through the entire body . . . from the head . . . into the neck . . . down the arms to the hands . . . back up to the arms . . . down the chest . . . both front and back . . . . down into the legs . . . the feet . . . and out the feet . . . into the ground. . . . Permit yourself not only to see the energy pour through the body . . . but feel it . . . and also hear it. . . . True health and wellness will be exemplified by a . . . free flow . . . of this fiery . . . radiant . . . white . . . light . . . energy through the body. . . . If there are problems in the body such as diseases or discomforts . . . whether they be consciously realized or not . . . they can be manifested by some impotence . . . or even a complete blockage . . . of the flow of this fiery . . . radiant . . . white . . . light . . . energy . . . through that particular area or areas of the body. . . . When these areas are perceived . . . you may be able to feel and see these areas being fragmented . . . and consumed . . . by this fiery . . . radiant . . . white . . . light . . . energy. . . . It is as though the debris and garbage of the body . . . were being incinerated . . . by this . . . healing force. . . . When the discomfort . . . disorder . . . or diseases have been fragmented and consumed . . . by this fiery . . . radiant . . . white . . . light . . . energy . . . the result will be . . . free flow . . . of energy . . . through this area. . . . Continue to feel . . . and perceive . . . through this downpour . . . coming from that sphere . . . above the head through the entire body . . . and out the feet . . . and into the floor . . . until the free flow . . . of this fiery . . . radiant . . . white . . . light . . . energy . . . has been established . . . it will represent the elimination of all toxins . . . wastes . . . and debris . . . that interfere with the . . . maintenance of health. . . .

When this free flow has been established . . . allow the sphere to close . . . and the downpour to cease. . . . Then allow the sphere . . . to get larger . . . approximately three feet in diameter . . . and allow it to rotate . . . very slowly . . . around its vertical axis. . . . As it rotates . . . allow it to descend . . . very slowly . . . so that it descends . . . around the entire body . . . from head . . . to toes. . . . The function of the sphere at this time . . . is to absorb any accumulated debris . . . that has been left behind by the radiant . . . downpour. . . . When it reaches the feet . . . the entire body should be cleansed of all debris . . . detrimental to maintenance of physical . . . and emotional . . . wellness. . . .

Now let the sphere begin to . . . slowly . . . rotate . . . in the opposite direction . . . around its vertical axis . . . and let it slowly begin to ascend . . . the body. . . . The function . . . of the sphere . . . at this time is to . . . instill . . . new . . . and vitalizing . . . energy . . . into the body. . . . Not only is the energy being instilled into the body . . . but it is being instilled . . . into a body . . . which has been completely freed . . . of all forces which would hinder the . . . complete assimilation and utilization . . . of this energy. . . . When the sphere reaches the top of the head . . . then ascends . . . above the head . . . the entire . . . body-mind axis . . . can be free . . . of all debris . . . and filled with a vitality . . . the energy . . . heretofore rarely if ever experienced. . . .

The sphere can now . . . stop rotating . . . and begin to . . . shrink . . . in size and eventually . . . return to the body as a point of . . . concentrated consciousness . . . in the forehead region. . . . Then, with a few deep breaths . . . this consciousness can travel throughout the body . . . and you can return slowly to the waking state . . . as you have done in previous exercises.

## REFERENCE

Korn, E. R., & Johnson, K. (1983). *Visualization: The uses of imagery in the health profession,* Homewood, IL: Dow Jones-Irwin.

## CHAPTER 4

# Imagery in Autogenic Training

ANEES A. SHEIKH
AND KAREN JACOBSEN

## HISTORY

Oskar Vogt, a brain physiologist who carried out his research on sleep and hypnosis at the Berlin Institute during 1890-1900, noted that intelligent patients who had undergone a number of hypnotic sessions were able to put themselves into a state that seemed to be similar to a hypnotic state. His patients reported that such "autohypnotic" experiences had a remarkable recuperative influence and enhanced their general efficiency (Jordan, 1979). Also, Vogt's patients consistently experienced sensations of heaviness and warmth. Stimulated by Vogt's work, Johannes Schultz, a psychiatrist, started to investigate, in 1905, whether hypnotherapy could be employed without cultivating in patients a form of passivity and a detrimental dependence on the therapist. Schultz noticed that during hypnosis his subjects experienced a feeling of relaxation, warmth, and heaviness in the extremities, as reported by Vogt earlier. In addition, his patients reported other sensations, such as calming of the heart and cooling of the forehead. Subsequently, without inducing a hypnotic state, he encouraged his patients to imagine that they were having the same physiological feelings. This method forms the basis of what is currently known as Autogenic Training (AT). Schultz first described it in 1926, and in 1932 his book *Das autogene Training* appeared. He published more than 400 articles and several books on the topic. Schultz collaborated extensively with Wolfgang Luthe who was instrumental in bringing it to the attention of the English-speaking parts of the world (Luthe, 1969-1973; Schultz & Luthe, 1959). But it was perhaps Hannes Lindemann who, through his book *Relieve Tension the Autogenic Way* (1973), did the most to make AT available to the Western world. After World War II, he worked closely with Schultz. Using AT, he sailed across the Atlantic Ocean in a 10-foot canvas boat in seventy-two days and was *Life* coverman in July 1957. He accomplished this feat by programming himself to endure extreme hardships through intensive AT before and during the trip. "There is no way I could have accomplished the voyage without AT," said Dr. Lindemann.

## AUTOGENIC TRAINING METHOD

AT is basically a relaxation procedure in which the subject mentally creates a peaceful environment and comforting bodily sensations. Presumably, it improves self-regulatory functions and not only enhances a person's overall capacity for psychophysiological adaptation, but also increases bodily resistance to all kinds of stress. Also, AT may render unconscious material more readily available. AT can be applied to about 80 to 90 percent of adults and can be used successfully with children, ages ten and over (Schultz & Luthe, 1959). "Physiologically, autogenic training is based on three main principles: a) the reduction of exteroceptive and proprioceptive afferent stimulation, b) the mental repetition or representation of psychophysiologically adopted verbal formulae and c) a mental activity conceived as passive concentration" (Luthe, 1962, p. 18).

Passive concentration is an important factor in AT. The client is told, "It is important that throughout this procedure you adopt a relaxed, passive, and casual attitude. You cannot force relaxation to occur. Just give up conscious control over your body, and allow your bodily processes to flow naturally. If the relaxation experience does not evolve exactly as you wish, do not become concerned but rather maintain your passive attitude. This will most likely ensure that you will eventually achieve the desired relaxation effect" (Luthe, 1963, p. 177). Before initiating the standard exercises, the client is also told about the importance of imagery:

Autogenic training relies upon your ability to focus on your body and imagine you are getting relaxed. An essential part of this process involves your picturing yourself in a comforting, peaceful environment. Most people choose a scene that is familiar to them, such as lying on the sand at a beach, or sitting in a meadow on a summer day. Take the next few seconds to choose your peaceful scene. . . . I am going to help you achieve relaxation by suggesting relaxing sensations for different parts of your body. I will repeat the feelings you are to focus on, and then you are to continue on your own until I suggest a new focus—imagining you are actually experiencing your relaxation scene, focusing on the identified body part, and sensing the identified feeling. To repeat, maintain a relaxed, casual, and passive attitude toward the procedure at all times. If your thoughts wander, or the relaxation is slow to come on, do not be concerned. Maintaining a casual attitude will hasten the eventual emergence of relaxation. (Schultz & Luthe, 1959, p. 24)

AT exercises should be practiced in a quiet room with reduced lighting. The preferred position is lying down; however, a comfortable sitting posture also is acceptable. In either position, the arms should be at the sides and the feet should be apart.

AT has a set of standard exercises that have formulae corresponding to various parts of the body. It is considered helpful to encourage the client to try to visualize the relevant parts of the body before he/she begins the corresponding formulae.

Once the client has assumed his/her training posture and has closed his/her eyes, the therapist starts repeating the formulae in a calm and suggestive voice for about thirty to forty seconds. Longer periods of time might provoke an undesirable state of tension. This therapist presentation should be followed by thirty seconds of silence, which gives the client an opportunity to continue the passive concentration on the formulae. Finally, the therapist needs to guide the client back to a normal state by telling him/her to: 1) flex the arms and legs; 2) breathe deeply; 3) open his/her eyes. This is called "canceling" and is deemed necessary by Schultz and Luthe. Note taking by the therapist and the client is also considered important. These notes can be used to monitor the progress of each autogenic exercise and can indicate when the client is ready to move on to the next exercise. The standard AT exercises follow.

## Standard Exercises

The standard exercises consist of the following six relaxation themes: heaviness, warmth, cardiac regulation, respiration, abdominal warmth, and cooling of the forehead. There are seven parts to each of the first two exercises, heaviness and warmth: right arm, left arm, both arms, right leg, left leg, both legs, arms and legs. Thus the standard exercises have a total of eighteen parts, seven for heaviness, seven for warmth, and one each for the remaining four. One or two training sessions are suggested for each of these components (Schultz & Luthe, 1959). "At this pace, approximately 6 months are required to master the standard exercises of AT. Although this may be the practice of AT's European orthodoxy, its American usage is markedly more compact" (Lichstein, 1988, p. 109).

Lichstein (1988) has developed an approximately twenty-five minute induction for the six standard exercises. According to him: "The procedure fairly reflects common practice among American therapists, and apparently induces deep relaxation state. The essential difference between the compact version . . . and the orthodox version is the elimination of prolonged repetition present in the latter. A deeper state of relaxation may be achieved by the orthodox procedure, but the cost in time is enormous" (p. 109).

Lichstein (1988) begins the first exercise by speaking the following phrase in a calm and soothing voice for about thirty seconds.

> I am at peace . . . My right arm is heavy . . . My right arm is heavy . . . I am at peace . . . My right arm is heavy . . . My right arm is heavy . . . My right arm is heavy. (p. 110)

At this point the client is asked to continue the exercises on his/her own for another thirty seconds. Then the focus changes to the left arm, to both arms, and then arms and legs. Similarly the therapist guides the client through the seven parts of the warmth exercise (exercise II). In the latter, the concentration is on warmth, but suggestions of heaviness also are interspersed.

In exercise III the formula, "Heartbeat calm and regular" is added to heaviness and warmth. Exercise IV adds, "My breathing is calm," and exercise V adds "My abdomen is warm," and exercise VI states "My forehead is cool." Exercise VI proceeds as follows:

> I am at peace . . . My arms and legs are heavy and warm, heartbeat calm and regular . . . I am at peace . . . My breathing is calm . . . My abdomen is warm . . . My forehead is cool . . . My forehead is cool . . . I am at peace . . . My breathing is calm . . . I am at peace . . . My forehead is cool . . . My forehead is cool . . . My forehead is cool.

After presenting each exercise, the therapist allows the client comparable time for quiet meditation. Total practice time for exercises I and II is sixty seconds each, for exercise III it is ninety seconds, for exercise IV it is two minutes, for exercise V it is two-and-a-quarter, minutes and for VI it is two-and-a-half minutes.

## Special Exercises

Schultz and Luthe (1959) suggest a few variations of the basic exercises to suit the specific needs of the clients. However, these should be used only after spending considerable time on the basic exercises. There are two general categories of these special exercises: Organ specific formulae and intentional or resolution formulae.

In organ specific formulae, the basic themes of heaviness, warmth, calm and regular, and coolness are adapted to the specific needs of the client (i.e., "my back is warm" for low back pain; "my nose is cool" for hay fever). "Creation of an individualized phrase should be guided by the psychophysiological process associated with the key term, for example, muscular relaxation (heaviness), vasodilation (warmth), and vasoconstriction (coolness)" (Lichstein, 1988, p. 112).

Intentional or resolution formulae aim at increasing or decreasing the occurrence of certain psychological functions. These formulae should be brief and to the point, exactly the result you want. Also, they should be positive, if possible. Instead of "I can't give up," it is better to use, "I shall pull through." Rhythmic and alliterative formulae also are considered particularly effective. These formulae should reflect an attitude of indifference rather than attitudes of fight and tension. "Cigarettes are unimportant" is better than "I will no longer smoke." This attitude of indifference is especially advisable during unusually intense emotional states. A few examples of useful resolution formulae to be used after the standard exercises follow (Parker, 1985):

Food addictions:       Alcohol (sweets, etc.) is completely immaterial.

Bowel regularity:      Bowel movement will be a half hour after arising (or whenever you wish). Colon retains (for diarrhea).

Remaining asleep:      I sleep deeply and soundly until I awake at 6 (or whatever time) and I wake at 6, fully rested.

Personal-social:       Neighbors are also people, I please them, they please me. Respect for my neighbor will make me well.

Ordering your life:    I am completely calm, happy, and free: I can be free only when there is good order.

Sexual tensions:       In the act of love I am free, active, and relaxed. My wife (husband) is pretty nice. I am a man and love as a man as long as I can.

## Autogenic Meditative Exercise

Schultz and Luthe (1959) recommended a number of meditative exercises to enhance visual imagery skills, but they cautioned that they should be employed only after the basic exercises have been mastered. A total of seven exercises are presented in order of difficulty and complexity. Only after successful practice of one, should the client move on to the next. Each exercise is to be practiced for approximately thirty to sixty seconds at a time. A description of exercises as summarized by Lichstein follows:

1. *Spontaneous experience of colors.* During periods of prolonged relaxation up to 60 minutes, vivid colors will spontaneously occur in imagination. Statistically, the first colors to appear cannot be predicted, although personal preferences do exist.

2. *Experience of selected colors.* The colors that most frequently appeared during level 1 are now produced on demand. The chromatic range may be extended until most colors are under control.

3. *Visualization of concrete objects.* The client is instructed to persevere with a passive attitude until an image of a concrete object spontaneously occurs. Training is continued until a variety of concrete objects can be imaginally generated with clarity on demand.

4. *Visualization of abstract objects.* The focus is now placed on abstract words, for example, truth, justice, friendship. Representations of this material often take a dreamlike form accompanied by auditory imagery.

5. *Experience of a selected state of feeling.* Emotions, desires, or moods having personal meaning to the client supply the imagery themes. The resulting imagery may take a realistic or symbolic form.

6. *Visualization of other persons.* At the beginning, the imagery subjects are people who are emotionally neutral to the client. Ultimately, clear, vivid imagery of personally significant people can be generated.

7. *Answers from the unconscious.* Here clients pose psychodynamically rich questions to themselves such as "Who is the one I love?" While in a state of meditations, the client awaits spontaneous emergence of the answer. This psychoanalytic preference in Schultz and Luthe's thinking need not limit the potential usefulness of the creative state attained in level 7. The attributes of unencumbered thinking and receptivity to diverse possibilities characterizing this level may also be effectively applied to pragmatic current concerns and problem-solving tasks. (Lichstein, 1988, pp. 113-114)

## CONCLUDING REMARKS

Luthe (1962, p. 182) asserted that "both clinical results and experimental data indicate that autogenic training operates in a highly differentiated field of bodily self-regulation and that with the help of autogenic principles it is possible to use one's brain to influence certain bodily and mental functions effectively." Luthe's claim has received considerable support from recent research that indicates that AT can, in fact, be beneficial in the healing of a number of physical and psychological problems (e.g., Aivazyan, Zaitsev, & Yurenev, 1988; Baily, 1984; Janssen & Neutgens, 1986; Linden, 1994; Pikoff, 1984; Schredl & Doll, 1997).

AT has also been expanded into a comprehensive therapy approach, known as Autogenic Therapy, wherein the standard exercises have been further elaborated and several new therapeutic procedures have been added. For details, the interested reader is referred to the six volumes of Luthe's (1969-1973) *Autogenic Therapy.*

It seems appropriate to end this brief discussion of AT with a few words from Murphy's (1981) *The Power of Your Subconscious Mind* which can act as a sort of all pervasive resolution formula to shield us from the daily strains and stresses:

> My body and all its organs were created by the Infinite Intelligence in my subconscious mind. It knows how to heal me. Its wisdom fashioned all my organs, tissues, muscles, and bones. This Infinite Healing Presence within me is now transforming every atom of my being, making me whole and perfect now. I give thanks for the healing I know is taking place now. Wonderful are the works of the Creative Intelligence within me.

## REFERENCES

Aivazyan, T. A., Zaitsev, V. P., & Yurenev, A. P. (1988). Autogenic training in the treatment and secondary prevention of essential hypertension: Five-year follow-up. *Health Psychology, 7,* 201-208.

Bailey, R. D. (1984). Autogenic regulation training and sickness absence amongst student nurses in general training. *Journal of Advanced Nursing, 9,* 581-587.

Janssen, K., & Neutgens, J. (1986). Autogenic training and progressive relaxation in the treatment of three kinds of headache. *Behavior Research & Therapy, 24,* 199-208.

Jordan, C. S. (1979). Mental imagery: European approaches. In A.A. Sheikh and J. T. Shaffer (Eds.), *The potential of fantasy and imagination.* New York: Brandon House.

Lichstein, K. L. (1988). *Clinical relaxation strategies.* New York: Wiley.

Lindemann, H. (1973). *Relieve tension the autogenic way.* New York: Peter H. Wyden, Inc.

Linden, W. (1994). Autogenic training: A narrative and quantitative review of clinical outcome. *Biofeedback and Self-Regulation, 19,* 227-264.

Luthe, W. (1962). Method, research and application of autogenic training. *American Journal of Clinical Hypnosis, 5,* 17-23.

Luthe, W. (1963). Autogenic training. Method, research and application in medicine. *American Journal of Psychotherapy, 17,* 174-175.

Luthe, W. (Ed.) (1969-1973). *Autogenic therapy.* Six Volumes. New York: Grune & Stratton.

Murphy, J. (1981). *The power of your subconscious mind.* New York: Prentice-Hall.

Parker, D. (1985). *The Power of Mind Workshop.* Presented at the Annual Conference of the American Association for the Study of Mental Imagery, Toronto, Canada.

Pikoff, H.(1984). A critical review of autogenic training in America. *Clinical Psychology Review,4,* 619-639.

Schultz, J. H , & Luthe, W. (1959). *Autogenic training.* New York: Grune & Stratton.

Schredl, M., & Doll, E. (1997). Autogenic training and drawn recall. *Perceptual and Motor Skills, 84,* 1305-1306.

# CHAPTER 5

# Imagery-Related Techniques in Neuro-Linguistic Programming

*MELISSA J. KLEIN, ADREANA A. SCIMECA,*
*AMARDEEP S. KALEKA, AND ANEES A. SHEIKH*

Neuro-Linguistic Programming (NLP) is a model of the structure of our subjective experience and how that experience influences our behavior. It was initially created in 1975 with the basic premise that "there is a redundancy between the observable macroscopic patterns of human behavior and patterns of the underlying neural activity governing this behavior" (Dilts, 1983a, p. 3). More specifically, the term can best be understood by breaking it into its parts as defined by Dilts (1983b):

> "Neuro" stands for the fundamental tenet that all behavior is the result of neurological processes. "Linguistic" indicates that neural processes are represented, ordered, and sequenced into models and strategies through language and communications systems. "Programming" refers to the process of organizing the components of a system to achieve a specific outcome. (p. 3)

Neuro-Linguistic Programming begins with Richard Bandler, a mathematics and computer science undergraduate at the University of California, Santa Cruz. He became involved in editing transcripts of workshop videotapes of the Gestalt psychotherapist, Fritz Perls. Through repeated viewing of these videotapes, Bandler absorbed the significant patterns of Perls' therapeutic interventions (Dawes, 1998). Bandler, in turn, organized his own Gestalt group, and he found that interventions that worked with one person did not necessarily work with another who had the same problem. "Given his background in mathematics and computers, it was more puzzling to him that these behavioral 'equations' did not produce identical 'answers'" (Dawes, 1998).

John Grinder was an Assistant Professor of Linguistics at UCSC when he first attended Bandler's Gestalt group. He also was skilled at absorbing and adopting other people's behavior. In addition, his particular area of expertise in linguistics was Noam Chomsky's Transformational Grammar which claimed to be a model of how language worked (Dawes, 1998). Grinder proposed to Bandler that they apply the same principles to understanding how the therapeutic process worked and what made an effective therapist. According to Bandler and Grinder (1979), the roots for all NLP work revolve around "figuring out what it is that effective therapists do intuitively or unconsciously, and to make some rules that can be taught to someone else" (p. 9). Gestalt therapist Fritz Perls was the first of many psychotherapists whose work Bandler and Grinder modeled. The best known of the others and the most influential in the development of NLP were hypnotherapist Milton Erickson and family therapist Virginia Satir.

As a result of the studies of behavior and linguistics, NLP became grounded on certain basic presuppositions which provide the foundation for the development and implementation of the various techniques which are used (Dilts, 1983b). These presuppositions include:

1. Communication is more than the words being spoken. The act of communicating involves many different tools.
2. Words are only inadequate labels for experiences. There is far more to the experience than is being expressed by words.
3. The meaning of communication lies in the response it elicits rather than in the intent of the communicator. The significance in any communication is in the meaning received by the listener.
4. There is no substitute in communications for clean, active, open, sensory channels which register the response in the listener at any given moment.
5. Human beings have the capability to learn from a single trial.
6. Individual skills are the result of the development and sequencing of representational systems which can be broken down into components. Any skill, talent, or ability that a person has can be broken down, and then it can be modeled and taught to anyone else.
7. People already have all the resources they need to effect change and achieve the desired outcomes.
8. Choice is better than no choice. Individuals make the best choice available to them at any time. When more choices are present, the chances are better that a good choice will be made.
9. Behavior is geared toward adaptation. Every behavior serves a positive intention and can be related to a context in which it has value. All feelings and experiences are positive in some way.
10. There is no such thing as failure, only feedback. Even a lost opportunity provides valuable information.
11. The map is not the territory. What a person subjectively perceives is not always actual reality.
12. If a communication is not eliciting the desired response, it is important to be flexible and to try many different things.
13. People work perfectly. There is no such thing as a broken person, only maladaptive behaviors.

The presence of these presuppositions in the model of NLP will be discussed in the following sections, beginning with the basis for the tools included in this method. In this discussion, the word "method" refers to the basic principles that initiate change underlined in NLP. The major methods include mirroring, meta-modeling, anchoring, reframing, overlapping, future-pacing, and therapeutic metaphor.

## MIRRORING

Therapists of many different persuasions feel that their first goal is to establish a positive connection or good rapport with the client. According to NLP, a harmonious relationship must be based on good communication, which is developed not only through language, but through the whole body (e.g., a smile, a wink of an eye, or hand movements). Recognizing each type of behavior, both verbal and nonverbal, is an essential part of the therapist's role of gathering information about the client's present state and desired state, evolving the client from the present to the desired state, and integrating experience of the desired state into ongoing behavior. Cameron-Bandler stresses the importance of rapport:

> To effectively gather information, or begin a process of change, it will always be important to establish rapport between yourself and your client, at both the conscious and unconscious level. An invaluable technique for doing just this is to generate verbal and nonverbal behavior that matches that of your client. This is called "matching." The client's subjective experience becomes one of being really understood. After all, you are speaking their language, verbally and nonverbally. (Dilts, 1983b, p. 23)

Once the therapist has understood the client's model of the world, he/she can enter and experience it. In NLP, body language is carefully noted and the establishment of rapport depends upon the therapist's ability to match or "mirror" the client's behavior. Also, it is important for the therapist to be able to hear the sensory-based words that a client uses and thus to identify the representational systems in which a client stores information.

It is believed that at any given moment, a person is conscious of a small portion of his/her experience; consciousness is a limited phenomenon. The portions brought into consciousness are determined by the interaction of present sensory capabilities and motivations, which are represented internally through different modalities. According to Lankton (1980), a representational system "is a sensory processing system that initiates and modulates behavior—sight, audition, feelings both visceral and tactile, gustation, and smell memories" (p. 16). A representational system is a way of representing the experience of the world internally and also of mediating behavior. The interaction with the external world translates through perceptions and images of that world. For example, a depressive client might hear only the negative things people say about him, and his representation system might consist of an internal voice that sounds slow and depressed and makes long lists of failures. He may bypass important perceptual data from the other sensory modalities. He might not fully focus on the positive feelings people try to give him, such as the kinesthetic experience of a hug from a friend, or a visual warm smile from a stranger. The perceptions affect the internal representations in the person and also the output behavior.

This depressive person's state is caused by an inaccurate view of reality. According to NLP, "we operate out of our sensory representations of the world and not on 'reality' itself" (Lankton, 1980, p. 17). Most of our behavior is mediated by internal constructions and subjective representations which we use to organize our experience of the world. Since the first goal of therapy is to achieve rapport, the therapist can make a connection with the client by interpreting his/her representational system and matching it. This is referred to as "mirroring." In order to achieve this goal, the therapist must be able to interpret the client. Bandler and Grinder set out to model therapists who were particularly skilled at achieving rapport in this way. They focused on three of the best therapists of their time, Milton Erickson, Virginia Satir, and Fritz Perls. As Bandler and Grinder describe (1979):

> If you watch and listen to Virginia Satir work you are confronted with an overwhelming mass of information—the way she moves, her voice tone, the way she touches, who she turns to next, what sensory cues she is using to orient herself to which member of the family, etc. It's an overwhelming task to attempt to keep track of all the things that she is using as cues, the responses that she is making to those cues, and the responses she elicits from others. (p. 9)

As Bandler and Grinder observed therapists, they noted that the most profound pattern had to do with the way in which the therapist connected with the client. In the book *Frogs into Princes,* the wrong way to communicate is demonstrated (Bandler & Grinder, 1979):

> Well, you know, things *feel* real heavy in my life, Dr. Bandler. You know, it's just like I can't *handle* it, you know . . .
> I can *see* that, Mr. Grinder.
> I *feel* like I did something wrong with my children and I don't know what it is. And I thought maybe you could help me *grasp* it, you know?
> Sure. I *see* what it is you're talking about. Let's *focus* in on one particular dimension. Try to give me your particular *perspective.* Tell me how it is that you *see* your situation right now.
> Well, you know, I just . . . I'm . . . I just *feel* like I can't get a *grasp* on reality.
> I can *see* that. What's important to me—*colorful* as your *description* is— what's important to me is that we *see eye to eye* about where it is down the road that we shall travel together.
> I'm trying to *tell* you that my life has got a lot of *rough edges,* you know. And I'm trying to find a way . . .
> It *looks* all broken up from . . . from your description, at any rate. The *colors* aren't all that nice. (p. 11)

In contrast, Virginia Satir shows how mirroring helps in establishing rapport (Bandler & Grinder, 1979):

> Well, man, Virginia, you know I just ah . . . boy! Things have been, they've been *heavy,* you know. Just, you know, my wife was . . . my wife was run over by a snail and . . . you know, I've got four kids and two of them are gangsters and I think maybe I did something wrong but I just can't get a *grasp* on what it was.

I understand that you *feel certain weight* upon you, and these kinds of *feelings* that you have in your body aren't what you want for yourself as a human being. You have different kinds of hopes for this. (pp. 10-11)

In the client and therapist's communication, a pattern develops. NLP acknowledges this pattern and attempts to explain it through the use of representational systems.

A client usually will use certain predicates, which in turn represent the way that individual creates his/her map. An NLP therapist is able to pick up these predicates and match them, so that both the client and therapist are on the same map. In the first, example, the client, Mr. Grinder is using words such as "feel," "handle," and "grasp." Dr. Bandler, the therapist, uses words such as "see," "perspective," "colorful," and "focus." Mr. Grinder is using predicates, which indicate that his map is based on internal feelings. The therapist is using predicates, which are mainly on the visual map. This basic incongruence hampers effective communication.

The use of predicates is only one means of mirroring. Other ways of mirroring include the use of eye accessing cues, interpreting body type, and using facial cues. Eye accessing cues were first presented in the way in which Milton Erickson utilized them (Bandler & Grinder, 1975a):

> ... each of us has developed particular body movements which indicated to the astute observer which representational system we are using. Especially rich in significance are the eye scanning patterns which we have deployed. Thus for the student of hypnosis, predicates in the verbal system and eye scanning patterns in the nonverbal system offer quick and powerful ways of determining which of the potential meaning making resources—the representational systems—the client is using at a moment in time, and therefore how to respond creatively to the client. Consider, for example, how many times you have asked someone a question and he has paused, said: "Hmmmmmmmmm, let's see" and accompanying this verbalization, he moves his eyes up and to the left. Movement of the eyes up and to the left stimulates (in right handed people) eidetic images located in the non-dominant hemisphere. The neurological pathways that come from the left side of both eyes (left visual fields) are represented in the right cerebral hemisphere (non-dominant). The eye scanning movements up and to the right conversely stimulate the left cerebral hemisphere and constructed images—that is, visual representations of things that the person has never seen before. (p. 182)

Therefore, according to Bandler and Grinder, eye patterns can reveal from which modality the person is accessing information. The eye accessing cue table for a right-handed person follows (Lankton, 1980, pp. 46-47):

Up and to the right = constructed visual image
Up and to the left = remember (eidetic) visual image
Neutral and to the right = constructed auditory sounds or words
Neutral and to the left = remembered auditory sounds or words
Down and to the right = kinesthetic feelings (also smell and taste)
Down and to the left = auditory sounds or words

A table for a left-handed person would be the opposite.

The use of eye accessing cues to mirror a client in therapy has been very beneficial to NLP therapists. For example, a client might say, "Doctor, I just don't understand what my wife wants from me anymore" (eyes look down and to the left). "Sometimes I wonder if she understands how she makes me feel" (eyes look up and to the left). A therapist trained in NLP would notice that the client is hearing an internal auditory tape, saying the word "feel," and seeing a remembered image. In other words, he is feeling and visualizing at the same time. His processing of experience is occurring in one representational system but is being consciously expressed through another system; the input and output systems are different.

The system which a person is using to process the information is the lead system. The overriding way in which the person communicates is called the primary representational system. In the prior example, the client is leading with a visual process and expressing a feeling, which is noted as the primary representational system. The mismatched connection between the lead and primary system is labeled synesthesia or "fuzzy functioning" (Lankton, 1980; Bandler & Grinder, 1976). In addition, the client first is in an auditory representation system and then he moves to a visual system. The therapist might respond, "Well, Mr. Roman, I can see how you might be made to feel this certain way, but what I was wondering about, was this . . . do you see a certain image or hear a voice when you think about this particular problem?" The therapist instantly mirrored the predicates and accessing cues, by using the words "see" and "feel." This would enhance rapport with the client, reassuring the client that both he and the therapist are on the same map. Then the therapist follows up with an important question, "Do you see a certain image or hear a voice when you think about this particular problem?" This question enables the therapist to double-check what the client accessed (i.e., an image and an auditory sound). The client probably will respond by sharing with the therapist his image and auditory sound, which would then lead into the NLP technique set up to deal with the problem.

In addition to using predicates and eye scanning patterns to match communication with a client, a therapist can also use overt body language, facial movements, skin texture changes, and voice tone changes. For example, if someone is asked to add the number 232 and 122 in his/her head the person may move his/her lips while looking straight up. This behavior indicates that the individual is leading visually and continuing auditorily. The NLP therapist uses the communication system (body language, predicates, or eye-accessing cues) that applies to and can be modeled for each individual client. At first, this style of communication is difficult to identify because subtle cues are overlooked; however, with practice this problem is overcome.

The goal of NLP is change from the client's present state to a desired state or outcome. The prerequisites for success are: the desired outcome must be explicitly represented; clean and active sensory channels must be maintained so that progress toward the outcome may be perceived, assessed, and responded to; and both internal responses and external behavior must be flexible, so that the outcome can be replicated in multiple contexts and situations (Dilts, 1983b). In NLP, a client's problems are defined in terms of behaviors and responses, rather than by a diagnostic label. Once the client's present state is determined, the therapist employs a set of tools to help the client achieve the desired outcome.

Since NLP is outcome oriented, the initial and most important step in therapy is to identify and define the desired state (Dilts, 1983b). The outcome must fulfill certain conditions: 1) it must be stated in positive terms; 2) it should be possible to test and to demonstrate it in sensory experience; 3) it must be initiated and maintained by the client and preserve any positive by-products of the present state; 4) it must be ecologically sound and possible future impacts of the outcome must be considered (Dilts, 1983b). Once the present state is known and the desired state explicitly defined, the therapist can then choose a set of tools and techniques to help the client achieve the goal. To better understand the language of the client and how his/her words relate to internal and sensory experience, Meta-Model can be helpful.

## META-MODEL

In childhood, a child learns to label everything with a word. Children also begin to attach experiences and associated feelings to specific words. The connection between words, experiences, and feelings varies for each individual. Language is not an example of the experience but is a representation of the individual's experience with a certain object or thing. According to Lankton (1980),

> the Meta-Model is a specific set of linguistic tools and categories that rests upon the premise that words only have meaning insofar as they are associated to internal representations or sensory experience. Meta-Model questions are designed to bridge the gap between language and sensory experience. (p. 50)

In other words, the therapist must be able to ask specific questions in order to understand fully what representational systems the client is using. Therefore, the therapist translates words into internal representations. In addition, this model also gives the client a better understanding of what he/she is saying.

NLP outlines many weak links in the language people use. Cameron-Bandler (1985) identifies nine of these weak links: deletion, lack of referential index, unspecified verbs, nominalizations, universal quantifiers, modal operators of necessity, cause and effect, mind reading, and lost performative.

Deletion occurs when a client leaves something out of a statement. If the client states, "I understand," then the therapist is not given the information about what the client understands. The client may too not fully comprehend what he/she has just said. Therefore, the job of the therapist is to Meta-Model a question in which the missing material is recovered (Cameron-Bandler, 1985).

Lack of referential index refers to the introduction of a person, place, or thing into a sentence without specifying it. This type of language problem revolves around generalization, which "limits a person's model of the world by leaving out the detail and richness necessary to have a variety of options for coping" (Cameron-Bandler, 1985, p. 227). To correct this lack of referential index, the therapist asks for the specifics involved. If a client says, "They hate me," the therapist would respond with "Who specifically hates you."

An unspecified verb is one which is introduced into the sentence but is not clarified. According to Cameron-Bandler (1985), "all verbs are relatively unspecified. However, 'kiss' is much more specific than 'touch'" (p. 227). For example, a client, might say, "I can change." The danger behind not specifying how and what lies in the probability that the client may not fully understand this statement. The Meta-Model question of the therapist will deal with specifically how the client can change. Therefore, the client is forced to deal with this issue overtly.

A nominalization is a word that is a process or a verb, which has been transformed into a noun; for example "love," "fear," "respect," "relationship," and "recognition." A nominalization is a negative structure because when an ongoing process becomes a noun, choices are lost on how the process is seen (Cameron-Bandler, 1980). In order for the therapist to transform a nominalization back into a "process" word, he/she uses the verb in the response. For example, "I need more strength," can be transformed by asking the Meta-Model question "How can you become stronger?"

A universal qualifier is a word that generalizes one specific event. These include words such as "never," "always," "every," and "none." A universal qualifier is dangerous because it automatically limits choices for the person. NLP is based on giving the client more choices. The NLP therapist would transform this weak link by challenging the universal. For example, a client might state that, "I am never going to smile again." This statement limits the happiness of the client. A Meta-Model transformation might be to sarcastically say, "You are never going to smile again," while the therapist is himself/herself smiling.

A modal operator of necessity expresses some limit on the nouns or verbs within the sentence. Again, this limits the client's choices. In order to transform this process, the therapist uses two very potent responses to these operators of necessity: "What stops you?" and "What would happen if you did?" (Cameron-Bandler, 1985); for example, if the client states, "I can't do it," the therapist could ask, "What stops you?"

The link of cause and effect "involves the belief that some action on the part of one person can cause another person to act in a particular way or to experience some emotion or inner state" (Cameron-Bandler, 1985, p. 230). This language process forces the person to respond without any choice. The proper Meta-Model translator is to simply ask, "How does X cause Y?" The cause and effect of "You make me hate you," can be challenged by asking, "How do I make you hate me?"

Statements referring to mind reading, such as, "I know what you are thinking," indicate that a client is acting on some delusion, rather than acting on information. Mind reading inhibits the usefulness of that person's model of the world (Cameron-Bandler, 1985). In order for the therapist to transform this process, he/she could ask, "How do you know this?"

In a lost performative statement, the speaker imposes a personal judgment or value on others. For instance, a client may say, "He never should have run away from his problem." This attitude is unhealthy because the client should be able to have his/her own views comfortably and permit the rest of the world the same right. A therapist should challenge a lost performative by a "for whom" question; for example, by asking, "Who should never run away" (Cameron-Bandler, 1985).

In conclusion, the ability to Meta-Model is a very important aspect of therapy because most translations give the client more choices. NLP rests on the philosophical assumption that if a person has more choices available, then he/she will be better able to cope with life's ups and downs.

## ANCHORING

An anchor is any stimulus which repeatedly elicits a response. The anchor can be an internal and/or external stimulus and the response can occur in any of the five sensory modalities—taste, feel, smell, hear, and see. When a person thinks of the word "dog," it might be anchored to an internal visual image of a person's pet dog. The person may hear it barking, may feel its soft fur, or even smell it. Similarly, if a person sees a dog visually, it might be connected to the memory of a pet dog that passed away years ago, which causes sadness in the present. Therefore, the external visual image is an anchor for the internal feeling of sadness. An internal anchor can also elicit an internal response; for instance, the internal visual image of a parent can make a person feel safe.

According to Lankton (1980), "the process of anchoring is designed to deliberately associate a stimulus to a particular experience" (p. 56). Therefore, the task of the therapist is to make those needed resources available to the client in the proper context. The anchor can be established either by sound, touch, sight, smell, or even a taste, or by using two or more modalities simultaneously. Many people can relate to the phenomenon of anchoring because, at one time or another, they have experienced it. For instance, the smell of freshly baked bread might bring back a host of vivid images.

Lankton (1980) describes an anchoring exercise which he frequently uses with his workshop participants:

> I have asked professionals to pair up and perform the following exercise: sitting face to face they are to take turns establishing kinesthetic anchors (a touch) for both a highly-valued positive experience and an anxiety producing one. As one person watches his partner's face intensely express the positive experience, he firmly touches a spot on the partner's knee. A few moments later after the negative experience has been recalled and the subject's face muscles, skin color, breathing, etc., have changed expression this is anchored with a touch on the other knee. The participants are then instructed to go back and touch the two knees in precisely the same spots sequentially and discover what happens. They are often amazed by the fact that their meaningless touches reproduce the facial expressions associated to the two experiences and the subjects report a parallel change internally. (p. 56)

As can be seen in this example, there are three general rules, which should be followed to anchor a response successfully: 1) The client should access the desired experience as powerfully and fully as possible. The more intense the recollection of the experience the stronger the anchor will be. 2) The therapist should insert his/her stimulus at the moment of fullest expression and most intense response. This timing is crucial. If the timing is off, the therapist ends up anchoring another feeling or experience. 3) The stimulus or anchor must be exactly reproducible. If there is a slight difference between anchors, probably no response to the stimulus will occur. Cameron-Bandler (1985) illustrates the use of anchoring:

A young woman, Melissa came to me for therapy because of sexual dysfunction. She became absolutely petrified when men approached her sexually. When asked to merely describe her experience as a man approached her, she became terrified. So, I anchored this response. Then, while using that anchor to trigger the same set of feelings, I asked her to go back through her past and to describe other times when she had those same feelings. (p. 136)

Then Cameron-Bandler was able to find Melissa's problem in her past and bring the specific cause into her conscious mind. In this example, Cameron-Bandler used anchoring to access experiences more readily.

The use of anchoring has recently evolved into the NLP allergy technique. Scientific research suggests that most allergies can be seen as phobias of the nervous system (Dilts, 1998). Since this is the case, a new NLP allergy technique involving imagery and anchoring has been formed.

The first step in the process of overcoming allergies is to have the client imagine or remember a salient memory of being near the allergy-causing agent. The client should access this experience as fully as possible, with the same emotional and physical reactions (eyes watering, blushing, coughing, etc.). The closer this imagery experience is to reality, the more effective this exercise. Subsequentially, the different submodalities are explored, which intensify and reduce the reactional discomfort. A submodality pattern is a way in which the brain sorts and codes experience. Varying the size, color, distance, depth, and clarity of a picture will intensify or diminish the response to it. Now an anchor must be established for a dissociated state, in which the client is seeing himself/herself as more relaxed. For example, a therapist might ask the client to imagine that a thick piece of glass separates him/her from the allergy-causing agent. Now the therapist might suggest that he/she imagine that he/she has just left his/her body in the seat and now is looking down on the body. At this moment, when the person's breathing is shallow and the facial muscles are more relaxed, the therapist will set the first anchor (A-1).

The next goal is to establish the second anchor (A-2) while the client is in a desired state. This goal is accomplished by helping the client to develop a positive reaction to the substance through the use of imagery. The submodalities that are discovered in the first step will become important during the building of a new imagined response. Once the person is able to imagine a positive response, the therapist can set the second anchor.

The next step includes the setting of an anchor (A-3) for what Dilts (1998) calls "counterexample reference experiences." By having the client access an associated memory of being close to the allergy-causing agent without experiencing the allergic reaction or by having the person identify some other substance that might be even more hazardous for the person, this counterexample reference can be experienced. For example, a person who is allergic to perfume might be asked to remember a time when he/she was close to cologne that did not cause the reactions. In addition, the client might be asked to imagine spilling a toxic substance like gasoline on his/her hand and to note that although it is toxic, it does not cause the allergic reaction. When the therapist notes that the client's eyes are clear, the breathing is normal, and the skin is the normal tone, the third anchor is set.

After all the anchors are set, the therapist fires off the dissociated state anchor (A-1) and has the client begin to imagine being near the allergy producing substance. Then the therapist fires off anchors for the desired state (A-2) and counterexample (A-3), making certain that the anchors are held long enough that the full physiological responses associated with the experiences as opposed to the allergy response are seen (Dilts, 1998). Gradually the client is introduced to the allergy-causing agent in separate stages. At each of these stages the firing process is repeated with the three anchors. In addition, the submodalities that were found in step one can be used again to decrease reaction.

Dilts (1998) claims that this "basic NLP Allergy Technique has now been applied thousands of times in clinical and training settings and has been effective in changing a vast majority of allergy symptoms. The types of allergies have included those to airborne material, such as smoke, pollen, perfume, etc., to various foods, and even in cases involving asthma" (Internet site). This technique is just one of the more recent applications of the basic method of anchoring.

· Sometimes anchors are tied to painful experiences. In this case, a therapist seeks to collapse the anchors. The reasoning behind collapsing anchors is that smaller pieces of unpleasant experiences can be handled more easily than one large unpleasant "chunk"; fear and pain is considerably less debilitating when taken in smaller proportions (Lankton, 1980). Therefore, in collapsing anchors, the chunks of a difficult memory are reduced, specifically by combining them with portions of incompatible experiences. The positive experiences of the visual, auditory, kines-thetic, and gustatory/olfactory systems, or taken collectively, the four-tuple, must have the strength to counter the negativity of the original experience. Lankton (1980) describes the steps in collapsing anchors:

1. Retrieve the unwanted experience. Get a sensory description of it that includes all the elements of the four-tuple. Anchor it.
2. Retrieve the necessary resources making certain that they are as intense as the problem four-tuple. Anchor them.
3. Have the client return to the problem state. Fire off both anchors at once. Hold them until sensory experience or feedback from the client tells you the integration has taken place. (p. 104)

This process can be compared to the experiences of letting memories of past achievements overpower a recent failure, or allowing the confidence earned from overcoming past difficulties to ease feelings of discouragement for when facing new challenges (Lankton, 1980).

## OVERLAPPING

Overlapping is a technique to assist a client in retrieving personal resources in the construction of new experiences by generating rich, full, vivid internal experiences, which involve all of the sensory modalities. Overlapping begins with a verbalization within the primary representational system and continues by guiding the client's awareness into another channel and another channel until all sensory modalities have been added. In a visual person, overlap would begin with a visual experience or an image, and then other sensory experiences are added to that image at the natural points of intersection. For example, with a client who is unable to access strong internal feelings, the therapist will use overlapping by starting from the client's visual image and leading him/her into experiencing the necessary internal feelings. Thus, the original representation is expanded to include all the sensory modalities within a vivid and intense internally generated experience (Cameron-Bandler, 1985).

In overlapping, internal experiences are constructed in the same manner in which the senses work naturally. To overlap effectively, the submodalities or sensory-specific characteristics of each system need to be in place. The visual experience includes such characteristics as color, brightness, texture, clarity, shape, and movement. The auditory submodalities include tempo, volume, pitch, location, and timbre. The kinesthetic system includes weight, temperature, location, and texture. The olfactory/gustatory systems include odor, essence, fragrance, taste, and temperature. Overlapping representational systems are designed to enrich a person's experience; as described by Cameron-Bandler (1985), "It brings portions of experience that were outside of conscious awareness into consciousness, and also serves to align the internal and external processes so that the experience becomes congruent" (p. 179). Overlapping is a means of accessing a client's useful experiences that were previously available.

## REFRAMING

It follows from the assumption that all behaviors have a positive intention, that even maladaptive behavior has some adaptive qualities. For example, a person who is afraid of success might be so because he is protecting himself from failure. Reframing is the process of taking an experience or feeling and turning it around so that it has a positive effect on the client. Dilts (1998) outlines the six step reframing system:

**1. Identify the problematic behavior.**
"What is the behavior or symptom you want to change?"

**2. Establish communication with the part of yourself that is responsible for the behavior.**
"Go inside of yourself and ask the part of you that creates this behavior, 'Please give me a signal if you are willing to communicate with me.' Pay attention to any internal words, images or feelings that might be a signal from that part of yourself."
2.1. If you do not get a clear signal, ask the part to exaggerate the signal. You may also use the symptom itself by asking "Please intensify the symptom if your answer is 'yes'."
2.2. If the part is not willing to communicate, ask "What is your positive purpose in not wanting to communicate with me?"
[If you have continued difficulty in establishing communication with the part, you may want to try a different change process.]

**3. Separate the positive intention of the part from the problematic behavior.**
"Go inside and thank the part for communicating with you and ask, 'What are you trying to do positively for me or communicate to me with this behavior?'"
3.1. If the intention of the part seems negative, keep asking "And what will that do positively for me? What is your positive purpose?"

**4. Find three other choices that satisfy the positive intention of the part but do not have the negative consequences of the symptom or problematic behavior.**
"Go to the 'creative part' of yourself and ask it to come up with at least three other ways to satisfy the positive intention of the problematic behavior."

**5. Have the part that creates the symptom or problematic behaviors agree to implement the new choices.**
"Go inside and ask the part responsible for the problematic behavior, 'Signal me if you accept the alternative choices'."
5.1. If any choices are not acceptable, or there is no signal, go to step 4 and modify or add choices.

**6. Ecology check. Find out if any other parts object to the new choices.**
"Go inside and ask, 'Do any other parts object to these new choices?'"
6.1. If yes, identify the part and go to step 2, repeating the cycle with that part. Implement the new choices. "Go inside and ask the part responsible for the problematic behavior."

(Internet site)

The goal of this six-step system is to overcome any maladaptive thoughts or imprints by finding the positive intention within them.

Another aspect of reframing deals with the newly formed NLP technique of reimprinting. According to Dilts (1998), "an imprint is a significant experience or period of life from the past in which a person formed a belief or cluster of beliefs, often in relationship to one's identity" (Internet site). The goal of this technique is to find the resources necessary to change the illogical belief. In order to achieve this goal, another NLP technique of Time Line therapy must be introduced.

Time Line therapy deals with the imagining of a line, which extends from left to right, on the ground in front of the client. This imaginary time line represents the client's past, present, and future. After this line is imagined, the client is asked to establish a "Meta-position" off the time line (Dilts, 1998). A Meta-position is the position in which the observer is dissociated from the events of his/her life. This position allows the client to see the events of his/her life, without reliving them or experiencing the emotions attached to them. Whenever the client moves forward on this time line, he/she is moving toward the future. Whenever the client moves backward on the time line, he/she should be reliving moments of the past.

Reimprinting involves the use of this Time Line therapy. In the first step of reimprinting, the client is asked to identify the problematic symptoms by standing on the physical location on the time line. The person should still be facing the future direction. Now, Dilts (1998) instructs,

> Focus your attention on the physical expression of your symptoms, and any beliefs associated with them, and walk slowly backwards pausing at any location that seems to be relevant to the symptom or the accompanying beliefs. Keep moving back in time until you reach the earliest experience associated with the symptoms and/or the beliefs. (Internet site)

After reaching this earliest point, while in the associated time line position, the client verbalizes the cluster of maladaptive beliefs that were formed during this experience. The client should be speaking in first person, present tense. After this has been done, the client steps backwards to the time line position before this negative imprint was experienced. The client should feel a difference, as if the event has not happened yet or has not affected him/her yet.

During the next part of this technique, the client is asked to step off the time line to the designated Meta-position and look back at the maladaptive experience. Next, he/she should note the effect these earlier experiences had on his/her life and verbalize any other imprints formed as a result of the experience. However, the client should be speaking in the third person, past tense. Then the client is asked to find any positive purpose or secondary gain from the symptoms or responses formed during the imprint experience (Dilts, 1998).

In the third part of this technique, the client is asked to identify significant others involved in the imprint. Toward this end, the client is asked to step back into the time line position and associate himself/herself with each of the significant others, one at a time. The client should describe, in first person, the experience of the imprint situation from that perceptual position. Then, the client should repeat the Meta-position step. He/she steps off the line and find the positive intention of past actions and responses (Dilts, 1998).

The fourth step, taken while in the Meta-position, is to identify the resources that each person, including the client, needed in the past. This resource is usually available in the present but was missing in the past. The client takes this resource and anchors it by representing it as an energy or light. Then, the client steps onto the first point discovered on the time line with the anchor in order to "'transmit' the resource back through time to each person in the system that needed it. This may be done metaphorically through the energy, light, or sound" (Dilts, 1998, Internet site). After this association has been made by the anchor, the client steps into the shoes of each person who needed the anchor and relives the maladaptive imprint experience from that person's point of view, while verbalizing the experience in the first person. The therapist continues using the anchor in order to reimprint many other different maladaptive beliefs.

## VISUALIZATION

The process of visualization is often associated with the achievement and maintenance of health in regards to the ability of visualization to have a physiological effect (Dilts, 1983b). In NLP, visualization occurs as the client creates visual representations of his/her desired state, and it is useful in helping the client move toward that state. More specifically, the client is encouraged to visualize the parts of himself/herself which are in a state of incongruence and then to visualize those same parts negotiating with one another (Dilts, 1983b). The client visualizes a healthy state not only in the visual system, but by using all of the senses in conjunction with one another. In this way, the person can more fully sense the desired outcome, thus making it more concrete and easier to achieve (Dilts, 1983b).

## THERAPEUTIC METAPHOR

The technique of therapeutic metaphor, developed by Milton Erickson, uses storytelling to provide important unconscious or conscious learning that causes new productive behaviors. Stories are effective methods for dealing with secondary gains from dysfunctional behavior. An effective metaphor is isomorphic, or of similar structure, to the problem content. It provides the opportunity to access previously unrecognized choices and to supply a solution or set of solutions that are generalizable to the problem so that appropriate changes can be made (Cameron-Bandler, 1985). Therapeutic metaphor is a non-threatening yet effective way to deal with problems not easily addressed by other techniques.

To construct a metaphor, first the problem is identified completely. The structural parts and pertinent characteristics of the problem are defined. Next, an isomorphic situation is imposed and a logical solution implied by the therapist. The useful lessons are identified and are used in the contexts in which they would be effective. This structure is placed in the context of a story, a form of indirect communications, in order to disguise the motive of the therapist from the client. To aid in extinguishing dysfunctional behavior which is continued because of secondary gains, those gains are identified and embedded into the story. The solution lies in providing a way of achieving those same gains but through healthy behaviors. Anchors are used in the process of story-telling to help make it effective, and the method of overlapping is used to enrich the metaphor.

The advantage of metaphors lies in the power of the unconscious; that is, people respond without trying. Cameron-Bandler (1985) explains that the client's "conscious processes do not interfere and while knowing that something happened, they really are not sure just what (or how) it happened" (p. 195).

## FUTURE-PACING

The test of any successful change work lies in the extent to which the learning created in therapy can be generalized to contexts and life situations outside of the therapist's office. The client should have a new set of tools or responses which can be utilized when needed. Future-pacing is the bridge between the therapist's office and the client's real world experience. It consists of anchoring a new set of behaviors to the stimulus that originally triggered the problematic behavior. The stimulus pattern that is responsible for the problematic behavior is asked to take responsibility for implementing the new behavior created in therapy. The new resources are then rehearsed for the future contexts in which they will be needed. When the situations are identified, the client creates an internal depiction of the circumstance in which he/she is able to access the needed resources. Thus, the resource behavior becomes attached to the circumstance to insure the full integration of new behaviors.

Future-pacing is important because it lies at the level of the unconscious. It cannot be assumed that the conscious mind will automatically take the accomplishments of therapy and apply them in everyday life. According to Cameron-Bandler (1985), "Although the conscious mind may try very hard, it usually recalls the new behavior only after it has already failed (by exhibiting the former behavior)" (p. 216). On the other hand, the unconscious mind does work automatically. Future-pacing is the final, and perhaps the most important, step in any effective therapeutic intervention.

## SOME NEW TECHNIQUES

NLP is a method which is continuously changing as brain functions and the ways in which they can be used are better understood. As a result, there are numerous new techniques, which have evolved from but maintain their basis in the original set of tools. These include Changing the Past, the Belief Change Pattern, and the Swish Pattern.

Changing the Past involves modifying past experiences through changing submodalities, which are "universal elements that can be used to change any visual image no matter what the content is" (Bandler, 1985, p. 22). These submodality patterns are ways in which the brain sorts and codes experience. Brightness is one such submodality of the visual modality. By increasing the brightness of an image, the intensity of feelings is also increased. Inversely, an unpleasant memory that causes bad feelings can be dimmed so that it is no longer bothersome. Varying the size, color, distance, depth, and clarity of a picture will also intensify or diminish the response to it.

The point of view that is taken when recalling memories can also affect the way in which the event-related feelings are re-experienced. Memories can be recalled either in an associated or disassociated manner. Associating involves going back and reliving an experience as it originally happened. Disassociation involves remembering the event from the point of view of an onlooker. It is beneficial to remember pleasant memories in an associated manner; however, by recalling unpleasant memories in a disassociated manner, all of the needed visual information is kept intact and can be dealt with in the future, but the unpleasant feeling response is avoided. The brain can be taught to associate with pleasant memories and to disassociate from unpleasant ones (Bandler, 1985). Similarly, the brain can be reprogrammed in regard to beliefs and habits.

Bandler (1985) proposes that changes in negative beliefs can be made by representing them in internal experience and modifying them to match the submodality properties of doubts through the Belief Change Pattern. Using another submodality, the content of the unwanted belief can be changed to the desired belief. In the Swish Pattern, which Bandler believes to be highly effective, the brain is directionalized so that the behavior tends to follow the same direction (Bandler, 1985). After the client identifies a behavior to be changed, he/she isolates a situation just before the behavior starts. This is the cue picture. The client also creates an outcome picture which is a view of the self after the desired change. The two pictures are then "swished" so that the outcome picture, which is initially a small and dark image, becomes big and bright and covers the cue picture. The "swish" occurs quickly and redirects the brain toward a new set of behaviors.

## CONCLUDING REMARKS

The tools of NLP are meant to be applied to changing old, unpleasant feeling responses in a very brief time, sometimes even in minutes. What people do has a structure, and once that is uncovered, it can be changed; people can be taught to use their brains in more functional ways. As Bandler (1985) proposes, "People aren't broken; they work perfectly! The important question is, 'How do they work now?' so that you can help them work perfectly in a way that is more pleasant and useful" (p. 143). People can change by reorganizing their experiences or by modifying the way in which they experience them.

NLP is the "briefest" form of therapy. According to Bandler (1985), change cannot occur slowly because the brain does not work that way. All of the information is set up ahead of time and then change is quick. In other words, "good NLP work is 95% information-gathering and 5% intervention" (p. 110). The phobic responds well to NLP and provides a good example as someone who has already proved to be a rapid learner; he/she has learned something quite ridiculous very quickly (Bandler, 1985). It is not surprising that the cure also can be achieved in a matter of minutes through neutralizing strong feeling responses by disassociation.

The method and tools of NLP are effective in creating quick change. However, the ability to use these tools effectively rests upon the skills of noticing nonverbal cues, linguistic patterns, verbal representations, and thought processes and formulating from them a model of a client within his/her world. NLP is not technique-oriented; its emphasis lies upon the therapist. The NLP skills are not easily learned and require a high level of dedicated effort.

For a dedicated therapist, the methods of NLP provide an opportunity for learning with every client. Bandler (1985) says,

> It is not a set of techniques, it's an attitude. It's an attitude that has to do with curiosity, with wanting to know about things, wanting to be able to influence things, and wanting to be able to influence them in a way that's worthwhile. (p. 155)

Thus, the changes that take place through NLP will always be different and will involve stepping into the client's world and creating reference experiences relative to him/her to change that client's map. NLP continues to evolve as more is learned about the nature and functioning of the brain.

## REFERENCES

Bandler, R. (1985). *Using your brain—For a change.* Moah, UTh: Real People Press.

Bandler, R., & Grinder, J. (1979). *Frogs into princes.* Moah, UT: Real People Press.

Bandler, R., & Grinder, J. (1975a). *Patterns of the hypnotic techniques of Milton H. Erickson, M.D.* (Vol. 1). Cupertino, CA: Meta Publications.

Bandler, R., & Grinder, J. (1975b). *The structure of magic I.* Palo Alto, CA: Science and Behavior Books, Inc.

Bandler, R., & Grinder, J. (1976). *The structure of magic II.* Palo Alto, CA: Science and Behavior, Inc.

Cameron-Bandler, L. (1985). *Solutions.* California: Future Pace, Inc.

Dawes, G. (1998). *The significance of neuro-linguistic programming in the therapy of anxiety disorders.* http://www.experiential-dynamics.org/nlp.htm

Dilts, R. (1998). *Articles.* http://www.scruz.net/~rdilts

Dilts, R. (1983a). *Roots of neuro-linguistic programming.* Cupertino, CA: Meta Publications.

Dilts, R. (1983b). *Applications of neuro-linguistic programming.* Cupertino, CA: Meta Publications.

Grinder, J., DeLozier, J., & Bandler, R. (1977). *Patterns of the hypnotic techniques of Milton H. Erickson, M.D.* (Vol. 2), Cupertino, CA: Meta Publications.

Lankton, S. (1980). *Practical magic.* Cupertino, CA: Meta Publications.

## CHAPTER 6

# Imagery Techniques in Cognitive Behavior Treatments of Anxiety and Trauma

## ROBERT J. LUEGER

Cognitive therapy and cognitive-behavior therapy emerged from two separate theoretical traditions, but have evolved to share many common features. Cognitive therapy originated in what might be called a "top down" approach in which thoughts influence feelings and behaviors. Cognitive behavior therapy emanated from behavior therapy, and might be considered a "bottom up" approach in which situational stimuli, responses (including thoughts), and consequences are at issue. One of the common features is the incorporation of imagery techniques in the treatment of affective disorders. In the past decade, significant advances have been made from these two perspectives in treatments of anxiety and trauma problems. The purpose of this chapter is to review the development of cognitive behavior treatments that have used imagery techniques.

### COGNITIVE THERAPY

Cognitive therapy (CT) originally was developed to treat depression (Beck, Rush, Shaw, & Emery, 1979), and was later extended to the treatment of anxiety disorders (Clark, 1986). Cognitive therapy is based on the assumption that it is the interpretation of an event, rather than the event itself, that determines the emotional state of the individual. Cognitive therapy focuses on dysfunctional, inaccurate, or extreme thoughts, on schemas that influence automatic thoughts, and on attributional styles that predispose the individual to interpret positive and negative outcomes in ways that result in distressful experiences. Specific thoughts are associated with particular types of emotional responses. Depression, with its accompanying sadness and guilt, involves dysfunctional thoughts of loss or of having acted wrongly. Anxiety is associated with thoughts of danger, and anger is associated with thoughts that the acts of others have wronged the individual.

The processes of cognitive therapy target these pathological thoughts, and typically involve cognitive restructuring and retraining. Cognitive therapy, like cognitive behavior therapy, is among the more directive therapies. That is, the therapist assumes an authority role in educating, analyzing, prescribing, and guiding the client through the change process. In cognitive therapy, clients are challenged to evaluate the validity of their thought-emotional reaction patterns. There are three phases to the treatment of an emotional disorder: 1) clients are taught to identify the dysfunctional thoughts that are associated with their dominant negative emotional states; 2) client and therapist together evaluate the validity of the thoughts; and 3) more adaptive thoughts are identified and inserted to replace the dysfunctional thoughts.

The following treatment of an experience of panic episodes illustrates the techniques of cognitive therapy. A thirty-two-year-old man employed as a marketing representative was referred to a mental health professional by his primary care physician following his second admission to a hospital emergency room for extreme breathing difficulty (shortness of breath), chest pain, racing heart, general weakness, and fear of dying. The first episode had occurred as he shopped in a mall, the second as he was being driven by his fiancee to a gathering of her family. The initial intake assessment clarified the absence of any causative physical condition, diagnosed the experiences and panic attacks, and focused on the dominant emotion of the experience, a fear of dying. In the first stage of the cognitive treatment, the therapist educated the client about the reactions that are common in a panic experience, guided the client through an analysis of the thoughts that preceded and accompanied the experiencing of fear, and targeted the critical dysfunctional thoughts that centered around financial ineptitude and physical and emotional vulnerability. In the second phase of treatment, the therapist helped the client challenge the exaggerated and unhelpful thoughts by examining the evidence for and against the validity of them in light of his current experiences. In the third phase, the therapist guided the client through the process of identifying alternative, more adaptive thoughts that emphasized the client's resiliency in the face of fiscal threats. The remaining therapy contacts reviewed the practice of the more adaptive resiliency thoughts, especially in contexts that involved fiscal challenge, and monitored treatment response.

## COGNITIVE BEHAVIOR THERAPY

Cognitive behavior therapies (CBT) evolved from behavior therapy and its antecedent-behavior-consequence analysis. Behavior therapies are based on stimulus-stimulus, stimulus-response, or response-reinforcement theories of learning. The different behavior theories give different status to thoughts. From the functional analysis perspective (radical behaviorism), thoughts are seen as behaviors that are cued by stimuli in a specific situation and are followed by emotional consequences of positive or negative reward. In the case of anxiety and trauma, the reward is usually negative in that it involves the dissipation of an aversive experience through avoidance. From the cognitive social learning perspective, thoughts are given a higher status as mediational events. Cognitive behavior therapies based on cognitive social learning theory attempt to: 1) enhance self-control strategies through stimulus control, self-monitoring, and self-reward; 2) establish alternative thought-emotional reaction sequences through covert conditioning, thought stopping, and covert sensitization; and 3) teach new cognitive behavioral responses through coping skills training, problem solving, and decision-making strategies (Mahoney & Arnkoff, 1978). Both behavioral analysis and cognitive social learning therapies begin with an analysis of the situation in which the problem behavior(s) occur, examine the behaviors and thoughts of the client, and identify the consequences following those behaviors and thoughts.

Cognitive behavior therapy conceptualizations of anxiety and trauma are influenced by the Mowrer's two-factor theory (1960) of fear responses in which fear is acquired through classical conditioning and maintained through operant learning principles. In this model, an initially neutral stimulus situation acquires negative emotion-provoking qualities because of its association with an intense negative personal experience. That stimulus situation evokes the negative emotional reaction, and a process of generalization occurs in which other feature-similar situations (same setting, same clothing or jewelry worn by the participant, same physical features of another person in that setting) elicit variations of the original negative experience. A general sense of loss of control typifies this response scenario. Avoidance behaviors follow because of the negative reinforcing properties of escaping the fear situation.

The goal of cognitive behavior therapy of fear responses is to extinguish the classically-learned associations and to replace those associations with more adaptive responses. CBT typically involves some element of progressive mastery of a hierarchy of avoidance inducing situations when anxiety and trauma are involved. Rehearsal and practice are key components of the continuing therapy contacts.

The case of a twenty-four-year-old woman traumatized by an attack outside the garage of her apartment while returning from grocery shopping illustrates the strategy of a cognitive behavioral treatment. The woman reported at intake that she feared leaving her apartment, avoided the specific grocery store at which she had been shopping as well as any of the stores of the same chain, and avoided wearing clothing that would make her look attractive. Since the attack, she had not worn any of the jewelry that she had worn the night of the attack. She also reported intrusive thoughts of guilt at how she might have contributed to her own vulnerability, and shame that she could not manage her independent living successfully. The cognitive behavior therapist initially determed that the woman suffered from Post Traumatic Stress Disorder (PTSD) and that a PTSD treatment was appropriate. The therapist then educated the client about the nature of the therapy including the schedule of sessions, skills to be learned, and the importance of completing homework assignments. Information was gathered about the assault situation, and the client was taught breathing exercises basic to a relaxation response as an adaptive response that is incompatible with the fear response. The therapist "normalized" the client's trauma responses by discussing common reactions of anger, guilt, depression, and shame. A representative hierarchy of fear producing situations/stimuli was constructed based on the client's rating of the fear of those situations. Progressive mastery began with use of the learned relaxation response to the least feared situations. Role playing and imaginal exposure preceded the use of in vivo exposure in subsequent sessions of therapy. The guilt and shame were addressed with cognitive restructuring in which she identified the thoughts associated with guilt and shame, examined the validity of those thoughts, and learned more logical and beneficial thoughts.

## IMAGERY TECHNIQUES IN COGNITIVE BEHAVIOR TREATMENTS

### Cognitive Therapy Imagery

The use of imagery in cognitive therapy is most evident in the identification of components of the self-schemas that contribute to maladaptive thinking or to the production of exaggerated thinking processes. Dysfunctional thought processes such as selective attention to failures, magnification of negative outcomes, minimization of positive outcomes, and arbitrary inferences about personal responsibility can be explored by imagining situations involving anxiety or trauma reactions. Active imagination and the production of fantasies can serve as a prime source for the identification of maladaptive cognitions and their accompanying mood components. A vivid fantasy account can illustrate for both client and therapist the sequence of thinking and feeling central to the dysfunctional affect. The cognitive therapist, in actively using the "Socratic" questioning procedure, attempts to facilitate the clients self-discovery of thinking and feeling connections.

In the example of the man experiencing panic previously described, the therapist might have asked the client to vividly recall the events surrounding the visit to the mall as well as the second panic episode's car ride with his fiancee. The client might have been guided to "slow down" a replay of these events in order to more closely examine thinking patterns, and to enhance the focus on components of the thinking. With regard to the identified problem thoughts, a minimization of financial successes and magnification of limits on autonomy became evident when these thinking processes were carefully examined.

### Cognitive Behavior Therapy Imagery

Imagery techniques are used in cognitive behavior treatments to achieve imaginal exposure in lieu of difficulties or unreadiness to achieve in vivo exposure. Two basic premises underlie the use of imaginal exposure. First, imagined situations sufficiently approximate actual feared responses so that active imagination results in an approximation of the avoidant response. Second, the imagined situation provokes a lesser fear response than the actual experience, and therefore is more readily managed with alternative adaptive responses. A third, more evident and practical reason for the use of imaginal techniques is their efficiency. In vivo exposure requires visitation of the eliciting situations, and actual visitation can be time consuming or even difficult to manage.

In the example of the traumatized woman above, imaginal exposure was used instead of actual visitations to generic grocery stores, another grocery store in the namebrand chain, and the neighborhood store itself. Imaginal exposure was combined with in vivo exposure in the processes of dressing in the feared clothing and jewelry.

## TREATMENTS OF ANXIETY

Anxiety disorders include a diverse array of syndromal presentations. Panic disorder often is considered the prototype of the anxiety disorders, although generalized anxiety and phobias, especially social phobia, have higher prevalence rates. Obsessive-compulsive disorders, although infrequent, have been treated with cognitive behavior therapy. Test anxiety is another problem that has been addressed with covert modeling techniques.

## Imaginal Exposure in Anxiety Management

**Social Phobia.** Social phobia has been described by some epidemiologists and the most prevalent of the anxiety disorders. CBT techniques have been successfully used to treat social phobia in group and individual modalities. The group modality offers more opportunities for in vivo exposure. In individual therapy, covert modeling, which is described more fully below, may be used in lieu of actual social encounters. This may be particularly useful when the fear response is most evident in a particular situation that does not generalize to a group context. CBT treatments of social phobia have achieved the status of "empirically validated" treatments.

**Panic Disorder.** A form of exposure that is used in the treatment of panic disorder symptoms is *interoceptive* exposure. In interoceptive exposure, the physical symptoms of racing heart, hyperventilation, and chest pain are confronted by practice exercises which induce mild forms of these symptoms. Cognitive restructuring techniques are taught to identify and modify cognitive misappraisals. Breathing retraining is provided to decrease the overbreathing that occurs during panic. Repeated exposure to the hyperventilation cues (interoceptive exposure) deconditions the fear reactions to panic-like sensations. Exposure is sometimes accompanied by modeling, first by the therapist, and later by covert modeling in the clients imagination.

**Generalized Anxiety Disorder (GAD).** CBT treatment of GAD is based on the premise that the disorder stems from constant perceptions of the world as a dangerous place. Negatively valenced images, worrisome thinking, and catastrophic imaging are a frequently-observed component of GAD. Clients are taught to attend to any subtle shift in their anxiety level and to note any patterns of worrisome thinking or catastrophic imaging. Clients are taught to intervene earlier and earlier in the response cycle by using relaxation and cognitive restructuring. In GAD, the images tend to be a major component of the feared stimuli, and so self-control desensitization is often used.

**Obsessive-Compulsive Disorder.** Exposure in obsessive-compulsive disorder is accompanied by response prevention of thoughts or actions that reduce anxiety. Foa, Steketee, and Grayson (1985) have provided an example of the use of imagery in treating obsessive-compulsive disorder with CBT. Using data from interviews in the initial sessions, six scenes were constructed for each patient. The scenes were organized in a hierarchy according to how many units of subjective distress (SUDs) that scene elicited.

> The first scene provoked 50 to 60 SUDs. A new scene was presented each day until a scene evoking 100 SUDs (the maximum number) was presented in the sixth session. From session 7 to 15, variants of the most disturbing of the scenes were presented. When additional feared material emerged during conversation or flooding sessions, this was also incorporated into the scenes.

> During imagery, patients were instructed not to fantasize themselves carrying out rituals. (p. 295)

Each of the flooding sessions lasted two hours, during which the patient reclined in a comfortable chair with eyes closed. The patients were instructed by the therapist to imagine the scenes described by the therapist as vividly as possible. Foa provided the following condensed example of one such scene:

> You just got up and finished putting on your clothes. The thought occurs to you that you need to undress, otherwise your husband will die in a car accident. You decide not to undress. You say to yourself, "I am not going to engage in any rituals, even if my husband dies." Suddenly the doorbell rings. You open the door and a policeman stands there telling you that your husband was involved in a car accident. He asks you to go with him to identify his body. Your daughter is already there. She accuses you of causing your husband's death. She says, "You should have undressed; you were selfish; you care only about yourself. Now because you failed to perform your rituals, Dad is dead. . . ." (p. 295)

### Covert Modeling

Another cognitive behavioral approach to treating anxiety or trauma symptoms is *covert modeling.* Covert modeling involves the mental rehearsal of a task to be performed in the future. Long popular in the enhancement of sports performance such as the "perfect" golf swing, tennis serve, or dive, covert modeling involves imaginal performance, self-induced relaxation, and covert reinforcement for desirable performance. Two types of covert modeling have been developed. In *mastery modeling,* the client repeatedly visualizes a perfect performance without any negative consequences and with positive consequences. In *coping modeling,* the client initially imagines herself or himself becoming fearful or anxious, then visualizes satisfactory performance. Coping modeling has been used to successfully treat social phobias (anxiety management) and to enhance resilience to future predictable stressors such as confronting a rejecting spouse or a work supervisor (examples of stress inoculation). Evaluation studies generally have supported the superiority of coping modeling over mastery modeling techniques.

Coping modeling is presented in three phases: 1) an educational phase, 2) a rehearsal phase, and 3) an application phase. In the first phase, the client studies and learns about his or her anxiety reaction. After learning the rationale for coping skills training, the therapist and client explore self-statements, thoughts, and images that precede, accompany, or follow exposure to the feared situation. One technique for making cognitions apparent is to ask the client to "run a movie" of reactions to the fearful situation, and to "stop the film" and do a "frame-by-frame" analysis of his or her behavioral response.

In the second, or application phase, the client is taught a variety of different techniques that can be used to manage and control his or her responses to fear-producing stimuli. Physical relaxation exercises are aimed at reducing arousal to manageable levels. The client also is instructed to select one or more positive experiences that are associated with states of relaxation, peacefulness, and tranquility by the client. Further, the positive image is developed and enhanced to increase its vividness and sensorial qualities to the point that the client can lose himself or herself in the image. Coping self-statements that are incompatible with fear cognitions also are taught to enhance the client's repertoire of positive self-talk.

In the application phase, the client practices these newly acquired coping skills while being exposed to imagined, role-played, or in vivo fearful stimuli. During this phase, the client learns which of the self-talk coping strategies works best for him or her. The following examples of positive self-talk have been successfully used in the cognitive behavioral treatment of test anxiety. Each illustrates one of the four phases of a stress response associated with test anxiety (Meichenbaum, 1977).

(1) I've prepared for this test. If I stay calm, I'll get through it just fine (preparing for the stressor).

(2) Take it one question at a time . . . Okay, now what is this question asking me to do? . . . I'm doing fine . . . relaxed . . . in control (being confronted with a fearful stimulus and feeling its impact).

(3) I know there might be some hard questions, but I'm not going to let that throw me. Don't let this test beat me . . . I'm prepared for it (dealing with the feelings of being overwhelmed).

(4) Sure I'm a little anxious, but I'm handling it okay. This test wasn't as bad as I thought it would be. I didn't let that tough question throw me. I stayed in control (evaluation of performance). (p. 17)

In summary, imaginal exposure, whether accompanied by cognitive restructuring or coping modeling, might be considered to be a therapy enhancing component in the treatment of anxiety. That is, it is a sufficient but not necessary way of presenting an essential component of therapy, exposure to the feared event.

## Imaginal Exposure in the Treatment of Trauma

The prospect of reliving a traumatic experience in memory is quite upsetting for most clients. To help the client control his or her anxiety response, the rationale of using exposure must be thoroughly discussed prior to the actual exposure, and this rationale must be repeated during the exposure process. The therapist must communicate her or his confidence in the procedure based on clinical experiences with similar cases and the results of empirical treatment studies, but should acknowledge that exposure can be difficult in the early stages of treatment. Client control of the exposure process also is important to the success of the procedure. The therapist ensures that exposures to increasingly stressful cues are conducted gradually. Respect of client control also requires balancing sufficient time to discuss each exposure experience with encouragement to try additional situations, and use of relaxation procedures as needed.

The following potential therapist-delivered rationale for imaginal exposure has been offered by Meadows and Foa (1998):

Today we're going to spend most of the session doing imaginal exposure, or having you relive the assault in your memory. I know that you think about the assault quite a bit, but in therapy we will confront this memory in a different way. Currently, when you think about the assault you feel upset and therefore try to push the thoughts away. It makes sense that you'd want to avoid thinking about it, since it was such a distressing experience. Unfortunately, as you've already discovered, trying not to think about it doesn't work very well, and it keeps coming back. Some of the symptoms of PTSD, like nightmares, intrusive thoughts, and flashbacks, are signals that you haven't yet dealt with the memories. So in imaginal exposure, you will deliberately confront the thoughts and memories without pushing them away. Reliving the assault in your memory lets you process the experience, so that you can file it away in your mind like any other bad memory, rather than having it be so real for you. It will also show that you can let yourself think about it and not lose control or go crazy, so that you end up having control over the memories rather than having them control you. You will also learn that the anxiety you experience when you think about the assault eventually decreases, just like it does when you stay in situations you were afraid of.

Get comfortable and close your eyes so you won't be distracted. Begin thinking about the assault, and when you talk about it, do so in as much detail as you can. Describe not only what's happening, but also what you're thinking and feeling. Talk about it in the present tense, as if its happening right now, rather than a story from the past. While you describe it I want you to visualize it in your head, describing what you're experiencing. We're going to do this for about 45 minutes, so that you have time for the anxiety to decrease, so you may end up telling the story of the assault several times. We'll hold off discussing it until the very end of the exposure rather than at the end of each retelling. Periodically, I'll ask you for SUDs ratings (subjective units of distress scale), so I know how you're feeling during this. The rating should be how you feel right now, sitting here, not how you felt at that time during the assault. Before we begin, do you have any questions? (pp. 111-112)

### Image Habituation Training

Imagery techniques also have been used to reduce or weaken the feared stimulus. Image habituation training (IHT; Vaughn & Tarrier, 1992) was developed as a flooding-like treatment of a traumatic response.

In IHT, each client audiotapes five or six self-descriptions of the recurrent trauma images being reexperienced. During the treatment, the patient listens to each audio-taped self-narration, and in the thirty-second silent period following each narration, the patient is asked to visualize the images evoked by the narration before going on to the next narration. The client then is instructed to listen to the tape for one hour each day over a ten-session period. The flooding principle of the treatment is that repeated exposure will reduce the stimulus-eliciting properties of the traumatic stimuli. An advantage of IHT is that the patient can implement the treatment outside the therapist's office.

## THE EFFICACY OF IMAGERY TREATMENTS OF ANXIETY AND TRAUMA

CBT treatments of anxiety and trauma have been evaluated in controlled studies and have been found to be quite successful (Barlow & Lehman, 1996; Foa &

Meadows, 1997; Tarrier, Pilgrim, Sommerfield, et al., 1999). For example, in the first study of exposure-based treatment of panic symptoms (Barlow, Craske, Cerny, & Klosko, 1989), 87 percent of the patients were free of panic symptoms at the end of treatment. These gains were maintained up to two years following treatment (Craske, Brown, & Barlow, 1991). In fact, all of the CBT treatments for anxiety and trauma disorders that have been reviewed in this chapter have been validated in at least two controlled studies conducted in different treatment clinics by different therapist- researchers, and accordingly have been listed among the "empirically supported therapies" (Chambless, Sanderson, Shoham, et al., 1996).

Nevertheless, CBT and Cognitive therapy treatments are not the only effective treatments for anxiety disorders. That is, the active ingredients of CBT treatments are sufficient to produce positive treatment responses, but are shared by other interventions given their success. The pluralistic nature of etiologies of disorders is upheld by the failure of treatments to be found to be superior to each other.

Imagery techniques, conceptualized as part of therapies, are incorporated into the delivery of treatments. For mild or very severe fear-eliciting stimuli, imaginal exposure may be as effective as in vivo exposure, although at moderate degrees of intensity, actual exposure may surpass imaginal techniques. Although there are a few studies of therapies that might be considered component analyses, there really has been little work to date on the comparative contributions of components, such as imaginal exposure or mastery, of successful treatments. Treatments often consist of multiple therapeutic techniques delivered in the most efficient manner possible, and the sequencing of those techniques in successful treatments would be of great interest to therapists. Components such as imagery techniques should be approached as sufficient but not necessary ingredients of treatments. Yet the inclusion of imagery techniques among the many empirically supported treatments for anxiety and trauma is strong testament to their overall clinical utility.

## REFERENCES

Barlow, D. H., & Lehman, C. (1996). Advances in the psychological treatment of anxiety disorders. *Archives of General Psychiatry, 53,* 727-735.

Barlow, D. H., Craske, M. G., Cerny, J. A., & Klosko, J. S. (1989). Behavioral treatment of panic disorder. *Behavior Therapy, 20,* 261-282.

Beck, A. T., Rush, A. J., Shaw, B. F., & Emery, G. (1979). *Cognitive therapy of depression.* New York: Guilford Press.

Chambless, D. L., Sanderson, W. C., Shoham, V., Johnson, S. B., Pope, K. S., Crits-Christoph, P., Baker, M., Johnson, B., Woody, S. R., Sue, S., Beutler, L., Williams, D. A., & McCurry, S. (1996). An update on empirically validated therapies. *The Clinical Psychologist, 49,* 5-18.

Clark, D. M. (1986). A cognitive approach to panic. *Behavior Research and Therapy, 24,* 461-470.

Craske, M. G., Brown, T. A., & Barlow, D. H. (1991). Behavioral treatment of panic disorder: A two-year followup. *Behavior Therapy, 22,* 289-304.

Foa, E. B., & Meadows, E. A. (1997). Psychosocial treatments for posttraumatic stress disorder: A critical review. *Annual Review of Psychology, 48,* 449-480.

Foa, E. B., Steketee, G., & Grayson, J. B. (1985). Imaginal and in vivo exposure: A comparison with obsessive-compulsive checkers. *Behavior Therapy, 16,* 292-302.

Mahoney, J. M., & Arnkoff, D. (1978). Cognitive and self-control therapies. In S. L. Garfield & A. E. Bergin (Eds.), *Handbook of psychotherapy and behavior change* (pp. 689-722). New York: Wiley.

Meadows, E. A., & Foa, E. B. (1998). Intrusion, arousal, and avoidance: Sexual trauma survivors. In V. M. Follette, J. I. Ruzek, & F. R. Abueg (Eds.), *Cognitive-behavioral therapies for trauma* (pp. 100-123). New York: Guilford.

Meichenbaum, D. (1977). *Cognitive behavior modification.* New York: Plenum.

Mowrer, O. A. (1960). *Learning theory and behavior.* New York: Wiley.

Tarrier, N., Pilgrim, H., Sommerfield, B. F., Reynolds, M., Graham, E., & Barrowclough, C. (1999). A randomized trial of cognitive therapy and imaginal exposure in the treatment of chronic posttraumatic stress disorder. *Journal of Consulting and Clinical Psychology, 67,* 13-18.

Vaughn, K., & Tarrier, N. (1992).The use of image habilitation training with post-traumatic stress disorders. *British Journal of Psychiatry, 161,* 658-664.

# CHAPTER 7

# *Imagery Rescripting Therapy for Trauma Survivors with PTSD*

## *MERVIN R. SMUCKER, JO WEIS, AND BRAD GRUNERT*

The use of imagery as a therapeutic strategy in treating trauma victims has been advocated by clinicians from a variety of theoretical orientations. Van der Kolk and van der Hart (1991) have noted that traumatic memories and their associated meanings are encoded as vivid images and sensations and are not accessible through linguistic retrieval alone, regardless of the victim's age at the time of the trauma. This finding corroborates the claims of many trauma victims who report difficulty with linguistically accessing and processing their traumatic experiences. It further has implications for the use of imagery as a primary therapeutic agent in the treatment of PTSD. Since much of the cognitive-affective disturbance associated with traumatic memories (e.g., intrusive recollections, recurring flashbacks) is embedded in the traumatic images themselves, directly challenging and modifying the traumatic imagery becomes a powerful, if not preferred, means of processing the traumatic material (Smucker, 1997).

Within this theoretical context, Imagery Rescripting Therapy (IRT) was developed in the mid-1990s by the senior author, initially for the treatment of childhood abuse survivors suffering from PTSD as adults, and is described in detail elsewhere (Smucker & Dancu, 1999; Smucker, Dancu, Foa, & Niederee, 1995; Smucker & Niederee, 1995). Numerous case studies as well as outcome data from an initial pilot project (Smucker & Dancu, 1999) offer empirical support for the efficacy of the procedure in reducing PTSD symptoms, eliminating recurring flashbacks and repetitive nightmares, and modifying traumagenic schemas. More recently, Grunert and colleagues have expanded the clinical applications of IRT for use with those experiencing PTSD symptomology resulting from other traumatic events, such as accidental injury, occupational injury, violent personal assault, and severe vehicle accidents (Grunert, Rusch, Weis, Smucker, & Mendelson, in press; Grunert, Weis, & Rusch, in press).

In short, IRT is a multifaceted, imagery-focused treatment designed to alleviate PTSD symptomology, alter traumatic beliefs and schemas (e.g., powerlessness, hopelessness, vulnerability), and enhance a trauma survivor's ability to self-calm and self-nurture. The treatment involves four essential components: 1) *imaginal exposure* (visually recalling and re-experiencing the iconic and kinesthetic components of the traumatic event together with the associated affect), 2) *imaginal rescripting* (replacing victimization imagery with mastery/coping imagery), 3) *self-calming/ self-nurturing imagery,* and 4) *linguistic processing* of the trauma (i.e., transforming the trauma into words such that thinking, talking, and/or writing about it is no longer upsetting to the victim).

The nucleus of the treatment involves activating and confronting the traumatic/ victimization imagery and replacing it with mastery/coping imagery, a process whereby individuals visualize themselves today responding in the traumatic scene(s) as empowered individuals no longer "frozen" in a passive state of victimization. Through the exposure and rescripting process, the traumatic images are identified, challenged, and modified along with the associated maladaptive beliefs, followed by the development of self-calming, self-soothing imagery. The use of imagery allows the traumatic material to be addressed directly through the eyes of the victim and then modified and reprocessed through the eyes of the empowered survivor.

Generally, four to eight imagery sessions (plus 1 to 2 follow-up sessions) are recommended for the most distressing flashback, although this format is open to modification according to specific client needs. Some victims of Type I traumas may require less than four sessions to eliminate PTSD symptomatology, while victims of more chronic Type II traumas often need eight sessions or more, especially in instances where the survivor was a victim of repeated childhood traumas.[1]

Before beginning with the imagery sessions, a pretreatment interview is conducted with an emphasis on assessing the client's current life situation, family, history of traumatic experiences, current psychological adjustment, overall physical and mental health status, alcohol and drug use, available family and community resources, severity of posttraumatic symptoms, and the appropriateness of IRT. Generally, if the client is recalling at least one traumatic memory via recurring visual flashbacks, repetitive nightmares, or other repeated intrusive recollections, IRT is likely to be appropriate.

Situations in which IRT may not be clinically indicated include: 1) current involvement in an ongoing traumatic situation (IRT is for recovering from post-traumatic stress, *not* from current, ongoing traumatic stress); 2) a diagnosis of schizophrenia, acute psychosis, or dissociative identity disorder; 3) current involvement in alcohol or substance abuse; or 4) the presence of vague or incomplete memories or the absence of trauma-related visual memories. Reconstructing memories, retrieving memory fragments, or altering original memories are *not* part of this treatment.

Near the end of the pre-treatment session, it is often useful to teach the client a brief focused-breathing exercise or some other self-calming technique. The therapeutic relationship can be significantly enhanced if clients can take something positive with them from the first session, e.g., a self-soothing strategy and the immediate benefits thereof.

---

[1] If the trauma was a relatively short-lived, one-time event (a Type I trauma), fewer IRT sessions are generally needed than if multiple, repeated traumas were experienced (Type II traumas).

If by the end of the pre-treatment evaluation the therapist has assessed the appropriateness of IRT, a brief description of the treatment is offered (may be paraphrased in the therapists own words):

> This treatment is designed to help you process and master your painful memories, so that you can feel more empowered and in control and be able to get on with your life in a more meaningful way. At the beginning of next session, I will discuss the therapy with you in more detail and address any further questions you might have at that time.

In the next session, the therapist presents a brief treatment rationale. Clients are informed of the heightened state of arousal and emotional distress that they will likely experience when the traumatic images are evoked in the session. Clients are likewise informed that activating their traumatic memories in a therapy session is quite different from experiencing them in their natural environment, that the trauma is not actually occurring at such times, and that throughout the imagery session the therapist's voice and supportive presence will provide a "therapeutic anchor." Following the treatment rationale, clients are taught to use a Subjective Units of Distress (SUDs) rating to indicate the amount of discomfort or distress they feel (Wolpe & Lazarus, 1966).

## IMAGINAL EXPOSURE

The exposure phase involves an imaginal reenactment of the entire traumatic event, as experienced by the client in the form of recurring flashbacks, nightmares, or other intrusive recollections. The client is asked to reenact the trauma (preferably with eyes closed) by visualizing and verbalizing aloud the entire traumatic memory in the present tense, as if it were occurring at that moment. If multiple recurring traumatic memories are reported, the most distressing one is generally targeted. The therapist inquires about the client's SUDs level every ten minutes or so throughout the entire imagery session. The SUDs ratings convey information to the therapist about the client's current emotional state, as well as the possible presence of any dissociating or numbing that may be occurring during the imagery.

The following instructions are offered by the therapist at the beginning of the imaginal exposure phase (may be paraphrased in the therapist's own words):

> I'm going to ask you to visually recall the memories of the traumatic event. It is best if you close your eyes so you won't be distracted. I will ask you to recall these painful memories as vividly as possible. It is important that you describe the traumatic event in the present tense as if it were happening now, right here. If you start to feel uncomfortable and want to leave the image, I will help you to stay with it. Every so often, I'll ask you to rate your discomfort level on a scale from 1 to 10. Please answer quickly and do not leave the image. Do you have any questions before we start? . . . What would you say your level of distress is at this moment? . . . I'd like you now to close your eyes, visualize the beginning of the traumatic scene, and describe what you experience, including

your thoughts and feelings about what is happening. (revised from Smucker et. al.,1995)

Any questions the client may have at this point about the imagery session are best addressed in a reassuring and succinct manner. A primary task of the therapist during the imaginal exposure phase is to provide a supportive, safe environment in which the client can visualize and verbalize the traumatic imagery while re-experiencing the associated painful affect. The therapist helps the client to "stay with" the effectively charged imagery as the client determines the level of detail included in the exposure description. Throughout the imagery session, the therapist's role is facilitative rather than directive. The therapist does not intervene other than to verbally reflect or restate what the client has just shared, or to ask the client for details of the traumatic scene (e.g., "And what's happening now?") or to elaborate on related thoughts and feelings.

When the reenactment of the traumatic memory appears to have ended, the therapist asks, "Is there anything more that happens in the imagery?" Once it is clear that the client has gone through and reexperienced the entire traumatic memory, the exposure imagery is brought to a close.

### Mastery Imagery[2]

Immediately following completion of the imaginal exposure phase, imaginal rescripting begins. This phase involves the creation of "mastery imagery." Initially, the mastery imagery phase closely resembles the exposure imagery. The client is asked to again visualize and verbalize the traumatic memory. This time, however, when the traumatic imagery is at its emotional peak (i.e., when the pain of the trauma appears to be most severe), clients are asked to visualize their "survivor" self today entering the traumatic scene to assist their "traumatized," "victimized," "injured" self. The therapist may facilitate this through such questions as:

Can you now visualize yourself as a survivor today entering the scene?
What happens when you, the survivor today, enter into the imagery?
What would you, the survivor, like to do or say?
Can you see yourself doing that?
How does the perpetrator respond to you, the survivor?
How does your "traumatized" (or "victimized") self respond to you, the survivor?
What would you, the survivor today, like to do or say to your "traumatized" self?

A primary aim of the mastery imagery phase is to replace victimization imagery with mastery/coping imagery. Thus, if there is a perpetrator involved in the traumatic scene, it is important that the survivor today be able to "confront" the perpetrator and "rescue" the "traumatized" self from the traumatic scene. It is crucial that clients

---

[2] Throughout the mastery and self-nurturing imagery phases, the therapist addresses the survivor today in the second person (as "you the survivor"), and addresses the "traumatized" or "victimized" self in the third person (as "your traumatized self" or "your victimized self"), so as to strengthen and reinforce the notion that the trauma survivor today is capable of coping and functioning as an empowered individual.

decide for themselves what specific coping strategies to use during the mastery imagery. In instances where clients are unable to visualize themselves as survivors today confronting the perpetrator and rescuing their "traumatized" self (which does happen on rare occasions), the survivor today may choose to imaginatively "bring in" additional support people (e.g., a police officer, friend, spouse, therapist) to help accomplish this task.

Throughout all phases of imagery, the therapist remains facilitative and non-directive while employing "socratic imagery" (as opposed to guided imagery), and is careful not to suggest, direct, or dictate to the client what to do or what should be happening. Socratic imagery is essentially socratic questioning (Beck, Rush, Shaw, & Emery, 1979) applied in the context of imagery modification whereby clients are encouraged to create their own mastery/coping imagery, as well as their own self-calming/self-nurturing imagery (Smucker, 1997). Client-generated coping imagery is thought to promote greater client empowerment than coping/mastery imagery that comes from the clinician.

### Self-Calming/Self-Nurturing Imagery

Immediately following completion of the mastery imagery, the therapist facilitates self-nurturing imagery during which the survivor today interacts directly with the "traumatized" self. The therapist may facilitate this "survivor-traumatized self" interactive imagery with such questions as:

What would you, the survivor today, like to do or say to your "traumatized" self?
Can you see yourself doing (or saying) that?
How does your "traumatized" self respond?
How do you, the survivor today, respond to your "traumatized" self's response?

When it appears that the survivor today has offered sufficient nurturance to the "traumatized" self and the client appears ready to end the imagery, the therapist asks if there is anything more that needs to happen in the imagery before bringing it to a close. When the client indicates a readiness to end the imagery session, the therapist says:

You may now let the imagery fade away, and when you are ready you may open your eyes.

### Processing and Debriefing

After the client is given a few moments to readjust, reactions to the imagery session are discussed and processed. The therapist may facilitate this by asking such questions as:

What was that like for you?
What was it like to see yourself today coping in the traumatic situation?
What was it like for you, the survivor today, to interact with your "traumatized" self?
What have you learned from the imagery session today?

The therapist also inquires about the client's ability to self-calm and self-nurture when feeling upset in general. The therapist and client may then collaboratively explore various self-calming strategies to experiment with between sessions. If there is any history of self-abuse, the client should contract for safety.

Homework is then assigned. Giving the client an audiotape of each imagery session (exposure and rescripting) for daily listening is a critical component of IRT. Listening to the audiotaped imagery sessions can be useful for facilitating further practice at home between sessions as well as generalizing these newly acquired mastery and self-calming/self-nurturing skills to other upsetting situations. The between-session homework generally involves asking the client to: 1) listen daily to the audiotape of the imagery session just completed, 2) write down SUDs levels (on a 0 to 10 or a 0 to 100 scale) every ten minutes or so while listening to the tape, 3) document in a journal efforts to self-calm and self-nurture when feeling upset, and 4) record number of recurring traumatic flashbacks, nightmares, or intrusive recollections experienced between sessions.

Clients need to accomplish four crucial tasks before the imagery work can be deemed successful: 1) replacing their traumatic/victimization imagery with mastery/coping imagery that they themselves create, whereby they can visualize themselves successfully confronting the perpetrator of the trauma (if an identified perpetrator is involved), 2) rescuing their "traumatized" or "victimized" self from the traumatic scene, 3) creating self-calming/self-nurturing imagery, and 4) activating and transferring the mastery imagery to other difficult, or potentially upsetting, situations outside the session.

If, after the initial four to eight imagery rescripting sessions, clients report experiencing additional recurring traumatic recollections, flashbacks, or nightmares, the most distressing traumatic memory is again targeted for rescripting. For each additional traumatic memory, two to four imagery sessions may be indicated.

### CASE EXAMPLE

Bob, a twenty-six-year-old, married, Caucasian male, was victimized in a robbery of the restaurant in which he worked as a manager. He and five other co-workers were at the restaurant and were closing for the night when three armed robbers entered the restaurant. Bob was forced at gunpoint to open the safe and registers in the bar and restaurant to provide the thieves with money. He presented for treatment ten days following the robbery.

During the robbery, Bob spent approximately ten minutes (by his estimate) with a gun held to his head, while he obtained money for the robbers. He vividly recalled both the terror that he experienced and the desire to just "act like Rambo" and assault the individual holding the gun. He states that during the robbery his primary concerns were for not only his personal safety, but for the safety of the five co-workers with him. When the police later apprehended the three suspects, they were returned to the restaurant for identification by the six employees involved in the robbery. The three suspects were accurately identified, and the money was recovered. Following identification of the suspects, each of the employees involved in the robbery went through a lengthy course of questioning by police department detectives.

Additionally, Bob met with the district manager early the next morning. Bob was immediately placed on suspension and later in the week was terminated for breach of procedure and for unlocking the back door where the robbers entered.

In the days and weeks following the robbery, Bob developed a number of clinical, PTSD-like symptoms that appeared directly related to his reactions to the robbery. He reported being unable to sleep for more than a couple of hours at a time, usually during day hours. In addition, he felt compelled to repeatedly check the locks on windows and doors throughout his house several times before retiring for the evening. He further reported becoming obsessed with thoughts of his own personal safety to the point where he could not go into a restaurant and sit anywhere where his back might be to other individuals without experiencing extreme anxiety. Bob also complained that his concentration had become significantly impaired and that he was suffering from repetitive intrusive thoughts of the trauma, including recurring flashbacks and nightmares along with accompanying startle responses. In addition, Bob reported a history of eczema and noted that, since the robbery, he had begun scratching his body. At the initial interview, Bob revealed how his recent scratching behaviors had resulted in a large raw area on each of his elbows, as well as on the back of his head.

When describing the incident at the first interview, Bob's reported SUDs were at a 10 (on a 1 to 10 scale) for all scenes of the robbery. The intrusive, repetitive trauma-related cognitions and visual flashbacks that he reported were of feeling the gun just behind his ear and having a profound fear that he was going to be shot and killed. Prior to the robbery, Bob reported having had no history of psychiatric difficulties, no history of alcohol or drug abuse, and had been employed full-time while pursuing a Master's Degree.

## Imaginal Exposure Therapy:  Eight Sessions

Bob's treating psychologist was experienced in employing prolonged imaginal exposure therapy, an exposure-desensitization based treatment for clients with PTSD (Foa & Kozak, 1986). Thus, Bob was initially treated with eight sessions of imaginal exposure only. During these sessions Bob visually re-experienced the entire robbery sequence, and between sessions he listened daily to an audiotape of the previous exposure session. While Bob was able to bring his SUDs levels down for the visual scenes that immediately preceded and followed the robbery, his imaginal exposure to the actual robbery scene itself did not lead to desensitization. The frequency and intensity of Bob's robbery-related flashbacks remained unchanged, and his SUDs ratings remained at a 10 while visually re-enacting the actual robbery scene, both during the eight imaginal exposure sessions and while listening daily to audiotapes of the exposure sessions. In addition, Bob was quite concerned about whether he would have to go to court and testify. His feelings of vulnerability and anxiety increased as he began to fear for his own safety.

## Imagery Rescripting Therapy:  One Session

After eight unsuccessful sessions of exposure therapy, a clinical decision was made to employ imagery rescripting as a means of coping with the continued PTSD symptoms Bob continued to experience, especially the recurring intrusive images. Thus, Bob's ninth therapy session turned out to be his first (and only) imagery rescripting session. The imagery session began with the robbers bursting through the restaurant door. As in previous imagery sessions, Bob felt immediate danger as he visualized the gun being placed next to his head. During the rescripting, however, Bob visualized himself as "an observer" on a shelf above and behind the robber. The following are excerpts from the imagery rescripting session.

Therapist: Can you visualize yourself, the survivor today, entering into the imagery?

Client: Yes.

T: Where are you now in the imagery?

C: I am imagining that there is a shelf right behind him that connects the oven to the wall.

T: So it's right behind the fellow holding the gun to your head?

C: Right. Right behind him. And I sort of like flick him in the back of the head, like you do to your little sister anytime that you want to irritate them.

T: So you are kind of snapping your finger against the back of his head? And how does he respond to that?

C: He looks around, he doesn't understand.

T: Do you think he understands what he has done by coming through that door?

C : I don't think he realizes what's about to happen to him.

T: What is about to happen to him?

C: He is taking the first step on the last journey of his free life.

T: So he has made a major blunder by coming through the door?

C: A huge mistake!

T: Are you able to tell that to yourself, your victim self, while the gun is to the back of your head? Can you give yourself that message?

C: I'm trying to.

T: What would you like to say to yourself when you've got the gun to the back of your head?

C: That this guy is making a huge mistake.

T: So even though when the gun is to the back of your head you may not feel like he has made a huge mistake, you are trying to keep him from doing anything stupid. Now you, the survivor today, can go back there and tell your victim self in that scene that he (the robber) has made a terrible mistake for his life. How do you feel about that?

C: I feel better.

T: In what way?

C: I can think about it and remember it, and that immediate knot seems to loosen.

Even while Bob is in the imagery and being victimized, he is able to recognize that the robber is making a terrible mistake about his own life that will have lasting effects. Bob begins to feel a sense of empowerment as he continues to confuse the robber by calling him "Sir." He feels that the robber cannot react negatively when Bob is being respectful to him.

| | |
|---|---|
| T: | And what would you today like to say to yourself back then in the imagery? |
| C: | You have control. |
| T: | How is it that you have control? |
| C: | Because you're not doing anything stupid. You are addressing him the right way. You're doing what he says. |
| T: | And how are you addressing him? |
| C: | Calling him sir. |
| T: | And how does he respond? |
| C: | I think it confuses him, placates him. I don't think he knows how to react. He just knows he can't react negatively to it. |
| T: | And how does that help you? |
| C: | It, it gives me a sense that he's not going to do anything more this time than what he is already doing. Now he is going to get down to business. Why is he there? What does he want? |
| T: | Okay. |
| C: | There is going to be no gratuitous violence, I don't think. As long as I can keep him calm. |

During the imagery that follows, Bob is able to make a decision that he will in fact identify the robber to the police and testify against him. Bob describes himself as giving the robber a false sense of security while recognizing that the robber is continuing to dig his hole deeper and deeper. Bob is able to picture himself on the shelf laughing, even though the robber is holding a gun to the victim's head in the imagery. It is this laughter that keys Bob into recognizing that he is okay and that he knows that he will remain so.

| | |
|---|---|
| C: | He doesn't understand what's happening to him. |
| T: | And what is happening to him? |
| C: | He's going to be put away, he's making a huge mistake. |
| T: | And how's that going to happen? |
| C: | Because I'm going to do the right thing, the smart thing. I'm going to survive and I'm not going to agitate him and we're going to get out alive. |
| T: | Okay. |
| C: | We're going to placate him for the time being. We're going to let him think he won when he's really going to lose in the end. |
| T: | And how is he going to lose in the end? |
| C: | Because even though he tells me not to look at him, I can still catch glimpses of his clothing and I can smell the alcohol on his breath and I remember approximately how tall he is. |
| T: | Okay. |
| C: | I'm going to tell the police when they get him and I'm not going to get upset. I'm going to be calm. |

T:     Okay. And what are you doing now?

C:     I'm placating him. I'm letting him have a false sense of security, that everything is going to be okay and that he's going to get what he wants and that they're going to be able to get in and get out of here.

T:     And what are you, the survivor, now doing on the shelf?

C:     I'm laughing.

T:     Why are you laughing? He's holding a gun to your head, isn't he?

C:     I'm laughing at him. I can't believe that anything is worth losing the rest of your life for, and that's what he's going to do. He's telling me he's going to kill me, but he's killing himself.

T:     And you're laughing at him?

C:     I can't believe he is so stupid.

Bob is now able, for the first time, to proceed successfully through the rest of the robbery scene and recognize the problem solving he went through while he was opening the safe, knowing that there would not be enough cash to satisfy the robber and that he could make plans to obtain additional cash for him from the other registers.

C:     He pulls me out and is mad because there is not enough money. I knew he was going to be mad, because who wants to walk out with quarters and dimes and nickels?

T:     So how did you prepare for that while you were opening the safe?

C:     That I was going to get him more money, that I know where there's more. And I tell him where there's more money and that I'll get it for him.

T:     Okay.

C:     He pulls me out of the office, pushes me over to the register, and has me open it. I ask him if he wants me to use my code or my keys. He just says, "open it, open it, open it!" I use my keys to open it.

T:     Okay.

C:     He asks if there is any more money. I tell him there is and that I'll get it for him. He pushes me head and face first into the door.

T:     Okay.

C:     It hurts a little. Then he says, "Are there any cameras here?" and I say, "No, there's not." He says, "Don't lie to me or I'll kill you!" I say, "No, I know there are no cameras in here."

Bob proceeds to open the second cash drawer for the robber and goes through the rest of the robbery imagery without fear, because his survivor self on the shelf continues to reassure his victim self that everything is going to be okay.

C:     You're going to be okay. These guys are done, they've cooked their own goose, they're done. Big tough guys, trying to get everybody scared and they're all going to jail.

T:     Because?

C: Because I wasn't stupid. I had control. I'm alive. I survived. And now I will testify against them according to the law, not like a punk, not like a thug, but with the legal resources that I have.

T: You know, the first time that we went through this I had the impression that you thought you should have physically reacted to them, like Rambo. What do you think about that now?

C: I think that if I would have done that, I'd be dead or someone on that staff would be dead. My actions impacted everybody in that room. They would have beat the hell out of me, but I think they would have hurt somebody else worse 'cuz they needed me.

T: So being the physical hero on the spot wouldn't have done what you needed it to do?

C: Not even close. I did the right thing.

T: You look pretty content with that.

C: I haven't always been sure.

T: And now?

C: I did the right thing.

T: Now you're sure?

C: Yeah, we're on the right path. I want that guy, I want him, I want him put away.

T: So when the court date rolls around, you're going to be there?

C: Oh yeah. Yes I am.

T: Are you going to feel intimidated?

C: No.

T: Are you going to be up on your shelf flicking him in the back of the head?

C: On that day I'm going to come off the shelf and let him see what happened and who's been messing with him.

T: That'll be his chance to understand?

C: I think that will be the worst part, the most painful part for him. It's like he was scaring me so bad and confusing me and making me wonder and threatening me.

T: Hmmm.

C: That all he was doing was adding to his own confusion and his own downfall. He thought he was strong; I was stronger. He thought he was smart; I was smarter. He thought he was in control; but I had the control, by the decisions I made, by the way I acted.

By the end of this one imagery rescripting session, Bob's SUDs ratings associated with the traumatic imagery, that had previously remained at a 10 despite eight sessions of imaginal exposure only, were reduced to a 3. Bob took the audiotaped imagery rescripting session home with him and listened to it a number of times over the following week.

When Bob came in for his next session a week later, his reported SUDs ratings were at a 0 for all of the robbery-related images. He could now freely think about, talk about, and fantasize about the entire robbery incident without feeling fearful or upset. His intrusive memories and flashbacks had ceased altogether and his sleep patterns had returned to normal.

He also reported being able to go into a restaurant and sit with his back away from the wall without feeling threatened. While he continued to check his windows and doors at night to make sure they were secure, he reportedly did this only once per night.

Shortly thereafter, Bob interviewed for a job with an alternate restaurant, accepted the job offer that was extended to him, and reported no on-the-job difficulties of any kind. Bob did decline the therapist's suggestion to go back and re-visit the restaurant in which the robbery took place. Although he was able to drive by the restaurant without anxiety and felt it would not be dangerous for him to go inside, he just felt no desire to stop or walk back into the restaurant.

All of Bob's gains were maintained at follow-up (at 3, 6, and 12 months). He eventually did get to testify in court against the robber which was, as Bob had predicted it would be, an empowering experience for him. Bob testified candidly and without fear and was able to look the robber directly in the eyes from the witness stand. As it turned out, Bob's testimony was critical to the case, as the robber received a life sentence.

The case of Bob offers an example of how such schemas as helplessness, vulnerability, and powerlessness can underlie PTSD symptomatology that develops following a traumatic event, and how an imagery-based, schema-focused cognitive treatment such as IRT can simultaneously alleviate PTSD symptoms and modify underlying traumagenic schemas. Since Bob's traumatic memories appeared to be encoded primarily in images (rather than words), imagery was used as a primary mode of intervention. However, when applied within the context of exposure alone, the use of imagery was unsuccessful. As noted above, eight sessions of imaginal exposure failed to reduce Bob's PTSD symptoms or modify his traumagenic schemas. By contrast, only one session of Imagery Rescripting Therapy (exposure and rescripting combined) was needed to successfully alleviate both his PTSD symptoms and significantly alter his trauma-based schemas of powerlessness and vulnerability.

## REFERENCES

Beck, A. T., Rush, A. J., Shaw, B. F., & Emery, G. (1979). *Cognitive therapy of depression.* New York: Guilford.

Foa, E. B., & Kozak, M. J. (1986). Emotional processing of fear: Exposure to corrective information. *Psychological Bulletin, 99,* 20-35.

Grunert, B., Rusch, M., Weis, J., Smucker, M. R., & Mendelson, R. (in press). Imagery, Rescripting for treating PTSD with industrial accidents following failure with imaginal exposure. *Cognitive and Behavioral Practice.*

Grunert, B., Weis, J., & Rusch, M. (in press). Early vs. delays imaginal exposure for treatment of PTSD following accidental injury.

Smucker, M. R. (1997). Post-traumatic stress disorder. In R. L. Leahy (Ed.), *Practicing cognitive therapy: A guide to interventions* (pp. 193-220). Northvale, NJ: Jason Aronson.

Smucker, M. R., & Dancu, C. V. (1999). *Cognitive behavioral treatment for adult survivors of childhood trauma: Imagery rescripting and reprocessing.* New York: Jason Aronson.

Smucker, M. R., Dancu, C. V., Foa, E. B., & Niederee, J. (1995). Imagery Rescripting: A new treatment for survivors of childhood sexual abuse suffering from posttraumatic stress. *Journal of Cognitive Psychotherapy: An International Quarterly, 9*(1), 3-17.

Smucker, M. R., & Niederee, J. (1995). Treating incest-related PTSD and pathogenic schemas through imaginal exposure and rescripting. *Cognitive and Behavioral Practice, 2,* 63 -93.

Van der Kolk, B. A., & van der Hart, O. (1991). The intrusive past: The flexibility of memory and the engraving of trauma. *American Imago, 48,* 425-545.

Wolpe, J., & Lazarus, A. A. (1966). *Behavior therapy techniques.* New York: Pergamon Press.

CHAPTER 8

# Imagery Scripts for Changing
# Lifestyle Patterns*

## JEANNE ACHTERBERG, BARBARA DOSSEY,
## AND LESLIE KOLKMEIER

### IMAGERY SCRIPT: WEIGHT MANAGEMENT

To reach your ideal weight, take time to create a relaxation and imagery tape and listen to it for twenty minutes several times a day. The following script helps you form correct biological images of being at ideal weight. It can also change your current eating and exercise patterns to reach and maintain your desired weight. Record a relaxation exercise, and then record the imagery script that follows.

As your mind becomes clearer and clearer, [insert your name] . . . feel it becoming more and more alert. Somewhere deep inside of you . . . a brilliant light begins to glow. Sense this happening . . . The light grows brighter and more intense. This is your bodymind communication center. Breathe into it . . . Energize it with your breath. This light is powerful and penetrating, and a beam begins to grow from it. The beam shines into your body now as you prepare yourself for reaching your ideal weight.

Just continue in your relaxed manner . . . Feel the deep relaxation from the top of your head all the way to your feet. Receive the inner message "I am calm and I am relaxed. I am excited about being consciously aware of healthy eating." With this inner feeling . . . you will feel good about yourself, just flowing with the challenges of each day. You will take this same feeling into your healthy eating. You will eat slowly and feel inner calmness.

Take a few moments to image yourself at your ideal weight. You are standing in front of the mirror. Look at each part of your body.

Your face looks just the way you want. And now looking at your whole body, part by part . . . your face . . . neck . . . arms . . . chest . . . waist . . . abdomen . . . hips . . . buttocks . . . and legs. Your body is at the ideal size for you. All parts of your body are taking on a new shape with your new eating and exercise program. Experience how this feels. Hear positive compliments about the new you from family. . . friends . . . and business associates . . . How does this feel?

*Reprinted with permission from Achterberg, J., Dossey, B., & Kolkmeier, L. (1994). *Rituals for healing: Using images for health and wellness.* New York: Bantam.

Choose the message that you want to give yourself at this new weight. Affirm to yourself that you are very wise and have the right to be at your ideal weight. You have the skills . . . and the knowledge . . . and you can listen to your inner wisdom that knows how to eat healthy . . . and how to maintain this new weight.

Rehearse the essential lifestyle patterns that will help you reach ideal weight and then to maintain this weight. Become aware of your signals of feeling hungry. With this awareness you are able to recognize true hunger and can eat healthy foods. Sometimes you may feel hungry with daily hassles or a tight time schedule. Remember . . . you can satisfy your mouth in a lot of ways that won' t involve a lot of calories. You may need just a drink of water or to suck . . . munch . . . or crunch something nutritious.

Mentally plan which food you will eat today—protein, dairy, complex carbohydrates, fruits, and vegetables . . . Now you are writing your food plan in your diary . . . As you keep your food diary . . . new awareness about your eating patterns comes to you. Your goal is to lose weight slowly, only a pound or two each week. You select healthy foods. You find time to eat. As you shop for food . . . see yourself reading food labels and checking for fat content. As you eat . . . you know the correct food groups . . . you know exactly how to create your nutritious eating plan.

You want to lose weight, and you can lose weight. You will not be hungry . . . the food intake that you have decided on will satisfy your hunger needs. You notice that there is plenty of time to chew each bite. As you eat slowly, enjoying every bite you take . . . you will recognize a full feeling sooner than usual. And with your new awareness, you now put your fork down and are pleased that you have recognized this full feeling. As you continue to move toward your ideal weight . . . you are proud of every pound that you lose. You will continue your new eating patterns and will keep the weight off.

Anytime that you want high-calorie, rich fat foods . . . these sensations will pass. If the thoughts of addictive candies, cookies, pies, and cakes come . . . say to yourself, "Stop." You will hear these words . . . "You are no longer overeating." . . . You do not need these foods. You are free of those past habits. You will drink water or eat a healthy snack or fruit . . . and be satisfied.

In your mind take yourself to your favorite restaurant . . . see yourself ordering from the menu. What do you need to eat? What can you eat that will satisfy you . . . and that will also make you feel good about yourself? Practice using your Bill of Rights. You have a right to eat just what you need . . . and to ask that your food be prepared just as you wish. Imagine that you are relaxed and at ease as you eat. If you are alone . . . you are enjoying yourself. If with friends . . . you are enjoying their company. You have now recognized that you are full and you still have half your food left. At this point you ask the waiter to take the food away and place it in a container for you to take home. You continue to sip on a nice beverage . . . and are thrilled at your new eating patterns.

Image yourself at home. You feel hungry . . . and are excited, for you have recognized your true hunger signals. You go to the refrigerator . . . and it is full of special, nutritious foods that you have bought and prepared. You choose a healthy snack and go and sit down to enjoy every bite. It feels so good to be using your conscious eating skills.

In your mind rehearse your exercise routine. Notice how you are enjoying exercise . . . Your body is stretching and gliding with every move you make. You feel light and energetic. As you increase your exercise, you speed up your body's metabolism and reset your fat thermostat to be more efficient. Many hours after exercising, you are still receiving the benefits of your exercise.

Once again . . . let your image of being at ideal weight be very present for you. Scan your body, starting at the top of your head. Take the time to see, feel, touch, and move each body part at ideal weight. You possess the knowledge . . . skills . . . and insight to be at this healthy weight . . . feeling alive with energy and wisdom with your new way of being.

Take a few slow, energizing breaths, and as you come back to full awareness of the room, know that whatever is right for you at this point in time is unfolding just as it should, and that you have done your best, regardless of the outcome. . . .

Note: Add your own special rituals for eating substitution, exercise program, and being at ideal weight.

## IMAGERY SCRIPT: SMOKING CESSATION

To enhance your healing and to reach the state of being smoke-free, take time to create a relaxation and imagery tape and listen to it for twenty minutes several times a day. The following script helps you form correct biological images of being smoke-free. It can be modified or expanded depending on your present habits and which new skills you wish to add in order to break your nicotine habit. Record a relaxation exercise, and then the imagery script that follows.

As your mind becomes clearer and clearer, [insert your name] . . . feel it becoming more and more alert. Somewhere deep inside of you, a brilliant light begins to glow. Sense this happening . . . The light grows brighter and more intense . . . This is your bodymind communication center. Breathe into it . . . Energize it with your breath. The light is powerful and penetrating, and a beam begins to grow from it. The beam shines into your body now as you prepare to focus on being smoke-free. . . .

In your relaxed state . . . affirm to yourself at your deep level of inner strength and knowing . . . that you can stop smoking. Say it over and over as you begin to image the words and feelings into every cell in your body. Feel your relaxed state deepen. You can get to this space anytime you wish . . . All you have to do is give yourself the suggestion and stay with the suggestion as you move into your relaxed state. This is a skill that you will use repeatedly as you move into being smoke-free.

Congratulate yourself for setting your stop date. You are aware of all your resources to quit. With your mind's eye now . . . see your calendar and experience yourself reading your quit date. With full intention to quit, mark your quit date on the calendar. Enlist the help of your family or a friend as you set your quit date.

It is now time to rid your body of toxins left from the cigarettes. Begin to cleanse your body . . . Feel the toxins flowing out of your body as you increase the liquids you drink. Practice your deep breathing exercises, remembering to exhale completely . . . enjoying this new awareness of how healthy your lungs will become with the cleansing and clearing of toxins. Experience your breath, skin, hair fresh as a spring breeze. See yourself making your surroundings smoke-free day by day. Notice the pleasant changes in your new, nonsmoking environment . . . First begin to notice that you are becoming more sensitive to smells . . . Enjoy the freshness of your clothes, home, office, and car being free of smoke.

As you keep your records become aware of your progress. Reward yourself regularly. Imagine you have had five smoke-free days. The worst of any withdrawal is over. What is your first reward going to be? Give yourself a big reward!

As you continue to deepen your relaxation, repeat the words "I am calm." Let your body experience these words in your own unique way. Register this feeling throughout your body. Begin to increase your awareness of feeling good about being alive, to be conscious of beginning new habits . . . free of smoking.

Starting now reflect on your wonderful decision to release the habit of smoking . . . a habit that could cause illness and take away your energy and vitality. Get in touch with your smoke signals. Is it a certain time of day, a person, a place, or social gathering? As you bring them into awareness . . . rehearse in your mind the healthy behaviors you will use to replace the urges . . . Is it drinking a glass of water . . . chewing sugar-free gum . . . going for a walk, listening to music, chewing on a toothpick, or taking a hot shower or bath? And as you think about smoking urges . . . those foolish habits . . . you can hear your powerful inner voice repeating clear affirmations . . . "I have stopped smoking . . . I am free of smoking . . . I feel strong and healthy . . . I can taste and smell fragrances. My cough has gone."

When you feel the urge to smoke, hear yourself saying "Stop. I don't need to smoke anymore. I am free." These words will become more powerful the more you say them. Remember this message is always with you . . . and you are no longer a smoker. That is behind you.

Hear your own voice saying, "I no longer crave a habit negatively affecting my health. This habit is diminishing steadily, and I can envision being completely free of this addiction. My mind is functioning in such a manner that I no longer crave tobacco . . . a habit that has affected my lungs and heart. I no longer place unnecessary strain on these organs so vital to life."

"As I stop smoking I will not be excessively hungry or eat excessively. Because of the power of my unconscious mind, I am free of my addiction. I am conscious of increasing my exercise to three or four times a week for twenty minutes or longer. I am increasing my fluid intake and chewing sugar-free gum. I am sleeping soundly at night. I am free of smoking . . . I am free." You can access this inner wisdom anytime that you wish . . . all you have to do is take the time.

Take a few slow, energizing breaths, and as you come back to full awareness of the room, know that whatever is right for you at this point in time is unfolding just as it should, and that you have done your best, regardless of the outcome. . . .

## IMAGERY SCRIPT: OVERCOMING ADDICTIONS

To speed up your recovery process, take time to create a special relaxation and imagery tape and listen to it for twenty minutes several times a day. The following script focuses on substance abuse and can be modified for other addictions. Record a relaxation exercise, and then the imagery script that follows.

As your mind becomes clearer and clearer, [insert your name] . . . feel it becoming more and more alert. Somewhere deep inside of you, a brilliant light begins to glow. Sense this happening . . . The light grows brighter and more intense . . . This is your bodymind communication center. Breathe into it . . . Energize it with your breath. The light is powerful and penetrating, and a beam begins to grow out of it. The beam shines into the core of your spirit. . . .

In your relaxed state . . . affirm to yourself at your deep level of inner strength and knowing . . . that you can stop drinking [or taking drugs]. Say it over and over as you begin to image the words and feelings in every cell in your body. Feel your relaxed state deepen. You can get to this space anytime that you wish . . . all you have to do is give yourself the suggestion and stay with the suggestion as you move into your relaxed state. This is a skill that you will use repeatedly as you move into your new healthy lifestyle patterns.

You have gone through detox . . . you are sober. Notice what you are feeling. Increase your awareness of deepening your relaxation. You have come a long way and are on your path toward healing.

Your craving for alcohol [or drugs] will diminish very, very rapidly . . . Anytime thoughts of alcohol [or taking drugs] come to your mind, you will say "Stop." Then repeat to yourself, "My craving for alcohol [drugs] is diminishing rapidly, very rapidly. I can drink water or other kinds of liquids that will satisfy my oral needs. I am secure in my inner knowledge that I no longer crave alcohol [drugs] which has such a negative impact on my life. I have the strength to give it up permanently." Repeat this paragraph several times.

Get in touch with your drink [or drug] signals. Is it a building, a time of day, a certain person, a social gathering? As you bring them into awareness, rehearse in your mind changing one of those signals. For example, if a certain bar is your signal . . . imagine you are walking down the street and you approach that favorite bar. But see yourself doing something different . . . as you pass by, you take a deep relaxed breath . . . and on the exhale . . . you have walked by the front door of the bar. Consciously affirm to yourself the choice that you have made. You feel confident, excited, pleased with your new patterns.

Imagine that you are with people who are drinking at a party. You have water or another nonalcoholic beverage in your hand. You are enjoying your friends, but in a new way. Experience how well you can talk and share some stories without alcohol [or drugs]. If any tension arises . . . once again, access your skills of relaxation and images of confidence . . . in control of your life, and free of addiction. Notice these new, sensory-rich images of awareness and being responsible.

See yourself attending an AA meeting [or another support group meeting]. You have opened your body and mind to receive many positive messages and support from others about being sober. Imagine now that you have entered the meeting room and are pleased with yourself for being there. Look around the room. Is there any one person that you might like to meet? If so, see yourself going over to meet this person and hear your voice as you introduce yourself. If there is no one you wish to meet, that is also okay. See yourself finding a place to sit and continue to focus on your relaxed breathing. With rhythmic breathing, you are able to be more present during the meeting . . . to be open to hear other people share their stories.

Imagine that you are ready to share part of your story. Remember there are many ways to share your story . . . sharing with a friend . . . a counselor . . . or your AA sponsor. Listen to your inner wisdom . . . you will know what is right for you . . . Can you imagine sharing something special about your healing journey? What would it be? How would you like to feel? The meeting is now over. Is there anyone that you wish to greet? If so, see yourself doing so.

Begin with some essential steps for giving power back to yourself . . . the steps of learning to trust and forgive yourself and others. What comes forth for you as you imagine forgiving yourself? What would this be like for you? Relive another aspect of your life's journey for a moment. Choose one person who has let you down or caused you turmoil in the past. Create your own healing images for loving yourself and this person. What are the new images? Let them spontaneously emerge from your spirit. . . .

Gather your family and friends in a healing image. What do you want to tell them? Listen to what they have to say. Listen to what you say in return . . . Know that as you continue to be aware of your special images . . . very healing images will continue to be present for you.

Allow the experience of letting old life programs emerge in your thoughts and then release them one by one . . . Release your intellectual level of being . . . and open to your Higher Power. Let yourself glimpse a space of your basic good self . . . It must occur . . . and every time it does . . . you open more of yourself . . . and your spirit sings its song. Remember, it is one day at a time toward recovery. Over time bring other people and other situations that need healing into your imagination. Let yourself continue to rehearse trust and forgiveness . . . your special touchstones on your healing journey.

Take a few slow, energizing breaths, and as you come back to full awareness of the room, know that whatever is right for you at this point in time is unfolding just as it should, and that you have done your best, regardless of the outcome. . . .

# CHAPTER 9

## *Imagery Exercises for Health*

### *GERALD EPSTEIN*

In this chapter I shall give some examples of my form of mental imagery process based on my understanding of how and why mental imagery works. You will notice in the succeeding exercises that the time recommended for them is short. This is a distinctly different approach than is commonly taught. The rationale behind the brevity of this approach is the notion that image is the language of no-time. This means that the image has to come as close to this no-time zone as possible. Lengthy imagery experience actually negates the nature of what is imagery. In addition, the quickness of imagery follows a homeopathic principle, namely that a small or minute amount of a substance produces a generalized internal healing response. Imagery, then, is a homeopathy of the mind. This molecular amount actually succeeds in giving a shock to the system, awakening it to respond at a higher level of functioning as it mobilizes its resources.

It is also worthwhile to consider my recommendation to do the exercises three times a day. It is by consistent repetition of the exercise that a new habit is created. Mental habits are created like physical ones—by repetition. By doing so, an actual biomental imprint is etched in our being.

Another reason for doing the exercises is to create a rhythm that has the effect of attuning the bodymind to a regulated order. With respect to this point there are certain times of the day that we have to be reminded to follow an intention to heal. These times of day relate to transitions—sleeping to waking, viz., sun-up; day to night, viz., sundown; waking to sleeping, viz., late night or midnight (high noon also figures in here; the time when the sun is at its highest point and is just on the verge of descending). Characteristically, around the world these times of day are dedicated either to prayer, meditation, or mental imagery. It is important that clients attune themselves to a regular rhythm or practicing imagery to ensure optional benefit. I believe this point must be stressed to them.

Also, I suggest to clients that they make a tape of their own voice giving themselves the exercises. They are told that eventually they won't need the words, but would just go and do this inner action, as they would any external action. With regard to the latter, they are reminded that they don't need words, for example, to get up from the chair, put on their coats, walk out the door to the car, open the car door, etc. Thus, inner imagery work becomes un-self-conscious, rather taking on the nature of an automatic process as in external, waking-life behavior. I don't provide tapes of my voice because I don't want them to become dependent on my voice, but instead their own voice as the healer. The one exception I make is for persons so debilitated by the illness that they cannot really muster the necessary strength and/or wherewithal to create the personal tape.

This focus on the clients' avoiding dependency on my voice coincides with the overall thrust of my work, which is to preserve their freedom, which includes the least possible intrusions I might make into their lives. My aim is to teach people to heal themselves, to become their own doctors, remembering that the root of the word *doctor* means "to educate."

The following exercises are extracted from my book *Healing Visualizations: Creating Health through Imagery* (Epstein, 1989) . This book has become a standard reference text for doing short imagery exercises for healing common physical and emotional disturbances. While the bulk of the book centers on daily ailments, there is a chapter on exercises for health for heightening and maintaining general health and well-being. You may notice there is a time frame given for each exercise. As part of our understanding for creating success in doing imagery, it is necessary before beginning an imagery exercise that you tell yourself the name of the exercise, its intention, and how long it is to take. By saying these things to ourselves silently, we are *giving an inner instruction* as to what has to take place. Saying the name serves as an orientation device that anchors us toward a healing intention. The intention we recite is geared toward directing our will in a certain direction with focused concentration. It in no way is a statement about an outcome of our efforts. While it is not the intent of this chapter to discuss the healing meaning of not focusing on an outcome in imagery therapy, suffice to say that focusing on an outcome or result of therapeutic process will negate the possibility for success of the work (for more in-depth description of this understanding, I would refer the reader to my chapters on the therapeutic relationship in my books *Healing into Immortality* (Epstein, 1994) and *Waking Dream Therapy* (Epstein, 1981). I would also recommend my chapter on the "Seven Keys to Healing" in *Healing into Immortality.* By stating the time for the exercise, we are setting our biological clock. This means that we will give ourselves the correct amount of time for the exercise, and we shall breathe out and open our eyes at the exactly appropriate time. I mention *"breathe out* and open our eyes" because it should stand as a usual aspect of imagery process to breathe out before opening eyes. Doing so brings us back naturally to our waking reality and creates the transition between the inner realm experience and our return to the waking world. It makes the return gentle.

I might also mention that I would recommend shortening the time of the exercises that I have in the exercises as written. Doing them anywhere from thirty seconds to one minute is sufficient. Half a minute to one minute is really a lot of imagery time and sustains the power of imagery. As patients become more familiar with their own process and develop facility with imagery, the time can even be further reduced.

## EXERCISES FOR HEALTH

Following are several exercises to help you maintain or heighten your general health and well-being. They are not aimed at specific maladies but rather at the processes by which we can all become more of what we are meant to be.

### A Bodymind Checkup

**Name: The Lake of Health and The Field of Health**
**Intention: To see your state of health.**
**Frequency: As needed, once for up to three minutes.**

If, besides visiting your doctor, you want to do some periodic checking on the state of your health, following are two imagery exercises you can count on to provide information. The axiom that holds true in the world of imagery is that the image doesn't lie. Becoming receptive to this truth can be immensely helpful in developing trust in yourself, and it will be especially beneficial in assessing your state of affairs.

A related imagery event that can reveal some oncoming trouble is your night dreams. Here you should pay attention to the appearance of individual, bright colors. A striking blue, red, green, orange, or yellow can bespeak some thyroid, vascular, gallbladder, liver, or kidney trouble, respectively. I would suggest that you go for a checkup when this happens. The one exception that I have found is the appearance of red in a night dream during menstruation. This is a normal accompaniment in dream life to the biological event of a woman's period.

**The Lake of Health.** Close your eyes. Breathe out three times and see yourself high up in the Andes at a lake that is at eighteen thousand feet. Tell the lake that you want to know the state of your health and that you want it to reveal your outer and inner body to you. Then look into the crystal-clear, quiet water and see yourself inside and out. (If you are healthy, you will characteristically see a golden color, pure pink, blue, or green. If you are ill, a gray, black, or bluish pink will appear at the site of the disturbance.) Then open your eyes.

**The Field of Health.** Close your eyes. Breathe out three times and see yourself as a general outside your tent at the head of the field of your body. Your bugler is next to you. You have a large golden flag blowing in the breeze at the top of your tent. At all important points on the field of your body are other tents with flags flying and buglers stationed next to them. Have your bugler blow his bugle and hear each bugler at each tent answer in turn. See the flags blowing at the same time and see their colors. Then open your eyes. If any sound is discordant, or a flag does not blow or shows a black or gray color, some change is taking place that bespeaks some disturbance or illness. It would be advisable then to consult your doctor.

### Burying the Past

**Name: Burying the Past**
**Intention: To remove the influence of the past.**
**Frequency: Once a week, for three to five minutes, for three weeks.**

Many people find that they cannot let go of the past. They may feel haunted by it, regret it, feel trapped by it, feel guilty about it, and so on. The intrusion of the past prevents us from being able to function productively. Harping on it can't change it; we seem only to keep experiencing more pain. The following exercise, aptly called Burying the Past, may help to relieve some of that tension and help to put the past to rest.

**Burying the Past.** Close your eyes. Breathe out three times. You are walking along a country path. The path is cluttered with rocks, which you clear in order to make it passable. At the end of the path you find a tree. Sit by the tree; from the ground, pick up a leaf and on it write all that has pained you from your past, all the regrets and all the obstacles from the past that inhibit you from going forward. Use the sap on the leaf as ink with which to write. Then dig a hole, knowing that you are going to bury the leaf and that the past, although buried, is still alive but will eventually disintegrate. Indicate when you want the past to disintegrate by writing a date on the leaf, then place the leaf in the hole, bury it with dirt, and quickly go back to where you started, seeing if there is anything different on the path. Then open your eyes.

## Cleansing

**Name: The Garden of Eden**
**Intention: To prepare yourself for everyday life in a positive way.**
**Frequency: Daily, in the early morning, for up to three minutes.**

This cleansing exercise is a wonderful way to start the day. It puts you in a good mood, and it also raises the level of your immune system. I often ask my patients to clean physically as well; clean out the clutter from their homes of an area in their homes on a regular basis, with the intention that they are cleaning themselves out internally at the same time.

**The Garden of Eden.** Close your eyes. Breathe out three times, and imagine yourself leaving your home and going out into the street (those of you who can descend a staircase should do so). Leave the street and see yourself descending into a valley, meadow, or garden, and go to the center of it. Find there a golden feather duster, whisk broom, or hand rake (depending on your preference, or the degree of cleansing you need). With this tool, quickly clean yourself thoroughly from top to bottom, including your extremities. See how you look and feel, knowing that you have cleaned away all the dead cells from the outside of your body and all the gloom and confusion from the inside.

Put down the tool and hear from your fight the sound of a flowing stream or brook. Go there and kneel by its edge. Take the fresh-flowing, crystal-clear, cool water in your cupped hands and splash it over your face, knowing that you are washing away all the impurities from the outside of your body. Then take the fresh-flowing, crystal-clear cool water in your cupped hands and drink it very slowly, knowing that you are washing away all the impurities from the inside of your body. Feel and sense yourself refreshed, tingling, energized, and more awake.

Get up from the stream and find a tree at the edge of the meadow. Sit under the tree that has branches hanging down with green leaves. Then with your back against the trunk, take in the pure oxygen that the leaves emit, together with the oxygen in the form of a blue-golden light from the sun and the sky that comes between the leaves. Breathe out carbon dioxide in the form of gray smoke, which the leaves take up and convert into oxygen. This oxygen is given off by the leaves and comes through the trunk, entering your body through your pores. You are thus making a cycle of breathing with the tree and are breathing as one with the tree. Let your fingers and toes curl into the earth, like roots, and draw up its energy. Stay there for a long moment, taking in what you need. Then get up from the tree and see how you look and feel.

Keep the image and feelings for yourself as you leave the garden and return to your street. Go back to your home by the way you went, and return to your chair. Then breathe out and open your eyes.

### General Well-Being

**Name: The Red Suit**
**Intention: To maintain general health.**
**Frequency: Once a day, for two minutes, every day.**

A simple way to produce physiological changes through imagery is imaginal jogging, a natural accompaniment to a physical exercise program that can improve its effectiveness. Even for those of you who don't exercise, or who find it boring, imaginal jogging can be beneficial. Recently a study was done at a Canadian hospital where patients undergoing rehabilitation from heart attack were divided into two groups. One group was given a typical physical exercise program; the other group was asked to perform the same program imaginally rather than physically. When the recovery rates of the two groups were compared, the imagery group was found to have recovered much more quickly.

**The Red Suit.** Close your eyes. Breathe out three times and see yourself putting on a red jogging suit and red sneakers. See yourself going out of your home or apartment and walking to the park. Enter the park and begin to run around it clockwise, becoming aware of everything you see. Become aware of what you sense and feel, of the wind passing by you. Become aware of your stride and your breathing. Notice the trees, grass, and sky. Complete the run by coming back to the point at which you started. Walk out of the park and back to your home. Take off the jogging clothes, shower, dry off, and see yourself put on the clothes you are going to wear for that day. Then open your eyes.

### Giving Yourself a New Start

**Name: Egyptian Rebirth**
**Intention: To give yourself a new start, a hopeful look to the future, a sense of purpose and meaning.**
**Frequency: Once, for five to ten minutes. This exercise is done only once every two years.**

This is a general healing exercise—healing in the sense of becoming whole—that will help you give yourself a new sense of purpose. Sometimes life can become routine or dull, or we are no longer inspired or satisfied by what we are doing. This exercise will enable you to shape new possibilities for yourself.

**Egyptian Rebirth.** Close your eyes. Breathe out once and see yourself as a scarab beetle deep in the earth at the base of a root, drawing nourishment from it.

Gather seeds from the surrounding earth. Take part of the root and make a ball, using saliva and earth to keep the ball together. Begin pushing the ball with your front legs upward and ahead until you reach the earth's surface. Find a soft spot and, tucking the ball against your abdomen, use your forelegs to make a hole in the crust, and come out onto the surface. Stay there a few moments, breathing now as an external creature and no longer an internal one. Feel the chest and lungs expanding and see the carapace (the hard shell equivalent to your back) looking straight and long as you stand up in your clear green casing. Next, feel the soft inside of your scarab body moving in a supple way within the rigid frame of the long backbone, which is seen as bright and straight. Then, using your faceted eyes, which can turn to look in all directions, see a river directly behind you and a mountain in front of you.

You have to climb the mountain and to push the ball in front of you, using your forelegs, shoulders, and lower back. The ball now has grass adhering to it, making it larger and larger in front of you, until you can no longer see where you are going. The ball is also getting heavier and heavier while you are climbing. Make sure that you don't lose the ball; otherwise, you will have to retrieve it and start over again. When you arrive at the top of the mountain, see, in the distance, the target or goal that you want. Then roll the ball down or off the mountaintop, seeing it hit the target squarely and exploding, sending all the seeds scattering, knowing that they must land and take root. Then stand upright as a human being, seeing your back becoming very straight.

Beginning with the lowest vertebra, touch each one, one by one, to see if they are in place. If they are not, clear off the thin tissue around the vertebrae, clean and stretch the vertebrae, and put them in place. Move up to the cervical vertebrae, coming now to the atlas (the second cervical vertebra responsible for turning the head) and adjust it so that you can turn your head completely around on the atlas. Then go to the axis (the first cervical vertebra, responsible for allowing the head to bend forward and backward), and adjust it so that you can bend your head completely forward so that your chin touches your breastbone. Afterward, you find yourself becoming, or have already become, very tall.

Your head is perfectly straight and your double chin (if you have one) has become flat. Feel every joint and articulation moving freely, beginning with the toes, to the bones of the foot, to the ankle, to the knee, to the tendons stretching behind the knee, to the pelvis and hip bones, feeling them rotate. Feel the tendons stretching along your spinal column. Now stretch all the way up to the sun and take some of it in your hands. When elongating to take the sun, feel your hands and arms stretching, knowing that your hands are your antennae. With the sun, burn off the fat from your abdomen (if you have any) and massage your back. Then burn off the fat from your double chin (if such exists). Warm the rest of your body with it. Place it in your solar plexus (about one inch below the lower end of your breastbone), giving heat to it, and the solar plexus sends this heat to the rest of the body. Wash your hands in the sun, and afterward throw it back in place.

Then look at the place of your goal and see how the trees and all other vegetation have grown there, knowing that all has come to fruition there, and see it bright. Run down the mountain lightly to the bottom, run to the river, and jump across into a bright, large, clear, open space and enjoy being there. Go now to the river and bathe in it, knowing that all is repaired. Bathe for a short time. Come out and sit under a tree to rest. Then physically open your eyes and see the river, space, mountain, and trees, with flowers and fruits. See your eyes without sadness and in a new way. Know that what you want to accomplish will be finished in two years.

### Relaxation

**Name: Becoming Blue Light**
**Intention: To achieve inner relaxation.**
**Frequency: As needed for one to three minutes.**

This exercise is for the occasions when the breathing-out exercise is not enough to produce inner relaxation, or in general when you feel you need to relax.

**Becoming Blue Light.** Close your eyes. Breathe out three times and see the oxygen you are inhaling coming in the form of blue-golden light formed by a mixture of cloudless blue sky and bright golden sun and the carbon dioxide you are exhaling going out in the form of gray smoke, like cigarette smoke being carried away in the air and disappearing. See the light become blue light as it enters your body, comes out of your heart, and travels evenly, gently, and smoothly through the arteries and capillaries, knowing that as it does you are becoming relaxed. When it has traveled throughout your entire body, open your eyes.

### Retracing the Past

**Name: Retracing the Past, Parts 1 & 2**
**Intention: To remove the influence of your past.**
**Frequency: Once a day, for seven minutes for each part, for twenty-one days.**

This imagery exercise provides a powerful way to wash out past influences and past traumas in your life. It is done in two parts. The first corrects the influence of the external world on you from earliest life until now, recognized as events and places. The second corrects your own internal influences on your life from earliest childhood until now, recognized as faults and errors. It is quite successful in helping you to wipe out persistent negative beliefs and experiences.

By correcting events, places, faults, and errors, I mean that you correct either your attitude or your beliefs regarding the experience, or you correct the experience itself. You can look at past events as beliefs that you have held on to in your memory. Through this exercise, you can remove the effects of these events by shifting your attitude or beliefs about them or by washing them away. You then create for yourself new beliefs by living the corrected events with a different past and a new present. Once the new beliefs are set in place, they will be expressed as new experiences in your life!

**Retracing the Past, Parts 1 and 2.** Close your eyes and breathe out three times. Looking into a mirror, see, sense, feel, know, and live in chronological order all the *significant* disturbing places or events of your life that you can recall from earliest childhood or infancy until the present moment. After completing that, keep your eyes closed. Breathe out once, and looking into the mirror see, sense, feel, know, and live yourself correcting these disturbing events and places in *reverse chronological order*, starting with the present moment going back to earliest childhood or infancy. For events and/or places incapable of being corrected, see yourself washing them out of the left side of the mirror using a fireman's hose. Keep your eyes closed. Breathe out once and, looking into the mirror, see, sense, feel, know, and live again these now-corrected events and places with a different past and a new now, seeing how you have to become in one year from now, two years from now, and five years from now. When you are finished, open your eyes.

Afterward, go through *exactly the same procedure* for part 2. This time, instead of considering disturbing events and places, the instruction is to see, sense, feel, know, and live the significant faults and errors of your life. After completing this part, open your eyes.

### Self-Renewal

**Name: Rejuvenation**
**Intention: To revive you, give you a sense of renewed purpose.**
**Frequency: Once a week for three weeks, thirty seconds to one minute for each exercise.**

When you're feeling uneasy and need a tonic to revive you, or if you need rejuvenating or a sense of renewed purpose, try the following exercises.

**Rejuvenation.**

1. Close your eyes. Breathe out once. Use a spade to dig up emotions in order to find something hidden. Take what you find for yourself. Then open your eyes.
2. Close your eyes. Breathe out once. Defuse a live bomb. Then open your eyes.
3. Close your eyes. Breathe out once. See an animal coming toward you on an incline. Then open your eyes.
4. Close your eyes. Breathe out once. Herd wild horses into a corral. Then open your eyes.
5. Close your eyes. Breathe out once. Be someone being someone else. Then open your eyes.
6. Close your eyes. Breathe out once. You are wrapped in bandages up to the neck. How do you feel? Unwrap the bandages and make them into a ball. Then open your eyes.
7. Close your eyes. Breathe out once. Make your way waling backward into a panther or leopard skin. See and sense what happens. Then open your eyes.

I hope that you have felt prompted to utilize these exercises in the way I have prescribed, and to incorporate the quickness of them in your work to ensure the power such a jolt can give to/for the healing process. Certainly, I would be quite interested in any feedback regarding responses your patients/clients have had. In line with this I shall be glad to give my input and the benefit of my twenty-five plus years of experience in this arena. I can be reached in New York City at: 212-369-4080, fax 212-369-5646, e-mail jerry@drjerryepstein.org.

## REFERENCES

Epstein, G. (1981). *Waking dream therapy.* New York: Human Sciences Press.
Epstein, G. (1989). *Healing visualizations: Creating health through imagery.* New York: Bantam.
Epstein, G. (1994). *Healing into immortality.* New York: Bantam.

# CHAPTER 10

# Imagery Techniques in the Work of Maxwell Maltz

## M. MICHAEL ISHII

Maxwell Maltz contributed much to self-image psychology by innovating many techniques arising from his observations as a plastic surgeon. He noticed many patients' personalities changed dramatically when facial defects were corrected. While personality improvements were easy to explain, "failures" were not. These patients would admit they looked better, but they complained that they did not feel better. He also discovered that some people sought plastic surgery when in actuality their physical appearance did not need improvement; he found that it was their self-image that needed work and not their physical appearance. From these observations, Maltz developed imagery techniques to improve the self-image, which he saw as motivating us all (Maltz, 1964).

According to Maltz, the self-image is composed of conceptions of who we are, conceptions arising from past experiences and other peoples' reactions to us, particularly in early childhood (Maltz, 1964). These past experiences and reactions can build a self-image which is actually false; the wrong emotional outlook can additionally bring on experiences which act to verify the false self-image. What is needed to change a pathological self-image is new insight, which can be brought on by the following exercises.

Many of Maltz's self-image exercises can be placed in two categories: improving self-image and relaxation. Key to both is activating imagination, which enters into every act, motivating us by giving goals to strive for. When used properly, imagination can set off an automatic mechanism changing the self-image. Pathologically used, imagination inspires worry, which is concern about things that may never happen (Maltz, 1964).

## IMPROVING THE SELF-IMAGE

*Exercise 1:* Since a self-image is formed through the use of the imagination, through mental images growing from past experiences; changing the self-image involves use of the same process. Maltz suggests that the client practice the following exercise for one hour each day.

Instruct the client to sit or lie in a comfortable position where the atmosphere is restful and quiet. Ask the client to let go and relax, to close his/her eyes physically and figuratively to any distractions.

Evoke the interior of a theater to the client, suggest that his/her mind is like an empty theater, and that he/she is the sole audience seated in a comfortable chair. Suggest that the movie screen curtain unfolds and that the movie begins. The movie is about the client: it depicts the client handling a problem situation successfully (one which the client had revealed to the therapist in a preliminary interview). What is needed here is an evocative, dynamic description by the therapist of a perceived success by the client. The success may be magnified and elaborated. Several successes may be used in order to make the daily visit to the "theater" more interesting and varied.

Once this "feature" has played on the screen, evoke a problem situation which the client perceives as a present failure. Have the client watch himself/herself handling the situation as he/she would like to handle it. Direct him/her to watch the success on the screen. Emphasize that he/she imagine that he/she is the person on the screen. Daily practice in watching self-success will result in increased faith in one's self as well as in an automatic change in one's self-image (Maltz, 1964).

*Exercise 2:* After determining what the client perceives as a problem situation, have him/her again visit the theater in his/her mind. When you feel that the client has changed his/her self-image enough to actually be successful through daily practices of Exercise 1, you should instruct him to take note of the steps his/her self-image took in resolving the problem. He/she should practice these steps in the theater over and over until these goals become definitive and realistic. The practice script should change gradually from fanciful to realistic means, so that the client is not disappointed when acting on these steps in reality. These steps must be within the client's potential (Maltz, 1964).

*Exercise 3:* Have the client visualize people whom he/she regards as successful. Evoke an image of the Declaration of Independence; make sure the client focuses strictly upon the words which insure equality for all. Now have the client visualize a situation in which he/she is surrounded by those people whom he/she regards as successful. This situation may be one taken from the client's life or may be one experienced by all, say a crowded department store counter. Have the client practice asserting his/her right to be served in turn, regardless of who follows him/her. Remind the client that he/she has all the rights that these highly regarded people do, that he/she is entitled to success just as they are. Such practice in imagery should elevate one's opinion of oneself and this often can be the difference between success and failure (Maltz, 1964).

*Exercise 4:* Emphasize the power of the imagination and the self-image by evoking images of important deceased people. These may be of historically important people, like Kennedy, or they may be of persons who have personal significance to the client. In either case, point out the client's vivid images of these people and the idea that these people, though deceased, are very much alive in his/her mind. Suggest that this power to bring people back to life can be used to bring past personal successes back to life, as vivid and as real as when they occurred. Doing so encourages the client to recognize the good in him/her (Maltz, 1964).

*Exercise 5:* Imagery can be used for happier living. Maltz suggests that the client evoke a happy inner world, a place where he/she can retreat in order to consolidate his/her resolve. Symbols of happiness, such as light, color, and personal meaning, can create an anchor point for the client to start successfully once again. The client also should wage war on negative feelings. The imagery that can be used here is one of battles with vermin and disease. Persuade the client that he/she has a natural right to happiness, and that unrealistic worries are like diseases invading the mind. Instead of allowing them to thrive like tapeworms, the client should cleanse the mind with injections of pride-bearing, successful memories. Also, the client should learn how to laugh again. Most adults chuckle or smile, but they have forgotten the childlike laugh which reverberates throughout the body and the mind. This is the laugh which brings a sense of release and freedom. Tell the client to visualize his/her elementary-school classroom and to remember a time when he/she really let go a laugh. Emphasize the vividness of the joke or situation which prompted the laugh, and encourage the client to let go once again. Show how this laughter is different from the laughter most adults experience. Laughing is one way to purify the mind (Maltz, 1964).

*Exercise 6:* Maltz stresses that people should accept that mistakes do occur and should not try to hide these mistakes from others. To aid the client in doing so, have the client relax with eyes closed and visualize that he/she is at a masquerade party. Emphasize to the client that although he/she knows everyone there, no one is recognizable due to the costumes. The evening is filled with merriment but when it is time for the party to end, everyone goes home wearing the masks, even the client. This imagery is to point out to the client that he/she hides feelings when there is no need to do so.

Have the client visualize the masks he/she wears to hide feelings from others and from himself/herself: tight-lipped masks of stoicism, an exaggerated expression of worry, a mien of acceptance. The vividness and details of these can point out to the client the extent to which he/she overuses them. Encourage the client to drop such masks which constrict growth (Maltz, 1964).

Learning acceptance of one's mistakes takes more than just dropping the mask. Have the client visualize making a mistake while moving toward a desired goal and accepting the mistake while moving on. Encourage the client to feel any natural embarrassment or despair, but underline the importance of moving on again toward the goal. Encourage the client to sit once again in the theater and to visualize a previous success where setbacks occurred. Point occasions when success would have come more readily if the mask had been discarded. By understanding and accepting previous setbacks on the way to success, present and future setbacks may be easier to accept (Maltz, 1964).

*Exercise 7:* This exercise is intended to strengthen the client to withstand minor crises. Have the client once again enter the theater in his/her mind and visualize a memory in which catastrophe seemed imminent. This memory should be one of those experiences where mountains are made of molehills. Encourage the client to relive the scene on the screen, to relive the terror associated with those inflated fears. Ask the client to recount all the dreaded possibilities he/she saw at this time. Underline the fear by encouraging the client to experience it as he/she had at that time: His/her heart is pounding, he/she is sweating and shaking all over.

Now tell the client to look again at the movie screen. Encourage him/her to visualize the resolution of this minor crisis and to understand how he/she had made such a mountain out of a molehill. Emphasize the relief the client felt when he/she realized that these fears were unfounded. Stress that it is negative imaging which is responsible for the panic. This will help to calm the client and shed light on the present from the past (Maltz, 1964).

*Exercise 8:* Sometimes the client must work on identifying what successes to strive for. The client should retreat to a relaxing empty place in the mind and ponder what success means. Random thoughts, impressions, and individual free associations about what success means to him/her often reveal what fundamental forces shape the client's self-image. Take note of these forces and help the client to understand what goals to work for (Maltz, 1974).

*Exercise 9:* This exercise could be practiced in the morning before the client arises. Encourage the client to relax with eyes closed, and to visualize himself/herself writing in huge block letters on the bathroom mirror the word IMAGE. As the client sees himself/herself through the word written on the mirror, have him/her hear the radio announcer say that he/she will not be 10 inches small with frustration, but instead will be 10 feet tall with self-confidence based on successes from the past (Maltz, 1974).

*Exercise 10:* Have the client once again go to a place of relaxation and quiet in the mind. Direct the client to focus on two questions: "What ten things do I like about myself, and what ten things do I detest about myself?" This is intended as an initial probe into the client's self-image and as a gauge of the client's ability for self-analysis. These responses can indicate the degree of self-affection the client has, as well as some of his/her preoccupations (Maltz, 1974).

*Exercise 11:* Maltz intended imagery to be growth oriented as well. Ask the client to relax in a quiet corner of his/her mind and to visualize writing the word EVOLUTION on a pad of paper. Emphasize that just as the client is able to "write" without writing, he/she is undergoing an evolution inside without outward signs. Underline that this evolution is just as important as the Darwinian form. This is an evolution from failure to success, to extending friendship to oneself as well as to others (Maltz, 1974).

*Exercise 12:* This exercise is intended to enable the client to track personal successes in life. Have the client visualize a chalkboard in his/her mind, a chalkboard which always will remain unerased. Direct the client to remember all the past personal successes and to write them down on this chalkboard. The only criterion for selection is that the success be important to the client and not necessarily to others. Now encourage the client to remember this chalkboard when faced by a seemingly difficult situation. Remind the client that there is room on the chalkboard for more successes (Maltz, 1974).

*Exercise 13:* Have the client once again enter the theater of the mind and relax in his/her private chair. Suggest to the client that it is dark but relaxing. A familiar voice tells the client that he/she will try and try again. The client will use his/her imagination creatively to spark journeys toward a goal. The client understands that the mind cannot really differentiate between a real and a vividly imagined event. Hence he/she will fill his/her mind with success images in order to change his/her self-image. Imagined success becomes real success. As the familiar voice relates the preceding creed, have the client probe whose voice it is. With practice, the client should recognize that the voice is his/her own, and not the therapist's. The goal of this exercise is to convince the client of the power of creative imagination (Maltz, 1974).

*Exercise 14:* The following is intended to give hope to the client and to point out a way to fulfillment. Have the client again visit the theater of the mind and wait for the silver screen curtain to open. As it parts, majestic music begins to play and light fills the screen. Suggest to the client that a wonderous epic is unfolding before him/her, a movie of a hero or heroine's success, a dramatic achievement of potential. Emphasize that the leads in the movie find a valuable lost treasure after a brilliant chase. Ask the client what tools the heroes used. React with disdain to any concrete tools the client may suggest and substitute for them the digging tool of clear creative thinking. Have the client watch the heroes open the treasure chest and find supreme spiritual riches: self-respect, peace, self-enrichment, fulfillment. Remind the client that he/she also can use this tool of clear creative thinking to find his/her own spiritual treasure chest (Maltz, 1974).

*Exercise 15:* After the client is in a relaxed position and is receptive to imagery, direct him/her once again to imagine standing in front of the bathroom mirror. Ask the client to write the word THINK with a crayon and then to stare at himself/herself and the word THINK in the mirror and to analyze its importance. Invite the client to bring the word to life, to give it real meaning.

Suggest that this process of giving life to the abstraction THINK also focuses on the client's own thought processes; the client should search for his/her own clear creative thinking.

Suggest now that the client write the words DO and NOW on the mirror. Remind the client that thinking is not sufficient for health, that immediate action is required as well. Remind the client that his/her daily goal should be to practice this exercise and to transform clear creative thinking into creative action (Maltz, 1974).

*Exercise 16:* Ask the client to relax in a quiet atmosphere for a few moments. Then suggest to him/her that he/she reflect on the meaning of the word "happiness." If the client is adept at imagery, ask him/her what he/she visualized. In responding, he/she will further explore whatever images developed. If the client is not yet adept, introduce some initial images of happiness, so that the client can reflect and develop images independently.

Some examples of happiness images are:

Happiness is a wholesome trinity: God, self, and man in a benign relationship.
Happiness is assuming that today and everyday is another day in the holiday season.
Happiness is being aware of and delighting in the little things in life.
Happiness is another view on love (Maltz, 1974, pp. 113-114).

*Exercise 17:* In another exercise in visualizing happiness, ask the client to relax and then to visualize that he/she is writing the word HAPPINESS on the bathroom mirror. Direct the client to reflect on the image. While he/she is focusing on the word happiness, he/she will listen to the following:

When you are happy, nature itself becomes glorious. Somehow flowers smell sweeter and life becomes more dynamic. When happiness washes over you, food is delectable, friendship holds you firmer, and your voice echoes with newly found strength.

However, when you are buried in misery, you are blind to any beauty within or without. Your hearing is blocked by earwax, flowers smell of decay, food is bland, and everything is tainted by flaw.

Remember that your happiness begins within you. It grows from clear observations and perceptions, to which you add promising visions of growth. Vow to youself that you will not refuse these visions. See how these visions are colored grey and blurred by inner cataracts when you are unhappy. Overcome these negative feelings and rise toward fulfillment. (Maltz, 1974, pp. 122-123)

*Exercise 18:* This exercise may be used when the client seems unaware of where changes are taking place. After an initial relaxation period, have the client focus on the word ACTION using the bathroom mirror exercise. Suggest that the client hold a dialogue with himself/herself while standing in the imaginary bathroom. Direct the client to say that he/she is like a funnel, the center of action. Have the client visualize that creative thinking is funneling and accelerating through him/her into creative action. Suggest that this action enables the client to change, even if he/she feels a failure (Maltz, 1974).

*Exercise 19:* This exercise could be used to find out what issues are important to the client. After an initial relaxation period, have the client stand in an imaginary bathroom facing a mirror. Suggest a happy thought to the client and ask him/her to visualize what facial reaction the happy thought brings. Suggest that not only events but also thoughts bring on imaginary facial effects, and these are just as important as the ones caused by real events. Have the client focus on the inner or outer facial scars in the mirror which are troublesome. What events have been traumatic? Remind the client that a scarred inner face can result in a scarred mind and soul. While facial scars can be endured, a scarred mind can be unbearable. Ask the client what scars are bothering him/her (Maltz, 1974).

*Exercise 20:* This exercise can be used to help develop the client's will power to accept success. After the client is relaxed, have him/her envision a closet in his/her mind, a closet to which he/she will be able to go in time of need. Instruct the client to open the closet door and to take out a movie projector which is always going to be in the closet. Ask the client to turn on the projector and to view pictures of success. Ask the client what he/she is viewing: These images can be of baseball pitchers striking out their opponents, of a great knockout punch, or of a marathon runner bringing down the ribbon.

Tell the client that he/she must use the imagination to project and build up these success images, and remind him/her that he/she can always go back into the imaginary closet to bring back these images when needed (Maltz, 1970).

*Exercise 21:* This exercise is intended to show the client the guiding nature of imagination. After an initial period of relaxation, instruct the client to envision himself/herself as an explorer, sailing through choppy seas of frustration for new horizons, to a new port: a new self-image.

Ask the client to continue his/her voyage, taking note of the ways the world is shaped. Suggest to the client that, like Columbus, he/she will find that the world is round; thus success and happiness can encircle it. Emphasize that this voyage should continue throughout life (Maltz, 1970).

*Exercise 22:* This exercise is intended to develop motivation to grow. Ask the client to close his/her eyes and to turn on the movie projector inside his/her mind. In the movie he/she sees, time is compressed. Direct the client to imagine a fetus, reaching out in the womb. Even in this confined space, it is growing, touching, seeing, probing, hitting, investigating. Note that in the movie, this exploration does not stop at birth. The baby continues to long for growth, what previously sufficed as boundaries now confines. Ask the client to reflect on the inertia which now besets his/her life and on the boundaries which now seem confining (Maltz, 1970).

*Exercise 23:* This exercise is intended for those clients who are inhibited from releasing anger. The client is seated, with eyes closed. Suggest to the client that he/she has an imaginary pencil and paper pad on an imaginary desk. Assure the client that, because they are hidden from all, even the therapist, no one save the client will know what is written on it. Encourage the client to write the nastiest letter possible, to use language which best expresses the anger felt, even if it is offensive. Instruct the client to write furiously until all seems to have been said. After doing so, have the client read and reread the letter. Ask the client if he/she understands and can accept what he/she has written. Then direct him/her to crumple up the letter and throw it away. Ask the client the meaning of such a symbolic act (Maltz, 1970).

*Exercise 24:* The individual should rule the self-image. But often the deflated self-image rules the individual. This exercise is intended to show the client this unfortunate process.

Have the client imagine that it is early morning, and he/she is relaxing in bed. It is now time to get up and to go to the bathroom to freshen up. Ask the client to imagine himself/herself walking into the bathroom and gazing into the mirror. Direct the client to picture himself/herself raising an arm to run a hand through his/her hair. Ask the client who is ruling whom; assert that the client is the source of action and not the self-image in the mirror.

Now suggest to the client that he/she closely examine the image in the mirror. Have the client pay particular attention to any exaggerated faults or characteristics. Ask the client, "Who is the source of action in working on this self-image?" The answer should be the same as above (Maltz, 1970).

## RELAXATION EXERCISES

*Exercise 25:* Have the client relax by sitting or lying in a comfortable position and breathing slowly and deeply. Direct the client to visualize a relaxing landscape. Give the client time to develop this landscape, and urge him/her to use all the senses and creativity to experience this relaxing scene. Ask the client after some time what this image is. Then help the client to repeat the image over and over, until he/she reports no further tension.

Once the client is engrossed in the relaxing scene, ask him/her to do some thinking about two stumbling blocks to relaxation: not accepting limitations and not learning the healing power of forgiveness. Tell the client that accepting limitations and using forgiveness can make the voyage to the relaxing scene easier (Maltz, 1964).

*Exercise 26:* Have the client stare into a real mirror periodically for six days. Instruct the client to try to notice signs of tension: a wrinkled forehead, clenched teeth, bitten lips, clenched fists.

Then direct the client to envision this image in his/her mind and to hold a conversation with it. The client should convince the image to drop troubles and to regroup strengths. Ask the client to turn away from this image in his/her mind, and to throw away the worried look while turning. Next, instruct the client to face the mirror again and gaze upon the image which now is wearing a smile. Ask the client what the smile means (Maltz, 1974).

*Exercise 27:* Ask the client to think of the most relaxing room that he/she has ever experienced. Now instruct the client to imagine being in that room. Tell him/her that he/she is free to change any feature in the room which does not contribute to the relaxing atmosphere.

Direct the client to envision a staircase which leads to this room. As he/she climbs these stairs, he/she will deposit a worry on each step. Suggest that the client walk up these steps to relax each day (Maltz, 1974).

*Exercise 28:* Have the client envision a geyser spouting steam. Ask the client to reflect on its symbolism. Suggest that he/she, like the geyser, should release tensions and distress. Tell the client to continue observing the geyser spouting steam while he/she is allowing tension to "blow off" (Maltz, 1970).

### REFERENCES

Maltz, M. (1964). *The magic of self-image psychology.* New York: Pocket Books.

Maltz, M. (1970). *Psycho-cybernetics and self-fulfilment.* New York: Bantam.

Maltz, M. (1974). *Psycho-cybernetic principles for creative living.* New York: Pocket Books.

# CHAPTER 11

## *The Oneirotherapies*

### *NANCY C. MUCH AND ANEES A. SHEIKH*

Oneirotherapy (from the Greek *oneiros* meaning dream) is known far more widely in Europe than in the United States. The term oneirotherapy will be used to refer to all three methods under consideration; as a proper name, however, Oneirotherapy belongs only to the school represented by Fretigny and Virel (1968), and the capitalized version will be used in reference to their method alone. At present, descriptions of three oneirotherapeutic methods are available in English translation. These are: the Oneirotherapy of Fretigny and Virel; the Directed Daydream (or Directed Waking Dream, in French le rêve éveillé dirigé) of Robert Desoille; and Hanscarl Leuner's Guided Affective Imagery (sometimes also referred to as cata-thymic imagery). The oneirotherapies are characterized by the comprehensive use of extended narrative visual fantasies with hypnoidal consciousness (deeply relaxed, subvigilant awareness). Oneiric reveries are alternated or in some way combined with interview sessions in which the fantasy contents are treated analytically or dialectically. In Europe, it is evidently a common practice for the oneirotherapist to act as a specialized technician among a team of practitioners in a psychological clinic (Fretigny & Virel, 1968).

Fretigny and Virel (1968) refer to Oneirotherapy as a "corpus of knowledge without postulates." This designation is intended to emphasize the pragmatic or clinical-empirical origin of the procedures. The history of psychotherapeutic image techniques in Europe has been researched and summarized by Fretigny and Virel. They feel that "the field of Oneirotherapy is far from possessing unity. It is a relatively recent development, born of the confrontation of the work of several experimenters in different countries who mutually ignored each other" (p. 255). These experimenters presumably include Desoille and Leuner whose methods are reviewed in this chapter. It should be recognized that, while these theorists may have had no contact with one another, their methods certainly appear to have common roots.

The oneirotherapists believe that imagery is a special language of the unconscious, and as such its natural function is to carry symbolically transposed affect. In the words of Fretigny and Virel, "the torrent of tendencies, inclinations, emotions and passion-directed elements determine the concatenation of figurative elements" (p. 55). The practice of oneirotherapy derives from the psychodynamic position, but the oneirotherapist may use induced images far more extensively than the psychoanalyst. The oneirotherapist undertakes a systematic exploration of the personality patterns through the analysis of extended image reveries. In most cases, a number of selected inducing images will be employed in order to initiate the imagery process or to introduce important elements into an ongoing imagery sequence.

## THE ONEIROTHERAPY OF FRETIGNY AND VIREL

### Basic Procedure and Rationale

The present discussion will be limited to the exploratory phase of oneirotherapy, insofar as this phase is separable from the therapeutic and reconstructive phases. In actuality, there is no well-defined division. A seemingly essential preparatory measure for extended reverie is the establishment of deep relaxation. The participant is usually given some instruction intended to help him/her achieve relaxation, and occasionally extended training is necessary. The oneirotherapist provides environmental conditions he/she believes will be optimal for maintaining a hypnoidal state without, however, creating the likelihood that the participant will fall asleep. The participant is acoustically shielded and exposed to minimal illumination. Usually, he/she reclines on a couch, unless he/she is more relaxed in a sitting position. Some therapists prefer to allow the initial image to occur without intervention; in this case the first images tend to be anodyne and appear in rapid succession unaccompanied by affective reaction. Eventually, significant effectively colored material appears spontaneously, often surprising the participant with its content. Fretigny and Virel favor the use of induction or "triggering" images for initiating, if not for directing the oneiric process. At the outset, the presentation of triggering images may accelerate the development of relevant content. It is held that certain images offered as therapeutic directives will evoke responses that have reference to predictable corresponding areas of experience. The extreme of this viewpoint is taken by Desoille (1965), who believes that each of his starting images asks of the unconscious a "rather precise" question (p. 3). Others, such as Leuner (1969), seek only to establish a rather vague and general projective field for the oneiric process. The difference in these approaches will be more evident to the reader after consideration of the respective methods. Fretigny and Virel prefer a variety of triggering images with flexibility in their application. The Oneirotherapist chooses triggering images best suited to the particular case and proceeds methodically. For each area he/she wishes to learn about, a triggering image can be offered, *if the relevant image does not occur spontaneously* in the appropriate oneiric context. Nevertheless, Fretigny and Virel prefer to intervene as little as possible beyond initiating the oneiric process and perhaps facilitating it at times with the introduction of new elements.

Fretigny and Virel recognize the practical and theoretical questions involved in the selection of triggering images. The choice of these images thus far has proceeded on both logical (theoretical) and empirical (observational) grounds. Some practitioners, influenced by Freudian and Jungian theory of symbols, derive a set of starting images which they assume will have the same basic meaning for all individuals (again Desoille's work is an example). In particular, mythical material common to persons of a given culture, or perhaps common across cultures, may be analyzed as to its psychological meaning (e.g., the witch and the Virgin as aspects of the mother) and then used as a kind of "universal language." Some therapists (Desoille, 1965; Fretigny & Virel, 1968) employ fairy tale scenes and magical resolutions freely, while others (Leuner, 1969) do not encourage these unless they spontaneously occur. If the therapist wishes to choose starting images on empirical grounds, he/she can make note of the images that frequently arise spontaneously in a variety of individuals during oneiric reverie, and note to what themes these are related. Or, images may be selected logically or on clinical hunch and then empirically validated.

Fretigny and Virel (1968) have used all possible methods for selecting their triggering images. They recognized the value of the traditional analogies expressed in mythology but at the same time, they prefer to let their choice be guided by empirical procedures—they refer to "statistical sorting" (p. 236), but they do not specify the procedure. In particular, they look for those images which occur spontaneously for many individuals during extended image reveries. They believe that the frequency (across subjects) of spontaneous occurrence is a necessary condition for any image which is to be considered a common element in a language of the unconscious. Accordingly, Fretigny and Virel have identified and listed elements which in fact have been observed to appear spontaneously under analogous conditions; these they have designated "crucial images." Some of the crucial images are: an octopus (in the "descent into the sea" condition), a cave, a treasure chest, a wise man, a monster, a veiled woman, and a witch. These images, if they do not occur spontaneously for a particular individual, can be introduced by the therapist in order to stimulate reactions to the theme they represent. On the other hand, Fretigny and Virel point out that there are certain excellent inductive images (e.g., a pitchfork stuck into the earth, a vase, or a key) which rarely, if ever, occur spontaneously. These are images which have been logically inferred or intuitively "happened upon" and later tested for their general usefulness. Broad and imprecise images involving common situations or scenes also may be used as starting points, for example, a beach or a train ride. Such images require the participant to impose his/her own structure upon the stimulus to a great extent; their vague demands offer the participant a wide range of possibilities.

Another distinction arises among the various kinds of inductive images. Some are images of objects (e.g., the key), others refer to general themes (e.g., ascending a mountain or following a stream), and still others specify only very general surroundings (Fretigny & Virel, 1968). The general supposition is that the more definite and limited the suggestion, the more precise the question represented by it. That is to say, the more explicit the limits of the starting image, the greater the pressure for the subject to represent specific preoccupations directly. Fretigny and Virel believe that too much pressure in this direction is disadvantageous because it is likely to lead prematurely to intense emotional reactions. Consequently they prefer triggering images which do not too tightly define the boundaries of the response.

Fretigny and Virel (1968, p. 65) remark (probably with reference to Desoille) that "it is tempting to imagine that 5 or 10 well-selected images would facilitate the exploration of 5 or 10 well-defined regions of the psyche (areas of psychological experience)." This presupposition, as interpreted by Fretigny and Virel, implies a certain invariability about the ordering of the human psyche and advocates a disregard for the specificity of the particular case. It seems however, that a theory of psychodynamic symbolism must presuppose a kind of lawfulness (which is invariability in another light) about the ordering of the human psyche, which achieves richness and variability with combinations and permutations of the basic elements. The invariability implied by a standard series of images (remember that these are not ends in themselves, but starting points) may be no more than is commonly assumed in psychology—that a person's relationship to his/her mother is rather important, that what he/she thinks of his/her ability to fulfill his/her sex role is important, and the like. The criticism of invariability applies more accurately to conditions in which the theme of the five or ten images is rather highly structured, which is, in fact, the tendency in Desoille's work. Desoille employs a series of mythical situations which place the individual within a somewhat predetermined plot. But this is a matter of directivity, the placement along a continuum from free to directed development. Fretigny and Virel are perhaps quite justified in pointing out the rigidity of Desoille's technique in comparison with their own. Desoille uses a standard, ordered series of images which are relatively structured and have certain specified successful conclusions, while Fretigny and Virel select triggering images from among the crucial images and key images mentioned earlier, as well as from nocturnal dreams, from spontaneous images from a previous reverie, and from special structured themes resembling Desoille's. Five cases are identified by Fretigny and Virel (1968), in which substantial directiveness is preferred.

1. The individual is of low intelligence and/or has very little education.
2. The individual has an impoverished imagination or a marked psychological lassitude (e.g., a psychaesthenic individual).
3. The individual has a recalcitrant obsessive theme.
4. The individual has excessively profuse imagery.
5. The individual tends to avoid, circumvent, or ignore crucial images (as in certain cases of resistance). (pp. 58-59)

It ought to be mentioned that the individual participating in Oneirotherapy is asked to write a report following each oneiric session. This report is then compared with the therapist's transcriptions of the same session. The participant is asked to include his/her recollection of the actual images, an account of the emotions experienced with these images, any memories of circumstances in his/her life when he/she had had the same feelings, and any associations which occurred to him/her either during the oneiric session or while writing the report. In this manner, the oneirotherapist solicits the individual's active help in explaining the cryptic elements of the imagery as these may relate to personal conflicts. By reading the participant's report, the therapist acquires information that relates the present affective patterns with historical events. By comparing the report with his/her own transcription, he/she observes how the participant has slanted his/her account. The lacunae, for example, are themselves meaningful in that they point to areas which need to be investigated.

## The Symbology of Significant Persons

The use of oneiric images for obtaining information about the personality of an individual requires a systematic approach to the interpretation of the image contents. Interpretation may proceed upon any of three avenues: 1) logical-theoretical analysis (as is the case with Freudian dream interpretation); 2) empirical evidence based on accumulated observations that certain symbolic representations usually refer to certain areas of experience, or that symbols are derived from their referents through certain mechanisms of transformation (e.g., the Freudian mechanisms for dreams); and 3) logical analyses of the idiosyncratic meaning of symbolic elements according to the individual's private associations and anamnesis. Fretigny and Virel evidently used all three of these approaches. They have not fully delineated their principles of interpretation, but they have given fairly complete treatment to the representation of significant persons; an account of this aspect of symbology follows.

The process by which an important figure or event is represented in another form is termed symbolic transposition. Fretigny and Virel (1968) have observed that persons who are emotionally very significant to the individual seldom appear in their direct form. The mother, for example, who is a crucial figure for most individuals, practically never appears in her own likeness; instead she may take the shape of a sorceress, a wrinkled old woman, a maiden, or some famous historical woman. Moreover, the individual will not, in most cases, recognize the reference to his/her own mother. The father figure, too, has a repertoire of usual symbolic representations including a king, the sun, and an oak tree.

According to the observations of Fretigny and Virel (1968), persons may be signified by animal, plant, or object images on the basis of some shared characteristic or meaning. For example, a person may be replaced by an object which displays one of his/her attributes, or by a symbol equivalent in affective value (for the subject), or by a situation analogous to one in which the person had had an important influence upon the psychological development of the individual. Fretigny and Virel (1968) recognize that symbolic transposition does not act in an unequivocal manner, hence that it is not possible to establish a completely reliable lexicon of image substitutions. Additional complexities, such as idiosyncratic meanings and a tendency for symbols to be condensed, are important variables in interpreting representations. Condensation refers to the common practice of projecting a whole group of diversely related elements into a single symbolic form. For instance, one symbol may represent all of the classes of persons toward whom an individual has a similar affective attitude (e.g., a rose may represent mother, sister, virgin, nun—females who are sexually taboo). The complete personal meaning of a symbol may be grasped through an analysis of its elements and of the attitudes the individual holds toward these.

An alternative or supplementary way to arrive at the meaning of a particular image is to simply wait and see whether spontaneous modification occurs. Fretigny and Virel (1968) give the example of the vase of roses which suddenly turned into a young girl—for the subject, these were two expressions of the same thing. Two types of spontaneous changes in the imagery are distinguished and named by Fretigny and Virel. An abrupt, unexpected change is called a "mutation"; a more gradual modification is a "metamorphosis." Fretigny and Virel supply no further rationale for making this distinction. Therefore it cannot be assumed that these two categories are functionally different.

The person figures appearing repeatedly in the imagery of a particular individual usually are found, upon examination, to be representations of the mother, father, spouse, children, or some other significant actual person. In general, it can be said that all figures appearing in imagery, whether they are part of the objective or of the mythical world, are interpreted to refer to persons within the actual experiential repertory of the individual. Animal figures of various kinds are rather common in oneiric imagery. Certain mythical animals seem to occur frequently as representations of corresponding affective qualities. But Fretigny and Virel (1968) find that hybrid animal-human forms are quite rare in personal imagery, although they abound in international mythology. Plant forms occasionally take on human significance, especially trees and flowers, but more typically they appear only as background. Inanimate objects also may represent persons. For one individual, a taper represented a father who was a candlemaker; for another, an empty liquor bottle substituted for an alcoholic father. Minerals, especially valuable metals, and gems may appear in oneiric fantasy and often have psychic qualities attributed to them. Animals, plants, and objects may mutate into persons, thus revealing their meaning. Mutations in the other direction are reportedly uncommon and usually involve one of two cases: a person changes into a crystal, indicating petrification (e.g., Lot's wife); or an unidentifiable person mutates into an animal form which represents one of the referent's personality traits as perceived by the subject.

Unidentified persons, nameless and faceless, or veiled persons, and persons visualized with their back always turned are frequent spontaneous occurrences. These figures are likely to be very significant; they point to important areas of conflict and represent particularly crucial persons, sometimes the individual himself/herself. When such figures occur, the Oneirotherapist attempts to maintain the individual's contact with the image. He/she encourages the participant to follow the movements of the image figure and observe it carefully. He/she tries to maximize the number of times the individual confronts the image figure in order to increase the likelihood that some modification of the image figure will eventually reveal the identity of its referent. Fretigny and Virel (1968) attribute the cryptic representation of person figures to resistance rooted in ambivalent feelings toward the person represented.

### Early Memories

According to Fretigny and Virel (1968), important early memories can be uncovered in oneiric reverie. Ordinarily memory images which represent early traumatic events do not appear directly, presumably because of their potential for creating emotional disequilibrium. However, Fretigny and Virel hold that certain conditions facilitate the recollection of these images: in particular, a special imaginary drama is supposed to be conducive to obtaining recollection. The participant is prepared with the following sequence of imaginary events: he/she is asked to imagine himself/ herself entering a building that is suggestive of hidden, secret things, such as a crypt or a pyramid. Then the participant is to imagine himself/herself wandering freely through the structure until he/she discovers a vault or chamber of some type, which he/she should carefully describe. At this point, the Oneirotherapist suggests that somewhere in the chamber there is a seat which has a solemn or ceremonial appearance with a tall back and massive arms, imparting a feeling of security. The participant is then asked to imagine himself/herself seated in the armchair, and when he/she actually feels secure, he/she is directed to allow a memory image (unspecified) to arise. The participant's success in recollecting an image from a much earlier period partly depends upon the completeness with which he/she has abandoned himself/herself to experiencing his/her identity temporarily *within* the imaginary events. Regression phenomena of the sort that occur under hypnosis also occur in oneiric reverie, provided that the involvement with the imaginary events is fairly complete, so that the individual is not bound to his/her awareness of the actual here and now. Involvement in the imagery depends in turn upon the success with which the participant is able to identify with his "Imaginary Corporal Ego," which is explained in what follows.

## The Imaginary Corporal Ego

The situation of the imaginary self within the image world is held to be a particularly important aspect for interpretation. The imaginary self is the imagined body with the feelings, sensations, and sense of spatiality that attend it. In Oneirotherapy, this image complex is known as the Imaginary Corporal Ego (ICE). Its experiential existence for the participant depends upon his/her ability to synthesize visual, kinesthetic, autonomic, and spatial images in such a way that his/her imaginary experience has a life-like quality. The ICE is a representation of the corporal pattern—the feeling of every normal individual that he/she "inhabits" his/her own body. As such, the ICE cannot be a purely visual entity; it involves an experiential sense of movement, autonomic reaction (e.g., the physical components of fear, excitement, or anger), spatiality, tension or tonus and, if all is well, a sense of coordinated wholeness. Since the ICE is part of the oneiric state, it escapes the constraints of the actual corporal-social self; it does, however, express the individual's fears and inhibitions insofar as they are not reality based, and it is considered an index of therapeutic change.

The projection of the ICE into the image reveries of the initial sessions is considered to be a critical task. During deep relaxation, the ICE must form with a kind of functional equilibrium which will allow the individual to use it as a vehicle for experiencing himself/herself with relation to the contents of his/her imagery, which are ultimately representations of intrapsychic elements and events. Therefore, the ICE ought to "hang together" at the outset. In theory, the totality of the imaginary space and the ICE are held to complementary aspects of the participant's psychic organization. The subject, lying on the couch in deep relaxation, is supposed to exprerience his/her self-awareness through the imaginary body with its attendant circumstances. The ICE registers the individual's reaction to the imaginary contents and acts as the vehicle through which he/she may resolve them.

The ICE reflects the participant's involvement in the imagery. Within the oneiric images, affective disturbances can be projected in two ways: they may register as deformations of the ICE, or the ICE may be kept intact while the disturbing affective components are projected as elements in the other parts of the image (e.g., threatening figures, monsters, and the like). Distortion in the ICE may take a variety of forms. The participant may experience it as lopsidedness or disconnection of head and limbs, or as whirling, sloping, expanding, contracting, or floating. Presumably it would be preferable that the individual maintain an intact ICE and express the distortions through the other parts of the image (this is not a matter of conscious choice, of course), since this would facilitate the kind of fantasy progression which would be likely to lead to insight and resolution. Mutilations of the ICE can be expressions of extreme feelings of inadequacy (Rigo, 1968). In that case, improvement in the ICE is indicative of therapeutic progress.

As mentioned earlier, the ICE is said to have an important function in the recapturing of significant early memories. It facilitates age regression phenomena which puts the individual in a position to relive events which occurred at a much earlier age. According to Fretigny and Virel, when the individual in oneiric reverie succeeds in experiencing entirely through his/her ICE, and consequently becomes detached from present reality, the significant events of his/her past become immediately available to him/her through age regression. That is, under the aforesaid conditions, by imagining himself/herself to be as he/she was at some other age, he/she is able to recollect the important experiences he/she had at that age. This is the same thing that happens during hypnosis when the hypnotist suggests, "You are six years old again . . ." (1968, p. 220).

## Resistances

Fretigny and Virel (1968) give a fairly specific description of the kinds of resistance phenomena that are observed in Oneirotherapy. These probably can be said to apply as well to the methods of Desoille (1965) and Leuner (1969), which are procedurally very similar. Two classes of resistance are distinguished by Fretigny and Virel—resistance toward initiating the oneiric experience, and resistance to full consciousness of certain important information that tends to arise within the oneiric experience. The most overt case of the first type is conscious opposition; in submitting to the exploratory phase of the oneiric process, the individual is asked to relinquish all control over his/her imagoic thinking.

The individual might be apprehensive about the therapist's possible ability to "take" information which he/she may not be fully willing to disclose. Fretigny and Virel (1968) observe that some persons feel less vulnerable if asked to deal with ideas rather than images, although the opposite is the case for others.

Occasionally it happens that the individual accepts the principle of the exploratory oneiric phase, feels comfortable about the use of images, accepts the particular therapist involved, and is generally willing to have the experience, but is unable to succeed in following the requisite instructions. This occurs presumably because the individual retains some unrecognized resistance. The simplest form of difficulty might be the inability to relax completely, or relaxation might be reached, but no images or free associations will come. Other individuals, who succeed in having images, do not permit the oneiric process to develop freely, but persist in directing their image-thinking in a rational, controlled manner. Or the participant will project himself/herself into the imaginary drama but will retain the role of a spectator, a protection against the potential anxiety related to becoming involved with the images.

It also happens that some genuinely willing and properly relaxed individuals do not succeed in their attempt at visualization. Fretigny and Virel (1968) attribute this to a rigid cognitive style inculcated by educational conditioning. Persons thus conditioned are unable to express their feelings in any but conceptual terms. However, if the therapist takes care in wording the instructions, he/she can help the individual to engage in visualization or its functional equivalent. The therapist should direct the individual to "conceive," say, a landscape; the kind of description which usually results may be regarded as "conceptual" by the subject, but for all practical purposes it is equivalent to an oneiric visualization. Consider the following example: "I imagine I am entering the sea ... I do not really see images corresponding to all this, but I quite easily imagine all that is to be seen on the sea bottom" (p. 117). According to Fretigny and Virel, such indirect descriptions do not differ in any way from the descriptions of visualizing individuals.

Fretigny and Virel (1968) have observed that once the imagery process is initiated, significant material comes forward immediately. But often resistance emerges to prevent the appearance of the significant image or to permit its representation only in disguised form. When the image is closest to revealing its referent, resistance will be at its maximum. A number of forms of resistance are reported to occur within the oneiric reverie. Nameless, faceless, or veiled person images, or person images that present only their back, already have been mentioned as resistance phenomena. Resistance may also cause the images to flow very slowly, become less clear, or fade away altogether. Ultimately the individual may open his/her eyes and abandon the oneiric state, with or without an experience of anxiety. In other cases, the images begin to flow in excessively rapid sequence, and the individual is forced to give up narrating them to the therapist. Resistances also may create mutations (the abrupt replacement of one image by another) to apparently unrelated images. Fretigny and Virel have found that resistance mutations usually produce a substitute image which, upon scrutiny, reveals direct relation to a suppressed underlying image; the appearance of the suppressed image itself probably would have disrupted the oneiric process. It also happens that resistances sometimes are objectified in the image as obstacles of various kinds. Such an expression of resistance can be helpful if the participant can be lead to its resolution through the oneiric process. At least he/she is made to encounter the fact of an obstacle in the context of a particular situation. He/she may be able to identify the meaning of the obstacle, or he/she may respond to it symbolically through the imagery. The success and realism with which the ICE treats the encountered obstacle will indicate the individual's capacity to successfully meet his/her resistances.

## Rationale

The basic elements and procedures of Fretigny and Virel's (1968) Oneirotherapy have now been given. What remains to be discussed is the rational-theoretical validation offered by the Oneirotherapists. Much of what will be said below also applies to the methods of Leuner (1969) and Desoille (1968), that is, to oneirotherapy in the broad sense. The following can be said in brief summary of the method of Fretigny and Virel: The Oneirotherapist, who is assumed to have a broad knowledge of psychological mechanisms, employs a dialectic with the participant in a mutual investigation of the latter's fantasy contents. The participant is asked to write a report of his/her oneiric reverie after each session. This report is compared with a recording or the therapist's transcription of the same session, and the comparison provides material for the next period of discussion.

According to Fretigny and Virel (1968), the use of this method allows the experienced Oneirotherapist to disclose the conflictual material present in the individual's fantasy themes and to discover the so-called structural details of the individual's personality (Fretigny and Virel do not specify what is meant by the latter, but in accordance with general technical usage, it might be surmised that "structural" refers primarily to any repetitive patterns of reaction, overt or covert, and especially to defense style). The method does not yield a typological or nosological report; Fretigny and Virel recognize this distinction and hold it to be of advantage that the technique bypasses typing and connects directly with the ontogenetic roots of the symptomatic feelings and behavior. Mental imagery localizes the difficulty, attaching it to specific fantasies or events. For example, Fretigny and Virel say that "where psychiatry may be unable to go further than the mere diagnosis of a state of shock, mental imagery can retrace and identify the nature of the affective traumatism, date it and lay bare its contents" (p. 178). Fretigny and Virel refer to this as "localization diagnosis" (p. 178). Their claim should be qualified, however, with the recognition that exploratory Oneirotherapy also is an exceedingly extended diagnostic technique. Thorough exploration of the important personality patterns of a given individual takes from ten to thirty oneiric sessions or more, and these are interspersed with additional dialectic or analytic interview sessions, and preceded by an anamnesis and relaxation training. The protractedness of the method is not necessarily a disadvantage, since the diagnostic and therapeutic phases are, in practice, not discrete and oneirotherapy reportedly often gives rather rapid symptom alleviation (note that symptom alleviation is not equated with resolution by most oneirotherapists).

The Oneirotherapists claim certain other advantages for their exploratory technique. These may be taken as applying to oneirotherapy in the broad sense. The following four points are stated by Fretigny and Virel (1968):

1. Mental imagery is oriented directly toward the individual's affective experience to a greater extent than traditional analytic therapy.
2. The use of imagery avoids the pitfall of encouraging predisposed individuals in sterile rumination.
3. It can be practiced with people who are incapable of systematic reflection because of their low level of sophistication.
4. It avoids the snares of "rational" thinking.

These points might be summarized by saying simply that mental imagery avoids the problems typically encountered with verbal expression in psychotherapy. However, each of these points deserves a modicum of individual attention. To begin with the clearest point, Number 3, it is quite reasonable to suppose that less educated or simply less verbally reflective individuals have trouble comprehending or fulfilling the requirements of analytically oriented therapy. The American behavior therapists use the same argument in support of their methods (many of which also rely heavily on imagery). It is simply much easier for the "average" individual to accept what he/she can readily understand and to understand what is most conceptually concrete. This may be one of the most compelling reasons for conducting psychotherapy though images instead of through words. But it should also be asked whether giving the average individual only what he/she can readily accept does not deprive him/her of an opportunity for enrichment. In other words, should psychotherapy not teach the individual something he/she did not know? Perhaps the psychodynamic image techniques, such as the oneirotherapies, are good middle ground. They do not demand much conceptual sophistication (average or above-average intelligence is still an important prognostic variable), but they do eventually lead the individual to more inclusive experience of his/her fantasy life, of the "inner workings" of his/her motivational system.

Point 2 listed by Fretigny and Virel does not seem very different from Point 4. Perhaps Point 4 refers to the necessity that verbal thought "make sense," and to the difficulty of representing certain complex perceptions within the confines of verbal syntax. Point 2 is self-explanatory but not self-evident. It is not possible that the individual could engage in the very same kind of rumination using imagoic thinking? In fact, Fretigny and Virel (1968), in their discussion of conditions counterindicating Oneirotherapy, cite cases in which certain individuals respond with a constantly changing profusion of facile images without affective involvement. It may be that persons who are predisposed to verbal ruminations are not disposed or not able to maintain this habit through imagoic thinking. That, however, is a question to be answered through observation; there are no logical grounds for supposing that the defense style involved should be inoperative in imagoic thinking.

In Point 1, Fretigny and Virel (1968) assert that oneirotherapy is oriented directly toward affective experience. This is the central claim of most therapists who prefer to use induced images at some point during therapy. It is this claim that is best substantiated by the testimony of a considerable variety of clinicians—even behavior therapists such as Wolpe (1969) and Stampfl and Levis (1967)—and their followers attest to the functional connection between visual fantasy and emotional reaction. The assumption under discussion is the heart of the hypothesis that imagery is a "special language of the unconscious"—that is, that it is a language whose elements and syntactical arrangement represent affective relationships.

## DESOILLE'S DIRECTED DAYDREAM AND LEUNER'S INITIATED SYMBOL PROJECTION

The methods of Desoille (1965) and Leuner (1969) are quite similar to the Oneirotherapy of Fretigny and Virel (1968) in both rationale and procedure, and for this reason they are given less extensive treatment. In this section, the focus will be on the particular stimulus images used by Desoille and by Leuner, and on their interpretations. Any features of the methods which distinguish them from Oneirotherapy also will be given, with one exception: Desoille ties his procedure theoretically to the Pavlovian theory of cortical excitation; this rationale will not be discussed. Certainly Desoille's theory represents a unique and interesting attempt to blend psychodynamic and conditioning models of pathology, but the subsequent discrediting of Pavlovian theory of cortical excitation would make this aspect of Desoille's rationale of little practical interest to contemporary clinicians. Furthermore, the theoretical tie to Pavlovian physiology has virtually no pragmatic importance for Desoille's diagnostic

method which rests, in actuality, upon clinical common-sense and analytical interpretation of symbolism. Therefore, the omission should not detract from an understanding of the procedures as they pertain to psychodiagnostics. The reader who
nevertheless is interested in an account of this part of Desoille's work is referred to the
monograph, "The Directed Daydream" (1965). A general difference between the
methods of Desoille and Leuner on the one hand, and Fretigny and Virel on the
other, is that the former work with a standard and invariant set of starting images
which are held to carry a more or less specific import. According to Fretigny and
Virel, flexibility is sacrificed by this procedure. But, of course, there remains latitude
in the individual responses to the given stimuli, which are developed in an extremely
extended fashion. There is considerable advantage in limitation for the theorist who
wishes to investigate the use of images as projective stimuli.

The format of Desoille's (1965) Directed Daydream (rêve éveillé dirigé) is similar
to Oneirotherapy: the participant engages in extended image reveries for which
he/she is prepared with a conducive environment and muscular relaxation; after each
reverie, he/she is asked to write a full report of his/her oneiric fantasy, which will be
analyzed at the next therapeutic meeting. Desoille believes that interpretations should
be made with the active collaboration of the participant and considers an interpretation valid only if the participant agrees with it. Interpretation is based upon the
anamnesis and associations which occur during the fantasy or while discussing it; this
is a clinical common-sense approach. But, in fact, the interpretation of the particular
images used by Desoille depends rather heavily upon a number of assumptions about
the meaning of symbols, taken mostly from the analytical theories of Freud and Jung.

Desoille (1965) prefers a systematic and directive style in working with images.
Six starting images comprise his stimulus repertory; these are administered in
invariant order, no more than one to a session. The images are held to be a series of
standard themes, each symbolically representing an area of psychological experience
of universal importance. Desoille suggests the starting image to the participant,
asking that he/she describe what he/she visualizes in detail. If the responding is
meager, Desoille will ask questions to stimulate further development. In systematically guiding the imagery, Desoille believes it is possible to uncover the full range of
the individual's habitual patterns of reaction, as well as unexercised potential modes
of reacting which later can be developed in a reconstructive phase involving both
fantasy and reality testing. The image stimuli themselves are thought to correspond to
"rather precise questions in the language of the unconscious" (1965, p. 3). Desoille's
procedure may be said to be more formalized than Fretigny and Virel's (1968)
Oneirotherapy. In addition, if one agrees with the symbolic significance imputed to
Desoille's six images, they then may be considered more structured than any of those
used by Fretigny and Virel; that is, Desoille's images may carry more precise import
and more limiting demands.

The six starting images employed by Desoille (1965) are listed and explained
below. The contemporary psychologist may find several of these too quaint; this
objection to the use of stimuli which are out of step with contemporary stylistic values
may seem trivial but it is not, since it is relevant to rapport and to the participant's
investment of trust in the technique. A contemporary adult, educated or not, may feel
foolish imagining himself/herself as the character in a fairy tale or myth which does

not make sense with respect to the world as he/she knows it. Simply stated, stimuli to which the individual relates with difficulty might be expected to reinforce his/her resistances. Another question, of course, is whether one is willing to agree with Desoille's symbolism. If not, what is the value of these particular image suggestions as projective stimuli? Unfortunately, there are few documentary response samples for evaluation by independent observers. This means that if the rationale for using the stimuli in question is unconvincing, there is no evidence in favor of these methods, save the enthusiastic testimony of their proponents, which in some cases seems very obscure indeed when so little is known of the general milieu of their practice. Still, the evidence provided by a variety of independent observers, who are not primarily concerned with the practice of image techniques, does suggest that images are natural carriers of important fantasy content and that it may be well worth the effort to develop systematic ways of tapping this source of information. With this task in mind, the reasonable point of departure is an examination of what already has been done; Desoille has been among the major contributors.

Desoille's rationale for each of the six images is given after the listing of the stimuli and their purported significance (Desoille, 1965).

| Number | Purpose | Theme |
| --- | --- | --- |
| 1 | Confronting one's more obvious characteristics | For a man, a sword<br>For a woman, a vessel or container |
| 2 | Confronting one's more suppressed characteristics | A descent into the depths of the ocean |
| 3 | Coming to terms with the parent of the opposite sex | For a man, descent into a cave to find a witch or sorceress<br>For a woman, a descent into a cave to find a wizard or magician |
| 4 | Coming to terms with the parent of one's own sex | The reverse of Number 3 above |
| 5 | Coming to terms with social constraints | A descent into the cave to find the fabled dragon |
| 6 | Coming to terms with the Oedipal situation | The castle of the Sleeping Beauty |

The following interpretations of the stimuli are given by Desoille in "The Directed Daydream" (1965).

1. The theme of the sword (a phallic or, more broadly, a virility symbol) presented to a man is equivalent to asking (in the unconscious symbolic language), "What do you think of yourself as a man, in the broadest sense of the term?" For a woman the vessel or container (a uterine symbol) asks the equivalent question. An individual

may visualize, for example, a substantial weapon, another ornate ceremonial instrument, another a blade with handles at both ends making it a useless weapon, and so on. When the initial image response is established, the participant is asked to describe in detail his/her imaginary location. Then Desoille suggests that the participant image himself/herself at the foot of a range of mountains, and that he/she should begin to climb one of them. At this point, individuals reportedly reveal differences in the ease with which they are able to imagine ascent; some will need considerable effort or will find their paths blocked by obstacles. When the pinnacle has been reached (Desoille sometimes continues the ascent up into the clouds, past the mountain peak), the sword or vessel is once again examined for changes in appearance. Changes, when they occur, are usually meliorative, and such changes are said to prognosticate beneficial development in therapy. Desoille considers this theme an indicator of the individual's capacity for "sublimation" or the "socialization of instincts" (presumably as indicated by the success in ascent).

2. In the second daydream, the participant is asked to imagine a seashore, a rocky coast where the water is very deep. He/she is to imagine wearing a diving suit and descending far into the water, reporting all that he/she visualizes as he/she proceeds. Desoille reports that under these circumstances, feelings of fear often arise rather quickly; the therapist makes no attempt to allay these feelings apart from forewarning the individual that they are to be expected. If necessary, the therapist even may suggest that something threatening is likely to appear; whereupon some kind of monster usually will take form, frequently an octopus. If such a creature appears, Desoille encourages the participant to subdue it with the power of a magic wand (a suggestion which he says is quite acceptable to most people). Then the participant should engage the creature as a guide in an exploration of the submarine depths. When the participant is ready to return to the beach, Desoille suggests that he/she take the creature along and, on land, tap it once again with the magic wand. The participant is told that doing so will cause the creature to metamorphose to reveal its true identity. As may be anticipated, when a metamorphosis occurs, the creature is replaced by a person who is a significant figure in the individual's life. In the final phase of the daydream, the participant and this person ascend a mountain which overlooks the sea. This theme is considered to be a random probing of the unconscious. Its corresponding question is "What is going on in the depths of your personality; what painful feelings are capable of upsetting you?"

3 and 4. The third and fourth themes bring the individual to confront figures which represent the range of his/her emotional response patterns to other persons. In Desoille's words, "One's memory is composed of a range of images which represent one's dealings with others. These images are related to feelings ranging from the most disagreeable to those capable of providing immense gratification, such as love." Graduated chains of images express this continuum. For example, the male images begin with a devil; then they change to something slightly less threatening such as a magician, thence to an "average fellow," and then they become progressively more positive: a hero, an angel, God. A chain of female images corresponds to this one. The various members of these chains (which Desoille calls "archetypal chains," after Jung's archetypes) reportedly occur spontaneously in the directed daydream. However, rather than waiting for them to occur, the therapist may use them to direct the

course of the daydream in order to explore the individual's habitual responses. (The implication, according to the listed purpose of these themes, seems to be that these responses are rooted in the relationship with the parents).

5. The fifth theme is an encounter with a dragon which must be sought in the depths of its cave. The dragon also arises spontaneously in directed daydreams. Jung interpreted the dragon as the mother who refuses to give herself to her son, that is, the son's incestuous desires toward his mother. However, Desoille rejects Jung's interpretation; according to the fable, "the dragon hoards a treasure and keeps captive a girl or boy who is eventually to be devoured by him, but who is rescued by a hero." Desoille suggests that the dragon represents all of the prohibitions imposed upon the individual by his/her cultural milieu—the family, social class, vocational commitments, and finally the nation. The treasure, then, represents the mental and spiritual potentialities the individual is unable to develop because of the countless prohibitions. The dragon's prisoners also are symbolic; the girl, for the male participant, represents his own sensitivity, the qualities which allow him to empathize with women; if he is not able to restore these, his heterosexual relations will be strained. Desoille does not comment on the meaning of a captive boy for a female, nor of the same-sex captives.

6. Finally, the sixth theme, is the story of "Sleeping Beauty"; it is conducted, as one might anticipate, differently for men and women. The male participant is asked to recall an actual experience he had with his mother, whether it was pleasant or unpleasant. Then his mother leads him into the forest where they look for the castle of Sleeping Beauty. When they find it, they enter, and the man leaves his mother in one of the reception halls. He goes upstairs by himself, finds Sleeping Beauty's bedroom and awakens her. If the sequence goes well, the subject will usually spontaneously feel that in playing the part of the prince, he is achieving sexual maturity. He then offers his sword to Sleeping Beauty as a token of his esteem and makes an ascension in her company. Then he descends to where he had left his mother and introduces Sleeping Beauty to her. Sleeping Beauty welcomes her future mother-in-law and leads her to a portion of the palace which has been reserved especially for her. Thus, the mother permits her son to take a wife. Desoille reports that this theme can elicit extremely dramatic scenes even with men who have had many sexual affairs without being able to choose a wife. For women, the Sleeping Beauty story is intended to represent their own awakening to sexual maturity. Here the woman herself is Sleeping Beauty. She is awakened, makes an ascent with the suitor, and returns to introduce him to her father, the King. According to Desoille, the sixth theme is directed toward the resolution of the Oedipal conflict.

Each of these themes may take more than one oneiric session to resolve, sometimes as many as four. Little remains to be said of Desoille's psychodiagnostic technique. It shares the aforementioned features of Oneirotherapy, as does Leuner's technique, which follows.

Leuner's (1969) psychodiagnostic method is known as Initiated Symbol Projection. The stimuli employed are identified by Leuner explicitly as projective stimuli, alike in principle to the TAT. According to Leuner, the images suggested serve to precipitate and structure fantasies which carry important psychodynamic material. The psychodiagnostic phase is differentiated from the therapeutic phase (symbol drama): in the former, only brief, limited responding to each of the presented stimuli is allowed; whereas in the latter, the participant is encouraged to dwell at length upon each of the same stimuli, in order to develop fully his/her affective response. Leuner considers the enhancement of the affective response central to the therapeutic phase; whereas, the diagnostic phase is adapted for acquiring as much information as possible within a short time. Thus, Leuner regards the two procedures to be almost mutually exclusive. Leuner seems to be the only oneirotherapist to separate these phases in this way. The distinction, while not particularly profound in a theoretical sense, seems very useful for purposes of controlled investigation.

Leuner employs ten standard starting images; these are intended to vary in degree of structure or specificity. Of the ten images listed, the first three form the invariant core of the technique. The first, the meadow, is also used as a starting point for each session: the other stimuli are introduced after the meadow image has been reestablished. The following are Leuner's standard stimuli:

1. A meadow
2. Climbing a mountain and describing the view
3. Following a brook upstream to its source and downstream to the ocean
4. A house which is to be explored
5. The appearance of closely related persons (usually the parents, but sometimes the individual's spouse, siblings, boss, or any other important person), in either literal or symbolic representation
6. The personification of the individual's ego-ideal
7. Situations which would evoke patterns of the individual's sexual behavior
8. A lion, representing the individual's feelings about aggression and his/her manner of dealing with it
9. Looking into a dark forest or cave
10. Watching a swamp. (Leuner, 1966, pp. 3-4)

Leuner describes and interprets his use of each of the stimuli:

1. The participant is asked to imagine a meadow, any meadow that comes to mind. Everything else is left as ambiguous as possible, so that the participant will not be influenced by suggestion and will be quite free to project upon the landscape his/her present affective quality. The participant is asked always to describe in detail all that he/she imagines, even the incidental details of the surroundings. According to Leuner, the meadow may represent a number of themes: it may represent a new beginning; or it may function as a screen onto which the individual projects his/her current life crises or his/her present mood; it may represent a Garden of Eden theme with deep connections to the source of emotional life.

Leuner (1969) provides some examples of responses to the meadow image:

> Sometimes a patient cannot visualize a meadow but can only see a desert . . . indicative of despair and loneliness. It is sometimes seen in cases of latent depression. An anxious patient described a meadow on a dark and stormy day. A 43-year-old married woman saw a summery meadow with a white bench . . . surrounded by flowers all in the shape of red hearts . . . she was falling in love with a wealthy old bachelor. The meadow may also be surrounded by a high fence with the patient standing caged within. (p. 6)

2. The participant is asked to imagine leaving the meadow and climbing a mountain and to describe the view from the top. The image is thought to relate to the participant's feelings about his/her ability to take control of his/her life; in addition, it may reflect any repressed wishes for fame. The altitude of the imagined mountain is related to the individual's level of aspiration. Leuner mentions that the mountain also may be interpreted, in psychoanalytical terms, as a phallic symbol, and as such, it may represent the introjected father. It might be added that the introject in turn presumably would be related to level of aspiration; in this case, the mountain also would evoke feelings about competition. When the individual has reached the top of the mountain, he/she is asked to describe the landscape below. What he/she visualizes refers to the way he/she feels about his/her own future.

Some examples of responses to the mountain image are as follows:

> A patient with a long-standing obsessive-compulsive neurosis visualized an extremely high mountain . . . he saw himself standing atop the mountain, surrounded by ice and snow. He was lonely and he was unable to climb down. He was actually a physicist who had often daydreamed about being an eminent genius like Einstein. . . . Depressed patients sometimes can not find the way up; in such cases , they may go deeper and deeper into a dark forest in the foothills. This seems to show a deep passive resignation to fate.

Leuner suggests that a major transformation in a landscape indicates that some corresponding change in the individual's perceptions, some interpretation made by the therapist, or some insight acquired by the individual has taken effect and is stimulating therapeutic development. For example:

> . . . 24-year-old female patient who suffered from psychogenic headaches . . . was unable to enjoy the view from the mountain because the ruins of an old medieval castle blocked her view. Her association showed that the castle was closely related to her early love for her father. When she was five her parents were divorced. The consequent separation from her father was a painful disappointment to her. As she got insight into her Oedipal problem, there was a simultaneous transformation of her image of the ruined castle. It gradually became smaller and smaller, and as it did so, the woman got a view of a very lovely green landscape in the springtime. This coincided with the development of an optimistic and promising feeling. (p. 7)

Assessments of the participant's progress are made from time to time by asking him/her to describe the view from the mountain. Changes also may reveal themselves in the features of the meadow or of the course of the stream (Image 3). On the other hand, when a prominent feature of the landscape is unchanging (particularly an obstacle, as in the example above), it may point to an issue which still awaits resolution, perhaps resistances which have yet to be overcome.

3. The image of a brook is the third stimulus. The participant eventually must imagine himself/herself following the brook upstream to its source and downstream to the ocean, but he/she may choose which way to go first. The brook itself is taken to symbolize "the flow of psychic energy and the potential for emotional development"

(p. 8). According to Leuner, the neurotic individual always visualizes obstructions in the downstream course: perhaps the brook flows into a hole in the ground, or its flow is dammed by a wall, or the stream diminishes gradually and comes to an end. These obstructions are interpreted as representations of resistance; their objectification in the imaging can give the individual some insight into matters which hinder him/her in living constructively. Leuner observes that most individuals have to follow the brook upstream first. This is the path back to the spring or, symbolically, to the very early mother-child relationship. Inadequacies in this relationship are indicated in the nature of the spring: perhaps the spring is meagre, or the water is dirty, or perhaps when the participant tries to immerse himself/herself in the water, it changes to sand which threatens to engulf him/her. On the other hand, the visualization of an ample and refreshing spring cannot be taken to mean that no serious difficulties arose in this stage of development; for the positive representation may be a fantasy of wish fulfillment. But in any case, it is a good sign when the participant is able to have a pleasurable visualization because it indicates at least some experiences of satisfaction involving a positive mother image.

Leuner considers the images of the meadow, the mountain, and the brook to be the core of his method. He points out that these stimuli make no attempt to introduce archaic material, although such is dealt with if it occurs. Also Leuner does not encourage fairy tales, archetypes, or mystical symbols.

> It would be wrong if we were to allow the patient to fly to the top of a mountain instead of doing the hard work of climbing. . . . We do not encourage the patient to imaging diving deep into the ocean. . . . We only encourage the manifestation of such fantastic imaging if the patient himself tends to produce it spontaneously in response to the standard situations, especially those which evoke symbolic figures from a forest, a cave, or a swamp. We believe that the patient derives more benefit from experiencing frustrations and resistances to his efforts than he would if he got miraculous support which led to a fantastic solution. We are aware of the opportunities to suggest all kinds of magical experiences in the course of a daydream . . . but we doubt that it really helps the patient to deal with reality and to overcome his neurotic maladjustment. (p. 10)

However, it should be noted that the technique known as Symbol-drama, which is a therapeutic manipulation used by Leuner as a part of his system of Guided Affective Imagery, does make use of symbolic solutions, including what he calls "magic fluids." Symbolic manipulation in the hypnoidal state is accompanied by intensified affect and seems to be taken by Leuner as the equivalent of what is known in traditional psychotherapy as "working through." (The interested reader is referred to (Leuner, 1969).)

But Leuner's distinction between "fantastic" solutions and legitimate solutions through symbolic acts remains unclear. The most reasonable assumption seems that the latter must involve effort and the arousal of affect and not merely the facile manipulation of fantasy contents.

4. The image of a house is the fourth stimulus. In accord with Freud, the house is considered a symbol of the individual's own personality. The individual may project onto it his/her wishes and feelings about himself/herself; for example, a palace might

indicate unrealistically exaggerated expectations, and a small hut may bespeak a limited self-concept. In addition, the various parts of the house should be considered. Leuner looks at the following features: the place where food is kept, the toilet facilities, the sleeping quarters with special focus on whether they have single or double beds, the content of the closets, the contents of the cellar and attic since they often contain childhood possessions connected with important events.

5. The fifth stimulus image involves the appearance in the meadow of a person closely related to the participant. The figure is visualized entering the meadow first at a distance. The participant observes the figure, describing its attitude and behavior. This image is intended to reflect the quality of the participant's emotional relationships. Sometimes Leuner permits the use of animal symbols which arise spontaneously to represent the parents, or he suggests the representation of a cow or an elephant. In this way certain resistances may be avoided.

> It is very meaningful . . . when a patient's elephant is at first a huge monument of marble, then comes to life. In the case of a female patient in her late fifties, the re-animated elephant stamped toward the patient as she was lying on the grass, then put a big foot on her breast. The patient reacted with anxiety and shortness of breath. . . . This daydream symbolized a traumatic event from her 13th year. Once when she appeared to be asleep, her father touched her breasts and commented on her attractively developing body to her mother. (pp. 11-12)

6. The sixth image is a figure which embodies the individual's ego-ideal (this term appears to be used not in the strict psychoanalytical sense). The participant is asked to say the name of a person of the same sex and then to imagine the person of this name. According to Leuner, the participant usually will imagine a person whom he would like to resemble. This image is used to help the participant work out his/her identity.

7. The seventh stimulus varies for men and women; in either case, it is designed to represent patterns of sexual feeling and behavior. For the male, the image is a rosebush in the meadow: picking the rose symbolizes sexual intercourse (a symbol from a poem by Goethe).

It is suggested that the male participant visualize a rosebush in one part of his familiar meadow. The description of the rosebush, and whether and how the rose is picked, is taken to reveal the individual's attitude about sexuality:

> It makes a big difference whether the rosebush is big or small, whether the roses are "those sweet, nice, tiny white flowers," as one young man put it, or whether they are deep red, full-sized blossoms. The essential test consists in having the patient pick one of the roses in order to bring it home and put it in a vase on his desk. The first young man of whom I spoke refused to pick the rose at all! An older man picked his rose so hastily that he got pricked by thorns. But it is not only the content of the response which interests us, the patient's resistances and his emotional reactions are also considered. (p. 13)

The female is directed to visualize that she is alone on a country road when a driver comes by and offers her a ride. Leuner lists some of the "innumerable possible outcomes" to this fantasy:

1. No car comes at all.
2. A little boy driving a toy car comes along.
3. The car is driven by a woman.
4. The car stops, but as the patient steps into it, it vanishes into thin air.
5. The driver of the car looks "very Italian." He is looking for sexual adventure, so he drives the car into a forest and the woman becomes awfully frightened. (p. 12)

It is quite unclear why Leuner has chosen stimuli of such a striking lack of parallelism for male and female participants. Why not, for example, have the male participant visualize driving along a country road and encountering a person who needed a ride? Not only are the images Leuner chose dissimilar, but the stimulus for male subjects is a very abstract and idealized representation of sexuality; whereas, the stimulus for the female is blatant. These two images have quite different demand characteristics, leading the respective participants in precisely opposite directions. The rosebush invites the male's feelings about an idealized sexual partner and what might be called a superego-dominated theme. The country road scene, on the other hand, seems to be inviting discussion of less socialized sexual fantasy. Also, the image for females is probably the better one. It allows, as Leuner himself has said, "innumerable outcomes"; there is more latitude and more opportunity for elaboration in the development of the theme. Perhaps both stimuli could be used for both sexes to represent the individual's idealized version of sexuality vs. his less socialized desire.

8. The eighth stimulus, the image of a lion, is intended to disclose the participant's manner of dealing with his/her aggressive impulses. He/she is to visualize a person he/she dislikes very much, brought face to face with a lion, and to watch and describe the lion's behavior. Leuner (1969) describes the response of one participant, a salesman with "cardiac neurosis and various vegetative disturbances":

These symptoms came on after a disliked customer had struck him lightly on the stomach. A year later he was still unable to work. When I tried to get the lion to confront my patient's adversary, the animal reacted like a shy dog. It became smaller and smaller and lay down at the feet of the patient. By the end of therapy . . . the lion was ready to attack the adversary and swallow him without resistance from the patient. (p. 13)

9 and 10. The participant is asked to imagine that he/she is watching from a concealed position 1) in a dark cave or dark forest and 2) in the muddy water of a swamp. The participant watches and waits for the emergence of any human figure, animal, or any other creature which might appear. These two stimuli are similar in intent to Desoille's descent into the sea. Both are purported to uncover deeply repressed fantasy material. Out of the cave or forest, says Leuner, come "Introjects which represent important parts of the individual's behavior patterns" (p. 13); from the swamp emerge animal or human forms symbolizing repressed sexual energy. Leuner (1969) interprets responses to these images in the following way:

The simplest way to deal with these symbolic figures as they develop and emerge from the patient's imaginary forest is just to let them come out. The woods and earth are excellent symbols of the unconscious and, therefore, the act of bringing up these figures to the surface is equivalent to bringing them into consciousness, and this is generally therapeutically profitable. These symbolic figures may be affect-laden animals which in terms of Jung's theory could be interpreted as archetypes. [However] . . . our experience converges with Boss who believes that these archaic affect-laden symbols can be explained in terms of the induction of a deep repression with marked intensification of emotional experiences from early childhood. This brief statement of our position still needs to be demonstrated through rigorous study. (p. 14)

This review of the methods originated by Desoille and Leuner has focused upon the stimuli they use and their lines of interpretation; in short, it has emphasized the distinguishing features of these methods. In summary, it probably will be well to recapitulate the common characteristics of oneirotherapeutic techniques. Fretigny and Virel's (1968) method was selected as an orienting model because their treatment of the oneirotherapeutic method was the most explicit and complete available. However, most of the procedural specifications made by Fretigny and Virel apply also to Desoille's and to Leuner's techniques.

All of the oneirotherapeutic methods use *extended* visual fantasies in *narrative* form to obtain information about the motivational system of the individual, including elements of conflict, perceptual distortion, self-perception, and early memories. The individual usually is prepared for using his/her visual imagination by conditions which promote relaxation; if necessary, preliminary training in muscular relaxation may be given. The reverie itself typically is accompanied by a hypnoidal state of consciousness—the participant focuses his/her attention on his/her fantasy experience rather than on his/her social-environmental and bodily conditions. Leuner does not necessarily take measures to prepare the participant with relaxation training. If the participant is able to involve himself/herself in his/her fantasy productions, the relaxation of bodily tension generally is concomitant. The oneirotherapists use the product of visual imagination in conjunction with associations, discussion, and interpretation. The participant's verbal contribution plays an important part in discovering the meaning of his/her imagery: Affective accompaniments of the imaginary experience are discussed along with associated ideas and memories; these are interpreted in the light of a detailed anamnesis. If a participant should have difficulty experiencing mind images, repetitive practice often helps him/her to do so, unless this inability is rooted in deep-seated resistances. The oneirotherapist may assume more or less directivity and may choose whether to introduce into the narrative elements which do not occur spontaneously. Desoille's technique is the most directive and structured of those reviewed. Usually in any form of oneirotherapy, certain standard images are presented to the participant as starting images. But Fretigny and Virel and Leuner allow for the use of free associative imagery in some instances; the starting images may be likened to projective stimuli (the stimulus being the *suggestion*). The response to any particular starting stimulus tends to be quite lengthy, and the diagnostic technique blends into other aspects of therapy-abreaction and insight. Leuner advocates separating the diagnostic and therapeutic phases by moving the participant quickly through the series of stimuli during the initial diagnostic phase, avoiding the development of full-blown affective reaction. The oneirotherapeutic method is generally a psychodynamic approach with respect to its assumptions and interpretations. The primary assumption is that the symbolism inherent in visual imagery constitutes an affective language which can express unconscious motives without causing them to fully impose themselves upon conscious recognition; for this reason, it is hypothesized, the participant will have less resistance to the expression of the underlying motives and will reveal them more readily than if he/she had to express and understand them verbally. The "language of the unconscious" hypothesis implies that some kind of symbolism is at work in the imagery. Most oneirotherapists take into account general universal theories of symbolism, such as Freudian dream symbolism and Jungian mythological-literary symbolism, as well as idiosyncratic symbols derived from the individual's associations and anamnesis. The advantages of these methods as diagnostic techniques lie in their independence of verbal facility, in the sense of abstractive sophistication and reflective precision. The disadvantages lie in the assumption of interpretive avenues without any compilation of supportive data which may be examined by independent observers. Desoille's (1965) method is probably least favored in this respect because of the precision he attributes to his stimuli and the directiveness he takes toward the participant's fantasy development. Leuner's (1969) stimuli, on the other hand, seem to appeal readily to common sense and perhaps also to more participants. Fretigny and Virel (1968) evidently prefer to choose stimuli according to clinical judgment of the particular case, and therefore no general criticism is appropriate. They appear to have attempted to systematically observe common meanings of fantasy elements; however, little documentation is actually available. Professionals wishing to evaluate the stimuli used in these methods will probably want to begin by taking little for granted.

## REFERENCES

Desoille, R. (1965). *The directed daydream*. New York: Psychosynthesis Research Foundation.

Fretigny, R., & Virel, A. (1968). *L'imagerie mentale* (F. Haronian, Trans.). Geneva: Mont-Blanc. (Unpublished translation in English by F. Haronian, New Jersey, 1970.)

Leuner, H. (1969). Guided affective imagery: A method of intensive psychotherapy. *American Journal of Psychotherapy, 23*, 4-22.

Rigo, L. (1968). *The imagination technique of analysis and restructuration of the profound*. Paper presented at the meeting of the International Society for Mental Imagery Techniques, Geneva, Switzerland.

Stampfl, T., & Levis, D. (1967). Essentials of implosive therapy: A learning theory based psychodynamic behavioral therapy. *Journal of Abnormal Psychology, 72*, 496-503.

Wolpe, J. (1969). *The practice of behavior therapy*. New York: Pergamon.

## CHAPTER 12

# Eidetic Psychotherapy Techniques*

## ANEES A. SHEIKH

In Eidetic Therapy, the diagnostic and the therapeutic procedures are inseparably intertwined. The eidetic procedures that have been developed help not only in understanding the underlying dynamics but also in drawing up the therapeutic plan.

Eidetic analysis has indicated that the symptoms are largely caused either by dissociation of the eidetic components, by fixation on the negative pole, or by a partial or complete repression of significant experience. Consequently, the aim of eidetic therapy is achieved mainly by the revival of the tripartite unity, by a shift of the ego's attention to the neglected positive pole, which brings about a more balanced and realistic appraisal of the experience, or by the uncovering of the repressed experience through progression of eidetic imagery. Since Ahsen (1968) considers an eidetic event in its full intensity to be the psychic equivalent of the corresponding actual event, the re-experience of personality multiples in the form of eidetics is the re-experience of the individual's history, which thus becomes available for change.

There are three main levels in the eidetic psychotherapeutic process. The first level deals with the symptoms of a psychosomatic or hysterical or phobic nature. Next is the developmental level, which pertains primarily to the widespread problems developed in early life with reference to the parents. Two major eidetic tests, the Age Projection Test (Ahsen, 1968) and the Eidetic Parents Test (Ahsen, 1972), form the basis for diagnosis and therapy at each of the first two states respectively. Ahsen also reports a third universal symbolic level of analysis that may help individuals to attain a deeper understanding and integration of meanings of psychic contents. However, as yet he has not presented this third level of analysis in detail in his published works. Consequently, the discussion of this level will not be included in this chapter.

Eidetic psychotherapy begins with symptom composition, which is accomplished through a structured interview during which the therapist tries to specify the exact nature of the physical (i.e., I ache all over) as well as the psychological (i.e., I can't

---

*Reprinted with permission from A. A. Sheikh, Eidetic psychotherapy. In J. L. Singer & K. S. Pope (Eds.), *The power of human imagination.* New York: Plenum, 1978.

think straight) elements of the symptom complex. The patient is also questioned about the worries or concerns that he may entertain about the symptom (i.e., I am afraid of going crazy). Worries and concerns about various parts of the body are also recorded. The symptom is composed completely in the language of the patient. Subsequent to the symptom composition, the therapist is ready to administer the Age Projection Test.

## THE AGE PROJECTION TEST

The therapist asks the patient to give his first, middle, and last names, nicknames, and any other names by which he/she has been called since childhood, for these names are assumed to refer to an individual's various identities. Next, the patient is asked to pay relaxed attention to what the therapist says. He is informed that when the therapist repeats certain words over and over again, he will see an image of himself somewhere in the past:

> The salient features of the symptom discovered during symptom composition are now reiterated to the patient in his own words in a repetitious manner. In the course of this repetition, the patient is addressed by his various names alternately. This repetition artificially activates the symptom to an almost unbearable acuteness. At this point five seconds of total silence are allowed to elapse. Suddenly the therapist starts talking about the time when the patient was healthy and happy. As the therapist talks about health in those areas where the symptom now exists, the patient spontaneously forms a self-image subliminally. The patient is now suddenly asked to project a self-image and describe the following: (a) the self-image itself; (b) the clothing on the self-image; (c) the place where it appears; (d) the events occurring during the age projected in the self-image; (e) the events occurring during the year following to the age projected in the image. (Dolan & Sheikh, 1977)

This procedure usually uncovers an event that precipitated the symptom or that began a series of events that eventually led to symptom formation. Once the self-image related to this event is formed, the patient is asked to project it repeatedly until it becomes clear, and then he is interrogated further about the critical period.

If no relevant event is discovered, the last portion of the test, called "Theme Projection," is administered. The patient is told to see the self-image standing before the parental images, crying to provoke pity and love. Then the self-image takes off one article of clothing and throws it down before the parent, saying, "Take it away, I don't want to wear it." The image proceeds: one of the parents picks it up and deposits it somewhere. The patient sees where it has been placed, what surrounds it, and what objects stand out. He is then asked to report any impressions or memories concerning the objects that stand out in his image.

Alternatively, an important image may evolve spontaneously during the dialogue on imagery between therapist and patient. Ahsen reports, however, that when the Age Projection Test is administered, the meaning and origin of a somatic or quasi-somatic symptom usually become evident. Based on the information revealed by the test, a therapeutic image is then constructed, and the patient is asked to project it repeatedly.

The therapeutic image may work in a variety of ways. It derives its therapeutic effectiveness from the four principles of "magical" functioning. Through these symbolic mechanisms, the image may prompt the release of repressed responses, lead to catharsis of accumulated affect, symbolically satisfy unfulfilled wishes, or correct an imbalanced ego interpretation of events by focusing on hitherto neglected aspects of the response (Panagiotou & Sheikh, 1974).

The Age Projection Test is a fascinating procedure with an intriguing rationale (Ahsen, 1968, 1977a). In the area of psychosomatic and hysterical symptoms, stunning successes in an astoundingly brief period have been reported. Numerous case histories are now available (Ahsen, 1968; Dolan & Sheikh, 1977). As these case studies demonstrate, frequently the symptom is dispelled during the first session. Even when this occurs, further analysis of basic developmental trends may be undertaken through another imagery test. Ahsen has developed a major instrument, the Eidetic Parents Test (1972), for analysis at the developmental level.

## EIDETIC PARENTS TEST

In eidetic therapy special significance is attached to the patterns of interaction between the patient's parents and the patient's perception of polarities that existed in their relationship. The Eidetic Parents Test (EPT) is designed specifically to uncover eidetics in these areas. They have been shown to reveal to a significant extent the quality of the familial relationships and their predominant pathological themes. This test provides not only the means for identifying areas of conflict, but also the format for therapeutic procedure. The test involves a systematic scrutiny of features of the parental images to determine the exact nature of the interparental and parent-child patterns of interaction. The first item on the test proceeds in the following manner:

Picture your parents in the house where you lived most of the time, the house that gives you the feeling of home.

Where do you see them?

What are they doing?

How do you feel when you see the images?

Any reactions or memories connected with the picture? (Ahsen, 1972, p. 52)

The entire EPT consists of thirty situation images in which various aspects of the parents and the parental relationships are visualized. In summary, the participant is asked to visualize the following items:

(1) How and where the parents appear in the house in which the patient was raised; (2) the left-right position of the parental figures in front of the patient;

(3) whether the parents look separated or united as a couple in the picture; (4) the feeling of an active-passive relationship between the two figures; (5) which parent seems to run faster in the image; (6) the pattern and purpose of the parents' running in the picture; (7) the freedom of the parental limbs, while running; (8) the comparative brillance of the parental eyes; (9) the object orientation of the parental eyes; (10) parental eyes—feelings they give, story they tell; (11) the comparative loudness of the parental voices in the picture; (12) the degree of meaningfulness in the parental voices; (13) the parental voices—the feelings they give, story they tell; (14) the degree of hearing by the parental ears in the picture; (15) the degree of understanding by the parental ears when they hear the patient speaking to them; (16) the parents sniffing the house's atmosphere, suggestive of whether they like or dislike the house; (17) the feeling of personal warmth imparted by the parental bodies in the picture; (18) the feeling of acceptance or rejection felt in respect to the parental skin; (19) how healthy the parental skin appears in the picture; (20) the extent to which the parents extend their arms to the patient; (21) the extent to which the patient extends his arms to receive from the parents; (22) the comparative strength of the parental hand grasp in the picture; (23) the parents' manner of swallowing food; (24) the parent's manner of drinking; (25) the pressure in the parental jaws while biting something; (26) the temperature of the parental brains; (27) the efficiency or inefficiency of the parental brains when visualizing as thinking machines; (28) the beating of the parental hearts, seen through a window visualized in the chest; (29) the appearance of the parental intestines, visualized in their abdomen; (30) the temperature and appearance of the parental genitals and their reaction to the patient's touching them. (Dolan, 1972, pp. 27-28)

Certain of these images perhaps require explanation. In particular, the use of various parts of the anatomy as image stimuli may seem to be a perplexing choice for focal inquiry. Generally speaking, they are utilized to elicit feelings about the soundness versus the infirmity of the parents, which may be apparent in characteristics of the skin, brain, heart, and viscera. The infirmity mentioned need not, of course, be an actual physical condition; these images are presented on account of their mundane symbolism; e.g. , the brain represents the thought processes, the heart the emotional processes, and so on. The pathology that shows up in the anatomical images usually ultimately refers to a psychological or emotional inadequacy.

The test includes standard verbatim instructions for presenting the stimuli. After the participant has been introduced to eidetics with a brief practice image, the test is administered in a "piccemeal, phrase by phrase enunciation of each item." If the participant fails to form an image in response to any test item, the instructions are repeated until he responds with an image. If he is totally unable to provide an image response, the cliniclan is expected to record the overt behavior of the subject.

Every image is repeatedly projected until its essential elements are sharpened and separated from its vague or changing aspects. The participant is allowed to acquaint himself thoroughly with his eidetic image before he is asked to describe it. It is essential to the effectiveness of the EPT that the participant be helped to see the image over and over again, and to describe his experience thoroughly. The examiner may need to do a good deal of rather directive and insistent questioning in order to pin down the core of the eidetic response. The participant is instructed not to force any aspects of the image, but to allow it to grow without any interference. He is encouraged to describe the image in "positive declarative statements."

It should be noted that eidetic responses, unlike oneiric reveries (Desoille, 1965; Fretigny & Virel, 1968; Leuner, 1969; Sheikh & Panagiotou, 1975), are not narrative. The repetitious, piecemeal projection of segments of the response is considered an important methodological feature in handling eidetics. It helps to construct the rigid sequence of what defines an eidetic area. Any attempt to project in a smooth, narrative fashion leads to a fictional response; the true eidetic, however, is not fictional.

It is apparent that the EPT stimuli are highly structured. The initial presentation of each stimulus permits only a brief response. Repeated projections allow no more latitude in responding; the image unfolds only under the guiding questions of the therapists. This limiting nature of the stimuli and the directiveness of their presentation have afforded a rigid basis for comparison between individuals and the possibility of using comparative data for establishing interpretive guidelines.

The faithful reporting of eidetic responses is aided by the fact that they are repeatable to the last detail. The reporting, however, is complicated by other matters, and the first response is rarely a pure eidetic. Ahsen (1972) has given the name "eidetic matrix" to the group of phenomena elicited during EPT administration. These include 1) the first response, 2) the primary response, 3) the secondary response, 4) the interjected response, 5) the underlying primary response, and 6) the overt behavior.

The first response reflects the participant's initial reaction to the instruction: this may take a variety of forms, including a manifestation of resistance, and, of course, will not always be an eidetic. The primary response is the true eidetic. It never fails to be repeatable and tends to recur in an almost mechanical manner. It is usually bright and clear, rich in emotional accompaniment, and has a meaning or set of meanings that the individual can usually recognize with some certainty. Any portion of the primary response may be repeated for elaboration or detailed examination. When repeated, it elicits feelings and memories, and after many repetitions, which may be punctuated by resistances and other types of behavior, it may spontaneously be replaced by a new primary that, in turn, through repetition, may give rise to still another primary. The primaries arising out of repetition of the first primary are termed "underlying primaries." The secondary response, interjected response, and overt behavior are types of reaction that frequently occur between primaries. After a few repetitions, the primary response may suddenly be replaced by material only superficially related to it, such as elements of the individual's ordinary fancy. Such responses are termed "secondary" and are usually used as a defense. Sometimes the individual punctuates the primary response with significant verbal or fantasy material. This behavior is called an interjected response and it occasionally contains important depth material that is of use in structuring therapy. Overt behavior refers primarily to the individual's facial expressions, postures, and other acts that express his attitude toward the imagery experience: for example, he may appear interested, indifferent, or irritated.

The repeated projection of the primary response along with the resultant affective elaboration and eventual replacement of one primary eidetic by another and another, is the crux of the full-length diagnostic-cum-therapeutic technique: it is actually through this process that therapeutic progress is made. The reader will recall that the primary eidetic is accompanied by somatic patterns and affective significations. It follows that the repetition of the primary results is a fuller experience of these, along with the visual component; this process implies the acquisition of a degree of conscious recognition of the connections involved, as well as a rather thorough working-over of the affective reactions. It has been observed that only when this process has been carried to completion for one eidetic, does it begin with another. Thus, each progression or change represents a step forward, a deepening and broadening of understanding and assimilation, an illumination of another aspect of the complex problem that the individual is not prepared to examine.

It has been noted above that image figures that are projected repeatedly tend to interact progressively. But at times, strong ego controls cause the images to become frozen at certain points of interaction, often when important trends are about to emerge. In order to break this immobility, the emanation technique is used. If the patient is projecting a visual image that holds a self-image ($p^1$) and an image of another ($F^1$), the therapist will request the patient to visualize "another self" ($p^2$) and "another figure" ($F^2$) emerge from the original images. The patient is then asked to describe the actions of $p^2$ and $F^2$ to the therapist. Any number of emanations may be elicited, but it has been found that more than two or three are rarely required in order to restore movement of the images (Ahsen, 1968; Panagiotou & Sheikh, 1974, 1977).

An individual's ability to produce a sufficiently rich eidetic response is interpreted as a sign of openness to his internal life. When the imagery reveals a "structural defect," it indicates a particularly problematic area. Two major forms of imagery defects are: meager responses and mutilated responses. Meager responses may occur in limited areas of eidetic imagery, and reflect the individual's particular problems in relating to those areas. However, insufficient responses may also be a general pattern and point to habitual suppression of emotional experiences. But, both the individual who gives meager responses in a restricted area and he who does so generally often learn to respond adequately, if they are repeatedly encouraged. Three sources likely to be the root of extremely persistent imagery repression are: 1) a perseverative fantasy theme, such as a phobia, which competes with the imagery, 2) religious or moral aversion to eidetic images, and 3) strong tendencies to acting out. To deal with the first source the use of the Age Projection Test is suggested: it will bring the dynamics of a perseverative theme to the surface. Ahsen interprets the second as a resistance of a disturbed patient to the experience, and suggests that the patient be instilled with an informed conviction that knowledge about his parents is absolutely essential to his well-being. The third source, the acting-out tendencies, is likely to be based upon an identification with the negative aspects of one or the other parent. It follows that in order for the individual to realize an internalized image of the parent, he must be able to differentiate himself from that parental image. The aforementioned three sources quite possibly do not exhaust all the causes of the inability to produce adequate imagery responses, and this inadequacy continues to be a nightmare for clinicians interested in using imagery as the main tool for diagnosis and treatment.

In contrast to meager responses, preponderant mutilated figures indicate "widespread trauma" in the history of the individual. Common mutilations are undersized, oversized, or entirely absent parent figures. Each of these is regarded to refer to a specific theme: undersized parents generally signify the individual's need to maintain a distance between himself and his parents; oversized parents commonly reveal that the parents are perceived as incorporative; and absent parents, in most cases, mean that the parents made themselves unavailable and the child wished them away or dead. Partially multilated images with, for example, vague eyes or limbs, faint voices, etc., usually represent related defects in parental behavior. However, grossly mutilated parental images, such as disembodied heads, limbs, or eyes, ghostly bodies, and the like, may indicate "terrorizing themes."

A number of inadequate and mutilated responses to the EPT should be expected. When these are elicited by only some EPT items and do not seem to be a pervasive tendency, they point to the areas of experience to which the participant relates with most difficulty, and which, therefore, are most in need of attention.

The therapists should perhaps be forewarned that it is not uncommon for participants to initially offer some resistance to the EPT. Several rather frequent manifestations of resistance are noticed. The first is "reality resistance": it refers to the participant's tendency to respond in a purely verbal-logical manner that is in accordance with facts rather than with his subjective experience. For example, he might say, "My father runs faster because he is a man"; whereas, if he attended directly to his image response, he would see that his mother was running faster. The individual who has the tendency to ignore the actual image will have to be continually reminded of it by the therapist. Another common form of resistance arises from apprehensiveness about relating to traumatic emotional experiences. The fear may be limited to only a few areas and their corresponding images or it may be pervasive. When the individual is confronted with the task of trying to understand his feelings, he may react by inhibiting his ability to experience his feelings. In such cases, one should attempt to facilitate the individual's reengagement with his emotional life by instructing him to consider and relate to the possible presence of emotion, even though he is not "feeling" any at the moment. A third form of resistance commonly encountered is a propensity for exaggerated verbalization. The individual tends to respond in a totally verbal manner and avoids seeing an image, or he may describe his image in such profuse detail that its reliability suffers markedly. Under these circumstances, the therapist must insist that the participant curtail his tangential or circumlocutory speech and limit himself to a concise description of what he sees and no more. In other cases, resistance manifests itself in argumentativeness; the patient does not comply with the instructions to visualize and report but instead challenges the therapist in various ways. The therapist obviously must avoid any arguments and again must find a relevant strategy to keep the individual on the track. Resistance can be expressed by deliberately providing misinformation. However, this form is relatively rare and occurs chiefly in individuals who have not sought therapy voluntarily. In still other cases, resistance takes the form of self-condemnation that stands in the way of cooperation in the assigned task. The therapist may be able to direct the individual away from this response pattern through repeated indications that his manner of response is inappropriate to the task and hence unacceptable. Furthermore, in some individuals, resistance stems from deep-seated inferiority feelings; they deprive the individual of the confidence to relate to his imagery in the necessary and decisive manner. If it is apparent, then the inferiority feelings must be treated before the images pertaining to the parents can become available for use. In general, any sign of apathy on the part of the participant should be countered by an active imagery approach by the therapist.

It needs to be highlighted that the experience that emerges in the eidetics often is at variance with the patient's conscious views of it. For instance, his experience of a parent in the imagery may differ radically from his conscious opinion of this parent. Generally, the Consciousness-Imagery-Gap (C-I-G) is caused by the need to repress a painful experience. Or, it may be the result of the parents' brainwashing of the patient.

Once the C-I-G has been uncovered, the next step is to challenge the patient's conscious beliefs and attitudes by confronting him with his contrary perceptions revealed in the eidetics. It is vital to take note of the patient's reactions to this procedure. Does he deny the existence of a gap and, thus, reject change? If he resists, what is the form of his resistance? Does he make an effort to bridge the gap? Or, is he eager to learn more about the unknown within himself? Evidently the nature of the patient's reactions to the C-I-G clarifies the problems under investigation (Ahsen, 1972).

The method is clearly a directive one. The directiveness is facilitated by the specificity of the instructions concerning the administrational procedures. Ahsen also recognizes the complexity of information that can be drawn from eidetic responses and is very explicit in orienting test users in the analysis of these responses. The repeatability of the images, as seen in the clinic (Ahsen, 1972; Dolan & Sheikh, 1976) as well as in the laboratory (Sheikh, 1976), leads to a high intra-individual reliability for the EPT. Among imagery techniques the test clearly has the distinction of being the best controlled and, therefore, the most feasible tool for research.

The interpretation for the EPT items may strike as surprising to some. A number of items are assigned meanings to which many investigators would readily agree, independent of theory-specific symbolism; these items include, for example, the image of the parents in the home, whether they appear separate or united, whether they look happy or otherwise, and so forth. Other items, however, such as anatomical details, have less logical appeal and may seem to be strange choices. Need for further research is obviously indicated.

## A CASE HISTORY

Numerous case histories of patients with a wide variety of symptoms are now available in the works of Ahsen and others. The following example is selected because it involves most of the major concepts and techniques of eidetic psychotherapy. It is summarized from a paper by Ahsen and Lazarus (1972).

Mrs. Jay, who was forty-one years of age, was suffering from pain in the upper left abdomen, chest, and left breast, from excessive irrational anxieties, including a fear of death, as well as from strong uncertainties and feelings of personal unworthiness. She had undergone behavior therapy with no gain.

After an initial composition of the symptoms, Ahsen administered the Age Projection Test. She reported a self-image around the age of twenty-six wearing a red blouse and a black skirt. She recollected that her father had died during the preceding year. He had suffered a fatal heart attack but was brought back to life temporarily through cardiac massage. She remembered begging the doctors not to massage the heart and let him die. She also mentioned that at the time she had felt extremely traumatized and had experienced choked hysteria inside.

From the patient's description, Ahsen selected two images dealing with the two opposed ends of the events: 1) massage of the heart (MH) and 2) death of the father immediately after cardiac massage (DF). In response to MH, Mrs. Jay developed the acute symptoms, and in reaction to DF, she became relaxed, though not entirely relieved of all symptoms. The hypothesis presented itself, that just as the doctors wanted to actively revive the father, Mrs. Jay wanted to actively let the father die. During further inquiry about this topic, the patient, on her own, saw images in which she suffocated her father with a pillow on the hospital bed. As she saw these images, she bitterly cried and then became completely peaceful and her somatic symptoms disappeared.

After the disappearance of her main debilitating symptoms, her past as well as her fantasy life started to unfold more freely. She remembered her father's two previous heart attacks. The experience of the images dealing with these events appeared to be laden with powerful affect which brought back the somatic symptoms. In the final analysis, these images, however, proved to be cathartic and strengthened the patient. Mrs. Jay showed keen understanding of the symbolism involved and clearly realized why she wanted her father to die during the cardiac massage.

The eidetics revealed not only her negative view of her father but also a positive one: she saw a jolly man, singing with her as he took her to school or for walks. She immensely enjoyed these images and they restored a feeling of worth in her.

The eidetics uncovered a number of other areas of conflict. An important one among these was her dread of school, where children persecuted her for being fat. Another was the anxiety caused by her first menstruation, her fear of conception and miscarriages, topics which had also emerged during Theme Projection. The EPT elicited many images which led her to the realization that many of her problems were related to her rejecting mother. She consequently felt very angry at her. In short, all three images, with the guidance of the therapist, enabled her to resolve her conflicts. Gradually she was relieved of all her symptoms. A follow-up after one year and another after two years revealed that her progress not only had been maintained but had advanced.

# REFERENCES

Ahsen, A. (1968). *Basic concepts in eidetic psychotherapy.* New York: Brandon House.

Ahsen, A. (1972). *Eidetic parents test and analysis.* New York: Brandon House.

Ahsen, A. (1977a). *Psycheye: Self-analytic consciousness.* New York: Brandon House.

Ahsen, A., & Lazarus, A. A. (1972). Eidetics: An internal behavior approach. In A. A. Lazarus (Ed.), *Clinical behavior therapy* (pp. 87-99). New York: Brunner/Mazel.

Biller, H. B. (1971). *Father, child, and sex role: Parental determinants of personality development.* Lexington, MA: Heath Lexington Books.

Desoille, R. (1965). *The directed daydream.* New York: Psychosynthesis Research Foundation.

Dolan, A. T. (1972). Introduction. In A. Ahsen (Ed.), *Eidetic parents test and analysis.* New York: Brandon House.

Dolan, A. T., & Sheikh, A. A. (1976). Eidetics: A visual approach to psychotherapy. *Psychologia, 19*, 210-219.

Dolan, A. T., & Sheikh, A. A. (1977). Short-term treatment of phobias through eidetic imagery. *American Journal of Psychotherapy, 31*, 595-604.

Fretigny, R., & Virel, A. (1968). *L'imagerie mental*. Geneva: Mont-Blanc.

Leuner, H. (1968). Guided affective imagery: A method of intensive psychotherapy. *American Journal of Psychotherapy, 23*, 4-22.

Panagiotou, N., & Sheikh, A. A. (1974). Eidetic psychotherapy: Introduction and evaluation. *International Journal of Social Psychiatry, 20*, 231-241.

Panagiotou, N., & Sheikh, A. A. (1977). The image and the unconscious. *International Journal of Social Psychiatry, 23*, 169-186.

Sheikh, A. A. (1976). Treatment of insomnia through eidetic imagery: A new technique. *Perceptual and Motor Skills, 43*, 994.

Sheikh, A. A., & Panagiotou, N. D. (1975). Use of mental imagery in psychotherapy: A critical review. *Perceptual and Motor Skills, 41*, 555-585.

# CHAPTER 13

# Techniques in Psycho-Imagination Therapy*

## JOSEPH E. SHORR

Psycho-imagination therapy uses four techniques, namely: 1) finish-the-sentence; 2) most and least question; 3) the self and other question; and 4) the imaginary situation (IS). However, it is the quality of ubiquitous waking imagery elicited through the imaginary situation that is the essence of the phenomenological method.

The theoretical purpose of using imaginary situations is based not only on seeing how the patient views his world, but also being able, in time, to "open up" the "closed system of internal reality." Fairbairn (cited in Guntrip, 1964) describes this internal world as a "static internal situation" that is precluded from change by its very nature so long as it remains self-contained. It is my contention that the better able the patient and the therapist are to see this "tight little inner world," the easier it will be to deal with the whole of the patient and his world.

When the patient is asked to imagine himself in certain structured situations, responses may be elicited that accurately bring into the "here and now" states of feeling that have their roots in the past. By stressing the situation with patients and encouraging them in their choice of action within the situation, they are ultimately helped to greater choice of action in their external reality.

Thus, although I had some interesting results from guiding a person in going into a house and telling me what he or she saw therein, far more was revealed when either I suggested introducing a significant "other" into the situation, or the patients did this for themselves. I could then urge the patient not only to tell me how he felt in the various parts of the house, but how he felt in relating to the other person in the situation.

Sometimes it is so urgent to develop a high degree of specificity that the imaginary situation will relate so specifically to one particular patient that it would never again be used with anyone else.

---

*Reprinted with permission from J. E. Shorr, Clinical Uses of Categories of Therapeutic Imagery. In J. L. Singer & K. S. Pope (Eds.), *The Power of Human Imagination*, New York: Plenum, 1978.

As the patient becomes accustomed to this kind of therapy it is less and less necessary to make interpretations for him. With specific cross-checking, including the most-or-least method, the finish-the-sentence technique, and the self-and-other technique, it would be possible to help focus the patient to greater awareness, where he would be forced to face the truth for himself.

Certain types of image categories were delineated from the imagery productions of hundreds of patients, imagery workshop participants, and university students in classes in the use of imagery. These specific imagery categories are separated for instructional purposes so that the trained therapist using imagery can have a systematic understanding of what certain kinds of imageries purport to do and what general expectancies of reactions appear to occur most consistently. The broad array of imagery instructions are intended to be a comprehensive and systematic guide for clinical use. I also encourage the therapist and the patient to use their own imagination in therapy to come up with imagery scenes that will lead to increased awareness.

Psycho-imagination therapy attempts to put the individual, through his own imagery, into a particular situation that would evoke a set of interactions that would be useful not only in revealing major problems in the areas of significance in the patient's life, but that would also permit him to relive experiences. Singer (1974) wrote, "Shorr uses an almost infinite variety of images geared very much to the specific characteristics of the patient and the specific developments in therapy."

The dialogical processes that result from the patient's imagery productions in interaction with the therapist to gain greater awareness and to focus for change are minimally included, since to include complete dialogue would be of a magnitude beyond the scope of this chapter.[1]

Another emphasis in psycho-imagination therapy is subjective meaning. Escalona (1973) suggests that it is mental imagery that may offer a unique opportunity to study the integration of perception, motivation, subjective meaning, and realistic abstract thought. In the course of describing his image, the imager begins to relate it to something of meaning in his personal life. Events, attitudes, feelings, motivations are attached to the image and can be used to explore further its interpersonal implications.

It is possible to achieve images that bypass the censorship of the individual in any type of imagery, daydream, or dream. What I am trying to show is that by asking the person to respond to specific types of imagery, certain kinds of reactions seem to emerge in their productions. Obviously, this is not an absolute since a person may reveal his areas of conflict, his style of defenses, and even focus certain images for change in any of the types of imageries I am categorizing. Yet, certain kinds of things are better revealed by offering one kind of imagery systematically than by offering another kind. For example, in self-image imagery I ask the person to imagine (IS): "There are two of you. One of you is looking through a keyhole at the other you." From the response of the person it is possible to get at not only self-image but areas of conflict, styles of defenses, and unconscious attitudes. Yet, I introduce self-image

---

[1] For verbatim therapist-patient interaction printed tapes, the reader would do well to read the author's *Psycho-Imagination Therapy* (1972) and *Psychotherapy through Imagery* (1974).

imagery as a separate category because it invariably adds a dimension of awareness that may be overlooked if it is not included, thus adding comprehensiveness.

The principle of categorization involves rules for grouping entities on the basis of some common or shared attributes. Here are the categories of imagery with common attributes.

## SPONTANEOUS IMAGERY

The use of spontaneous imagery is generated in two ways. One method is to ask the patient to allow any images that he "sees" to emerge and then to report them. As the sequence of images flows, certain ones can and often do become affect laden. These images can then serve as a vehicle for further dialogue or possible release of feeling.

A second method is to ask the patient to offer the next five consecutive images that occur to him. He is then asked which of the five gives him the most reaction. From the one selected, a dialogue or release of feeling may occur. On occasion, the therapist can ask the patient to "become" in his imagination the image that he had the strongest reaction to, and to complete certain sentences as if he is the image. It is possible to have the patient finish the same sentences for each of the five images.

Here is the actual example of a male, thirty-three years old, with a history of violent behavior.

The five consecutive images are: 1) a lake; 2) a tree; 3) a motorcycle; 4) a woman; and 5) death in a hood similar to the one that danced in the Woody Allen movie.

I then asked him to imagine he was Death, since he immediately responded that it was the fifth image that caused a very strong reaction in him and to finish these sentences as if he were the image.

I feel lonely.
Adjective that best describes me: power.
I wish I had something to do besides collecting bodies.
I must collect bodies.
I need a vacation.
I secretly don't like this job, but God gave it to me.
I will do my job.
Never refer to me as irresponsible.

From those responses we were able to get into a meaningful dialogue. I will not attempt interpretation but, as you can see, a lot can be revealed in a short time.

Another possibility with five consecutive images is to ask the patient if he can find some sense out of the pattern of the five images. It is also fruitful at times to ask for an additional five consecutive images either at the same session or at later sessions.

In addition, spontaneous imagery can be stimulated by suggesting that the patient image walking down a road and reporting everything he sees.

The most common form of imagery in man is spontaneous and arises before our "inner eyes" without any apparent stimulus from any specific course. Augusta Jellinek (1949), originator of the term "spontaneous imagery," put it most aptly when she stated, "These images are experiences as they would originate independently as though we were only spectators, and not the source of these productions." Anyone who has asked a person to "just imagine anything that comes to you," with no regard for directions or specific content, will know that surprises never cease for the person imagining, who may express discovery, amusement, or shock, and for the therapist himself, who may be quite astonished by the unexpected nature of the imagery. Most frequently the imagery seems to flow into a continuous stream of scenes and actions.

As a person grows to trust his spontaneous imagery during the therapeutic dialogue and begins to see meaning and direction from it, he can begin to trust his spontaneous imagery when he is outside the therapy situation and can begin to derive his own meanings and directions.

## DIRECTED IMAGERY

Directed imagery is the primary method used, except where spontaneous imagery is used or where patients volunteer images that are "now" occurring to them or images they have had in the course of time that they wish to examine for meaning. Certainly intrusive images the patient presents should be examined for meaning and release of feelings, as it would preclude the need for directed imagery.

Directed imagery can capture the flow of imageries that are constantly going on in our minds. There are certain times when the spontaneous flow of images may seem to be without theme or apparent coherency, going on in an endless fashion of shots and sequences. The intervention of directed imagery can be used then to capture the flow and bring coherency and integration to the production. My experience validates those of Horowitz and Becker (1971), who say that the specificity of instructions for reporting visual images increases the tendency to form as well as to report images.

The therapist is urged to allow the flow of imagery to go as far as it seems it can go before offering new imaginary situations. Dialogue should be engaged in when the flow appears to stop.

The incidental remarks the patient makes while imagining are not to be ignored. I will offer one of many possibilities. For example, there are persons who are competitively motivated to offer only seemingly creative-sounding imagery. Such persons might say they are offering boring imagery, and they must be reassured to report all and be told, too, that no imagery is insignificant and all have potential meaning.

## SELF-IMAGE IMAGERY

All of us have a theory of ourselves, about what kind of person we are. Our self-concept of competent or incompetent, attractive or repulsive, honest or dishonest, etc., has an enormous effect on our behavior. Personality theorists have suggested concepts such as self-esteem, self-confidence, self-negation, self-doubt, self-respect, etc. There is considerable evidence to support the belief that each of us has a self-system, a set of attitudes we have about ourselves. This self-system is how we define ourselves. Yet, inextricably bound to our self-definition is our perception of how others see us. Sullivan (1953) has stated that even when we are alone, our thinking, images, and behavior always relate to other people, real or imaginary.

The individual's self-image or self-definition may be revealed in any type of imagery, daydream, or dream. Yet, an even more clear picture with accompanying feelings may emerge if the effort is made to concentrate on the person seeing images of himself alone, in a situation.

Self-image imagery can be categorized in the following manner:

1. Those imaginary situations in which the patients are asked to imagine there are two of them. Then they are asked to imagine such things as "kissing yourself," "hugging yourself," "sitting on your own lap," "holding yourself up," etc. Attitudes of self-acceptance or nonacceptance, shame, or self-revulsion may emerge. This self-observation may reveal conflicts and style of defenses heretofore concealed to the imager.

2. Those imagery situations again in which the persons are to imagine there are two of them. Then they are to imagine "looking through a keyhole and seeing yourself," or "two of you sitting in easy chairs facing each other in a dialogue." This helps us see ourselves and talk to ourselves.

3. Those in which there are two of you but with one of you in need of help, i.e., "you are in a boat—another you is in the water in the middle of the ocean. What do you do?" Often this imaginary situation and other variations of the same phenomenon indicate a person's attitude toward self-help or accepting help.

4. Still another group of imagery situations that tends to elicit self-images combined with reminiscent images are, i.e., "image of yourself in a classroom," "image of yourself in a child's playground."

## DUAL IMAGERY

Psycho-imagination therapy is predicated on the premise that a person's inner conflicts are brought about by the opposition of two strong and incompatible forces, neither of which can be satisfied without exacting pain, fear, guilt, or some other emotional penalty. Of course, to become aware of these antithetical forces within oneself, these ambivalences, is to begin to recognize the complementary opposites within experience. Once this can be accomplished the patient can attempt to change his reactions to reality situations, can, in effect, negate conflict, can indeed actualize his own personality.

A rather remarkable phenomenon appears to occur when a person is asked to imagine two different forces, dolls, trees, animals, impulses, etc., and then to contrast each of them with each other. In the great majority of the reported imageries (but not all), there appears to be some form of bipolarization between them. This can be better demonstrated when one asks the imager to assign an adjective to each of the two images. The adjectives may reflect opposite forces of some kind. To enhance the opposing or contrasting forces, one can ask the person to imagine one of the images speaking to the other image, then to imagine the answer back to the first image from the second image. Again, this can be reversed, with the second image speaking to the first image and the first image's remarks back.

Dual imagery is so fertile that from here it is possible to develop it in many directions. I will demonstrate a few directions:

| First Image | | Second Image |
|---|---|---|
| | the person | |
| Statement to person from image | | Statement to person from image |

Another direction:

| First Image | | Second Image |
|---|---|---|
| | the person | |
| Statement from image to person | | Statement from image to person |

Another direction:

Suggest that the first and second image walk down a road together (or appear together in some way) and become aware of what their interaction appears to be.

Another direction:

| First Image | | Second Image |
|---|---|---|
| | the person | |
| (M/L) The most unlikely (or difficult) statement from the image to the person | | (M/L) The most unlikely (or difficult) statement from the image to the person |

Another direction:

| First Image | | Second Image |
|---|---|---|
| | the person | |
| Statement from the image to a significant person in the person's life | | Statement from the image to a significant person in the person's life |
| or | | or |
| Statement from the significant person in the person's life to the image | | Statement from the significant person in the person's life to the image |
| or | | or |
| Statement from the therapist to the image | | Statement from the therapist to the image |
| or | | or |
| Statement from the image to the therapist | | Statement from the image to the therapist |

There is no absolute formula for using dual imagery. When I suggest that a patient image two trees, or two animals, or two women I usually find that some items are neutral and others are affect laden. It is difficult to tell in advance what the patient will respond to with strong emotion. Thus, I suggest that you engage the patient first with what seem to be neutral images and work into the affect-laden imagery according to the patients readiness to deal with sensitive material.

The major emphasis is on awareness of conflict; the particular way in which the patient views his world; the dialogue that may ensue; the release of feelings; and the readiness to enter into the focusing approaches such as cathartic or task imagery.

Experience with dual imagery as a means of discovering areas of conflict and expanded awareness seems to fall into the following general groupings:

1. Those that compare two images of things: two rocking chairs, two tables, two rooms, two bathtubs, two houses, etc.

2. Those that compare two images that are alive but not human: two flowers, two trees, two animals, etc.

3. Those that compare two images that are human: two women, two men, two children, etc.

4. Those that compare the person in relation to forces or impulses. Those include: Above you is a force. What do you feel and do, etc.? You awake from sleeping in a field at night and there are footsteps over your body. Over what part of your body are the footsteps, and to whom do they belong? Or: You walk down a road and somebody taps you on the shoulder, etc.

5. Those that compare two of you: You are in a cave. You are also outside the cave. Call to yourself. Or: You are in a boat in the ocean and you are also in the water. Throw a rope from that you in the boat to the you in the water, etc.

6. Those that compare two body parts of one person: Imagine what your heart says to your head. What does the left side of your brain say to the right side of your brain, etc.?

7. Those that compare body parts of one person to another person: What does your heart say to the heart of another person, etc? What does the heart of the other person say to your heart, etc.?

8. Those that compare differences in physical space directions: You walk down a shallow river and you see something on each side. Or: You look ahead and see something; then turning, what do you see, etc.? Image in front and image behind.

9. Combined categories of dual imagery: Imagine two different animals in human situations, or any other possible combination of dual imagery conceptions that may occur creatively in the operational use of imagery that seems to help delineate conflict areas.

The dual images frequently represent the two parts of self in conflict, that is, self versus self. Then, at other times it is the self versus the other person. In any case, dual imagery can serve to make a person aware of his internal conflicts and those conflicts with other persons. A dialogue is a natural outgrowth of the reporting of the dual images leading to further meaning of the conflicts.

When a person is asked to image two bipolarized images together and then to imagine them as one image, he may experience great difficulty as he attempts this. Some persons protest and say it is impossible. One person brought the two images together and then exploded them in his imagery so that they would disappear. Apparently, the more bipolarized the dual images, the more difficult it is to imagine them in a unitary manner.

In the use of dual imagery with detached or schizoid persons, I have observed changes in their imagery when the detachment lifts. What appeared in detachment as dull and limited seems to enlarge and expand and become more vivid. At other times, with some detached people, one of the dual images has upon examination revealed itself as the "secret self" of that person.

## BODY IMAGERY

All of us tend to look at our body image through the eyes of others so, for example, what we see in a mirror is interpreted through a set of social values. We invariably evaluate our body images against an ideal of preferred standard reflecting a cultural bias.

The idealized body image also relates to those body images we may have of ourselves with our eyes closed. Such self-observation may reveal internal satisfaction or its opposite, self-hatred.

Empirical evidence indicates that persons tend to be able to sense a body-part core of their identity when asked to identify such a body correlate.

Furthermore, introjection of parental figures can be evidenced when persons are asked to imagine in what part of their body their parents reside. They can see their parents in their heart, guts, arms, etc. Most patients are not overly surprised by the body reference to particular organs and respond quite naturally to such a question.

In the developmental process, if a person has been falsely defined by the significant other, false definition may take on bodily form. The mother or father who "resides" in the patient's chest appearing hostile is in reality the false identity or the neurotic conflict internalized.

The patient is asked to "exorcise" the bad parental figure out of his body and to remove the influence of the other; and when accomplished, it can lead to a healthier, more independent identity.

The following are thirteen examples of different types of body imageries:

1. In what part of your body does your body-part core reside? Statement from core to other.
2. In what part of your body does your anger, love, joy, guilt, shame reside?
3. In what part of your body does your mother or father reside? (Introjection-body exorcism)
4. Enter your own body. Describe the journey.
5. Have mother or father, etc., enter your body. Describe their journey.
6. Enter your mother's or father's body. Describe your journey.
7. Dual body imagery: image of chest; image of back. A force that goes into your head; a force that comes out of your head.
8. Statement from your own: head to heart; head to guts; head to genitals—statements back.
9. Statement from you to other person: head to head; head to heart; head to guts; head to genitals, etc.—and all can be reversed in direction of other to you and their statements.
10. Imagery that relates to "buffer-zone" areas and self-touching: What is the closest you will allow a stranger to come near you? Imagine what parts of your body you find easiest to touch and what parts do you find most difficult?

11. Imaging one's own body in relationship to attractiveness, size and shape, masculinity or femininity, and strength: Sensing your body, which part seems most attractive or least attractive? Sensing your body, which part of your body are you most aware of? Sensing your body, what is the most secret part of your body, etc.?

12. Body-holding imagery involving others: Imagine holding your mother's or father's face in your hands. Reverse and imagine them individually holding your face in their hands.

13. Composite imagery: your parent and your body as merging and then separate out your own.

## SEXUAL IMAGERY

Individuals can fantasize or imagine sexual happening from memory images nearly congruous in feelings to their past actual occurrence. Empirical evidence indicates that sexual imagery can be so vivid that the physiological response can cause increased heartbeat rate, a rise in temperature, rapid breathing, vasocongestion, and even orgasm. Of course, other imageries besides sexual ones can be near-re-creations, but sexual images are certainly the example par excellence.

In fact, my experience indicates that when persons say they cannot have images, they will respond when I ask them if they can imagine sexual scenes or recall sexual memories. So far this has resulted in no failures.

Sexual themes are a fertile area for the imagination to play upon. They have power because of their importance in our lives. Images of sexuality we have during intercourse or in place of it, as in masturbation, are as common as rain. Then there are other images related to the strategies of interaction between men and women that anticipate sexual outcomes, acceptance, or rejection.

Sadistic or masochistic images may emerge, as well as images of dominance, rejection, jealousy, unfavorable comparisons, feelings of heartbreak, joy, sin, being dirty, etc.

Since sexual conflicts deal with the most vulnerable, the most tender, the most shame-inducing, and the most guilty feelings, they are the most difficult to disclose to oneself and others. In order to get at these conflicts, I start with general imagery situations that have no obvious sexual overtones, but that have, through clinical use, proved to be sexually revealing.

The range of sexual images is so vast that one would have to be encyclopedic to categorize them. I offer the following categories as the most productive from my clinical experience.

The imageries can be systematically categorized in the following manner:

1. In about 98 percent of the persons who are offered the following imagery situation, sexual feelings and attitudes are expressed. The 2 percent of individuals are those who relate this imagery to death or burial and those, like prisoners, who regard it as an escape hatch. Since 98 percent do respond to it and reveal themselves sexually, it can be a powerfully important sexual imagery: Walk into the middle of a room.

There is a hole in the floor. Look through the hole and tell me what you see. Then imagine going down into the hole and tell me what you feel and do.

Here is an actual response from a thirty-year-old woman. I will not attempt interpretation or patient-therapist dialogue. "The room is dark—it's very hard to find the hole. When I look through I see a crocodile. Wow! I just can't go down—but I'll try. Whoo, my dress flies up—I'm an easy target (laughs). Roger the crocodile will do me in—I don't belong there."

2. There is a special imaginary situation in which the person is asked to imagine three doors—a left, middle, and right door—and then to imagine entering. Experience indicates that nearly always the response to the middle door relates to either sexuality or love relationships or the lack of them even if the manifest content is not explicitly sexual. The left and right doors do not follow a predictable fashion, but can be used for further information and awareness in any case.

3. There are those imageries that ask the person to image sexual parts. Examples are: Imagine an animal that comes out of a penis and an animal that comes out of a vagina. Remove lint from the navel of _____ (someone the person is intimately involved with).

4. Certain sexual imageries that are useful to attitudes between the sexes are as follows: Escort a group of women (or men) prisoners one mile away to another station. What happens? What do you do and feel, etc.? Imagine a woman (or man) on a six-foot mound of earth, etc.

5. Imageries that involve parents such as: Take a shower with your father or mother. Stare at the naked back of your father or mother. Have each of them stare at your naked back, etc.

6. Imageries that relate to sexual fantasies such as: Imagine the fantasy a person of the opposite sex would have about you. What is your sexual fantasy about an ideal sexual partner, etc.

## PREDICTING IMAGERY

To predict the reported imagery production in another person one has encountered for the first time would be virtually impossible. Yet, when two persons, intimately involved, are asked to predict each other's imagery in separate and private reports, surprising results may occur. For example, I have asked married couples privately and silently to report five consecutive images and then to write them down on paper. I then asked each partner to predict the imagery of the other. A bimodal distribution of predictions seems to occur. That is, some couples were able to predict a good many of the other partner's imagery while others seemed to have little awareness of the other's imagery. The results of the dialogue that follows when one partner reveals his or her own imagery to the other partner can be of great therapeutic value. It can heighten the degree of awareness for the person and the partner. Increased communication invariably results because the partner is seeing the other through his or her way of viewing the world. Even those who are poor at predicting the other's imagery now have a chance for awareness of the other that has been heretofore overlooked.

## TASK IMAGERY

Other investigators have indicated that higher therapeutic results can be achieved when a patient is asked to face difficult symbolic forces and "transform" them into images that are more readily handled. The various forms of confrontation, whether it be staring, killing, exhaustion, magic fluids, etc., are designed to "transform" the symbolic demons, thus reducing anxiety and sometimes terror.

My own experience indicates it is possible to offer certain imagery that I refer to as task imagery, that can offer the possibilities of "working-through" a conflict. These imaginary situations involve him in mastering a piece of work or action. Invariably, this is followed by asking the patient to redo or reexperience the imaginary situation. This very often results in a changed self-concept in the person.

While Leuner (1969) uses a standard set of confrontation imagery, I use a great variety of imagery. For the most part, the task imagery involves nonsymbolic or concrete imagery, though it may take on symbolic forms at certain times.

My own use of task imagery stresses the use of dialogue between myself and the patient.

As the therapist utilizes and gains experience with task imagery, he may develop his own creativity and flexibility in the choice of imaginary situations.

Task imagery may reveal the patient's internal conflicts, his style and manner of approach, his defenses and fears; and also it can serve as a vehicle for focusing for a changed self-concept in the "working-through" of the imaginary task. Task imagery affords the possibility of a patient's facing himself and then attempting to change his self-concept. The important ingredient following the initial flow of imagery is to reexperience or redo the imagery in a manner that leads to a possible healthy conflict resolution.

In repeating the same imaginary situation with a person, one can attempt to increase the intensity of the desired response, focusing for greater feeling response each time. This is especially true when the feeling response seems devoid of affect. In repeating the same imaginary situation, one may offer the instruction to "say something with more feeling." An example of this was asking a man, "to imagine two different rocking chairs and then to imagine somebody different in each." He imagined an old man in one rocking chair and a young man in the other. I then instructed him to make a statement to each of the men. He started with an abstract statement in his initial response. His second response was a factual statement about the furniture. I repeated the imaginary situation, urging him to make an emotional statement about each man. This time, he had more feeling in his statement and expressed some concern about "the other man's son who was lost in Vietnam." From this initial-feeling spark, more profound expressions of feelings emerged.

All of these and many more are helpful and offer the patient the possibility of working for change. But it must be remembered that the patient must be ready to focus for change. The elements determining this readiness are the patient's awareness of his internal conflict; the release of feeling connected with contributory traumatic incidents; cognizance of the undermining strategies of behavior of the significant others; and recognition of his counter-reaction strategies.

Gardner Murphy (1947) anticipated the concept of the transformation of imagery when he stated, "But images . . . are manipulable just as muscular acts, to give new and better satisfaction."

Here are some of the main types of task imageries that can be used with reference to what it purports to do and to the "working-through" of some form of conflict resolution and enhanced self-image.

1. Those task imageries that are related to the achievement and power motive: Imagine climbing a thousand steps to the top; imagine building a bridge across a gorge.

2. Those task imageries that allow the person to fight powerful forces: You are caught in a blizzard and you must find your way to safety. Herd a group of horses into a corral one mile away.

3. There are those task imageries that allow the person to fight for a new start against guilt and shame: You are an embryo about to birth. Imagine taking your first steps as a baby.

4. To fight against loss of control and return to your own mastery are these task imageries: Imagine backing through a paper wall. You are stuck on the top of a ferris wheel and you are to get down safely.

5. One of the most powerful task imageries relates to fighting rotten feelings about oneself. Here are two such imageries: You are in a tank of the foulest liquid. How does it feel? You must get out. You are in a sewer full of rats. Get out.

6. Creating order out of disorder through imagery exercises such as: Imagine cleaning an oily, scaly piece of metal until it is clean; Imagine a very knotty rope and unravel it.

7. Imagery related to rescuing oneself and others: You are asked to fight and overcome danger. Lead people out of a swamp. Imagine successfully removing the fuse from a bomb.

8. To feel greater control over overpowering forces: Ride a Sherman tank over bumpy fields, control a steel ball swinging into and felling buildings.

9. Transforming weak or negative images into strong or positive images. For example, if there is a rabbit or snake in one's guts, one can concentrate on transforming it into a more positive or stronger image.

## CATHARTIC IMAGERY

There are certain kinds of imaginary situations in which the patient is asked to imagine the "bad" parent in front of him and openly, in psychodrama fashion, to define himself in a positive manner. Imagination can substitute in many persons for actual face-to-face confrontations. Obviously, this kind of focusing procedure requires a supportive therapist aligned on the side of the patient, and equally important, a readiness on the part of the patient to liberate himself from a false identity. Of necessity I will not discuss patient readiness but will limit my remarks to the imagery approaches. The following are types of imageries that lend themselves to cathartic expression on the part of the patient:

1. Those imageries relating to being wrongfully accused of a non sequitur accusation: Imagine the parental figure accusing you and then reverse the process by accusing the accuser to the point of rightfully asserting your true position.
2. Certain finish-the-sentence items may be used as: I am not _____: I am _____: Never refer to me as _____, etc.
3. Certain traumatic incidents recalled in reminiscent imagery may also be used in this fashion.
4. Parental imageries: You and your parent in a dry well a hundred feet down with a ladder to the top. Describe the reactions, etc.

## DEPTH IMAGERY

Depth imagery is not an accurate descriptive term since any imaginary situation can cause a person to react from the very depths of his feelings, which appear to come from the unconscious forces within. Yet, there are certain imageries that seem to get at depth or unconscious forces, nearly always eliciting a profoundly deep set of actions, no matter who the patient may be.

These highly emotionally charged imaginary situations should be employed with caution and with awareness of what the patient is ready to face.

Here are a few examples: Imagine that you are a child and you are crying. Now imagine your mother or father "licking" away your tears. Your mother or father walks into a room and finds you dead on the bed.

In addition to these are those imageries that seem to plumb the unconscious forces within but do not involve parental figures: Imagine a sealed can underwater. Open it. What do you see, feel, and do? Imagine putting your hand into a cave three times, each time going a little deeper. What do you do, see, and feel?

## GENERAL IMAGERY

For purposes of categorizing therapeutic imagery, there are those imaginary situations that are not specifically dual imagery, task imagery, body imagery, sexual imagery, self-imagery, etc., and yet exist as a vast area of the function of the imagination. These imaginary situations I refer to as general imagery. Again, as with any other type of imagery, meaning and dialogue leading to awareness and change are most important. Here are a few examples.

1. Try to imagine an image of a "molecule of you"; "your conscience"; or "Paradise." What do you do and see and feel?
2. Imagine you are a walnut, or an amoeba, or a sandwich on a plate, etc. Speaking as that image, what do you do and see and feel?
3. Allow yourself to have a fantasy or daydream.
4. Image of a pair of scissors cutting something; image of a fire end of a stick; image of a knife, etc. What do you do and see and feel?
5. (IS) Imagine a light beam and follow it up into the sky. What do you do and see and feel? (IS) Stare into a fire. What do you do and see and feel?

6. The creative possibilities are so vast and the directions that general imagery can go in are so various as to defy ordinary classification. As a therapist, you may find unchartered imagery areas so fertile and new that may carry with them wonderment and excitement. New possibilities can and do occur.

## DETECTION OF RESISTANCE IN IMAGERY PRODUCTION

Clinicians using imagery generally agree that patient responses can bypass the censorship of that person to reveal hidden aspects of personality. It is this special ability of reported imagery that provides us with therapeutic awareness that verbalizations alone may not reveal. Despite this, imagery used in therapeutic interactions is not free of resistance.

Resistance is the patient's mechanism in the service of keeping buried repressed material because he wishes to avoid the anxiety that would ensue were this material revealed. The concept of resistance is so complex that I am restricting my remarks to the detection of resistance in imagery production.

First we need to distinguish between those who consciously resist, and those who, despite honest attempts, seem not to have any images—those who will not and those that cannot. Both are resisting. Those who will not will do so in a more conscious style. Those who cannot will resist for more hidden or unconscious reasons.

Individuals who will not image are aware of their fight against revealing themselves. Among the enormous variety of reasons for actively refusing to respond we find: fear of exposure, fear of not being able to compete with the assumed high level of other persons, hostility to the therapist and the idea of therapy, fear of loss of control, or the belief that imagery is just another trick to entrap him, etc.

To the refusal to image must be added the dimension of defiant imagery. There is a defiant imagination that, in open opposition, may defy the therapist by showing him that none of his efforts can bypass the patient's resistance.

Certain patients will report fake imagery—they fabricate or manufacture imagery. I find this occurring only rarely. However, the falsely reported imageries are still subjective productions and must be examined for possible meaningfulness. The detection of such false imagery is difficult and requires that vaguely defined skill called clinical experience.

Moreover, one must not overlook voice cues since much is revealed in the telling of imagery. Raised and lower tones, sudden silence, hesitancies, changes in volume must be individually examined to reveal defiance and resistance.

In my own work, perhaps because of selective factors, those who will not image comprise a very small percentage of the therapeutic population. The following, obviously incomplete list of resistance patterns should aid in detecting resistance among the overwhelming majority of patients who readily involve themselves in imagery. I must reemphasize that these kinds of resistances appear in the imagery productions of persons who ordinarily have good imagery flow.

1. Unreported imagery: If certain imagery sequences seem to bring up feelings of great anxiety or shame and guilt, the person may say he has images but is having great difficulty revealing them at this time. Encouragement by the therapist or a temporary

shift into dialogue may break this barrier and eventually allow the patient to report the imagery.

2. Foggy, clouded, or vague imagery: This is especially revealing when it occurs only sporadically as a general phenomenon. Feelings states such as anger or joy may be resisted by the individual when this occurs.

3. Stick figure or cartoon imagery: If this occurs only on occasion, it probably indicates resistances are in operation at those periods. Sometimes the patient may recognize his own resistance. One, for example, told me, "I'm getting those cartoon images again. I'm probably resisting."

4. Distancing themselves from the therapist: The patient may say that during his imagery responses he imagined the therapist at a great distance. One patient, whenever her imagery had a sexual content, told me, "You are a mile away." Yet, in her other imagery productions, I appeared a few feet from her.

5. Diversionary imagery: Specific kinds of imagery recur as a diversion when the patient is resistant. One patient said that whenever he was involved in difficult imagery he saw food. A typical statement from this man was "I know I'm resisting, because I'm getting those food images again."

6. Reduced images: This is manifested in imagery productions where the patient suddenly sees tiny images, almost microcosmic in size. When this is contrary to their ordinary imagery flow, it may represent aspects of themselves they do not wish to see.

7. Inability to image the self: The inability of persons to see themselves in imagery is sometimes evidence of resistance. For example, some patients have difficulty seeing their faces in imagery. Some can see only their backs. Often this is a resistance to feelings of shame and guilt. When these feelings are eliminated, they are usually able to see their faces and the front of their bodies.

8. Lack of affect: When persons offer imagery without the concomitant matching feelings, they are probably expressing resistance. When in time, their imagery productions and feelings merge and feelings are expressed, resistances are usually overcome.

9. No imagery: If no imagery occurs after repeated attempts in a relaxed state, the patient may be feeling depression, or emptiness of existence, or feelings of nothingness. This is an example of "cannot" rather than of "will not."

## GROUP THERAPY IMAGERY

It would be neither appropriate nor practical to attempt here a comprehensive analysis of group therapy and its myriad forms. I shall restrict my remarks to psycho-imagination group therapy as it relates to the use of imagery.

Psycho-imagination group therapy emphasizes the patient's self-definition and the degree to which his self-concept permits or constricts his behavior vis-a-vis the other group members. His awareness of how others in the group define him becomes crystallized. Furthermore, the group can become the arena for re-enactment of old family interactions that molded the patient's false positions and negative self-image.

The overall purpose of interaction within the group is to help each and every patient become aware of his or her conflicts and then take the risks inherent in focusing for change. While, broadly speaking, nearly all of the imagery approaches suggested for individual therapy can be utilized in group therapy, there are several factors that must be taken into account. First, groups involve interaction between men and women together; some patients find it considerably easier to express feelings and imagery to members of the same sex, and sometimes find it difficult to express feelings to members of the opposite sex. This is especially true of those persons with problems relating to exposure of sexual inadequacy. Overcoming this kind of reluctance, permitting oneself the free flow of imagery and emotional expression without the feeling that one is weird, is a barometer of the patient's growth.

Second, the factors of peer competition and belonging, while not always evident in one-to-one therapy, may surface in group contact. The disclosure of such feelings and the coping with them are part of the group process. Also, basic trust of authority figures and basic trust of one's peers are areas that may be subjected to considerable emotion and conflict within the group setting. By example, by identification, by stimulating one another, by giving increasingly free play to their fantasies, dreams, imagination, and unconscious production, co-patients often afford the conflicted group member a chance to develop and nurture the courage for new alternatives.

The use of imagery in group therapy may take the following directions:

1. Imagery within the person subjectively experienced.
2. All the persons in the group engaging in imagery about a single member.
3. That member's reactions and imagery in response to the others' imagery.
4. One person engaging in imagery about every other person in rotation.
5. All of the other people, then, engaging in imagery about that one person in return-reaction imagery.
6. All of the persons engaging in imagery about each of the group members at various points in their past or present lives (or the future).
7. The therapist engaging in imagery about each of the group members at various points in their past or present lives (or the future).
8. All of the persons interacting in imagery without any directed consecutiveness, but yet having its own internal consistency in the sequences of reactions, depending on the particular group.

While the main thrust of this discussion involves imagery, it would be unwise to assume that imagery is the sole method used in group therapy. I have found that the "finish-the-sentence" questions can also be of invaluable help as "group starters." Among these "FTS's" are:

1. The more I know you the more I _____.
2. I cannot give you_____.
3. The most difficult thing to tell you is _____.
4. If only you would _____.
5. I like you best for your _____.
6. The adjective that describes you best is _____.
7. Sooner or later you will find me _____.
8. Never refer to me as _____.
9. I will not allow you to define me as _____.
10. My best defense against you is _____.

11. I have to prove to every woman or man _____.
12. Your strongest point is _____.

There are countless other "finish-the-sentence" approaches that can be used. Not only are they useful group starters, but they can also be used at any time in the group interaction for the purpose of clarifying reactions and feelings. They may also very well serve as leads into imagery if they result in particularly strong reactions. There are times, especially in the focusing approaches, that certain imagery may lead back to an appropriate "finish-the-sentence" question, as in cathartic imagery. The possibilities are extremely varied and can be created effectively at almost any moment of feeling and interaction.

Group imagery in which the entire group is simultaneously presented an imaginary situation permits participation of each person's imagination for a time and then the imagery is shared by all. Following this, interaction usually occurs on many levels depending on the particular group. Examples are: Imagine the entire group is in prison and then imagine that we all find a way out. We are all in a stagecoach and we are going on a journey. What do you imagine will happen to us as we go?

A use of dual imagery might be for each person in the group to react to a single patient, as in: imagine standing on Steve's shoulders. How would it feel and what do you imagine will happen? Bipolarization of feelings and conflicts may be indicated between the central person of the situation and each of the other members in the group. For example, John's response was "I can't get on Steve's shoulders because my heels would dig into his shoulders and hurt him. I will be too much of a burden on him." I then asked Steve what he would feel if John were standing on his shoulders. "I'd be in competition with him," Steve said, "I'd have to show him I can carry him with ease and never flinch even for a second. I can never show another man I'm weak. That's unmasculine."

As the group members take turns giving their imagery in standing on Steve's shoulders, and as he responds to them, it will be quickly revealed with whom, among them, he is in greatest conflict. At any point in time a sequence of intense interaction may occur between two persons, or among several. The emphasis, to reiterate, is on helping the individual become aware of his internal conflicts, his negative self-image, his own self-definition, and the difference between how he defines himself and how others define him. This awareness may serve to engender in him the strength to attempt behaving differently, more in line with his "true" identity. If, as a result of the reactions to an imagery situation, anyone in the group is being defined falsely, he or she must of course be encouraged (by me as well as the other group members) to assert himself or herself and insist, "You cannot define me that way."

In group therapy it is also possible to combine imagery with some form of psychodrama to help increase patient awareness of internal conflicts. I asked one man to imagine two different animals, and he visualized a koala bear and a panther. I then asked him to imagine that he was a koala bear and then to make a statement as the koala bear to each group member. When he had finished, I asked him to imagine he was the panther and then to make a statement to each group member as the panther. Without going into the details of his responses, I can say that his experience was highly therapeutic and effective both for him as well as the other group members.

Needless to say, such combined use of imagery and psychodrama can be utilized with effectiveness in other imaginary situations. The group therapy setting helps focus and crystallize the reactions for greater awareness and therapeutic change. For example, one person in the group is to imagine himself as a child and acts out how he attempts to get adopted by two other group members who act as a couple who may want to adopt him.

Body imagery can be introduced into the group interaction by the following imaginary situations. This is directed to one person in the group: Imagine handing your heart to each group member in turn. Say what you feel, see, and do.

Of course, each group member will likely react to accepting or rejecting, etc., the heart of that one person. Following the same procedure, one can have each person in turn imagine holding the face of each group member in his hands and telling the group what he sees, feels, and does. Then each group member can share his reactions to that person, etc.

Self-image imagery can be introduced by asking the group as a whole in turn to look through a keyhole and imagine seeing a group member in the room. Each person then reports his or her imagery and that person then reacts to the individuals in the group. Another form of self-image imagery is to ask each group member to imagine he is in a child's playground alone. Then each group member is to report his or her imagery, which subsequently leads to interaction, possible reminiscent imagery, or other imagery productions.

Sexual imagery can be introduced by asking each person to imagine picking lint from the navel of _____ (a group member). The interaction of that person and the other group members tends to follow naturally. This can continue in turn with all the group members and their interactions. Another sexual imagery that can be introduced in group therapy is to ask each person to imagine escorting a group of women or men prisoners to another area one mile away. After each group member reports his imagery, interaction at many levels is possible, leading to awareness and changed self-concepts.

General imagery of an infinite variety is possible in group therapy. I shall only mention a few: One group member imagines a bird on the head of each other group member. Their reactions in turn to that person's imagery again serve as a point of reference for interaction. One group member imagines an image on the chest of each person in turn, etc.

Depth imagery can occur in any of the previous dimensions of imaginary situations. Those that seem nearly always to elicit reactions of a profound nature invariably leading to the focusing approaches, including cathartic imagery, are as follows: imagine you are a baby and you are being passed from one group member to another in turn around the group. What do you feel and see and do? One group member is to imagine being chained to the leg of each group member in turn. The reactions of the other group members to him are important as well as the feelings and actions, etc.

Task imagery can be utilized in group therapy by asking each person to imagine being seated on a gold throne and then coping with the group in any way the imagery directs. The reactions in return from the other group members may result in either a certain kind of interaction or in redoing the imagery within the framework of a healthier self-concept.

Each person in the group is to imagine himself as an embryo about to birth itself. The imagery can be shared and interactions at various levels usually occur. I must emphasize that the group sessions are not so structured that imagery is the only function involved. Anything may be brought up at any time: a particularly traumatic situation or decision a person is involved with; carry-over reactions from previous sessions; thoughts and feelings people have had about some of the others in the days between group meetings. Also included may be awareness and feelings patients have gleaned from individual sessions and wish to bring up spontaneously in the group situations. Nothing, certainly, should deter spontaneous behavior unless the spontaneous behavior is used as a cover-up for some difficult internal conflict. To keep the structure and the spontaneity of the group unfettered is a fine goal for any group therapist.

## REFERENCES

Escalona, S. K. (1973). Book review of Mental imagery in children by Jean Piaget and Barbel Inhelder (New York: Basic Books, 1959). *Journal of Nervous and Mental Disease, 156*, 70-71.

Guntrip, H. (1964). *Personality structure and human interaction.* New York: International Universities Press.

Horowitz, M., & Becker, S. S. (1971). The compulsion to repeat trauma: Experimental study of intrusive thinking after stress. *Journal of Nervous and Mental Disease, 153* (1), 32-40.

Jellinek, A. (1949). Spontaneous imagery: A new psychotherapeutic approach. *American Journal of Psychotherapy, 3* (3), 372-391.

Leuner, H. (1969). Guided affective imagery (GAI): A method of intensive psychotherapy. *American Journal of Psychotherapy, 23* (1), 4-22.

Murphy, G. (1947). *Personality: A biosocial approach to origins and structure.* New York: Harper.

Shorr, J. E. (1972). *Psycho-imagination therapy: The integration of phenomenology and imagination.* New York: Intercontinental Medical Book Corporation.

Shorr, J. E. (1974). *Psychotherapy through imagery.* New York: Intercontinental Medical Book Corporation.

Singer, J. L. (1974). *Imagery and daydream methods in psychotherapy and behavior modification.* New York: Academic Press.

Sullivan, H. S. (1953). *The interpersonal theory of psychiatry.* New York: Norton, W. W. Col.

# CHAPTER 14

# Imagery Techniques in the Work of Mike and Nancy Samuels

## JOHN S. KRUCK

In the mid 1970s, Mike Samuels, a physician and photographer from the West Coast, co-authored three books that still enjoy a great deal of popularity. The titles include *The Well Body Book* (Samuels & Bennet, 1973), *Be Well* (Samuels & Bennet, 1974), and *Seeing with the Mind's Eye* (Samuels & Samuels, 1975). The first two titles are companion volumes which outline an easily understandable approach to holistic medicine. The third title of the trilogy is an in-depth study of visualization from a variety of perspectives. Visualization exercises from all three books will be described here.

### SEEING WITH THE MIND'S EYE

*Seeing with the Mind's Eye* is written in three sections. Section I is a cultural history of the phenomenon of visualization from ancient to modern times. Section II is a practical and systematic guide to the development of visualization skills. Section III is an examination of the role of visualization in everyday life, psychology, parapsychology, medicine, creativity, and spiritual practices. It should be noted that an outstanding feature of this oversized paperback is its many photographs and drawings that add a graphic dimension to the descriptions of visualization exercises found in the text.

The summary of *Seeing with the Mind's Eye* will be limited to visualization exercises that appear unique and original. Most of these descriptions are found in Section II of that book. The interested reader is referred directly to Section I for a historical approach to visualization and/or Section III for a general summary of work done by other investigators. These techniques can also be found in other chapters of this book.

The authors take the position that visualization is a skill that we are always using unconsciously. However, the capacity for visualization can be consciously enhanced through practice. Visualization skills consciously developed can be used to promote self-growth, psychosomatic health and healing, daily problem-solving, and spiritual practice. Like any skill, it is helpful to break down visualization ability into its component parts, which can then be practiced in a systematic manner. Like other authors on the subject, Samuels characterizes deep relaxation as a necessary prelude to any form of visualization practice. Usually a form of Jacobsen's progressive muscle relaxation (1942) or Luthe's autogenic suggestions (1969) are recommended. Deep relaxation with breathing not only minimizes distraction from unwanted muscle tension, but also tends to quiet the mind allowing greater receptivity to images.

## I. Concentration Exercises

A first step toward building the skills needed for visualization is developing an ability for single-mindedness and concentration. Samuels' exercises for developing concentration are inspired by the discipline of yoga, one of the oldest and most effective methods of teaching attention and concentration.

**Concentration on Simple Objects.** Find a small object of simple design and construction. A book, pen, ashtray, bottle, etc. would do nicely. Place the object a few feet away from where you are seated. You should be able to see the entire object from your position. Look intently at the object with eyes open. Try to keep attention centered on the object. If thoughts begin to wander away from the object, simply bring your attention back to the object and begin the concentration exercise once again. Initially the exercise should be structured as one-minute trial periods. As the ability to concentrate becomes easier, the duration of the exercise can lengthen.

**Concentration and Breathing.** Counting breathing cycles is, in itself, another method of building the powers of concentration. An easy way of using breathing this way is to count the first inhalation cycle as one, the second cycle as two . . . and so on. Again the main difficulty with this method, as with any concentration exercise, is interference from unwanted thoughts and images. Samuels and Samuels suggest a couple of different procedures for dealing with thoughts that break down concentration. The more "active" of the two is described as a thought-stopping technique. Using this method, the subject is instructed to immediately and abruptly stop the flow of thought as soon as he[1] becomes aware that concentration has been broken. The counting of breaths is reinstituted as quickly as possible after the thought is stopped.

The other approach of thought interference can be described as "passive" or even Zen-like in quality. This approach calls for the cultivation of an attitude rather than a special technique. Subjects are instructed to "maintain an impersonal attitude toward their thoughts, as if they were someone else's. They neither grab hold of the thoughts nor chop them down. They neither stop them or pursue them" (Samuels & Samuels, 1975, p. 113).

---

[1] Please accept the outdated "he, him, and his" when it appears in my writing, reflecting either/or both genders. I use these words rather than gender-free language in order to avoid distracting from the original message for the sake of another, important as that one is.

## II. Seeing

Another series of exercises designed to help in building the component skills required for effective visualization is the practice of "seeing." If a subject can consciously become more aware of the elements that constitute his immediate environment, this ability will generalize to the surroundings in the imaginal environment. The exercises the authors outline are similar to the concentration exercises. Rather than merely avoiding the interference of outside thoughts, the primary emphasis in the practice of seeing is to allow consciousness to completely fill up with the perception of an object.

**Seeing and Attitude.** The first exercise is global in its approach. It is an effort to integrate a concern with active awareness of one's surroundings into the continuity of everyday life. The subject is encouraged to become more attentive to the objects that inhabit his environment wherever and whenever a moment of reflection is possible. When viewing an object, the individual attempts to suspend his natural attitude or conventional notions that define the object. He tries to focus purely on the phenomenal presence of the objects that are given to perception. Special attention to density, texture, spatial configurations (lines, contours, curves, contrast , depth, etc. ) as well as light and color, may be suggested. While focusing on the different perceptual dimensions of the object, the individual is encouraged to "feel" the visual images rather than interpret them. The experience is an attempt to get in touch with the object itself as opposed to grasping it through cognitive categories.

**Seeing: Fixating on an Object.** The key element in learning how to see is the capacity to allow an object to flood conscious experience. When this is achieved, both the field of perception and the field of consciousness converge upon the object, acting as complements to each other. In order to obtain this experience, the authors suggest positioning the body close to an interesting object of your choice. Your eyes should be close enough to the object so that, as much as possible, the object itself is the only percept in your visual field. When this is accomplished, fixate your attention on a particular detail that you see. As you do this, allow consciousness to fill up with the object so that now both external and internal awareness share a common focus. Once this alignment of perspectives is experienced, it will become easier to reproduce. Eventually a subject can learn to get this same effect even when body proximity to the object of perception is more distant. For example, say that a person focuses in on an object across a room allowing it to simultaneously flood perception and consciousness as described above. He can now use this state to "zoom in" on the object similar to the effect of a telephoto lens. As the object fills awareness, the size is expanded. Likewise "zooming out" on an object creates an imaginal distance which shrinks the size of the object. Samuels and Samuels state that this technique can bring new knowledge and awareness of our environment.

**Imagination and Seeing.** The seeing exercises described so far emphasized the perceptions of actual objects. The imaginal perspective, however, can be integrated with the act of perception as another form of practicing seeing. For example, a subject could take an ordinary object and while focusing in on that object, imagine various scenarios in which the object ordinarily appears. The authors use the example of an apple to illustrate how this exercise can be done.

The first step is to outline a series of common situations in which an apple appears: 1) an apple can be eaten by a hungry person; 2) an apple can be the subject of an artist's painting; 3) an apple can be picked off a tree by a migrant worker; and 4) an apple can be bobbed for by a playful child, etc. Once the subject has assembled a series of appropriate scenarios, he is instructed to concentrate his focus on an actual apple. While viewing the apple the subject is instructed to imagine and "see" the apple from the point of view of the main character in each scenario. Starting with scenario 1) he tries to perceive the apple in a manner that a hungry person would look at an apple. After developing scenario 1), the subject rapidly jumps to scenario 2) and develops that image. Successive scenarios follow in similar fashion. According to Samuels, this exercise will help a person break free from automatic associations and labels we give to objects.

**Seeing in the Here and Now.** Other exercises are designed to teach the centering of consciousness in the here and now. Borrowing an idea from G. Gurdjieff (Ouspensky, 1949), Samuels and Samuels (1975) suggest walking down a street while concentrating only on what is presented to one's perceptual field. This exercise has some similarities to the concentration exercise described above. If thoughts begin to stray while walking, the subject simply recenters his attention to the task-at-hand. As the person moves, his surroundings change, yet consciousness should stay with immediate perception so that "all there is at any one moment is the present image" (p. 116). If a person can hold consciousness to the here and now, the ordinary experience of time as a series of successive moments is suspended. Likewise, the perception of individual objects as a sequence of discreet events is surpassed. The only object is the object immediately perceived.

**Seeing and Visualization.** A variation of the above exercise is to become aware of your environment while walking, sitting, or standing. While observing the objects of the environment, note the different things that you see. Then stop, close your eyes, and try to remember as many objects as you can. This exercise can also be done in a more structured manner. Collect a number of diverse objects small enough to fit on a large tray or table, positioning the collection of objects at eye level. Study them intently for a minute to two. Closing your eyes, try to form an image of the array of objects. The idea here is not to create a running list, but rather to form a valid image. Open your eyes and compare your actual perception to the image you had just created. With practice, the discrepancy between the internal and external will become less and less.

**Seeing: DaVinci's Device.** Another excellent method of practicing was inspired by Leonardo DaVinci. Aptly named DaVinci's device, this exercise uses ambiguous stimuli to trigger spontaneous imagery. Leonardo found that when he stared at a plaster wall that was cracked and covered with peeling fragments of paint it would become a projective screen for the imagination. While fixing his vision on the wall, images would spontaneously appear on the wall. He found that he could focus upon and watch the images which often gave him problem-solving clues. This type of exercise can be practiced on any large two-dimensional area, the surface of which creates a random design or pattern.

## III. Visualization Techniques

The authors describe the process of visualization as "creating a mental image, creating a picture in the mind, seeing with the mind's eye" (Samuels & Samuels, 1975, p. 121). Once a student has mastered some basic relaxation and concentration abilities, he is ready to move to the practice of visualization. Although a few visualization techniques have already been introduced, Samuels and Samuels designate the following exercises as a method of systematically teaching or learning how to create internal pictures.

**Visualizing a Geometric Design.** The first technique in this section involves picturing a two-dimensional geometric design. Although any geometric figure will do, they use a triangle to demonstrate the technique (Samuels & Samuels, 1975, p. 121). Their figure emerges from a gray background with black horizontal lines which provide a marked contrast to a white triangle which stands out in the foreground. A similar stimulus can be easily constructed using any geometric figure as long as there is a good contrast between the figure and its background. Different colors could easily produce an effective contrast.

Initially the subject is asked to spend a few moments doing some breathing and calming exercises. Then he is instructed to stare at the geometric design for a minute or two. After fixating on the design, the subject closes his eyes and images that he is still viewing the actual stimulus. The subject should be told to focus in on the imaginal figure noticing the shape and contrasting background that surrounds it. After viewing the internal image, the subject opens his eyes and returns to the actual stimulus. He compares the two images, the external stimulus with his internal picture, and then closes his eyes visualizing the figure once again. This time, however, the subject is told to imagine the geometric design about 1.5 feet in front of his closed eyes. As the image is projected outward it can be focused upon as if it were an external perception. Again, the subject closely examines the internal figure and background. This exercise should be done with minimal preconceptions or expectations. It should be explained to the subject that there is no "correct" image, rather any image produced at this point is a "good" image.

**Visualization and Three-Dimensional Objects.** Samuels and Samuels (1975) point out that motivation and a person's involvement is of primary importance in image-making. If the two-dimensional exercise above is too abstract and acts to minimize involvement, a three-dimensional object can be used. For example, a flower may have more meaning for you than does a two-dimensional design. If this is the case, you can take the flower and place it at eye level in front of you. Again, after briefly relaxing, look intently at the flower until you feel that you "know" the flower. Then close your eyes and let an internal picture of the flower develop. While imagining the flower try to picture it about two feet in front of your eyes and face. Scan the details of the flower image as if you were looking at the actual flower. Notice the petals, leaves, color, and shape of the flower. Open your eyes and compare the internal picture you were viewing with the actual flower. Try to add details to your image while you try the exercise again.

**Visualization and Past Memories.** In the last exercise visualization and short-term memory were combined. In the following exercise the subject will create a visualization using long-term memory and images from the past. Movement within an imaginal scene is also introduced here. The subject, as always, begins the exercise by practicing relaxation. As the subject closes his eyes relaxing more deeply, he is told to picture himself standing in a room that is familiar from childhood. As the room image begins to develop, it is suggested that the subject visualize the wall of the room directly in front of him. He is told to look at the wall in the same way that he would look at a wall in an actual room. Then the subject scans the room noticing the furnishings around him: chairs, tables, lamps, paintings, pictures, etc. As he finishes scanning the room, it is suggested that he focus on the floor and notice how it is treated. After viewing the floor, the subject is asked to focus in on the wall to his right. Then, reversing the procedure, he focuses in on the wall to his left noticing any important details on the wall. At this point, the subject is told to move his perception of the room 180° and focus in on the wall directly behind him.

**Visualization and Movement.** The following exercise is intended to add to the ability to move from one perspective to another while engaged in an imaginal scenario. In this exercise you will learn how to "move" your focus around a three-dimensional object. Upon relaxing, you should try to build an image of a house. The house could be a composite of memory images or an imaginal house. You should picture yourself outside the front of the house allowing the front facade to capture your entire perceptual field. When the front of the house is in focus notice some of the details. Look at the front door, the windows, steps, porch, and the color and composition of the outside finish. Looking at the outside finish move your focus in closer to the house. Examine the finishing boards or siding more closely. Take a more detailed look at doors and windows and any other details of interest to you. Now begin to walk around the house starting from your position in the front. As you walk around the house completing a circle, you are all the while viewing the outside of the house from various angles. Return to the front of the house where you began.

**The Experience of Movement.** When a perspective is changed or moved while viewing an internal picture it is often experienced as a movement in consciousness. Unless special efforts are made, the subject does not see his own body moving relative to the viewed object. It is more of a felt shift in his awareness of the object. When mastered, movement is an immediate response to the internal image. Samuels and Samuels (1975) describe it as a disembodied movement. The following exercise encourages the development of this skill. The subject relaxes while focusing upon an actual kitchen chair placed directly in front of him. He is instructed to study parts of the chair. He should attend to how the back of the chair appears as well as the sides, legs, and seat. After a period of study with eyes open, the subject closes his eyes and starts to picture the chair. He sees the internal chair in the same perspective as the actual chair. He views as many details as possible, color, shape, composition, texture, etc. Now changing his internal perspective, the subject is instructed to move his focus to one side of the chair. When this is accomplished, he moves his focus to the other side and examines the profile of the chair. Then he moves to the back of the chair visualizing what it looks like from this perspective. Returning to the front of the chair, it is suggested to the subject that he can now picture the chair as if he were standing above the chair looking down upon it. The last movement involves a shifting of perspective to the underside of the chair. If this type of exercise is practiced consistently, imaginal movement can be learned to be produced at will.

**Imagination and Movement.** The next exercise in the series combines the use of images from the imagination with movement. Images from the imagination are internal pictures that portray events that are outside of ordinary reality and consciousness. Images from the imagination are not bound by the limitations and laws of causality experienced in non-imaginal experience. The following exercise will be completed by picturing an image from the imagination.

The subject should find a three-dimensional object that has a unique and interesting shape. Samuels and Samuels (1975) suggest using a tea kettle. The subject relaxes and studies the details of an actual tea kettle that is placed before him at eye level. He closes his eyes and is instructed to picture the tea kettle in front of him. Then he is asked to shift his focus to one side of the kettle. The subject continues to study the shape of the kettle as he "moves" around the kettle. It is suggested that special attention should be placed on the transformation of shapes, the shapes that appear and disappear as the movement around the kettle is in progress. For example, the subject should notice how the spout slowly disappears as he moves his focus from front to back of the kettle. Changing perspective again, the subject imagines himself looking down at the kettle. What is seen from this point of view? Now he switches perspective again picturing the teapot in front of him at eye level. When this is achieved the subject is asked to imagine the tea kettle itself rotating around in a slow circle. The subject should, as he did earlier, pay particular attention to the spatial transformations as the kettle rotates. Since the tea kettle moves as if it had its own power to do so, it can be called an imagination image.

**Imagination and Memory.** Another exercise in the series is designed to combine "imagination images" with memory images from the past. The subject is asked to lie down and practice relaxing as preparation for the visualization experience. Closing his eyes, the person is told to recreate the childhood room image described in an earlier exercise. As the subject refamiliarizes himself with the room, it is suggested that he scan surrounding walls until a light switch is found. The subject is instructed to turn on the light and focus on the burning bulb. The subject is asked to turn the light on and off a couple of times while looking at the bulb. The person is then instructed to find a table or desk in the room and move himself toward it. When the subject gets to the table it is suggested that he will find an object on the top. The object is an object common to a desk, like a pencil, pen, or book. The subject is asked to pick the object up and take a good look at it. The object is then returned to the tabletop.

Using the imaginal scene, it is suggested that the object rises up from the table and floats to the ceiling where it makes contact. Now the subject is told to watch the object hover on the surface of the table. The next step is to suggest to the individual to turn toward a wall with a window. When the window is seen, the subject should imagine himself floating toward the window, through which he passes. Still floating outside the window, the subject looks around to see what is now on the horizon of vision. It can be suggested that the person sees houses, roads, landscape, sky, etc. in the immediate distance. Then, the subject should look down and visualize the ground beneath him. Details should be momentarily studied. Ending the exercise, the subject feels himself floating to the ground where the feet make contact with the earth.

This exercise is an excellent way of developing control over imagination images.

**Imagination Images and Control.** Another exercise for the development of imagery control is as follows.

With eyes closed imagine an airless red balloon. Picture blowing up the balloon until it starts to become round. It should not be completely inflated. Tie the balloon off at the stem and begin to throw it in the air. Imagine the balloon floating up to the ceiling where it stops. While the balloon is resting up against the ceiling, picture the balloon spinning on itself. Watch it as it picks up momentum spinning faster and faster. Now stop the spinning and picture the balloon hopping along the ceiling. Again stop the balloon and imagine it floating down so that the balloon is at eye level. Try to change the red balloon into a yellow balloon. When this is accomplished, turn the balloon blue. Watch the blue balloon fall to the floor and bounce upon contact. Picture the balloon continuing to bounce along the floor. Stop the movement of the balloon and concentrate on the image of the balloon growing in size; double the original size of the balloon. Then reverse the image, picturing the balloon becoming very small as it rests on the floor.

**Visualization of Other Persons.** The next exercise in the sequence goes beyond the visualization of things, objects, or landscapes. The following exercise introduces the visualization of other people. Again you close your eyes and relax as preparation for the practice session. When you are completely relaxed, begin to picture a familiar person out of your past or present standing a few feet away from you. Notice the details of your person's face. Focus in on his eyes; see their shape and color; notice skin, hair, and the shapes of lips, mouth, nose, chin, and head. Scanning the rest of the person's body you should notice the person's position and posture. Focus in on their clothing, noting familiar details associated with the other person's style and appearance. Picture a familiar scene in which your person is involved in some mundane familiar activity such as making a telephone call.

Study your person intensely as you picture him talking on the phone. Notice the way your person positions himself while speaking. Notice the way the phone is held. Listen to the person's voice and see if you can make out what is being said. While you do this, pay special attention to vocal inflection, speed, and vocal tone. Picture the person closing the conversation and hanging up the phone. The exercise is completed.

**Visualizing One's Self.** The next exercise in the teaching method goes beyond third person visualization to visualization of self. The authors point out that this may be a particularly difficult exercise to master because of the natural tendency toward self-evaluation and judgment. With practice, however, most people will develop the capacity. In the following exercise, the self is pictured as embodied. The subject becomes an observer to the image of himself. In exercises described previously, the observing self has been more of a hidden observer with bodily images assumed or absent. In the following, subjects are required to "step outside themselves," while at the same time developing a picture of their presence in the image. This shift is from "it" to "I," third person to first person.

Because most people lack a clear detailed image of their bodily selves, the authors suggest that some preparation for this exercise may be helpful. Preparatory work can include using a mirror to notice more details about one's appearance or viewing photographs, home movies, or videos. The exercise itself is as follows.

With eyes closed and in a relaxed state, the subject imagines his face. He should focus in on facial structure: eyes, hair, mouth, and nose. Next, looking at his body, the subject should study how the hands, arms, legs, and feet appear. Then, as in the previous exercise, the subject should imagine himself performing an everyday activity. Again, if a scene of a phone conversation is used, the subject focuses in on body posture as he answers the phone. He should carefully listen to his imaginal voice making notice of inflection, tone, speed, etc.

**Visualization and Use of Sensory Images.** The next exercise is designed to expand the use of sensory images while developing a visualization. Up to this point, image making has been limited to the use of visual and auditory senses. Expanding the use of sensory capabilities will increase the vividness and effectiveness of the imaginal experience. A typical exercise created for sensory enhancement of images is as follows.

Imagine a scene from the past which evokes good feelings of inner warmth, peace, comfort, or tranquility. Once the image emerges, view the landscape around you. If, for example, you are at a seascape, *see* the waves breaking on the sandy beach, *watch* the clouds waft through a blue sky, *view* the seagulls overhead, *hear* their calls breaking through the *sound* of the surf. *Feel* the sensation of the sand conforming to the shape of your body. *Feel* the grain-like quality of the sand against your skin. *Feel* and *see* the sun pouring out of the sky giving a bright glare to everything around you. *Feel* the sun's warmth as it dries and heats the surface of your body. *Smell* the odors of the seashore: the water, the smell of fish, the lotion you use to keep your body moist. Call from memory those good body feelings as you breathe and enjoy yourself, at peace with your surroundings. Eventually, with practice, you will be able to easily return to this "place" and recreate those good feelings at will.

**Visualization and Bodily Sensation.** The next exercise uses various sensory modalities in combination with imagined body sensations. While sitting and relaxing, the subject projects his arms straight out in front of his body. It is suggested that the left arm feels very heavy. The subject should picture a heavy object, maybe a book, on top of the left hand. The individual should feel the weight of the object wanting to "push" the arm down. At the same time it is suggested that the right arm is extremely light. A helium balloon is pictured. It is attached with a string to the right wrist. The subject should feel the balloon's buoyancy making his right arm feel remarkably light. Samuels and Samuels (1975) state that most people's left arms will drop while doing the exercise. The right arm often moves upward.

## IV. Receptive Imagery

In this sequence of exercises, the authors introduce the use of spontaneous non-directed imagery. Emphasis is on expanding the use of imagination. They call this type of picturing "receptive visualization" (Samuels & Samuels, 1975, p. 131).

**Workshop Image.** Closing the eyes and relaxing, imagine a place or a room that could be described as a workshop. This room should not be a scene out of the past but a unique and original place that belongs to your inner world of imagination. Once the image develops, see yourself in the space of the room. Scan the place in which you find yourself. You will begin to see some of the details in the room. Try to focus in on the layout of walls, doors, windows, ceiling, and floor. Do you see furniture? What kind? What are the objects in the room made of? What is the feeling or atmosphere of the place? As you explore the room you will notice a comfortable place to sit, perhaps a chair, the floor, pillow, or rug. Activity in your workshop does not necessarily conform to the laws of physics. Objects may be juxtaposed in fantastic positions. A chair may be floating, or perhaps there are things you have never seen before. Get familiar with your place. You may want to add some things to your room like a clock and/or viewing screen that you can use when you return to this room. You may even see a friendly stranger in your room who can guide you in this inner space. You may want to study what he looks like. You can ask for a name which may lead to further communication. Before leaving your room, look around again. Is there anything else you would like in the room? Try to visualize it. The room can be a place that you will continue to get more comfortable with as you return to it. It can be used for work or leisure, but remains a special place of your own.

**Elevator Image.** The next exercise is also designed to provide the experience of receptive visualization where images from imagination can be created and explored. In this exercise the mental screen which was mentioned above is used. Samuels suggests that before getting involved with this visualization a modified progressive relaxation exercise is helpful. The subject should be in a prone position with legs uncrossed and arms next to the sides of the body. The subject combines deep breathing with systematically letting go of muscle tension from toes to head. When deep relaxation has been achieved, the subject is instructed to imagine himself in an elevator car. The subject sees the doors close and looks at the number panel above the door which tells what floor the elevator is on. It is suggested that the elevator is on floor ten, as indicated by the number ten illuminated on the panel. The subject feels the movement of the elevator as it starts. He realizes it is on its way down and the number nine lights up on the panel. It is suggested that the subject will continue to become more and more relaxed as the elevator descends from floor to floor. The panel light changes from nine to eight and the suggestion is made that the subject's relaxation is getting deeper. This is done for each successive number until the first floor is reached. The subject is told he is deeply relaxed in body and mind as the doors to the elevator open. The subject finds himself in a comfortable room that is dim but not completely dark. He sees that the room contains a comfortable chair that is situated in front of a large viewing screen. The subject is instructed to visualize himself sitting in the chair facing the screen.

At this point the subject is told to give himself the following suggestion, "I am deeply relaxed. My mind feels clear and tranquil. I can visualize vividly and easily. My mind is open and receptive to images that will be helpful to me. I can look at the screen and see images come into view and disappear. If I wish to, I can hold the images on the screen or look closely at them. I can even influence what type of image will appear on the screen. If I have a question, I will see images that will help me find the answer. If I'm working on a problem, I will see images that will help me with its solution" (Samuels & Samuels, 1975, p. 152). When the subject wants to return to normal consciousness, he re-enters the elevator. Doors close. He feels the elevator slowly climb as the panel numbers change from one to ten. When he arrives at the tenth floor and the doors open, it is suggested that the subject feels refreshed, rested, and healthy.

**Deep Space.** Another way to accomplish a highly receptive state is to use images of light and space. This exercise again begins with progressive muscle relaxation and breathing. When the body is totally relaxed, the subject is instructed to imagine himself moving into deep space. He should view and feel himself as weightless as he hovers through space. It is suggested that the subject sees that blue-black color of space surrounding himself. As he is floating through the darkness, it is broken by the light of stars and planets. The subject notices how a planet or star grows smaller as it becomes more distant. As these lights in the distance recede further and further, the subject becomes more and more relaxed. At this point it is suggested that there is an area of vague diffused light ahead. As the subject gets closer to the massive white light, it gets brighter and more intense. As the subject enters the light, he should feel the light flooding with energy. He continues to move toward the center of the light which is "beyond light and darkness" (Samuels & Samuels, 1975, p. 156). As the center is reached it is suggested that the clear light is the center of openness and receptivity. The subject is told that he will spontaneously begin to see pure images that will automatically appear and disappear. The subject should let the images come and go as they please. When the subject wants to return, he travels through space back to his point of origin.

**Change: Internal and External Images.** The next exercise uses the ability to receive receptive images and applies this ability to solving problems in everyday life. This exercise combines most of the various techniques so far described. The exercise is outlined as follows: Upon relaxing the body, let yourself go deeper to a level of relaxation where images can be freely received.

Try to imagine a living space or home where you know you would be completely at ease. As in previous exercises, notice the details of this living space. If you find yourself in a particular room, examine the details of that room including ceiling, floors, appointments, walls, and windows. Walk around the house from room to room. Give yourself time to "feel" as well as see the room. Smell the room, what does it remind you of? Focus on the lighting in the room. What is in the room? Go around the room touching and feeling the objects in it. At this point leave the interior of the house to explore what is outside. Pay attention to where the house is located. What kind of land is it situated on? What is the yard like? Is the yard landscaped? How? What does the house itself look like? See if you can identify the architectural style and detail of the building. Once this imaginal space becomes familiar it can be returned to. Upon return you may want to make some decorative or structural change more in tune with your own likes and dislikes. Practice making these changes. When the image becomes clear and familiar to you, compare it to your actual surroundings . . . the dwelling where you currently live. According to the authors, if there are discrepancies that you would like to change "you can choose aspects of your inner vision which you wish to make real in your external world" (Samuels & Samuels, 1975, p. 157).

Samuels and Samuels are suggesting that by working with the appropriate inner images a person is participating in the process of making the inner vision a reality. Demonstrating this idea, they use the example of wanting to move from one city apartment to a country house. Once a firm decision is made to move from city to country, visualize the country house as clearly as possible. Add as many details as possible using all the sensory modalities to explore the house you desire. Add movement while you walk through the house. Visualize yourself living in the house comfortable and happy, etc. The notion here is that receptive imagery can be used in combination with a more directed and pragmatic approach to visualization to assist in bringing about a desired result. Structured or directive imagery is not better than receptive imagery nor vice versa. Both types of imagery are usually combined in practice.

## THE WELL-BODY BOOK

*The Well-Body Book* is an excellent introduction to holistic medicine. It not only provides a foundation for understanding holistic principles and philosophy, but is a practical workbook and reference for the prevention, diagnosis, and treatment of disease. The primary tenet in a holistic approach to medicine is the continuous interaction between mind and body. It is because of this interaction that visualization techniques can be effective in promoting optimal health and/or healing. In *The Well-Body Book*, Samuels and Bennet (1973) develop a number of interesting healing images which are summarized here.

### The Imaginary Doctor

Samuels and Bennet (1973) suggest that the script to the imaginary doctor be taped so that interference from unwanted cognitions are minimized. They also suggest taking one-half hour in a quiet comfortable place to practice the exercise. Once preparations are made, the subject does a series of relaxation exercises. The authors describe a technique that combines progressive relaxation with a breathing technique. In this exercise, the muscles of the body are relaxed systematically by starting with the feet and muscles of the legs and moving up the body to buttocks, stomach, chest, hands, and face. Each muscle group is contacted mentally while doing a cycle of breathing. While exhaling, the subject sends his breath to the area to be relaxed. This is repeated for every muscle group.

When the subject is relaxed, he is instructed to imagine a house. He notices the architecture and landscape surrounding it. It is suggested that he proceed up to the door and go inside. He is told that there is a special room in the house that is his own. The subject begins to search the house for his room. Walking down a hallway, he finds the door, he lets it swing open, and looks into his room. He is encouraged to add to the room anything that would make it more comfortable. It is suggested that he visualize some furniture in the room including an easy chair to sit in. He enters the room, takes a seat in the chair, and becomes peaceful, relaxed, and secure. Scanning the room, the subject notices an unusual sliding door. It opens and closes vertically from top to bottom. The subject imagines that his doctor inhabits the space behind the door. Although the door is closed, the subject is instructed to open the sliding door by merely willing it. Then he closes it in a similar fashion.

The subject is encouraged to imagine what kind of personal qualities his doctor will have. Samuels and Bennet suggest (1973) that the doctor is humane and understands the functioning of your body very well. He is good at comforting fear. The doctor is also firm and honest. He not only understands the body but also understands how feelings, thoughts, and body interrelate. He may say things difficult to accept but always for the benefit of his patient. He also has a good sense of humor that adds a balance to his more serious side.

The subject now imagines himself sitting in his chair that is directly in front of the closed sliding door. He imagines the door opening and sliding downward from top to bottom. The door opening reveals the top of the doctor's head. The subject is told to notice the hair and its color. Is there hair or not? He can already tell if his doctor is a man or woman. The door slides down a little further and now the doctor's face is visible. The subject is instructed to pay attention to the contours of the face and to examine eye color, brows, nose, mouth, and chin. The subject is asked to feel what is projected from the doctor's facial expression.

The door continues to slide down to the doctor's waist. The subject focuses in on the doctor's apparel noticing his shirt or jacket. The subject is told to imagine the doctor's body beneath the clothing. He asks himself, is it muscular, well developed, thin, etc.? He notices the doctor's posture while the door slides down revealing the rest of the doctor's body. The subject again focuses in on clothing. He is asked to see if the doctor has a belt. Looking at the belt, he notices the belt buckle. He sees the doctor's pelvic area and is asked to see how the doctor carries this area. Focusing on the hands now, the subject looks at their size, especially the fingers. He should notice if they are hairy, smooth, or rough. He can see if the doctor is wearing jewelry.

Now the subject looks at the doctor's legs. He notices the thighs and their size, then the lower legs, and finally the doctor's shoes. If there are no shoes, the subject should notice the skin color and texture. If there are shoes, he should notice the color and style. Are they polished? Can the subject tell if they are new or well worn. He should notice how weight is distributed on the shoes or bare feet.

The subject should now take in the doctor's entire presence as he stands in the door. The subject should try to feel the presence rather than interpret it. Can the subject feel a sense of grace or clumsiness? Can he feel the weight of the doctor's presence? What kind of immediate feelings does the subject himself experience? Still looking at the doctor, the subject is encouraged to fantasize about what the doctor's presence represents. Is he old? Young? Where did he come from? What kind of background, etc.? The subject should once again scan the doctor's appearance with special attention to details in clothing.

The subject should indicate to the doctor that he is welcome. As he enters the room, his hand can be grasped, body embraced, or perhaps the subject just watches him. The subject should introduce himself and see what kind of response is given. The subject may want to ask the doctor his name or ask him a question. Communication might be verbal or appear to be telepathic. If the subject has difficulty in getting started with the doctor, it can be suggested that the subject tells him he needs his help. He can feel free to reveal any feelings he might have to the doctor. He can tell the doctor he wants help in keeping well and that his emotions sometimes interfere with this goal. At this point it really is up to the subject how he wants to deal with the image; it is his personal physician and healer that can be called upon for any problem-solving situation.

When the subject is ready to return to ordinary consciousness, he should thank the doctor and have him move back to his space. The subject should imagine the door closing from the floor up. Now the subject imagines himself getting up from the chair in his room. He leaves the room, closing or locking the door behind him. He follows a hallway out to the door through which he entered the house. Suggest to the subject that he count from one to three before returning to normal consciousness, feeling refreshed and relaxed. The imaginary doctor can be summoned whenever the subject needs him. This will get easier the more it is practiced.

## Health Color Chart

The health color chart is a device that has two main purposes: 1) it is a map to an individuals own physiology—it brings together what a person knows about his own bodily functions and presents it as an image; and 2) the health color chart is also a tool that helps a person tune in or become more aware of his physiological functions in an intuitive feeling way.

The health color chart is based on simple schematic drawings of the human body (Samuels & Bennet, 1973, pp. 45, 47). Before using the diagrams, however, the authors have their patient do a systems review of body organs. The patient notes what type of symptoms are familiar to him and in which part of the body they present themselves. After completing the systems review, the patient is asked to color in the organs represented in the body diagram with colored pencils. The important point here is that the patient choose the colors which he feels are most appropriate for him and his symptoms. Upon completing the color chart, the patient is told to study the chart focusing on the various colors and organs until a clear image is created.

Once the image is created, it can be used in conjunction with the imaginary doctor visualization. Samuels and Bennet (1973) suggest to the patient that he should go back to his imagery room and hang the color chart on the wall. It should appear exactly like the chart he completed earlier. The patient can then summon the imaginary doctor and use the chart in working with him on personal health issues.

## Bright Life Chart

In this exercise, the patient again uses a schematic body diagram to build a positive image of optimal health. The idea is to get the patient to create a color image of his body and organs that evokes a feeling of vitality and well-being. The colors, again, should have personal meaning for the patient as he develops his image of ideal health. When the diagram is finished, the patient is instructed to study the organ colors with eyes open. When he is familiar with the image, he closes his eyes and develops an internal picture of the chart. As he visualizes the chart, he is told to breathe a little more slowly and deeply. With each exhalation, it is suggested that his breath is bathing the image with more vitality and energy. Continuing to do deep breathing, he should try to expand the size of the image while noticing the colors becoming more brilliant. As the visualization is focused upon, the colors continue to grow in intensity and liveliness.

### The Bright Life Chart: Using a Mirror

This exercise involves standing naked in front of a mirror that reflects your entire body. Looking at yourself, close your eyes and recreate the image of the Bright Life Chart. When the picture is clear, open your eyes to see your own reflection. Study it. Now close your eyes and try to picture your own body emanating the colors of the chart. See the colors coming from the center of your body becoming more intense in color. Try to feel the colors filling the cells of your body with energy until the entire body feels full of vitality. Focusing in on your breathing, inhale and exhale. As you exhale, the colors continue to become more luminous. With each breath you take, the colors radiate out from the center of your body moving out into space. Each time you breath, the colors continue to expand out in all directions. This exercise is excellent for feeling of depletion and can be done with or without a mirror.

### Mirror Visualization

Relaxing while closing your eyes, picture the reflection of your body in a mirror. It doesn't matter if you see yourself naked or clothed, just concentrate on your self-image. Then try to get in touch with your bodily feelings, as you imagine yourself growing larger, more healthy, and bright. Continue growing in size and health as you breathe. This exercise can help with self-confidence if practiced in situations where you want and need to make a good impression.

### A Short Healing Exercise

If a person is feeling ill at ease, the following exercise may be helpful. The subject is first instructed to relax while doing some deep breathing exercises. When relaxed, it is suggested to the subject that he can see a mental picture of his own body. He is told to look at his body and its various parts focusing in on an area that he feels needs energy. It may be a sick part of the body or, perhaps, just a tired part of the body. The subject is told to choose a color that he associates with aliveness. He then imagines that pleasurable color filling the part of his body that needs revitalization and/or healing. As the color permeates the body part, it is suggested that he feel very healthy. He is told to move back to the feelings of this actual body and to feel the new sense of health. The subject begins to concentrate on his breathing and with each exhalation he sees and feels the color becoming more vivid and strong. He then pictures the healing organ becoming relaxed and emanating healthy energy.

### Visualization and the Elements

Using the images of light, air, water, and earth can provide a way of calming the body quickly and effectively.

**Light.** Relax deeply. Concentrate on your breathing cycles. As you do an inhalation, try to feel as if you are drawing energy from the universe into your body. Each time you exhale, concentrate on the bodily feelings of tension leaving, being replaced by relaxation. As you relax further, picture the interior of your body becoming filled with light. The source of the light begins in the center of your body and is getting more and more radiant and bright. Enjoy this feeling. Sense the relaxation and light energy.

**Air.** Relaxing, close your eyes, and begin abdominal breathing. As you take in air, imagine that energy from the universe is filling your body. With each exhalation you feel more and more peaceful and relaxed. Picture a line of light around the contours of your body. Think of a color that is pleasant to you and imagine the light around you radiating that color. Each time that you breathe out, picture the colorful area becoming more vivid and bright. See if you can enlarge the area surrounding your body. Watch and feel it expand further and further in all directions. Next picture the aura as a magnetic type of energy that seems to pulsate as it continues to expand into space.

**Water.** Relax and breathe deeply from your stomach. The energy of the universe is drawn inside of you each time that you inhale. Each exhalation is a feeling of deeper relaxation and lack of tension. Picture a pool of water or a pond. Imagine that next to the pond is a ledge of rock from where you are viewing the still, peaceful pond. Now visualize yourself picking up a big round, dense, heavy ball. You lift this heavy ball up over your head and then heave the ball into the pool.

Picture the ball as it splashes into the water sending droplets into the air. Try to imagine the splash occurring in slow motion. The ball begins to sink into the pond. As the ball submerges, the water comes rushing over it covering it completely as it sinks to the bottom of the pool. Now you see the ripples moving out in circular waves from the point of contact. Watch the rippling motion repeating itself. The ripples get smaller as the pool begins to become more calm. View the pool until all the ripples have faded and the water surface is still and peaceful once again. Tell yourself you are relaxed and feel new energy.

**Earth.** Close your eyes and relax. Practice abdominal breathing as your body begins to calm. Each time that you breath in, you are drawing energy from a universal life force. Each time that you exhale, you allow your body to become more and more relaxed. Picture yourself sitting in a landscape that is a special place to you. It gives you warm feelings of contentment and pleasure. Imagine your body as vital, beautiful, and alive, as you sit there feeling good. Visualize your landscape, whatever it may be, as inviting and alive with an energy of its own. Note the feelings of harmony and oneness with your environment that you experience. As you calmly sit, imagine the energy of the earth streaming up into your body and filling it with feelings of strength and health. You feel relaxed, refreshed, and at ease.

## THE *BE WELL* BOOK

*Be Well* (1974) was written as a complement to *The Well-Body Book*. The main theme in *Be Well* is that we all have access to a life energy which is the essence of all healing. Our thoughts, feelings, and attitudes interact with our bodily reality in ways that can either encourage or discourage that universal life force to perform its healing functions. *Be Well* attempts to teach an individual how to get in touch with his natural healing energies that will maximize his healthy condition and minimize his dysfunctional states.

### The Feeling Pause

Samuels and Bennet (1974) suggest that there is a deeper part of ourselves, a universal self that is constantly in tune with a healing life-giving force. If a person can contact and listen to the universal self, it can guide to health, harmony, and feelings of ease with his environment. The universal self can also give messages about imbalance and corrective actions that may be needed. Messages from the universal self may emerge as emotions, images, and/or bodily feelings and sensations. If the feelings are comfortable, ease and comfort are what is indicated by the universal self. If feelings are anxious and uncomfortable, the message is disease or imbalance between body and mind. The questioning of feeling images is called the feeling pause. Performing the feeling pause is quite simple. A person needs only to relax and quiet his mind while asking himself how his body is feeling at a given moment.

The authors use the example of finishing a telephone call that leaves a person with mixed feelings. Where did the conversation take the person? Ask the person to close his eyes and to get in touch with immediate feeling or emotion. Is he happy, sad, disgusted, angry, full of joy, etc.? Can he name the emotion he is experiencing? Ask the individual to interrogate various parts of his body while paying close attention to the sensations found there. For example, how do the person's ankles, legs, stomach, chest, shoulders, arms, etc. feel right now? Each body part will produce a feeling or sensation. Ask the subject to articulate and name the sensation for each part of his body. Is the general feeling one of ease or discomfort? Tell the subject to feel his heart beat and to observe his breathing process. Are these rhythms slow and easy? Is there tension or relaxation? Tell the subject to focus in on his thought process. What emotion does his self-talk portray? The overall idea here, once again, is to become more aware of the relationship between mind and body. As this awareness grows, the message from within can become more useful in a practical and meaningful way.

The feeling pause can also be expanded by associating images and visualization experiences with the "pause." The feeling pause can be imagined to be a place or space where questions can be asked and answered. The notion of the feeling pause should be explored with images provided earlier in this chapter. This will allow the imaginal scenario or visualization to become a vehicle for the universal self and the messages it is attempting to communicate.

### Feeling Pause and the Body

Another important dimension of using the feeling pause is to understand the physiological strengths and weaknesses of the body proper. Samuels and Bennet (1974) state that the body can be divided into seven discreet anatomical/functional divisions (pp. 88-89): 1) skeletal muscles, 2) genital regions, 3) digestive organs, 4) heart and lungs, 5) throat, nose, mouth, 6) eyes, ears, head, and 7) mentation. According to Samuels, the strength and sensitivity of these areas vary from organ to organ and person to person. By using the image of the seven body divisions, a person can learn which areas of the body are the strongest sources of disease and comfort. The areas which attract and produce stimulation are called receiver areas. Receiver areas, sensitive to both feelings of ease and disease, will produce information useful to the subject while performing the feeling pause.

## Using the Receiver Areas for Healing

To explain this concept, Samuels and Bennet (1974) use the example of a headache. If you had a headache, you might lay down and relax as a first step. Then go into your feelings pause state, tuning into your bodily sensations. Then you could locate a receiver area that to you feels strong and comfortable; perhaps, it is the area of your chest and lungs. As you continue to relax, imagine the easy feelings in your chest areas moving up toward your head. Move the good feelings over the back and shoulders and up the neck. Let the good feeling flow into your head area. You can use an image of warmth to enhance the feeling of ease and comfort.

## Visualizing the Healing Process

Visualizing the actual physiological functions involved in healing a given disease state can promote and encourage the healing process. Samuels and Bennet (1974) describe the use of this exercise in regard to a sinus infection. If a person has a sinus infection, he could be shown a picture of the sinus passageways and cavities. He could then try to imagine the passageways dilating and opening up. He could imagine the infection and blockage of mucous beginning to drain through the cavities and out his nose. Images with regard to healing, however, need not be literal. Images can be metaphorical and symbolic. Samuels and Bennet (1974) gives the example of a virus. One could imagine the virus as little spots on a blackboard the subject is erasing. Any image that corresponds to the basic structure of healing action will do. Samuels and Bennet give the following as foundations for building healing images: erasing bacteria, building new cells, making rough smooth, changing hot body areas to cool areas, sore areas to comfortable feelings, tension to relaxation, draining inflamed or swollen areas, wet to dry, dry to wet, moving cleansing blood to target organ or area, and opening up pressures areas.

## REFERENCES

Jacobsen, E. (1942). *Progressive relaxation.* Chicago: University of Chicago Press.
Luthe, W. (1969). *Autogenic therapy.* New York: Grune and Stratton.
Ouspensky, P. D. (1949). *In search of the miraculous.* New York: Harcourt, Brace and World.
Samuels, M., & Bennet, H. (1973). *The well-body book.* New York: Random House, Bookworks.
Samuels, M., & Bennet, H. (1974). *Be well.* New York: Random House, Bookworks.
Samuels, M., & Samuels, N. (1975). *Seeing with the mind's eye.* New York: Random House, Bookworks.

# CHAPTER 15

## Gendlin's Focusing Techniques

### JULIE H. TYNION

Since the 1960s, Dr. Eugene T. Gendlin and his colleagues at the University of Chicago have explored questions relating to the outcome and efficacy of psychotherapy. Their early work centered on identifying those aspects of psychotherapy and the therapeutic relationship that are most predictive of success on outcome measures, regardless of the therapeutic technique employed. A number of questions were considered, e.g., "Why doesn't therapy succeed more often? Why does it so often fail to make a real difference in people's lives? In the rarer cases when it does succeed, what is it that those patients and therapists do? What is it that the majority *fail* to do?" (Gendlin, 1981, p. 3).

This research considered many forms of psychotherapy, including Psychoanalysis, Gestalt Therapy, Behavioral Therapy, Client-Centered Therapy, and Primal Therapy (Gendlin, 1996). Outcome measures included client self-report, therapist ratings, and independent, standardized psychological tests (Cornell, 1996). When the outcome measures agreed as to whether a particular client's therapy had, or had not, been successful, that client's individual sessions were analyzed for content. Literally thousands of hours of tape-recorded therapy sessions were studied. Entire courses of therapy were considered, from a client's first session through his or her last session. What emerged was a portrait of successful therapy that was quite different from that which was hypothesized.

Gendlin and colleagues (1968) found that there was a significant difference between successful and unsuccessful clients, and that this difference, once defined, could be spotted in the first or second session. However, the hypothesis that differences between individual therapists' behavior or therapeutic techniques had an effect on outcome was not supported. Instead, the researchers found that successful clients, themselves, *do* something different in therapy than do unsuccessful clients, and that this "crucial difference" is remarkably easy to identify. The difference is irrespective of therapist characteristics, therapeutic method, or even session content. Instead, it is a characteristic of the client him/herself. "The difference is in *how* they talk. And that is only an outward sign of the real difference: *what the successful patients do inside themselves"* (Gendlin, 1981, p. 4).

It became apparent through the study of the successful psychotherapy clients that, . . . at some point in the session, [they] would *slow down* their talk, become *less articulate,* and begin to *grope for words* to describe something that they were feeling at that moment. If you listened to the tapes, you would hear something like this: "Hmmm. How would I describe this? It's right *here.* It's . . . uh . . . it's . . . it's not exactly anger . . . hmmm." Often the clients would mention that they experienced this feeling in their bodies, saying things like, "It's right here in my chest," or "I have this funny feeling in my stomach." (Cornell, 1996, p. 4)

The thing that distinguished the successful therapy clients from the unsuccessful ones seemed to be their tendency or ability to acknowledge a vaguely described *body awareness* that they were able to tap into during the session. The less successful clients, on the other hand, were those who either remained articulate and analytical or who became caught up in emotional catharsis.

Gendlin could find no existing terminology which adequately encompassed this vague body awareness, so he coined the term "felt sense" to describe it. A felt sense is an awareness *in the body,* a *physical sense* of a problem or a concern, rather than a thought or an emotion. It can be thought of as an unclearly defined "edge" of a feeling (Gendlin, 1996, 1981). A felt sense, though, is not merely a "gut reaction" to a problem. Rather, it is "the broader, at first *unclear,* unrecognizable discomfort, which *the whole* problem (*all that*) makes in your body" (Gendlin, 1981, p. 69).

To illustrate the concept of the felt sense, Gendlin (1981) suggests thinking of any two people who are significant in your life. As you let your mind move back and forth between them, you will begin to notice an "inner aura" when you let your attention concentrate on first one, and then the other. You will notice that the sense of "all about" one person is quite different from the sense of "all about" the other.

Once the felt sense had been identified, Gendlin centered his efforts on finding a way to describe, operationalize, and to teach the inner act of contacting and utilizing the felt sense to bring about emotional change. He termed this act "Focusing."

"Focusing is a body-oriented process of self-awareness and emotional healing. It's as simple as noticing how you feel—and then having a conversation with your feelings in which *you* do most of the listening. Focusing starts with the familiar experience of feeling something in your body that is about what is going on in your life. When you feel jittery in your stomach as you stand up to speak, or when you feel tightness in your chest as you anticipate making a crucial phone call, you are experiencing what we call a 'felt sense'—a body sensation that is meaningful" (Cornell, 1996, p. 3).

The Focusing process consists of six steps, or "movements." With some practice and experience, the movements will evolve into a fluid process, but for now it will be helpful to explore each of the six movements in some detail.

## FOCUSING MANUAL

Before beginning, make yourself as physically comfortable as possible. Any restrictive clothing, such as belts or shoes, should be loosened or removed. The temperature of the room should also be comfortably warm. Then, sit back and relax.

Take a few deep breaths. It is not necessary to sit still, or in any particular position. The goal is to have a sense of general physical comfort and calmness, but not to go into a deep or meditative state. It is important not to become too relaxed, as you need to be aware of sometimes subtle bodily sensations (Cornell, 1996; Gendlin, 1990). Cornell (1996) suggests keeping a Focusing journal at hand so that you can, if you like, keep a record of your Focusing sessions.

### First Movement: Clearing a Space

Next, ask yourself, "How am I feeling right now? Why don't I feel great? What is getting in the way? What is bothering me right now?" Then, *stay quiet.* Simply listen to what comes. Any number of problems might present themselves, from trivial ones to major life issues. Do not try to come up with an exhaustive list; just let what comes, come. Anything that interferes with your potential for tranquility should be acknowledged.

At this point, simply let the problems surface. Acknowledge each one as it comes, but do not dwell on any of them. Do not allow yourself to delve into any of the things that surface, either intellectually or emotionally. Simply allow each feeling to be there, and say, "Yes, that feeling is there right now." "DON'T GET SNAGGED ON ANY ONE PROBLEM. Just list the problems mentally, the big and the small, the major and the trivial together. Stack them in front of you and step back and survey them from a distance" (Gendlin, 1981, p. 52).

It might be difficult, especially at first, to do this. Many people tend to critique their feelings as soon as they are aware of them. Thoughts like, "It's ridiculous for me to feel that way!" or "It isn't logical for me to react like this," or, even, "*Why* am I feeling this way?" are counterproductive.

Instead, try to remain "cheerfully detached" from the problems as you list them. Mentally take them and stack them to one side, clearing a space for yourself as you go. Say to yourself, "Yes, those things are there, but except for them I'm fine. The list might be long, and terrible, but that is all that is between me and feeling fine." Continue listing and stacking the problems "until you hear something say, 'Yes, except for those I'm fine'" (Gendlin, 1981, p. 53).

### Second Movement: The Felt Sense of the Problem

Ask which problem feels the worst to you *right now.* If nothing on the list stands out as being the most painful, or the biggest, or the heaviest, or the prickliest, or the most "stuck," etc., simply choose one problem to explore. Ask yourself, "What wants my awareness now?" or "How am I about that issue?" (Cornell, 1996, p. 28).

Do *not* "go into" that problem as you usually would. Stand back from it for a moment, and let your body get a sense of how the *whole problem* feels. Ask the question, "What does this whole thing feel like?" but do not answer in words. "Feel the problem *whole,* the sense of *all that*" (Gendlin, 1981, p. 53). *Wait.* The felt sense is a *physical* experience, not a mental one, and usually requires about thirty seconds before it begins to take shape. Allow the answer to come from your body, not from your head.

This can be especially difficult to do, particularly at first. It is in the second movement that "old tapes" start to play in one's head, e.g., "Here I go again, complaining about my dead-end job. If it's so bad, why don't I just quit?" If such thoughts come up, try to dismiss them politely, saying, "Yes, I know, I've been all over that. But I'm going to set it aside, for now. Perhaps I'll deal with that later." The goal in the second movement is to "let your sensing go inwardly down past all the details that can distract and sidetrack you, past all the squawking and jabbering, *until you feel the single great aura that encloses all of it*" (Gendlin, 1981, p. 54).

The felt sense can reside in any part of the body, but usually is felt most clearly in the middle area: the throat, chest, stomach, and abdomen (Cornell, 1996). If you are having difficulty locating the felt sense, it may help to begin by sending your awareness to this middle section. For some people, even this type of attention to the body may be problematic. If so, it may help to try the following exercise:

> Put your attention in your left big toe; wiggle it if necessary. Press it down. Now feel the sensation in it. Now come up to your knee. This time don't move your knee, just see if you can find it from inside. Then move to your groin, and from there move up into your stomach. There you are. (Gendlin, 1981, p. 91)

In the second movement of focusing, the felt sense is always unclear or fuzzy at first. It does not lend itself easily to definitions or labels, but it has a distinct feel of its own. Gendlin (1981, 1996) describes this quality as "the edge" of the problem.

### Third Movement: Finding a Handle

The next step after contacting the felt sense is to describe it (Cornell, 1996; Gendlin, 1981, 1996). Try to imagine how you might describe the felt sense to another person. Usually, a word or phrase (e.g., "jumpy," "heavy," "an empty feeling," etc.) will present itself, although the description might also be in the form of a sound or an image. Try to find a handle that gives the sense of *all that* about the felt sense. Avoid letting your head or your emotions dictate the handle; instead let it come from the felt sense itself. Try the handle on for size, and do this gently. When the handle is right, you will know it. The feeling is similar to the common experience of running into an acquaintance and forgetting his or her name. As you mentally scan through any number of names, you somehow "just know" when you have hit upon the correct one.

As you search for the proper handle for the felt sense, you may feel the quality of the problem beginning to change.

> As you say the words (or as you picture the image), the whole felt sense stirs just slightly and eases a little. This is a signal, as if it said, "This is right" . . . You know that any number of perfectly sensible ideas are not part of the feeling and you drop them, until you get something the feeling itself opens up to. (Gendlin, 1981, p. 56)

The most important thing to remember during the third movement is to stay in touch with how your body feels (Cornell, 1996). It is easy to get so involved in searching for the proper descriptive word, phrase, or image that you remove your attention from the physicality of the felt sense. If this happens, bring your attention back to the inner area of your body where your felt sense resides, and then let the handle come.

## Fourth Movement: Resonating the Handle and the Felt Sense

Apply the handle you received in the third movement to the felt sense, and check to see how well they fit together. They should "click precisely into place—a perfect fit" (Gendlin, 1981, p. 56). As words, phrases, or images come up from the felt sense as possible handles, they should then be checked back against the felt sense for confirmation. One of three things might then occur.

First, you might feel an inner sense of fit; a feeling of "Aha!" or "Yes—that's *it!*" In this case, there is a sense of satisfaction and completeness, as the essence of the felt sense has been identified. Second, you may feel as though the handle you have found is only partly right; that there is more to the felt sense than that handle conveys. Wait again, and another handle might come up that, in addition to the first handle, pinpoints the essential quality of the felt sense. Third, you might find that the first handle you try is on the right track, but not exactly right. As you check this word, phrase, or image with the felt sense, it will lead you to another, more precise handle. Check this with the felt sense to see if it resonates (Cornell, 1996).

Continue this process of waiting for a handle to present itself and checking it against the felt sense until you feel you have achieved true resonance; a perfect fit. When you have found an exact match between the words and the feeling, *stay* with that for a bit. Allow yourself to experience the sense of rightness. "The sense of rightness is not only a check of the handle. It is your body just now changing . . . Give it the minute or two it needs to get all the release and change it wants to have at this point. Don't rush on. You just got here" (Gendlin, 1981, p. 57).

## Fifth Movement: Asking

Usually, finding an appropriate handle will produce a *felt shift,* i.e., a physical sensation that feels like a release. If such a shift has already occurred during the previous four movements, go right into the sixth movement, receiving. If however, you felt only a tiny shift (one that does not change the quality of the problem), or no shift at all, enter into the fifth movement, asking.

In this movement, "ask the felt sense, directly, what it is. Usually this consists of *spending some time* (a minute or so, which seems very long) staying with the unclear felt sense, or returning to it again and again" (Gendlin, 1981, p. 58). Using the handle as a way to check back with the felt sense can help you do this. The handle is a way to get back in touch with the essence of the felt sense, in the here and now. It is not adequate to simply remember what the felt sense was like. If the felt sense is not vividly present, you will not be able to ask it what it is.

For example, if the handle for your felt sense was "heavy," repeat that word to yourself until the felt sense is saliently there. Then ask the felt sense "What is it about the whole problem that feels so heavy?" Often, you may feel flooded with answers in your head. If so, just let them go by. These answers are "old tapes" that come from your mind. Wait, and repeat the question if necessary. "The felt sense itself will stir, in answer, and from this stirring an answer will emerge" (Gendlin, 1981, p. 58). The words and images that come from the felt sense, not from the mind or the emotions, will produce a bodily *felt shift*. The felt shift is "a time when everything in your body/mind, in your whole organism, is rearranging itself to accommodate the new understanding you have received" (Cornell, 1996, p. 45). The felt shift is your body's way of telling you that a fundamental change has occurred. This change will be accompanied by a feeling of relief or discovery, which, without exception, feels *wonderful*. Even if the felt sense brings up unpleasant or difficult things that you must consider or do, the *physical* release of the felt shift is a "marvelous" and pleasurable feeling (Cornell, 1996; Gendlin, 1981, 1996).

If you do not experience a felt shift, it may be helpful to ask one of the following questions:

1. "What is the worst of this?" (Or, using the handle "sticky," for example, "What is the 'stickiest' thing about this?")
2. "What does the felt sense need?" (Or, "What is needed to make this OK?")
3. "How would my body feel if this whole thing was OK?"

If you ask these questions of the unclear felt sense, wait a minute or two, and do not experience a felt shift, it may be a good time to stop Focusing, for now. The answers cannot be forced (Cornell, 1996; Gendlin, 1981, 1996). "Focusing is not work. It is a friendly time within your body. Approach the problem freshly later, or tomorrow" (Gendlin, 1981, p. 60).

### Sixth Movement: Receiving

If you have experienced a felt shift—even a very small or unclear one—it is very important to take the time (which may be only a minute or two) to receive it. Greet this message from your body in a friendly way, and you will be likely to continue to experience other felt shifts (Gendlin, 1981).

This does not mean that you must take action, or even agree with, the felt sense. Successive shifts are steps that are linked together. Each new message is contingent on the receipt of the previous one. "It is very important to protect this first form, in which your new life-direction can be sensed. . . . Your body is changing, your life-direction is appearing, this is only one step" (Gendlin, 1981, p. 60).

After you have taken time to receive the felt shift, you may wish to stop Focusing, or to go another round. If you decide to stop for now, know that you can "bookmark" the place in your "inner landscape" that you are leaving and return to it at any time. If your body urges you to continue, you might ask your body "Does that take care of the whole problem? Is it solved?" and then wait for the felt sense of all that. Then proceed through movements 2 through 6 as you did before. Another approach is to continue from the last felt shift and ask, "What is the whole sense of *that?*" (Cornell, 1996; Gendlin, 1981).

### Focusing: Short Form

Gendlin (1981, pp. 173-174) provides the following distillation of the six movements of Focusing:

1. Clear a space

    How are you? What's between you and feeling fine?

    Don't answer; let what comes in your body do the answering.

    Don't go into anything.

    Greet each concern that comes. Put each aside for a while, next to you.

    Except for that, are you fine?

2. Felt Sense

    Pick one problem to focus on.

    Don't go into the problem. What do you sense in your body when you recall the whole of that problem?

    Sense all of that, the sense of the whole thing, the murky discomfort or the unclear body-sense of it.

3. Get a handle

    What is the quality of the felt sense?

    What one word, phrase, or image comes out of this felt sense?

    What quality-word would fit it best?

4. Resonate

    Go back and forth between word (or image) and the felt sense. Is that right?

    If they match, have the sensation of matching several times.

    If the felt sense changes, follow it with your attention.

When you get a perfect match, the words (images) being just right for this feeling, let yourself feel that for a minute.

5. Ask

    "What is it, about the whole problem, that makes me so _____?"

    When stuck, ask questions:

    *What is the worst of this feeling?*

    *What's really so bad about this?*

    *What does it need?*

    *What should happen?*

    *Don't answer; wait for the feeling to stir and give you an answer.*

    What would it feel like if it was all OK?

    *Let the body answer:*

    *What is in the way of that?*

6. Receive

    Welcome what came. Be glad it spoke.

    It is only one step on this problem, not the last.

    Now that you know where it is, you can leave it and come back to it later.

    Protect it from critical voices that interrupt.

Does your body want another round of Focusing, or is this a good stopping place?

Although Focusing does not require the presence of another person, e.g., a guide, a listener, or a psychotherapist, it can be quite useful in psychotherapy (Cornell, 1996; Gendlin, 1996). Gendlin argues that

> ... therapy ... does not consist mainly of the familiar, already defined kinds of experience, whether dreams or emotions, actions or images. Therapy is rather a process that centrally involves experience *before* it becomes one of these defined "packages" and again *afterward* when it dips back into the prepackaged zone at the edge of consciousness. (Gendlin, 1996, p. 4)

Focusing can help the client and the therapist move past two kinds of "dead-ends" in therapy. The first, which Gendlin calls the "Dead-End Discussion," occurs when the therapist and the client become locked into a pattern of intellectualization and logical (or Freudian, or Jungian, or common-sense, etc.) analysis of the problem. The worst example of this scenario occurs when the therapist is content to "impose interpretations that seem plausible only to [him/her], not to the client. Then [s/he sends] the client home after an hour of arguing" (Gendlin, 1996, p. 8). Another example is "cognitive restructuring," or "reframing": this can be effective *only* if a bodily shift has occurred in response to the cognitive restructuring. Real change can occur only if a new way of physically *having* the problem, not merely a new way of thinking, has taken place.

The second dead-end occurs when the therapist and the client become locked in an endless rehashing of the same strong emotions. "Despite the fullness of [the] emotional content, it does not change; they feel the same feelings over and over again" (Gendlin, 1996, p. 12). The goal of therapy, therapeutic movement, generally occurs in small, progressive steps, not in one great cathartic moment. It is in the sensing of the *unclear* edges of the client's feelings and experiences that these steps come (Gendlin, 1996). Gendlin (1996) states that these steps always occur in the direction of growth, echoing Carl Rogers' construct of the self-actualizing tendency (Rogers, 1959).

Focusing can have a greater role in therapy than just helping to move past a dead-end. It is a way to help the client begin to sense him/herself differently; to perceive his/her centered *whole self.* "Nothing is more important than the person inside. Therapy exists for the person inside; it has no other purpose. When that inner being comes alive, or even stirs just a little, it is more real and important than any diagnosis or evaluation" (Gendlin, 1996, p. 23). This is true regardless of the therapeutic orientation of the psychotherapist. To facilitate Focusing, however, the therapist must be an *active* listener.

Active listening, as described by Rogers (1957, 1980), requires that the listener empathically reflect what the focuser is saying. "Without reflecting, bit by bit, neither therapist nor client can easily discover what is really meant and felt, let alone what might come further at the inner edge that opens once a message has been fully received" (Gendlin, 1996, p. 297).

Through actively listening to the client, and reflecting back to him/her, the therapist can help the client to become aware of his/her bodily sense of the edge of the problem. "Listening is therefore the foundation which makes therapist-aided focusing possible. If a therapist listens, swiftly asks for the client's feeling, and responds exactly to it without arguing, editing, or adding—always returning to this between any two moves—then [even] mistakes will result in an especially good process" (Gendlin, 1996, p. 111).

## CHAPTER 16

# Imagery Techniques in Emotive Reconstructive Therapy

## JAMES K. MORRISON

Before detailing the imagery techniques used in emotive-reconstructive therapy (ERT) (Morrison, 1979), a brief exposition of the theoretical propositions underpinning those procedures seems appropriate.

### THE THEORETICAL APPROACH

ERT is based on a cognitive model of personality (Kelly, 1955; Piaget, 1972; Sarbin, Taft, & Bailey, 1960) and incorporates the view that there are interpersonal variations in the level of Reticular Activating System (RAS) arousal (Fiske & Maddi, 1961; Schachter & Singer, 1962). The individual is thus viewed as an active person constantly engaged in the process of monitoring and interpreting experiences so as to maintain an orderly view of the world and, concomitantly, an "optimal level of arousal" (Fiske & Maddi, 1961).

Within ERT, clients are viewed as individuals "victimized" by their apparent inability to construe themselves and others in a congruent, personally satisfying manner. Thus, their predictions about self and others are frequently invalidated by life's experiences. The behavior of clients reflect, to some extent, the adoption of certain roles as a means of coping with stress. Finally, I assume that these inadequate self-constructs and often dysfunctional roles have their source in early childhood experiences (Morrison, 1977) which are poorly encoded in a person's memory, and thus are retrievable only with difficulty.

The theoretical position of ERT places great importance on the key concepts of *stress, memory,* and *early childhood experiences.* It is precisely through the use of imagery procedures, as well as some ancillary techniques (e.g., deep breathing exercises, role playing), that clients learn to probe their memories of early childhood experiences, especially those that caused stress. Once those events have been construed in more complex, understandable, and explanatory ways, clients are often able to then construe themselves and other key persons (e.g., parents, siblings) in such a way as to reduce stress. So, for example, if a client has always lived in conflict with a father, often a "life review," especially of appropriate childhood events, may (depending on what that client remembers) provide him or her with the opportunity of construing that father in a more rational, complex, and unstereotypical fashion. Thus, a client often will remember in ERT incidents which contradict simplistic constructs formed in childhood. He or she may be able to elaborate a new construct system to account for this "lost information," resulting in a less negative and less stereotypical view of such a father. And this new view can lead to a more constructive relationship with that parent.

## THE IMAGERY PROCEDURES

Most clients come for ERT once a week for a forty-five minute session. In the *emotive* or first phase of a session, the emotive-reconstructive therapist attempts to recreate the physiological and psychological stress events of early childhood through facilitating imagery and, when needed, by asking the client to hyperventilate or to engage in deep, regular breathing for short periods of time. For example, clients are asked to sensorially immerse themselves in past events by focusing on the contextual surround (colors, noises, odors, texture) of early experiences, and then to provide the therapist with a minimal verbal description of the same. To bring about hyperventilation, clients are requested to breathe deeply and rapidly for twenty- to thirty-second time periods; this is done when the therapist judges that hyperarousal would enhance the vividness of the imagery and/or facilitate the expression of a certain feeling. At times, deep regular breathing is substituted for hyperventilation, especially where hyperventilation might be contraindicated for reasons of health. Often neither type of breathing exercise is necessary, because the imagery alone is vivid enough to induce strong feelings.

Thus, primarily through vivid mental imagery, a client is aided in re-experiencing the type of hyperarousal encountered in childhood. During the recreation of early stress, the client can now be assisted by the therapist in applying adequate constructs in order to reduce stress. While actually feeling the stress, a client can learn effective ways of coping with it.

It is important to note that in ERT the client is helped in recalling certain sensorial, especially visual, information which is not often considered in traditional verbal therapy, as Singer (1974) points out. With *eyes closed* and with a focus on the contextual surround of an event, the client begins to recall more and more detail about early events. Soon the client begins to experience some strong feelings about these early events and the persons connected with them.

When clients have great difficulty eliciting vivid images, some imagery training or use of hypnosis can often resolve the difficulty. The hypnotic procedures I most often use are those of "levitation" and "reverse levitation." Such hypnotic techniques are, of course, also useful in inducing the type of "time regression" necessary for ERT.

A further word is in order about the major procedures used in ERT, the mental imagery techniques. There are three basic imagery techniques:

1. *Sensorial recreation of a perceived event.* Through mental imagery, clients are helped to more fully recall partially remembered, *anxiety-arousing events* (e.g., death of a parent or a severe beating). Sensorial recreation of perceived events can also be used to help the client recall *pleasurable* events of childhood. At times, such recreations are helpful to prevent clients from falling into the trap of construing their

parents in completely negative terms, or of blaming parents for all problems. Taking responsibility for one's past, however minimal due to a child's inadequate coping strategies, is important in ERT. Accepting major responsibility for one's present experiences is essential.

2. *Sensorial fantasizing of symbolic events.* Again, these procedures can deal with either anxiety-arousing or pleasurable events. A few examples will clarify how anxiety-arousing imagery can often be used in symbolic ways. One client was asked to imagine herself standing in the middle between her parents, looking back and forth between them, and being forced to go in one direction or the other. This fantasy was highly anxiety-arousing and helped the client to remember the terrible feeling of being caught in the middle between two parents, each of whom was constantly trying to use her against the other.

Other clients have been asked to imagine inanimate objects (e.g., a teddy bear), expressing feelings for them when they are unable to do so themselves in certain therapy sessions. At times, after expressing feelings, some clients are asked to imagine the reaction of their parents. Lastly, still other clients seem to gain a great deal of insight by imagining a dominant mother or father shrinking in size, while they grow in size so that they can feel powerful enough to express the anger they feel toward such parents.

3. *Some recreation of a perceived event combined with fantasizing a symbolic event.* For example, after clients remember an experience where a parent had induced rage in them, and after they have expressed that rage, these clients are asked to imagine a parent's reaction. Such imagined reactions often lead to new discoveries about how clients construe parents.

At the beginning of therapy, I ask clients to list as many early and emotionally upsetting experiences as they can remember. After going through a standard sequence (see Morrison, 1977) of scenes common to most children (e.g., upsetting scenes at school, with mother, with father, etc.), I eventually try to recreate some of the experiences which the clients had listed. I do not believe that with most clients there is one key scene or event which must be discovered and re-experienced. I usually find a whole host of scenes which carry with them the type of content and affect which enable clients to figure out the basic dysfunctional patterns of their lives.

At times during the emotive phase of therapy, in addition to the above techniques, I will also use "gestalt-like" techniques (e.g., pounding on a chair to facilitate release of verbal anger), verbal confrontation (e.g., "You're lying to your mother!"), directed role playing (e.g., "Tell your father how you feel."), and other ancillary techniques. Such techniques, although not apparently as essential to therapy as is the focus on imagery, nevertheless are helpful, inducing clients to express intense and complex feelings which are difficult to define until they are expressed. Along with the feeling of release which often follows the expression of heretofore anxiety-arousing feelings, clients often perceive that they have discovered new self-conceptualizations. These new self-constructs, along with the subsequent adoption of appropriate roles, enable clients to effectively cope with stress.

It is actually during the *reconstructive* or second phase of an ERT session that clients focus on the reconstruction or reconceptualization of their lives. After recall and expression of feelings, clients are asked to open their eyes. Then the therapist's primary task is to facilitate the integration of new data. With assistance, clients are usually able to bring a more complex system of constructs to bear in interpreting events which were previously of a global, vague, and hyperarousing nature. In so doing, clients are able to suspend those dysfunctional constructs which were previously employed in futile attempts to resolve problems. In my opinion, in order to successfully avoid repetitions of dysfunctional behavior patterns, one must retrace and then understand basic life patterns. If those basic patterns are understood, the rest of the client's life offers opportunities for him/her to continually clarify those patterns through frequent insights or subtle modifications of the therapy-induced reconstructions.

Before a therapy session concludes, the therapist provides support to clients by means of self-disclosure and reassurance. Such therapeutic interventions are aimed at comforting clients after a moment of often dramatic and painful discovery. No one who has done this therapy has any doubt that clients' feelings of pain and distress are clear and genuine. Nor is there any difficulty for the therapist in emphathizing with such clients.

## A CASE STUDY

A case study will help illustrate the clinical use of some of the above techniques. The client, John, was a thirty-nine-year-old married artist (painter, sculptor) who had requested individual psychotherapy from the author because of severe, prolonged depressions which periodically led him to seriously consider suicide. His depressive periods had for a long time negatively affected his work productivity and self-image. In the initial interview, the client agreed that there were a number of unresolved conflicts resulting from childhood which he needed to confront.

In his first therapy session, John recalled a number of very pleasurable events from the age of four, a time before his father returned from World War II and before his younger sister was born. When I asked him to try to clearly visualize his mother's eyes, he quickly felt intense pleasure remembering this time when he was the sole object of his mother's love. He could also clearly hear a particular piano piece his mother used to play, and that music was always a joyful experience.

In the next therapy hour, John remembered how life changed when his father returned from the war. Various vivid images of objects (a toy plane, his father's medals, ribbons, and police uniform) helped him remember how negatively he and his father began to view each other. John and his father viewed each other as rivals for his mother's affection. A boxing match, during which his father tried to unsuccessfully prod him to violence, was terribly anxiety-arousing and caused each to lose respect for the other. John was asked to breathe deeply and feel intensely what he felt toward his father during that boxing match. He was also encouraged to role-play with his father. Suddenly he said, with great anger:

> Why are you making me do this? I hate this. I hate you for making me do this.
> Leave me alone!

John never could have expressed this kind of anger at his father when he was small.

In the next session, John began to imagine the toys he had at the age of six, and felt so joyful at remembering them that he laughed and laughed for about five minutes. At the end of that session he began to realize that his mother had encouraged a conflict between him and his father, hoping her son would side with her in her conflict with her husband.

In the fourth session, I asked the client to form images connected with the anxiety-arousing death, wake, and funeral of his father who died four years earlier. The session was a dramatic example of how imagery can provoke powerful emotions. John realized he really always wanted his father to love him, and ceased to think of his father as the "bad guy." After this session, the client felt hope for the future. He reported he felt like he "was coming out of a fog." His self-destructive urges were greatly reduced.

In subsequent sessions, issues with his sister, mother, and father were explored with increasingly positive results. Sessions eight, ten, and twelve are especially illustrative of the varied uses of imagery procedures in ERT. In the eighth session, I asked this artist to focus on the images of water connected with his childhood, since I sensed water themes were important to his painting. These images (floating in water, fishing, favorite pond, etc.) were varied and extremely vivid, and the entire session was an incredibly pleasurable and uplifting experience which had a long-lasting effect, even months later. The images, he felt, had caused him to feel "happy, safe, carefree, and joyful," feelings he had forgotten were part of his repertoire.

Because the client was still having some difficulty being as relaxed as he desired, in the tenth session I used a "reverse levitation" method of hypnosis. Once John was deeply relaxed I had him imagine he was soaring into space and looking down at earth. He saw himself there and remembered again how insecure he was as a boy. He remembered vividly the smell of cut grass, and how he'd try to get away from cutting the lawn for his father so that he could run down to his favorite creek in the woods. It was only there that he could feel free by escaping family conflict.

Session twelve was devoted to an exploration of ways to increase productivity in art. I asked John to spend time forming vivid images of his workshop-studio. Once those images were so clear he felt he was actually there, he realized that it was in this room that he always experienced a deep sense of aloneness. When he tried to create, sad and lonely images from childhood would always intrude. I asked him to use the positive images which he had been remembering from his childhood to fight the feelings of loneliness. Images of water and certain toys took on a great power, and he realized that with these images he was powerful enough to destroy the negative, intrusive images. He described the feeling thus:

> I'm winning. Oh! I'm going to beat it. No one can stop me now. I'm flying. Oh! I'm sorry I always felt helpless. Now my hands are feeling strong. I'm not a nothing [as his father had often told him]. I'm a warrior, not a mouse!

Later in the session, he described this feeling as like "being born again." He felt really free, like a "soaring eagle."

Especially after this session, John began to report that he had reached his major goals for therapy. He was no longer depressed or suicidal. He was relaxed, felt extremely productive in his painting and sculpting, and felt more serene about both parents. After three more imagery sessions of little consequence, we decided to complete therapy. An eighteen-month follow-up meeting confirmed the stability of these changes. He continued to grow in many ways.

Those who are more interested in ERT, besides the references already mentioned above, might consult some of the following articles: Morrison, 1978, 1980, 1981; Morrison and Cometa, 1977, 1980, 1982; Morrison and Heeder, 1984-85; Morrison and Teta, 1978. Other references are also available from the author.

## REFERENCES

Fiske, D., & Maddi, S. (1961). *Functions of varied experience.* Homewood, IL: Dorsey Press.

Kelly, G. (1955). *The psychology of personal constructs* (2 vols.). New York: Norton Co.

Morrison, J. K. (1977). The family heritage: Dysfunctional constructs and roles. *International Journal of Family Counseling, 5,* 54-58.

Morrison, J. K. (1978). Successful grieving: Changing personal constructs through mental imagery. *Journal of Mental Imagery, 2,* 63-68.

Morrison, J. K. (1979). Emotive-reconstructive psychotherapy: Changing constructs by means of mental imagery. In A. A. Sheikh & J. T. Shaffer (Eds.), *The potential of fantasy and imagination.* New York: Brandon House.

Morrison, J. K. (1980). Emotive-reconstructive therapy: A short-term, psychotherapeutic use of mental imagery. In J. E. Shorr, G. E. Sobel, P. Robin, & J. A. Connella (Eds.), *Imagery: Its many dimensions and applications* (Vol. 1, pp. 313-320). New York: Plenum.

Morrison, J. K. (1981). Using death imagery to induce proper grieving: An emotive-reconstructive approach. In E. Klinger (Ed.), *Imagery: Concepts, results, and applications* (Vol. 2, pp. 303-310). New York: Plenum.

Morrison, J. K., & Cometa, M. C. (1977). Emotive-reconstructive psychotherapy: A short-term cognitive approach. *American Journal of Psychotherapy, 31,* 294-301.

Morrison, J. K., & Cometa, M. C. (1980). A cognitive, reconstructive approach to the psychotherapeutic use of imagery. *Journal of Mental Imagery, 4,* 35-42.

Morrison, J. K., & Cometa, M. C. (1982). Variations in developing construct systems: The experience corollary. In J. C. Mancuso & J. R. Adams-Webber (Eds.), *The construing person* (pp. 152-169). New York: Praeger.

Morrison, J. K., & Heeder, R. (1984-85). Feeling-expression ratings by psychotherapist as predictive of imagery therapy outcome: A pilot study. *Imagination, Cognition and Personality, 4,* 219-223.

Morrison, J. K., & Teta, D. C. (1978). Simplified use of the semantic differential to measure psychotherapy outcome. *Journal of Clinical Psychology, 34,* 751-573.

Piaget, J. (1972). *Judgment and reasoning in the child.* Totowa, NJ: Littlefield, Adams & Co.

Sarbin, T. R., Taft, R., & Bailey, D. E. (1960). *Clinical interference and cognitive theory.* New York: Holt, Rinehart & Winston.

Schachter, S., & Singer, J. E. (1962). Cognitive, social and psychological determinants of emotional state. *Psychological Review, 69,* 379-399.

Singer, J. L. (1974). *Imagery and daydream methods in psychotherapy & behavior modification.* New York: Academic Press.

# CHAPTER 17

# *Imagery in the Work of Ira Progoff*

## *LAREE D. NAVIAUX*

The process by which the image making faculty of man unfolds and fulfills itself is central in the life of the psyche and in human development. (Progoff, 1969, p. 192)

## BACKGROUND

Over a thirty-year period, Ira Progoff has worked with imagery. It is an intrinsic part of a process which in the past decade has developed into the "Intensive Journal." What initially appear as simple techniques and activities are part of a process that is comprehensive, encompassing, and profound.

This process is described as a method for reconstructing and integrating life's experiences. "It does so in a neutral open-ended way without imposing external categories, interpretations or theories on the person's experience. While maintaining the persons integrity, it draws along the life process" (Naviaux, 1980, p. 84).

In *Depth Psychology and Modern Man,* Progoff (1969) developed concepts to describe the depths of an individual and to enable those depths to unfold amidst the pressures of modern civilization. A connection between depth psychology and a variety of divergent viewpoints was sought. Edmund Sinnott, a biologist, proposed that the protoplasm of each living organism is a "system working toward goals according to its nature" (Sinnott, 1967, p. 205).

Mind is thus defined in terms of inner regulation and directiveness toward goals that work within the protoplasm. With this inherent purposiveness and formative tendency of protoplasm, two different directions become manifest in the human mind. There is a self-conscious awareness and a spontaneous expression of goals. This latter direction lies latent in a nonconscious flow of protoplasmic imagery from which ideas emerge spontaneously. Thus, the source of man's conception of reality is in the nonrational depths of the psyche. Below the surface and at all levels of the psyche is a flow of imagery. It is constantly in movement. "*Imagery in movement is the essence of the psyche* and of all the processes by which it reaches fulfillment" (Progoff [1959], 1969, p. 165).

The images can vary from those close to conscious awareness that can be easily translated into rational terms to those at a deeper level where the symbolism is more obscure. The unifying principle of these various levels is the essence of organic individuality. This principle works toward integration, so that all of the separate processes and the wholeness of the person draw their pattern from it. From the outset, it was there as a seed image of the individual personality. It has a pervasive unifying function throughout the individual's life. Imagination, the depth process of image making, thus has its roots in life as a basic process of protoplasmic unfolding. Image making at the deepest levels of the unconscious is the goal of the formation and integration of personality (Progoff, 1973).

## TWILIGHT IMAGERY

For clarification of this important process, each aspect will be presented.

### Twilight

"The primary quality of Twilight Imagery lies in its *twilightness,* the fact that it takes place as though by itself, on the intermediary, or twilight level of consciousness" (Progoff, 1975, p. 78).

In this intermediate state of consciousness, between waking and sleeping, the usual busyness of the mind is quieted and slowed down. Instructions are given to get comfortable, close our eyes, and breathe deeply and slowly. Attention is turned inward, we wait in stillness for the various forms of images to appear.

### Imagery

Imagery is presented as inward symbolic perceptions of all kinds. These include bodily feelings and awarenesses, sounds, smells, subliminal thoughts, hunches, intuitions, phrases, ideas, or visual images. The varied aspects of the contents of our life experienced at levels below our mental consciousness are reflected to us in many forms. Both the nonvisual senses and vision express representational, symbolic experiences. They are perceptions and awarenesses that come unguided from our inner and outer senses.

### Beholding

An attitude of beholding what comes while in the twilight imagery state is necessary. Images come of themselves and are not to be bidden, forced, or guided. It is inappropriate to consciously or deliberately determine what perceptions to experience or to direct what is being perceived. With a quiet, passive attitude we turn our attention inward and in the stillness observe them and perceive them as they take shape, appear, and move on. We follow the direction of their movement, being open to what we are experiencing. At naturally convenient points, we record the observations and beholdings.

Persons with vivid imaginations, with special skills such as editing, or with a special problem may try to direct the twilight imagery experience. It must be stressed that this resource is not something to direct or guide, and that its content must not be consciously or deliberately altered. Such efforts will interfere with the process. The main purpose is to tap the resources just below and beyond our conscious awareness.

It is rich with potential in its natural spontaneously-occurring flow. If the imager wants to be directive, he/she should seek other procedures.

### Recording

Because the twilight level experiences are spontaneous and unguided, they occur differently each time. Thus, we have to be free and flexible in relation to the depth of ourselves as it is manifested. It is important to record what we can while we are in the midst of an imagery experience.

Eyes closed, notebooks open on our laps, we open our eyes only enough to enable us to record what we can as we are in the midst of the experience. As legibly as we can, we quickly jot down the perceptions as they come. At times the experience is so strong that it keeps us caught up in it. In such a case, we have to retain in our memory what we experienced, and when the experience has run its course, we proceed to develop more fully what we recall and have recorded.

The recordings are dated and kept in the twilight imagery section of the "Intensive Journal." This section is used at various times during workshops and as needed or desired for individual use.

### Reading

An important aspect of the "Intensive Journal" and of twilight imagery is reading. This can be done silently or aloud. It is important feedback. Reading aloud adds a special dimension to the process. That which came freely and spontaneously may be painful in the reading. On the other hand, an experience that may have been difficult loses its emotional hold on us as we read aloud.

As we read the experiences back, feelings stir within us, new thoughts or perceptions and insights are evoked, awarenesses strike us, sometimes we can see new possibilities for our future. These responses, in turn, require recording.

### Correlation of Inner and Outer

The next step is to raise questions and be reflective about what we have experienced and recorded. These inner experiences from twilight imagery add an important dimension to the outer movement of our lives. An integrative principle lies beneath the surface.

Our conscious and nonconscious perceptions and experiences each need to be considered in their own right, placed side-by-side and allowed to balance. We pose questions of whether they are the same, opposite, parallel, or tangential to one another. Do they confirm or contradict each other? The task is to look objectively at our subjective perceptions and experiences.

As the inner and outer perceptions are allowed to fit together of their own nature, an inner correlation may appear. This is not a task of thinking or analyzing. Rather, it is a process of feeling the quality and tone of each of them. By coming together within us, they balance themselves in relation to one another. It is a process of inner life balancing and nonanalytic self-integration. As the opposites of our outer and inner experiences are set side-by-side in a neutral, noninterpretative way, they can meet, balance, and integrate. This life correlation allows for progressive integration of these two dimensions of our lives. "Together they form a *whole message* which can speak to us. . . . There is an *organic inner continuity* in the movement of our lives and it is expressed both inwardly and outwardly" (Progoff, 1975, pp. 83-84).

## USES

Twilight imagery is used to quiet and deepen the atmosphere and our inner awareness before starting on a specific activity. One of the first activities used in the Intensive Journal Life Context Workshop is the "Period Image." Another activity from the Depth Feedback Workshop is "Twilight Dreaming." These two activities will be presented in detail, followed by several other uses.

### Period Image

After having completed a description of the present period or time of our life, there is a time of focusing inward at the twilight level.

We breathe slowly, softly, letting thoughts drop away without our thinking about them. . . . We remain in quiet calmness.

Sitting in quietness, our eyes close. We let this take place gradually. It is as though the stillness and the softness of our breathing draw our eyelids together so that they seem to close of themselves. We realize that when our eyes close gradually and softly in this undeliberate way the darkness we enter is not unpleasant. It is, in fact, rather comfortable. It carries an atmosphere of calmness with it as we let ourselves quietly drift into the twilight level. Our attention has naturally readjusted itself and has turned by its own tempo to an inward dimension. Here we may perceive the realities of life, in the varied aspect of their symbolic forms. This *inward beholding* gives us the added vantage point of a depth perspective.

As we are doing this, we let ourselves *feel* the tone and quality of the period we have described. We do not think about it, we do not evaluate nor make judgments about it. Having described in the Period Log the main factors that come to our mind, we do nothing further on the conscious level. We merely sit in the quietness, our eyes closed, our attention turned to twilight level of experience. Here we let images come to us again, images of every kind. We do not specify what kind of images they shall be, whether we will see them, smell them, hear them, interpret them, feel them in our body. Whatever their form, they will be twilight images coming to us out of the middle level of consciousness between waking and sleeping, and just presenting themselves to us so that we can observe them in a natural way and record them. . . . We merely let ourselves feel the content of the period that we have described, and with that as the background, we let the imagery form itself out of its own nature. We specifically wish to keep our conscious mind out of the way, so that our imagery will reflect the flow of our life, and will not be slanted to reflect our subjective desires. (Progoff, 1975, pp. 80-81)

### Twilight Dreaming

In the Depth Feedback Workshop the twilight imagery state is used in reviewing a series of recorded dreams of the "Intensive Journal." Dreams and dream fragments are simply, objectively, and factually described from recollections of them. Of more importance than the content of each dream, is the process that is moving toward life integration at the depth level. Within this continuous record of dreams lies the integrity of their movement. Thus, dreams are not analyzed by any of the traditional or popular methods. Rather, they are allowed to remain on the depth level, where they can be continued from within themselves and can extend their movement and unfolding.

> We read the series of dreams until we feel ourselves to be within their movement. It is a stream that carries us along with it. Our eyes are closed. . . . Now, on the screen of our mind's eye, the dreams continue themselves. Some of the scenes from the dreams may reappear, but not necessarily the scenes nor their contents as they originally took place. It is not our specific dreams that we are continuing, but the inner process of our dreaming as a whole. We are letting it move freely out of its own context so that it can reach and reflect the full range of its possibilities.
>
> Images and feelings and actions continue for us now, just as would be the case in our sleep dreaming. We let the inner movement of our Twilight Dreaming move on by itself. We do not guide it. We do not direct it. We do not restrict it. We encourage it to move on its own and in its own way wherever it wishes to go. Inwardly we follow it. With our emotions and inner participation, we freely go with it. We let our Twilight Dreaming proceed as fully and as long as it wishes. We behold it, accompany it, and let it carry us as a vehicle driven by its own inner guidance.
>
> As our Twilight Dreaming continues, it is often helpful for us to speak out the experiences that come to us . . . to articulate them so that they can be heard seems to make them more tangible for us so that we do not lose them in their wispiness, but can take hold of them and record them. (Progoff, 1975, pp. 238-239)

### Other Uses

Twilight imagery is used as a means of setting for recalling and remembering the facts about a certain period in the past, and in reviewing the life of another person or an aspect of our life, feeling the movement of their development through time. In the Process Meditation Workshop, the twilight imagery state is used to create an atmosphere for reviewing our life and establishing the spiritual stepping stones or the development of our search for meaning.

Apart from its place within the specific activities of the "Intensive Journal," twilight imagery can be used as a means of quieting one's self, focusing inward, experiencing the flow of images, gathering them through recording, and refreshing or renewing oneself. When used this way, the recording remains important for catching the imagery in movement and later reading and reflecting.

### BENEFITS

In *The Practice of Process Meditation*, Progoff (1980) identifies the molecules of thought and imagery as a modality for obtaining information regarding the movement of the subjective process. Correspondences between physical reality and human existence are made. Just as there is molecular movement in the depths of matter, there is also movement of images and subliminal thoughts in the depths of consciousness. At times they come together to form new combinations.

This imagery that moves within us at levels deeper than our mental consciousness has the inherent human capacity of inward perception. It is a natural mode of awareness. When we establish an atmosphere that makes it possible for attention to be turned inward in a quiet way, this capacity shows itself to be strongly present. Often it expresses itself in such a way that it catches us unaware.

From the depth experiences with the unconscious, there can occur an unexpected reversal in the quality of our awareness. There is an enlightening and even an inspirational power in this awareness. We may possess greater perceptual acuity, our thought processes may move more quickly and relevantly with insights, intuitions, and recognitions of all kinds. These may be related to our life in general or to specific projects.

When these new patterns of images and thoughts develop below the surface, new qualities of behavior and action are soon reflected on the surface of our lives. This is the rich benefit of the twilight imagery process.

## REFERENCES

Naviaux, L. (1980). The intensive journal process: A method for integrating life's experiences. *Journal of Mental Imagery, 4,* 83-86.

Progoff, I. (1969). *Depth psychology and modern man.* New York: McGraw-Hill.

Progoff, I. (1973). *The symbolic and the real.* New York: McGraw-Hill.

Progoff, I. (1975). *At a journal workshop.* New York: Dialogue House Library.

Progoff, I. (1980). *The practice of process meditation.* New York: Dialogue House Library.

Sinnott, F. (1967). *Matter, mind and man.* In R. N. Anshen (Ed.), *World Perspective* (Vol. XI). New York: Harper & Bros.

# CHAPTER 18

# Animal Imagery, The Chakra System, and Psychotherapy*

## ELIGIO STEPHEN GALLEGOS

Contemporary Western culture has characteristically viewed the human being in terms of physical body parts (medical model), social/biological function (e.g., id, ego, superego), behavior patterns, emotions, aspects of awareness (conscious, preconscious, unconscious), or elements of imagination (archetypes).

By contrast, traditional Asian cultures have derived a view of the human being as comprised of energy, its movement and blockage. This is the view upon which acupuncture and the chakra system (Motoyama, 1981) are based. In Kundalini Yoga, for example, energy is said to be raised from the root chakra up through the various chakras to the crown chakra, with the energy in each chakra influencing attitudes, behaviors, and awareness (Radha, 1978). The first chakra is centered at the base of the spine and is concerned with one's groundedness and relation to the earth, security, and physical survival. The second chakra is centered in the gut, a few inches below the navel, and is the source of one's emotions and passions. The third chakra is located in the solar plexus and is concerned with power. The fourth is located in the heart and is the source of love and compassion. The fifth is in the throat and is involved with communication. The sixth is centered in the forehead and concerned with the intellect. The seventh is located at the top of the head and is concerned with one's relation to God, the Universe, the Eternal. Western psychologists have some difficulty accepting such theories, given the dominant culture's concern with philosophical materialism and skepticism about the transferability of Oriental conceptions to Western therapeutic practice.

Recent work by the author attempts to combine both Western visualization therapy techniques (Assagioli, 1971; Shorr, 1983) with certain aspects of chakra theory in the psychotherapeutic diagnosis and treatment of Western clients in a Western setting. Specifically, a method of using animal symbolism and imagery in the expressive imagination of the client has been developed for use in an otherwise standard therapy context. This method produces metaphoric descriptions related to the chakra system in a form that is readily understandable to the Western client and therapist, and

*Reprinted with permission from Gallegos, E. S. (1983). Animal imagery, the chakra system, and psychotherapy. *Journal of Transpersonal Psychology, 15,* 125-136.

which can serve as both a vivid diagnostic tool and a medium for effecting therapy and growth.

## PROCEDURE

If the client is already experienced in visualization, the procedure may be entered into immediately. If not, then training in relaxation is necessary as well as some initial introduction to the process of visualization. The introductory procedure I characteristically use is that of having the client imagine he or she is a seed that has been embedded in the earth through a cold winter. Gradually spring comes, the sun warms the earth, and a warm gentle rain begins to fall. The earth soaks up the moisture as does the seed. The seed casing then pops open and the seed begins to grow roots. The roots are nurturing, anchoring, and provide an intimate relationship with the earth.

Then a shoot begins to grow upward, breaks through the soil and begins to absorb the warmth and energy of the sun. As the energy is absorbed, the stem grows taller, eventually developing leaves and then a bud. The bud gradually opens to reveal a beautiful blossom. The blossom stands before the sun and thanks it for its energy. The sun replies, thanking the flower for its beauty.

This visualization can itself be used diagnostically in terms of the richness of the soil, the depth, strength, and breadth of the roots, the strength and height of the stem, and the color, size, number of petals, etc., of the blossom, plus any interesting deviations that the client describes as having occurred in the plant's growth. The purpose of the imagery in this procedure is for the client to learn to allow the imagery its process while observing and reporting to the therapist.

The system and procedure developed for contacting what I think of as the personal characteristics of the chakra system are as follows: With the client fully relaxed with eyes closed, he/she is asked to concentrate his/her attention in the center of the forehead, and to become aware of all of the feelings in that area. The client is instructed to tell the therapist when attention is fully concentrated in the forehead. Upon this indication, the therapist instructs the client to spontaneously allow that area and the attendant feelings to turn themselves into an animal in his/her imagination. The client is asked to tell the therapist what animal it is and to describe what it is doing. The animal is also asked its name and whether it has anything to tell or teach the client at this time. Following this, it is asked if there is anything it needs or if there is anything the client can do for it.

The client is then asked if he/she is willing to do this for the animal, and if the response is positive, encouraged to do so. If the response is negative, the request and negativity are explored further. The animal is then thanked for being there and told it will be seen on a later occasion.

The procedure is repeated for the throat, heart, solar plexus, gut, and the pelvis-legs-feet. This provides a representative animal for the energies of the intellect, communication, heart-compassion, power, emotions, and grounding-security. To date, only a minimal amount of work has been done exploring the spiritual or crown chakra.

In subsequent sessions, the animals are introduced to each other to observe how they interrelate and they are helped to work through any conflicts. Their counsel is then sought about which one of them needs most to grow, and the others are asked to support that growth. The animals can also be used as a support system in working with any other material that emerges. One other avenue appears to be helpful in the clients' growth: having the client become each of the animals, one by one, to gain an experience of that particular animals' acquiescence. Each animal is always treated with respect and dignity. The therapist must always remember that what is being ultimately dealt with are elements of the individual which may have been rejected and/or negated, and which need to be welcomed back into a harmonious integrated whole.

The growth that the animals undergo may be a growth in size or a transformation into a completely different animal. This growth has characteristically been followed by changes in the client's relationship to the environment in terms of thought, feeling, and behavior. The reverse is also true; changes that the client has undergone in everyday life may be reflected in changes in the animals or in their relationship to each other.

## GENERALIZATIONS

The Intellect animal has characteristically been observed to be a bird, frequently an eagle or a hawk, or a large cat such as a lion or a lynx. It has also not infrequently been a monkey. Beyond this, individual aspects appear to be characterized. One of our clients was a young lady just graduating from college, whose head animal was a fox. She had used her intellect very adaptively in learning to take tests and give teachers feedback they sought but had never encouraged her intellect to grow into its own dimensions. It roundly chided her for her neglect.

The Communication animal has generally been the least developed of the animals, frequently appearing as a snake, a turtle, a caterpillar, etc., indicative of primitiveness and defensiveness. This is usually one of the first animals to undergo growth and transformation: a snake becoming a bird, a turtle becoming a dolphin, a caterpillar becoming a white crane. It is possible that this lack of development is a cultural phenomenon: we may not learn to communicate as much as we learn how to not communicate, which is the origin of deception.

The Heart animal (love, compassion) has varied greatly and, in the few cases where there have been similarities, is either a lion or a bear. Beyond this, individuality emerges: a fish in an intensely Catholic person, a dove in a peacemaker, a chicken in a young teenager afraid of his emerging passions. Occasionally two, or even three, animals appear at a single chakra. This is possibly indicative of a divided energy which needs to be healed. The two animals may be indicative of a divided orientation or polarization; a perplexed husband with a lover whose bear animal is both a turtle deep in a canyon and a fledgling eagle on a high ledge. Circumstances may be that both animals are willing to merge voluntarily, in which case a third animal emanates from their union. But most frequently there is a conflict that needs to be resolved first.

The Power animal seems highly individual, perhaps a wild stallion that needs to be tamed, or a sleek, black panther, or a rabbit. In several instances it has been a dragon.

One minor generalization is that women appear to have a power that is hidden (a raccoon, an ostrich, a teddy bear) and which needs to be unmasked or developed. A young lady whose power animal was two rams butting heads had given half of her power to her lover and found herself in frequent conflict with him.

The Emotional animal appears frequently as a large or spirited animal (a whale, a gorilla) and occasionally as an animal that is restrained: a caged tiger, a tethered or hobbled wild horse, a hibernating bear. One of the first tasks at hand may be to free or awaken the animal, but this is done only after conferring with the animal as to why it is restrained. Typically the other animals rejoice at the freeing of their colleague.

The Grounding animal has usually been an animal that is sure-footed or that lives close to the earth: a prairie dog, a rabbit, a mountain goat, a deer, antelope, or kangaroo. This is characteristically a beautifully supportive animal, and may teach the client how to run or how to be at home in nature. One individual whose other animals were all large, powerful animals had as a grounding animal a rabbit. In an imagined council of the client's animals the rabbit expressed a fear of the others because they were all so big and powerful. The others all expressed support and encouraged the rabbit to grow to be their equal, whereupon the rabbit grew to be a giant rabbit, ten feet high, who was extremely settled and no longer afraid.

Mention must be made of the intensity of feeling and emotion that these animals draw up and of the deep warmth and support that is felt from them. Of course, this is a factor that appears to be characteristic of visualization in general, that feelings are much closer to images than they are to words or descriptions.

Frequently the animals will bring up unfinished business. One individual, whose head was an owl looking at the full moon, had as a heart animal a raven that seemed to be alternately black and white, and who was quite angry. When the raven was asked what he needed, he said he wanted the client to give him his head. The client suddenly recalled a situation of several years past where he had decided to allow his heart to be his guide, but after getting into a dangerous and frightening situation, became very calculating, always seeking reassurance. Upon questioning about this old event, the raven indicated that he had specifically led the client into that situation to teach him how to surmount fear but the client had not trusted him adequately. They had been at odds since that time. The client apologized and acknowledged that he had gone back on his commitment to his heart, whereupon the raven became settled, took on a brilliant black sheen with feathers tipped in white, and took the client for a long flight. From that day the client's relationship to his wife changed from apprehensiveness to rich involvement.

One exciting aspect of this work is that the client is well able to observe *where* a difficulty occurs and can marshall the support of the remainder of his energies rather than nebulously identifying completely with the difficulty. This more direct use of the client's energies is also extremely helpful for the therapist and it is not unusual for significant changes to occur in a single session.

Another area where this approach is extremely helpful is in understanding relationships between individuals. Frequently, people who are close will observe that they have similar animals. Or, if there are areas of conflict, they can localize them specifically. A man and wife who frequently argued were found to have as

Communication animals a snake which was frequently sneaky and a white stallion that tended to stomp on snakes. In processing, the snake encompassed her Power and Emotional animals, whereupon it turned into a bird. The bird and stallion got along well and the couple's arguments came to a halt.

## CASE STUDY

As an illustrative example, I present here a case study of Jane Doe. When I met her she had been in therapy for five years. Her symptoms were depression, self-negations, and suicidal tendencies. A previous therapist had encouraged Jane to enter into "non-suicide" contracts and she admitted to me at the end of her therapy that she had restipulated the contract almost daily in order to keep from committing suicide. She was thirty-four years old, divorced, with two children. Her manner was intense and her voice was high-pitched. She initially expressed fear of me. I assured her that I respected her and trusted her ability to grow, and would do nothing to threaten or pressure her, which she accepted. She told me at the time that she hated herself because she was not perfect. I told her that I felt each human being was a beautiful flower deep inside. She replied that she was sure there was no flower within herself. I had her do a visualization for getting in touch with that inner flower. Jane expressed surprise at what she had seen: a tiny baby.

At our next meeting I explored her history. She had grown up on a remote ranch in northern Wyoming. Her mother was dominating, usually angry, and defensive. Jane felt she had never been good enough for her mother and had not been wanted from the time she was born. Her older sister had a personality similar to that of her mother. Her father was passive and quiet.

She said she felt like she was nothing. Her existence was a deep dark well with a lid over it. The only delight there had been in her early life was when her father took her hunting or fishing with him. Although he was also reticent with her, on these occasions she felt he truly cared for her. When asked if she could give each of these little girls a different name, this one she called "Richness." The other's name was "Nothing."

She also expressed a tendency to want to withdraw into a corner where she would be safe. I assured her she was free to retreat to the corner whenever she wished and she was also free to come out of that corner, and I encouraged her to practice both of these movements so they could both become voluntary.

At our next individual session I asked her to place the chairs in the room to represent the positions of family members at home. Mother and sister chairs were placed in the center of the room, her own and her father's were placed in two corners. As a newborn baby her position was at the center of the room, but in that position she immediately felt jealousy from her mother and sister. As she removed herself to the corner, she felt her father also move to a corner in silent support of her.

In the Visualization—this was done in a group setting resulting in less initial information than is usually derived from an individual setting—Jane's intellectual animal was a giant eagle. She was standing below it and could only see its legs and lower body. Its first words were to tell her how dumb and stupid she was. In dismay, she asked why it was saying that to her. It replied that it wanted to give her an example of what she does to herself.

Her Communication animal was a weasel, and at this she felt demeaned.

Her Heart animal was a dead dog, encrusted with a fungal growth, lying on a stone slab in a cave. She was visibly disturbed at this.

Her Power animal was a white bird in a cage which, when released from the cage, became a large dragon roaring in anguish. Its anguish was over the dead dog.

Her Emotional animal was a small fuzzy bear who reached inside of her and removed a small blue stone which he then showed her. Its soft glow illuminated the room with a good feeling.

Her Grounding animal was a porpoise.

At their first council meeting the animals agreed that their first task was to bring the dead dog back to life. They all gathered around the dog, whereupon an infant child appeared. Jane immediately recognized the infant as a fetus she had aborted at the age of nineteen and over which she had come to feel extremely guilty and had continuously condemned herself. There was also a fifteen-year-old boy present whom she recognized as the aborted fetus had it been allowed to live and grow. The boy told her that he was not angry at her, that he was comfortable where he was, and that Jane had to accept what she had done without condemnation. After great internal struggle, acknowledging her immaturity at the time she had the abortion, she "owned" her part in it.

Upon this, the dragon ceased its lament, the weasel turned into a swan, and the dog regained its life. The animals rejoiced in celebration. Her voice developed a mellow gentleness.

On a subsequent occasion, Jane came to see me quite depressed. She said the fifteen-year-old boy had been presenting himself in imagination, wanting her to go with him. She refused and was quite fearful. In a visualization she agreed to go with the boy only if she could take the dog with her. He agreed and led her over a hill. At this point the boy began to change, growing large and frightful. Jane recognized him as her anger against herself. Her initial response was to attempt to suppress him but he only grew larger. Her other attitude was to escape from him but she knew he would pursue her. At my encouragement she asked him if he would be willing to help her grow and he agreed, whereupon she *embraced* him and he immediately dissolved. She felt strong and settled, and the dog took on an extraordinarily beautiful glow.

At a subsequent meeting, Jane confessed that she was upset because her dragon, to whom she had become fondly attached, had begun to change and she was trying to resist the change, wanting to keep him as he was. He had already lost his scales and his body had become rather hairy; she knew his legs were trying to grow longer. She was very sad at this and demanded that he stop changing, upon which all the other animals became passive and unresponsive. We discussed her difficulty in letting go, and she agreed to engage in a visualization where she allowed the dragon to leave. She told him goodbye and he went over a hill. I encouraged her to fully experience the sadness of letting go and she cried. A moment later a brown-winged horse flew toward her and she knew this was her power animal transformed. He took her for a ride to a distant valley where she found a small girl named Richness who was herself.

A month later she came to see me and reported that her thoughts of suicide had become very intense. In discussing them she also revealed to me that they had always been accompanied by a feeling of terror. Upon closer questioning, she revealed that whenever she felt the terror her thoughts immediately went to suicide. We agreed to meet the following week to do a visualization where she would encounter her terror directly, and I asked her to reaffirm her non-suicide commitment.

When we next met, she reported having experienced intense anxiety during the intervening week, with several sleepless nights.

In the visualization, we first gathered all her animals together and asked them if this would be an appropriate time for Jane to encounter her terror. All acknowledged that the time was propitious, except for the eagle—he remained silent. They were all then asked if they would support her in the encounter and they all said they would.

I then asked her to allow her terror to present itself to her as an image in her imagination. It appeared immediately as a large, bearded man cracking a whip. He looked much like her father. She asked why he was cracking the whip. "So you'll be afraid," he replied. She asked what he wanted of her. He replied, "I want you to disappear." When she asked if he would be willing to give her his energy for her growth, he answered that he would not. I then had her ask him to tell her when he first appeared in her life. She immediately saw herself as a very small child, together with her sister, jumping on a bed, making noise, and having fun. Her mother was sick in bed in an adjacent bedroom. Her father suddenly appeared in the doorway, enraged. He removed his belt and whipped them both brutally, leaving welts and blisters on her body.

I then asked her to take any animals with her that she wished and return to that early scene to heal the two girls and the father. She took the dog and flying horse with her. The dog licked both girls' wounds, which healed them, and the father was also healed of his rage.

She returned to the cave with the animals where Terror was also waiting. He was now tiny. She asked again if he would give her his energy for her growth. He refused and grew big again. I had her ask him to show her the second time he came into her life.

She saw a scene of herself as a small child with her hands tied behind her back. She didn't know the circumstances. I had her see the scene just prior to this. She saw many people at her parent's home. It was a party. She went to the bathroom by herself, proud that she was doing this alone, but she emerged without her panties. Her parents were shocked, spanked her and tied her hands behind her back. She didn't understand why they were upset as she thought she was doing something good.

I had her return to the scene, taking any animals she wished, to heal the little girl and the parents. She took the swan and the bear and at the last minute had the dog come also. There were so many people that she couldn't seem to do anything. The swan then engaged them and kept them occupied while she untied the girl's hands and soothed her. She had both parents lie on the floor. The bear unzippered their chests and with his jewel erased something from the heart of each.

Upon returning to the cave I had her ask Terror to show her the third time he entered her life. She then saw numerous events of chastisement, punishment, rejections, as if they were being projected on the wall of the cave. I had her ask all the animals to stand with her and beam a healing light on the scenes. At the end of this procession of events Terror was gone, the whip lying on the floor, and her father, clean-shaven, was standing before them, hat in hand, staring at the floor. The animals informed her that she needed to unravel the whip and macrame it into a wall hanging. She engaged her father's help in doing this. It became a wall hanging that she suddenly recognized as one she had made five years earlier while in a psychiatric ward. All the animals then danced in celebration with Jane and her father.

When I saw her two weeks later, she was amazed that there had been no further thoughts of suicide, as these had been so omnipresent for the past five years. There was a clear, direct look in her eyes, her voice was calm and settled, and she told me that several friends had commented on how changed she looked. The small fuzzy bear had grown to full size, and each animal had a blue, glowing jewel in its heart. She felt deeply joyful.

## DISCUSSION

The uniqueness and individuality of each of the animals is difficult to convey in words. The animals have their own personalities and specific orientations as much as individual human beings do, but they seem naturally oriented toward preferring cooperation with each other. They are occasionally overjoyed when first encountered, as having finally been given recognition, and they are quite aware of their value to the individual. One woman's emotional animal was an octopus. She was horrified because she interpreted that as meaning she was emotionally clinging and she began to cut the octopus' arms off. It was horrified at this, chastised her, and told her that it was through the tentacles that she maintained contact with others and should be appreciative of them.

The animals also become intimately comforting and the client gains a great sense of richness from their presence. As the animals learn to love and support each other, love and care appear more frequently in the client's life. In fact, some very recent work has involved asking the animal that most needs to grow to stand in the center of a circle with the client and the other animals around the periphery. The peripheral participants are asked to beam their love and support at the center animal as if it were a light. In some cases this alone has been adequate to induce a transformation.

The transformation can be sudden—a turtle suddenly exploding into an elephant, for example. Or it may also take some days to occur, during which the client is aware that the animal is changing, and may be aware of certain parts, but is unable to tell what the animal is becoming. Not infrequently the animal will disappear, only to reappear later as a different animal.

And the animal is also independent of memory. Occasionally a client will forget what a certain animal was, especially early in the imagery, but when he goes to meet the animal, recognizes it immediately when it is seen.

## CONCLUSION

This therapeutic process was initially developed when the author observed similarities between the chakra system and the totem poles of the Northwest Coast

American Indians. This therapeutic process also acknowledges a relationship between those tribal Indian transformation rituals and modern psychological transformation. This relationship is being explored in a separate paper. In any case, it is possible that the use of animal imagery, as metaphoric description, may be of therapeutic value in other systems as well.

## REFERENCES

Assagioli, R. (1971). *Psychosynthesis.* New York: Viking.
Motoyama, H. (1981). *Theories of the Chakras: Bridge to higher consciousness.* Wheaton, IL: Theosophical Publishing House.
Radha, S. S. (1978). *Kundalini: Yoga for the West.* Spokane, WA: Timeless Books.
Shorr, J. E. (1983). *Psychotherapy through imagery* (2nd ed.). New York: Thieme-Stratton.

# CHAPTER 19

# *Tsubo Imagery Psychotherapy**

## *SEIICHI TAJIMA*
## *AND GOSAKU NARUSE*


This is a report on a new type of imagery method whose therapeutic manipulation is chiefly to control the experiential distance between the self and visual imagery. Our method, called Tsubo Imagery Therapy, consists of the following steps: 1) preparation; 2) passive visualization of several tsuboes; 3) minimal feeling in each tsubo; 4) rearrangement of the tsuboes; 5) maximal feeling in each tsubo; 6) sealing the tsubo; 7) distancing; and 8) entering the next one, or finish. In addition to the control of experiential distance, other major characteristics of our method are: first, the imaged tsuboes have the function of a safety device or capsule which protects the patient from being directly exposed to intense critical experiences; second, special attention is paid to somatic experiences while imaging the tsuboes; third, the therapy proceeds in small steps set by the patient's own preferences. Our method, effective and with the least danger, is applicable to cases of neurosis and also to relatively serious problems such as borderline or schizophrenic.

In psychotherapeutic process using free imagery, the authors have observed that the patient's visual imagery, which initially may be symbolic and incomprehensible to that patient, eventually presents its kernel and becomes understandable to him.[1] With this change in meaningfulness, the experiential distance between the visual imagery and the patient who looks at it as a vision is reduced. For example, the patient may at first be looking at the image as an outside observer, but will eventually begin to be absorbed into the image and will vividly experience emotions and bodily sensations related to the imagery. This consequently enables the patient to experience new kinds of feelings (Tajima, 1980a, 1980b; Tajima & Naruse, 1978). These observations lead us to the following hypothesis: one of the chief curative mechanisms in imagery therapy is this change of experiential distance (or mode) and, therefore, the control of experiential distance can be an important therapeutic

---

[1] He, his, and him are used interchangeably with she and her. We use these words rather than gender-free language in order to avoid distracting from our essential message for the sake of another, important as that one is.

*Reprinted with permission from Tajima, S. & Naruse, G. (1987). "Tsubo" imagery therapy. *Journal of Mental Imagery, 11*(1), 105-118.

manipulation. There are many different imagery methods for psychotherapy. Among those which have been developed are Ahsen's Eidetic Psychotherapy (1968, 1972, 1977); Guided Waking Daydream by Desoille (1966), Oneirotherapy by Fretigny and Virel (1968), and Guided Affective Imagery by Leuner (1969). These imagery methods appear to have been successfully applied to neurotic patients; however, application to more serious cases such as those patients diagnosed as borderline or schizophrenic have even been thought to be contraindicated due to these patients' ego weakness. In America, Ahsen has reported cure of such cases, and similar results by nonverbal psychotherapy such as imagery methods and focusing have been reported in Japan (Masui, 1977; Ohta, 1981; Tajima, 1976). It appears from our studies, however, as also noted by Ahsen, that the application of imagery therapy may cause a sudden intense critical experience or presage of it in more serious cases. As the result of this, a worse condition may develop or a breakdown of the relationship between the patient and his therapist can occur. These problems are probably not specific to imagery therapy but can occur in any kind of therapy dealing mainly with nonverbal experience. Therefore, in our view, it is necessary that such therapies be partly modified so that they can be effective not only for neurosis-level patients but also for more serious cases as those diagnosed as borderline or schizophrenic. In our view, therapeutic manipulations that control the pace of the patient's experiencing are necessary, otherwise therapy may rapidly promote critical experience within his inner world. In imgery therapy, this can be achieved by controlling the experiential distance between the patient and his/her visual imagery. In addition, some kind of safety device that protects the patient from directly being exposed to his/her experience is also necessary. From this point of view, the authors developed a safe and effective method for such purpose (Tajima, 1976, 1980a, 1980b, 1982, 1983a, 1983b, 1983c, 1984; Tajima & Naruse, 1978). The following is a report of our own method for such a purpose, employing the imagery of tsubo.

## THE INITIAL CASE

The tsubo imagery method was developed in the course of working with imagery therapy by the first author. A tsubo is an oriental container made typically of earthenware which corresponds to a jar or a pot. It is quite similar, for example, to a Chinese jar.

The initial case using tsubo imagery was with a male patient, age twenty-six. The patient, having failed in his entrance examination to a university, wanted to try again but he instead got a job due to strong pressure from his parents. After changing occupations several times, he became employed in a hospital. Although he had no license, he was put to work as a lab technician. Sleeplessness and delusions of persecution were apparently triggered by media reports of unlicensed medical technologists working in hospitals, and he was subsequently admitted to a mental hospital due to his delusions and also violence to his mother. When interviewed by the first author, he was found to have fewer delusions of persecution; however, he did have ideas of persecution and insomnia. At several interviews he frequently used difficult words and appeared to be employing intellectization for defense. The therapist, therefore, decided to apply the free imagery method in this case. The patient developed a strong interest in this method. His free imagery at the tenth interview consisted of many tsuboes placed in a cave from the entrance to the bottom. He explained that the contents in the tsuboes near the entrance were resolved and the contents in those near the bottom were unresolved. The therapist said: Something is coming out of the tsubo; and there appeared an armbone and a skeleton. At the next imagery session the therapist told the patient to enter a tsubo; this instruction brought on a reaction in the patient that was different from the one at the previous interview. Inside the tsubo the patient had considerably less visual imagery than before and, instead, he experienced bodily feeling such as unpleasantness in the chest and stirring around the arms, having been unable to enter the tsuboes near the bottom also. In one of them he experienced a feeling of sleeplessness which dissolved his actual sleeplessness. In the eighteenth imagery session he reported: Uneasiness . . . in my loins . . . a heavy burden in my loins . . . (a pause) . . . anger, terrible anger! . . . that's why I've been violent to my mother! Following this, his ideas of persecution disappeared and have not reappeared in his daily life. At the twenty-fourth interview he experienced feelings of being blamed and fear of being attacked while inside the tsubo. He then sealed the tsubo to store it away somewhere, stating that he would never again need to open it.

In this case tsuboes appeared to be acting both as safety devices and capsules which protected the patient from being directly exposed to his experiences. He could not enter the tsuboes near the bottom of the cave at the beginning of the therapy, for these gave him greater pain than did those near the entrance. His feelings, as experienced both mentally and bodily, were stronger in the tsuboes than in the visions obtained using the method of free imagery. This case inspired us to devise a new type of imagery method. This technique, which we have named Tsubo Imagery Therapy, consists of following steps: 1) preparation; 2) passive visualization of several tsuboes; 3) minimal feeling in each of tsuboes; 4) rearrangement of the tsuboes; 5) maximal feeling in each tsubo; 6) sealing the tsubo; 7) distancing; and 8) entering the next one, or finish.

While experiencing the imagery, the patient went through physical and emotional responses which led to a mental set and/or meaning through which he was able to seal away the tsubo. This gradual process of opening and revealing was especially effective with this patient. In addition, we have observed that this method is successful with various mental disorders, for example, neurosis, psychosomatic disorder, borderline cases, and some cases of schizophrenia. It is also useful in the training of therapists and for self-actualization in those without any mental troubles.

## INSTRUCTIONAL PROCEDURE

Following is the standard procedure for Tsubo Imagery Therapy along with typical reactions of patients.

### Preparation for Tsubo Imagery

Many patients do not realize that the cause of their problems, or symptoms, originates in their own inner worlds. Usually they direct their attention to the outer world or to others. They are eager in therapy to complain of these things; however, their mental set needs to be changed at this stage, so that they learn to tune in to their inner world. We refer to this as inner world set. If applied too early in therapy, patients, especially the more serious or borderline cases, tend to regard the tsubo method as a trespass into their inner worlds by their therapists. They feel fear or anxiety that they will lose themselves when they find that they are the object of another's interest, attention, or affection. This makes difficult and also prolongs formation of the relationship between the patient and therapist, a relationship which is required for the investigation of the patient's inner world through a joint effort. This therapy needs to be applied carefully to such patients.

## Passive Visualization of Several Tsuboes

In this stage, the patient, sitting on a chair in a quiet room, is taught to relax using a shortened form of Jacobson's (1934) method of progressive relaxation. Then the therapist tells him to close his eyes and to visualize passively in his mind some tsuboes or tsubo-like containers which contain something. The passively visualized tsuboes are different for each patient in number, form, material, arrangement, etc. Some patients visualize only one. The therapist should be careful, especially when only one tsubo is visualized, as the tsubo may contain something extremely significant and quite critical to the patient, it is often difficult for the patient to enter the tsubo or to leave it. (Countermeasures for these reactions will be mentioned below.) In most cases of only one tsubo, the patient can be regarded as excessively fixated upon something in it. As for shapes and materials, not only do tsuboes appear in the imagery, but also vases, bottles, barrels, and many other containers. For convenience of exposition, all such containers will be referred to as tsuboes in this chapter. Some tsuboes are colored, some have decorative patterns on them, and some have attachments such as handles, etc. As for arrangement, some patients passively visualize their tsuboes as being lined either lengthways or sideways, and some visualize their tsuboes in the shape of a pyramid or lozenge. The therapist needs to be careful at this stage not to ask the patient what he feels about his tsuboes; this sort of question should be asked only when the patient is inside his tsubo or else the tsubo will lose its function as a safety device or capsule.

## Feeling a Little in Each Tsubo

Next, the patient is instructed to enter each of the passively visualized tsuboes for a moment and to get a little impression of it. Then he is told to get out of the tsubo immediately and to seal it. While the patient visualizes many tsuboes, some of them are chosen. The patient and his therapist should discuss which and how many to choose; about three appears to be a favorable number in our experience. There may be some tsuboes that the patient cannot enter or refuses to enter, which suggests that they contain something he does not want to feel. In such a case the therapist does not compel the patient to enter the tsubo but tells him to seal it; such a tsubo, in most cases, is too small to enter or too narrow at the mouth. The patient can seal it in various ways: he may use a lid made of paper or wood, he may use a cork, or he may cover it with an iron plate and, in addition, may wind a chain around it and lock it. The more critical the contents are, generally speaking, the more tightly the patient seems to seal his tsuboes.

### Rearrangement of the Tsuboes

The patient is told to rearrange his tsuboes in a comfortable order according to his short-stay impression in them. The tsuboes should be, however, carefully rearranged without destroying the original form of arrangement.

### Maximal Feeling in Each Tsubo

The therapist tells the patient to enter the tsuboes in order, from the most comfortable one to the least comfortable one, and to feel passively the contents as sufficiently as possible in each imagery session. The patient in a tsubo informs his therapist of his various visual images, emotions, feelings, both mental and bodily, and bodily sensations. It is important in this step to allow the patient inside the tsubo to feel its contents passively and as sufficiently as possible in each session and, in addition, also somatically, if possible. The therapist can ask him, for example, as follows: How are you feeling now?; What is it like inside?; Which part of your body is feeling the impression (or imagery)?; How are you feeling in your body now?

Since verbalization often prevents the patient from sufficiently feeling the contents, the therapist may help by suggesting that the patient should be silent to feel sufficiently. When visual imagery is abundant, the therapist lets the patient freely expand his visual imagery. Moreover, the therapist encourages the patient to direct his attention to his feelings and bodily experience, allowing him, when he presents an intense emotional reaction such as crying or shouting, to discharge his emotion. After such intense emotion almost subsides, the therapist should tell the patient to feel with his body again so that the bodily feelings or bodily senses are not interrupted by intense emotions. A patient who was diagnosed as a borderline case, for example, described her bodily feelings and senses for the first time after she had presented intense emotion in her tsubo for several months.

### Sealing the Tsubo

After the patient has experienced his feeling as sufficiently and as passively as possible, he is told to get out of the tsubo, leaving his experience there, and to seal it.

### Distancing

The patient is now instructed to distance himself sufficiently from the tsubo. He may place it away from him, put it away somewhere, or he himself may go away from it.

### Entering the Next One, or Finish

The patient is instructed to enter the next tsubo, or to make that imagery disappear. This concludes the tsubo imagery exercise.

## SOME PRINCIPLES FOR APPLICATION OF TSUBO IMAGERY THERAPY

There are three principles for the application of the tsubo imagery method. The first principle is to adopt the patient's pace, to pay respect, for example, to his own decisions. These decisions may involve whether this method will be applied at each interview, whether the patient will enter the tsubo or not, whether to continue to stay in the tsubo or get out of it, etc. The second principle is to help the patient develop resourcefulness. The patient may sometimes face various difficulties at each step; the therapist, in the event of difficulty, helps the patient discover ways of dealing with it. In case the patient has no idea, the therapist suggests some possible devices. The third principle is to proceed in small steps. It often takes the patient a long time to be able to fully feel the contents in the tsubo: it is necessary to advance gradually in order to attain a maximum level of feeling. Applying the tsubo imagery without the principles mentioned above may have hazardous effects to the patient. Some difficulties and ways of dealing with them will now be discussed.

### Being Unable to Enter Tsuboes

When the patient cannot enter a specific tsubo, she should be treated with great care, for such a tsubo usually contains something she does not want to feel. The therapist, in such a case, should not force the patient to enter it; the therapist, instead, tells the patient to seal the tsubo properly. Continual sessions in this way enable most patients to try to enter the specific tsuboes. Moreover, the therapist trains the patient to be resourceful by asking the patient both in verbal interviews and imagery sessions questions such as these: What might happen if you enter the tsubo?; What might you need to enter it? An imagined rope or a ladder often helps the patient to get into the tsubo or he might enter it by joining hands with her therapist. If the patient herself does not think of these possibilities, then the therapist can suggest them. Proceeding in small steps is also useful: first, for example, the patient tries only to seal the tsubo; next, she tries to come close to the tsubo and tries to look into it, when she can do that, she tries to put a part of her body, her arms or legs, for example, into the tsubo; finally, she tries to fully enter the tsubo.

### Intense Emotion

When the patient experiences intense emotion outside the tsubo, the therapist advises her to put the emotion into the tsubo concerned or into an empty one. The therapist can, for example, tell her to wrap her emotion and bodily experiences in something and to put them into a tsubo. This technique is based on Masui's (1982) technique which is based on clearing space in focusing (Gendlin, 1981). Masui instructed the patient to choose a troublesome problem, find a body sense for it, and then enclose it in a box and put the box away.

### Appearance of Dangerous or Dreadful Objects

The patient often meets dangerous or dreadful objects in a tsubo. The therapist tells her to leave the tsubo and to seal it after she experiences the feelings, both mentally and bodily, toward the objects as sufficiently as she can in each session. Repeating this process, her fear for the objects usually decreases and the original forms of the objects appear. Here, again, the therapist helps the patient find some effective way to deal with the objects; for example, gradually advancing toward the object is usually effective.

### Being Unable to Get Out of Tsuboes

When it is difficult for the patient to get out of the tsubo, the therapist, in most cases, needs to help her rapidly and actively; the therapist can, for example, suggest to the patient that he can use some implements around her such as a rope or a ladder; the therapist can tell her to breathe deeply or to relax; or the therapist can pull her out of the tsubo by the arm. Verbal interview after such an imagery session is important so that the therapist and patient can determine what brought about such experiences. Such experiences are often brought on when the therapist and/or the patient conduct the treatment too hurriedly.

### Lingering Uncomfortableness

In case some uncomfortableness experienced in the tsubo remains in the patient even after she leaves the tsubo, the therapist helps her try to get rid of it. The therapist, for example, can tell her to repeat going in and out of the tsubo several times; can advise her to enter the most comfortable one again; or the patient may successfully escape from her uncomfortableness by wrapping it in something and putting it into a tsubo. After each imagery session, a verbal interview is carried out in which the patient and therapist discuss the imagery session. In situations like the one mentioned above, the therapist should discuss with the patient whether any better measures might have been possible.

## CASE REPORTS

Following are two case reports exemplifying the Tsubo Imagery Therapy.

### Case 1

A female patient, age thirty-two, was diagnosed as a borderline case by a psychiatrist. This patient, born of a concubine, was separated from her mother a few weeks after her birth and taken into the care of the legal wife of her father. Having married at eighteen, she lived with her spouse in the home of her parents-in-law (a traditional custom in Japan). The suicide of her mother-in-law when she was thirty-three years old triggered her symptoms of sleeplessness, loss of appetite, withdrawal, and delusions of persecution. She was sent to a mental hospital, where her condition entered a state of remission within four months. After two years, however, she fell into the same condition again when her husband was transferred. Weekly psychotherapy was begun while she was staying at a hospital. After several interviews, she directed extroverted erotic feelings toward her therapist and manifested also a violent trust-distrust conflict toward him. Supportive verbal interviews for about one year revealed that the patient had felt hostility toward her mother-in-law for several years prior to her mother-in-law's suicide. Consequently, she felt as if she herself had killed her mother-in-law. The therapist inferred that her illness may have originated from her early object relationship. Her delusion had disappeared around that time, and yet she was suffering from depression, abelia, and suicidal thoughts.

Psychotherapy by free imagery was employed as the next step. The patient was excessively frightened by a devil or a black object in her free imagery but this therapy, which lasted two-and-one-half years, produced no evident effect on her. Then Tsubo Imagery Therapy was applied to her for eighteen months. She passively visualized several tsuboes, which included one in which she was holding her therapist and another in which a devil appeared. At the beginning she could enter the former, which gave her a feeling of safety, but she could not enter the latter. In the eighteenth session of tsubo imagery, she could get into the latter for the first time, where she was overwhelmed by a devil and a black object, which made her unable to stay for a long time inside. Gradually, however, she came to be able to stay longer inside and to feel more, and, in addition, her three-year-old depression disappeared.

In the twentieth tsubo imagery session she described the following:

| Patient: | (In the tsubo of a devil) . . . it's dark . . . a devil! . . . horrible! |
|---|---|
| Therapist: | How are you feeling in your body? |
| Patient: | As if my chest were pressed. |
| Therapist: | Feel it as sufficiently as possible. |
| Patient: | It's thrusting my throat . . . (covering the wound) . . . (groans) . . . my pain's gone somewhere. |

In the twenty-fifth session of tsubo imagery, the devil which had been troubling her changed into its original form:

| Patient: | A devil, there . . . it's stabbing me . . . terrible . . . it stabbed me in the breast . . . (pressing her breast) it hurts me . . . |
|---|---|
| Therapist: | Feel it as sufficiently as possible. |
| Patient: | Why! That can't be! . . . I hate to say it . . . it cannot be a devil . . . my mother who has brought me up [that is, the legal wife of her father] . . . so sad . . . somewhat murky feelings. |

In the twenty-eighth session she experienced: a dreadful feeling in my mind which was almost making me mad. She confessed to her therapist that she disliked telling him about that. In the thirty-second session it occurred to her to seal the tsubo and to make the therapist keep it. Having done this, she was not troubled by the dreadful feeling any more. This effect was probably due to the therapist keeping the tsubo, which enabled her to keep enough experiential distance from it while keeping the contents secret from the therapist.

## Case 2

A male patient, age thirty-two, was diagnosed as schizophrenic by a psychiatrist. His parents, having lived separately for approximately two years, began to live together again soon after he was born. He passed his childhood without a feeling of security due to the bad relationship between his parents. His father and elder sister mostly took care of him on behalf of his mother, who did not like to care for children. Having graduated from high school, the patient wanted to go somewhere away from home to live and work, but he had to stay home because of his mother's opposition even after he had begun to work. He quit his job and made an unsuccessful attempt to marry a woman, and this appeared to trigger auditory hallucinations, delusions of persecution, broadcasting of his thoughts, experiences of being influenced, and guilt feelings. He was admitted to the hospital four times in three years. During a fifth stay at the hospital, his auditory hallucinations, delusions of persecution, broadcasting of thoughts, and experience of being influenced had disappeared, and yet he was being troubled with unaccountable guilt feelings, gloominess, and insomnia. Weekly psychotherapy sessions were begun to deal with these symptoms.

After supportive interviews for three months, Tsubo Imagery Therapy was initiated. The patient visualized passively three tsuboes which he called, after staying inside each for a while, a tsubo giving no feeling, a comfortable tsubo, and a gloomy tsubo. The remarkable thing is that he concluded that the tsubo giving no feeling was easier to stay in than the comfortable one, that is, he was being troubled by too much feeling. He decided to stay for a long time only in the tsubo giving no feeling. The therapist suggested to him: This tsubo is the one where you will be allowed to stay without feeling anything. You can stay inside until you feel enough. For the following two months his sleeping difficulties decreased a little. Next, he began to try the other two tsuboes. In the gloomy tsubo he felt as if he had been sinking deep, pulled and swallowed into the depths; he could stay there only for a moment but, little by little, he became able to stay longer. He realized that the impression there was nothing but those of his home. This realization led him to decide to leave home and get a job. At the thirty-sixth interview those impressions largely decreased, which consequently enabled him to sleep better and made his gloominess and guilty feelings decrease.

At the forty-sixth interview a certain feeling occurred to him. He said that he would not like to explain it if the therapist didn't mind. The therapist agreed and asked him to put the feeling into an empty tsubo. This feeling, which he managed to put into the empty tsubo, consisted of a pressing on his mind and a seizing of his throat. The therapist promised not to make any further inquiries about it. Since leaving the hospital, the patient has been working without symptoms.

## DISCUSSION

Tsubo Imagery Therapy has three chief aims: 1) nonverbal experience in tsuboes; 2) self-control of experiential distance by the patient; and 3) a trusting therapist-patient relationship.

### Aims

**Nonverbal Experience in Tsuboes.** The experiences in the tsuboes are different for each person and for each tsubo. For each patient, visualized tsuboes are classified usually into three groups: comfortable tsuboes, neutral tsuboes, and uncomfortable tsuboes. The patient often experiences his illness or problems while imaging himself inside his tsuboes: a patient of phobia, for example, vividly experiences a feeling of phobia and a patient with psychosomatic disorder experiences the ill condition itself. One of the aims of our method is to help the patient fully receive impressions in the tsuboes in order to bring about change. In the experience, the patient 1) becomes aware of feelings that he had not experienced before, that is, he experiences new feelings; 2) becomes able to stay inside the tsubo longer than he did before because the uncomfortable or painful experiences inside a specific tsubo disappear or diminish; and 3) becomes aware of the meaning of his experiences inside the tsuboes.

These changes are accompanied by the disappearance or decrease in the illness or problem of the patient. What brings about these changes? We have inferred that it would be the change in the mental set of the patient to his experiences; that is, a receptive set toward his mental or bodily experiences is formed, which we call the set oriented to the self. Also, the integration of his imagery with related feelings and meanings, as discussed by Ahsen (see Ahsen, 1984, ISM: The Triple Code Model for Imagery and Psychophysiology) provides a solid, unified base on which to develop more strength and sense of self.

**The Self-Control of Experiential Distances by the Patient.** The patient can shorten the experiential distance between the contents of his tsubo to feel its contents. He can, on the other hand, lengthen the distance by getting out of the tsubo to seal it and then place it at a distance. Another aim of our method is, therefore, to help the patient learn how to control this experiential distance through his visual imagery of the tsuboes. It is, in other words, a technique for dealing with or getting along with each experience inside the tsuboes, as a result of which the patient will not be influenced or troubled by such experiences any more. For this aim the patient usually needs to be trained to be resourceful. Since the patient, in most cases, can present only a stereotyped reaction, the therapist helps him devise ways to lengthen or shorten the experiential distance. We regard the ability of the patient to control the experiential distance between himself and his imagery as related to his ability to handle interpersonal relations.

This is an especially important aspect regarding serious cases such as borderline ones, that is, once the patient learns how to get impressions inside a tsubo to some extent, the therapist should help him devise ways for being apart from the tsubo. The necessity of this process is exemplified by Cases 1 and 2.

**A Trusting Patient-Therapist Relationship.** It is no exaggeration to say that the patient-therapist relationship is important for every kind of psychotherapy. Our method also requires a trusting relationship which should be established preceding its application. Moreover, the application of our method brings on feelings of trust and safety in the patient, which assures the patient that the therapist will never trespass on his inner world without his permission. This feeling of trust is an important contributing factor in the success of the therapy.

## Characteristics

The characteristics of the Tsubo Imagery Therapy are in the following paragraphs.

**The Control of Experiential Distance as the Chief Therapeutic Manipulation.** The experiential distances of the patient are controlled through the tsubo imagery of the patient. Experiential distances are more easily controlled by our method than by ordinary imagery techniques.

**The Importance of Bodily Experiences of the Patient.** The patient is likely to become more aware of bodily feelings and senses in the tsubo. Our method utilizes such bodily experiences for, in our opinion, they will be more vividly felt by the patient and easier to deal with by both the patient and therapist. Our method is, as Kira and Murayama (1982) and Masui (1984) have pointed out, quite similar to felt sense in Gendlin's focusing (1981). The remaining task for us will be to compare our method with others: Eidetic Psychotherapy (Ahsen, 1968, 1972, 1977, 1984), Guided Waking Daydream (Desoille, 1966), Oneirotherapy (Fretigny & Virel, 1968), Guided Affective Imagery (Leuner, 1969), Focusing (Gendlin, 1981), etc. These comparisons may lead to a more precise theory of tsubo imagery therapy. For such a theoretical consideration, Ahsen's theory of ISM unit seems to be useful.

**The Use of Tsuboes as Containers of Imagery.** The third characteristic of our method is that the patient is required to visualize specific imagery, tsuboes or tsubo-like containers, for treatment. Such imagery has a function of a safety device which protects the patient from being directly exposed to severe experiences or from having a fear of that kind. Such a safety device tends to enable the patient to produce deeper imagery of his inner world and, furthermore, to experience it bodily. The authors call this phenomenon the *safety device effect* in imagery.

In Japan, Nakai (1974) observed a similar phenomenon in art therapy which he called the *fence effect*. He discovered that the fence technique, namely the therapist's marking a fence on a sheet of paper, had a facilitating effect upon the schizophrenic patient's drawing of it. Moreover, he reported that the content of the patient's drawing emerging from the fence technique was more internal, centripetal, secret-confessing, and regressive, with more projected expression of dependency and ego identity and more confusion or diffusion than the content elicited in drawing without the fence technique.

A safety device is a closing device and, at the same time a disclosing device.

**Proceeding in Small Steps and at the Patient's Pace.** The patient, in most cases, visualizes passively more than one tsubo, from which the therapist selects the most comfortable one to begin treatment with. The decision of the patient is valued in the therapy situation. One of the principal rules for dealing with tsuboes too difficult to enter is to go in small steps according to each patients preference. This avoids processing too hastily, beyond the ability of the patient. These therapeutic manipulations function as pace controller in this therapy.

Our method is, in one respect, similar to systematic desensitization in behavior therapy, that is, with tsuboes in order, from the easiest one to the most difficult one. They are, however, extremely different in another respect: unreal or symbolic imagery is usually employed in the former, while imagery based upon actual experiences of the patient is adopted in the latter.

Due to the four characteristics mentioned above, our method could prove to be one of the safest and most effective among the many imagery techniques. Moreover, our method, which brings on unnecessary and unfavorable reactions in the patients less frequently, has proved to be effective for treatment of those patients diagnosed as borderline or schizophrenic. In our opinion, some form of therapeutic manipulation which functions as a safety device and pace controller will also prove to be necessary for other kinds of psychotherapies, particularly nonverbal psychotherapy. Further, carefully conducted investigations will be necessary to determine how effective tsubo imagery will be for various types of disorders. Our method, although an independent therapy in its own right, can also be successfully applied in conjunction with other therapies.

## REFERENCES

Ahsen, A. (1968). *Basic concepts in eidetic psychotherapy*. New York: Brandon House.

Ahsen, A. (1972). *Eidetic parents test and analysis*. New York: Brandon House.

Ahsen, A. (1977). *Psycheye: Self-analytic consciousness*. New York: Brandon House.

Ahsen, A. (1984). ISM. The Triple Code Model for Imagery and psychophysiology. *Journal of Mental Imagery, 8*, 15-42.

Desoille, R. (1966). *The directed daydream*. New York: Psychosynthesis Foundation.

Fretigny, R., & Virel, A. (1968). *L'imagerie mentale*. Geneva: Mont-Blanc.

Gendlin, E. T. (1981). *Focusing*. New York: Bantam Books.

Jacobson, E. (1934). *You must relax*. New York: McGraw-Hill.

Kira, Y., & Murayama, S. (1982). Waga Kuni ni okeru Focusing Kenkyu no Ayumi to Kongo no Tenbo [The steps and perspectives of studies on focusing in Japan]. The Faculty of Education, Educational Psychology Section, Kyushu University, *Research Bulletin, 27* (2), 47-54.

Leuner, H. (1969). Guided affective imagery (GAI): A method of intensive psychotherapy. *American Journal of Psychotherapy, 23*, 4-22.

Masui, T. (1977). Imi Imeijio Teikyo shita ichi Chiryo Katei ni tsuite: Furue to Moso Kibun ga Tsuyokatta Ichi Shorei [On the therapeutic process adapting imagery of meaning: A case with tremor and sense of delusion]. In H. Kawai, M. Saji, & G. Naruse (Eds.), *Rhinsho Shinri Keisu Kenkyu (Case studies on psychotherapy)* (Vol. 1). Tokyo: Seisin Shobo.

Masui, T. (1982). *Shin-Shin Imeiji o MochiitaügMa o Toru KotoühtoügOite Oku Koto no Shinri Chiryo no Kokoromi* [Trial on psychotherapy by mind-body imagery: Distancing and Putting aside]. Paper presented at the 28th annual meeting of Japanese Society of Hypnosis, Fukuoka.

Masui, T. (1984). Tsubo Imeiji Ryoho no Shokai to Focusing [Introduction to the tsubo imagery therapy and focusing]. In S. Murayama et al. (Eds.), *Focusing no Riron to jissai* (pp. 133-138). [Theory and practice in focusing]. Tokyo: Fukumura Shuppan.

Nakai, H. (1974). Wakuzukeho Oboegaki [A note on fence technique]. *Geijyutsu Ryoho* [Japanese Bulletin of Art Therapy], *5*, 15-19.

Ohta, T. (1981). *Seinenki bunretsubyo-ken Kanja eno Focusing Giho no Kokoromi* (pp. 88-97). [Trial application of the focusing technique to a patient diagnosed as adolescent schizophrenia]. Rinsho Shinri Kenkyu [The Studies on Clinical Psychology], Sophia University.

Tajima, S. (1976). *Hiteikeiseishinbyosha no Imeiji ni yoru Chiryo Jirei* (pp. 107-120). [A case of imagery therapy on a patient diagnosed as atypish psychosis]. Archives of Psychological Clinical, Kyushu University.

Tajima, S. (1980a). Imeiji Ryoho ni okeru Chokumen [Confrontation in the imagery therapy]. In G. Naruse (Ed.), *Saimin Symposium* (pp. 238-255). (Symposium on hypnosis), Vol. X: Imeiji Ryoho [Imagery Therapy], Tokyo: Seisin Shobo.

Tahima, S. (1980b). *Hannya to Kannon* (pp. 143-150). [Hannya and Kannon]. In G. Naruse (Ed.), Saimin Symposium [Symposium on hypnosis]. Vol. X: Imeiji Ryoho [Imagery Therapy], Tokyo: Seisin Shobo.

Tajima, S. (1982). *Imeiki Ryoho Kenkyu 1. Tsubo Imeiji-ho no Hyojun-teki Tetsuzuki* [The studies on imagery therapy: 1. Standard procedure of tsubo imagery method]. Paper presented at the 28th annual meeting of Japanese Society of Hypnosis, Tokyo.

Tajima, S. (1983a). Tsubo Imeiji Ryoho [Tsubo Imagery Therapy]. *The Bulletin of the Humanities and Sciences, Hiroshima Shudo University, 24* (1), 71-93.

Tajima, S. (1983b). *Tsubo Imeiji Ryoho: Hikaku-teki jyutoku na Kesu ni taisuru Giho-ron* [Tsubo Imagery Therapy: Some technical consideration on its application to relatively severe cases]. Paper presented at the 47th annual meeting of Japanese Psychological Association, Tokyo.

Tajima, S. (1983c). *Tsubo imeiji-ho ni yoru Kyokairei no Chiryo Jirei* [A case of tsubo imagery therapy on a borderline patient]. Paper presented at the 2nd annual meeting of the Association of Japanese Clinical Psychology, Nagoya.

Tajima, S. (1984). Tsubo Imeiji Ryoho [Psychotherapy by use of tsubo imagery]. In K. Mizushima & K. Ogawa (Eds.), *Imeiji no Rinsyoshinrigaku* (pp. 54-60). [Clinical psychology of imagery]. Tokyo: Seisin Shobo.

Tajima, S., & Naruse, G. (1978). Imeiji Ryoho no Ichi Jirei [A case report of image therapy]. The Faculty of Education, Educational Psychology Section, Kyushu University, *Research Bulletin, 22* (2), 31-40.

# CHAPTER 20

# Conception Imagery Exercise: Journey to Beginning

## BEVERLY CAROL STOKES
## AND LOUIS STOKES

We shall not cease from exploration
At the end of all our exploring
Will be to arrive where we started
And know the place for the first time.
Through the unknown, remembered gate
When the last of earth left to discover
Is that which was the beginning;

T. S. Eliot: "Little Gidding" Part V, 239-245
from *Four Quartets,* Faber and Faber (London)

The Conception Imagery Exercise is part of the Psyche/Soma Imagery Series which we have been developing over the past fifteen years. This series combines movement, color expression, and connective language exercises designed to develop an individual's confidence in their own ability to express inner feeling, sensing, and intuiting processes. The movement and color expression exercises are simple in process and require no prior training in movement or drawing experience. The result is that participants are able to move and to create visually in personally satisfying ways and the exercises are rich enough in potential to be relevant to their personal growth process.

The Psyche/Soma Imagery Series finds its psychological roots in a Jungian approach to working with imagery and the unconscious and its movement roots in the work of Bonnie Bainbridge Cohen's approach to the interrelationships between the major body-mind systems. Marion Woodman, Jungian analyst, writes that ". . . some means must be found to create an adequate image—physically as well as psych-ically. . . . What is at stake is the integration of body, soul and spirit" (Woodman, 1985, p. 35). She stresses the importance of the image in personal growth and integration: "It is the contained energy of the images that constitutes what Jung, drawing upon an ancient tradition, called the 'subtle body' or 'breath soul' . . . which holds the physical and psychic tensions and acts as a catalyst releasing energy to both sides" (Woodman, 1985, p. 63). Hillman writes that seeing through an event to its image releases the individual from the search for literal understanding into a mythical appreciation in life—realization of the soul. He explains that the image is "the only way in which one sees," and that it "can only be perceived by an act of imagining" (Hillman, 1983, p. 7; 1979). He further writes that the archetypal image ". . . is not given simply as revelation. It must be *made* through *image work* and *dream work.* The modes of this work may be concrete and physical as in art, movement, play and occupational therapies" (Hillman, 1983, p. 14).

Marion Woodman has found that ". . . releasing the body into spontaneous movement or play constellates the unconscious in precisely the same way as does a dream" and that body movement ". . . can be understood as a waking dream" (Woodman, 1982, pp. 78-79; 1980, 1984). Joan Chodorow, a Jungian analyst and dance therapist, writes ". . . self directed movement tends to develop a relationship to both sensory and imaginal realms. . . . When felt body sensation emerges as physical action, an image may appear that will give the movement meaning" (Chodorow, 1982, p. 198; 1984).

Bonnie Bainbridge Cohen approaches movement and imagery through the differentiation of, and extension of awareness to, the major bodymind systems and their interrelationships. Each system, with its separate function, is essential to the others in providing a complete framework of support and expression. Her work is based on our developmental process through movement and perception, human development (ontogenetic), and the evolutionary (phylogenetic) progression through the animal kingdom (Cohen, 1983, 1985). Based on her findings, we use a movement process of experiencing and differentiating that expands each individual's matrix of movement, feeling and expression.

D. W. Winnicott (1974) provides the important psychotherapeutic framework for the Psyche/Soma Imagery Series in his position that it is *only* in playing that the child or the adult is able to be creative, to use their whole personality, and to come ultimately to discover the self. The Psyche/Soma Imagery series has developed based on the three fundamental therapeutic principles that he has espoused: relaxation and trust, creative play activity, and reflection of the experience back to the individual.

- The first principle of relaxation and trust is essential to any therapeutic or educational approach using imagery procedures. Dora Kalff refers to this environment as a "free and sheltered space" within which to establish ". . . an inner peace which contains the potential for the development of the total personality, including its intellectual and spiritual aspects" (Kalff, 1980, pp. 29-30).
- The second principle of creative mental and physical activity manifested in external play forms the core of the Psyche/Soma Imagery Series—the expression of the image through physical movement and color/form expression.
- We approach the third principle to be grounded in a *non*-interpretive reflection of the client's experience of their primary process movements and drawings. Our orientation is to assist clients, through movement, color expression, and connective language, to come to *their own realization* of the meaning, significance, and relationships in their primary expressed material.

The core of the Psyche/Soma Imagery Series is creative mental and physical activity manifested in the play of spontaneous movement and color expression. Our central belief is that our internally expressed imagery must serve as the motivation, or impulse of intention, for focusing our externally directed communication; otherwise the imagery process remains merely the creation of a mental fantasy world with no communication to the external world, or to the inner world of the body. Marion Woodman cautions against a solely mental approach to the dream image (and, we would say, to images in general):

> The goal is to integrate body and psyche: to take the healing symbols from the dreams, put them into the unconscious body areas and allow their energy to accomplish the healing work. One of the dangers in analysis is that we imagine we have done our work when we think we understand the dream images; we become fascinated by the interpretation. If the symbol is not contemplated, however, its healing power is lost. It has to go into the fire of the heart in order to be transformed. (Woodman, 1982, p. 87)

Jean Houston writes that ". . . research into imagery was opening other pathways of tapping into the body's basic wisdom, which in turn can guide the natural healing process," and speaks of the ". . . charged imagery that then creates those channels of communication for dialogue with our innate body wisdom" (Houston, 1982, pp. 11-12). In the Psyche/Soma Imagery Series, the movement or dance, the visual image of the subtle body drawn on paper, and the connective verbal expression combine in a synergistic force which creates a "charged image." This image, tempered by the "fire of the heart," has the power to unlock the inner and outer communication channels of the body and, in the union of psyche and soma, to initiate personal growth.

The Psyche/Soma Imagery Series is an evolving collection of exercises which use movement and color expression, combined at specific times with language association, in different sequences for particular therapeutic and teaching situations. Such exercises as the Conception Imagery Exercise presented in this chapter are potentially very powerful and we advise their use only in appropriate therapeutic settings with properly trained practitioners and prepared clients. Other exercises in the Series are suitable for applications in either therapeutic or educational environments.

## THE CONCEPTION IMAGERY EXERCISE

Procedures for this exercise are designed to be carried out within specific space and time frameworks. Participants lie down on the floor within the boundary defined by a large, blank piece of paper during the imagery instructions. The deliberate passage of time during instructions, as well as the spatial arrangement on the floor, allow the process of the more subtle preverbal and nonverbal body images, sensations, and feelings to develop as the imagery instructions proceed (Dossey, 1982; Sheehan & Bayliss, 1984). Thus, a state of awareness is developed in which the imagery can transform into active expression more readily than if quicker states of preconsciousness were achieved, e.g., in direct mental visualization.

By going back through time in the Conception Imagery Exercise, we stimulate sense perceptions stored in specific bodymind systems and finally in the cells themselves. Thomas Verny (Verny & Kelly, 1981) postulates a third avenue of communication or memory in addition to the physiological systems (the central and autonomic nervous systems). What was called intuition in the past, Verny would call sympathetic communication which is encoded in individual cells as an "organismic memory." Thus, even a single cell, such as a sperm or ovum, would have memory. This, he feels, could be the physiological basis for the Jungian concept of the collective unconscious. Adopting this bipolar model of memory is, he believes, the best way to explain the existence of reported prenatal and birth memories. These preverbal memories are invested with psychic energies which can be expressed through the body movements and the colors and forms in the drawings.

Developing the work originated by Bonnie Bainbridge Cohen (1983, 1985), we utilize the fundamental building blocks of our evolutionary origins: the movements observed in the animal kingdom and the early developing human. In the Conception Imagery Exercise, we focus specifically on the first two neurological patterns (of 14 patterns identified by Cohen):

- The first neurological pattern, breathing, can be explored phylogenetically through one-celled animals (amoeba) and ontogenetically through the ovum and cellular breathing.
- The second neurological pattern, navel radiation, can be experienced phylo-genetically through the starfish (adult stage) in radial symmetry with the center of control in the middle of the body. Ontogenetically, in the human the navel functions as the primitive control center as movement is initiated from the navel and spreads outward.

Exploring the body systems through movement and initiating movement from the specific body systems is expressing the "mind" of the point focused in that system. We come to know the skeletal muscular system as the container and the organs as contents. By locating the place of an organ and following an impulse to move from that point, we experience the mind-state and feelings of that organ. Before beginning the imagery exercise we prepare the participants by moving their awareness from their outer environment to their inner environment. The movement exercises develop a new connection to the self, through which participants can explore new points of initiation from the prenatal systems.

The two developmental movement patterns, "breathing" and "navel radiation," are introduced. Spinal and homologous patterns are experienced in this process but not focused on. At the conclusion of the session the change of perceptual level from inner focus to outer is achieved through the "coming to standing" movement sequences, which bring the participant to the vertical position, and aligns perception with this level. (Those practitioners familiar with this work will note that we do not go through all the developmental movement and evolutionary patterns in this exercise.)

The individual's movement and color expression process invokes a new, uniquely personal awareness of the bodymind. As Arnold Mindell writes, "The real body is the product of cultural concepts. . . . In contrast, the dreambody is created by individual experience, personal descriptions of signals, sensations and fantasies which do not necessarily conform to collective materialistic definitions" (Mindell, 1982, p. 11). The full scale body drawing gives a view *of* the self, a type of inner psychic mirror, rather than an impersonal drawing which has been created *about* the self. This is one of the most important therapeutic points in the development of the Psyche/Soma Imagery Series. The color/form expression and movement process, which demands intuitive choices and commitments from the individual, "charges" the inner image with the personal energy needed for external expression—"fired by the heart's emotion." As von Franz points out: ". . . emotion is the carrier of consciousness, there is no progress in consciousness without emotion" (von Franz, 1980, p. 252).

The inner image contained in the recesses of the bodymind now takes on another dimension, a dimension of separateness. Within this distance, a creative dialogue can be established between the participant and their "dreambody" image which carries the potential for change through inner and outer action. This "objective" external personal image of the individual is invested with an emotional quality which cannot be as easily ignored or forgotten as the inner image memory.

## MATERIAL AND SPACE REQUIREMENTS

We work with double-weight white craft paper in rolls four feet wide which can be cut to size for different types of exercises. The Conception Imagery Exercise requires four-foot lengths, creating a square format. We use ordinary crayons and water-based color markers. Large size children's crayons are useful for filling in large areas of color and smaller crayons for increased color range and detailing. Broad and medium point color markers also work very well for drawing on this scale. Since participants will be lying and moving on top of their colored drawings, other art materials such as pastels, chalk, and charcoal are not suitable.

The color expression exercise is done directly on the floor. Hard-surfaced floors such as linoleum or wood (in a gym or dance studio) work best. We have been successful drawing on top of the tightly woven carpeting used in schools and other public spaces, although the crayons will sometimes tear the paper if pressed on too hard. There is not a set square foot requirement for space, although there has to be enough room for each participant to lay paper on the floor with sufficient space around it so that he or she can move and draw without impediment.

## RELAXATION AND MOVEMENT—
## PREPARATORY EXERCISES

Our preparatory exercises form a continuing series of pre-imagery exercises designed to enhance the participant's receptivity to inner feeling, sensing, and intuitive states during the imagery exercise which will follow. These exercises are presented in three sections:

- Section 1: traditional forms of relaxation technique, such as progressive relaxation and autogenic training,
- Section 2: general movement relaxation techniques and movement group dynamics,
- Section 3: specific movement sequences to be used as a prelude to the imagery exercise.

It should be noted that this preparatory relaxation and movement section is discussed only in relation to the core session of the Conception Imagery Exercise; other general relaxation and movement would be advised in prior sessions with the group or individual, based on the practitioner's own background experience.

### Section I: General Relaxation Exercises

Anyone working with imagery techniques in a therapeutic environment will have developed their own particular sequences of exercises for client relaxation prior to using imagery procedures. It is assumed that readers will have sufficient skills to do general relaxation exercises. Breathing techniques would usually form an essential component, and we would recommend that a procedure such as progressive relaxation, in which the body is directly relaxed, also be used as preparation for the deeper levels of somatic memory that will be invoked by the imagery exercise. We would also recommend using prior sessions in an all-day or weekend workshop, or in ongoing individual or group therapy, for general relaxation training so that all participants would have adequate experience in relaxing before the imagery session itself. Participants should reach a level of relaxed receptivity to the sensing and feeling processes of the inner mind and body systems in preparation for their expression.

### Section 2: General Movement Exercises

This sequence of movement exercises initiates changes in the participant's mind and somatic awareness in preparation for the age regression imagery instructions. It is assumed the practitioner has practical group experience and can modify and sequence the movement exercises according to group dynamics. This exercise increases awareness of the verticality of the body, the body's relationship to space and to its own kinesphere. The kinesphere is the space that is defined by the reach space around the body: up/down—the vertical axis; right/left—the horizontal axis; and forward/back—the sagittal axis.

Direct participants to begin walking around the room. You may suggest they stretch up high and, at an appropriate time, reach down low, or stretch to the side. At intervals, and allowing time between directions, suggest they walk slowly . . . quickly . . . backwards . . . sideways . . . centrally . . . peripherally. Walking through space, in and around others, leads to awareness of the straight and angular pathways created by moving forward, backward, and sideways. Moving quickly through space, participants find that movements and responses become more automatic as speed increases. The pathways created are now curves and arcs, and participants become more attuned to the kinesthetic experience. When these ideas have been explored, suggest that movements come to a close. Request that participants remain standing, with eyes open or closed, and focus on their breathing rhythm. Then they can sit in a circle and share this experience. This entire sequence should take between fifteen to twenty minutes including time for sharing.

Alternatively, you may ask them to form a cluster together in the middle of the room. Instruct them to move closer together until all are touching someone else with a part of the body. You can then instruct each individual to close their eyes and focus on his or her own breathing. At an appropriate time, you would then ask the whole group to expand their focus and become as one organism breathing. Then instruct them to allow their eyes to open and to gradually move apart and create a circle of sharing. When moving apart the group may feel they have been connected by invisible "threads" and, as they sit in a circle, will continue to feel the connection. At this point, a few minutes spent sharing the movement experiences verbally creates a group cohesiveness which will support and contain the energy during the following Conception Imagery experience.

## Section 3: Specific Movement Exercises

The "mind state" of the room changes as participants change the spatial level from the initial vertical position as they walk around, to sitting while sharing verbally, and now to lying on the floor. One's sensory awareness shifts from the outer (air environment) to the inner (fluid conception environment). It is important to align the level of sensory perception to the infant and prenatal levels by doing the following preparatory movement and relaxation exercises of cellular breathing and naval radiation.

**Cellular Breathing Exercise.** This pattern can be explored through one-celled animals (amoeba) and will be experienced as the baby in utero (embryo). Have the participants sit in a circle after sharing the previous movement or relaxation experiences. Allow a few minutes between each instruction. First ask that they *imagine* their hand and arm breathing and then to *imagine* their hand and arm moving. After an appropriate time ask them to *feel* their hand and arm breathing at a cellular level and to move their hand and arm from the knowledge it has of itself. You might add that this is not just an image but a physically felt sensation. After an appropriate interval, ask the question: How did you feel the two experiences were different?

Movement is like breathing—expanding and contracting. Sensory awareness of external stimuli (touch and vibration) are a function of the surrounding membrane (skin), and are precursors of the future special senses. Participants should now be lying down on the floor at this point. Then, ask that they: *Feel* the inside and outside of themselves—at the skin level and then feel the cells expanding and contracting. Allow a few minutes between instructions.

**Navel Radiation Exercise.** Phylogenetically this pattern is experienced through the adult stage of the starfish in radial symmetry, with the center of control in the middle of the body. Since this potential extension is in all directions, the pivot point is central. Ontogenetically, in the human the navel functions as the primitive control center. Breathing is the underlying function from which navel radiation develops. Movement is initiated from the navel and spreads out from the center. The human has six extremities—head, two upper limbs, two lower limbs, and a tail (coccyx). All extremities have equal importance in locomotion and in exploring the environment.

Participants are lying on their stomachs (prone position). Give them the following instructions: Allow all extremities to have equal energy as you raise your extremities while keeping your balance centered in the navel. The head is not given more importance and the tail is felt to the end of the circle. It is important to feel the diagonals across the body (e.g., left hand to right foot, and right hand to left foot). This exercise should be done slowly and mindfully several times.

## CONCEPTION IMAGERY INSTRUCTIONS

When the relaxation and movement exercises are finished, participants are each given a single sheet of paper (approximately 48" × 48") and asked to lie down on the paper so that all of their body is contained within the paper boundaries. The paper is cut to this size so that participants have to assume some type of fetal position to fit onto the paper. While they are settling onto the paper, supplies of crayons and water-based markers are placed around the room near participants so that several people can use each supply conveniently at the end of the imagery visualization. Participants are instructed to allow their body to spontaneously move within the paper boundary in whatever manner they wish during the visualization period. This instruction may be repeated several times during the imagery session to assist participants in keeping their movements as flexible and fluid as possible.

At this stage, they are also reminded to focus quietly on their breathing, allowing themselves to gently take fuller and fuller breaths as they become more and more relaxed lying on the paper. At an appropriate time, when all participants are suffi-ciently relaxed, with their eyes closed, the first imagery instruction is given. Request participants "to imagine spontaneously a personal experience that occurred *today.*" They are given the general instructions that any personal image is appropriate. They are not to be concerned if the image does not appear to match the chronological sequence of the instructions; they are to allow whatever image or images spontaneously to appear without any judgment or evaluation. They are simply to observe the image or images.

After a pause of approximately forty-five seconds, they are instructed to allow an image to appear, or to evolve, from the *previous day,* from their personal experience (45 second pause). Continue, asking for: An image from the *previous week* (45 second pause). An image from the *previous month* (45 second pause). An image from the *previous year* (45 second pause).

The participants are now acquainted with the imagery procedure, and further instructions concerning their imagery responses can now be mentioned. The most important concept to emphasize at this time is that images arising might not be visual, but rather a body sensation or emotional feeling might emerge, with or without a clear visual image. It might be an auditory, tactile, taste, or smell sensation that occurs, again with or without a visual image. The only essential procedure to follow is allowing whatever image, sensation, thought, or feeling that arises to occur without evaluation; to simply observe it until the next instruction is given. Mention that participants may experience a drifting in and out of a quasi-sleep state, and assure them that they will still respond to instructions in a satisfactory manner.

Before continuing the instructions, mentally establish an approximate age baseline (e.g., age 30, 35, 40, 50, etc.) which the majority of the participants have reached. Instruct the group as a whole to recall spontaneously an image from that year. Younger participants should go back one year at a time from their present age after each instruction until the year mentioned includes them as well. If someone is particularly young relative to other group members, ask them to recall different images from the previous year until the year mentioned includes them.

Pause forty-five seconds. Instruct participants to recall an image from five years before the baseline age, and allow a forty-five second pause. Continue in five-year blocks until age twenty is reached, with a forty-five second pause between each block. Reassure participants that any image, feeling, or sensation that comes to body or mind is appropriate. If no particular image appears, the focus should go to their breathing, with awareness of the movements and sensations of their body, until the next instruction is given. Participants should allow the body to move spontaneously within the paper boundary. Inform participants that images may appear as fields of color, or light, or sound, or taste, or as a twitch or feeling from part of the body, as well as a personal image memory.

From age twenty, go back in two-year intervals until age ten is reached, allowing forty-five second pauses after each instruction. Participants may be concerned that images are coming from photographs that they are remembering, or stories that they may have been told about their childhood, and that these are not "real" images. Assure the group that any spontaneous imagery is appropriate, regardless of source. Repeating these instructions prepares participants for the time sequences prior to the first year and into prenatal time.

Count back from ten years to one year in one-year intervals, with a slightly shorter pause of thirty to thirty-five seconds after each instruction. After one year has been reached, begin counting back from eleven months in one-month blocks, with twenty second pauses between each block. Remind participants that as they become younger their image modalities might change, and that any experience of sensing, thinking, or feeling is appropriate. All they need do is allow and observe any spontaneous occurrence in the bodymind.

After one month, start at twenty-eight days and go back in two-day intervals until day ten is reached, pausing fifteen seconds after each interval. From day ten, count back one day at a time, with intervals of ten seconds after each day. After day one, start at twenty-two hours and go back in two-hour intervals, with five-second pauses, until the tenth hour. From hour ten, count back one hour at a time, with three- to five-second pauses, until hour one is reached. After the first hour, begin counting in five-minute blocks, starting at fifty-five minutes, pausing three to five seconds between each block, until the ten minutes is reached. Continue in one-minute intervals, with three- to five-second pauses, until one minute is reached. Continue counting from fifty-five seconds, in five-second blocks, to ten seconds, allowing approximately two to three seconds for each interval.

Count from ten seconds, in one-second intervals, with one-second pauses between each, until one second is reached. Then simply announce: "This is the time of your birth." A smooth transition from perinatal to prenatal is very important so that participants do not feel the imagery exercise is completed at the moment of birth. The therapist therefore must not linger at this point, but should allow only a three- to five-second interval before continuing the instructions. Care must be taken to maintain an even pacing of instructions so that there is no speed up or anticipation created as the moment of birth approaches.

We then continue: It is now one second *before* your birth (pause 2 seconds). One minute *before* your birth (pause 3 to 5 seconds). One hour before your birth (pause 5 seconds). One day before your birth (pause 10 seconds). One week before your birth (pause 15 seconds).

Now, clearly change references to time from *"time before birth"* to *"time after conception."* The next instruction is given: It is now eight months *after your conception* (pause 20 seconds). Continue counting down, one month at a time, to the first month, allowing a twenty-second pause after each month. After the first month, count the days from twenty-eight days in two-day intervals until the tenth day, with fifteen second pauses. At the tenth day, go back one day at a time, allowing ten seconds after each day, until day one is reached. Count from twenty-two hours after conception, in two-hour intervals, with five-second pauses, to the tenth hour after conception.

From hour ten, go back in one-hour intervals, with three- to five-second pauses, until the first hour after conception is reached. After the first hour, begin at fifty-five minutes after conception, go back in five-minute intervals until ten minutes after conception is reached, with three to five seconds between instructions. At ten minutes, change to one-minute intervals, with three- to five-second pauses, until one minute is reached. Beginning at fifty-five seconds after conception, go back in five-second intervals, allowing two- to three-second pauses, until ten seconds is reached. Continue in one-second intervals, with one-second pauses after each count, to one second after conception. Then announce: "This is the moment of your conception." Take particular care *not* to develop a "count down" quality in the voice during this final period before conception.

## DRAWING AND COLOR EXPRESSION EXERCISE

After a fifteen- to thirty-second pause, instruct participants to allow feelings, movements, sensations, and images to transform into colors, lines, patterns, and forms emanating from their bodymind. As these visual forms of expression emerge, the participant should experience them as transferring onto the blank white paper under the body. We describe the paper as blank photographic paper, ready to receive their color images and impressions. Tell the participants they will have approximately two to three minutes to allow their image to appear and to allow their body to assume their most natural position on the paper. At the end of that time period, announce that you (and your assistants, if any) will trace the body outline of each person onto the paper they are lying on.

The therapist (and assistants) then begins tracing each participant's body outline directly onto the paper. This tracing by "the other" is critical to the participant's success in color expression because it serves as a witnessing and also an "objective" boundary which each participant can respond to personally. The objectively drawn outline cuts through the tension of the large blank expanse of white paper, allowing the participant to "continue" the drawing. The outline also sets the kinespheric scale of the drawing and opens up the movement of the entire body as the participant completes the color expression process.

Outline the form of each participant with light brown crayon as he or she lies on the paper. This is done lightly so that participants can reinforce the body boundary or easily change the outline. Keep the crayon perpendicular to the paper so that the outline, especially of arms and legs, is not too skinny (or fat) because the crayon is too far inward (or outward). It is useful to imagine a light source directly above the part of the body that you are working on which casts an imaginary shadow onto the paper. (If, for example, the leg is raised at the knee, not touching the paper, it would still cast a shadow outline onto the paper which could be traced.) Tell them after their outline is completed, they may begin drawing their image, using as many colors of crayon and marker as they wish

Tell participants they will have approximately twenty to thirty minutes to draw and color. If someone does not start drawing right away, or if someone was "asleep" and didn't hear the instructions, suggest lying down on the paper in the same position as the body outline and to allow or imagine any colors, lines, shapes, and patterns that emerge into the consciousness to transfer onto the blank white paper. These same instructions would be given to a person who has drawn briefly, and is now looking at the paper without further drawing. In addition, he or she should be asked to experience an active dialogue, directly through the body, with the colors, lines, and patterns that have already been drawn onto the paper. Any additional images that spontaneously emerge could be transferred onto the paper in a continuing, active, process. This procedure can be repeated until it is felt that the drawing has been completed.

When almost all participants are nearing completion, or have finished drawing, instruct those still coloring that there are three to five minutes remaining before the next instructions will be given. Timing for the closing instructions will vary from group to group. When the majority have finished, bring the others to completion so that group energy does not dissipate. It is important to have all participants finish before the next series of instructions is given so that they can respond immediately and spontaneously.

## CONNECTIVE LANGUAGE EXERCISES

At the end of the drawing period everyone is given another sheet of paper (approximately the same size, 48" × 48") to work with. Ask that they respond to questions you are going to ask by writing with crayons or markers on the new sheet of paper, using any form of written language response that they desire, any grammatical form that they wish, without concern for correctness of spelling or syntax. It is important to respond spontaneously, without evaluating what is written. However, some form of intelligible language should be used, even if it is another language from childhood.

Ask each participant to choose the "*most important color*" used in the drawing and for them to allow "*that color*" to write on the paper any words, phrases, or sentences which spontaneously come to mind. This instruction is given in this format to give permission to the participant to continue responding from their intuitive function even within the more rational method of writing words. It is also the reason of continuing to use the large sheets of paper and crayons/markers rather than a pencil or pen. Tell participants they will have four to five minutes to write. At the end of that time, or when the majority have finished writing, give those who are still writing another half minute to finish.

Then instruct them to choose another color used in the drawing and use it to write down *"what they feel about the drawing,"* again allowing the color to write spontaneously without evaluation.

Allow a three- to five-minute interval for completion, and ask them to choose any color from the drawing and use it to write down *"what they see in the drawing."* Again allowing three to five minutes for their responses.

With some groups or individual clients, other or additional questions might be asked at this point. We have found these three general questions to be most useful and suitable for any general group format. Now participants are requested to clear the floor in preparation for the closing movement exercise.

## CLOSING MOVEMENT EXERCISE— NAVEL RADIATION VARIATION

All participants begin lying on the right side, curled in a fetal position. Movement is initiated from the navel, beginning on the in-breath. Instruct them to reach up and back with the upper limbs and head. The lower limbs and tail (coccyx) lengthen and reach back as the limbs extend. The upper and lower limbs reach toward one another. The shape created by the body in this extended state is like an arc or bow. At the point of full extension, the feeling in the body is like a pod bursting, allowing the exhalation to curl the body into flexion. The body shape changes from growing to shrinking as movement is synchronized with the incoming and the outgoing breath. This movement should be done five times or more, allowing a rhythm to develop. Participants will then roll on their backs to the left side and, from the fetal position, will begin this movement sequence again.

Now instruct participants to slowly roll from the fetal position onto their hands and knees. Then from this position, ask them to: "Slowly come to standing with their eyes closed following their body's natural movements." You could add that this sequence of movements, culminating in coming to verticality, recapitulates our early developmental experience of the self as it expresses *"Here I am . . . I am here."*

## CONCEPTION IMAGERY EXERCISE INTEGRATION

How the therapist proceeds from this point is mainly dependent on whether the exercise has been given as part of a one-day or weekend workshop, an ongoing workshop series, or as a session in an ongoing individual therapeutic relationship.

The Conception Imagery Exercise takes between one-and-one-half hours to two-and-one-half hours to complete, depending on group dynamics or the individual client. In an all-day or weekend workshop, individuals would have the next hour or so to spend by themselves reflecting on their images, movements, and words and writing down any feelings or thoughts on their experience in a journal. At the end of this individual period of time, depending on the theme and objectives of the workshop, we would either allow participants to voluntarily discuss the responses that they wrote down in answer to the three (or more) questions, share observations from their journal, or discuss their whole experience in general. Or we might continue exploring other imagery and movement exercises from our Psyche/Soma Imagery Series with a later sharing session.

In any case, we deliberately avoid any type of "show and tell" rational explanations or any type of interpretation about each individual's primary material of the actual drawing, either by the therapist or any other participant. If it seems required, depending on the group of participants, we would even tell participants to focus on their own drawing and not to compare their drawing with others, nor to offer any interpretations to others about their primary expressed drawings. Any type of interpretation by the therapist or others would stifle the internal processing within each individual as they continue integrating the drawing and words they have expressed. They would be asked to continue keeping a journal on any other intuitive sensing, feelings, and thoughts that might arise in body manifestations or other images throughout the rest of the day and in their dreams. Most of our participants are accustomed to keeping a dream journal and are involved in some form of ongoing analysis, therapy, or exploration with a qualified professional.

If the exercise has been given as a single session in an ongoing series, participants would be advised to take their drawing and written responses home with them so that they could have the opportunity to review and reflect on the images, movements, and words they have created during the session. They would be asked to note in their journal any other intuitive sensing, feelings, and thoughts that might arise in dreams, body manifestations, or other images before their next session. Occasionally, if the therapist and an individual decide that the power of the expressed imagery is too strong for an individual to integrate alone, they might begin the process of integration immediately or arrange a subsequent therapeutic session on a timely basis.

## REFERENCES

Chodorow, J. (1982). Dance/movement and body experience in analysis. In M. Stein (Ed.), *Jungian Analysis*. La Salle: Open Court Publishing.

Chodorow, J. (1984). To move and be moved. *Quadrant, 17* (2), 39-48.

Cohen, B. B. (1983). Letters to Bonnie Bainbridge Cohen. *Contact Quarterly*, 6-7.

Cohen, B. B. (1985). *The basic principles and techniques of body-mind centering*. Amherst: The School for Body-Mind Centering.

Dossey, L. (1982). *Space, time and medicine*. Boulder, CO: Shambhala.

Hillman, J. (1979). *The dream and the underworld*. New York: Harper and Row.

Hillman, J. (1983). *Archetypal psychology: A brief account*. Dallas, TX: Spring Publications.

Houston, J. (1982). *The possible human: A course in extending your physical, mental and creative abilities*. Los Angeles, CA: Tarcher.

Kalff, D. (1980). *Sandplay: A psychotherapeutic approach to the psyche*. Santa Monica, CA: Sigo Press.

Mindell, A. (1982). *Dreambody: The body's role in revealing the self*. Santa Monica, CA: Sigo Press.

Sheehan, P., & Bayliss, D. (1984). Time estimation, imagination, and hypnosis. In A. Sheikh (Ed.), *International review of mental imagery* (Vol. 1). New York: Human Science Press.

Verny, T., & Kelly, J. (1981). *The secret life of the unborn child*. New York: Delta.

von Franz, M.-L. (1980). *Alchemy: An introduction to the symbolism and the psychology.* Toronto: Inner City Books.

Winnicott, D. (1974). *Playing and reality.* New York: Penguin Books.

Woodman, M. (1980). *The owl was a baker's daughter: Obesity, anorexia nervosa, and the repressed feminine.* Toronto: Inner City Books.

Woodman, M. (1982). *Addiction to perfection: The still unravished bride.* Toronto: Inner City Books.

Woodman, M. (1984). Psyche/soma awareness. *Quadrant, 17* (2), 25-37.

Woodman, M. (1985). *The pregnant virgin: A process of psychological transformation.* Toronto: Inner City Books.

# CHAPTER 21

# *Images and Depth Psychology: The Legacy of Carl Jung*

## *DOROTHY SAWYER*

What follows is for those who can adopt a "beginner's mind." It is a starting point, a kind of map showing high points, an overall view that can be of use to a layperson or professional caregiver who is not yet acquainted with the ways of Carl Jung.

Carl Gustav Jung (1875-1961) was a Swiss physician whose contributions on the uses of imagery have importantly influenced Western notions about how the mind works. During a lifetime of observing his own images and those of patients, he created a specialized language for the imaginal life. History, literature, art, and folklore added richness to the background from which this language emerged. Some of Jung's vocabulary for confronting unconscious images moved into common usage (e.g., *introvert* and *extravert*).

In addition to language, Jung's techniques on the uses of imagery have penetrated the working styles of three generations of psychotherapists. There may no longer be a real "Jungian," and perhaps there never was; but Jung's creative approach brought permanent changes to the professional and personal worlds of those seriously interested in the human psyche and how it functions. It is helpful to know at the outset that a single chapter can only be an indicator for further study. Just as any map is an interesting beginning for study, it is not equivalent to the bigger experience it represents.

Although dream work was the most common way that Jung worked with images from what lies below consciousness, an introduction to his uses of imagery might best begin with *active imagination.* Those who have used imagery for purposes of personal growth, physical change, or performance will recognize aspects of this technique.

## ACTIVE IMAGINATION

It cannot be said that Jung invented this method for interacting with unconscious images; but he gave it a name and elevated it to an important status in his psychotherapy practice.

*Active Imagination* refers to an interplay or dialogue between the conscious ego and unconscious contents. This is a way of getting in touch with the ongoing drama that continues below consciousness while we are awake, of which we are usually unaware. There is a kind of internal activity going on behind normal consciousness at all times. *Active Imagination* is not the same as day-dreaming, which is less purposeful. In *active imagination,* one can work with images from dreams, fantasies, free drawing, story telling, spontaneous movement, or other creative endeavors.

In *active imagination,* one is dealing with a middle ground, where "neither conscious nor unconscious has an unfair advantage over the other" (Spoto, 1989, p. 114).

Andrew Samuels, an analyst in London, writes

> The idea of active imagination derives from Jung's discovery that the unconscious has an independent symbol-producing capacity. Jung found that this could be used analytically and designated working with such material *active imagination* [author's emphasis] to distinguish it from passive fantasizing and also to emphasize that the patient may have to make choices based on the outcome of his active imagination. (1985, p. 12)

To prepare for *active imagination,* it is necessary to bring one's self into a quiet state of mind in a place free of interruptions. One can begin with a mood, a dream to dream onward, a part of the body, an illness . . . the choice is up to the imager, possibly in cooperation with a therapist.

Quietly bringing attention to the image will usually activate it. Some responsive "others" exist in that subliminal world; they are not really "other" and can converse with the ego. It is not necessary or desirable to push or force or hurry anything along. The images have their own time. Characters emerging from that mostly ignored world of the psyche can be witty, surprising, instructive, or very wise. In relating to them, the ego maintains its own boundaries and identity. These kinds of relationships can be compared to the way an analyst enters into a patient's drama but retains personal boundaries (Samuels, 1985, p. 202). An example of a first try at active imagination from a participant in a group is quoted below.

> It took many trials before I met with success. When it finally came, it was most dramatic, like a floodgate bursting open. The torrent of imagery which flowed was striking and intensely vivid, sometimes unfolding like a narrative story. It lasted five minutes and took me an hour to record.

Los Angeles analyst Janet Dallett has written about this kind of experience:

> To permit that other point of view to come up, most people have to find a way to set aside that critical judging mode of the ego. At this stage, the ego must simply observe uncritically what comes up, remaining alert, but not filtering out anything. (Dallett, 1982, p. 178)

Jung comments:

> We must be able to let things happen in the psyche. Consciousness is forever interfering—helping, correcting and negating—never leaving the psychic process to grow in peace . . . To begin with, the task consists only in observing objectively how a fragment of fantasy develops. (Jung, 1929, p. 16)

Warnings are sometimes given about using the process of active imagination. A more conservative view suggests doing this only with a trained helper. The reasoning is that without responsible guidance, the opening of an unconscious store of images can be overwhelming, particularly for those whose ego structures are not very secure. Others suggest a serious do-it-yourself approach. Analysts may suggest that issues for which there is not sufficient time in the analytical session be addressed by the client between sessions through active imagination. The results are then addressed in a therapy session in the same way as dream images, described below in the sections on dream work.

Several more frequently used forms of active imagination are those connected with spontaneous drawing, movement, working with clay, and other free-form activities that can also be called dialogues with aspects of the unconscious (Matoon, 1978; Stein, 1982).

## FREE DRAWING

At times this is done with the non-dominant hand to avoid automatic and structured responses. In using drawing to evoke images from the unconscious, one is not trying to produce a work of art. Drawing can be done with or without color, can be done in isolation or with a group, or with a partner, and is best done with minimum planning and thinking. A young man in his late twenties experiencing this form of activity for the first time, reports

> When I was done, I had a black and white drawing of a wheel with eight spokes, each holding a figure of special significance. This was a very personal statement of myself at that time, yet I was not yet satisfied with the result. Something was missing—COLOR!
>
> My third and final drawing I colored in crayon . . . Without knowing why, I kept enlarging the center of the wheel, and finally realized it was taking the shape of a butterfly. This was a very emotionally moving experience. As I completed my final drawing, I felt in some way that I had emerged from a cocoon and was now much freer in my ability to express my feelings to the others in the group.

The words "without knowing why . . ." suggest a quality that is wanted—of something emerging on its own, not governed by conscious ego intentions. Surprises of this kind are a good sign that a two-way conversation is going on. Conversing with unknown or little known parts of the self begins to integrate those aspects of our selves that need our attention. We can begin to see *complexes* which were invisible or unclear before the imaging experience. Non-verbal forms like drawing can move an imager in ways different from those of mere verbalizing.

## SAND TRAY PLAY

Two trays can be provided: one with dry sand, another with damp sand, which is more moldable. There is also a collection of small objects which can include people, buildings, vehicles, rocks, animals, demons, trees. . . . This form of active imagination has been used successfully with very young children as well as adults. Here the interplay between conscious and unconscious may be done in silence, or with the player conversing between the conscious self and the images. If it can be said that there is a technique, it is simply that of allowing play with the sand and figures. Done for a part of continuing sessions, it is often possible to see a developmental aspect as the play/work continues. A sense of purpose often emerges. The helper/analyst is a supportive presence, just being there as the arrangements in the sand speak for themselves.

## BODY MOVEMENT

This form, like the other non-verbal forms of imagining, is usually facilitated by a therapist or group leader. In actual experience, it is not unusual or difficult to elicit responses from the body in the form of movement. A mood or emotion can be felt by any or all body parts—arms, legs, chest, right side, left side, elbows, knees.

It is possible to portray symbolically a current situation which exists in the conscious life. An example is the feeling of being trapped. What posture does one take? How does one explore this trap? Is it a cage, a box, or what? How does one move within it, if at all? How can one explore it? In what ways might one find escape? It may not even be necessary to ask these questions, as movements arise spontaneously.

> The therapist most often suggests a structure for self-directed movement that will enable discovery and development of themes from the unconscious. The movement process may produce an overall impression, a repetitive gesture, a certain body state or image that invites further exploration . . . Verbalization is an important part of the process. There is usually some verbal expression and exchange before, after, and occasionally during the movement. (Chodorov, 1982, p. 196)

The movement experience may be only a few minutes in length, or twenty minutes, or more. It is natural to have a quiet, reflective pause when the movement is over. Drawing, poetry, or just sitting quietly can be a bridge to talking about the experience. As in other forms of active imagination, talking may be necessary.

## MUSIC

The use of music with imaginal activities is debatable. Indeed, it is used by some therapists to evoke images and responses. However, it can be convincingly argued that culturally conditioned music denies one a direct experience with one's own unconscious contents. There is something to be said for the pure experience without the kind of powerful emotional prompting that music has built into it.

## MOLDING CLAY

The clay is soft and workable. Time must be taken to let the form or forms emerge. Let the clay become alive in one's hands. It has its own way of growing or diminishing here and there. The result does not have to look like something in the outer world to have meaning.

Sometimes when partners work together facing each other as they mold clay, complementary objects emerge, to the surprise and satisfaction of both partners.

## OTHER FORMS OF ACTIVE IMAGINATION

Story telling, creating songs with or without words, writing poetry or original personal myths, psychodrama—all can be useful ways of actively imagining. When work is done in a group, teams of players can produce collective dramas or games. Among other benefits, spontaneous play can be a remarkable release of energy after a long day's journey through the psyches of all present.

## JUNG'S LANGUAGE

Language can be called "a way of looking at things." Mathematics is a language, "a way of looking at things." There is also a language of science and one of music. "Freud and Jung are also two ways of speaking," says James Hillman in *The Myth of Analysis* (1972, p. 118).

There is much diversity of style among those who have written about how Jungians treat images. But language may be what unites them most—even if parts of that language are hotly debated. If he were alive today, Jung doubtless would not be a "Jungian," if by that one means inflexible and unchanging. He did teach many independent personalities during his lifetime, perhaps no one of whom would meet a preconceived notion of what it is to be "Jungian."

The ideas described by Jung were not new with him; many of the concepts are ancient. His unique contribution was to organize words and concepts in a way that "rings true" when used in psychotherapy, with implications for health as well as pathology. The framework "works" for those who are profoundly disturbed, but also for those who are functioning well and wish to pursue an individual search for wholeness and balance.

### Individuation

An individual search for meaning, Jung thought, was the task of the second part of life. He called it the *individuation* process. The first large task in life, he said, is to strengthen an ego structure through which one can relate to people, objects, and events of the world around one. Somewhere in mid-life, the individual starts an inward journey to find meaning—throughout the aging process and, finally, death. Among other ways of standing alone in his time, Jung was unique for developing a language particular to mid-life and beyond.

### WHO ARE WE? EGO, PERSONA, self, Self?

### Ego

While some have called the ego the center of conscious life, Jung declared it cannot be called the center of the psyche. "This entity is responsible for identity and personal continuity in time and space . . ." (Samuels, 1985, p. 56). The *ego* can be considered as a sense of "I" that relates us to conscious life. It can also be called an interface between what is conscious and what lies below consciousness. It is what, in common everyday terms, we view as a *self* with a lower case s. The Self (capital S), of which the mandala is a symbol, is the archetype of unity and totality. The term can refer to the psyche as a whole, functioning as a unit, to the central archetype of order, when viewed from the point of view of the ego, and the archetypal basis of the ego.

> The reality that is described by the theoretical relationship between the ego and the archetypal Self is one of the most mysterious in all of human experience. It is paradoxical. In one sense the ego is the Self, at least that part of the Self that exists in empirical consciousness, acting and living in the world of consensual reality. But in an equally profound sense, the ego is as subordinate to the Self as man is to God in traditional theological terms . . . the archetypal Self is quite a different concept from the uncapitalized "self" of everyday usage in such phrases as "I am not myself today." (Hall, 1986, p. 41)

The *dream-ego* refers to the character in the dream doing the dreaming. The *dream ego* may be viewing the dream, or participating in the action, or both. It is only a part of the "I" which is the center of consciousness.

## Persona

Persona, from the Greek word for mask, is the appearance one presents to the outer world. The role mask might be that of "teacher," "nice guy," "good mother," "statesman." It is an interface between the inside and outside. Images with an interfacing function can appear as symbols in dreams and fantasies. Some such images could be clothing, buildings, or vehicles.

## Conscious

*Consciousness* is a strange phenomenon. The *conscious* can be used as a noun, meaning that of which we are aware. The *conscious* is what is readily available in ego life. We cannot be conscious of much at any one time. It is an "intermittent phenomenon" (Mahoney, 1966, p. 40). On diagrams or maps of the psyche, it is usually depicted as a space in which the *ego* is a central figure. The *collective conscious* refers to shared cultural values, assumptions, and forms.

The *unconscious,* all that is below consciousness, has retrievable aspects, such as personal memories and learnings from the past, things that can be brought to mind with some effort. This part of the *unconscious* is called the *personal unconscious,* a store of memory from each individual life.

Deeper still lies what Jung called the *objective unconscious* or the *collective unconscious.* It is that part of the psyche which all human beings share by virtue of their humanity. Here, as in an underground stream, is a deeper way of knowing. Here, he said, lie those patterns which are comparable to instincts in animals, the patterns he called *archetypes.*

## ARCHETYPES

An *archetype* can be understood as a potential for experience. Though archetypes might be named and talked about, they can never be made fully conscious. Jung associated them with the material in myth, fairy tales, and other folklore, as well as with bigger-than-life images that human beings sometimes report from their dreams, fantasies, and creative works. *Archetypal* images can have a special awesome quality, a deeply moving significance. Jung assigned the term *numinous* to that quality. *Numinosity* is commonly attributed to religious experiences, not necessarily connected with a conventional belief system.

The Greek pantheon is a collection of archetypal patterns, as is a deck of Tarot cards. It can be said that some forms of mental illness result from an individual's belief that he/she has *become* the archetype; this resembles a kind of possession. It can also be said that for every extreme found among the Greek gods, there is a compensating opposite, just as there is in the human psyche.

One of the relatively familiar archetypes is that of the mother. As infants, there is something within each of us, a felt sense of something or someone who nurtures, protects, allows us time and space for growth, is moist, dark, warm, and permissive. In the infant's life, the biological mother or a substitute provides enough of these qualities for something in the infant to attach a deep potential for *mother* to the person who carries these traits. Language confirms the impression by providing words for the experience—mama, mommy, or mother. The archetype is bigger than the actual person can be, the merely human one who assumes the role. But a child attaches bigger-than-life qualities and usually bigger-than-life expectations to that finite mother. Variations on the mother archetype are the *earth mother, bad mother, devouring mother, virgin mother.*

Some other archetypal potentials are father, wise man, clown, magical child, "trickster," priest, healer. Part of the individuation process is to realize that these potentials are within us all, to become aware of them and their power to move in us, at the same time knowing that we are not ourselves the archetypes.

### Shadow

Parts of one's personality that have been driven inward, those traits one considers undesirable, that which is disowned, unrecognized, undeveloped, or unfamiliar, are called the *shadow.* Shadow figures may appear in dreams or be the object of one's conscious derision or criticism, usually viewed as existing in someone other than one's self. *Shadow* does not necessarily mean undesirable, however; shadow figures in dreams can provide for us a more complete view of our own possibilities. "Shadowy" figures such as a black shark or a dark brown bear can suggest a concentrated form of life energy which would be of much value in a life of unassertive other-directedness. A dream personality of a different nationality or sex can possess traits that, if developed, could enrich and add depth toward more conscious living. More about the *shadow* is described in the section on typology (p. 263).

### Anima and Animus

In each person, male or female, is an inner presence of the opposite sex. Jung called that presence in a male the *anima,* and for a female he called the inner male presence the *animus.* This kind of (mostly unconscious) presence may, like the *shadow,* have qualities that would be of much value to conscious life. In dreams, the *anima* or *animus* can, like the *shadow,* have qualities of being disowned or under-developed.

The terms *anima-ridden* and *animus-ridden* suggest that the *anima* or *animus* as much as possesses a person, *has* that person, rather than the person having it. An anima-ridden man, according to earlier Jungian thought, can behave as an inferior female—touchy, gossipy, moody or "bitchy." An animus-ridden female can, similarly, be like an inferior male—critical, pushy, opinionated, or life-stopping.

A man in whom an unconscious anima is very strong can seem to lack clear boundaries. He may at the same time be compassionate, nurturing, and able to express tenderness without embarrassment. A woman with a strong animus may seem argumentative and often missing the mark, but she may also be able to exercise her assertive intellect effectively and understand a man's point of view enough to be a friendly and comfortable companion to men.

Since Jung and his early students lived in a time that differed dramatically from our own in concepts of what it is to be female or male, notions about *anima* and *animus* are evolving. Our ideas about *anima* and *animus* are culturally driven, and even now history is casting new light on what it is to be masculine or feminine.

The *anima* or *animus* has the role of connecting a man or woman with unconscious life. Consequently, dream or fantasy images involving this kind of archetype can at times have a *numinous* quality. At best, these figures can lead an individual to enrichment of life and progress on the individuation journey. At worst, left unconscious they can cause havoc. It is not the maleness or femaleness of the traits that causes severe misunderstandings; it is the unconsciousness behind the behavior.

## ATTITUDE TYPES

### Introvert and Extravert

Much of the imbalance and emptiness in the lives of his patients Jung attributed to a tendency to become one-sided, valuing one version of truth over another. He perceived that Freud and Adler had valid but seemingly opposing points of view, and that their use of language attributed value in different ways. From these examples, along with many others, Jung concluded that there are two major ways of viewing reality, and that extreme reliance on either one leads to imbalance. One major way he called *introversion,* the other *extraversion.*

*Introversion* is a movement of psychic energy inward, toward the subject; *Extraversion,* a movement of psychic energy outward, toward the object.

> The introvert . . . remains within himself, putting together a system of his own with which to cope with the outside world. The extravert . . . goes out to the visible

world with complete assurance, drawn as by an irresistible attraction . . . Introspection, he feels, is unhealthy. . . . (Martin, 1955, pp. 18-19)

No one person can be purely either introvert or extravert. Usually one side
predominates, but it is possible for a personality to favor both attitudes about equally.
It is also possible for individuals to change during a lifetime, from one attitude to the
other, or to shift back and forth from time to time, seeming to prefer first one point
of view, then another.

The importance of these concepts in imagery is that frequently dreams and
fantasies will depict attitudes of a type compensatory to that of the conscious life.
Memorable examples of compensation from literature have depicted a quiet and
retiring man or woman who has fallen desperately in love with an outgoing night-club
singer or con artist.

## JUNG'S TYPOLOGY:
## DOMINANT AND INFERIOR FUNCTIONS

### Psychological Functions:
### *Thinking* and *Feeling; Intuitive* and *Sensing*

These are two pairs of opposites. Jung noticed that people appear to process
reality in one of four major ways, in addition to introverted or extraverted attitudes.
The most favored function he named the *dominant* function, the least favored, the
*inferior* function.

A *dominant* function is supported by the next strongest function, called an
*auxiliary* function. There is no special name for the relatively weak function which is
weaker than the auxiliary function and almost as weak as the most primitive, or
*inferior* function.

*Thinking* and *feeling* are *judging* functions, and are also called *rational* functions.
*Intuitive* and *sensing* functions are termed *perceiving* functions, also called *nonrational* functions.

A person with *thinking* as a *dominant* function defines, names, and categorizes—
observes the world and tries to have it "make sense." A *feeling* person's way of
processing is to make a decision about value: "I like it" or "I don't like it;" "It is good"
or "It is bad," "acceptable" or "disagreeable." Thinking persons judge their experience in one way, feeling persons judge in another.

Those who are strong in the thinking function do have feelings, and a pre-
dominantly feeling person can think. Each one tends, however, to be somewhat
compulsive when using an inferior function, and also very sensitive about the
results. Marie Louise von Franz amusingly suggests that, just as a thinking person
can easily have his feelings hurt, so can a feeling person have his thinkings hurt.
If the pressures of life are such that it becomes absolutely necessary to mobilize
an inferior function, the effort can be made; however, if a flaw is found in the
effort, there is a tendency to want to dump the whole thing. "It is like walking on eggs;
people cannot stand any criticism here" (von Franz-Hillman, 1971, p. 9).

Besides super-sensitivity around one's inferior function, there is also distrust of those who have that function as a strong one. One is suspicious of someone whose values appear to be so markedly and annoyingly different from one's own. Also, one can tend to over-value such people. On such overvaluing has many a love affair or promotion been based! A corporation executive used to thinking and sensing facility can be deeply impressed with an employee's easy communication style with factory workers; a creative intuitive thinker can be overly impressed with someone who organizes and sorts with ease (or knows where the car-keys are; see *intuitive* and *sensing*).

The *inferior function* can on rare occasions have a quality of being unspoiled, fresh, and lively. It is practiced much less often than the easier functions, but sometimes it can come through with a remarkable purity. A person with thinking as a dominant function may have an occasional impressive power to express feeling. A dominantly feeling person may write a thesis of exceptional intellectual impact.

*Intuitive* and *sensing* are types that get their information either from the unconscious or directly from the senses. The *intuitive* can seem to predict events before they happen, or to know what nearby people are going to say before the words are out. This kind of person seems to get an enormous amount of information very quickly, from "one knows not where." In fact, intuitives can be so good at their hunches that they can tend to become over-confident and be very wrong when they are wrong.

Someone who has a dominant *sensing* function perceives through the senses. What one can see, hear, feel, touch, and taste in the here-and-now has reality and that can seem to be the only reality. This sort of person is not likely to think that dreams and fantasies are of much value, and may report that they never dream, or just cannot see visual images when nothing is there. If life events push this sort of person into an experience involving the intuition, there can be an instant conversion (a result of overvaluing what the intuitive accepts as ordinary). The intuitive, on the other hand, may tend to overvalue those aspects of sensing that would make everyday life easier—for instance, knowing with certainty where physical effects are. Lost objects are a constant source of pain to the intuitive, who may repeat, "Now, where did I put my glasses?" while the glasses are perched on that same person's forehead. Both intuitive- and sensing-oriented persons are *perceiving*—one from the unconscious, the other from the senses.

One type usually cannot easily understand or patiently tolerate the apparent clumsiness of a person with an opposing dominant function.

It is usual in describing a client in terms of psychological typology to assign an *attitude type*—introvert or *extravert*—together with a *dominant* function and an *auxiliary* function; for example, an *introverted thinking/sensing* combination or an *extraverted feeling/intuitive.* . . . There are a number of possible permutations.

Qualities associated with an inferior function may appear in fantasies as figures of the same sex or opposite sex as the fantasizer/dreamer. A figure of the same sex Jung referred to as a *shadow* figure. Images of the opposite sex were called *anima* or *animus* figures. The following are examples of both shadow and animus from the dream of an introverted intuitive/thinking female.

I am in a school and I enter a classroom. Marilyn Monroe is there. She is a housekeeper, and has in her hand a note, a testimonial from a male rock star, in appreciation to her for having cleaned his apartment.

The dream image of Marilyn Monroe as a housekeeper can be called a *shadow* figure, being of the same sex as the dreamer. The male rock star, though not seen in the dream, is an *animus* presence. Actors and actresses often have a strong *feeling* function (opposing the dreamer's *thinking*), and certainly good housekeeping tends to be something requiring special effort for an intuitive person. A rock star is extremely *extraverted,* in opposition to the *introverted* conscious life of the dreamer.

Archetypal figures like the *shadow, anima,* or *animus* have qualities that are less conscious than, and in contrast to, the conscious orientation. As the lesser known, unknown, undeveloped, or disowned qualities, shadow figures can appear in dreams and fantasies as persons of a minority race or nationality. At times they may wear dark clothes or have an atmosphere of foreignness to the imager. Though these figures may appear as creatures other than human, the term *shadow* does not necessarily imply "better" or "worse" than the conscious attitude; it is simply the less conscious. Since these images are compensatory, they can bring powerful new insights for a better-balanced life.

## COMPLEXES

In the Jungian definition, *complexes* are entities sometimes consisting of a great number of elements clustered around a nucleus: the original disturbance point.

> The term *"complex"* is one that has suffered considerably in the "intolerable wrestle with words and meanings". . . As Jung originally used it, the meaning was exactly that of the roots from which the word derives: something *com-plex* twisted together . . . The personal unconscious . . . is full of such twistings together: sore points, explosive topics, earlier attitudes we have failed to assimilate. And there are other "twistings together" of a more permanent kind, essential parts of the human psyche, which behave like so many independent personalities. . . . (Martin, 1955, p. 71)

*Complexes* have a repetitive or cyclic quality. They keep coming around to interfere with living one's life freely. A few examples are "mother complex," "Christ complex," "victim complex," "Oedipus complex." Complexes seem to have wills of their own, invading conscious intentions and even physiological processes (upsetting digestion, causing the heart to race, tensing muscles, causing other stress reactions). Events in childhood, and an individual's childhood responses to those events, result in *complexes* that remain part of adult life. Andrew Samuels, London analyst, writes

> The concept of a complex was Jung's way of linking the personal and the collective. Outer experiences in infancy and throughout life cluster round an archetypal core. Events in childhood, and particularly internal conflicts, provide this personal aspect. A complex is not just the clothing for one particular archetype (that would, more accurately, be an archetypal image) but an agglomerate of the actions of several archetypal patterns, imbued with personal experience and affect. (1985, p. 47)

Complexes seem to swallow large amounts of psychic energy, or *libido.* This use of the word—*libido* as psychic energy—differs from Freud's use of the word as sexual energy.

The unconscious, Jung said, serves to compensate for the one-sidedness of the conscious life. The demands of consciousness, plus one's need to keep up a *persona* and keep down the *shadow,* can lead us away from sanity and life. In a technical society that richly rewards strong *sensing* and *thinking* functions, the contemplating and relating parts of life are easily undervalued. Emphasis on "tangibles only" overrides attention to the inner life, and at times the imaginative life.

Powerful images contacted through dreams, active imagination, fantasies, drawing, and other means can provide a necessary balance for sanity. Life can then be more than mere survival.

## ATTITUDE IN WORKING WITH IMAGES

In learning something of the Jungian glossary of terms, we already have some clues as to how therapists using Jungian techniques work with images. Besides presupposing a working knowledge of these terms, there is also an attitude of not presupposing what the image means to the imager. The dreamer knows better than anyone if an interpretation fits, and it may take some time to find a good fit. Great care is taken not to cut off the life of an image with a hasty interpretation. One learns to respect the image, to stay with it, to let it have its own life. Letting the images become conscious, learning to live with them, allowing them their own rhythm—all are a part of a hold-it-lightly attitude. As with holding a handful of sand, clutching causes the images and their unique potential to be lost.

## TECHNIQUES LEARNED BY THE CLIENT

Some techniques, such as recording personal dreams and images, must first be acquired by the client, who is called the *analysand* in a one-to-one analytic consultation. The terms "client" and "patient" are also used. Study groups, therapy groups, and unled informal groups may be found which call themselves "Jungian." As with individuals, informal groups not led by an analyst/therapist use whatever resources their earnest and sincere efforts find available, perhaps including occasional visits from practicing therapists or other expert speakers and leaders.

Dream work is a major way in which Jung-oriented therapists work with images. Dreams come to us relatively intact from the unconscious. A personal journal, with pen or pencil, is left handy at the bedside so that dreams may be recorded as soon as possible after they occur. A small tape recorder has been found useful by many people who find that dreams escape easily. It can help to lie quietly for a while upon awakening. Movement or an abrupt entry into the objective world can cause a dream to slip away. Dreams can be recorded in as much detail as can be remembered, leaving out nothing. If the image was one of a gate or door, what size was it? What style? What shape and age? Of what materials? In what surroundings? Connected with anything? Is anyone or anything else there? Is something that would appropriately be there absent? Reporting the dream in great detail means taking care to notice textures, temperatures, color or the absence of color, and any peripheral objects or people seeming to want to escape notice.

Include the emotional tone of the dream; and thoughts and feelings upon awakening. It is helpful to date the entries and describe briefly the conscious situation of awake life at the time of the dreaming. Experienced analysts advise: don't edit, sweeten, or in any way change the dream as you write. Do not try to interpret at this stage. Simply record the dream or the fantasy as it occurred. Be faithful to the images just the way they are.

The necessity to record a dream immediately must be taken seriously. People with excellent memories have believed that an extremely vivid dream will surely be remembered in the morning, but that is often not the case. It happens often, too, that people will record dreams in a half-asleep state in the middle of the night, to find that their own writing looks strangely alien in the morning. None of it would have remained conscious, had the dream images not been recorded immediately. Some people will report that they never do dream. This has been proved not to be possible; everyone dreams. Learning to capture dream images can be helped by continuing to pay attention to whatever does occur, even if it is only an emotional tone upon awakening. Usually, efforts are rewarded with more vivid dreaming and more frequent remembering.

Even a tiny fragment of a dream which seems of no use to the dreamer can be amplified and made meaningful. The example below demonstrated this point.

The dream of a thirty-year-old woman: "I am sitting with my sister." End of dream. Question: How do you feel when sitting with your sister? Answer: "Warm and comfortable." Question: What is it like to be with your sister? Answer: "Right now I miss my sister. She is thousands of miles away, and I miss her. But when I'm with her, this is how I feel—warm and supported, and someone will pick up the pieces. It feels as though, if I were to get to the end of my own resources, there will still be someone there to see that things will be all right. It feels as though I am not the only one in the world to do the things I must do."

The dreamer reports that since the dream, she has been able to "let go," at those times when there is simply not much more of her to give. There is a kind of quiet knowing that the world will go on even if she does not hold it together personally. A sister part of herself just lets her be, supporting her when needed.

A certain area of the journal or dream log is set aside for relevant associations that come up in the recording of the dream. Even a brief fleeting image of a relative, a friend, or a work location can be useful. By recording the dreams faithfully, one may notice the emergence of a dream series from time to time. A series refers to repeated dreaming about similar themes, which may or may not be presented in the same kind of images. Sometimes the dream life seems to say, "Let me put it another way." It is also possible for several themes to interweave. Dreams in a series can be interpreted first as a single experience, then with a long-term perspective.

The same kinds of questions are asked if images come from *active imagination,* guided imagery, meditation, free drawing, finger painting, or any of the many ways of experiencing less conscious material. One must, however, remember that these other (non-dream) methods are partly conscious or consist of a dialogue between the ego and the spontaneous evocations of the unconscious. One is then working in a borderline area between conscious and unconscious. The work is then with some ego involvement and one must be aware of possible ego contamination. There is also the obvious fact that we are not working with material from so deep a level of the psyche as are dreams. We are more likely to get archetypal material from dreams. And yet, examples of archetypal significance have been evoked through non-dream images. It is also possible to approach episodes in the waking life as though they are dreams, with often surprising and helpful results.

## A SESSION WITH A JUNG-ORIENTED THERAPIST

Some facts about daily life—especially concerning the forty-eight-hour period just before the time of a dream to be discussed—may be reviewed before or after the relating of a dream or dreams.

The images, from whatever source, are reported by the client as well as can be remembered, or are conveyed from a dream log. Sometimes the dreams or active imagination experience will have a clear outline or form, with a *setting* and a *cast of characters*, an *exposition,* or description of a situation. The *dream ego* may have been watching the action or may have been a part of the action, or both simultaneously. The dream can have a *development*, gradually leading to a *crisis, a culmination,* or *peripeteia,* and finally, a *solution* or *lysis.* If the dream has these features, they are noted. Many dreams and other forms of imaging, however, do not have that clear a pattern. Whatever the images were, it is still possible to proceed with the next step of *amplification.* Even the absence of a dream is something to work on.

*Amplification* means enlarging upon the associations of the imager with the images. What feelings were evoked? What memories? What connection with what significant others? What relationships with previous images? Amplification is made through personal associations, especially those connected with a current situation, through cultural associations, and finally, through archetypal associations.

Body language, tone of voice, gestures, or facial expressions might all give cues to a dreamer which he would be lacking on his own, for he cannot see himself as he relates the dream. Omissions (upon repeating) or mispronunciations might also be cues. Sometimes lively responses will indicate that something almost got away—"Oh! I almost forgot something!" or "Well, there was something else, but it isn't important, so I won't even mention it." Experience shows these are often important additions.

The dream reporter may use certain words or a family of words repeatedly, even in describing differing images or differing situations within the imager. Without making assumptions or premature interpretations, it is possible to report such repetitions to the client in addition to body language, facial expressions, or gestures—simply and objectively. For instance, "I noticed that when you said someone called you a perfectionist in your dream, you had a little smile," or "Several times as you were describing your brother in your dream, your hand made a downward pushing motion." Surprising or incongruent gestures can be especially interesting, for they suggest that something unconscious is going on.

In listening to dream reports, the sounds of the words—puns—may supply important clues to the symbolic meanings of images. Someone dreams of walking about without feet. Is one then "de-feeted" or lacking in stand-points, or what? Strangely, these are not at all absurd pursuits. Words are themselves images and can resonate on the level of what they sound like rather than their dictionary meanings.

The analyst will know something of the life history of the analysand, and both can be aware of the life context at the time of the imaging or dreaming. By virtue of training and experience, the analyst will also have a background in myth, fairy tales, and powerful cultural symbols.

*Amplification* is not the same as free association, which is one association followed by another and another, moving away from the original image. In amplification, one stays close to the image. Personal associations are sought. What comes to mind with this image? Of whom am I reminded; in what context? Do colors, numbers, or moods connected with the image bring further associations? Jung believed that dream images were not a disguise for something else, even though presented in symbolic language. Remember, too, that the images belong to the imager. The dream belongs to the dreamer. "Only the imager knows for sure" applies to interpretations; no matter how beguiling it is to speculate on "interpretations of convenience," it is only the one who has the images who can, finally, know what fits and what does not.

Besides personal association, cultural associations are sought to amplify the image. Archetypal associations may also be found. This is where one can most fairly assume that the analyst has more to offer than the analysand, for his training would have given him/her access to myth, folklore, and religious symbolism, where archetypal images abound.

Facile interpretation is to be avoided in favor of letting the image have its own development. A number of Jungians have suggested that the image is often powerful enough to work its own healing without much help from interpretation. Finding quick answers can close off the life of the image before its full meaning can be felt. If an interpretation does seem to fit, it must fit the whole dream or the whole situation. Some images from dreams or active imagination continue to yield magnanimously for years, during which time newer images can also be explored.

It is always helpful to have a written record of what transpired, along with amplifications and possible interpretations.

### JUNG GROUPS

A group provides a kind of laboratory in which to test new ways of relating or being. It makes it possible to address interpersonal issues, by virtue of the availability of many personalities with whom to explore transferences and projections. Some group leaders with a Jungian orientation will not hesitate to adopt methods from other therapies—for instance, Gestalt dream work, bioenergetic therapies, sensory awareness, or encounter group exercises. There are wide differences of opinion concerning the use of such techniques, as well as differences in the use of group therapy itself. Some analysts report good results from a combination of private and group sessions.

The frequency and length of meetings vary. A group might meet on week-ends, once or twice a week, or for a week-long or even a month-long experience. Doing group work is a subject requiring its own chapter—or book—of descriptions and techniques. Recruiting, method of payment, confidentiality, and safety issues must be responsibly confronted and decisions made.

## FINAL THOUGHTS

Carl Jung's ideas on the uses of imagery have made a deep impression upon twentieth-century psychology. Although debated even among devoted Jung-oriented practitioners, they continue to yield results not found in other ways. His respect for the image just as it emerged from the imager's unconscious leads to some important conclusions. One conclusion is that the cleverness or inventiveness of the therapist is not what matters most. The image comes from and belongs to the imager. No amount of outside creativity can match the imager's own store of personally connected material that is owned only by that person. Urges toward rapid solution, rather than evolution, will bring the psyche to repeat the same messages again and again, perhaps in differing forms, until they are understood more clearly by the one who owns the images.

## REFERENCES

Chodorov, J. (1982). Dance movement and body experience in analysis. In M. Stein (Ed.), *Jungian Analysis* (pp. 193-203). LaSalle and London: Open Court.

Dallett, J. (1982). Active imagination in practice. In M. Stein (Ed.), *Jungian Analysis* (pp. 173-191). LaSalle and London: Open Court.

Hall, J. A. (1986). *The Jungian experience: Analysis and individuation.* Toronto, Canada: Inner City Books.

Hillman, J. (1972). *The myth of analysis.* Evanston: Northwestern University Press.

Jung, C. G. (1929). Commentary on "The secret of the golden flower." In *Collected Works* (Vol. 13, pp. 1-56). Princeton: Princeton University Press, 1967.

Mahoney, M. F. (1966). *The meaning in dreams and dreaming.* Secaucus, NJ: Citadel Press.

Martin, P. W. (1955). *Experiment in depth.* London: Routledge & Kegan Paul.

Mattoon, M. A. (1978). *Applied dream analysis: A Jungian approach.* Washington, DC: V. H. Winston & Sons.

Samuels, A. (1985). *Jung and the post-Jungians.* London and New York: Tavistock/ Routledge.

Spoto, A. (1989). *Jung's typology in perspective.* Boston: Sigo Press.

Stein, M. (Ed.) (1982). *Jungian analysis.* LaSalle and London: Open Court.

Storr, A. (Ed.) (1983). *The essential Jung.* Princeton: Princeton University Press.

von Franz, M.-L., & Hillman, J. (1971). *Lectures on Jung's typology.* New York: Spring Publications, The Analytical Psychology Club of New York.

# CHAPTER 22

# Imagery Techniques in Psychosynthesis

## L. MARTIN MOLESKI, M. MICHAEL ISHII, AND ANEES A. SHEIKH

Psychosynthesis is a therapeutic system that was originated and developed by the Italian psychiatrist, Roberto Assagioli (1888-1974). Assagioli felt that psychoanalysis was incomplete because it did not give sufficient attention to the "higher" aspects of human consciousness, particularly to the natural tendency toward positive psycho-physical growth. Assagioli maintained that a truly inclusive conception of the human being had to take into account not only the development of the personality, but also the "transpersonal" dimension of experience.

Assagioli sought a more comprehensive conceptual framework that would include all the dimensions of human experience—physical, emotional, mental, and spiritual. Toward this end, Assagioli added meditative techniques from the East to the analytical, behavioral, and humanistic methods of the West. Psychosynthesis became based on the principle of synergy—the coming together of divergent aspects at higher levels of organization; yet at the same time the approach utilized many practical methods for fostering human potential within contemporary society.

Like other European clinicians, Assagioli found that imagery techniques were beneficial in tapping many aspects of the total personality. In Assagioli's major works, *Psychosynthesis* (1965) and *The Act of Will* (1973), he discusses theoretical aspects of the nature of imagery and laws that it follows, and he demonstrates how it can be utilized in the clinical setting.

In this chapter, only the basic techniques are presented. The interested reader is referred to other sources for further details (Assagioli, 1965, 1973; Brown, 1983; Ferrucci, 1982; Gerard, 1964).

## TECHNIQUES OF VISUALIZATION

Assagioli noted that imagination is itself somewhat synthetic in that it integrates several levels of sensation, emotion, cognition, and intuition. Assagioli suggested that visualization be used as an initial means to develop the ability of imagery in the client. The following exercise could be used:

First imagine the setting, which is a classroom with a blackboard, grey or dull black. Then imagine that in the middle of the blackboard appears a figure; let us say the number five, as if written with white chalk fairly large and well defined. Then keep it vividly before your inner eye, so to speak; that is, keep the image of the five vivid and steady in the field of your conscious attention. Then on the right of the five visualize the figure two.

So, now you have two figures, a five and a two, making fifty-two. Dwell for a while on the visualization of this number, then after a little while, imagine the appearance of a four at the right side of the two.

Now you have three figures, written in white chalk, five, two, four—making the number five hundred and twenty-four. Dwell for a while on this number.

Continue adding other figures until you are unable to hold together the visualization of the number resulting from those figures. (Assagioli, 1965, pp. 146-147)

Since the numbers will change in size, color, and location, the result of the exercise is the client's realization of what little control he/she has over imagination and concentration. Also, the exercise serves to indicate an initial ability level in imagery, and a repetition of this visualization at a later date can be used to gauge the client's progress. The improvement will not be solely in the ability to maintain imagery but also will be in imagination, concentration, and in development of the will.

After sufficient skill is attained in the first exercise, Assagioli suggested that color be introduced in a second exercise. The client is asked to visualize simple geometric forms: a square, a triangle, a circle, and an oval in *color*. By imagining and trying to maintain a red square, a green triangle, an orange circle, and a blue oval, the client can discriminate his/her abilities to visualize form and color. The client, by using simple geometric forms, also is prepared for another imagery technique, symbol utilization (Assagioli, 1965).

The symbols used in visualization can be chosen for therapeutic value as well as for developing imagery ability. Gerard (1964) suggested the use of synthesis symbols. The integrative meaning of synthesis symbols, such as a sunflower or the sun, resides in the geometric form within the image—that of the mandala. Recreating and embellishing the image over and over will develop imagery ability as well as help to integrate the will with other inner dynamic forces. Other symbols which can be used in visualization include: symbols of harmonious human relations (2 hands holding each other), symbols of masculinity or of femininity, and symbols of emotion. Colors are strongly suggested for the latter class.

Assagioli called a third exercise "mental photography." The client is asked to behave much as a camera does: He/she is presented with an image, such as a photograph, a mathematical formula, or a painting, for one minute. Then he/she is asked to close his/her eyes, to visualize the image he/she has just seen, and to describe it with as much detail as possible. This exercise also can be used to measure a client's progress, but it is valued more for developing mnemonic retention, because an image based on reality must be maintained (Assagioli, 1965).

Visualization can be used to develop dynamic imagery as well as static imagery. Unlike the three introductory exercises, this one allows the client to develop a suggested image acting according to a *predetermined* sequence. The initial effect may be the client's realization that control needs to be developed, not only along static dimensions of an image, but also along a dynamic, time-oriented line. The advantage of developing dynamic imagery is that *living* symbols can then be used.

## TECHNIQUES OF AUDITORY EVOCATION

Another imagery technique which Assagioli developed was the evocation of sound images. The client is instructed to evoke sounds of the sea, of the wind, or of a river. Whether instructions are given to exclude or to incorporate the accompanying visual images depends on the goals of the therapist. If improved concentration and developing of the will is desired, then instructions to exclude visual images should be given. But if the goal is to observe the spontaneous processes in developing such an image, then no such exclusion should be suggested. Music also can be evoked, with the advantage of progressively incorporating chord, rhythm, melody, and instrument (Assagioli, 1965).

Another exercise exactly opposite in intent is to exclude all sound from the mind. A metronome can be placed near the client and he/she can be instructed to listen to it for a short time. Then the client is told to "erase" the sensation and instead to substitute the auditory image of silence. Another way to help exclude distractions of sound from the mind is to ask the client to imagine entering a building of silence, such as a temple, church, or library. The focus on being in the building and on the silence can aid in excluding outside distractions and in bringing up subtler sounds from within.

A parallel to mental photography is Assagioli's auditory registration. The client is presented with a short music piece and is asked to immediately hear it again in imagination. Like mental photography, auditory registration is to be valued for maintaining an image based on reality. In addition, reintegration of some of the accompanying emotions experienced while listening to the original piece can be undertaken. This reintegration can be valuable in lessening the tension of a client, for example, by re-evoking soothing music or bird songs (Assagioli, 1965).

## TECHNIQUE OF EVOKING OTHER SENSATIONS

Evocations of tactile, gustatory, olfactory, and kinesthetic images are easily made, if the client actually experiences them first and then imagines them. The processes involved largely parallel those underlying mental photography and auditory registration. Tactile images, for example, can be developed by having the client pass his/her hand over a textured surface and then asking him/her to evoke the tactile image repeatedly. Similar procedures can be devised for the remaining types of images. These techniques are indicated for those clients who focus too strongly on their emotions, and for those who do not pay attention to their bodies or to the range of images available (Assagioli, 1965).

## OTHER INTRODUCTORY IMAGERY TECHNIQUES

Other introductory imagery techniques are somewhat less directive and more individualized. For example, after an initial session, a client can be asked to write about a major concern, a precipitating emotional trauma, or recent growth. Suggestions to focus on subjectivity encourage the emergence of verbal images which are used naturally by the client. Noting figures of speech, as well as the modalities of these natural images, often can point out avenues of approach in developing a client's imagery (Brown, 1983).

Drawing also can be used to help develop imagery. The client is asked to relax in a comfortable position with eyes closed and to wait for images to develop in response to the therapist's description of an important emotional issue. After the client has translated these images into a drawing, further impressions and associations can be developed by studying the drawing. Free drawing also can capture spontaneous images for later examination. The use of drawing to record important images also allows the client to chart progress in the development of the self.

Spontaneous images may arise in the course of guiding a client through predetermined image development. At first, spontaneous images may be distracting and discouraging to the client, but they can be helpful if they are recognized as symbolic of an issue of importance. The self is less in control of these spontaneous images than of predetermined static or dynamic images; thus, a client may at times encounter a spontaneous image which he/she finds terrifying. Unexpected images can be very useful after the client has demonstrated reasonable imagery development. Spontaneous imagery can be evoked effectively by the use of open-ended settings, such as waiting for something to emerge from a cave. Often the image is of a frightening nature; therefore, the therapist must guide the client to confront the image and to integrate it.

## TECHNIQUE OF IDEAL MODELS

The above techniques generally involved the sensation and perception of reality-based images. Assagioli intended these techniques to be introductory exercises, that is, aimed at developing a client's imagery abilities. Assagioli emphasized that the mental and emotional creativity of the imagination could be used in turn to change the self-image of a client by the following exercise. The client is asked what particular quality or ability he/she desires to possess. Then the client is instructed to visualize himself/herself actually demonstrating that quality in as many modes as possible. The client is encouraged to imagine this self-image in different settings playing various roles, so that unforeseen qualities in the self-image can be brought out and developed. Short, vivid repetitions are more effective than a prolonged and persistent image.

Gradually the client should be able to incorporate the quality into his/her actual life (Assagioli, 1965). Ideal models also can be evoked by asking the client to gaze into an imagined mirror or reflecting pond. The imagined reflected self-image often is either an idealized or a self-depreciating image. Encouragement to incorporate the idealized image into the self or to understand the self-depreciating image often will lead to an improvement in the client's self-image.

## TECHNIQUES OF SYMBOL UTILIZATION

From the development of imagery abilities and the improvement of the self-image, Assagioli turned to spiritual development. Assagioli suggested several methods of using symbols as images. The therapist can offer a symbol chosen from the six classes: symbols of nature, of animals, of humans, of man-made things, of religious/mythological content, and of abstractions. Secondly, the therapist can use spontaneous symbols discovered during treatment. Thirdly, the therapist can suggest a symbol initially but then allow the client to freely develop a symbol out of it. The choice of the symbol as well as the manner in which it is presented depends on what has been most effective in the past and on the stage of treatment at which the client is. Presentation of the image can be done by either naming the symbol and describing it, by showing the client a picture of the symbol, or by visualization alone. How the client redescribes the symbol, what meaning he/she attaches to it, and what dynamic changes occur in the image can indicate to the therapist the progression of the integrated personality toward a spiritual realization (Assagioli, 1965). An example of symbol utilization follows:

> Let us imagine we are looking at a rosebush. Let us visualize one stem with leaves and a rosebud. The bud appears green because the sepals are closed, but at the very top a rose-colored point can be seen. Let us visualize this vividly, holding the image in the center of our consciousness.
>
> Now begins a slow movement: the sepals start to separate little by little, turning their points outward and revealing the rose-hued petals, which are still closed. The sepals continue to open until we can see the whole of the tender bud.
>
> The petals follow suit and slowly separate, until a perfect fully-opened rose is seen.
>
> At this stage let us try to smell the perfume of this rose, inhaling its characteristics and unmistakable scent, so delicate, sweet, and delicious. Let us smell it with delight.
>
> Let us now expand our visualization to include the whole rosebush, and imagine the life force that arises from the roots to the flower and originates the process of opening.
>
> Finally let us identify ourselves with the rose itself or, more precisely, let us introject it into ourselves. Symbolically we are this flower, this rose. The same life that animates the universe and has created the miracle of the rose is producing in us a like, even greater miracle—the awakening and development of our spiritual being and that which radiates from it. (Assagioli, 1965, pp. 214-215)

An elaboration of symbol utilization is the guided daydream. After an initial relaxation period the client is asked to imagine a setting such as a meadow and to describe it. The therapist attempts to incorporate meaningful archetypal or spontaneous symbols to evoke images which suggest further work. Movement within the setting often indicates the direction of imagery growth. Ascent from the meadow often evokes transcending, peaceful, joyful images, while descent often brings repressed and painful images. Upstream explorations of brooks, which symbolize energy, often lead to the discovery of sources of strength, while downstream voyages lead to where energy is expressed. Other landmarks or figures suggested or spontaneously incorporated often aid in breaking down resistance.

Another variation of symbol utilization involves the visualization of not only symbolic topography but also of symbolic events, such as patiently untangling a massive knot, taming a wild horse, lifting an immense weight, restoring a temple, or reaching the safety of a harbor. A gradually improved scene resolution, achieved possibly after many repetitions, can result in a gradual improvement in the relevant aspect of the personality.

Assagioli offers another technique utilizing symbols to effect change: The client is instructed to discover images for conflicting forces within himself/herself and to then allow these images to interact with each other. The client can gain insight by taking on the role of each image separately or by observing the conflict from a third perspective. In this manner, transference is minimized because it occurs with the images, not with the therapist. At the core of this technique is the process of symbolic identification: The client is asked to identify with every element in the conflict.

Other techniques involving symbols also utilize symbolic identification. Clients who have somatic complaints often can evoke images which associate their complaints with visual or kinesthetic analogues. Withdrawn clients may find it easy as well to associate depersonalized qualities of themselves with separate visual images. For example, if a client suffers from somatic stomach cramps he/she may report images of tightly tied knots. The therapist's role is to then guide the client to imagine that the knots are loosened and untied (Gerard, 1964).

It is possible to symbolize troubled emotional states also. Imagining a door with the word of the troubled emotional state on it and opening it can release emotion-laden images which can be used later. Imagining a huge heart and entering it through a door also can evoke imagery which represents emotional states. The responses found in TAT or Rorschach tests also can reveal symbols of troubled emotional states.

Using light in imagery also involves symbol utilization. A client fearful of death can be encouraged to enter an imagined globe of radiant fire. Experiencing the destruction of the body teaches the client that the self is not identified with the body. An imagined approach toward an area of bright light and merging with the light imply a merging of the self with enlightenment and spiritual growth. Another exercise designed to lead to self-discovery is one in which the client imagines himself/herself to be like an onion: He/she gradually peels away the superficial layers of the personality. Or the client can be encouraged to imagine a wise man, such as Christ, Buddha, or an old king, and to engage in a dialog with this figure, which often is a personification of the ideal self. The advice of the wise figure often is accepted by the actual self and hence leads to spiritual growth.

## TECHNIQUE OF IMAGINATIVE EVOCATION OF INTERPERSONAL RELATIONSHIPS

The previous techniques have focused on the enhancement of imagery ability, on the development of the self-image, and on spiritual realization. Evoking interpersonal relationships is a way for the client to develop an effective inner attitude toward others. This is accomplished in two steps. The first step is to ask the client to describe in detail an interaction with another which arouses fear and anxiety. After the client has done so and has become relaxed again, the therapist repeats the description to the client. The client is instructed to incorporate these details into a vivid image of the feared interaction and to react freely to it. Assagioli termed this first step "imaginative desensitization." The reactions become weaker as the first step is repeated, and the client is then ready for the second step. Now the therapist asks the client to visualize various types of interactions with others. After repetition, the desired attitude and relationships will be visualized and should be emphasized. It is through imagery then that the often automatic, maladaptive reactions are extinguished and effective inner attitudes toward others emerge (Assagioli, 1965).

## INNER SILENCE

The goal of this exercise is to quiet the body, the emotions, and the mind and thus to render you aware of the more subtle aspects of your nature.

1. Select a quiet place. Keep paper and pencil within reach. Assume a comfortable position. Close your eyes, take a few slow, deep breaths, and relax.
2. Imagine that it is a beautiful sunny day and you are standing in a meadow, at the foot of a mountain. There is a path leading to the peak, and on it is a clearing in whose center stands a temple, the temple of silence.
3. Start to climb this path. As you progress, become aware of the heightened feeling of elevation and expansion. As you draw near the clearing, note the stillness, the energy of silence emanating from the temple.
4. Let your body absorb this relaxing silence. Slowly approach the temple's entrance. Now enter the temple, and let the energy of silence penetrate your feelings, rendering them serene. As you reach the center of the temple, which is open to the sky, silence permeates your mind—it becomes quiet, yet alert and lucid.
5. At the center is a beam of sunlight, and from here the energy radiates. Stand on this sunlight and let silence fill your entire being. Let the energy from the sun flow through you; take time to experience its quality.
6. Retaining the awareness of the silence within you, become conscious once more of your body, then of your environment, and then open your eyes.
7. Write the experience down. Some aspects which you could explore are: What was the most meaningful facet of this experience? What does silence mean to you? How would your life be changed if the experience of silence were with you more of the time? (Adapted from Sloan, 1977, pp. 136-137.)

## A LETTER FROM THE HIGHER SELF

This exercise provides an opportunity for a deeper experience of the Higher Self.

1. Close your eyes and focus on your breathing pattern.
2. Now follow the breath inside your body. Do you feel a sensation of pleasure anywhere in your body? Go to these places and enjoy the feeling. Now slowly

move the sensation of pleasure to the tense parts of your body. Allow the feeling of openness and pleasure to permeate your entire body.

3. Certain feelings may have arisen as you focused on the discomfort in your body. Identify these feelings. What feelings resulted from the sensation of pleasure? Let these feelings blossom and enjoy them.

4. As you concentrate on your feelings, thoughts may come to your mind. Notice which ones go with the discomfort and which ones go with the pleasure. Focus on the latter.

5. These are all facets of who you are. Focus on them and be aware that it is you who is focusing on them and who chose the aspect on which to focus.

6. Now step back—step back as far as you can to gain the widest perspective.

7. Imagine that you are the one who elected to be born, to have this body, these feelings, this mind. Can you remember making that choice? Go back to that time and recall the purpose that brought you into this world and the love you have for the form you selected. Claim the love, wisdom, and clarity which are your birthright.

8. From this position of acceptance, look at the person as he/she is today, at all the events that have shaped him/her.

9. Do you wish to say anything to this person you chose to be? Write this person a letter.

10. Place it in an envelope, seal it, and address it to yourself. Ask a friend to mail it to you, when the time is right. You will receive the letter when you best understand its message (Adapted from Brown, 1983, p. 99).

## SUBPERSONALITIES

These two exercises are designed to help you recognize, accept, and integrate your subpersonalities.

### The Door

1. Make yourself comfortable and relax. Close your eyes and breathe deeply. Imagine in considerable detail a big wooden door before you. It bears the sign SUBPERSONALITIES. Visualize them all behind this door.

2. Open the door and let some of your subpersonalities come out. Observe them carefully, but do not become involved with them.

3. Gradually focus on the main or the most interesting one.

4. Now strike up a conversation with it.

5. Ask it what it wants, and then find out *why*. Ask it what it *needs,* and why it needs it.

6. Now *become* this subpersonality. Focus on how you feel as this subpersonality. How does the world look to you? Ask yourself, "What do I want? What do I need?"

7. Now step back from the subpersonality and ask yourself, "What would my life be like if this subpersonality dominated all the time?"

8. Scrutinize this subpersonality again and note what you value and what you dislike in it.
9. See yourself with the subpersonality outside on a beautiful, sunny day. A special ray of sunlight envelopes you and your subpersonality. This energy from the sun will bring some changes.
10. Has the subpersonality changed? Relate to it again and try to improve your relationship with it.
11. Write down your experience in detail. You also may find it useful to make a drawing of your subpersonality (Adapted from Carter-Haar, 1974, pp. 93-95).

### The Loyal Soldier

1. Relax, close your eyes, and be aware of only your breathing.
2. Now review your life of the past several weeks. Begin with the present and move backwards until you find a time when you felt frightened or upset or restricted. Select an occasion when you were not in immediate physical danger.
3. Relive this experience with all its attendant feelings, thoughts, and sensations. How would the world look from this viewpoint? How do you feel about yourself? What actions would you like to take?
4. Now in your imagination, step back and see yourself as another would see you. Observe impartially—just see with which subpersonality you were identified on that occasion.
5. Observe what this subpersonality is attempting to do for you. Ask it what it is attempting to do, and listen carefully to the reply. Thank this subpersonality for its loyal efforts to take care of you.
6. But also take note that this subpersonality restricts you, when it is in charge. It has limiting beliefs about you and the world. Maybe you know what qualities it needs to be more effective. Can you fill its needs? Imagine doing so, and notice its response. Make any agreements which you feel would help to integrate this loyal soldier into your personality.
7. You may wish to write the experience down in your journal (Adapted from Brown, 1983, p. 19).

## EVOKING AND DEVELOPING DESIRED QUALITIES

The aim of this exercise is to create inner and outer conditions which aid in fostering and enhancing a desired quality within yourself. It is suggested for daily practice. In this outline, the quality of serenity will be used, but the technique can be employed for other qualities, such as gratitude, courage, patience, joy, compassion, etc. It is vital that the choice of the quality to be enhanced come from within you, it should have real meaning for you personally.

The procedure for this technique follows:

1. Relax and take a few deep breaths. Then reflect on the idea of serenity: Hold the concept "serenity" in your mind, and think about it. What is its nature, its meaning, etc. As this concept evokes insights, ideas, or images in you, record them in your workbook.

2. Open yourself to other ideas or images related to serenity that may arise from your unconscious, and write them down as well.

3. Dwell upon the value of serenity, especially in this hectic modern world. *Praise* serenity in your mind. *Desire* it.

4. Take on a physical attitude of serenity. Relax all muscular and nervous tension. Breathe slowly and rhythmically. Allow serenity to express itself on your face, and try to visualize yourself wearing that expression.

5. Evoke serenity directly. Imagine that you are in a place which renders you serene: a beach, a temple, a cool forest, possibly a place where you have felt serene in the past. Try to feel it. Repeat the word SERENITY several times. Let serenity permeate you. If possible, identify yourself with serenity.

6. Imagine yourself in situations which in the past tended to irritate you: dealing with a hostile person, or facing a difficult problem, or feeling rushed. Then *see* and *feel* yourself calm and serene. (You may postpone this step until you have acquired some familiarity with the exercise.)

7. Resolve to stay serene throughout the day . . . to be a shining example of serenity . . . to emanate serenity.

8. Make a sign with the word SERENITY, using the color and lettering that you feel express this quality the best. Place this sign where you can see it often and if possible at the times when you are most in need of serenity. Whenever you look at it, evoke the feeling of serenity within yourself.

This exercise to foster a desired quality can become the nucleus of a more extensive program. You can collect poetry, music, drama, artwork, photography and dance, which evoke serenity, and use them to create a more comprehensive experience. Also you can utilize all aspects of your environment which foster a sense of serenity.

*Note:* A few individuals may react negatively to the exercise; that is, attempts to evoke serenity may bring tension, anxiety, etc. This usually means that a core of negative emotions blocks the development of the desired quality. This reaction is most likely to occur during Step 6 of the exercise. If the negative reaction is strong, it is best to abandon the exercise, to explore the negative feelings, and then to release them through catharsis. Thereafter, this exercise can be resumed. Now it will be particularly valuable; for, it will help to fill with a positive quality the psychological "space" left by the release of the negative feeling (Adapted from Assagioli, 1965).

## WHO IS AWARE?

### Part 1

The purpose of this exercise is to gain awareness of the experience of "I," by being an observer. By focusing on specific sensations and images, the experience of self-identity is captured.

1. Assume a comfortable position and sit quietly. Breathe in deeply, and as you exhale, become more relaxed. Look around you, in all directions, and become *aware* of everything you see. *See* everything you observe in all its detail. . . . See as clearly and as vividly as possible. Allow yourself a few moments to do

this. Now close your eyes and feel your own breathing rhythm. As you inhale, breathe in this vivid, visual awareness, and as you exhale, ask yourself, "*Who is aware?*"

2. Now with your eyes still closed, become aware of what you *hear. Listen* to what you hear . . . to the sounds as well as to the silence. Continue feeling your natural breathing rhythm. Inhale deeply, and as you slowly exhale, ask yourself, "*Who is aware?*"

3. With your eyes still closed, imagine in front of you a blackboard, and that you are drawing a white circle with chalk on the blackboard. Look at the circle . . . become aware of it. Now take a slow, deep breath, and as you exhale, ask yourself, "*Who is aware?*"

4. Let the circle gradually fade away, and as you breathe in your natural rhythm, focus on your self as the one who is aware. Allow yourself to really experience being yourself. Take all the time you need to get as clear a sense as possible of this experience . . . the awareness of yourself as the one who is aware.

5. Practice this experience of being an observer until it becomes spontaneous and can be achieved at will.

### Part 2

The purpose of this second part is to move beyond the experience of self-identity to the experience of self-awareness. While the experience of "I" is valuable in increasing one's ability to distinguish the difference between inner and outer events, the progression to the experience of "the true and unchanging self" is the foundation for experiencing the "will," a key concept in all psychosynthesis exercises.

1. Once again find a comfortable and quiet spot. Look around you and become aware of what you see. Look at things in detail, and see everything as clearly and as vividly as possible. Now close your eyes and feel your natural breathing rhythm . . . breathe in slowly . . . and exhale slowly and completely. As you inhale, take in this whole awareness, and as you exhale, ask yourself, "*Who is aware?*"

2. With your eyes still closed, become aware of what you *hear.* Listen to all the sounds and to the silence around you. Now take a slow, deep breath . . . and as you exhale, quietly ask yourself, "*Who is aware?*"

3. With your eyes still closed, imagine in front of you a blackboard, and that you are drawing a white circle with chalk on the blackboard. Look at the circle and become aware of it. See as much detail as possible. Now take a slow, deep breath, and as you exhale, ask yourself, "*Who is aware?*"

4. Again let the circle gradually fade away, and as you breathe in your natural rhythm, focus on your self as the one who is aware. Allow yourself to really experience being your self. Get as clear a sense as possible of this experience . . . the awareness of your self as the one who is aware.

5. Now try to experience clearly what it is like to be your self, become aware of the *stability* of the self, of its permanency. Allow yourself to experience your self as the stable state of consciousness that is *always* there. Even in the midst

of change, full awareness of your self is always available as a source of stability and as a source of clear perception.

6. Retain this awareness of being your unchanging self, and focus your attention on your body. Allow yourself to experience your *body*. What you experience is that your body changes. The sensations of your body are different this moment than they were just a few moments ago, and they will be different a few moments from now. Your body is different now than it was when you were a child, and it keeps changing with every year. But your self does not change.

7. Once again, focus on your self, on the stability of the self. Now direct your attention to your *feelings*. Become aware that your feelings also are changing all the time. But your self does not change.

8. Focus on your self and on the permanence of the self. Now become aware of your mind. See how your thoughts change. They change from minute to minute, and as you grow, your ways of thinking change. But your self does not change.

9. Once again focus on your self. As you do this, become aware of your body, your feelings, and your mind. Become aware that you *have* these three aspects to yourself, they are *yours*. Realize their value as a means of expression. Realize that you have the capacity to direct and regulate these parts of yourself at will. But they are not you. You are your self, the one who is aware.

10. Now take a few minutes to become aware of what you have gained through this exercise. You may want to write down a few notes (Adapted from Vargiu, 1975, pp. 95-97).

### The Sun

The aim of this exercise is to attain inner peace and self-renewal.

1. Visualize yourself walking along the beach just before dawn. The sea is calm and almost motionless as the last bright stars fade away.

2. Feel the purity and freshness of the air; breathe it in, as you watch the water, the stars, the dark sky. Take time to experience the silence before the sunrise. Feel the stillness. Feel the predawn moments filled with all possibilities.

3. The darkness begins to melt, and the first hint of color appears over the horizon. You stand and face the sunrise; red hues glisten in the distance, then golden light spills over the horizon. The sun's first rays reach you and fill you with a certain excitement and a sense of awe.

4. As the sun rises higher over the horizon, rays of golden, shimmering sunlight reach out over the water directly to you, filling your heart and your whole being with radiant sunlight, the dawning of a new day.

5. As you watch the sunrise, become aware of the feelings deep within you.

6. The temperature of the water is pleasant and you decide to go for a swim. You walk in slowly and start to swim in the golden radiance. A sense of great joy fills your being. You can feel the water, filled with light and radiance, bathing your whole body. You feel yourself moving effortlessly and gracefully in the sea.

7. As you swim toward the sun, the light around you increases, and you are less aware of the water. You feel permeated by a wondrous, golden light. A sense of joy overwhelms you, as you bathe in the vitality of the sun. As your feelings are pervaded by warmth and radiance, your mind is illuminated by wisdom and light (Adapted from Ferrucci, 1982, p. 122).

## OWNING A PEAK EXPERIENCE

This exercise is designed to achieve personal growth.

A. *Embracing yourself, gathering yourself together*

1. Focus on a time when you experienced great joy, peace, excitement, vitality, and tranquility, when you experienced *who you are* (a peak experience). Experience that moment. Experience the *quality* of the energy.
2. Separate the energy from the actual experience. See that the experience of the actual moment and the quality of the energy can be separated.
3. Let a separate image or symbol form in your inner consciousness, that represents the quality of the energy of the peak experience.
4. Realize that this image or symbol is a part of your being, a part of your inner essence.

B. *People you admire*

1. Visualize people who represent the qualities and the energy that you have identified.
2. What do these persons represent?
3. Now realize that these qualities are a part of you, that they exist in you. To be able to see a quality in someone else, you first must have that self-awareness, that awareness of having it yourself.
4. Hold in your consciousness all these thoughts, all these feelings, all these energies—the experience of joy and aliveness, the people they represent, and the awareness of these qualities in you.

C. *Saying "yes" to life*

1. Experience a time when you felt that things were right, a time when you said "yes" to life!
2. Experience that moment fully, focus on it vividly, energize it.
3. Feel that experience to be at the center of your being. own it completely (Adapted from Yeoman, 1986).

## REFERENCES

Assagioli, R. (1965). *Psychosynthesis*. New York: Hobbs, Dorman & Co.
Assagioli, R. (1973). *The act of will*. New York: Viking.
Brown, M. Y. (1983). *The unfolding self*. Los Angeles: Psychosynthesis Press.
Carter-Haar, B. (1974). The door. *Synthesis, 1,* 93-96.

Crampton, M. (1977). *Psychosynthesis: Some aspects of theory and practice.* Montreal: Canadian Institute of Psychosynthesis.

Ferrucci, P. (1982). *What we may be.* Los Angeles: Tarcher.

Gerard, R. (1964). *Psychosynthesis: A psychology for the whole man.* New York: Psychosynthesis Research Foundation, Issue No. 14.

Sloan, H. H. (1977). Inner silence. *Synthesis, 3-4,* 135-143.

Vargiu, J. G. (1975). The observer and the consciousness of "I." *Synthesis, 2,* 94-100.

Yeoman, T. (1986). Personal communication.

*Note:* The reader is also encouraged to consult various issues of the journal, *Synthesis: The Realization of the Self,* published by the Synthesis Press, 830 Woodside Road, Redwood City, CA 94061.

# CHAPTER 23

# Imagery Techniques in the Work of Jean Houston

## SHIRLEY BANKIER

Jean Houston, along with her husband Robert Masters, is one of the founders of the human potential movement. Past president of the Association of Humanistic Psychology, she has spent the last forty years investigating human consciousness. With an academic background that included professorships in philosophy, history, and psychology it is apparent that Houston's fascination with the human mind began long before her explorations into its inner processes. In fact, it was because of her broad range of expertise in the humanities that she was asked, in the early sixties, to become part of the research team studying the effects of LSD on the human personality. Over the next few years, she and her husband studied the mythic, cross-cultural, and symbolic themes that repeatedly surfaced as they guided hundreds of subjects under the influence of this powerful psychedelic.

> What has been abstract and exclusive in my philosophical and historical studies became extremely concrete in my LSD work. In the process of taking depth soundings of the psyche, it was as if a lifetime of witness to the spectrum of human behavior and possibilities was condensed in the experiences of a few years. (Houston, 1980, p. xiii)

Their work during these years is the subject of their book, *The Varieties of Psychedelic Experiences*. Among the incredible range of phenomena that they observed and describe are: sensory changes and conscious awareness of internal bodily functions; alterations in the experiencing of time, space, and body image; hallucinations and eidetic imaging; heightened capacity for memory, concentration, and suggestibility; and intense awareness of psychodynamic processes with affective swings from extremes of anxiety to extremes of pleasure. When this work was forced to an abrupt halt because of the misconduct of several researchers, Houston and Masters were too intrigued by what they had witnessed to abandon the subject. Instead, in 1965, they founded the Foundation for Mind Research to conduct research on non-drug induced altered states of consciousness.

By studying ancient as well as contemporary cultures, and investigating both orthodox and esoteric methods of altering consciousness, they discovered procedures that had been used by different societies to expand their awareness beyond the narrow range of perceptions acceptable to the rational Western mind. These methods of expanding consciousness, which were always highly valued by the cultures that used them, were thought to result in a deeper understanding of the Self. Houston and Masters combined ancient teachings and modern research methods to study "the experiential and pragmatic value of altered and expanded states of consciousness, alternative cognitive modes, new styles of learning, thinking in images, thinking kinesthetically, time distortion, and the evocation of the creative process" (Houston, 1980, p. xv).

As they concentrated on expanding and refining sensory and perceptual potentials as well as the self-regulation of pleasure and pain, they arrived at what became the major focus of their research at the Foundation, the body-mind continuum. They developed a system they call Psychophysical Reeducation which forces a conscious reintegration of the mind and the body through the practice of specific exercises. These exercises allow the individual to unlearn those patterns of body movements that contribute to disease and learn new patterns that can lead to psychophysical rehabilitation of physical problems as well as to increased potentials for optimal physical functioning. This work is the subject of their book, *Listening to the Body* (Masters & Houston, 1978). It soon became obvious that their subjects who were doing the psychophysical work were also demonstrating evidence of improved memory, multiple track thinking, and the ability to connect, at will, with the symbolic and mythic dimensions of their consciousness. As Yogi Masters have so clearly demonstrated by their well documented control over their autonomic nervous systems (a skill gained on their path to spiritual enlightenment), mental, psychological, and spiritual potentialities are intimately connected to physiological processes. More exercises were then developed which integrated "movement, imagery, intense concentration and creative intentionality." These exercises seemed to have "profound consequences upon the conscious repatterning of both physical and mental lives" by somehow bridging and connecting right and left hemispheres, older and newer neural structures, brain and consciousness (Houston, 1982, p. xx).

The significance of this work represented a radical departure from modern Western thought with its belief in the supremacy of the logical, rational mind and its contempt for the physical, intuitive, and emotional. Our culture's unwillingness to validate other ways of knowing, other ways of perceiving reality, is a "direct outgrowth of the loss of awareness of sensori-motor functions, as is its inability to use a larger range of body-mind perceptions for more subtle understanding and complex problem solving" (Houston, 1982, p. xix). Houston believes that this has led to a deterioration of the physical body and a real loss of intellectual abilities for us as individuals and as a culture. More critically, now faced with Star Wars technology and life threatening environmental and social problems, the linear problem solving strategies that are fundamental to rational thought seem inadequate to deal with the complexity of contemporary crises. Houston and Masters seem convinced by their research that, given the opportunity and the education, people have the capacity to attain the levels of understanding necessary to meet these crises by developing new problem-solving strategies. These strategies would be based on the creative and conceptual leaps made possible by the conscious reintegration and development of the body and mind.

The Foundation has had many opportunities to make practical applications of its research. It has been involved in setting up model schools with curriculums based on new ways of learning that use a broad range of sensory and cognitive abilities. Houston and Masters have applied their discoveries about brain functioning to work with retarded, autistic, and brain damaged individuals. They have been successful in helping geriatric patients regain failing skills and learn new ones. They have also conducted seminars for public administrators and bureaucrats that have allowed the participants to expand their visions of the ideal society by gaining insights into their ideal selves. In 1975, the Dromenon Center, named after the ancient Greek rites of growth and transformation, was established to provide training seminars for educators and those in the helping professions. In 1977, Jean Houston began conducting Dromenon seminars and New Ways of Being Institutes all over the world.

Most of the exercises in this chapter come from Houston's book, *The Possible Human*. It is a comprehensive introduction to her work on human potentials based on her workshops. *Mind Games* (1973) and *Listening to the Body* (1978), coauthored by Houston and Masters, and her other book, *Life Force: The Psychohistorical Recovery of the Self* (1980), will be described later.[1] These earlier books offer opportunities for more intense work in the areas of imagery and altered states of consciousness and psychophysical reeducation. Many of the following exercises were designed for groups with one member acting as a guide. All of them can still be very meaningful experienced alone although directions will sometimes have to be pretaped. Dancing, drawing, or writing, any form of creative expression, is encouraged as a natural extension of the exercises after they are completed. These exercises are meant to be enjoyed. Acknowledging the need for more significant research in this area, psychological and physiological explanations are offered only as informed speculations. No promises are given about personal transformations, only the knowledge that through this work "many thousands of people have regained or enhanced their understanding of themselves and their capacity for growth" (Houston, 1982, p. xxv).

\* \* \*

The exercises in the first section of *The Possible Human* are used to increase consciousness of the relationship between the mind and the body. Eastern and Western traditions have long held that each individual possesses a secondary, non-physical, "subtle body"—the kinesthetic body. By developing awareness of this kinesthetic body, the body of the muscular imagination, one can achieve a wider range of movement and attain conscious involvement and control over physical processes usually unaccessible to consciousness.

## THE KINESTHETIC BODY

Individuals should be guided through this exercise or the directions should be put on tape. It is an exercise in movement and attention and should be discontinued whenever attention wanders.

---

[1] Houston's imagery work in the area of what she calls sacred psychology is not covered here. The reader is referred to other sources (Houston, 1987).

Stand comfortably with eyes closed, paying careful attention to your breathing. Consciously release any tension you feel in your body. Starting with your dominant side, raise your arm, being aware of any muscular sensations in your body as you do this. Lower your arm with the same focused awareness. Repeat this several times. Now do the same thing with your kinesthetic arm, mentally visualizing the action as clearly as possible, again noticing any muscular sensations. Alternate stretching your real and kinesthetic arm several times. Do the same thing with your other arm.

Repeat the exercise, this time alternately rotating real and kinesthetic shoulders first forward, than backward.

Next make a fencing lunge to the right with your real body. Return to center and repeat several times. Now lunge to the right with your kinesthetic body. Alternate lunging the two bodies to the right several times before repeating the exercise, this time lunging to the left. Next, you are going to lunge to the left with your real body while you are lunging to the right with your kinesthetic body. Come back to center before repeating, this time reversing the directions of your lunges. Stop and notice how your body is feeling.

Raise and hold your real arms in the air, maintaining awareness of your kinesthetic arms hanging at your sides. Now slowly and consciously raise your kinesthetic arms while lowering your real arms. Stop and rest.

Jump as high as you can into the space in front of you with your real body, then jump back. Do the same thing with your kinesthetic body. Alternate and repeat several times. Finally, jump forward with your kinesthetic body and stay there while you jump into your kinesthetic body with your real body. Before opening your eyes and moving around, breathe deeply and notice how your body feels.

Once the kinesthetic body sense has been developed, and this may take a great deal of practice, it can be used as a form of skill rehearsal for any sport or physical discipline.

## THE IDEAL BODY

After a kinesthetic sense has been established, this exercise can be used to increase body awareness by revealing unconsciously held negative body images and replacing them with positive ones. It will hopefully allow an integration of real and ideal body images.

Begin by standing comfortably and breathing deeply with your eyes closed. Starting with your dominant side you are going to scan your body, slowly and intimately, starting with the toes of one foot and finishing at the top of your head. If there are areas that are difficult to visualize, contract the muscles in those areas to increase awareness. Rest for a moment when you are done.

Now return your attention to your feet and quickly go over your body with your mind's eye from your toes to your head, then back down again. Repeat this several times.

Having thus inventoried your real body, imagine in great detail your ideal body. Place your ideal body in front of you so that you are looking at its back. Now jump into it. If it does not feel comfortable, jump out of it and adjust it, perhaps by making it more realistic. Jump into it again. Repeat this adjustment of your ideal body until you feel comfortable in it. When that occurs, move around in your ideal body as you begin to sense it becoming integrated with your real body.

## CONTACTING YOUR BODY WISDOM

In this exercise an attempt is made to initiate a dialogue with the personification of your innate body wisdom, one whom Houston calls "The One Who Knows Health." By giving voice to the stresses that our bodies are consciously and unconsciously subjected to, we are forced to become more conscious participants in our own health.

Begin this exercise by establishing contact with your kinesthetic body for a few minutes while you mentally focus on a question about your health. According to Houston, there is a definite relationship between the quality of the advice you receive and your commitment to acting upon it.

Lying or sitting comfortably, spend several minutes relaxing your body. Imagine, as clearly as you can, that you are on a mountaintop looking for a way down. Now, having discovered a rocky stairwell, imagine yourself descending until you reach a doorway at the bottom that leads into the mountain. Go through the door and down a hallway, all the while being aware that you are entering a place that contains special knowledge about your body.

At the end of the hall is a door with a sign that says "He who knows health." Enter the room and meet the being who knows all about your body and its needs. Sit down, still very relaxed, and ask any questions that you have. Be receptive to any message that you might receive—words, images, muscular sensations, or feelings. When you sense that the messages are done, ask "What can I do for you?" Receive the answer and sit quietly, focusing on your breathing for a few minutes.

When you are ready to leave, thank this being for knowledge offered and received. Close the door behind you and retrace your steps up to the top of the mountain. Open your eyes and experience your body.

This exercise may have to be repeated several times before contact can be made with your body wisdom. This wisdom may be personified as an animal or a child instead of an adult. In time, your body can become a powerful ally in attaining physical health and well being.

In the next section of *The Possible Human*, called "Awakening the Senses," the exercises attempt to increase sensory awareness to allow a more complete experiencing of reality. Houston believes that as most people learn to conceptualize and abstract, the quality of their perceptions are diminished. "Conceptualization isolates consciousness from its object, thought from experience, and the local consensual reality from the larger Reality" (Houston, 1982, p. 33). Not meaning to deny the importance of conceptualization for intellectual processing, her argument is that any one way of knowing is limiting. Citing Margaret Mead's capacity for sensual detail and Michael Faraday's multi-modal perception of space and energy as examples of the merger of conception and perception, she argues that the conscious development of all modes of knowing lead to real understanding and creativity.

## CLEANING THE ROOMS OF PERCEPTION

Begin by spending a few moments focusing on the different ways each sense allows you to experience your environment. Then close your eyes, breathe slowly and evenly, as you imagine yourself moving through one of your blood vessels, starting in your toe and ending up in the cerebral cortex of your brain. Now travel to your pineal gland, right between your eyes, where you will come to the House of the Senses. Turn the key in the door and put it in your pocket. Turn on the light and you will find yourself in a hallway full of cleaning supplies. You are going to clean up your senses and their neurological bases. The first room you will enter is the Room of Vision. Thoroughly dust and scrub this room, throwing out garbage and opening windows. When you are done, be aware of the light flooding your sight and notice that, looking out the window, you can see for miles.

At the end of this room is the door leading to the Room of Hearing. Go in, always remembering to leave the doors open between the rooms you enter. Now visualize yourself slowly and methodically cleaning this room. When you are done, walk around and listen to your footsteps. Stand by the open window and hear the wind in the trees, children laughing, and animals playing.

Now enter the Room of Smell. This is a very old room, filled with trunks and old bottles of deodorant and air freshener. Clean it and clear it out. Then open the window and smell the outdoors. At the end of this room is the door to the Room of Taste. This room is filled with all the debris from junk food you have ever eaten. Get rid of all the grease and grime. Then take an apple out of your pocket and eat it. When you have finished, notice another door at the end of the room. Go through the door into the Room of Touch. When you are done cleaning out this room, walk barefoot on the floor, touch the walls and window frames.

When you have finished, notice another locked door, go through it and back into the hall where you will leave all your garbage. Go up a stairway leading to the floor above and, feeling your senses refreshed, go up the stairs. This is the room of the Sixth Sense, home of all the senses not encountered below and the place where all the senses come together. Open the windows and make yourself at home before you start to clean out debris accumulated from your childhood. This room has a balcony which allows you to look down into the rooms below which are all connected by their open doors. Aware of the warm breeze blowing through the open windows and doors of your senses, inhale the fresh air of the Room of the Sixth Sense and swinging your head down, blow through all five rooms. Repeat circling with your head and blowing through all the rooms at least a dozen times.

Relax and become aware of the sensations in your body. Promise these rooms that you will keep them clean and come back often. Now go down the stairs to the front hall and get rid of the garbage. Open your eyes and be very conscious of your total environment as experienced by all your senses. The clarity of any particular room can be used as an indicator of your primary sensory mode.

## FINE TUNING THE SENSES

This exercise is to help you "tune" your senses in order to control the amount of stimulus that they bring you.

Imagine a dimmer switch that controls your sense of hearing with numbers on a dial going from 1 (softest) to 10 (loudest). Five will represent your usual level of hearing. Focus on some fairly even sound in your environment. Notice that it seems to get louder as you pay attention to it. Give this background noise the value of 3. Concentrate on the dial and turn it to 8, listen, then 9, listen, and then all the way to 10. Now turn it back to 3. Slowly turn it to 2, then 1, now quickly back to 3, then 2, then 1. Slowly move the dial around, listening to the changes in the volume of the sound until you can go easily from 1 to 10 and back, conscious of all the gradations in between.

## LISTENING TO MUSIC WITH YOUR WHOLE BODY AND SYNESTHESIAS

Pick up a piece of music to listen to that is not too familiar. Lie down on the floor, barefoot, dressed in loose, comfortable clothes. Focusing on your breathing, let go of any tension in your body.

As the music begins, allow it to flow over you, touching and caressing your entire body. Experience it moving around and through you. Do this for a complete piece of music and then change it. When you are able to really experience music in this way, allow yourself to feel the colors and the textures of the music, its smells and tastes, its temperatures, its light. Allow the music to seep through all your senses until you feel a part of it.

This exercise has been used by therapists to stimulate creativity.

## PLEASURES AND THEN SOME

Make a list of your personal pleasures. Then choose one that is especially vivid for you and visualize it as completely as possible, using all your senses. Let it fill your body. Maintaining awareness of the pleasure that you are experiencing, look at a problem that you had before you started this exercise. How does it look now?

In her next section, "Awakening the Brain," Houston suggests that it is possible to exercise the brain to prove its functioning, much the same way that one exercises the body. Because of Western culture's emphasis on rational, logical thinking, usually associated with the left hemisphere of the brain, the right hemisphere, the site of creative, non-linear, non-verbal information processing, is typically underutilized. Furthermore, the tremendous capacity for complex interactions between the two hemispheres is not being developed. By stimulating conscious use of the whole brain, the following exercises are meant to improve the quality and complexity of our intellectual functioning by increasing conceptual and perceptual fluidity.

## LEFT BRAIN/RIGHT BRAIN

This exercise was created by Robert Masters and first appeared in Listening to the Body. It tries to integrate many different brain functions: words, images, emotions, and senses. This exercise will have to be put on tape if it is to be done alone, otherwise it should be read to you.

Close your eyes and direct your attention to your breathing. Allow the rhythm of your breath to become regular. As you do this, allow your consciousness to rest in your solar plexus and gradually move up through your body, passing through your lungs and then your heart, moving up the left carotid artery to the left side of your brain. Move your awareness forward now to your left eye.

Keeping your eyes closed, look down with your left eye. Now up. Look to the left . . . and to the right. Keeping your awareness in your left eye, allow that eye to circle clockwise . . . and counterclockwise. Which direction is easier? You may find it easier if you are looking at a clock and follow the numbers of the clock as you move your eye.

Now shift your attention to your right eye. Keeping your eyes closed, look down and then up. Repeat this several times. Now move your eye from right to left. Allow your right eye to circle to the right and then to the left, clockwise and counterclockwise. Is this easier with the right eye than the left?

Relax your eyes, feeling them get soft and releasing the muscles around the socket. Rest for a minute.

Keeping your eyes closed, direct your attention to the right side of the brain . . . and now to the left. Shift back and forth easily a few times, noting any differences between the two sides of your brain. Does one seem more accessible than the other?

Keeping your eyes closed and relaxed, imagine the images that will be suggested as vividly as possible. Don't strain as you do this.

On the left side of your brain, imagine the number 1 . . .

And on the right side the letter A . . .

On the left side the number 2 . . .

And on the right side the letter B . . .

On the left the number 3 . . .

And on the right the letter C . . .

On the left the number 4 . . .

And on the right the letter D . . .

On the left the number 5 . . .

And on the right the letter E . . .

Continue with the numbers on the left and the letters on the right, going toward the number 26 and the letter Z. You don't have to actually reach 26 and Z. Just continue for a minute or so. If you get confused or lost, go back to the place where the letters and numbers were clearly together and begin again.

Rest for a minute, relaxing your attention as you do so.

Now reverse the process you have just done, putting the letters on the left and the numbers on the right.

On the left image the letter A . . .

And on the right the number 1 . . .

On the left the letter B . . .

And on the right the number 2 . . .

Keep going toward the letter Z and the number 26.

Stop and rest for a minute. Note whether it was easier on one side than the other, whether numbers or letters were more clearly imagined.

Continuing with your eyes closed, on the left side of your brain imagine a festive outdoor scene with a big picnic and fireworks.

On the right image a couple getting married.

Let that image go and, on the left, imagine a procession of nuns walking two by two through a lovely medieval cloister.

On the right there is a hurricane sweeping through a coastal town.

On the left is an atom.

On the right is a galaxy.

On the left are fruit trees bearing new blossoms.

On the right the trees are weighted down with frost and snow.

On the left is the sunrise.

On the right is the sunset.

On the left is a green jungle forest

On the right is a snow-covered mountain in the Alps.

On the left is a three-ring circus.

On the right is a thick fog.

On the left is the sensation of climbing rocks. Try to capture the feeling and sensation of the rocks and breathe easily as you experience it.

On the right, imagine how your hand feels caressing a baby's skin.

On the left, the feeling of plunging your hands into warm soppy mud.

On the right, that of making snowballs with your bare hands.

On the left you are pulling taffy.

On the right you are punching a punching bag.

Now, on the left hear the sound of a fire engine.

On the right the sound of crickets chirping.

On the left the sound of a car starting.

On the right somebody is singing in a very high voice.

On the left the sound of ocean waves on a beach.

On the right the sound of your stomach growling.

Now on the left the smell of a pine forest.

On the right imagine smelling freshly brewed coffee.

On the left the smell of gasoline.

On the right the smell of bread baking.

Now on the left brain, the taste of a crisp, juicy apple.

On the right the taste of hot buttered toast.

On the left the taste of a lemon.

On the right the taste of nuts.

Now on the left side of the brain, experience as fully as you can the following scene: you are riding a horse through the snow and sleet carrying three little kittens under your coat, and you are sucking on a peppermint.

On the right side of the brain, you are standing under a waterfall singing "You Are My Sunshine" and watching a nearby volcano erupt.

Now, eyes still closed, with your left eye look up toward your left brain. Move the eye so that it circles and explores this space. Roam around for a while.

Now do the same thing for a while with your closed right eye on the right side of the brain.

Now with the left eye trace some triangles on the left side of the brain. Now make some rectangles. Now make some stars.

Now with the right eye trace some triangles on the right side of the brain. Now make some rectangles. Now draw some stars.

Now make many overlapping circles on the left side, leaving spirals of light streaming from these circles into the left side of the brain. Imagine the brain as charged with energy by this light.

Make many overlapping circles on the right side with the right eye, leaving energizing light streaming from these circles.

Now, with both eyes, circle vertically just in the middle of the head. You should circle along the corpus callosum, the ridge where the hemispheres of the brain come together. With both eyes together, circle as widely as you can inside your head.

With both eyes, create spiraling galaxies throughout your brain. Fill the whole of your brain space and the inside of your head with them.

Stop and let your eyes come completely to rest.

Try to make horizontal circles with both eyes just at the level of your eyes, and circling as widely as possible inside your head. Now try making smaller circles horizontally at the level of your eyes. Make them smaller . . . and smaller . . . and smaller . . . until you get down to a space that is too small for circling and then you will want to fix on that point and try to hold it. Continue to breathe freely with your muscles relaxed as you do this. If you lose the point, make more large circles, letting them become smaller and smaller until you get back down to a point, staying fixed on that point for as long as you can easily.

(Circling inward and holding on the point in the center is an excellent meditation exercise when done by itself.)

Rest for a moment. Then, in the middle of your forehead, imagine a huge sunflower. Then erase the sunflower.

Simultaneously, imagine a sunflower on the left and some green damp moss on the right. Let them go.

Imagine that there is a big tree growing right in the middle of your forehead.

Let go of that, and imagine that there is a golden harp on the left, and just a little to the right of the harp is a drum. Try to hear them as they play together.

Let them go and imagine on the left an eagle, and on the right a canary, both of them there together at once. Let them go now, and imagine the canary now on the left and the eagle on the right.

Let them go, and imagine two eagles on the left and two canaries on the right. Let them fade away.

Breathe easily, and if you need to adjust your position to be more comfortable, do so.

Now, in the middle of your forehead, imagine a small sun. Then imagine the sun just inside the top of your head. Try to roll it down the inside of your skull to the inside of the back of your head, so that if your eyes could turn completely around in your head, they would be looking at it.

Now raise the sun along the back of your head to the top and then down to the forehead. Now raise it along the inside of the head from the forehead back to the top and then to the back of your head, and then to the top of the head and back to the forehead. The sun should be making vertical semicircles on the inside of your skull.

Now let that sun move out in front of you and see it setting over the sea. From somewhere in the direction of the sunset comes a sailboat. From what direction is the sailboat coming? From the left, from the right, or from some other direction?

Let that image fade away and imagine an elephant walking. Try to become more and more aware of him as he walks. He stops and eats something, pushing his long trunk into his mouth, then he walks some more, then he sees you and breaks into a run. He slows down and then he stops and eats some more.

Let the elephant go, and imagine seeing Santa Claus in a sleigh pulled by reindeer. Observe the sleigh and watch it accelerate, then slow down and stop, then start up again, going faster and faster as it circles around and down a spiral track that is inside of your head.

Starting from your chin, the sleigh spirals up and around and around and around until it reaches to the top of your head. Then it spirals down and around and around and around to your chin. Then it rushes up and around and around and around to the top of your head. Then it circles down and around and around to your chin. Circling now up and around and around and around to the top of your head. Let it stop there poised on the edge of the front of the top of your head.

Now yawn and let Santa and his sleigh and reindeer drive down over your nose and into your mouth, swallow the sleigh, and forget all about it!

Now focus your attention on the left side of your brain for a while. Concentrate on it and try to see or imagine what your brain looks like on the left side. Be aware of the gray matter and the convolutions of the brain. Concentrate in the same way on the right side of the brain. Pay attention to the thick bands of fibers that connect the two hemispheres of the brain.

Now try to sense both sides at once, the whole brain. Sense its infinite complexity, its billions of cells intercommunicating at the speed of light. Meditate on it as a universe in itself, whose dimensions and capacities you have only begun to dream of.

Now breathing very deeply, imagine that by inhaling and exhaling you can expand and contract your brain. And do this for a while, expanding your brain when you inhale slowly and deeply, and contracting your brain when you exhale slowly and completely.

Let your brain rest now and, holding its image, speak directly to your own brain, suggesting, if you wish, that its functioning will get better and better.

Suggest that you will have more brain cells accessible to you and that the interaction of the cells and all the processes of the brain will continuously improve as time goes by.

Tell it that the right and left hemispheres will be better integrated, as will older and new parts of the brain.

Advise your brain that many of its latent potentials can now become manifest and that you will try to work together with the brain in partnership to allow these potentials to develop in your life.

Listen now and see if your brain has any messages for you. These messages may come as words or images of feelings. Give the brain time to respond, withholding judgment. Does your brain want something from you? What does you brain want to give you?

Again being aware of the whole of the brain, begin to feel a real sense of both communication and communication with your brain.

Think of it as a new friend and of this friendship as a profound and beautiful new fact in your life. In the weeks to come, spend time nurturing and deepening this friendship so that the two of you (your brain and your consciousness) can work together in useful ways. But now, spend some minutes communing with your brain. Images may come to you, or feelings, or words, as together you move into a more complete partnership and friendship.

If you wish, while you do this, place your hands about half an inch above your head and have the sense that you are caressing the "field" around your brain, in the same way that you might pat or stroke the hand of a dear friend. (Allow about three or four minutes for this to happen.)

If you have some special intention for your brain, offer it now.

Continuing to feel a communion with your brain, open your eyes and look around. Observe whether there are any changes in your sensory perceptions. How do you feel in your body? What is your mood and your sense of reality? Do you feel that your possibilities have changed? Observe these things.

## MULTITRACKING

This exercise is an attempt to gain some conscious control over our brain's capacity for processing dozens, perhaps hundreds, of different functions and ideas at the same time. By learning how to use our conscious multiple tracking skills, they can be put to use to improve the quality and efficiency of our mental and emotional lives.

To begin, stand up and make sure you have enough room to move freely. Get centered and balanced.

Let your head and shoulders move from left to right together in an even swinging movement.

Now let your head and shoulders swing apart—that is, your head and shoulders are moving in opposite directions from each other, your head going left while your shoulders go right, and your shoulders going right while your head goes to the left.

Now your head and shoulders swing together . . .

And apart . . .

Together . . .

And apart . . .

Now, with your head moving in the opposite direction from your shoulders, let your eyes follow the shoulders. It's rather like flirting!

Don't get cross with yourself if you can't do this. Remember that we are just playing a game as well as asking you to awaken circuits in your brain that may never have been used before.

Now return just to the head and shoulders moving in opposite directions, your eyes doing anything they like. At the same time, tap dance.

At the same time sing a song like "Tea for Two."

Stop at the end of the song and rest for a minute.

Now let your head go right and your face go left.

Now reverse and let your head go left and your face go right.

Keep on doing this, reversing the order each time.

Add a little jog and snap your fingers. At the same time move your hands in circles.

And hum "Yankee Doodle Dandy"!

And, simultaneously, think about a hive of bees, a spiral staircase, and a bowl of Jell-O!

Stop and rest for a minute.

Now let your hips and arms swing back and forth together.

Now let your hips and arms swing in opposite directions.

Now together again.

And now in opposite directions.

At the same time, jump up and down.

Add a boxing movement with your hands.

And whistle "Dixie."

And think about Marie Antoinette, a ski slope in the Alps, and a giraffe.

And a giant traffic jam and buttered popcorn.

Stop and rest for a minute.

Lie down on your back on the floor with your knees bent, the soles of your feet on the ground, and your hands on your chest.

Begin to raise and lower your elbows in a flapping motion.

At the same time bicycle with your legs.

Now put your feet on the ground and open your knees wide and bring them back together in a flapping motion while you bicycle with your arms.

Now flap with your arms and bicycle with your legs.

Change.

Change once again.

And sing "A Bicycle Built for Two" or "Row, Row, Row Your Boat," changing the movement of your arms and legs at the end of each line.

Stop and rest for a minute after you have done this for a while.

Still lying down with your knees bent and your arms at your sides, begin beating very slowly on the floor with your right hand.

Now add a fast beat with your left hand while your right hand continues to beat slowly.

Keeping these two motions going, let your right foot begin to tap a slow beat.

Keeping all these motions going, let your left foot begin to tap a fast beat.

Stop.

Let your left hand beat a slow beat.

Now add your right foot tapping a slow beat.

Now add your right hand beating a fast beat.

Now add your left foot tapping a fast beat.

Keep all of this going for a few minutes.

Stop and rest.

Stand up now, and again let your head go right and your face go left.

Now reverse and let your head go left and your face go right.

Keep on doing this, reversing the order each time.

Add a little jog and snap your fingers.

At the same time move your hands in circles.

And hum "Yankee Doodle Dandy."

And, simultaneously, think about a hive of bees, a spiral staircase, and a bowl of Jell-O!

Stop and rest for a minute. Be aware of any improvements you have noticed.

Now for the most interesting and subtle of the sequences:

Standing in a comfortable and relaxed position, close your eyes and become totally centered and balanced.

Take four steps forward and imagine, kinesthetically and actively, that you are taking four steps backward.

Now take four steps backward while thinking four steps forward.

Keep repeating this for a few minutes until it seems natural.

Now, as you move forward, allow your arms and hands to move in clockwise circles.

As you move backward, reverse the direction of your arms and hands.

Continue to do this for a while.

Now, keeping all of the motions and thoughts going, think counter-clockwise while you are making a clockwise motion with your hands, and think clockwise when you are making a counter-clockwise motion.

At this point you are taking four steps forward and making a clockwise circle with your hands while you are thinking four steps backward and thinking a counter-clockwise circle for your hands. Then you are taking four steps backward and making a counter-clockwise circle with your hands while thinking four steps forward and clockwise with your hands.

Continue to do this for five to fifteen minutes, until it becomes a simultaneous dance of movement and thinking. Should you lose one or more of these tracks, stop and begin again, adding movement and thinking sequences gradually until you are comfortable with all of them.

One of the greatest human gifts, a gift that continues to elude scientific understanding, is our capacity for memory. Brain research seems to indicate that memories themselves are never lost but that retrieval systems vary greatly from individual to individual and generally seem to deteriorate with age. The tragedy is that by losing our memories, chances are we have also blocked or lost those times of our life" (Houston, 1982, p. 83). The exercises in "Awakening Memory" are meant to help us recapture the missing spaces in our lives in order to reexperience and learn from those that were positive and, also, to try to somehow come to terms with those that were painful or traumatic.

## PRIMING THE MEMORY BANK

This exercise is based on Houston's observation that activating early sensory memories seems to improve memory in general. The exercise should be done with a partner. One person, the rememberer, lies on the floor with eyes closed. The other person reads the directions. Later they will reverse roles.

Part 1. The reader says "Tell me about . . . from your childhood," completing the sentence with each of the phrases from the list that follows allowing two minutes for each response: a very young boy, an old lady, your favorite foods, a favorite or hated teacher, eating an ice cream cone, your bedroom, climbing a tree, what you usually ate for breakfast, some favorite shoes, a family vacation.

Now switch roles and continue. "Tell me about . . . a balloon, going to the store, going to the beach, favorite songs you sang, a birthday party, blowing bubble gum, a very young girl, an old man, interesting smells you remember, a favorite cartoon character.

Stand up and notice how your body and head feel.

Part 2. These directions can be put on tape or two people can take turns reading them aloud. Sit down with your eyes closed. Now without speaking, as vividly as you can remember, allowing one minute for each memory, "Remember getting up this morning, what your were doing at this time yesterday, high school graduation, hearing about JFK's assassination, some event from last summer, the first time you fell in love, your first day at school, the last time you went to the grocery store, your earliest memory ten years from now, the signing of the Declaration of Independence, William Shakespeare watching a performance of Hamlet at the Globe Theatre, Joan of Arc leading the Armies of France, Cleopatra floating down the Nile on her barge, building the Great Wall of China, the giant dinosaurs dragging their huge bodies across the earth, the creation of the earth, the creation of the universe, a million years from now, yourself at this moment. Open your eyes and share your experiences.

## RECALLING THE CHILD

This exercise allows you to reenter the past, from the present, and helps heal your early traumas by integrating your past and present selves. It should be done with one person acting as guide. It is also suggested that a drum be used to mark the passage across time.

Sitting comfortably with your eyes closed, become aware of your inhalations and exhalations. Do this exercise pretending that you still exist somewhere as a child, a child who does not know it has grown up in another reality.

With the sound of the drum, call your child to come to you from wherever it exists. When you feel the presence of your child, respond and interact with the child, in whatever ways seem appropriate to you. Take the next fifteen minutes to befriend and love your child, allowing yourself to receive the child's love and friendship as well.

This exercise can stop here, after saying good-by to your child, perhaps promising to visit again, or you can go on to the next stage.

## BECOMING BEFRIENDED BY YOUR EXTENDED BEING

In this part of the exercise you are a child to the extended version of yourself, who you would be if all your potentials were fully realized. Close your eyes and again focus on your breathing as your fully realized self enters your reality and comes to meet you. (Sound the drum 10 or 20 times.) For the next five to ten minutes allow yourself to be nurtured by your "High Self," acknowledging the caring and power that are the embodiment and fulfillment of your own beauty and strength.

Now call forward again the child that you were. Hold the child in your arms as your other Self holds you, creating a perfect trinity. Experience the love and support that flows between you. Allow five minutes for this part of the exercise.

Let your child and your High Self return to their own realities, knowing that you can call them back whenever you need to. Know, also, that you carry around both these selves within yourself and that this connection must be acknowledged frequently to be truly realized.

The exercises in the next chapter of *The Possible Human,* "Awakening Your Evolutionary History," will not be included here because they are not primarily imagery exercises. They are still very interesting and can be a meaningful part of the sequence of this work. Interested readers are encouraged to refer to *The Possible Human.*

## DYADS OF ACKNOWLEDGMENT AND COMMUNION

This exercise is an invitation to overcome the competition, jealousy, guilt, and all the other negative attitudes that so frequently affect our relationships with each other. Instead, this is an opportunity to experience a totally different way of relating to each other, to experience the pleasure that comes from exercising "the potential of each one of us to acknowledge and empower another" (Houston, 1982, p. 123).

This exercise is done with a partner. Sitting across from each other with your eyes closed, let your fingertips touch throughout the exercise.

You begin by breathing deeply and evenly, focusing your awareness on your fingertips. Noticing the heat, muscular sensations, and pulses, feel the flow of energy between your fingers. Do this for two minutes.

Keeping your fingertips together, open your eyes and look into the eyes of your partner, seeing the fully realized being that exists there. Still conscious of the energy flow, receive the universal humanity of the other knowing that yours is also being received.

Now close your eyes and imagine yourself as a unified receiving station on reality. For the next few minutes, allow yourselves to receive everything present in the room whether it is physical, emotional, or spiritual by nature.

Now be a receiver for the neighborhood, the country, the Western hemisphere, the planet earth, the solar system, the galaxy, the Universe, and the mind of God. Allow sixty seconds for each experience.

Slowly open your eyes, again receiving your partner but this time receive the everyday self, the eternal self, and your fellow traveler. Do this for two minutes.

Close your eyes and bring your foreheads together, deeply acknowledging the power and beauty that flow between you. Do this for one minute. Now pull your heads back and look into each other's eyes.

Although imagery techniques are used throughout her work, it is in the chapter called "The Creative Realms of Inner Space and Time" that Houston directly addresses the subject of imagery. Describing the natural human capacity to use imagistic thought as the simultaneous patterning of ideas and images, she explains how this capacity, so pronounced in children, gets inhibited in most of us by the accepted emphasis on the development of verbal thinking. The following findings that came out of her imagery studies, conducted with hundreds of subjects, all point to the potential for enriching our lives inherent in the imagery process: "that the visual-imagery process seems to be essentially creative, tending to gather meanings and seek out solutions"; "that prolonged vivid narrative imagery, especially if it is repeatedly experienced, increases motivation to do creative work and also sometimes breaks through creative blocks"; and "that there are imagery experiences that, liberating and serving the needs of autonomy or self-actualizing tendency, leads to a higher order of creativity as a consequence of maturation and growth" (Houston, 1982, p. 145). The exercises in this chapter attempt to begin the reactivation of our typically diminished imagery capacities.

## BECOMING UNITS OF TIME

Since imagery is essentially a right hemisphere process and the right hemisphere is not time bound, images are not related to serial clock time either. Rather, they occur in what Houston and Masters call ATP, alternate temporal process, the time of dreams, altered states of consciousness, and, frequently, creative experiences. During ATP, a great many ideas and images are experienced simultaneously, extending in consciousness for hours, days, or longer, yet actually occurring in only a few minutes of objective clock time. This exercise is used to restore a sense of fluidity to the experiencing of time by allowing you to become a unit of time.

Before the exercise begins, you must practice moving into a hyperalert state by making a buzzing sound like a bee—zzzzzzz. Allow this sound to resonate through your body. Stay relaxed and focused as you repeat the sound. This exercise is done in a comfortable and supported position. You will try to look at reality through the eyes of a person whose being is structured by units of time. With eyes opened or closed, make the zzzzzzz sound resonate through your body.

Begin with and alternate the buzzing sounds (allowing 30-60 seconds) with each of the following images (allowing 15-60 seconds for each image). Zzzzzzz. You are now one second, experience reality from the perspective of being one second. Zzzzzzz. Then be one minute, then one hour, then one day, one week, one month, one year, 100 years, 1000 years, 10,000 years, one million years.

Look around and describe your experience of being one million years.

## THE YARDSTICK OF TIME

According to the work of Dr. Humphrey Osmond and Dr. Bernard Aronson, when you change time, you change reality. This exercise helps you learn to control your experience of time in order to influence your mood and perceptions by giving you some understanding of where you seem to live on the time continuum.

Seated comfortably, imagine a yardstick, 36 inches long with the first 12 inches representing time past, the next 12 inches, time present, and the last 12 inches, time future. Determine where you live on the yardstick, in the past, present, or future. Now breathing deeply, exhale, and let go of time. Repeat this for several minutes. Imagining the yardstick, visualize the divisions changing as the past and present shorten to only 8 inches, allowing 20 inches for the future. Focus your awareness on experiencing yourself in the realm of expanded future. Open your eyes, look around and move your body, still aware of living in future time.

Close your eyes, breathe, exhale, and once again, let go of time. Now repeat the experience, assigning 20 inches of the yardstick to time past. Finally, expand present time to 30 inches, allowing only 3 inches for the past and future. Experience yourself in the powerful expanded present.

## THE ARCHAEOLOGY OF THE SELF

Houston's research on imagery uncovered four levels of the psyche: the sensory, the recollective-analytic, the symbolic-mythic, and the integral-religious. Each level is characterized by its own style of imagery and content, logic, and psychological dimensions. This exercise can help you live your own reality more fully by allowing you to probe these different levels of the self. This exercise works best when you are guided through it.

*The sensory level:* Sitting or lying comfortably, close your eyes and breathe deeply. Inhale, holding an image of air rising into and energizing your brain. Exhale, maintaining the sense of your brain being aerated. Continue breathing like this for a minute, all the time aware of a deepening sense of self. You will repeat this breathing at the beginning of each level.

You are walking down the street when a large crocodile comes toward you. You have one minute of clock time, all the time that you need, to find out what happens.

*The recollective-analytic level:* Again, energize your brain with conscious breathing for one minute.

You are standing in front of a full length mirror that shines with an inner light. Reaching out and touching the mirror, your hand slips through the glass. You follow your hand to the other side of the mirror. You have two minutes to explore the other side.

*The symbolic-mythic level:* Energize your brain for one minute. Now you are walking in the forest and you hear the sound of hoof-beats behind you. You turn and on a majestic black horse sits a distinguished, benign looking skeleton in armor. Bowing to you, he presents you with a golden chalice. You have three minutes of clock time to finish this adventure.

*The integral-religious level:* Breathe for two minutes, sensing that each breath is taking you deeper inside of yourself. You are on a tourist bus traveling in the Holy Land. The bus stops on the outskirts of Jerusalem. You take advantage of some free time to wander off by yourself in the hills. Suddenly the air and light change and the road beneath your feet disappears. All signs of modern culture are gone and you become aware of a powerful silence. Looking around, you notice a large stone wedged into the hill in front of you. Pushing the stone away, you discover the entrance to a cave. Inside is a human figure wrapped in a blood stained shroud. Knowing who it is, you lean over and tell the figure that it is time to wake up now.

You have four minutes of clock time to finish this exercise.

## SKILL REHEARSAL WITH A MASTER TEACHER

In this exercise you evoke someone who will be a symbolic representation of all the knowledge and artistry of a skill you have learned but still need to perfect. This master may be someone you know or a historical figure like Mozart or Einstein.

Begin by actually going through the motions of your chosen skill, then repeat the motions kinesthetically. Go back and forth several times. Then run around for a few minutes—actually jumping, running, or tumbling. When you are totally exhausted, lie down and listen to the following instructions.

Imagine yourself alone, lying in the bottom of a rowboat. You are very relaxed, even drowsy, as you sense the gentle waves carrying you further and further out. Slowly you become aware of the boat going down and around, deeper and deeper into the ocean. The water is not closing in on you, it is creating a tunnel of spinning water through which you can still see the sky. Finally, you land on the ocean floor. Getting out of the boat, you see a circular door with a bronze handle. Opening the door, you can see a stone stairwell leading to a world under the ocean. Going down the stairs you find yourself in a cavern filled with beautiful stalagmites and stalactites. You wander through the cavern until you come to a corridor. At the end of the corridor is a door over which is written, "The Room of the Skill."

Behind the door is a room whose atmosphere is permeated with the presence and spirit of your skill. Your Master Teacher is here and will give you powerful instructions to improve your skill. The teachings may just be feelings or muscular sensations, verbal messages or images. Just be receptive to whatever happens, knowing that the skilled person within you is undergoing some very intensive training. You have five minutes of clock time but you know that is all the time that you need.

Now you must leave. Thank your Master, knowing that you can return as often as you like. Before you go, look up and notice the stream of light that is coming through the ceiling. This is the light of confirmation of your skill. Go and stand under it.

Leave the room, close the door, and quickly run through the corridor. With the constant awareness of your skill growing inside of you, go up the stairs and when you reach the ocean floor, get back into the boat. Feel your skill becoming more and more powerful as it moves through your entire being. The vortex of water pushes you to the ocean's surface and the waves carry you back to shore. Anxious to try your new skill, you leap out of the boat and pull it in.

Open your eyes. You are wide awake and eager to really try your skill. First, practice for awhile physically, then, kinesthetically. Go back and forth until you feel the full integration of the two.

In her final chapter, "Toward a New Natural Philosophy," Houston describes her vision of the possible humans. They are those individuals who have learned to think in multimodal ways, who have been able to recognize their "psychospiritual and neural functioning to bypass the cerebral, cultural and psychological reducing values" (Houston, 1982, p. 193). Using the metaphor of the hologram, she explains that we are all really a part and the whole of a much larger reality. The natural conclusion of an expanded consciousness, then, is the ability to experience the fundamental connectedness of Life while using personally developed sources of creativity and energy to effect important changes in society. Although she clearly acknowledges the spiritual and mystical foundations for her ideas, Houston cites a great deal of research from physics and neurology to defend her vision. For her, science and religion are not incompatible, rather, they are different means, both equally valid and very compatible, of exploring and understanding reality.

## ORCHESTRATING THE BRAIN AND ENTERING THE HOLOVERSE

This exercise was originally created by Robert Masters. Like his other exercise, "Left Brain/Right Brain," this one also has you "talking" to your brain. This time, however, you will be trying to extend your vision to the universe and beyond.

Sit comfortably, close your eyes, and breathe deeply. With a great deal of awareness, move your right hand over your skull where your brain is. Now, using both hands, hold as much of your skull as possible. Gently massage your scalp for several minutes. Stop and notice how your scalp and hands feel.

Now look inside your brain at your left hemisphere and then your right hemisphere. Try to find the corpus collum that connects the two hemispheres, like a bridge. Imagine yourself going up and down this bridge. Now imagine yourself walking through your brain, feeling your brain expanding with each deep inhalation and contracting with each deep exhalation.

Knowing that your mind directs the brain to produce different kinds of wave patterns, suggest to your mind and your brain that, acting together, they produce alpha waves, the waves associated with meditation and serene states of consciousness. Breathe and maintain consciousness with your brain as it produces the long amplitude waves of alpha. Next, tell your brain to produce the slower waves of theta, the waves of creativity. Now delta waves, the sleep producing waves. After several minutes, direct your mind to the production of beta waves. These much faster waves make you very alert. See if you can tell the differences between the different kinds of waves.

Now suggest to your brain that it produce endorphin, the natural painkiller that also produces euphoria and pleasure. If you are experiencing any pain in your body, direct it there. Next, direct your brain to activate its pleasure centers. See if you can feel the pleasurable sensations flowing into your body.

Again, tell your body to produce alpha waves, then theta waves, then delta waves.

Tell your brain to stimulate and activate those parts responsible for imagery. Stimulate your senses by intensifying the activity of your nervous and sensory systems. Focus on each of your five senses.

Massage your scalp again, as in the beginning, aware of the shape of your skull underneath. Be aware now of your whole brain.

Now focus your attention on your spine. Notice where it joins your skull and follow it down to the coccyx. Go up and down your spine several times. Next, concentrate on the space between your eyebrows, the location of your pineal gland, sometimes identified with the third eye. Try to stimulate that gland, the third eye, knowing that you are activating your visionary potentials. Pretend that a third eye really does exist in that place. Open and close it, think about its shape and color. What does it allow you to see?

Again suggest to your brain that it become more alert, that it is responsible for the optimum functioning of the systems of your body. Allowing your body image to enter your awareness, be conscious of your body as part of all that exists. Now visualize your hands extending into space and time, your arms spanning the universe. Your pelvis is the source of all creation and your heart the center of existence. Your shoulders hold up the world and your head holds the "continuum of totalities." Your breath is the breath of Life and in your head, your friend, your brain, begins to play a symphony.

All your brain waves become one wave, one melody. The song is the song of the Holoverse, the song of being. Receive the Source, the Holoverse, the beginning and totality of all things and of God. Receive everything. Allow five minutes for this.

Begin to come back now, knowing you can plug into the Source whenever you need to. Suggest to yourself that you are waking up and becoming more alert. Direct your mind and brain to work together, to help you become so alert that your former existence feels like a dream. You are no longer vulnerable to social, biological, or unconscious pressures. You are awake and free to control your own life, to experience yourself completely, to consciously connect with the Holoverse, with all there is.

Your unconscious and conscious minds, your body and body image, are moving toward unity and awareness. Who you are in time and space and who you are in the larger reality are coming together so they can communicate with each other. When you are ready and you feel these connections and their power, wake up and open your eyes. Continue to allow what you have learned and experienced to affect you.

This concludes the imagery exercises from *The Possible Human*. More complete directions as well as numerous suggestions for variations on each exercise are to be found in the original, as well as extensive discussions of relevant research and theory. At this time, the three books that preceded *The Possible Human* will be described and some of their imagery exercises will be presented. Examining Houston's work in this way makes it possible to understand the evolution of her ideas and techniques.

*Mind Games* was the first book by Houston and Masters to come out of their research on non-drug induced altered states of consciousness. It is an ordered collection of mental exercises meant to take individuals to increasingly higher levels of awareness by allowing them to experience different states of consciousness. It is intended to be used by groups of individuals, led by a designated guide, who are committed to participating in all the exercises. *Mind Games* is organized into four sections, or Books. The introduction makes it very clear that every game should be played in sequence and the order of the Books themselves should be maintained. A great deal of research went into the ordering of the games so that each one builds on the experiences of those preceding as it takes participants further along the continuum of consciousness.

Many of the exercises in *Mind Games* use imagery techniques to expand consciousness, but it is impossible to describe them all here. Several of the exercises will be presented to allow the reader to see how the authors use imagery to induce ASCs (altered states of consciousness) and increase the experiential capacities of the mind. The following exercise appears in Book One and is the first method used to induce ASCs.

After being led through a deep relaxation, you will be guided back through a dream that you once had as a child, a dream that may have been forgotten but will now be remembered. In the dream, you leave your bed and go through a secret door in the back of your closet. On the other side of the door is an ancient stone staircase that takes you down to the edge of a pool of dark water where you find a boat. Lying in a bed of blankets on the bottom of the boat, you are gently rocked by the water as you move toward a light coming through an opening in the distance. Finally, you reach and go through the opening and you find yourself being bathed by warm sunlight. Still being rocked by the water, feeling very peaceful and content, you notice birds singing, fish jumping, the smell of flowers and grass.

Continuing to float, your boat finally reaches shore at the edge of a meadow. You leave the boat and walk through the tall grass, conscious of the life all around you, the breeze and the sun's heat, conscious of your body moving. You approach a large tree and set down beneath it. Relax and enjoy your surroundings. Sit in total harmony with the world around you, feeling the connectedness of everything as you prepare to play the games.

## THE ALICE GAME (FROM BOOK ONE)

You are lying on your back and ASC's have been induced. You are guided through a deep relaxation, focusing on how heavy the different parts of your body become as you relax them. When you are feeling very heavy, the experience is reversed. Now you become aware of getting lighter and lighter, until you feel so light that it seems difficult to maintain contact with the ground. Next, you are shrinking. You get smaller and smaller until you are just six inches tall. Take your time experiencing each of these changes. Now you are starting to grow. You get bigger and bigger until you are eight feet tall. Experience and enjoy your strength and energy. Slowly return to your normal size. You will now be guided through several more transformations. You will be a rock, then metal, then a piece of wood that turns into a tree that blows in the wind. Then you become the wind itself, blowing over the earth until, transformed once again, you return to your own body.

## THE SMASHING OF THE ENSLAVING IDOLS
## (FROM BOOK TWO)

ASCs are induced and deepened. Know that your capacity for experiencing the world through your senses has been diminished. It is as if you see the world through a thick transparent substance. Imagine a beautiful scene from Nature for a minute. Now watch yourself placing a thick sheet of a glassy substance between yourself and that scene so that you can no longer sense it completely. Next, imagine yourself picking up a sledge hammer and smashing that obstruction, knowing that what you are destroying represents all the impediments to awareness that interfere with your experiencing of life. You have five minutes to destroy any other crippling, negative symbols, or idols that have prevented you from realizing your potentials, any values, attitudes, or expectations that have stunted your personal growth.

## THIS EXERCISE, FROM BOOK THREE,
## HAS NO NAME

ASCs have been induced and deepened. You are walking on a path in a jungle until you come to a clearing where a primitive people are involved in a powerful, wild ritual. There is a great deal of chanting and drumming. At first, you are just a spectator. You watch the fire in the center of the circle and see the naked dancing bodies as you listen to the throbbing of the drums. Soon, you become a part of the ritual, you know everything the others know and become part of the collective experience. Allow several minutes for this part of the exercise.

Now you are going to be transported to a mountainous region that looks like Tibet or India. You are approaching a large stone temple, very high in the mountains. Going deeper into trance, you go up the steps into the temple. Inside you see a group of monks that have come to sing and pray. The songs that the monks sing are prayers that have been sung by their order for thousands of years. They use their music to make direct contact with God. Experience their God meeting them through their music as you listen. Now give yourself up totally to the music so that you can experience their God yourself.

By the time that the players have reached Book Four, they are functioning at a very deep level of trance. They are able to induce and deepen ASCs without the guide. At this point, there is very little need to suggest images to them, since powerful images are now being generated by the participants' own altered states of consciousness.

In Houston and Master's next book, *Listing to the Body*, the focus shifts to the other end of the mind-body continuum. As previously discussed, this book is an introduction to their system of Psychophysical Reeducation. The primary imagery technique used in this work is the mental visualization of physical movements of the body. This technique is the same one that was used in the "Kinesthetic Body" exercise of *The Possible Human*. While most of the book is devoted to exercises that involve physical movements, real and imagined, there is one group of exercises that rely much more heavily on the "subjective" component with very little movement of the body in space. Several of these exercises will be presented below.

## STIMULATING THE NERVOUS SYSTEM

This exercise attempts to explore the brain's connection with various parts of the body through the nervous system. Seated comfortably with your eyes closed, you begin by focusing your awareness on the interior of your mouth. Then you move on to your nasal passages and then to your eyes. This is all done slowly and consciously, trying to sense each of these parts and their component structures very distinctly. Attention is then focused on each part of your brain, ending with the brain stem. Imagine a line running from the base of your brain to each of your eyes. As you breathe, imagine the impulses moving between them. Now move your attention to the space behind your eyes, inside your head, and imagine impulses moving between that part of your brain and eyes. Now look at the top of your brain, right under your skull, and again imagine impulses from the pupil of each eye to the center of the upper brain. Next, connect the following three points into a triangle and send impulses through it with your mind, letting your eyes follow. Look toward your right eye, then to the top of your head, back to the left eye, and over to the right eye. Now do it again, reversing directions.

Now focus your attention on the left side of your brain. Look from the inside of your head at your ear and nasal passages and at your eye. Imagine the whole physical brain as clearly as possible while you think of it as the complex dynamic structure that it is. Try to think of your brain as a relay center for your directions as you speak to it. Still concentrating on your brain, just visualize your right hand clenching into a fist. Imagine the signals from your brain going down your arm telling your hand to make a fist. Try to sense your hand responding, be aware of the slightest movement in your muscles, even though your hand is not really clenched. Now send a message to your hand to relax, then to make a fist again. Remember to keep your hand motionless. Repeat this several times, trying to become more and more aware of the impulses, the messages, between your right hand and your brain.

Concentrate on your brain and notice if your awareness is more on the left or right side of your brain, your arm, your hand. Look to the left with your eyes and again sense your brain inside your skull. Now focus your awareness on the base of your spine, then up your spine to the top of your brain and back down again. Do this several times, conscious of your spine as a connection between the top of your head and your genitals.

Now let the mind suggest to the brain and nervous system that energy is gathering at a point near the base of your spine and genitals, and that this energy will move into and up the spine, through the brain to the top of your head and then all the way back down. Bring the energy back up to the brain and imagine it swirling around, energizing your brain. Watch it move to the point between your eyes, circling and swirling, then moving up and circling in a horizontal plane below the top of your head. Use your eyes to watch it swirl.

Know that you can make changes happen in your brain just by imagining them, just as you did with your hand. These changes will occur whether you can sense them or not. Again, sense the energy swirling and getting stronger, stimulating brain cells and improving their functioning, improving the functioning of your entire nervous system. Feel the energy moving down your spine being conducted to every part of your body through your nerves.

Breathe deeply and pull yourself up so that you are sitting more erect. Does that increase your awareness of the internal movement of your nervous system? Watch the energy concentrate there and move to your brain, stimulating your nervous system. Contract your rectum several times to see if that further stimulates the energy flow. Now let the energy rise to your brain again and then slowly open your eyes. Sitting quietly, notice how you feel.

## USING WORDS AND IMAGES TO ALTER THE BODY

Lie down with your arms at your sides and your palms down. Now scan your body image. Notice what areas you can sense quite strongly, which areas are difficult to sense. This exercise should cause very recognizable changes in the body and the body image. Slowly scan your body again.

Focus your attention on your left foot, flexing the toes several times. Now imagine flexing them, ten or fifteen times, maintaining normal breathing throughout. Now actually flex your foot four or five times, then imagine flexing it ten or fifteen times. Now imaging doing it ten or fifteen times. Now actually bend and raise the knee, then let it drop. Do this ten or fifteen times, noting all the sensations it causes in your leg and hip. Repeat the movements in your imagination, still aware of the sensations. Next rap just your left palm on the floor five times. Then imagine doing it fifteen or twenty times. Then rap with your hand, this time bending it at the elbow. Now imagine it. Now rap with your hand by raising and lowering your whole arm off the floor. Repeat this movement in your imagination.

Next, stroke the left side of your face with your left hand, noticing the sensations in your hand and face. Then imagine doing the same thing. Now, only in your imagination, move your left hand up and down the left side of your body, from the top of your chest all the way down your body to your foot. Then imagine your left leg being stroked by someone else's hand, then by two hands, one on the outside of your leg and the other on the inside. Now imagine the bottom of your left foot being stoked and then gently stimulated by someone's fingernails. One hand now takes hold of your foot and the other massages each one of your toes. Now imagine your masseur (or masseuse) using a soft brush to methodically stimulate the whole left side of your body. Then rest for a moment and notice if you have more sensation on one side of your body than the other. Open your eyes and look directly at the ceiling. If either eye seems to be straining, it means that your head is leaning to one side. If this is the case, adjust your head and then close your eyes again.

Bend your left leg so that the foot is flat on the floor and your knee is pointing to the ceiling. Now sense your entire left side, one part at a time, starting with your toes and ending with your left eye. Rap the bottom of your left foot on the floor several times. Now, imagine it. Rap your left hand, bending your arm at the elbow. Now imagine rapping with your left hand, bending first at the wrist, then the elbow, then lifting the whole arm. Extend your left leg and lay it on the floor.

Your masseur is going to massage your left side again with warm oil, starting with the foot. Next, hot wet towels are applied, this time starting at your head. Take all the time you need to imagine these processes vividly. Now, your side is briskly dried off with a towel, starting at the feet. Finally, the hands go all over your body, still on your left side, gently slapping your skin.

Rest for a few minutes and, with your eyes closed, notice where your eyes are looking. Focusing attention on your left leg and foot, suggest to yourself ten times, that your leg feels heavy and warm, that the blood is flowing through your left leg and into your foot. Do this all over your left side. When you are done, repeat ten times, "My left side is heavy, warm, and relaxed." Next, suggest to your foot that it is feeling more and more alive. Notice that your awareness of your foot is increasing. Picture your foot, based on your sensing. Fill in any gaps with your memory. Do this with your entire left side. Notice where your eyes are looking.

Now imagine a line dividing your body in half. Sense the left side and imagine how it looks. Imagine flexing your toes, your foot, your ankle. Imagine rapping the back of your knee on the floor, then your hand. Then imagine and sense your arm as you lift it off the floor.

Now imagine flexing your foot, rapping your palm on the floor, and bending your arm at the wrist all at the same time. Then flex your left toes and fingers simultaneously, then imagine flexing them alternately. Breath normally as you do this. Open your eyes and make sure you are looking straight up. Move your head if there is any strain. Observe your body image again. Compare how the two sides of your body are lying on the ground. After you are done, roll over to one side and slowly get up.

Houston calls her next book, *Life Force: The Psycho-Historical Recovery of the Self,* a "journey of transformation" (Houston, 1980, p. 29). Like *Mind Games,* its exercises are meant to be experienced in a particular sequence by individuals in a group. Here the focus is not on mind expansion or physical functioning but, rather, on psychological development. The book evolved out of Houston's studies in history, philosophy, and psychology and is based on the idea that the stages of an individual's psychosocial development from infant to adult recapitulates mankind's psychosocial evolution.

Houston perceives the history of the individual and society as being divided into five related stages. The first stage, primitive, pre-individualistic society, corresponds to infancy. This stage is followed by the Heroic Age of Man, a period of self-assertiveness and differentiation. This historical period corresponds to an individual's childhood. The next stage is marked by self-consciousness and the search for identity. It is the period that saw the emergence and development of the transcendent religions and philosophies of the world and corresponds to adolescence. The fourth stage, which began in the beginning of the fifteenth century, was the Age of the Individual. Self-sacrifice for God or society was no longer the ideal as capitalism and technology created a new ideal of self-sufficiency. This age corresponds to what Houston calls the first maturity. The final stage is just evolving historically and corresponds to the later years of life, the second maturity. Based on a vision of responsible, global interdependence and cross-cultural learning, it is an age of post-individual man.

## BIRTH AS TRAUMA

This exercise is done on the floor in pairs. One person acts as the parent-womb and curls around the other who is the fetus. This is meant to be an reenactment of a typical hospital birth before the influence of the natural childbirth movement. The guide leads the participants through the birth, instructing each pair to act out their appropriate parts. The birth begins peacefully in the womb but quickly changes to the painful, frightening contractions of birth. After birth, you reexperience being held upside down and slapped to make you breathe through your lungs. Your eyes are assaulted by bright lights and stinging drops. Then, after further probing and handling, you are wrapped in a blanket and left alone in a bassinet.

## THE BLESSED BIRTH

The partners switch roles as they are led through a "rebirthing" based on the Leboyer Method of Childbirth outlined in *Birth Without Violence*. Again, this exercise begins in the womb, but there is a greater emphasis and longer experiencing of prenatal pleasures. The pain and terror of contractions and birth are repeated but this time you are born into a darkened, silent room. You are placed on your mother's naked stomach immediately and your cord is not cut until your lungs have begun to respirate on their own. Your mother massages your body and then you are placed into a warm pool of water, reminiscent of the womb. After a comforting period of weightlessness, you are carefully wrapped in a blanket and placed next to your mother.

These two exercises were from section one, called "The Cradle of Awakening." The next two exercises come from section two, "The Shining Hour."

## THE PROTEST

This exercise is almost identical to the one in *Mind Games* called "The Smashing of the Enslaving Idols." An imaginary sledge hammer or mace is used to destroy the symbols or forces that have prevented you from reaching your potential as a human being, all the restraints and limits that have been put on you since childhood.

## I BECOME WHAT I BEHOLD

The exercise begins by having the group gather around an old weathered log. You are to call out anything that you see in the log—faces, animals, etc. Now look more closely, and from a deeper level of yourself, try to perceive mythic or symbolic patterns. Finally, look for patterns of your own life. The group is now divided into pairs. Each pair must find its own object from nature. Look at your object for ten minutes, breathing deeply, allowing yourself to become the object. Take turns speaking as your object, first generally, then in terms of a specific problem or question that you have. Resist any temptation to enter into a dialogue with your partner.

The next exercises, the last ones to use imagery in the book, come from the third section called "The Search for the Grail."

## THE DUNGEON OF THE CASTLE OF CONSTRAINTS

Close your eyes and focus your awareness on your breathing. You are locked up in the dungeon of constraints. It is an awful place, but terrible as it is, you know that it is a prison of your own creation. Each bar represents the negative restraints that you allow to influence your life. Try to see those images of yourself in each bar that keep you from freedom. There is a legend that once in awhile, a cake with a file is delivered to the occupant of this cell. Look around until you find this cake. Now you must decide if you are going to remove the file and saw your way out, recognizing the implications for your freedom that go with your decision.

If you decide to escape, make actual filing movements with your hand and arm as you cut through each bar. Breathe and saw, breathe and saw, trying to connect with any fears or anxieties that you are experiencing. When you have finished sawing through as many bars as necessary to get out, crawl or walk through the opening. Standing up, know that you are now freer than you were before but that you are still not free enough. The dungeon leads to a room filled with an immense spiderweb, the symbol of further restraints to growth and fulfillment.

## THE SPIDERWEB

It is suggested that throughout this exercise, the guide plays some music that suggests struggle within the web and eventual triumph.

It is impossible for you to pass through this room without getting trapped by the web. You quickly find yourself pulled into its center. These powerful threads represent the people or events from your past that still exert a significant, negative influence on you. These forces do not have to control you any longer. Their strength lies in your acceptance of them, an acceptance that is more often based on habit than on weakness. Pull gently on some of the weaker threads until they break.

This web is the result of error and confusion. You are going to pull out those threads, spun long ago by yourself and others, that have resulted in poor self-esteem and crippled your capacities. Follow each thread to its source, to the person or experience that generated it. Try to see if it was your error, your own misunderstanding, that created this negative influence. Or, if you were truly wronged, try to express forgiveness to another or to yourself so that you can let go of the self-destructive resentments and angers that are still part of you. Keep moving toward those sources, pulling and breaking threads, becoming much freer and much more human by this symbolic battle. You have ten minutes to complete your escape. Do whatever is needed—pull, confront, forgive—until you are free.

## THE DARK FOREST

This is the last exercise in this trilogy of freedom. In it you battle the forces of jealousy, evil, guilt, and despair that surround the castle of constraints. Finally, victorious, you enter the Kingdom and you are really free. Because this exercise involves some very powerful breathing techniques that are not recommended for individuals with cardiac or respiratory problems, readers are referred to the original text for complete instructions and cautions.

It is clear from their books that Houston and Masters have succeeded in developing material that allows their readers to explore the meaning and limits of consciousness. This is apparent even though almost all the exercises presented here have had to be adapted in some way and space permitted only a brief presentation of their theories and research. The fact that imagery plays an important role in many of their exercises attests to their belief in its potential power to effect changes at many different levels of the body-mind continuum. This is especially true in *The Possible Human*, which manages to integrate so much of their previous work into an introductory exploration of human potentials. Obviously, a great deal of research about personal transformation remains to be done.

## REFERENCES

Masters, R., & Houston, J. (1973). *Mind games*. New York: Delta Books.
Masters, R., & Houston, J. (1978). *Listening to the body*. New York: Delta Books.
Houston, J. (1980). *Life force*. New York: Delta Books.
Houston, J. (1982). *The possible human*. Los Angeles: J. P. Tarcher Inc.
Houston, J. (1987). *The search for the beloved: Journeys in mythology and sacred psychology.* Los Angeles: J. P. Tarcher Inc.

# CHAPTER 24

# *Transformational Fantasy*

## *JOHN T. SHAFFER\**

Although fantasy has been used as a therapeutic aid for decades, only since the 1960s has its use become relatively widespread. As therapists experimented with it, they usually named their particular variety. The result has been a whole array of labels: "directed daydreams," "guided imagery," "symbolic visualization," "psycho-imagination," "guided fantasy," and "twilight imagery," to name a few. I believe that fastening a label on the process is not as important as gaining the best possible understanding of the dynamics at work within the process. Still, a name is convenient. I decided to call my particular use of fantasy "transformational fantasy."

In working with this fantasy process, I assert that the psyche, or some higher aspect of mind, creates an ongoing fantasy story within our lives—a drama with which most of us never communicate. This fantasy story is like a series of scenes from a mystery or acts from an ongoing play. The play, however, has no set script—the person experiencing the fantasy improvises as he/she changes with the spontaneous development of the plot. Solving the plot of the fantasy symbolically usually produces a transformation which yields a solution to a real-life problem. The transformation is part of a process that avoids any kind of predetermined framework. Each person's experience with transformational fantasy is as unique as his/her fingerprints.

This chapter will outline the process of transformational fantasy. It will explain how the subject and guide work together within a common framework in the fantasy process. It will describe the concept of staging areas in the left brain, right brain, center, and the hallway of the mind. Finally, it will explore the common emotional experiences and stages of growth experienced by a wide variety of people.

The fantasy experience may be loosely described as "induced." I do not over-emphasize this quality because it implies hypnosis or manipulation—something on which the fantasy experience does not depend. The fantasy is also "shared" between the guide and the client. I often call it "guided fantasy" although, as we shall see, the guide does not lead the fantasy as much as *follows* it very closely.

## SETTING THE SCENE FOR FANTASY

The room is calm and peaceful, dimly and soothingly lit. The person chooses either a comfortable chair or a couch and loosens any snug-fitting clothing. The subject listens to the following explanation.

*The author wishes to express his appreciation to Dr. Gordon Cook for his help in editing this chapter.

What you are about to experience is similar to a dream because you will be caught up in your fantasy as you are in a dream. You will have a very real sense of "being there." You are not "creating" the dream. Instead it just happens, entirely of its own accord. You will experience the fantasy from two points of view. One part of you is caught up in the fantasy experience. At the same time, another part of you is objectively looking at the experience and is able to report both feeling and content to me without shattering the fantasy. You will be able to live completely inside the fantasy, and at the same time, you and I will be sharing. The simplest way to understand what fantasy is like is to experience it.

When beginning the fantasy, the guide and subject have complete freedom to choose the stage setting or starting point. They should agree before beginning. Once this is done, the instructions to the subject are simple:

Close your eyes. Relax in you own way as much as possible. . . . Breathe deeply several times using your diaphram. . . . You are walking down a strange road or strange street. Look around and observe where you are. As you walk along, you come to an unusual house. . . . Tell me about it when you are ready.

Most subjects have little or no difficulty entering the fantasy quickly. Some report in immediately. Others may take up to a minute. The reporting involves a surprisingly easy process of disengaging the conscious mind. If the person does not report in fairly soon, the therapist asks, "What's happening?" In a few instances, the subject may have trouble seeing the house or in experiencing the particular stage setting agreed upon. If this happens, the guide begins where the subject is. The therapist asks what the person is experiencing and seeks to help him/her in exploring it.

Generally, the subject in a fantasy is able to slip into and out of altered states of consciousness at will, in a way that allows him/her to interact creatively with his/her own internal resources. As stated earlier, the subject in fantasy finds that there is a split between one part of him/her which is free to report objectively and precisely what is being experienced without shattering the fantasy or its development. A good example of this subjective/objective split in experiencing the fantasy at two different levels is found in the following excerpt from my first visit to my own body more than a decade ago:

I had felt during the entire visit the presence of an unseen guide. I told my guide that I wanted to visit my prostate and quickly I found myself in the presence of a green balloon about eight inches long. It was filled with something and closed with a cork stuck in the mouth of the balloon. "That's my prostate—a balloon?" I thought to myself with a feeling of shock. "Am I supposed to believe that this green balloon is actually my prostate?" So my objective self said to the unseen guide, "That's my prostate?" The guide replied, "Do you know what a prostate looks like?" My objective self had to reply that I did not. "Then," said the unseen guide, "what the hell's the difference?"

Once again I had to admit the truth of this logic. My subjective self looked at the green balloon with considerable interest. I somehow knew it would be good to take the cork out of the balloon because I also knew it was filled with stuff that should come out. I started to look around for a corkscrew. At this turn of events, my objective self said with complete dismay and disbelief: "A corkscrew? Where do you expect me to find a corkscrew in here?" My subjective self spontaneously began to reach inside my pockets looking for a corkscrew. Witnessing that, my objective self almost went through the roof. "You dummy! The odds of you finding a corkscrew in your pocket are one in a billion. Besides you don't even know how to use one." My objective self was having fits! He could not understand what was going on!

Not to be deterred for anything, my subjective self took out the cork, emptied the balloon of all the gunk in it, and watched with satisfaction as it drained down a hole. I had done what I had innately sensed was the "right" thing to do. At the time, it never occurred to the guide or to me that healing had occurred. I was totally unprepared for what happened afterwards. I went home thoroughly exhausted. I had been taking a nightly sitz bath to ease the prostate pain. That night I forgot to take the bath, and the next. It finally dawned on me a week later that I had no longer had pain in the prostate and didn't have to take any more sitz baths.

I still recall with considerable amazement my first experience with this split-level observation between my logical self on the one hand and my fantasy self on the other. But when I became the guide, I observed hundreds of subjects experiencing fantasy in a similar way.

## THE GUIDE IN FANTASY

The subject's partner in fantasy actually *follows* him/her closely. The guide's principal task is to understand all the nuances of what the subject is experiencing within fantasy. From time to time, the guide may need to ask questions for his/her own clarification. In this sense, it is the subject who is leading the guide in order that the latter may participate meaningfully in the experience. This feeling of mutual participation is basic to the success of fantasy.

The second task of the guide is to communicate his/her understanding of what the subject is saying and experiencing. This is different from the first form of clarification, in which the guide seeks to understand. In the second task, the guide translates his/her understanding into the subject's terms. This process helps to reassure the subject that the guide is following sensitively and knows what is going on. Such a translation of understanding is important in helping the subject gain insight into his/her own feelings as the process unfolds.

The final task of the guide is to help move the experience along. In the early sessions especially, the subject does not know what to expect in guided fantasy. He/she has no idea of the creative possibilities of his/her own resources. This is especially true in dealing with strange and unexpected events or objects having a symbolic quality. The guide assists by offering various procedural aids to expedite the subject's progress: "Talk to the house. Tell it you want to be friends," "Ask the monster for help," and "Be the dark pit." The guide assists the subject in experiencing the full depth and breadth of his/her fantasy.

Sometimes the subject becomes blocked and does not know what to do. In this case, the guide simply can wait and see what will happen. The subject usually experiences some cue within the fantasy and a new direction and movement emerges. Many times, however, the subject is really blocked. Experiencing and then overcoming the blocking may be the important thing for the subject. As this happens, the client gains confidence and experience in taking control of his/her life.

Although the guide strives to experience the emotional feel of the subject's fantasy, he/she must maintain his/her objectivity. He/she needs to be able to survey the emerging plot, or plots, of the fantasy in order to be able to help the subject when blocking of some kind occurs. In such a case, the guide's sensitivity to the subject's present state, along with his/her memory of what has happened earlier, enables him/her to give good procedural guidance. In addition, the fantasy experience tends to be self-correcting as far as the guide is concerned. The subject will either ignore or refuse a suggestion that is not consistent with the inner movement of the fantasy.

## THE BASIC STAGING AREAS OF FANTASY: THE LEFT AND RIGHT HEMISPHERES OF THE BRAIN

My favorite process model is taking the person on a "visit" to either the left or right hemisphere of the brain, depending on which seems to be most open to the subject. It is relatively easy for the client to disengage the conscious mind from the concerns of the day by focusing on what is literally going on inside his/her head. An example is given below:

Guide: Be in your left hemisphere . . . when you can, tell me what you are experiencing.

Client: Surrealistic, spacious, stark, surrealistic figures, sharp focus and detail.

Guide: How do you feel in there?

Client: Not uncomfortable, but a little uneasy. It's difficult to get into a relaxed mood.

Guide: Well, that's a good beginning for the left hemisphere. Now be in the right.

Client: It's totally different. Tropical, lush, sunny, soothing, sensuous. Reminds me of Jamaica, totally relaxing. I feel totally at ease.

Guide: What do you feel like doing?

Client: I thought I felt like painting but I don't want to do that. I just want to explore the beauties of all this. I just want to enjoy it.

The variety of experience is enormous. Some subjects have difficulty entering one of their hemispheres. For example, while Lynn's right hemisphere was comfortable, spacious, and peaceful, he was denied access to his left hemisphere. However, after exploring the right hemisphere for a while, he found a window opening onto the left hemisphere. He could not open the window, but he could look through. Various machines were working fast and furiously on the left side. A great throbbing sound came through the wall and window. "Everything is too fast," he said, "much too fast." He later learned how to slow things down.

## BASIC STAGING AREAS:  THE CENTER

Sometimes the guide can suggest doing a favorite activity in each hemisphere and finally moving that activity into the corpus callosum, the narrow interface between the two brain hemispheres. Here, the guide invites the subject to create a personal "center" linking both brains. The brain, of course, is automatically doing all these functions to some degree. However, the experience of the person visiting his/her brain may point up problems between the two hemispheres defined by a lack of integration in the center. To illustrate the different quality of an experience in each hemisphere and then in the center, consider what happened to Joe. He decided that he would play the piano and sing. In his right brain, the notes were "taut and difficult to hold in tune." "I'm constrained," he remarked. In his left brain, things flowed better. "It's freer, easier, and I have a small audience of friends. They are listening appreciatively." When Joe played in the center, something remarkable happened! A huge grin spread over his face, his cheeks flushing in surprise. "I'm on the stage at the Metropolitan Opera," he reported. "The house is full and everyone is cheering!"

This leads me to the importance of working with a process of centering. The expression, "I've got to get my head together" may mean far more than many people realize. Centering is getting one's head together, getting the left and right brain to work out a synergistic process of interaction and coordination. The purpose of centering is to assist the subject in establishing the center of the corpus callosum as a personal sanctuary, one of the most basic and most natural functions of the center. Generally, the process of centering is easy. The subject is asked to be in the center of the corpus callosum and to become acquainted with the area. The subject may furnish the area as designed, or the center may furnish itself. I often suggest a table and chair, a bed, or a recliner. The experience of resting or sleeping in the center is refreshing and renewing. The center serves both as a conference area to discuss problems between left and right brains and a place of peace in which to meditate and integrate experiences.

Much self-healing takes place at the center. Most subjects are able to look down through their bodies from the center. They can see and talk with their organs, identify trouble spots, and often can heal the troubled area. An example of identifying a trouble spot may be seen in Sandra's experience. Toward the end of a group session, she looked down through her body and saw a strange sight. She could see her whole circulatory system extending all the way to her wrists and ankles where for no apparent reason it ended. "No wonder I have such cold hands and feet," she exclaimed.

## BASIC STAGING AREAS:
## THE HALLWAY OF THE MIND

A fourth staging area for fantasy learning is the "hallway of the mind." It is located down a corridor behind the center to the rear of the head. Along the hallway will be doors leading to rooms representing physical, emotional, or learning problems of concern to the subject. For example, there may be a pain room, an anger room, a grief room, a self-esteem room, a hate room, a sex room, a math room, a weight control room, an archive room, or any room the subject and guide agree to explore or that the subject happens upon spontaneously. Sometimes unmarked but inviting rooms are found in the hallway of the mind. One woman had complained of physical exhaustion centered entirely in the calves of her legs. Checking the muscles out in fantasy, she found them extremely tense. Furthermore, they were protected by armor.

She did not know it, but in her mind she had been wearing iron calf-guards. Try as she might, she could not understand why her calves were so tense and why she needed to protect herself with heavy armor, until she explored her hallway. She found an unmarked room with a three-year-old girl inside who asked her how she could have forgotten that she had been attacked by a rooster that had viciously pecked all over her calves. The realization was immediately picked up by her calf muscles. She could feel them relax and watched as the calf guards "melted away."

Generally, visits to these rooms do not solve mysteries all on their own. They are like pieces which fit into a larger puzzle. A few examples will give something of the flavor of the various experiences. Marlene had decided to visit her guilt room:

Marlene: I'm looking at a great, big, black door. There's a skull and cross bones on it. It's ugly—made of heavy iron. I can hear me inside screaming at someone, but when I go in all I see is piles and piles of paper. No, over in the corner is a little man sitting all by himself. He's just sitting there holding a 100-year candle.

Guide: Ask him why it's a 100-year candle.

Marlene: He says it will probably take 100 years to get the room cleaned up! He's all worn out. There are filing cabinets all over and the shelves on the walls are crammed full of papers.

Guide: It's really a mess.

Marlene: Yes, it is. He wants to know what I want. I don't really know. I'd like to throw everything away, but I can't really do that.

Guide: Tell him that you weren't aware of the mess, and that you've come to help him clean it up.

Marlene: I did and he's happy about my offer. He says he's ready to work with me.

In less than five minutes, Marlene has illuminated constructively a whole set of feelings that had been festering unattended. When subjects have had sufficient experience with transformational fantasy, they often are able to relax and experience self-guided fantasy on their own. One such person, Susan, wrote to me at length about her experience:

I decided to visit my Fear and Restriction Room. When I opened the door, the light was very dim. There was the desk and the dark heavy curtains, closed tightly. As my eyes grew used to the dark, I could make out a figure sitting there in the chair behind the desk. Large and strong, all covered with hair, it remained silent and still in its place behind the desk. Although it neither threatened me nor tried to scare me, its appearance was that of a big scary, hairy monster.

At first I was reluctant to reach out and touch it, but, as I sat there and looked at it, I felt there was a kindness and goodness deep inside it. I reached out and took its hand. We became friends. I introduced the monster to Miss Prim (a self-explanatory aspect of my character whom I had met in an earlier fantasy). When I urged them both to go out to the playground, the monster declined at first, saying the bright light would hurt its eyes because they had been in darkness for so long. After Miss Prim and I gave it a large hat and huge sunglasses, the monster grudgingly agreed to go out into the light.

As soon as they were gone I went over to the windows and opened the dark curtains. They were on the swings and Miss Prim was really letting go, laughing and having fun. She wasn't at all worried about getting her clothes dirty or her hair messed. The monster went clumsily along with this and looked like it was beginning to enjoy it. Finally, as I left the window, they were holding hands and spinning round and round, fast as they could go, screeching with delight.

In a later fantasy the monster's fur fell away, revealing a battered woman with deep wounds all over her body. Miss Prim dressed the wounds, made a stretcher, and helped Susan carry her "battered self" to her center where she could heal and grow strong. This return to the center illustrates one of its important functions—a place of sanctuary and regeneration.

## THE FUNCTION OF CENTRAL CONTROL

The concept of a "central control room" where all body-mind functions are coordinated is an important starting image. Generally, it is located either in the center itself, or below the center, or in the hallway of the mind. The function of central control usually takes time to clarify. It often is seen as a big computer room, and more than once subjects have gasped in amazement: "Why, the computer is running amuck! No one's in control!" Ann's experience was somewhat different. She found "a big computer in the center, surrounded by a circle of small computers." Suddenly she remarked, "The big computer is working very hard while the little computers are just sitting there. Some of them seem broken and none of them work. . . . Oh! I understand! The big computer is TOO BIG! It's TOO HEAVY! None of the little computers like him at all. He does all the work. BUT HE'S TOO BIG AND HEAVY!"

The following case, which involves the image of central control, illustrates the coaching function of the guide. It also shows how staging areas may be integrated to restore the balance of bodily systems (homeostasis), leading both to healing and to an improved sense of well-being. Bertha had been hospitalized for angina pectoris and an erratic heart beat. A complete physical examination was made and nothing was wrong. She visited central control and reported:

Bertha: It's a large darkened room with a peculiar-shaped person there. He's like a triangle person. I tell him I am visiting my body to find out what's the matter with my heart and why I'm in so much pain. He doesn't know anything about it. He seems disinterested.

Guide: Can he help you in any way?

Bertha: No, he doesn't seem to know anything and doesn't want to.

Guide: Tell him you are leaving, but you'll be back later. Now, be in your left brain and when you are there tell me about it.

Bertha: It's like the last time. A large empty room. Rather cloudy or misty. It's somewhat pleasant. But, the right brain is much smaller and darker. There's this sharp knife sticking up through the bottom near the entrance. That's why I'm having my headaches!

Guide: Can you do anything about the knife?

Bertha: No, I tried to pull it out and it won't come. I'd like to cover the sharp edges.

Guide: Is there anything around that you could use—anything in your pocket book?

Bertha: Some bee's wax. I'll coat the edge of the knife with that. Ah! That feels much better.

Guide: Great! Now go back down the hallway of your mind and this time go to your pain control center.

Bertha: It's a dark room. There doesn't seem to be anything in it. I'm inside now, and even though it's dark, I know it's empty.

Guide: O.K. Now, go to central control and report in with all your experiences. Bring the triangle man up to date.

Bertha: He seems interested in what I am telling him.

Guide: Ask him why the pain control center is dark.

Bertha: He says there's a light switch there and when I'm ready to find it, I will. He also just said it won't be today.

At the end of this session Bertha reported that her headache had almost disappeared. She felt an improved sense of well-being. She returned the following day for another session. But a pain in her heart and arm left her unable to do anything to improve her situation. The triangle man in central control was somewhat more interested and responsive, but he volunteered no further suggestions. The guide then sent her on a visit to her grief room. (Her youngest son had been killed in an accident and other family deaths had disturbed her.):

Bertha: I'm there, but it's so crowded. I'm almost smothered because it's too full of people and past events.

Guide: Ask the room to make some space for you, to clear the air. How about putting in a window?

Bertha: It can't do anything about its present condition, it says. But wait, the people and events just did move back a bit. It's a little more open. They are standing there looking at me and I find it not so bad in here now.

Guide: Good. Now go down the hallway to your pain control center.

Bertha: I'm there and, damn if there isn't a light switch right by the door? I'm turning the light on. (Bertha paused. Suddenly she smiled and gasped.) Oh! When the light is on, the pain is under control! When it's off, the pain comes back. That's the way it works!

Guide: Well! Thank the pain control center for its help and go back to central control and brief triangle man.

Bertha: I'm telling him all about it. He's really interested. He's aware of what I am doing and thinks that it is good. I even think that he's beginning to get the idea that he should be in charge and keep an eye on things.

Guide: Ask him if he will do just that on your behalf until you see him again.

Bertha: He says he will!

Bertha's problems were not miraculously solved. However, over the time that the therapist remained in touch with her, she reported a lessening of pain and an improved ability to cope. Others with whom I have worked have had far more formidable problems with central control. For example, a highly stressed person may be unable even to enter central control because it is "on untouchable automatic." On the other hand, one person suffering from great stress and tension found a huge computer in control, saying in a most authoritarian and ominous tone, "It's about time you reported in!"

## THE ROLE OF THE PSYCHE:
## "THE REAL IS WHAT WORKS"

Carl Gustav Jung was one of the first persons to investigate the relationship between fantasy and the workings of the mind. Jung suggested that fantasy could take three different forms: voluntary, passive, and active. Voluntary fantasy was that produced by the mind *consciously* at work at "telling a story." Such artificially created fantasy was of no interest to Jung. He was concerned with fantasy which was "an eruption of the contents of the unconscious into the conscious mind." The way a person reacts to this eruption of unconscious material determines whether the fantasy will be active or passive. If the subject does nothing more than witness the on-rushing material as in a dream, the fantasy is a passive one. If, however, the person steps out and interacts with the material in order to alter it, the fantasy is an active one.

The fantasy material that wells up from the unconscious, according to Jung, or from the superconscious, has its origins in the psyche—a personal "story teller" possessed by all people—something roughly equivalent to the spirit, as opposed to the mind and the body. I feel that in guided fantasy the conscious mind willingly receives the mythology of the psyche, learns new meanings and possibilities for growth and expansion, and then is able to change naturally in the desired growth direction. The Jungian concept of the psyche seems to be the richest word for describing the inner guiding of a higher mind at work. My experience has shown that the psyche does not tell just a story here and an entirely unrelated episode there. Instead, although many fantasy experiences seem unrelated, there is a thread that ties them together. They are part of an unfolding story plot. Some case material illustrates this.

Consider, for example, the experience of Mary who, over a period of several months, spent eighteen sessions in a house fantasy developing her house in great detail. In the early stages, Mary moved very slowly; she had a great deal of difficulty even getting into the house. Once she was in there, she had trouble seeing what was in each room. Gradually, however, the contents of the rooms emerged. The living room was completely bare, but the dining room had an attractive table. What at first appeared to be a big glass window, became a glass door leading from the dining room into a beautiful, completely furnished patio with a lovely back yard. In her exploration of the dining room, there was another important item that she could only sense but not find. This missing item was a mysteriously hidden door leading to her bedroom. She was intensely interested in the hidden door, and she completely ignored the patio and back yard in her search for it.

For several sessions three "plots" seemed to intertwine. First, each time she visited, she noticed something new in her living room. Secondly, she would remark how beautiful the patio and backyard were but would show no interest in going out for a visit. The third and central plot was finding the hidden door to the bedroom. When she finally found the door and visited the bedroom, she was very surprised. It was the most luxurious, most feminine bedroom one could imagine!

She was astounded and overjoyed at the same time! She expressed her surprise to her guide by sharing with him her expectation that her bedroom would be a dingy, unromantic place. She looked around at the large sunken tub, the imposing four poster with ornate hangings, and a lovely dressing room. Her attention was caught by a strange mirror. She walked over and saw the beautiful room reflected in sharp detail. Then tears came into her eyes and she said with great sadness, "There's no reflection of me in the mirror; I'm not in the picture!"

She came out of the fantasy experience weeping. "I knew that bedroom was too good to be true," she said. I suggested that although this was a real blow to her self-confidence, it was also a great promise. After all, it was a dream bedroom; now she had to make it her own. In the following fantasy experiences the first two subplots helped her gain some confidence.

She had visited the patio for a few minutes each time, had managed to furnish half her living room, and had discovered her family room. The latter was the only room which she had found comfortable from the beginning and which she had found complete except for a sewing machine! Where was her sewing machine! She found it in a new room off the bedroom, but it would sew only for enjoyment, it told her quite emphatically! The patio also told her that she must learn to enjoy herself.

Meanwhile, over in a corner of her bedroom, a stage setting for a series of subplots had developed. The setting was an easy chair, a reading light, and a table with a book. She went over to the table and found that the book was a Bible which she could not open. Eventually, she learned what book in the Bible she was to read. In doing so, she experienced a whole sequence of developing events. First, she walked over to the mirror, and there she was reflected as a lovely woman! Furthermore, by this time, her living room was fully furnished. She was able to relax on the patio and to move freely about her entire house. The results astounded her. With the help of a body fantasy, she was able to overcome her frigidity, develop a better overall relation with her husband, deal flexibly with her teenage son, and change from a mousy person into a more outgoing, secure individual. Mary's house fantasy was a developing series of plots and subplots. The meaning of some of these for her life were clear to her. Others never became clear to her or to the guide.

Transformational fantasy can achieve its most long-lasting and most positive effects when it is applied to the unfolding of a personal plot or "life script" over a period of time. This will be more clearly illustrated by some lengthy, complete case studies presented later. In the meantime, the case of Lois will be a useful way to clarify some of the ways in which the fantasy plot can unfold. During twenty-four sessions spread over a period of six months, Lois worked on the exploration of a recurring nightmare that had troubled her greatly over a period of many years.

I am retelling her story in shortened form; nevertheless, the sense of growth and development is retained. This is her nightmare:

I am walking toward a garden. There are several rows of various vegetables. I come to several rows of cabbages. I notice one particular cabbage which seems larger than the others and to which I am attracted. I go up to it and begin to pull back the cabbage leaves. When I reach the center of the cabbage, I find an imp sitting upright on an elegant little chair with a spear in one hand. I am startled. The imp is arrogant and triumphant. He frightens me.

Lois's psyche narrated a life script that took on the form of a drama.

## ACT ONE: THE ENEMY

When Lois entered fantasy, the nightmare came alive exactly as she had described it, only it continued past the point where she ordinarily would have awakened.

The imp immediately begins to throw spears at me. I am pained and shaken. I curl up in order to protect myself and wait for it all to go away. Finally, he quits. I ask him why he threw the spears at me, and he says that it is the only way to get my attention because I just won't listen to him.

In another session, as she approached the cabbage, the imp begins a dance filled with life, joy, and exultation. In a variety of ways, the imp begins to reveal his role in Lois's plot. He finds a stone which has special powers. Both he and Lois are in awe of it. In a later session, he encroaches on Lois's identity by picking up her violin and playing it gayly. She is both frustrated and angered by this. Step by step, the imp leads Lois toward the realization that she has never before properly valued her own spirit and energy. A few sessions later, Lois wishes to examine the imp's stone but she is afraid of it. The imp will help her only if she will join him in approaching the stone. She fears both the imp and the stone; yet, she is willing to take the risk. As she and the imp approach the stone, she experiences a feeling of great awe mixed with a desire to flee. The stone, it seems, represents a responsibility that she would rather not assume.

## ACT TWO: THE IMP AS TEACHER

Roughly midway through her fantasy sessions, she described the change that had taken place in her feelings toward the imp:

My feelings toward him had been ones of extreme horror. Here was someone or something in my life demanding to be dealt with, pressing itself on to my conscious mind. The imp was a strong aggressive force that seemed to say, "Look I'm here and you have no choice but to deal with me." He had so much vitality and drive that I didn't see any way I could come to grips with him. During the weeks that followed, my fear of the imp grew in leaps and bounds, and the rigidity of my determination to fend him off grew so that, sometimes, just to take a step toward him could only be accomplished through a great act of will. His ways of getting my attention seemed cruel and hurtful. At times, my greatest desire was just to roll up in a ball and hope he would go away. However, despite everything, I had the feeling that he was not going to go away by himself and that I must either find some way of coming to terms with him or must somehow root him out of my existence.

That is, her fear turned to anger, which provoked the imp to tease and mock her.

## ACT THREE: FRIEND AND TEACHER

During the final stages of her encounter, she developed the feeling that the imp had been reaching out to her in an attempt to communicate something of value. "He had been trying to cajole me into a kind of self-freeing or awakening," Lois said. As these feelings grew, she came to understand that the imp had been an ally the whole time. The real purpose of the imp was to make her aware of her own needs—needs that she had not allowed herself to experience or meet. By the end of the sessions, she had developed a great admiration and affection for her imp. There seems to be little question that the process of learning to deal with her imp represented the discovery and integration of a completely unknown and ignored self. This was the message of her plot. There is a unifying plot behind all guided-fantasy experiences. Following the story of the fantasy over multiple sessions is one of the principle roads to growth and self-healing.

## THE INTERACTION BETWEEN THE FANTASY PROCESS AND THE GUIDE

We have seen how the psyche becomes a spontaneous storyteller. Like the waters of an underground spring which flow to and fro and finally bubble up through fissures in the overlying rock, so the psyche's "plot" seeks to bypass conscious and unconscious resistance. There appear to be two functions of this blocking. A learning dilemma, that is, a problem to be solved, is the most common reason for the appearance of a block. The psyche seems to be testing the will or the strength of a person. In doing this, it also forces the individual to stop and really become acquainted with the whole area. Then he/she will discover many reasons for the block, and this discovery opens up many new possibilities for growth and learning. A second function of a block is best illustrated by the ending of the old Looney Tunes films: "That's all folks!" The psyche, for some reason, is closing out the fantasy experience. It is my hypothesis that the psyche carefully protects the person from going too far, too fast in a fantasy. We have come upon this phenomenon many times. Gloria experienced both the "That's all folks!" ending and one of an entirely different kind. She was on a path leading to a desired goal, when she was suddenly confronted with a large plastic shield blocking her way. Nearby was a ladder; she placed it against the shield and climbed up. To her surprise, the ladder curved backwards and unceremoniously deposited her behind where she started. Not to be outdone, she began to dig a tunnel under the shield, but instead of coming up behind the shield, she came up in front of her starting point. With more stubbornness than ever, she looked for another way. It appeared that there was a path leading off to the left around the shield. She followed the path, but it brought her back to the starting place again! At this point, she gave up with the remark, "I guess I'm not supposed to go out there today."

Another type of blocking, which appears to be a signal of the psyche to stop, is blackness, or a light so bright so that one cannot see. Such hindrances appear often in fantasy but usually last only for a single episode. Indeed, by the time the person comes back to the next session, the block may be completely gone. When structures of resistance are encountered, it may be necessary to call upon the resources of the guide. Sometimes his/her role is to get the subject to do what he/she at first doesn't want to do. For example, Tom had been bothered by a dream in which he was imprisoned in a room covered with a wallpaper full of snakes—live snakes! These snakes wanted to bite Tom, and he was continually dodging them.

Guide: O.K. now see the big one that's trying to bite you. Are you game for the experiment?

Tom: I don't know. Snakes aren't my particular thing.

Guide: Look, that snake really wants to bite you. How about letting him?

Tom: Let a snake bite me? Letting that thing bite me?

Guide: Well, yeah. It seems that he really wants to. Please him. Give him the satisfaction.

Tom hesitated, and so the guide asked him to become the snake. He could not do it very well, but he did begin to get the feeling that it was very important for the snake to bite him. Tom let the snake bite him and when its fangs were in his arm, the guide directed him to pet it. With effort, he reached out and patted the snake on the head. As he did so, a big smile came over the snake's face. Tom was fascinated. "You know," he said with amazement, "this isn't so bad, the snake kind of likes me!" Tom's nightmare never returned. This episode reflects only a way of getting rid of the symptom that is expressed in the nightmare. A prolonged exploration in fantasy almost certainly would lead to an understanding of why the nightmare occurred in the first place.

We have discussed many of the common experiences of subjects and their guides in fantasy. While virtually everyone needs the guide for assistance in getting around blocks, many need the presence of the guide for security and reassurance. Consider Dianna. She had explored the basic fantasy staging areas. In addition, she had visited her cosmic center located at the very top of the head above the normal center. This is the area where subjects are most likely to experience peak feelings, or what Abraham Maslow has called the oceanic feeling—a sense of oneness with one's surroundings. In an earlier session, Dianna had described her cosmic area as a "very pretty scene with high skyscrapers, millions of stars and snow-covered mountains." One of the biggest mountains attracted her. She wanted to climb it, but she sensed that she was not ready yet. At the same time, she expressed a fear of participating in any of the fantasy without a guide to help and protect her. About three weeks later, she decided to climb her mountain:

Dianna: The mountain is so steep and smooth that I can't get a foothold.

Guide: Be the mountain and tell me how you feel.

Dianna: I feel that it would be nice to be climbed, but I don't know how to help her climb me.

Guide: Would it be all right if she chopped some steps in you?

Dianna: Yes.

At this point, Dianna took over the fantasy herself and reported the following flow of events to her guide:

I don't really want to cut into the mountain, so I will ask my shoes to grow spikes, which they obediently do. I can climb pretty well now. Because the mountain is terribly steep, I can't climb very far without stopping to rest. Feeling safe, I rest for awhile and then go on. Finally, I start feeling dizzy and think about stopping. The mountain assures me however that everything is okay and urges me to continue. Suddenly I'm at the top and looking all around at a most unexpected sight! There is a big shopping mall on the top of the mountain. Being the mall, I feel uncomfortable about my mountain-top location. Being the mountain, I don't like having the mall sitting on my summit. I ask who put the mall there and get no response. I call the same question out to the skyscrapers, but they don't know either. I ask them if they would like to have the shopping mall. They would love it.

Now, determined to find out about the mall, I go back in time to the last day that my mountain top was vacant. I do my climbing over, and I run smack into a little boy building the mall right on top of my mountain! I asked him why he did such a thing. All he says, with a mischievous grin, is, "Because I wanted to." I ask him if he would mind if we moved the mall down to the skyscrapers. He says he will do it and, before I know what's happened, he has folded up the mall into a black suitcase and skipped on down the mountain.

Dianna felt that only in the guide's presence could she work freely and creatively on her own. Generally, the more experienced the subject, the less he/she needs the guide during the fantasy itself.

## THE USE OF ALL THE SENSES TO EXPERIENCE THE FANTASY

Clients who use only the sense of sight often feel that they are just a spectator; therefore, I encourage my clients to use all their senses in experiencing fantasy. As a result, doors talk and darkened tunnels in the floor of a hemisphere of the brain emit enraged roaring and bellowing. Once, on exiting from the body via the anal tract, a subject was encouraged to breathe deeply and report on the smell. A look of disgust was replaced by pleasure as he did so and announced, "Honey!" Travelers inside the stomach, lungs, heart, and intestines sometimes find unsuspected textures and other tactile surprises.

Indeed, the physics of the senses themselves can be warped in strange and unexpected ways. Leslie's house fantasies illustrates this:

Guide: What kind of blackness do you have this time?

Leslie: A fearful blackness. The blackness is afraid of me. It just said to me, "You come to destroy; you come to bring light."

Guide: So you will destroy by bringing light?

Leslie: Yeah and I asked it why it was afraid of light, and the answer came back, "Light always pushes me away." Evidently that gives me courage, because I am going to take a step toward the blackness now, and as I go, the blackness seems to be careful to keep its distance. Now all this is very odd because the blackness seems so much larger and so much more powerful.

Guide: Yet the plain fact is, it retreats.

Leslie: Right.

Guide: From you?

Leslie: Right, and it keeps its distance because where I stand, it's light and yet I can see the blackness. It is kind of like a wall moving back. And I've gotten to the door now, in the bedroom, and I'm opening the door and going into the blackness. Oh! This is a blackness very different from the kind in the hall. This is a very stubborn blackness, because when I opened the door, it didn't back away from me. . . . But wait, all along the baseboard, all the way around to the bed, for some reason that blackness hasn't gone there.

Guide: So! You have a little room to move into.

Leslie: Yeah, I've just checked it out. It seems like the blackness is a thick heavy blanket thrown over all the furniture. It's a very heavy thing.

Guide: Then you can see the nature of it. It doesn't fill the room. It's just a heavy blanket like essence, and it's too heavy to move of its own accord.

Leslie: Yeah. While you were talking, I explored the corner and moved in under the bed. It's the largest piece of furniture in the room and has the most space under it that's free of the blackness.

Guide: Ask the space if it can help you. It seems to have some muscle of its own.

Leslie: It will help. I asked, "What will we do?" And I get the feeling it said, "I do like you, only I'll make myself thin." And look at that! It's moving out very slowly under all the blackness. It has become shiny and it just keeps on moving. Oddest thing I've ever seen. It's like . . . like . . . it's a sheet!

Guide: A shiny, moving sheet.

Leslie: Yeah, and now it's gone all the way to the four corners of the room, and at the corners it is sort of coming up the wall like it's going to encompass it—and that's exactly what it's doing and it's going to grow."

Guide: Under, around, and over.

Leslie: Yeah, and now I have a big, huge bag, and it has tied itself in a knot. And there's a little more space in the room now. I've crawled out from under the bed. I've got space now to be myself. I've got all the blackness tied up in this huge sack which suddenly starts to shrink, sack and all, and settle on the bed like a pile of laundry. My impulse is to just pick it up and throw it out the window but the sheet-become-bag says, "No, carry me out." So I've picked up the bag and am now standing out in the hall. I start downstairs but the sheet says, "No, not there. Go through the blackness." So I start into the blackness and find that there seems to be another room. I get a real sad feeling from the room. I can't tell what the room is.

Guide: Can you respond somehow to the sadness? It seems very, very sad.

Leslie: And the sheet says, "That's why I have come." I get the feeling it's the room of death that I was in once before, but it doesn't make any sense. I tell the sheet, "if that is where you have brought me, I don't understand." It says, "We have two more rooms." I say, "Two? Why two?" It doesn't respond. But I have this strong feeling that I'll have to enter the sad room. I'm trying, but I can't seem to get into the room because the blackness is so thick. I'll be the blackness and see what it feels like. Whew! It's thick, and spongy, yet solid. It's very heavy. I get the feeling it couldn't get out of the room even if it wanted to. Earlier I thought it refused to budge because of stubbornness.

Guide: So it feels confined and so utterly squeezed into the room. That is its real nature. It's not stubborn after all.

Leslie: Yeah. And I ask how I can help it, and it says that it doesn't know because it is so bulging at the seams that it can't see. I'm standing here thinking how to help it and suddenly I'm beginning to get real, real tiny. You know what! I'm so small, I can step between the tiny cracks between it and the wall. I slip around and under it and I go through the door into another room. I get a very strange feeling. This must be the second room, and it doesn't have any darkness at all. I get the feeling that this is the little boy's room. I can't see any furniture, but the room does have a joyous feeling. I say to the sheet , "You said there were two rooms and stuff to do in each room. What do I do here?" And the sheet says that all I have to do is look and remember the joy. The sheet says the joy is the one thing that will help me when I go back to that other room, and I say that I still don't want to go back to the other room. But the sheet remarked, "You must. And the joy is coming too, so it won't be too bad."

Guide: So you have two rooms, side by side. One of great joy and one of great sadness. Both of these you are experiencing and will experience and the joy will carry you through the sadness.

Leslie: Yeah. Who'd believe that could be the message of a bed sheet?

## THE LOGICAL ILLOGIC OF FANTASY

Transformational fantasy operates in a realm of complete illogic. Anything can and does happen, but no one is harmed by any happening. Indeed, in the illogic of guided fantasy, fearsome events or creatures may be faced one-on-one. When this occurs, the fearsomeness often evaporates.

Consider Sam, who was deathly afraid of bears in his dreams. He had a recurring nightmare in which grizzly bears were continually on the prowl outside his house. He wanted to be free to leave his house to go to town, but he never could because those bears were always out there. One big bear was particularly terrifying, although, in his dreams, he could never see it clearly. As Sam was reliving the nightmare in fantasy, the therapist asked him to call out to the fearsome bear and ask it to have a chat. So Sam said to the bear, "Why are you bothering me this way?" "Because you're a coward," snarled the bear in reply. "Can't I ever be free to leave this house?" "No, you're too cowardly," growled the bear.

At this point, the guide suggested that Sam open the door and go out to face the bear. He was very reluctant but finally agreed. The bear growled menacingly in front of the open door. The guide suggested that Sam take a step toward the bear. The bear kept growling but did not move. Sam took another step and then another and one more. Suddenly, he was only a few feet from the bear and could see it clearly for the first time. "Why it's only a teddy bear," he gasped. Facing up to this bear helped him to overcome his passive relationship with people. He never had the dream again.

Subjects often find themselves in dire positions during their fantasies. Many times they need to look for resources to help them out of jams. Such resources appear with an illogical logic all their own. Consider a brief episode experienced by Tina as she worked out a nightmare that involved a monster in a cave.

She found herself in the center of the cave with the monster between her and the cave entrance. Although she was very scared, she looked around, found a torch, and a flint to light it and, protected by her torch, started edging toward the cave entrance. Suddenly the monster grabbed the torch and extinguished it. She could hear him breathing right in front of her. She was frantic. There were no resources handy, just the darkness and the cave. The guide suggested that she ask the darkness for help. It agreed and wrapped a "double strength darkness" around her and she walked out right in front of the monster.

Harry's fantasy furnishes another example. He was making his first body trip and was fascinated by his appendix. At first he casually remarked that he had a healthy appendix. One would think that would have been the end of his interest. But no, he walked around his appendix, looking at it from all sides and remarked, "My, that's a healthy appendix! I think I'll go inside it and see how it looks in there. . . . Well, it's healthy inside too." After a few seconds of silence, he suddenly groaned as if in deep pain. His guide could not comprehend what was happening and asked what was the matter. Harry replied, "I just took a rusty nail and gouged my appendix. I just wanted to see what an appendicitis attack looks like." Having learned to go along with whatever happens in fantasy, the guide said, "Don't you think it is time to sound the alarm? The rest of the body is probably not expecting an appendicitis attack." "Yes, that's right. Here's the alarm." He reached up and yanked at an alarm. "Boy look at those white corpuscles coming to the aid! Too late! I'm going to the hospital. Wow! They are cutting right through!" He described the operation to remove his appendix in considerable detail. Finally everything appeared to be all right. But he wanted to be certain so he dived into the bloodstream. He did not like swimming and wished for something to ride on. At once he spotted a raft and hopped on board. However, as he did so, two great white corpuscles sped toward him. Just as he thought they were going to devour him, they dove under the raft and ate it out from under him. One got on one side of him, and one on the other, and they scolded him. "What do you mean, an honored guest of the body, pulling this stupid trick! First puncturing your own appendix, and then the raft. . . . Don't you know that raft you so innocently rode on could have been the cause of a blood clot? Pulling such a stupid trick! What's the matter with you?" He got a fearsome dressing-down. However, after apologizing, he was able to continue on a rich journey.

## GETTING THE SUBJECT'S ATTENTION

Transformational fantasy offers significant learning opportunities to nearly all who participate in it. Many of the events taking place in fantasy occur because the psyche is trying to focus the attention of the subject on a problem. Recall, for example, the case of Lois whose frightful imp was throwing spears at her to induce her to explore the ignored facets of her personality.

Zelma's experience offers another example. When I met Zelma, she was fifty years old. At the age of three, she had had a nightmare that she remembered vividly forty-seven years later. She dreamed that she was going to visit a friend. Dressed in especially nice clothes, she set out on her journey. Rounding a curve in the road, she encountered a donkey with the most horrendous set of teeth she had ever seen. Before she could cry for help, it took a large bite out of her chest. She awoke screaming and has carried the memory with her ever since.

I instructed her to close her eyes, to go back in her life, and to meet the scared little girl again. She found that the little girl was drenched in perspiration and badly in need of a bath. She first comforted the child by holding her close, and then she gave her "child-self" a bath. I then advised Zelma to tell the little girl that the time had come to visit the donkey. When she did so, the child immediately jumped into her arms and clung to her fearfully. The little child held on with all her strength. Zelma remarked: "She's squeezing the life out of me." I ignored this inviting opening and insisted that her mission was to face the donkey. So, with the child hanging on tightly, she went out to look for the donkey. Soon she found him and tried to threaten him into submission by saying: "If you bite this little girl again, I'll hit you with a two-by-four." The donkey seemed to sneer at her in defiance. She tried various approaches to put the donkey in its place, but no matter what she said the donkey spit back at her.

At this point, I instructed her to come out of the fantasy and tell me her impressions of the donkey. She answered: "Well he's mean. He is just starved." At my suggestion, she returned to the fantasy with the little girl hanging on. Only this time, she procured a bucket of oats with which to feed the donkey. It devoured them and asked for more. It was insatiable and ate at least 100 additional buckets of oats! Toward the end of this process, something began to change. Finally Zelma said in astonishment, "I just can't believe it. The little girl is loosening her hold and is reaching out toward the donkey. Suddenly both of us are petting it!"

Then Zelma asked the donkey why it had done such a terrible thing. It answered, "I got your attention, didn't I?" For forty-seven years, it had been getting her attention without any resultant learning on her part! But it did not give up until she came to terms with it. Zelma as a small child had been hurt and deprived in some fashion. As the donkey needed to be nurtured, so did both the girl and the adult into whom she had grown.

## THE PSYCHE'S GIFT OF INSIGHT

Generally, the psyche calls attention to a problem in such a way as to offer an insight into the problem's solution. We have just seen how Zelma came to realize that the ravenous donkey represented a part of her childhood-self that had been malnourished.

Henry's exploration of the psyche led to an understanding of the origin of two brain tumors. Henry was in his early twenties. To investigate the origins of his tumors, the guide asked him to go back to a time when the tumor was fully formed but still benign. He regressed to an awkward thirteen-year-old adolescent. The guide then suggested he go back to the very beginning of the tumor—to the event that triggered its growth. Suddenly he remembered. White tennis shoes flashed through his mind. He pursued the shoes and reported the following:

I was about eight or nine years old. I would race different people down the block, and always I would win! One day, for the first time, I was racing a girl whom I liked very much. I remember now that she was really fast. When we started out, we were side by side. Then I saw her gain a little bit and started to get a little tense. I really had to beat this girl. I tried harder, but all I could see were her white tennis shoes pulling away from me. It's just amazing reliving the whole thing! Everything seems normal for a few years inside my brain. But then suddenly, I believe it's not long before my thirteenth birthday, *I see one little cell begin to shiver and shake. And then more little cells around it begin to shiver and shake. The tumor is beginning to grow!* I think that losing that race caused me to get more and more tense—especially since I lost to a girl! I wasn't supposed to lose to anybody. But to lose to a girl! Wow! It was like a vicious circle as it began to build up greater and greater anxiety.

Guide: Then you mean to say that the picture of those cells quivering was the beginning of your tumor? That all the anxiety of those years was eventually caught up in that cell and the others?

Henry: Exactly. That's right.

Guide: One cell quivering with anxiety.

Henry: Yeah. And I could see that cell too.

Guide: But the insight was to connect the two experiences, to see that it began with the loss to the girl and the destruction of your macho image and then crystallized into the experience with the cell.

Henry: It was bad enough in my family to be beaten, let alone by a girl. I guess the tumor was calling my attention to the fact that there was something radically wrong with me. Something wrong with my way of thinking.

Guide: Well let me add this, it was calling your whole life style into question. It was forcing you to come to terms with a new way of understanding yourself, other than the old macho image.

Henry: Yeah. That's true.

Guide: O.K. Now, a few years ago you had an operation to remove that first tumor. During this time, your girl friend was a tower of strength for you and became more involved with you than you could handle. She got too close to you.

Henry: That's right. She said that I was repulsive to her and all this stuff. I remember that I walked out of her room after she said that. I was so mad! I couldn't really handle what she had told me. I took all the bedboards out of my bed, and I beat the shit out of everything in my room. I had never felt so torn up in a long, long time. And you know, it came to me later in our last fantasy—I saw it clear as could be: As soon as she said that I was repulsive to her, that is when the cells in my brain began shaking and quivering again. It was the rebirth of the tumor. I didn't know how to let the anger out in any constructive way. That cell was shaking and didn't know where to go. Literally, it just didn't know where to go.

Guide: That, then, was the inception of the second tumor. Both of them were related to traumatic failure experiences with women. Those were the focusing events that started a sequence of events that culminated in the two tumors. So now this second tumor is growing and becoming more noticeable to you. What is it doing to you?

Henry: I figure it is saying that all the anger I was feeling was definitely not good for my health. It's telling me to save some time for introspection and to slow down. It's telling me to take a lot of time to think about my relations with other women.

About a month later, a long session was held. Unfortunately, it a not taped, and the notes have been misplaced. Here is the construction of the session:

> I am in my head on the left side, where the new tumor is supposed to be. The doctors are not sure, but a brain scan seems to indicate the possibility of a tumor. I really don't want to look, for fear they are right, but I must face up to it. (Pause) Yes, there appears to be a very small tumor beginning to grow. I just can't let that happen. I cannot face another brain operation. I'm just going to have to do something about it.

He called for his inner brain surgeon to cut it out. However, they both believed it should be kept in safety somewhere. So he found a lead strongbox in a supply cabinet, and they put it in the box for safekeeping. Henry felt a sense of relief, but something compelled him to look into the empty place where the tumor had been.

> He continued: Why, it's full of little eggs, which could grow into tumors. I'll have to do something about that, or it won't be safe in the future. I'll always be worrying about tumors growing. I know what I'll do; I'll call for some maggots to come and clean this whole area out. They are eating away, and now the area is safe. Whew, that was something. I need a long rest.

Since we had no access to medical records, we do not know if a second tumor had developed. Nevertheless, in the two years since the fantasy operation, Henry reports that he feels better, and better both physically and mentally.

The fantasy process helped Marla focus on her frigidity problems and it led to immediate and lasting progress. Marla was quite willing to visit various parts of her body: She entered her mouth and went down through her lungs and stomach. But then she bypassed all of her sexual organs and went down in her leg. She kept on traveling down the leg and finally ended up in her big toe. All of a sudden she said, "I am not going to climb up all that long way to get out again." The guide asked how she was going to get out, and she replied: "Through my big toe." She tried, but in her tiny state, the big toe was like a tower 40 feet high and her toenail was like a far-off skylight. She could not get up to and through the skylight, no matter how hard she tried. Then she exclaimed, "She's running, she's running. She's fallen down and scraped her foot on a rock. Now I can get out." She dived into the bloodstream and came out through the wound.

At this point, Marla still seemed lost in deep thought. When the guide prompted her, she revealed, "I'm sitting on this giant's toe and he, he, he . . ." She was very embarassed and could not finish the sentence. The guide finished the sentence, "And he's naked."

"Yes," she agreed. "And he doesn't have . . ."

Again the guide finished the sentence, "And he doesn't have any sexual organs?" "No he doesn't."

The guide suggested that she enter into a conversation with the giant to find out what the reason was for his condition. He would say only that he was "born that way." This was the end of the opening session. The experience illustrates in two different ways how the first fantasy had picked up her sexual problem. First, she simply ignored her sexual areas in her body fantasy. Second, fantasy made for her a giant without any sexual organs. Now all this did not solve her problem. It simply brought it to her attention.

In later sessions, in several conversations with the giant, she was able to deal with the feeling that she was somehow different from other women and that she had no natural sexual nature. Then, a few weeks later, in another body fantasy, she was walking down one of the Fallopian tubes. About halfway down, she came to what she called a "closed hole." She explored this closed hole through four sessions, and finally she managed to open it halfway. She felt elated about this. In her next visit, she proudly shared the fact that for the first time in intercourse with her husband, she was able to respond in a positive way, although not as fully as she thought she might be able eventually.

## ENABLING THE SUBJECT TO CREATE
## HIS/HER OWN SOLUTION

A major goal of transformational therapy is to develop internal resources. These are never constructed according to any kind of predesigned framework, nor are they imposed on the subject from outside. The subject and the guide need only to agree on the use of starting images for fantasies. They attempt to avoid, wherever possible, any kind of predetermined agenda, so that the subject is free to create his/her own solutions naturally and spontaneously. The importance of this is illustrated by Carla's experience.

Carla was able to uncover powerful internal resources of which she had been unaware. She was a thirty-one-year-old, self-conscious and sexually insecure, but attractive woman. During a regular checkup, Carla's physician discovered cysts in both her breasts. He instructed her in breast self-examination and told her not to worry. But she became very upset and finally mentioned her problem to me. I suggested fantasy as a way to deal with the cysts. Carla summarizes how she was able to use her own inner resources to turn what she described as a precancerous state into a physically harmless and emotionally fortifying growth experience:

> The first time I entered my breasts, I sensed both heat and redness—the tissue was angry. I could immediately relate this to some situations in my life which were (and still are) a source of conflict and pain. I sensed that my breasts were demanding attention, just as my life situations were. When I asked my breasts why they were angry, they said because they felt useless. I was able to soothe them, to say aloud, "I'll attend to you. I promise you I will. It will be all right."
>
> The next time that I visited my breasts, I saw the cysts, flat, round, whitish-yellow structures. By this time, I had learned that they were made of connective tissue that is always present in the breast, which turns in upon itself to form cysts. I sensed that my breasts were less angry than before, but still wanted a function. Then it occurred to me that perhaps this connective tissue could serve a

supportive role—something I would certainly appreciate since, after breast-feeding three children, my breasts were not very firm. I blessed them, however, for the nourishment they had provided my children, something they'd done almost in spite of me, since I'd not been too keen on breast-feeding and had done it mainly to please my husband. I now also blessed my breasts for the increased pleasure they provided me during lovemaking. Now I asked them to use the connective tissue in them for added support and shaping, so that they and I would be more attractive and desirable. I was amazed! I could almost see it happening, the tissue turning outward, spreading through my breasts, unraveling the cysts right before my eyes. The reaction was so positive that I felt my breasts were telling me that I had had a most clever idea. The pain and soreness in my breasts disappeared immediately. Within a period of weeks, my breasts were firmer than they had been in years.

The change is definitely noticeable. I experienced no weight gain. In fact, due to a rigorous schedule, at one point I lost almost five pounds, but from my hips and thighs—not from my breasts. I have a new confidence and poise, and an appreciation of my own sexuality—due to other changes and growth, but also due to this experience. Perhaps most important is the therapeutic value. In a sense, I feel that through fantasy I have eliminated an imbalance in my body which could have been very dangerous, perhaps precancerous. The masses which were so painful have disappeared. I feel a new sense of oneness with my body.

What had happened? Carla had used her own inner resources for self-healing, and she had built up a working coordination between her body and her mind.

The matter of tapping internal resources is too important to leave to a single illustration. Therefore, we shall take a quick look at Martha, who was suffering from a kidney infection caused by her inability to completely eliminate the fluid wastes processed by the kidney. She visited her kidney and called for her personal physician, with whom she had talked earlier in her health center (one of the rooms of the hallway of her mind). Her physician came immediately. At first glance, she thought that there was a tear in the kidney, and she guessed that her physiclan would want to sew it up. However, neither she nor her physician had any thread. In previous fantasies, she had seen six angels flying overhead, so she appealed to them for help. They immediately came to her aid. Martha told her angels that she needed some thread, and they began at once to spin both gold and peach-colored thread. But the strands became wider and wider, and to her dismay, they eventually turned into pieces of coth, gold and peach in color. She could not imagine, nor could the guide, how the physician was going to sew the kidney with strips of cloth.

Seated across the room was a real physician, a friend of the guide. She was listening to the conversation and shaking her head to indicate that in her judgment, the procedure was not going to be medically correct. The guide did not convey this information to Martha. Instead, he waited to see what would happen. What did occur was very surprising, both to the guide and to the observing physician.

The inner physician began wrapping the strips of cloth around the kidney like a cocoon. At this point, the medical doctor nodded her head approvingly. She knew that the kidney was not adequately supported by its fatty capsule and tended to tilt forward and constrict the flow of urine through the ureter. When the inner physician had finished, Martha seemed pleased with the situation and said, "That's much better."

Then she went to the bladder and saw that the tube between the bladder and the kidney was kinked. To her surprise, one of the angels threw a golden spear up to the ureter in order to straighten it out. Standing back and looking at the result with satisfaction, she thanked her inner physician and the angels, as well as both the kidney and the bladder. The fantasy was over, but within thirty minutes Martha urinated twice. She announced that, in her estimation, she had regained full bladder function. Previously she had been unable to urinate in any quantity without pain.

This story of the inner doctor is very important to our understanding of the impact of fantasy on self-healing. Fantasy is there to be used to free the inner physician. The strength of the doctor who resides within is a crucial determinant of our ability to fight diseases. Norman Cousins made this point quite eloquently in his best-seller, *Anatomy of an Illness* (1980). He mentions an experience that he had had when he visited Albert Schweitzer at his African jungle hospital. The discussion turned to witch doctors, and Cousins made a disparaging remark about their quackery.

> "Some of my steadiest customers are referred to me by witch doctors," Dr. Schweitzer said with only the slightest trace of a smile. "Don't expect me to be too critical of them."
>
> When I asked Dr. Schweitzer how he accounted for the fact that anyone could possibly expect to get well after having been treated by a witch doctor, he said that I was asking him to divulge a secret that doctors have carried around inside them ever since Hippocrates. "But I'll tell you anyway," he said, his face still illuminated by that half smile. "The witch doctor succeeds for the same reason all the rest of us succeed. Each patient carries his own doctor inside him. They come to us not knowing that truth. *We are at our best when we give the doctor who resides within a chance to go to work.*" (Italics ours)

## CREATING A WORKING UNITY OUT OF BODY AND MIND

In a general sense, the use of transformational fantasy provides an experience of overcoming the dichotomy between mind and body. It is different from biofeedback because it provides an experience of "being there" in any part of the body, rather than receiving some mechanical signal and then having to learn the meaning of that signal and how to use it. Of course, both biofeedback and the use of transformational fantasy to obtain what might be called psychefeedback are built on the assumption that the mind can be trained to control bodily processes.

Building a working coordination between body and mind is the ultimate goal of transformational fantasy. Each subject will experience this coordination to some degree, since each is learning how to modify behavior that falls short of achieving the goal, in such a way as to bring the self closer to the goal. Sometimes the process is arduously complex. On other occasions, it is astonishingly simple.

For example, consider what happened to Barbara, who said in total frustration, "I am never going to diet again. When I diet I lose weight in the breasts, where I don't want to, and none in the hips where I really am much too big." I suggested she walk down the hallway of her mind to her weight control room. She did, and when she entered, the first thing she saw was about thirty thermometers all around the room.

This certainly caught her interest. She explored and found that each thermometer had a different temperature reading. This further intrigued her. Then she traced one of the thermometers to her heart. It was not a thermometer at all; it was the fat-burning control. Furthermore, since the heart was a lean muscle, she saw that it had a high fat-burning temperature. In fact, the highest of all. Then she looked at the one leading to her hips—it was 22°; the one leading to her breast read 66°! "My poor breasts are on 66°—and my fat hips on 22°!" she exclaimed incredulously. She sat quietly with a frown on her face. Then she yanked both wires from their sockets and interchanged them. "That's that," she said proudly, "now we'll see how they'll work."

I could not really believe that such a trick would work. A month passed before I saw Barbara again. When she walked in, she stood and turned around several times and looked at me. Her pants were baggy and I asked, "What happened?" She replied, "I lost about 2 inches around my hips and not a bit around my breasts."

Andrea was able to gain important integrating insights from fantasy in a short period of time. She had complained of a bad pain in her neck. The therapist instructed her to be in her neck where the pain was at its worst. She reported the following:

Andrea: There's green stuff under the muscle. Now there's a flow of green stuff. It feels kind of sicklike. Yuck! But it's beginning to move fast. It's loose enough now to come out. It appears to be in the spinal cord, that's like two cords seeping out through the muscle. It's concentrated in my neck. The green stuff should be flowing freely up and down my spine and not seeping out.

Guide: Call for your medical specialist to help you.

Andrea: He says the two cords are two columns representing energy moving up and down the spine. The leaks are caused, oddly enough, by some lack of mental discipline that manifests itself as physical illness. I'm not channeling energy properly and this shows up as leaks in the spinal column.

Guide: Let's experiment again. Have you ever visited central control?

Andrea: No, I don't think so.

Guide: Go to central control. It's an area where all the mind and body functions are integrated.

Andrea: Why, it's like a boiler room! It feels like it is really trying to do well. I don't see much wrong with it. Just little things here and there.

Guide: Things are in pretty good shape?

Andrea: Yeah.

Guide: Try to see where the relationship with the brain is.

Andrea: Ohhh! It's rusted. That's it! The little things wrong here and there are not just little things. They are proof that the equipment is faulty—old and rusty. But I could put new and old parts together. I'm going down to the supply room to get some new parts. I think central control is glad I'm here. It's neither a roaring welcome nor a cold reception. It's more like a close collaboration. I think the way to repair it is to run new parts up through the old parts and to replace the old parts that way! Hm. It looks like that ought to work. . . .

Guide: There's an intercom in central control. Say hello to all parts of your body on this first visit, and thank them for cooperating.

Andrea: Hey! That's really nice. You know what the intercom system is? It's a conch shell. When I talk, it magnifies my voice. Still, it's very soothing to all concerned. I feel very relaxed. My neck is not as painful.

Guide: Is that enough for today?

Andrea: Yeah.

Our last illustration of the power of transformational fantasy to bring about a greater state of coordination and unity between mind and body is the experience of someone who was able to use a symbolic body analogy to solve a psychological problem. Tom had been plagued by a periodically recurring state of deep depression. He chose to embark on a body fantasy, and he was surprised to see a shiny, oily, black film coating every organ of his body. He looked inside his chest cavity and found a furnace burning out in the middle of nowhere producing black smoke in profusion. Trying to reason with the furnace produced no results. It refused to respond to him and maintained a kind of arrogant independence. "I burn. I burn. I burn, and you can't do a thing about it," it said. Faced with such arrogance, Tom felt completely helpless. He wanted to smash the furnace, but he could not do it because he was afraid that the ashes might burn him. I asked Tom to check where the fuel supply was. He found that it was a big strip-mined coal vein and saw an endless succession of trucks hauling the coal to his noxious furnace. When I suggested to Tom that he might have a truck driver's license in his wallet, he was skeptical—but on checking, there it was! At this point, Tom went to look for an empty truck. He found one and climbed in. He picked up a load of coal and instead of dumping it in the furnace, he dumped in on the ground behind the furnace.

He got out of the truck and went over to check the furnace and, sure enough, found it burning less violently. He asked what had happened and was told, "I've had a temporary interruption in my fuel supply, nothing to worry about." It was Tom's first clue that he could exert some control over the furnace. Eventually, in a series of body fantasies, he completely mastered the furnace and tied it in as an auxiliary heating plant for his body's primary metabolism or "main heating plant."

His was a symbolic body fantasy. In no way did he see an anatomical body, but the effectiveness of what he did see was without question. It short-circuited the depth and duration of his periods of depression. For the first time, he felt that he had some ability to deal with the depression which previously had completely overwhelmed him.

These complex, bewildering, and often humorous journeys into the self point to a number of basic conclusions. First, the world of guided fantasy has simultaneously the qualities of the real world and the dream world. Second, these qualities are woven into a coherent, unified mystery-drama of the self by some higher mind or aspect of the mind. This inner guide, which we call the psyche, is absolutely trustworthy and is the prime resource for growing in understanding.

## REFERENCE

Cousins, N. (1980). *Anatomy of an illness.* New York: W. W. Norton.

# CHAPTER 25

## Good Health Imaging

*ANEES A. SHEIKH AND*
*KATHARINA S. SHEIKH*

The mind is its own place and in itself
Can make a heaven of hell and hell of heaven.
(John Milton in *Paradise Lost*)

How much sway does your mind have over your body? Try this simple experiment. Imagine that you are holding a plump yellow lemon. Picture it in your mind until you can smell its fresh scent. Then imagine picking up a knife and cutting into this ripe lemon. You slice off a thick, juicy wedge, and then you take a big bite of it. You feel the lemon juice in your mouth flooding every taste bud. Your cheeks curl and your lips pucker.

The lemon image probably triggered substantial salivation; for, the autonomic nervous system, it appears, readily responds to the language of imagery. The effect of imagery is not limited to the salivary response. Mental images can bring about rapid and far reaching emotional, psychological, and physiological changes. In fact, it now has become clear that imaginal events can have an impact which is as forceful as that of reality. In recent years, it has been convincingly demonstrated that in addition to the salivary response, numerous other bodily responses are influenced by mental images. These include: heart rate, blood flow, electrodermal activity, activity of the voluntary muscles, various aspects of body chemistry, body temperature, blood pressure, dilation of the pupil, electrical activity of the retina, and other ocular effects. Also, the effectiveness of mental imagery in the treatment of a wide variety of health problems has been documented. These include: obesity, insomnia, phobias and anxieties, depression, sexual malfunction, chronic pain, fibroid tumors, cancer, and a host of other ailments.

Is the use of imagery in healing a recent development? Not really. Throughout the ages and in numerous cultures, imagination has been regarded as a powerful agent in the healing process. The mind's ability to alter bodily condition through imagery was recognized by the Egyptians over 4,000 years ago. For centuries, the Tibetan, Chinese, Ayurvedic, and Yogic systems have been utilizing images to influence the flow of life energy which is believed to determine health and illness. The American Indians practiced rituals to induce visions of guidelines for future action, including treatment methods of illness. The Polynesian Kahunas used elaborate imagery-based

341

procedures to combat various ailments. The Greeks came to the Temples of Asclepius to pray for healing visions; discarded crutches and other artifacts left along the temple walls attest to the efficacy of their visions. The famous Greek physician Galen employed dream imagery for the diagnosis and treatment of physical illnesses. Paracelsus, a Renaissance physician and founder of modern chemistry, believed that "man is his own doctor and finds proper healing herbs in his own garden; the physician is in ourselves, and in our own nature are all things that we need." He called imagination the "sun in the soul of man" and believed that "the power of imagination is a great factor in medicine. It may produce diseases . . . and it may cure them. . . . Ills of the body may be cured by physical remedies or by the power of the spirit acting through the soul" (Sheikh & Sheikh, 1996, p. 484).

In Western medical tradition, imagination continued to be considered a leading factor in health and illness until the seventeenth century. However, when Descartes' dualism assumed supremacy, imagination was excluded from the physicians concerns. Now the mind and body were considered to be separate entities which did not affect one another. In the early 1920s, the Behaviorists too did their part in discrediting imagination. Watson called images "mere ghosts of sensations with no functional significance whatever."

After 300 years of neglect, images have finally made a remarkable comeback. More and more health professionals are becoming disenchanted with treating the body as a unit divorced from the mind, and holistic medicine is again drawing many followers. Health professions again have begun to heed Plato's words: "The cure of many diseases is unknown to the physicians of Hellas, because they are ignorant of the whole which ought to be studied also; for the part can never be well unless the whole is well. It is the greatest mistake in the treatment of diseases that there are physicians who treat the body and physicians who treat the mind, since both are inseparable."

With this change in the *Zeitgeist,* mental imagery is firmly assuming its rightful role in the attainment of health and growth (Sheikh, 1984). What makes imagery such a valuable tool? Based on recent research, here are some of the properties which render images singularly effective for achieving health:

1. Experience in imagination can be considered to be psychologically equivalent, in many significant respects, to the actual experience; imagery and perception seem to be experientially and neurophysiologically similar processes. Thus, the consequences of imagery can be similar to the consequences of actual experiences.
2. Images are a source of extensive details about past experiences.
3. Imagery provides an easier access to significant memories of early childhood when language was not yet predominant.
4. Imagery appears to be very effective in bypassing resistances and defenses.
5. Imagery has been referred to as a direct voice of the unconscious.
6. The imagery system helps us to experience more fully a range of emotions. Hence, imagery is capable of producing diverse physiological changes.

A lot has been written lately about the use of imagery in eliminating or ameliorating various health problems. The techniques included in this chapter are primarily for those who are not suffering from any serious illness but are interested in maintaining health and enhancing growth, and fulfillment, and enjoyment of life. These are based on age-old wisdom and have been found to be generally beneficial. Most health professionals are convinced of undesirable effects of negative imaging on health. It follows, then, that the reverse also is true. It seems that, in a very real way, we are what we image. So, as Nathaniel Hawthorne says, let us "keep the imagination sane; that is, the truest condition of communion with heaven."

Some of you may find it helpful to read a given technique several times, until you feel that you have absorbed its essence and can then practice it with eyes closed. Others may prefer to have someone read it to them while they image. Still others may want to record the image and then listen to it as they practice it. At the conclusion of each imagery, we recommend that you slowly count up to five, and then bring yourself back to your surroundings. Take a few minutes to orientate yourself before your return to your usual activities.

## AT PEACE WITH YOURSELF AND AT PEACE WITH THE UNIVERSE

Loosen any tight clothing and assume a relaxed position. Take a deep breath and hold it for a while . . . and now let go. Take another deep breath and hold it. . . . This time when you let go, try to empty yourself of all stale air and make the sound "Haaaaaa." . . . Now breathe normally for a few moments and concentrate on nothing else except your breath. . . . Now when you inhale, tell yourself, "*I am,*" and when you exhale, tell yourself, "*relaxed.*" "*I am*" (inhaling), "*relaxed*" (exhaling). Repeat this a few times. . . . "I am . . . relaxed . . . I am . . . relaxed . . . I am . . . relaxed . . . I am . . . relaxed." When you say the word "relaxed" to yourself, let your body sink deeper and deeper into the chair or into the rug or the bed . . . Deeper and deeper.

During the day, you spend a great deal of your energy fighting the force of gravity. Now for a few moments, let that force of gravity take over completely . . . Let every muscle . . . every fiber . . . every cell in your body be pulled down and down . . . further and further down . . . Feel your body slowing down and your mind slowing down. There is no rush . . . no hurry. There is nowhere you have to go . . . nothing you have to do. Just feel that wonderful sense of relaxation throughout your body. Tensions and frustrations are gradually seeping out of your system. Every time you breathe in, imagine that you are breathing in a wonderful glow of relaxation, and every time you breathe out, imagine that you are breathing out tensions, fatigue, frustrations. . . . As these tensions leave your mindbody, your whole being becomes so calm, so tranquil . . . so silent. . . . A feeling of peace washes over you and through you. It is so calm, so quiet . . . so silent . . . so silent. The silence feels so warm and comfortable and so healing . . . so deeply healing. You feel at ease . . . at peace . . . at peace with yourself and at peace with the universe . . . deeply at peace.

## IMAGINE YOUR BLESSINGS

Most of us have the unfortunate tendency to focus on the unpleasant events in our past and to forget the happy ones. If someone does us both a good turn and a bad turn, we probably will focus on the bad one and erase the good one from our mind or interpret it negatively. Shakespeare already noted this human trait in *Julius Caesar:*

The evil that men do lives after them;
The good is oft interred with their bones.

Perhaps at one time there was some survival value in being more aware of the threats in the environment than of the promises. However, now this awareness seems to be a source of much unhappiness. We would do well to consciously fight this tendency and thus develop a more positive outlook on life. The following exercise promotes this attitude.

Make yourself comfortable. Take a deep breath, hold it for a while and then let go. Repeat several times. Now breathe normally. With every breath, feel your body slowing down and your mind slowing down. Feel any outside noises and the verbal chatter in your mind fading away. They are becoming fainter . . . and fainter . . . and fainter.

A number of happy events occurred in your past. You have not thought of some of them for a long time. Some were big events . . . others were just incidents. But they all made you feel happy . . . joyful . . . made you feel good in the very core of you. . . . Perhaps it was your wedding . . . or the birth of your first child . . . or the recognition of your achievements by someone whose opinion mattered a great deal to you . . . or the warm hug your grandmother gave you when you were a child . . . or the contentment and security of sitting in your father's lap listening to a bedtime story . . . any scenes of events when you experienced others' kindness, compassion, and love . . . when you, in turn, felt kind, compassionate . . . loving . . . serene . . . secure . . . elated . . . successful . . . on top of the world. . . . Do not merely watch a ray of these events, relive them in your mind. Relive the event in all its richness. Reexperience the sights . . . the sounds . . . the smells . . . the textures. Do not rush. Dwell on each image until it revives the original feelings in the very center of your being. Enjoy your feelings thoroughly before you move on to the next event. Remember that we are not asking you to *count* your blessings, but rather to *imagine your blessings.*

We recommend that you spend about fifteen minutes in the beginning of the day and fifteen minutes before going to sleep imagining your blessings. Also you might find it helpful to record your reexperiences of happy events in a journal, adding a few each day. Your initial response to this suggestion may be that you will run out of material very soon. We assure you that you are in for a surprise. Once you start emphasizing the positive, you will find much of it in your past and in your present, and your outlook on life will most likely be transformed.

## THE DANCE OF LIFE

Close your eyes. . . . Relax. . . . Become aware that your body consists of trillions of cells next to one another. But if you looked at the body tissue through a powerful microscope, you would discover that the cells are not tightly packed but have some space between them.

Now imagine that the space between the cells is being squeezed out and the cells are crushed together. From head to toe, your body is now a tightly packed mass.

Now let some space creep back in between the cells, restoring the original condition.

Now create a little extra space between all the cells. All of these trillions of cells that make up your body now have some room to breathe . . . to move around.

Imagine that all of these cells throughout your body . . . are beginning to move in a very rhythmic way . . . beginning to dance. You can feel this beautiful dance of life going on throughout your system . . . from head to toe. Each and every cell is participating in this dance . . . perhaps a sacred dance . . . dancing to the rhythm of life . . . dancing to the music of heavenly silence.

You feel full of energy . . . joy bubbles up in you. You may feel like a bottle of champagne that has just been opened.

After you have fully experienced this joyful dance, retain the wonderful feelings it has left in you. Then gently bring yourself back to your surroundings and open your eyes.

## IMAGINE HEALTH

A number of our physician friends have been using images, with or without medication, to heal various physical disorders. The assumption is that vividly imagining the physiological function underlying the healing of a diseased organ can encourage and expedite recovery. For example, if you have a sinus infection, the physician may show you a picture of the sinus passageways and cavities and ask you to imagine that the mucous is beginning to drain and that your sinus passageways are beginning to open up. Or if you have a kidney problem, the physician may show you a picture of a sick kidney and one of a healthy kidney and ask you to imagine that your sick kidney gradually is beginning to look healthy. However, the healing images need not be literal; metaphorical ones may be equally effective. For example, you could imagine the virus as tiny spots on a blackboard which you are erasing. Samuel and Bennet, in *Be Well* (1974), suggest a few guidelines for developing healing images. These include: erasing bacteria, building new healthy cells, making a rough surface smooth, changing tension into relaxation, changing the temperature of a body part, sending cleansing blood to the unhealthy organ or area, and opening up pressured or blocked areas.

## CREATING YOUR OWN SAFE PLACE

Sit or lie comfortably. . . . Close your eyes. . . . Relax. . . . Think of the words safety . . . comfort . . . warmth . . . joy . . . love . . . security . . . peace . . . freedom . . . creativity. Meditate on their meanings for you, and let the images which they evoke freely go in and out of your mind.

Now visualize a beautiful natural setting. This can be a place you have actually visited or a product of your imagination. Here you feel serene and safe. To accentuate these feelings you may add to your image a hospitable cave or a treehouse or a fort. For added protection you can surround your dwelling with a medieval moat or a magic circle, or place it in a bubble of golden light. You may wish to leave your safe place unfurnished or you may add to it items which represent security, comfort, and joy to you. Now visualize this place as clearly and vividly as you can, involving all your senses, and savor the feelings which are evoked.

Practice this several times, until the vision of safe place becomes imprinted on your mind and you can summon it quickly in fairly elaborated form.

If your safe place is readily available, you can retreat to it and be strengthened by the positive feelings it nurtures in you, whenever you feel anxious, frightened, restless, or sad.

## CLEANSING LIGHT

A number of ancient approaches, including the Hindu, Buddhist, and Sufi traditions, have employed images of cleansing light to promote healing and personal growth. This is one version of that exercise.

Relax and imagine that you are sitting in a beautiful landscape on a perfect day. The sky is filled with rainbow lights, and one shaft of the white light has found you. It is brighter than one hundred suns. You feel it warming the top of your head. It now penetrates your skull and flows into your body. You feel it illuminating and pleasantly warming your head, then it flows down your neck, into your chest. It radiates into your arms, into your hands, right down to your fingertips. This light continues to flow through your abdomen and into your legs, feet, and toes. You feel that you are brimming over with light. The light is thoroughly cleansing you, and your body is becoming luminous. All your negative emotions, such as jealousy, anger, fear, your negative thoughts, your bad habits, and your physical ailments are being dissolved by the light. If you have a mental or physical affliction which does not readily respond, imagine that it is flooded by more and more light until it starts to heal. You may now imagine that the impure elements are leaving you in the form of dark smoke which is quickly blown away by a gentle breeze. You are left feeling free and joyful.

You can use this exercise whenever you wish to rid yourself of negative elements.

## MENTAL COCKTAIL

The following technique is an adaptation of a procedure found in the book *Superlearning* by Ostrander, Shroeder, and Ostrander (1979).

Get comfortable and relax. Now imagine that you are sitting at a table and on it are a number of small bottles and an empty glass. Each bottle is filled with a liquid representing a personality trait; the labels on the bottles read: self-confidence, freedom, love, assertiveness, and so on. Prepare a cocktail of your choice. Pour in the liquid of any characteristic that you wish to strengthen or add to your personality. After you have prepared your cocktail, sip it slowly. Imagine that as you drink this liquid, it spreads throughout your system and begins to take effect. You have a deep feeling that you gradually are changing in the desired direction and becoming a more balanced person. The more you sip, the more you change. After you have finished the drink, continue, for a few moments, to concentrate on its effect. Then let the image fade away, and gently bring yourself back to your surroundings.

But keep in mind the contents of the drink that you just finished, so that it may continue to have its beneficial effect. To reinforce its power, you may want to repeat this exercise and enjoy several more cocktails. Also, you may wish to vary the type and proportions of the liquid characteristics.

## INNER WISDOM

Many Eastern and Western traditions indicate that the human organism is much wiser than we believe it to be. Unfortunately this wisdom often is inaccessible to the conscious mind. But there is an ancient technique which is helpful in connecting with this inner wisdom. This technique, along with its many variations, is one of the most frequently used imagery techniques, and the numerous claims of its efficacy are found in the literature. This is our version:

Close your eyes and relax deeply. Now imagine that you are in a beautiful natural setting: The lush green grass is dotted with bright blossoms . . . brightly colored song birds dart in and out of majestic trees . . . sunbeams dance in the cool clear water of a stream. At a distance lies a mountain chain. On top of one of the mountains, you notice a moving white speck. It is radiating clear bright light, and it is slowly moving down the mountain toward you. You are intrigued by this light and you start walking toward the mountain. As the distance decreases, you begin to sense that it is a wise and compassionate being that knows you completely—your past, your present, your future. You keep on moving toward this being until you are face to face. He/she is your inner guide or inner advisor. Enjoy his/her presence, as you talk about issues in your life. Feel free to ask any questions about anything that is on your mind. Wait patiently for the answer. When the experience of being with this inner guide appears complete, express your appreciation for his/her company and advice and perhaps make arrangements to meet again. Then gradually let these images fade away but hold on to the advice that was offered. Open your eyes.

The guide may take the form of someone familiar to you or he/she may be a stranger. This guide may even be nonhuman or may not take on a distinct form but merely be a wise presence. Also your communication with this advisor may not be in words, but you will nevertheless be aware of this message.

It is not advisable to follow the suggestions of the inner guide without first evaluating them carefully. If they seem to make sense and the risk is minimal, you may want to put them into action and see how they work.

## THE TRUE SELF

Views of human beings range from a notion that they are machines made of meat to the belief that they are sparks from the divine fire. We tend to believe that human beings were indeed fashioned in God's image. If this were not so, how would we be capable of comprehending such concepts as love, saintliness, and divinity? Our view of the nature of human beings also radically influences our attitude toward our fellow beings. We cannot possibly muster the same regard for a machine made of meat as for a creature who reflects the divine. The Indians have a wonderful way of greeting one another: "Namaste"—I greet the god within you.

The following imagery is designed to help us focus on the divine aspect of our nature. It is an adaptation of a technique we learned from Pir Vilayat, Head of the Sufi Order of the West (Khan, 1982).

Relax and imagine yourself in a sacred place. As you look around, you become aware of a majestic figure who seems to have changed the surroundings with her magnetism. She radiates divine power—you recognize it as the same force which moves the planets and tells the seed to grow.

She is looking at you, or rather into your very soul, with profound understanding, and in the light of her wisdom you see all things more clearly. Her total awareness reminds you to be more fully aware.

She seems to be above all suffering, yet also exquisitely sensitive to it and deeply compassionate. In spite of her awareness of sadness, she is bubbling over with joy. You sense that she is truly at peace and truly free, not only from the world but also from herself. Contact with her absolute freedom, in turn, liberates you.

She is all-knowing but also innocent, and her purity gradually cleanses your soul of all inauthenticity. She has shown you that you too share in the divine. You feel that you harbor a divine power, and that you radiate light and life. You have tuned in to the suffering of all creatures, yet you are joyful. Also you are at peace—a peace born of absolute freedom. You are infinitely above and beyond the forces that once held you.

Do you realize that this is your being, your true self?

## THE HOUSE OF LIFE

Relax and imagine that you are at the seashore. It is a balmy, sunny day. The sky is blue and the water is a deeper blue with bobbing white caps. The music of the waves, and a gentle breeze, and the cool sand under your feet caress and soothe your senses. It feels so good to be alive.

Rising behind the beach are beautiful mountains. As you look up, you see a house perched on top of one of the peaks. What a delightful spot for a house! You are drawn to this house as if it were a magnet, and before you realize what you are doing you are making your way toward it. Finally, you stand before it and you are aching to step inside. You knock on the door and it is opened by a very kind person who does not hesitate to invite you in. You have never seen or even imagined a house so exquisite in every respect, and the view from the large windows is breath-taking.

As you are drinking in the delights of this place, the owner tells you that he has to go on an important mission, which may take a week, a month, a year, ten years, fifty years, or even longer. He makes you an offer: you may live in the house during his absence, but you must vacate it upon his return. Take note of your reaction to this offer.

You accept the terms and the owner leaves. The house is now your home and time flies by. A few months . . . a few years have passed. Assess the quality of your life during this time.

Just as you are in the midst of doing something very important, . . . at least it seems important to you . . . , you hear a knock at the door. You open the door and see the owner. Notice how you react to his return.

Now let these images fade away. Take a deep breath and open your eyes.

You can consider this house as a metaphor for life. It has been given to us on uncertain terms. Are you enjoying your stay in this exquisite house . . . or is uncertainty in the way of fully living your life? When the time comes for that knock at the door, will you feel angry and will you tell the owner, "Why didn't you drop dead someplace . . . I was just beginning to enjoy my stay" . . . or will you welcome him back with a sense of gratitude for letting you be in this heavenly place?

When death beckons, some of us may be resentful, others may feel like the Indian Nobel laureate Rabindranath Tagore (1962, p. 88):

> When I go from hence let this be my parting word, that what I have seen is unsurpassable.
> I have tasted of the hidden honey of this lotus that expands on the ocean of light, and thus am I blessed—let this be my parting word.
> In this playhouse of infinite forms I have had my play and here have I caught sight of him that is formless.
> My whole body and my limbs have thrilled with his touch who is beyond touch; and if the end comes here, let it come—let this be my parting word.

We would like to end this chapter with a word of caution. These imageries should be practiced only when you are able to relax and give them your undivided attention. Doing them while driving is not a good idea. Anyone with a serious physical, mental, or emotional problem should consult a physician/therapist concerning the use of these techniques. Although most readers will readily relax and begin to benefit from these techniques, a few may find that their imageries persistently evoke anxiety and discomfort. If this occurs, they should stop practicing them and seek professional guidance on the use of these methods.

## REFERENCES

Sheikh, A. A. (Ed.) (1984). *Imagination and healing.* Amityville, NY: Baywood.

Achterberg, J. (1985). *Imagery in healing.* Boston: Shambhala.

Sheikh, A. A., & Sheikh, K. S. (Eds.) (1996). *Healing east and west.* New York: Wiley.

Khan, V. I. (1982). *Introducing spirituality into counseling and therapy.* Lebanon Springs, NY: Omega Press.

Ostrander, S., Schroeder, L., & Ostrander, N. (1979). *Superlearning.* New York: Dell.

Samuels, M., & Bennet, H. (1974). *Be well.* New York: Random House.

Tagore, R. (1962). *Gitanjali.* New York: Macmillan.

## CHAPTER 26

# Guided Meditation*

## RAM DASS AND STEPHEN LEVINE

Sit straight, so your head, neck, and chest are in a straight line. Start by focusing in your heart area, in the middle of your chest where the Hridayam, the spiritual heart, is located. With your mouth closed, breathe in and out of your chest, focusing on your heart as if you were breathing in and out through your heart. Breathe deeply.

Imagine a substance, a golden mist which fills the air. With every breath, imagine you are pulling into you this golden substance. Fill with it; let it pour through your entire body.

Breathe in the energy of the universe. Breathe in the breath of God. Let it fill your whole body. Each time you breathe out, breathe out all of the things in you that keep you from knowing your true self, breathe out all of the separateness, all of the feelings of unworthiness, all the self-pity, all the attachment to your pain, whether it's physical or psychological. Breathe out anger and doubt and greed and lust and confusion. Breathe in God's breath and breathe out all of the impediments that keep you from knowing God. Let the breath be the transformation. Now let the golden mist that has poured into your being focus in the middle of your chest; let it take form as a tiny being, the size of a thumb, sitting on a lotus flower right in the middle of your heart. Notice its equanimity, the radiance that makes it bright with a light that comes from within. Use your imagination. And as you look upon this being become aware that it is radiating light. See the light pouring out of its every pore. As you meditate upon it, experience the deep peace that is emanating from this being. Feel as you look upon this being that it is a being of great wisdom. It's sitting quietly, silently, perfectly poised. Feel its compassion and its love. Let yourself be filled with its love.

Now, slowly let that tiny being grow in size until it has filled your body so its head just fills the space of your head; its torso, your torso; its arms, your arms; its legs, your legs. So that now in the skin of your body sits this being, a being of infinite wisdom, a being of the deepest compassion, a being who is bathed in bliss, self-effulgent bliss, a being of light, of perfect tranquility. Let this being in your skin begin to grow in size.

---

Experience yourself growing until your head reaches the top of the ceiling and you are sitting beneath the floor and all of the beings gathered within this room are within your body. All of the sounds, even the sound of my voice, are coming from inside you. Feel your vastness, your peace, your equanimity.

Continue to grow. Your head goes up into the sky, blueness all about, until all of your town, your environment, is within you. Look inside and experience the human condition, see the loneliness, the joy, the caring, the violence, the paranoia, the love of a mother for her child, sickness, fear of death, see it all. Realize that it is all within you. Look upon it with compassion, with caring. At the same moment with equanimity, feeling the light pouring through your being, inward and outward.

Now grow still larger, feel your vastness increasing until your head is among the planets and you are sitting in the middle of this galaxy, the earth lying deep within your belly. All of humankind lies within you. Feel the turmoil and the longing. Feel the beauty. Sit in this universe, silent, huge, peaceful, compassionate, loving. Let all of the creations of human beings' minds be within you; look upon them with compassion.

Continue to grow until not only this galaxy but every galaxy is within you, until everything you can conceive of is within you. All of it inside you. You are the only one. Feel your aloneness, your silence, your peace. No other beings here, all of the planes of consciousness are within you.

You are the Ancient one. Everything that ever was, is, or will be is part of the dance of your being. You are all of the universe and so you have Infinite Wisdom; you appreciate all of the feelings of the universe so you have Infinite Compassion. Let the boundaries of your being disintegrate now and merge yourself into that which is beyond form, and sit for a moment in the formless, beyond time and space, beyond compassion, beyond love, beyond God. . . . Let it all be, perfectly.

Now very gently, very slowly, let the form of the boundaries of your vast being, the one, be reestablished. You are vast, you are silent, all is within you. Come back from beyond the One and slowly come down in size, come down through the universes into this universe, until your head is once again among the planets and the earth is within you. Until your head is once again in the heavens and the cities are within you.

Come down in size until your head is at the top of this room. Stop here for a moment. From this place, look down into the room and find the being who you thought you were when you began this meditation. Look at that being, bringing to bear all of your love and compassion. See the journey of that being as it is living out this incarnation, see its plight, its fears, its doubts, its connection. See all the things it clings to which keep it from being free. See how close it is to knowing who it is. Look within that being and see the purity of its soul.

At this moment reach down from your vast height and very gently, very delicately, with your mind, place your hand very gently on the head of this being, and bestow upon it your blessing, a blessing that in this very life, it may fully know itself. At this moment you are that which blesses and that which is being blessed. Experience both simultaneously.

Come down in size now until you are back into the body which you thought you were when you began. You are still flesh surrounding a being of radiance, of wisdom that comes from being in tune with the truth, and of a love for all things. Feel the love and peace pouring out of you. Use the light that is coming through you now for transmitting that energy, that blessing, to all beings everywhere. Become a lighthouse and send peace and love to all those who suffer.

Think of all the people whom you have felt less than love for, look to their souls and surround them with light, with love and peace at this moment. Let go of the anger and the judgment. And then send the light of love and peace out to people who are ill, who are lonely, who are afraid, who have lost their way. Share your blessings, because only when you give can you continue to receive. And you will find that no matter how much you give, you will receive tenfold. As you go on this spiritual journey you must accept the responsibility to share what you receive, for that is part of the harmony of God, that you become an instrument for the manifestation of the will of God.

Now let the radiant perfect being once again assume its diminutive form, the size of a thumb, sitting upon a lotus flower in your heart, in your spiritual heart in the middle of your chest, radiant with light, peaceful, immensely compassionate. This being is love, this being is wisdom. This is the inner Guru, this is the being within you who always knows. This is the being whom you meet through your deeper and deeper intuition when you've gone beyond your mind. This is the being who is the flow of the universe, the tiny form of the entire universe that exists within you. At any time, you need only sit and quiet your mind and you will hear this being guiding you home. When you have finished the journey, you will have disappeared into this being, surrendered, merged; and then you will recognize that God, the Guru, and self are one.

# CHAPTER 27

# *Imagery-Related Meditations**

## *PIR VILAYAT INAYAT KHAN*

### MEDITATION PRACTICE

First, relax the muscles of the back, the spinal cord, the arms, and the legs. Then sit in a very upright position, the spinal cord absolutely straight. If you sit on a book or cushion, that is best, for then your knees are on the ground. If once you have done this, you will realize how very comfortable it is. It forces the spine to be straight. Otherwise the knees are a little too high, and the spinal cord is not straight. Now you are ready for the takeoff. You leave everything behind, and assume an attitude of total detachment. You do not give up the impressions from the outside world—that is, the perception—you leave the mind behind. Then you give up your physical or egoic consciousness. Tune your soul to a very fine pitch. Now give up the frontiers of your being, whether they are the physical body or the mind, and imagine the tremendous richness that flows through you and that is you. Imagine that you are the incorporation of the whole universe. You are continually capturing elements out of space. You begin to assume cosmic dimensions.

Now let cosmic consciousness flow through you without appropriating it; you experience an awareness of cosmic consciousness—consciousness frees itself from its support. This is the time to launch yourself upwards: identify yourself with pure, luminous consciousness. You become totally transparent, and the consciousness is egoless. At this point, you feel the pull of the gravity of the earth and you also feel the buoyancy of the soul. The farther the buoyancy of the soul draws you upwards, the more you become aware of the jubilation and glorification of the higher spheres. It is sublime; you cannot experience it from your egoic consciousness. Your consciousness must be freed from that center. You have lifted yourself beyond the realm of thought. The next thing to do is to glorify yourself—partake in the glorification. Raise your consciousness and attune yourself to the highest point, where your whole being becomes an act of glorification. You experience the peace of this high altitude; you seem to feel a tremendous power—a very subtle and sublime power. You are now imbued with this power.

---

*Reprinted with permission from the following books by Pir Vilayat Inayat Khan: *The Call of the Dervish*, Santa Fe, NM: Sufi Order Publications, 1981, and *Introducing Spirituality into Counseling and Therapy*, Lebanon Springs, NY: Omega Press, 1982.

Now you redirect your consciousness downward, and bring down your vision of beauty and your sense of peace and the very subtle power of the higher planes—the nobility and the sovereignty—and radiate it as you move downward. You feel a rejoicing of the planes through which you have passed, and you feel committed to manifest that which you have experienced. The moment of the blessing descends upon you—the moment to renew the covenant and link yourself with the masters, saints, and prophets of the great hierarchy of the government of the world, united with all the illuminated souls who form the embodiment of the master, the spirit of guidance. You feel the influence of the higher spheres still working around you; you are carrying the atmosphere of the higher spheres with you, and it is as though you were entrusted with something very sacred.

You can always recapture your contact with the higher planes. Bring your consciousness down by allowing the pull of responsibility—the feeling that you have something to do and accomplish—to draw you back. Maintain that state of awakening, of acute awareness, of high-powered sensitivity—the power of the divine beings, the peace, and the sovereignty—but do not lose the common touch. A channel has been opened up, and once it has been cleared you can always establish communication upwards at any time. Keep the line of communication open.

## A MEDITATION ON ECSTASY

Toward the One: make your soul as high as you can reach; extend your consciousness to incorporate and embrace the entire universe. Make your heart like an ocean of love, encompassing all beings by its breadth, its depths, and its all-accommodating compass. Extend the roots of your being right down into the fabric of the universe. Shake away all the trammels that curtail your freedom—freedom of thought, freedom of understanding—so that you may awaken to cosmic consciousness. Let your heart be lifted by your intuition and your divine beauty, which have been buried under the layers of make-believe and illusion in which we have been caught in our everyday picture of the world. Recover the memory of what you have always been since the beginning of time—what you are and always will be beyond time—and watch the forward march of becoming unfolding itself beneath you while you remain suspended, immobile in eternity, in a state of immunity from agitation and emotional turmoil. Take the wings of independence and detachment: on these wings you can take flight. They are the way to freedom. They give access to the planes beyond your normal purview, so that you may leave your body behind to take care of itself. Leave your body consciousness behind; leave your mind behind. Let your consciousness of the mind take care of the mind, of the thoughts, until you are able to see without eyes and hear without ears and walk without feet and understand without the mind—and experience the ecstasy of cosmic beauty in the soul rather than wallow in the emotions of the heart.

Let your understanding be annihilated in the mystery of the unknown. Face the reality that cannot be grasped with the mind by letting yourself be shattered; enjoy the shattering of your being in its encounter with a reality so glorious, so all-encompassing, that we have no measure with which to account for it. We have no means of grasping it except by allowing ourselves to be totally annihilated by it, thereby being resurrected with a power we never knew: the power that runs the universe, the power behind the giddy rotations of the planets and the galaxies and the great spirals of stardust in the heavens; the force within the atom and the force within the sap of the plant; the force that is carrying you forward toward unknown horizons. Be part of it so that the power of God inhabits you, transforming and strengthening you beyond any conception—and then rise to an ever-wider consciousness so that when you look back upon your life, your little problems and your little concepts, you realize how you've been caught up in the whirlwind of an illusion. How is it possible that you can let yourself be browbeaten into accepting the evidence of the immediate environment when the universe is speaking from its far corners, telling you that what you think you are is simply the crossroads where every atom of the universe meets every other—a juncture, a knot in a network whose end cannot be found?

The secret of increasing the magnitude of your consciousness is to look upon it as a capacity or an accommodation, like a chalice, starting out from the heart center, in the middle of the chest. You don't radiate from the heart center, you simply find room for more and more beings—starting with those beings you find difficult to love and then reaching out farther and farther with the power of the heart—a cosmic emotion beyond human emotion. Sense the compassion of the Mother of the world—the emotion of suffering being transformed into joy. Then awaken to the consciousness of the soul instead of the heart, beyond emotion. You discover the divine perfection in you and watch yourself speeding toward the awareness of divine perfection. Then you realize the One behind all multiplicity, the spaceless behind space, the timeless behind time, the numberless beyond multiplicity, and participate in the great celebrations when all beings converge in the measure of their awareness in the great rejoicing, where they are celebrating the overcoming of limitation and of illusion in the crowning of the King of the universe.

Toward the One, the perfection of Love, Harmony, and Beauty, the Only Being, united with all the illuminated souls—you unite yourself with all the illuminated souls—who form the embodiment of the master, the spirit of guidance—all the illuminated souls, whom you reach not only by the power of your thought, but by that great cosmic law of invocation whereby the soul of every creature can find a resonance in the soul of every other creature simply by turning toward him. You stir the hearts of the prophets and the masters and the saints, of all the heavenly beings and all the hierarchies of beings, just by your invocation.

## COSMIC CONSCIOUSNESS MEDITATION

Imagine that you are a pilgrim, you have left the world behind and are loosening the invisible strings that are holding you back. You have reached a deep state in retreat, where you find you have become like a deer in the forest: you are so much a part of nature that your consciousness reaches into the consciousness of the trees and the flowers, the wind and the sun. This is cosmic consciousness: consciousness that is no longer centered in the person. Imagine walking in the forest and becoming totally immersed in the whole scene by losing your personal consciousness. You experience what it is like to be a tree, a bird, a butterfly, an insect, a snake, an animal, a rock. We know that consciousness does not have to operate from the vantage point of the body. You can experience yourself as a rock by getting into the consciousness of a rock, experience yourself as a dog by getting into the consciousness of the dog, experience yourself as a flower by getting into the consciousness of a flower, or experience yourself as a person you know by getting into the consciousness of that person.

You can begin by getting into the consciousness of a crystal. A crystal is a very special form of matter. In most matter, the molecules are rather randomly distributed, but where matter has become very purified, as in a mineral crystal like quartz, all of the molecules are disposed in absolute geometrical constructs, some of them rather simple, others more complicated, but always strictly geometrical. This is because all the molecules pulsate at the same frequency so that the optimal position in which they can be packed is orderly. If you could get into the consciousness of each molecule, you would find that it has found a way of relating to the other molecules in a state of resonance—it is locked into a cosmic harmony. Inasmuch as there is any personal consciousness in the molecule, in the atom within the molecule, or in the electrons within the atoms, it is expressing a harmony far beyond its own volition, the cosmic harmony. It is simply fitting into the resonancy and continuing to pulse without any variation in time and space, as if time and space had been suspended. In this case, overall consciousness is more important than personal consciousness, there is very little personal consciousness, so the overall consciousness comes out more strongly in the form of what we might call the symphony of the spheres. You can experience what it would be like to be a crystal—that wonderful readiness to oscillate at the frequency it is supposed to oscillate at by the conjunction of forces.

Because of its oscillation, the crystal lends itself to the rays of the light of the sun passing through it; if you get into the consciousness of a crystal, you experience what it is like to be so much in sync with the cosmic harmony that you also become an instrument of the light of the universe. You feel yourself totally clear and luminescent, effervescent. It is really a sacrifice of freedom, initiative, complexity, variety, fluctuations from sclerosed order—except that if the crystal is exposed to the energy of light, then some of the electrons may tear themselves away from the sclerosed order and fluctuate, taking a certain amount of freedom by traveling away from their orbitals; when they run out of energy, they have to fall back again into their orbitals, and at that time they radiate light: they have been activated by light, and now they themselves radiate light. You can experience the moment of glory when an electron is able to free itself of that sclerosed order, and then the joy of itself giving off light as it falls back into place again. Our bodies are like that—are partly crystals—so getting into the consciousness of the crystal will enable us to get deeper into the mystery of the very fabric of the planet, of which we are part.

Now you can get into the consciousness of a flower. Here there is a much greater degree of consciousness because the very substance of the flower is organic: it does not have to subject itself to such rigid laws as the crystal. Each molecule has its own contribution to the cell; it is given much more free choice and responsibility in the whole, and is also able to understand something about the other molecules—how they all fit into a purpose. The consequence is that the consciousness of a flower as a whole is much more advanced. You can get into that consciousness, as a whole, while at the same time being conscious of all the cells and molecules, and then you will see how the flower is delighted by having an opportunity to manifest beauty, to display beauty; in fact, the beauty of the cosmos is coming through it. You can feel how this beauty manifests as form and as shades of color, and you may also experience how precarious the flower feels: it is short-lived, and it is delivered into the bands of the environment, so that it can suddenly become too cold and be frozen, or have too much heat from the sun, or suffer from a drought, or be stepped on by animals or by people. It is very precarious, although it has so much to bring through, and the only way it can survive its precariousness is to produce perfume—to transmute its molecules into perfume, so they can continue to express its beauty when it can no longer survive in the form in which it was living before. Of course, the flower has divine consciousness. All the beauty, and also the power, that are coming through are beyond its own personal consciousness, and where the personal consciousness is not strong, then the divine consciousness comes through more strongly.

In the dog, personal consciousness is much stronger, so the divine consciousness gets a bit bogged down. It comes through as the dog's instinct—sometimes overwhelmingly. Here it is easier not only to experience him or her through his or her own eyes, but also to experience yourself through the eyes of the dog. What do you look like to a dog? He is excited, so enthused by your intelligence, and he would so much like to understand why you do things the way you do. This is why he is capable of deferring to your judgment, which sometimes makes him look subservient. It is because he cannot quite grasp your intelligence, but knows, perhaps from experience, that your intelligence usually proves to be right, or to be operative. We must look very different in the eyes of a dog than the way we have become accustomed to picturing ourselves. If we can really see ourselves as we would look to a dog, or to a lion or some other animal, we would be adding a whole new dimension to our experience of ourselves and to our self-image.

Now you might try getting into the consciousness of a person—a friend, someone very close to you. Here, there are some reservations to make, and rightly so, because some people would not like other people to be able to know all they think or how they feel. This is because many of us were hurt when we were children: we've been laughed at. Perhaps we think that people might not value some of our thoughts or would even consider them objects of derision. We might feel that some of our feelings are so sacred that perhaps people would either not understand them or not value their sacred nature. It may have been the case that we have confided in another person and that person has betrayed our confidence, with disastrous consequences. In wartime, for example, keeping a secret can be a matter of life and death. If a person comes to us in confidence and reveals to us a secret of his soul, we have no right to shout it from the rooftops. This is why doctors are under the rule of professional secrecy. There are many reasons why some people would not like everyone else to be able to read right into their hearts and souls, or into their thoughts, and it would be an indiscretion to try to probe behind their curtains of privacy. This is a practice that you can carry out with human beings only if you choose a person who is so close to you that you feel that person would have no objection to your looking right into his soul. Of course, there are different levels of the beings that might be involved; there should be no objection to reaching into the higher consciousness of any person—to experience what that person is experiencing when he is in a very high state of meditation. Very often, the murshids, or Sufi teachers, call their pupils when they are in a very high state of meditation, because they want to share it. When one experiences something very beautiful, one wants to share it, particularly when it is an impersonal experience. So I suggest that you think about people who are very close to you—but try to get into their real being rather than their personalities. What would their sense of identity, their self-image, be if they really knew themselves as they truly are in their non-manifested being—that aspect of themselves that has not yet manifested in their personality? This is a most important practice for counselors, gurus, and lovers, because anyone who loves another person can make that love creative by helping the person to be what he is. The only way to do that is to discover the real person. Then that person will discover himself through your eyes, and you will help him to become what he is.

You can think about one person after another, and imagine them in a very high state of consciousness. Then try to get into their consciousness. That high state of consciousness is actually the real foundation or ground out of which the personality of the person has grown, just as a crystal grows out of its foundation; and that foundation is really impersonal. So when you get into the consciousness of a person in his highest state of consciousness, you cannot say that you are getting into his personal consciousness. What you are getting into is a cosmic or transcendent state that is coming through that person, right down into his personality. At the time when you are reaching him, you are really reaching into the cosmic dimensions behind the personality. That is why many Hindus and Sufis say, "I see God in him. All that I see is God." At that level, what you see is divine attributes coming through the person.

This is a practice that I recommend doing every day—getting into the higher consciousness of all the beings around one. The next half of it is to see how you appear to each person. If that person is in his or her higher consciousness, then he or she is able to assess the non-manifest in you, which is those qualities that are on their way into manifestation in your personality but that have not yet come through fully. You realize right away that the very perception that person has of your higher being hoists your consciousness into its higher regions and makes you aware of those qualities that are the essence of your being and are trying to come through your personality.

We now come to the more general attunement of the contemplative who is on retreat, walking through the forest, or even walking through the city. His consciousness is distributed throughout and around him, instead of being centered in his person. Instead of judging people or animals or trees from the vantage point of his person, his consciousness is everywhere in all beings. This attunement brings about ecstasy. You can sit with your back against a tree and experience how the tree feels with your back against it. This consciousness may reach beyond the planet into the sun; it is consciousness of the sun that makes the rishis and dervishes so powerful. They experience what it is like to be the sun. According to the Sufis, the sun is a being—Prince Hurakhsh, the archangel of the sun—who is burning himself in sheer bursts of energy and, because of that, giving life to the entire planetary system. The sun embodies a life-giving, energy-giving disposition. So if you get into the consciousness of the sun, you yourself become life-giving. Having experienced the condition of the sun, you become like the sun.

You can even go beyond the sun to the consciousness of the distant stars. Then you can begin to see yourself from the point of view of the cosmos. Einstein, for example, when he was pushing a stroller in New York, could see himself pushing that stroller. In the middle of the enormous, overwhelming motions of the stars, and seeing the planet Earth as being just a little grain of sand in the whole vast mechanism of the universe, he could see himself pushing a stroller in New York with reference to the whole majestic motion of the stars. This is how you can see yourself: instead of being the center of the universe yourself, or thinking, "My body has emerged from the universe," you can think, "It is the universe that emerges as my body." That is a different attitude altogether.

The Sufis say that you get into the consciousness that links all things together. What does a leaf know of another leaf of a tree, except through the fact that both of them are part of the consciousness of the total tree? A leaf cannot reach another leaf through space; it reaches the other leaf because it has access to the consciousness of the whole tree, which includes the consciousness of all the leaves. In the same way, you can reach all beings by getting into the consciousness of all the collective beings together, instead of trying to reach each being through your eyes, through space and time, from outside. You see the bark of the tree if you reach a tree through space and time, but you can reach into the consciousness of the tree from inside.

The practices we are doing lead to becoming immersed in the total consciousness of God in the universe—not the consciousness of God beyond existence, but right in existence. This is what the contemplative does when he turns his attention inside instead of outside. It is more difficult to experience the consciousness of the tree if at the same time you are aware of how it looks in time and space. If you close your eyes, and therefore discard your picture of the tree from the outside, it is easier to get into the consciousness of the tree from inside and to experience what the tree experiences. That is why it is easier to experience what a person is like when you are not sitting in the presence of that person talking, although you can sometimes experience what a person is like by sitting in his presence without talking and with closed eyes.

This is why, as Buddha says, the contemplative places a sentinel at the doors of perception and turns within. Of course, you must be very careful that you do not encapsulate yourself in your own person. What is aimed at is to discover the whole universe from inside. To begin with, close your eyes, so that you are not picking up information through the senses any longer. If you do this, you will generally find yourself caught in your thoughts, so the next stage is to do with your thoughts exactly what you did with the perception of the objects around you. You consider the thoughts as being external to yourself. Generally, we adjust ourselves to the thought process, but here you have to offset consciousness from the thought process. The thoughts will continue to function, just as the objects around you keep on moving, but you don't pay attention to them. It is just as if you were able to find a space within that is quite different from the space without. Hazrat Inayat Khan, the founder of the Sufi Order, says that the perceptions of the physical world tend to pull one's consciousness to the surface; when one resists that, then one finds oneself immersed in the depth. In this inner space, you are in the collective consciousness of all beings. We are all communicating from inside.

All the radio waves in the universe interpenetrate one another at every point in space, whereas the electrons occupy separate spaces. The waves are all co-present at one point of space, which means that all reality that appears in different locations in space is co-present in the inner space, irrespective of location. You can find everything everywhere—or, perhaps more accurately, nowhere, since this reality is not found in the space that is outside. There is no being, no thought, no happening in the universe that you cannot tune into, because it is all co-present in the inner space. You cannot reach it by going anywhere or by turning outside through your senses; you can reach it only by turning inside and getting into the divine consciousness.

## MEDITATIONS WITH ENERGY

Relax the muscles of your back: the bottom of your back, the bottom of the spine, the middle of the back, the shoulder blades, the shoulders; relax the jaw and the inside of the skull.

Exhale very deeply and inhale without effort. Then exhale still longer and inhale without effort.

Scatter your consciousness into the vastness as you exhale and experience yourself as a convergence of the universe as you inhale. Then think of your body as dust that is scattered in space as you exhale, and think of it as being coagulated as you inhale. Let your thoughts be scattered or "spaced out" as you exhale, and then reformed as you inhale. Let your personality be dismantled as you exhale, and let the forces of nature build it up anew in a rebirth as you inhale.

Once more, extend consciousness as you exhale. This time, you get into the divine consciousness, you merge into the divine consciousness of the total universe, and then as you inhale you experience your consciousness as an eddy, or vortex, or whirlpool that has formed itself in the ocean of consciousness. Then you go back into the ocean again.

### Earth Energy

We want to work with energy, to dynamize ourselves with fresh energy; and we want to go through an absolutely total purification at all levels of our being, becoming refreshed, renewed, and regenerated. So first of all, we have to re-establish our contact with Mother Earth. Concentrate on the energy that arises from the earth in the bottom of your spinal cord (the muladhara chakra), and then you can drain out polluted magnetism into the earth. You will have to feel the electromagnetic field around your body, particularly around your arms, like a zone of charged particles around your body.

As you exhale, you must feel how this zone, or area, or etheric body, or whatever you may wish to call it, is drawn into the earth, downwards, and drained from your body; and the essential point of contact is, of course, the muladhara center at the bottom of the spine. As you inhale, you should be aware of the magnetism of the earth. It is very slight: it is not a very powerful force. It is the force that is used by mariners when they use a compass to steer their course.

You could concentrate on both the chakra at the bottom of the spine and also the chakras in the hands, so as you inhale you are drawing this energy from the earth. While you are radiating energy out through your hands, you let the polluted magnetism of your body be drained through the muladhara chakra back into the earth field. By this time you should feel a very high intensity field of magnetism around your body, which also permeates the cells of the body, continually drawing fresh energy from the magnetic field of the earth and draining itself back into the magnetic field of the earth. It is your contact with Mother Earth—your covenant with Mother Earth.

### Energy of the Spirit

Now, having worked with earth energy, we shall work with celestial energy. In its highest form, this is the energy of the holy spirit. It is associated with the crown center.

As you inhale, you must turn your eyeballs upwards and press your tongue against the palate. Attune your whole being to this very fine, very subtle form of energy. Just imagine walking in a landscape of ice and snow; and you need not only to be wary of cleaning the mud off your shoes because you don't want to pollute the snow, you must also strip yourself of most of yourself, so that only the very finest, gossamer quintessence of your being is able to reach into these spheres. It is as if you were jettisoning ballast from a balloon so that you are able to rise higher.

Now you have to concentrate on the aperture at the top of the head. Imagine that the crown center is as the yogis describe it—a million-petalled lotus—and it opens up. The whole lotus opens up under the action of the rising magnetism of the earth that is triggered off by your thoughts, your concentration. This allows that very subtle quintessence of your being to rise.

This is just a model, because, in fact, you are not being displaced in space. There is only a switch in the focus of consciousness into high levels of the universe, or into universes other than the physical one. There is no displacement in space: I am saying this so that you can avoid doing astral projection. What you are doing is becoming conscious of something that is, and that is all here; at least, it is not somewhere else in space. In fact, it is not in space at all, as we understand it.

You have an image of landscapes of snow and ice, just in order to make you feel intensely purified and very peaceful, to the point that you enjoy the cold. In fact, you open the pores of your body to the cold and let all that energy seep right into the pores of your skin, and then deep into the bones, so that you are just part of the immaculate scene. You are a pilgrim in the high Himalayas—stripped bare, purified, free, immaculate, disintoxicated, anesthetized, depersonalized—in search of the waters of life, which is pure energy, or, rather, the life of life, the catalyst that triggers off the latent energy in all things: pure spirit. And you have to touch upon it; you have to reach that part of yourself that is spirit and reestablish the connection.

Just think of yourself as being pure spirit. You have arrived at such a fine state of stripping that you are just spirit. And the only way to reconcile the thoughts of any denseness of the body is to think of the body as different layers that you have incorporated in the course of your descent. Now you are reversing the course of descent, so think of the layers as being just formations with which you have established some kind of connection; but the quintessence of your being is pure spirit.

As you exhale, you experience your descent: the descent of spirit. This is not the same as imagining that you are being quickened by the spirit, because then you would be identifying yourself with the transient layers of your being. As you rise, you discover; to discover means you uncover, and finally you realize your real identity. It is all in the mind: it is all a matter of realization. You rid yourself of your opinion about what you are, and discover another way of looking upon yourself, which is more reliable because it is unchanging. All the things you thought you were are changing and are, therefore, formations. Now as you exhale, and while you experience yourself as descending, you have a feeling of quickening the flesh with what you are, which is pure spirit. You are catalyzing its setting, triggering off latent energy, vivifying every cell of the body. That is the last stage at the end of the exhalation. On the way down, there is a descent through all the different bodies: the body of light, the mind, and the etheric and astral bodies—all the different bodies are dynamized.

The consequence is that the cells begin to dance. That is one of the meanings of the "dance of Shiva." Everything springs to life under the action of the spirit: it is like awakening the sleeping princess. The rays of the sun awaken the little shoots that are frozen through the night and are now drinking the dew; all things spring to life.

It is very useful to become aware of the cells of the body, of all the activity that is going on in them: mitosis, the proliferation of the cells, the flow of blood through the cells, the ionic flow of magnetism through the cells, and the activity of the cells metamorphosing the environment, which is the food, into their own material (what is called replication). You can experience all these phenomena, and you can experience how the whole process is triggered off by the magic wand of spirit. It is a kind of magic, how all this takes place.

Now, every time you inhale and turn your eyeballs upward, the lotus opens up at the top of your head and you strip—you become pure spirit. And every time you exhale, you infuse all the different bodies, including the physical body, with pure spirit. At that time the whole process of life is spurred, intensified, enhanced, dynamized.

Now you can combine the two poles of your being—the bottom of the spine and the top of the head. As you are drawing earth energy through the bottom of the spine, your consciousness is free to rise in the crown center, above the crown center, and go through the immaculate state, while your body is being dynamized by the earth. Then, as you exhale, you can concentrate on being pure spirit infusing the body, while all the polluted magnetism is being drained through the bottom of the spinal cord, the muladhara chakra.

You could also think of the linkage of the magnetism of the earth and the magnetism of the heavens. You could pull energy in at both ends at the same time as you inhale, and you would find that these two forms of energy—celestial energy and earth energy—mingle just like hot and cold water in the faucet in the solar plexus.

### Prana Energy

What I would advise doing now is incorporating a third form of energy, the energy of prana, which also flows into the solar plexus, so that you have three sources of energy, or three portals or inlets through which energy is drawn into the body. Prana energy is neither earth energy nor celestial energy. You could, perhaps, call it energy from outer space. Scientifically, it is gravitational energy, which is a much greater power than electromagnetic energy. It is like the deformation of space through its condensation due to matter; the presence of matter will always deform space or cause stress upon space's landscape. Your body, for example, is like a dry patch in an orange, which draws the rest of the orange into itself; it stresses the orange. In that sense, that point of stress is linked with the whole rest of the universe, so you are able to draw the power of the universe into yourself by your sense of yourself, which is the ego.

Then you can do the opposite: when you lose the sense of your ego, then you reach out into the vastness of space. There is even a change in the cells of the body that are not under stress anymore—in the proteins. There is a deconformation of the cells. There is something that happens to the cells that get into a different phase as your consciousness scatters in the universe: they change again. There is a conformation pattern that takes place in the nerves as you inhale—as you become aware of your ego—and at that moment, as you inhale, you are drawing energy from outer space. It is best to think of yourself as a vortex—a whirlpool. Forces are set up in a whirlpool; the energy of the whole lake, or ocean, is converged in the whirlpool. And, in a sense, that is something that happens to your consciousness: by thinking of yourself as being a point of convergence in the whole universe, you unleash the forces of the universe in yourself. You allow the forces of the universe in yourself to build up, and you experience the whole universe converging in you—the whole ocean heaving up in one wave.

### Combining Earth, Spirit, and Prana Energy

Now you can combine all three forms of energy at the same time as you inhale: you can inhale through the bottom of the spine, the top of the head, and the solar plexus, drawing in all three forms of energy. But a far better way of putting it is to say that you are each of those forms of energy. You are not just the magnetism of the earth, which is really the transmutation of mass into energy; you are the power of the whole universe. As you exhale, you not only reach out into the vastness; your consciousness reaches beyond space—not in any direction of space, but beyond any spatial extension—and also deep into the earth.

### Light Energy

Now we can work with the transmutation of fire into light. As you exhale, you can enhance the burning process in your body by thinking of your body as being like hot coals; you are blowing upon those coals, and consequently they burn more brightly. You produce heat in your body, and you should feel a flush of heat around your body, like an infrared radiation, as you exhale. As you inhale, concentrate first of all on a golden color, like the sun, in your heart center, then blue in your eyes, violet in your third eye, and a diamond-like hue in the crown center, with all kinds of reflections of all the colors of the spectrum in it. Then, as you exhale, you experience not so much a hot infrared radiation anymore, but a radiation that has become much more light than fire; and it gives you a feeling of coolness rather than heat.

Now we shall have to halve the inhaling and the exhaling. In the first half of the inhaling, you are burning intensely, but are also drawing radiation from the atmosphere. In the second half of the inhaling, you concentrate on the higher chakras—the golden, blue, and violet light. In the first half of the exhaling, you are radiating light, the light of the aura, and in the second half, you are radiating heat and infrared radiation as you enhance the burning process in your body. Now, in the first half of the inhaling again, you draw radiation from outer space, and in the second half concentrate upon the higher chakras, enhancing their light rather than their heat. Then as you exhale, in the first half you are radiating light and the second half heat. As you inhale, you are drawing in radiation in the first half, and in the second half transmuting fire into light—transmuting light in the higher chakras. In the first half of the exhalation, radiate light again, and then continue in the cycle.

What we are learning to do is to work with energy and dynamize ourselves. And it is that energy that transmutes consciousness, or shifts consciousness from its very narrow purview into higher states of awareness leading to awakening—which is our ultimate goal.

# CHAPTER 28

# Imagery and the Conquest of Time: Selected Therapeutic Techniques from Various Sources

## SUNDAR RAMASWAMI

It has been said of mental imagery that it makes us the people we are in all aspects of our lives, that our realities exist in our minds which, to use Milton's felicitous phrase, can make a heaven of hell and hell of heaven. The implication here is that the physical world which we inhabit is but a pale copy of a truer, separate reality which is accessible only through the contemplative power of the mind. Thought makes the present absent and the absent present. It is this capacity of the mind to transcend time and hence mortality that gives it the power to heal. The riches accessible to the mind are nowhere described more splendidly than by Plato (Kaplan, 1950):

> This, my dear Socrates said Diotima, the stranger of Mantineia is that life above all others which man should live, in the contemplation of beauty absolute, a beauty which if you once beheld you would see not to be after the measure of gold and garments and fair boys . . . . But what if man had eyes to see the true beauty—the divine beauty I mean—pure and clear and unalloyed, not clogged with the pollutions of mortality and all the colors and vanities of human life—thither looking and holding converse with the true beauty simple and divine? Remember how in that communion only, beholding beauty with the eye of the mind he will be enabled to bring forth not images of beauty but realities and bringing forth and nourishing true virtue, to become the friend of God and be immortal, if mortal man may, would that be an ignoble life? (p. 218)

When Plato referred to bringing forth realities and nourishing virtue he was expressing the Greek preoccupation with self-improvement. Using one's imagination, one can transcend the physical to access a timeless, beautiful realm coterminous with Godhead. And this communion can nourish us. It is but a short step to develop specific techniques of imagery to heal us or, as the ancient Greeks saw it, to make mortality more bearable and less mortal.

Borysenko and Borysenko (1994) describe a technique of using the mind's eye to access the inner beauty which is also a source of wisdom. They encourage us, in imagination, to chance upon a door behind which are several masks that we wear. Is the door easy to enter? Or is it difficult in a rigid way? Is the mask we encounter on entering familiar to us? Is it a thing, an animal, a feeling, a wish, a pose? Can we reach behind the mask and take the core wisdom center in it and imagine it to be a sunlit summer meadow? "Spend a moment appreciating the lushness of the grass, trees, and flowers that shine inwardly with a living light . . . the fragrances, the colors, the warmth of the sun . . . the more you open to the beauty, the more you can feel the sacred presence of your own Higher Self and the Beings of Light who are always ready to come to your aid. Feel the sunlight shining down upon you and washing over you . . . feel it running through you, filling you with vitality, clarity, and compassion . . . feel it filling your heart and emerging through your eyes. . . . Now, look at your mask, also bathed in light . . . the light pouring over it and shining out through it" (p. 162).

The authors encourage us to communicate with this deepest level of our being, to love and know this aspect of the self and finally to seek its assistance in reordering our lives. These may be accomplished by asking how it came about and was born and how it has been trying to help. This exercise is concluded with a request that this inner self always operate from its highest potential. This conversation with one's higher self may be finished by taking the beautiful, loving being which was the core of the mask and nestling it in one's heart.

Getting in touch with the innermost layer of our being is but a preliminary step in harnessing its heating potential for which many techniques have been developed.

One such technique is that of the Golden Image introduced in the Silva Basic Lectures in 1966. The technique involves "white framing" those things you want to enhance and emphasize and "blue framing" those you want to eliminate. When something causes one to be fearful or guilty or angry, one creates an image of that thing as well as an image of its opposite. Someone who feared public speaking would create an image of speaking before a large audience and being applauded for it. Silva and Goldman (1988) illustrate the technique with the example of someone who wishes to substitute sipping a glass of water for smoking.

> Sit comfortably and visualize yourself smoking. Put a blue frame around the scene. Make the scene large, colorful and dynamic. Give it movement. Bring in as many senses as you are able. Get a sense of the odor of cigarettes, of touch, taste. Make the scene three-dimensional. Next, create a white framed image of the thing you wish to substitute for the habit. Make the white framed image quite small, about a tenth of the size of the blue framed image. Imagine the white framed at the lower left hand corner of the large blue framed image. In the white framed image put a picture of you sipping from a glass of water. Leave the scene fuzzy, black and white, flat and small. When you have both images set, count to yourself, "one, two, three." At the count of three, say "switch" and switch images. Now the blue framed image with the picture of you smoking is the smaller and the white framed image with the picture of you sipping a glass of water is the larger. Put the smaller, blue framed image at the lower right side of the now larger, white framed image. The right side represents the past, the left side represents the future. (pp. 53-54)

The white framed images are always those that one wishes to enhance and the blue framed ones those one wishes to diminish. The next steps in this technique involve enhancing the ambience of the white framed image, the one in which you are seen sipping water. The scene is made three dimensional, more color, depth, texture, and space are added. With the blue framed image, on the other hand, the opposite is done. It is deliberately diminished, made fuzzy, out of focus, small, flat, one-dimensional. Silva and Goldman (1988) conclude thus: "You see yourself smoking in the blue frame but the scene is getting so small that soon it is the size of a bean. In the meantime, the white framed image is growing larger, brighter, sharper. The blue framed image disappears from the scene. That is how you can deal with a fear or a habit" (p. 55).

The authors go on to describe the use of the Golden Image technique in helping a person with the problem of procrastination. Stanley, the Silva Dynamics student, was 240 pounds and five feet eight inches. He sat around watching TV because he put off doing the things he enjoyed such as fishing, going to the movies, or going on a trip to the Caribbean which he had wanted to do. In addition, Stanley lived and worked in an area that was very cluttered and which he had wanted to straighten out but had put off. The Silva instructor asked Stanley to come up on the podium and imagine that he was back home and to describe what came to his mind. Stanley described the cluttered space and the TV show he usually watched, Star Trek. On questioning, he said that the image of the cluttered space was fuzzy while that of the TV show was clear and bright. The instructor asked Stanley to put a blue frame around the image of the TV show and a white frame around the image of the clutter. He then counted to three and instructed Stanley to switch the images. The image of the office clutter was now clear and large, multidimensional and that of the TV show fuzzy and unclear and weak. He reported that the office space looked clean and neat, spotless as if a tasteful decorator had arranged everything. He added that he couldn't wait to get back home to spruce up his den.

What happens in procrastination is the diminishing of the image of the activity that one has no desire for and the enhancing of the image of the activity that one wants to do. Procrastination is a substitution and the creation of a powerful, bright image of the substitute. The Golden Image technique can be used to change habits such as overeating and drinking as well as negative feelings like anger and jealousy by turning down the image of the unpleasant activity and enhancing the image of the target behavior. With practice, one can eventually use the blue-framing and white-framing techniques consciously in daily life.

The Golden Image technique, the educated reader would have guessed, is but an elaboration of a saying of the philosopher Epictetus: "What, aid, then is it possible to discover against habit? The contrary habit. Oppose to one habit the contrary habit" (Gill, 1995).

Miller (1987) describes an exercise specific to healing. He begins with mental relaxation. "Imagine you are standing at the top of a circular staircase at the edge of a beach. Count from ten down to zero. As you count, imagine you are descending the staircase, walking slowly down and around. Feel yourself going deeper, and any time unnecessary thoughts enter your mind, imagine an ocean wave washes through, erasing the thought like words being erased from the sand. You should feel extremely calm when you reach the count of zero; if not, you may take ten slow steps along the beach, sensing the soft sand and the warm water and letting them relax you" (p. 259).

After inducing a calm state of relaxation one then extends the imagery to healing the desired organ. Imagine being able to visualize in detail the organ you wish to heal. This may be accomplished by imagining one's consciousness to become a pinball and entering a submarine the size of an aspirin. This submarine is then swallowed and travels inside a blood vessel to the site in question. Scan the area carefully and imagine what it would look like when completely healed. For example, many individuals visualize cancer cells as an army of invading soldiers all dressed in black. Now try to imagine how the area will look after being fully healed, viz, the soldiers are all dead. Next, imagine how this process of healing may be accomplished. Perhaps an invading army of soldiers dressed in white will kill the soldiers dressed in black. Perhaps there would be increased blood flow together with healing antibodies to the site of the cancer. After several minutes of visualizing this transformation it is important to visualize the area of the body to be fully healed and restored to optimal functioning. Imagine using the organ in new, healthy ways.

Miller (1987) concludes this exercise by encouraging a visualizing of the way one would like to be in the future. "Now form an image of yourself several months or years in the future. Imagine yourself looking the way you'd like to look, feeling the way you'd like to feel, and dressed the way you'd like to be dressed. Imagine yourself doing whatever it feels most pleasurable to be doing. Let yourself into this image, allowing yourself to have the mind, the body, the emotions and the spiritual awareness that you would really like to achieve. This is the person you really are down deep inside, and each time you allow yourself to see this person, you will become more and more like the person you want to be" (p. 261).

Miller (1997) also describes an exercise to enhance self-esteem. The core sense of "I AM" evolves with growth and maturity as one becomes less and less identified with possessions, titles, and accomplishments. The superficial self-identifications with jobs and skills ease their grip and the pure self begins to emerge, the sense of "I AM" which may be experienced as pure light or peace. In this exercise, adopt a comfortable position and turn your awareness inward. Feel yourself floating, light and fluffy, floating through time and space, gradually. Experience the harmony and beauty and peace of a special place with different blooms, of many different colors, all specially arranged for you. You see a cool, inviting spring with a wise old tree next to it. As you seat yourself against the tree you go to your center that is all still and quiet. "What is the deepest sense of yourself you can be aware of right now? At your essence, who are you? Let go of the superficial images of yourself, drop the roles you sometimes have to play and sense who you really are. For a few moments, let go of your professional position, your family identity, even your name. . . . Keep going deeper, beyond the more superficial definitions of yourself to the most profound level you can reach. Who are you? Let that question be answered from deep within. "I Am. . . ." What word or phrase best completes this sentence for you? . . . Feel that sense of power and richness, the sense of really being in touch with yourself . . . the pulse of life within you. . . . Now, repeat silently to yourself, with a deep recognition of their truth, the following: I accept myself exactly as I am at this moment and time. I am learning to trust myself. Within me there is a great power in which I am learning to release through my daily practice" (Miller, 1997, p. 377). This exercise may be concluded by gentle stretching and by extending the centering achieved into everyday activities.

Siegel (1989) describes a healing meditation that can be used along with the one described above. Begin with deep breathing, breathing out conflicts and fears. As you silently mouth the words "peace" or "relax" let the tension go out of your neck and shoulder muscles. Imagine sitting in an old-fashioned classroom with wooden desks with names carved onto them. The teacher wipes the blackboard clean after filling it with lessons. Similarly, imagine wiping the blackboard of your mind clean and thus readying it for new experiences and learning. Now you are ready to go on a journey to the middle of nowhere, to your own special corner of the universe. When you arrive there take in the energy of the universe, of the earth and sky. Use this energy to eliminate any problems you are experiencing. Siegel then goes on to lead a guided imagery exercise that concludes with refashioning a new self. The exercise involves building a bridge from your corner of the universe to the rest of the universe. The journey starts with an awareness of the weave, fabric, and texture of one's life.

> Then take a look at the bridge you've built as you walk across it: how wide, how long, how strong? What kind of connection do you have with the universe? As you cross the bridge to start down your path to begin your journey all of the people in your life will be present—family, friends, coworkers, people you have all kinds of relationships with. Stop and touch them and talk to them. See what changes occur in your feelings and theirs as you all come together. . . . As you walk down the path you will see an old house off to the side with a garden and a porch. Walk through the garden, up to the porch steps and into the house and find the living room. And when you find the living room look around in it for a chest. . . . When you find your chest, open it and see what lies within, what your heart would like to tell you. What gift or message does your heart have for you as you look inside your chest? When you find the message within your chest make it part of you and then come out onto the porch and back to the garden. Find a place where you'd like to plant a seed to create more beauty. And prepare the soil and take the seed and plant it. And then become that seed, sitting in the dark, paying attention to what it feels like to be that seed. . . . So put down roots to give yourself the nourishment and strength you need to get a grip on things. And then grow, pushing aside problems and obstacles until you break out into the sunlight and then stretch your limbs to the sky. Grow and bloom and blossom. Become that unique beautiful individual that you already are. . . . Go through your body, opening every cell to light, to love. Harmonize the organs, and listen to what they have to tell you. Go through your body, repairing, rebuilding, recreating. Walk the corridors of your mind and brain, opening doors, cleaning the shelves of old material, turning the valves and switches in the different rooms to create the changes that you want to create in your body so that you create a new self, a new you, a new I. (pp. 262-263)

For those of us interested in improving our relationships with friends and family, Ostrander and Schroeder (1979) offer an exercise specifically geared for this. The preliminary step is to use a preferred relaxation technique to reach a comfortable state of relaxation. Then, say the authors:

> visualize yourself in a park. It's evening, and there's going to be a fireworks display. You spread out a blanket on the grass and lie down on it. You feel very

relaxed and comfortable. You look up at the clear night sky. There's the sound of the first fireworks and a rocket of red shoots up into the black darkness. A fountain of brilliant red color cascades across the sky. You enjoy the vivid display. Another rocket takes off. A display of luminous orange fireworks showers down bright sparks. With each color you feel more and more relaxed. There's the whoosh of a roman candle and cascades of golden yellow ripple against the blackness. You feel steadily more calm and centered. Now there's a green rocket. It spirals up into the heavens lighting up the entire sky with rich emerald green. You feel very, very comfortable and relaxed now. A blue rocket takes off. The sky lights up with streamers of shimmering blue color. A roman candle shoots up. Fountains of purple color fill the sky. You feel very relaxed, breathing deeply and easily. The last fireworks display of the evening shoots up into the dark sky. It's a beautiful violet-pink color. Galaxies of violet light up the night. You watch the last sparks of violet color fade into the darkness.

Feeling very, very relaxed you count from 1 to 3 and imagine yourself resting on your rug in your own get-away place—in your own room. You get up and sit in one of the chairs. At this time, you are going to select a person with whom you want to develop more effective communication. It can be a friend, family member, instructor, co-worker, or boss with whom you might be having a disagreement. It can be anyone with whom you wish to establish more effective communication and understanding. Count from 1 to 3 and the person whom you have selected will walk through the door into your room. The door opens and the person enters your room. He/she closes the door and comes over and stands in front of you. Look at this person. Begin to see him as a fellow human being with feelings, attitudes, and emotions. Focus in on every detail of the person—the face, hair, forehead, cheeks, lips, eyes, ears.... Now both of you walk to the desk and sit down on chairs facing each other. At this time, in your own words, tell this person what you feel is the cause of the lack of communication or understanding between the two of you. Be clear and complete and honest in your description of this problem. Take your time. Now have the other person tell you in his own words what he feels is the problem. Listen carefully to what he has to say. Try to understand and feel what the person is feeling. If you would like some help, ask a third person to come in as a fair witness. This person will come through the door into your room. Ask for his opinion. Now turn to the other person and this time acting as a completely objective third party, express the situation as you now understand it. Be as clear and as honest as possible. You and the other person stand up. Face each other and mentally see yourselves having the kind of communication and understanding that you are capable of having. See yourselves having complete understanding and feel the feeling of hurt or anger or mis-understanding dissolve as you smile at this person. If you are having any problem becoming friendly with this person, ask another person or expert for advice. (pp. 285-287)

According to Ostrander and Schroeder (1979) this exercise will help develop a better perspective about the other person and result in improved communica-tion. And if at any time one wishes to increase one's understanding of a relation-ship or problem one needs to have the other enter the get-away place and engage in this exercise. The authors also recommend the ancient Pythagorean exercise of reviewing the day before falling asleep. Pythagoras is said to have advised his disciples on entering their homes at the end of each day to pose the questions, "Where have I gone wrong? What have I done? What duty has not been carried out?" (Rutherford, 1989, p. 15).

Naparstek (1994) describes imagery techniques to help connect with one's feelings, to develop healthier boundaries and to be kind and forgiving to oneself. The technique to connect with one's feelings begins with the client taking a full, deep cleansing breath, exhaling, then taking a deep breath deep into the belly, then breathing out completely. The client then focuses attention inward, scanning how one is feeling, a curious inventory of how and what one is doing. With the detached, disinterested eye of a neutral observer, the client senses his or her energy level, mood and well being. This awareness also takes into account those places where one is tight or tense, soft or relaxed. This scanning is extended to the head, a gentle inventory of how one is feeling inside. Then it is extended downward, to the neck and shoulders, noticing tension, then down toward the heart, noticing heaviness or palpitations or agitation. The scan then moves down the chest and rib cage again noticing without censure any constriction, all the while taking in deep breaths and exhaling fully. This inventory is now extended to the full length of the legs, down to the tips of the toes. "And asking your body to show you what it's feeling . . . asking your feelings to show themselves to you . . . breathing out fully and easily . . . asking to see where they are held in the body . . . staying open and curious to sense their location . . . and what these emotions look and feel like . . . so just letting the intelligence of the body show them to you . . . clearing away a space and letting the wisdom of the body answer . . . showing you a place that might be denser, heavier than the rest . . . maybe it's a feeling of excitement and joy or perhaps you find yourself holding tight to a clenched anger in your legs . . . ready to take a closer look at this feeling or mix of feelings . . . curious about the texture, size of it, it's taste and smell. . . . And asking the body to continue to show you whatever you need to know about this . . . trusting it to reveal what you need to see. . ." (pp. 141-142). Throughout this scan the client continues to breathe deeply, with slow breathing in and exhaling fully. No praise or blame is engaged in, no reactions to how and what he or she is feeling. As one repeats this exercise one develops the capacity to trust this process of knowing oneself better, of connecting more deeply with oneself.

The exercise to develop better boundaries also begins with deep breathing, breathing deeply into the belly and expanding the entire diaphragm and belly. The warm energy of the breath is sent to any part of the body that is tight or tense, loosening and softening them up. Any unpleasant thoughts that occur are also exhaled with the breath along with any emotions so that both the mind and the emotional self are quiet pools. As in the previous exercise a gentle curious awareness is extended from the head to the toes, taking in the neck and shoulders, the chest and abdomen, the small of the back, the pelvis and the entire length of the legs. Each area is gently scanned, an inventory taken of how it's feeling, tight or tense or rigid or relaxed, any emotions associated with the part, noticing without praise or blame any thoughts that arise that are connected to that part, all the while breathing in and out deeply. Also, one is encouraged to take note of the interface of the surrounding air and one's skin, aware of where and how the air touches the skin, noticing that remarkable boundary. Naparstek (1994) goes on:

And perhaps beginning to perceive a vibrating cushion of energy . . . surrounding and protecting you . . . breathing in and out and sending your breath out into this cushion . . . making more and more palpable this cushion of energy . . . feeling it tingle and vibrate all around you . . . while inside you can feel safe and protected . . . able to take in what is nourishing to you . . . but insulated from what you don't want or need . . . send the powerful energy of the breath out into it . . . understanding that this is part of who you are. And now see if you can imagine that this cushion of energy is drawing to it all the love and sweetness that has ever been felt for you by anyone at any time . . . feeling it pull in all the caring and loving kindness that has ever been sent your way . . . every prayer and good wish, permeating and filling the field of energy surrounding you . . . pulling it all in like a powerful magnet . . . calling every good wish home . . . and so increasing the powerful, protective field around you even further . . . And perhaps even sensing the presence of all those who have ever loved or nurtured you . . . those who believed in you . . . loved and protected you . . . or guided you well . . . or perhaps special animals, guardian angels, or magical beings . . . it doesn't matter . . . just so you feel their protection and support. . . . (pp. 156-158)

When the client comes out of this state he or she can retain or call up when necessary this state of protection and grace.

The exercise to enhance self-esteem and to see oneself with kinder eyes also begins with deep breathing. The client is encouraged to breathe in deeply and send the breath to those parts of the body that seem tense or sore. As in the previous exercise any unwelcomed thoughts or feelings are exhaled with the outgoing breath. The client is then asked to imagine a safe and peaceful place, real or make believe just as long as it feels safe and peaceful. Then the client familiarizes himself or herself with this special place, gradually allowing it to become real. This may be accomplished by appreciating the colors and scenery, the sounds of the place, the music of wind or rain or birds and crickets, the night sounds, the texture of the ground, whether it be sand or grass, feeling the air on one's skin, either brisk or breezy, gentle or still, fragrant or odorless. As one becomes more and more attuned to the beauty of this special place there occurs a tingling sensation, an intimation of something magical about to occur. "You begin to discern a kind of transparent screen shimmering there . . . getting more and more opaque and solid as you look at it. . . . And as you watch the screen you gradually become aware of the form of a very special someone . . . perhaps someone who loved you well from your past . . . maybe a special guide or teacher . . . a parent or grandparent. It could also be an angel or spirit or special-power animal . . . someone or something good and wise and kind and loving . . . with the ability to see from the heart into the truth of things" (pp. 161-162). As one watches the screen and this person becomes more and more defined, one can easily enter the screen oneself and take a reverential walk around this special person, noticing the individual from all angles, what he or she is wearing, the pose and expression, sensing the air and special energy surrounding the individual. And, then, somehow, for a short while one is able to slip out of one's body and boundaries into the body of this other being, feeling and sensing the world as this person does, seeing the world as he or she does, gaining perspective. "And perhaps even seeing you over there . . . with these other eyes . . . looking over at you . . . and seeing who you really are . . . looking under, around, and through your surface . . . to the essence of who you really are . . . and seeing all the hidden splendor . . . all the vast beauty of your being. . . . And perhaps seeing what you are here to do . . . with all your unique gifts and special abilities . . . appreciating what you were born to do . . . in your own way . . . in your own time" (pp. 163-164). And then, when one has savored this experience and wisdom fully, one takes leave of this awareness, wishing the other body well but sliding back into one's own body. Finally, one slides out of the translucent screen back to the special place even as the screen fades away. Whenever one allows oneself to slowly return to the room where one started this exercise there will be the sense that one is better for this.

Gawain (1978) describes a set of imagery techniques that enhance the energy of the body. The first is a visualization technique to get one's energy flowing and dissolve any blocks.

> Sit comfortably with your back straight . . . . Close your eyes, breathe slowly and deeply, counting down from 10 to 1 until you feel deeply relaxed. Imagine that there is a long cord attached to the base of your spine and extending down through the floor and way down into the earth. This is called a "grounding cord." Now, imagine that the energy of the earth is flowing up through this cord (and up through the soles of your feet if you are sitting in a chair) and flowing up through all parts of your body, and out through the top of your head. Picture this until you really feel the flow well established. Now imagine that the energy of the cosmos is flowing in through the top of your head, through your body and down through your grounding cord and your feet into the earth. Feel both these flows going in different directions, and mixing harmoniously in your body. (pp. 85-86)

Gawain (1978) then goes on to describe a meditation for purifying one's body.

> Lie down on your back with arms at your sides or with hands clasped on your stomach. Close your eyes, relax and breathe gently, deeply and slowly. Imagine that there is a glowing sphere of golden light surrounding the top of your head. Breathe deeply and slowly in and out five times while you keep your attention on the sphere of light, feeling it radiate from the top of your head. Now allow your attention to move down to your throat. Again imagine a golden sphere of light emanating from your throat area . . . . Allow your attention to move down to the center of your chest. Once again imagine the golden light, radiating from the center of your chest. Again take five deep breaths, as you feel the energy expanding more and more. Next put your attention on your solar plexus; visualize the sphere of golden light all around your midsection . . . . Now visualize the light glowing in and around your pelvic area. Again take five deep breaths, feeling the light energy radiating and expanding. Finally, visualize the glowing sphere of light around your feet, and breathe into it five more times. Now imagine all six of the spheres of light glowing at once so that your body is like a strand of jewels, radiating energy. Breathe deeply, and as you exhale, imagine energy flowing down along the outside of the left side of your body from the top of your head to your feet. As you inhale, imagine it flowing up along the right side of your body to the top of your head. Circulate it around your body this way three times. Then visualize the flow of energy going from the top of your head down along the front of your body to your feet as you slowly exhale. As you inhale, feel it flow up along the back of your body to the top of your head. Circulate the flow in this direction three times. Now imagine that the energy is gathering at your feet and let it flow slowly up through the center of your body from your feet to your head,

radiating form the top of your head like a fountain of light, then flowing back down the outside of your body to your feet. (pp. 87-88)

Gawain (1978) describes an exercise to create one's own sanctuary, a safe, trusting place of tranquillity to which one can go any time.

> Close your eyes and relax in a comfortable position. Imagine yourself in some beautiful natural environment. It can be any place that appeals to you . . . in a meadow, on a mountaintop, in the forest beside the sea. It could even be under the ocean, or on another planet. Wherever it is, it should feel comfortable, pleasant, and peaceful to you. Explore your environment, noticing the visual details, the sounds and smells, any particular feelings or impressions you get about it. Now do anything you would like to do to make the place more homelike and comfortable an environment for you. You might want to build some type of house or shelter there, or perhaps just surround the whole area with a golden light of protection and safety, create and arrange things there for your convenience and enjoyment, or do a ritual to establish it as your special place. (pp. 89-90)

Finally, Gawain (1978) describes a technique to connect with what the ancient Greeks called one's daemon, the inner presiding genius also known as one's counselor or master or guide.

> Close your eyes and relax deeply. Go to your inner sanctuary and spend a few minutes there, relaxing, getting oriented. Now imagine that within your sanctuary you are standing on a path which stretches off into the distance. You start to walk up the path, and as you do so, you see in the distance a form coming toward you, radiating a clear, bright light. As you approach each other you begin to see whether the form is a man or woman, how they look, how old they are, and how they are dressed. The closer they get, the more details you can see of their face and appearance. Greet this being, and ask him or her what their name is. Take whatever name comes to you first, and don't worry about it. Now show your guide around your sanctuary and explore it together. Your guide may point out some things that you've never seen there before, or you may enjoy just being in each other's presence. Ask your guide if there is anything he or she would like to say to you, or any advice to give you at the moment. If you wish, you can ask some specific questions. You may get immediate answers, but if not, don't be discouraged, the answers will come to you in some form later. When the experience of being together feels complete for now, thank your guide and express your appreciation, and ask him or her to come to meet you in your sanctuary again. (pp. 91-92)

Sometimes one may not perceive one's guide clearly and distinctly. The guide may present as a ball of light or take the form of someone you know. If this person happens to be someone that you do not care for, you can repeat this exercise and request that the guide be someone you can relate to positively. Your guide may be unusual in many different ways; what is important is that you sense their power, presence, and love. And your guide may change form and name from time to time; it is also possible to have several guides. Gawain concludes "Your guide is there for you to call on anytime you need or want extra guidance, wisdom, knowledge, support, creative inspiration, love, or companionship. Many people who have established a relationship with their guide meet them every day in their meditation" (p. 93).

Prather (1981) describes a set of games for healing. He refers to a Master, presumably the Demiurgos of the universe, who has installed a mind projector in one's head, at the center of the forehead. This projector is thought activated and has two features, a light signal and a corrector switch. The light signal reveals the inner nature of the flow of external events. Old judgments are replaced by the projector's quiet evaluation of the inner tone of the situation one is in. This inner tone is signaled thus: a continuous gently expanding light signals total love. Light flashes alternating with darkness with the latter increasing signals conflict and fear. The content of the present situation can be changed by activating the corrector switch. The appearance of the situation is left unmanipulated, for it to change naturally and of its own accord, with only the content changed to reflect comfort and happiness. As Prather says "Merely wish the corrector switch on and immediately the content of your thought and therefore the content of the outward situation will turn from fear to love, from conflict to comfort. But remember, please, you must wish it activated for everyone in the situation. Thoughts set the goal and therefore start the traveler on his way. Thoughts make the pathway smooth or rough and determine the time of arrival. Every thought is but a step in some direction and a destination reached through pain or peace" (Prather, 1981, p. 49).

Another game involves thinking of one's mind as a circular pond or reflecting pool into which God shines continually. In order to have the peace of God deep within it is only necessary to eliminate from the mind the ripples of fear, agitation, and longing. A quiet attentive inventory of the state of the mind will enable the ripples to subside, for dark images to be wiped clean so that the mind is restored to its pristine state of purity, a still mirror of clarity, a perfect surface that reflects God's smile.

Yet another game is the dream game. When a person wakes up in the morning he or she did not awake so much as passed from one dream to another. The dream dreamt last night was no less real than the "waking" reality of today's awake "dream." Everything occurs in the mind, both last night's dream and today's waking "reality." And if a person wants the world to be different he or she in fact wishes the contents of the mind to be different because the world that is experienced is but the dream that eternally goes on in the mind. "As a dreamer you cannot be happy unless the contents of your mind are happy. Therefore, wish the whole to be at peace. Suffer not at all one unforgiving thought. . . . And now bless everyone you see and everything. Today no darkness is outside your reach. . . . You live the contents of your mind today and only that. Today, there are no other minds. So be still a moment and forgive each thing within your mind. You wish a dream of love in which to move about, not a dream of angry judgments and of hate. Today, an entirely different goal is yours: You rule the world. And you will the world into a kingdom of light" (Prather, 1981, p. 64).

Any therapy that claims to confer perfect mental health needs to offer a framework for anticipating and coping with events and injuries that have not yet happened, that are yet to come. Alvin Toffler's phrase "future shock" refers to our inability to anticipate and assimilate crucial future events. When the future arrives we are overwhelmed and distressed. As we live into our nineties and even beyond it is more important than ever before to develop an armamentarium to help adapt to the changes wrought by the advancing decades of life. "For thought's life's slave, And life's Time's fool, And Time, which takes survey of all the world, Must have a stop"

(Shakespeare, First Part, King Henry IV, Act 5, Scene 4, Black's Readers Service, New York, 1965). Time is the ultimate disease and here imagery offers a way to cope.

Lazarus (1977) describes how he was alerted to the phenomenon of the future overwhelming an individual. A client he was seeing for acute depression appeared to have many enviable life circumstances—a good job, good family life, good physical health—and yet had lapsed into a depressed state on learning that his favorite restaurant was closing down. He realized that things were not the same any more: his youth was gone, his childhood home in Chicago had been razed to the ground only to be replaced by a huge apartment building, his daughter announced that she was getting married, etc. He had last "known" his daughter as a thirteen-year-old and she was now a twenty-one-year-old woman!

This client prompted Lazarus (1977) to follow-up on former clients. He found that several clients who had made good recoveries relapsed when some future significant but eminently predictable event had overwhelmed them. One young woman, for example, who had been successfully treated for anxiety relapsed when her father, who had previously had two heart attacks, had a third heart attack and died. Lazarus asks "What would have happened if, before discharging her from therapy the first time, we had done something more than merely talk about her feelings regarding the fact that her father might soon suffer a fatal heart attack?" (p. 169).

Mental rehearsal through projected imagery is an obvious technique. Apart from helping clients resolve current problems, it is possible to predict and anticipate future problems. For example, for young couples in marital counseling it can be anticipated that many would face the stresses of parenting and some of them would go through divorce with its attendant problems. For those in business and the corporate world, new future stressors would stem from being promoted to higher and more demanding roles or being passed over for such promotions. Some are likely to face job losses and lay-offs. The middle-aged clients can prepare for the empty nest when children go off on their own; in some cases, they will have to anticipate the grown children returning home with children after the break-up of their own marriages or even returning with their new spouses because of economic issues. Older clients can be prepared for illness, the death of loved ones, and to face their own mortality.

Lazarus (1977) states that actively planning for and rehearsing future scenarios helps prepare the client to cope with the future-to-be. It is crucial to picture possible future scenarios that are likely to unfold in one's life and vividly imagine oneself dealing with these situations.

The old truism that "time heals" is slightly misleading. It is not the mere passage of time that heals. A person who lapsed into a coma and awoke ten years later or Rip van Winkle who awoke twenty years later are both likely to remember acutely and relive any hurts they may have experienced immediately prior to falling asleep. What the passage of time does is offer us ample opportunities to re-integrate the slings and arrows of time. That is, to engage in healing responses which enable us to view, think about, and experience the hurts in newer and different ways. To think of injuries in new ways, indeed to imagine them in new ways hitherto unimagined, offers the clue to healing. This should not surprise us since some sort of reprogramming seems to be at the heart of mental health and creativity. Dreams are beneficial to mental health. Schizophrenics in remission show a particular need for REM sleep while those exhibiting gross symptoms do not suffer from REM rebound, suggesting that schizo-phrenia is "dreaming whilst awake." For normal mortals dream deprivation, as in REM sleep deprivation, results in a variety of symptoms (Storr, 1988). It is reasonable to hypothesize that some sort of scanning and re-programming of daily experience goes on in dreams.

Arthur Koestler (1969) has described how re-sorting and re-ordering of experience lies at the heart of the creative process. Evelyn Underhill (1990) intimately describes the processes of incubation and illumination that are the essence of mystical experience. Storr (1988) suggests that what is common to dreaming and creative incubation is the inhibition of motor activity. According to Anthony Storr, the capacity not to respond automatically and instinctively to a stimulus is essential if one is to develop alternate, intelligent, and adaptive modes of responding. "The inhibition of motor activity which occurs in dreams can be seen as one way of delaying immediate responses so that some kind of sorting activity can occur in the brain. A comparable inhibition of motor activity occurs when we are awake and engaged in thinking. Thinking can be regarded as a preliminary to action; a scanning of possibilities, a linking of concepts, a reviewing of possible strategies. . . . Prayer and meditation facilitate integration by allowing time for previously unrelated thoughts and feelings to interact. Being able to get in touch with one's deepest thoughts and feelings, and providing time for them to regroup themselves into new formations and combinations, are important aspects of the creative process, as well as a way of relieving tension and promoting mental health" (pp. 27-28).

The time projection or time tripping described by Lazarus (1977) takes advantage precisely of that unique aspect of time that permits re-sorting. In this technique, when one is upset over an important letter lost in the mail, a minor damage to one's car, or losing a research grant time tripping into the future allows one to view this from the vantage of one year later. In other words, it tries to do here and now the re-sorting that one year's passage of time normally does. Viewed from the vantage of a distant future, say five or ten years hence, many current upheavals would appear trivial. Lazarus goes on to describe time tripping into the past using a personal example:

> Often by going back in time and picturing oneself doing things differently, important insights and constructive feelings emerge. . . . A few months ago I was discussing some formative events and encounters in my professional develop-ment with an interviewer. During the interview I said that in retrospect I regretted having spent three and a half years in Philadelphia and if I had known then what I know now I would have avoided going there. . . . One of my colleagues suggested time tripping. I agreed and under his direction I pretended that the year was 1967 and instead of going to my new position in Philadelphia I elected to go elsewhere. I rewrote my ticket, by-passed Philadelphia, introduced some pleasant events, remained in California and then pictured myself toward the middle of 1970 after not spending three and a half years in Philadelphia. In the imagery, I saw myself feeling relieved and happy at missing the negative events that had really taken place during the period I had spent in Philadelphia. The time tripping sequence involved a series of events that all added up to having a much better time personally and professionally in California. . . . As the time projection brought me nearer and nearer to present time I realized two important things. First, it struck

me that without having experienced certain negative things in the past, I would be less able to appreciate certain positive ingredients in the present. . . . Second, I saw that the seeds of some very special present-day friendships were sown in Philadelphia, and that by eliminating those three and a half years I would be losing some vital links to the present. The immediate and lasting impact of that time tripping exercise was to wipe away my regrets at the so-called wasted years I spent in Philadelphia. (pp. 134-135)

Lazarus (1977) describes several additional applications of time tripping. The first clinical example involved an obsessional female client who was preoccupied with the feeling that she had married the wrong man. The woman had been engaged to a man for over two years but he had kept postponing their wedding date. Her family had not liked her fiancé. She broke up with him, started dating again and married her current husband. Two weeks before the marriage her former fiancé had come to her and asked her to marry him. She had refused whereupon he had said "You are making a serious mistake." Now, happily married with a three-year-old daughter, the woman was haunted by the notion that she had made a terrible mistake and had indeed married the wrong man. In a time tripping exercise into the past, Lazarus asked her to imagine that she had in fact married her former fiancé. She was then asked to imagine what living with him would have been on a day-to-day basis: sleeping with him, making love, dining out, doing the various chores, raising children, visiting her family, and so on. She imagined them dealing with various household matters such as money, religion, child-raising, etc. After the exercise this patient stated that she would have been miserable had she married her former fiancé and was no longer troubled by the notion that she had married the wrong man.

The second clinical example involves the application of time projection to broken romances. This is one area in which the exercise is particularly effective. When a romance ends it is particularly devastating. It prompts the rejected party to engage in self-doubt and intense self-questioning. The rejector becomes invested with special qualities. He or she is seen as a prince or princess that the rejected party must have. To break this compulsion it is useful to employ time projection by asking the sufferer to move forward in time and visualize himself or herself engaging in a variety of rewarding activities. At first, the rejected party would be very resistant to the exercise, choosing to mope and cry. He or she is likely to find no activity rewarding, claiming that the only satisfying mode of life was one in which he or she was reunited with the rejector. It is therefore particularly important to use a variety of potentially rewarding activities such as painting, horseback riding, playing music, traveling to exciting destinations, etc. to help the rejected person imagine himself or herself experiencing joy and fulfillment in ways other than being with the beloved. "When one views a broken love relationship from the vantage point of 'six months into future time,' most people discover that there are 'many pebbles on the beach' and that it is rather silly to pine over one pebble in an overpopulated world. Clinically, I have observed that as soon as I can get a depressed person to admit that some sort of pleasure may be derived from a particular activity, there is an excellent chance of helping that individual overcome the depressed feelings. . . . Many people automatically discount the events that can bring joy into their lives. When they feel 'down in the dumps,' they forget that many enjoyable and fun-filled events are available for their pleasure. Time projection forces them to reconsider these pleasurable stimuli and to stop nursing their misery and gloom" (p. 139).

Time projection, of course, can be used with rejections and failures of all kinds. For example, if a student at a University is despondent over the unusually long time it was taking him/her to complete their studies, time tripping five or ten years into the future and imagining himself/herself working successfully at a chosen profession would help lend the perspective that an extra semester or two to complete a college degree is a minor event in the context of one's life.

## REFERENCES

Borysenko, J., & Borysenko, M. (1994). *The power of the mind to heal.* Carlsbad, CA: Hay House.

Gawain, S. (1978). *Creative visualization.* Mill Valley, CA: Whatever Publishing.

Gill, C. (Ed.) (1995). *The discourses of Epictetus.* New York: Everyman.

Kaplan, J. (Ed.) (1950). *Dialogues of Plato* (Jowett translation). New York: Pocket Books.

Koestler, A. (1969). *The act of creation.* New York: Macmillan.

Lazarus, A. (1977). *In the mind's eye.* New York: Rawson.

Miller, E. E. (1987). *Software for the mind.* Berkeley, CA: Celestial Arts.

Miller, E. E. (1997). *Deep healing: The essence of mind/body medicine.* Carlsbad, CA: Hay House.

Naparstek, B. (1994). *Staying well with guided imagery.* New York: Warner Books.

Ostrander, S., & Schroeder, L. (1979). *Superlearning.* New York: Dell Publishing.

Prather, H. (1981). *A book of games.* New York: Doubleday.

Rutherford, R. B. (1989). *The meditations of Marcus Aurelius: A study.* New York: Clarender Press.

Shakespeare, W. (1965). *King Henry IV,* First Part, Act 5, Scene 4. New York: Black's Readers Service.

Siegel, B. (1989). *Peace, love, and healing.* New York: Harper and Row.

Silva, J., & Goldman, B. (1988). *The Silva mind control method of mental dynamics.* New York: Pocket Books.

Storr, A. (1988). *Solitude.* New York: Ballantine Books.

Underhill, E. (1990). *Mysticism.* New York: Doubleday.

# CHAPTER 29

# *Techniques to Enhance Imaging Ability*

## ANEES A. SHEIKH, KATHARINA S. SHEIKH, AND L. MARTIN MOLESKI

As researchers are furnishing more evidence of the effectiveness of imagery-based methods in the educational and clinical process, educators and clinicians are becoming increasingly interested in implementing them in the classroom and in the clinic. But, of course, the success of these procedures is dependent upon the learner's ability to form vivid images. A number of studies have demonstrated that significant changes in experiential, behavioral, and physiological measures can be produced in subjects who experience vivid images but not in those who can muster only weak ones (Marks, 1977; Richardson & Taylor, 1982; Sheikh & Kunzendorf, 1984). The crucial question that comes to mind at this point is: Are weak imagers condemned to remain so, or can they learn to reduce or even to eliminate their handicap?

Already in 1883, Sir Francis Galton, in his *Inquiries into Human Faculty* (1883), indicated that practice in forming mental images can strengthen this ability. Galton referred to a French educator who trained his students to visualize objects so clearly that they could draw these images. He began by urging his students to examine the object carefully, so that they could form a clear visual image. Next, he directed them to "draw" it in the air, so that they might retain "muscular memories" of it. Finally, he required them to draw the object from memory. He claimed that after his students had been trained in this manner for three to four months, they could summon images with ease and could hold them steady enough to draw them.

Imagery researchers agree that everyone has the capacity to imagine. Marks comments, "While the ability to generate and employ mental imagery varies across people, the potential to do so is probably universal. Given appropriate and optimal conditions of thinking and performance, it is likely that all persons could utilize imagery-encoded information" (in Korn, 1983, p. 61). Kroger and Fezler state, "Many believe that once sensations have been experienced, they are retained somewhere within the system and that the ability to recall and experience the situation and its associated sensations is available to all of us, although we rarely take advantage of these possibilities" (in Korn, 1983, p. 61). Imagery ability is an innate potential like drawing or the use of language, or any other skill that improves with practice. Since the potential is there, it is possible to develop it through training. Of course, not all people can become superimagers, any more than they can learn to draw like Leonardo da Vinci or write like Shakespeare, but everyone can improve his/her skill over what it is at the present (Sommer, 1978). In short, the main ingredient in improving imagery appears to be "practice, practice, and more practice" (Sommer, 1978, p. 139).

Conversely, neglect eventually will lead to the inability to summon images. Korn (1983) states, "Any system or ability that is not nurtured tends to atrophy. When we do not utilize the birthright of imagery experience, we eventually 'forget' the experience entirely" (p. 62).

The next question that arises is: Have researchers provided evidence that practice can improve imagery ability, and have they identified specific methods? Unfortunately, systematic research in the area of the enhancement of imagery has been very limited, but a number of useful suggestions and some indirect evidence are scattered throughout the literature. The purpose of this brief review is to bring these together and to offer recommendations for further research.

## METHODS FOR IMPROVING IMAGERY VIVIDNESS

The salient factors that seem to lead to improved imagery vividness include: relaxation, concentration, body position and sensory input, sensory training, practice in imaging, multimodal training, convincing the client, developmentally determined images, increased right-hemisphere activity, somato-affective states, overcoming resistances, drugs, and certain developmental factors. This section provides a brief discussion of all of these factors.

### Relaxation

Relaxation appears to be one of the most important prerequisites for the experience of vivid imagery (Bakan, 1980; Gendlin, 1981); for, it seems to allow the process of becoming aware of internal states to begin.

Imagery, a symbolic mode of representation, to be distinguished from the verbal symbolic mode (Paivio, 1971), is produced throughout the waking hours. But generally we are unaware of our imagery because it has to compete with the live broadcasting of everyday experience. We constantly are bombarded by stimuli, and the preoccupation with filtering out the superfluous ones among them renders us unaware of the internal stimuli which are of a relatively less dramatic nature. Furthermore, in Western cultures, the tendency has been to emphasize verbal, rational, secondary thought processes at the expense of imaginal experience—most people literally lose sight of their imagery.

During relaxation, the noisy, hectic world is shut out, and the inner world, the realm of imaginal experience, has a chance to become the focus of attention. Gendlin (1981) notes, "Imagery comes very well and very richly during highly relaxed states" (p. 71). Singer (1974) concludes that relaxation is "conducive to the occurrence or awareness of imagery and ongoing daydreaming" (p. 226). Relaxation reduces "hyperalertness to external stimulation that would blur the vividness of imagery and overload the visual system which must handle both imagery derived from long-term memory and incoming stimulation" (Singer, 1974, p. 226). Bakan (1980), too, focuses on the central role of relaxation: "It is evident to people who work with imagery that relaxation is conducive to the experience of imagery." He explains, "The left hemisphere appears to have a closer relationship to motor activity than does the right hemisphere. Perhaps imagery activity, associated with the right hemisphere, is incompatible with a high degree of motor activity" (p. 40). It may be more accurate to say that imagery is incompatible with *changes* in sensory input or in motor activity. Many long-distance runners have reported that they have experienced highly vivid imagery, often of a creative or problem-solving nature, while running. Their imaginal experience appears to be related not to speed or distance but to length of time: Generally it occurs when they maintain a steady pace. This finding is in harmony with Shapiro's (1974) observation relative to the psychology of meditation: he states that meditation involves habituation to any single stimulus which has been the primary focus of attention.

Numerous relaxation procedures have been developed over the years. For detailed information about these methods the reader is referred to other sources (Korn, 1983; Lichstein, 1988; Samuels & Samuels, 1975; Sheikh, 1984).

## Concentration

Relaxation is a necessary preliminary step to visualization: it clears the mind and dispels distracting muscular tension. But another prerequisite for vivid imagery is the ability to concentrate. Generally, an endless procession of thoughts files through our mind, and we seem to have little control over their occurrence or their nature. But obviously this lack of thought control must be overcome by anyone who wishes to focus on one image.

Yoga (Samuels & Samuels, 1975, pp. 111-113) offers a variety of suggestions to develop the powers of concentration:

1. Concentration on a small external object: The student attempts to think only of the object, and each time a different thought intrudes, he/she pushes it aside and returns to the object.
2. Counting breaths: The student tries to ban all thoughts and to focus on counting breaths. Every time a thought does arise, he/she returns to the count. One way of dealing with these unbidden thoughts is to cut them off as quickly as possible, before they have a chance to unfold. Another approach is to let the intrusive thoughts pass unheeded, as if they belonged to someone else. A Zen metaphor likens thoughts to birds flying across the sky of one's mind—one simply watches them appear and then disappear.

Regular practice of such exercises enables a person to better ward off intrusive thoughts and to hold an image for a longer period (Samuels & Samuels, 1975). Detailed discussions of numerous exercises in concentration are available elsewhere (Goleman, 1977; Ostrander, Schroeder, & Ostrander, 1979; Samuels & Samuels, 1975).

## Body Position and Sensory Input

The supine body position has been found to facilitate the experience of vivid imagery, and it probably was by design that Freud directed his patients to the analytic couch. Pope (1978) has stated that the recumbent posture can markedly increase the experience of visual imagery and influence the flow of consciousness and the quality of our imagining experience. Kroth (1970) reported that individuals who were reclining, free-associated more freely, more spontaneously, and generally more effectively than those who sat up. Unfortunately, Kroth did not present data on imagery per se. Morgan and Bakan (1965) determined that subjects who were lying down produced reports that rated much higher on vividness of imagery than subjects who were sitting. In a subsequent study, Berdach and Bakan (1967) elicited memory material from subjects in a reclining or sitting position, and they found that the reclining subjects produced earlier and more copious memories than the comparison group.

Segal and Glickman (1967) produced some very objective evidence by means of the Perky phenomenon. Subjects, who were either lying down or sitting, gazed at a blank white screen, onto which they were directed to project certain images. Unknown to them, the experimenter projected comparable images onto the screen. The investigators found that reclining subjects were much less likely to become aware that an external image had been projected. That is, their own images were sufficiently vivid to preclude awareness of the external ones.

A number of researchers have proposed explanations why imagery is enhanced in the reclining position. Berdach and Bakan (1967) suggest that this is so due to the decrease of tension in the head and neck muscles, a condition which prevails also at the onset of rapid eye movement sleep. Singer points out that the reclining position is associated with sleep and hence with dreaming and daydreaming. Most people report that the greatest part of their daydreaming occurs while they are preparing for sleep (1978).

Rychlak (1973) proposes that the effect may be due not to the reclining position as such but rather to the reduction in complex external stimulation that accompanies this posture—a blank ceiling simply is not very distracting. As Richardson (1969) indicates, imagery is more likely to manifest itself when we are awake and when external stimuli are not functionally operative.

## Sensory Training

On the basis of extensive interviews of women who had been rated as excellent hypnotic subjects, Wilson and Barber (Barber, 1984; Wilson & Barber, 1983) concluded that a hallmark of these individuals is their profound fantasy life. These people (who constitute approximately 4% of the population) fantasize much of the time, and they do so very intensely—that is, they generally can "see," "hear," "smell," "feel," and fully experience what they are imagining.

These fantasy-prone individuals experience more vividly in all the sense modalities not only their fantasies but also the real world around them. Wilson and Barber (1983) hypothesize "that vivid sensory experiences, vivid memories, and vivid fantasies are causally interrelated as follows: individuals who focus on and vividly feel their sensory experiences, have relatively vivid memories of their experiences; and individuals with vivid memories of their experiences are able to have relatively vivid fantasies because they can use their vivid memories as raw material from which they can creatively construct their fantasies" (p. 380).

This relationship is corroborated by what is known about the manner in which creative persons approach the world. It seems that they experience the world with a certain innocence and consequently more intensely. Vivid sensory experience engenders vivid sensory-based memory, which in turn provides the material for vivid fantasies.

In other words, it appears that sensory training leads to improved imagery abilities (Galton, 1883; Richardson, 1969; Wilson & Barber, 1983). Samuels and Samuels (1975) state, "The better people train their minds to perceive external images, the easier it becomes for them to imagine internal images as well" (p. 114). For instance, "learning to see directly affects the ability to visualize. In seeing the images are external; in visualizing the images are internal. But the process and effect are similar" (p. 116).

Many psychologists believe that congenitally blind persons have no visual images. Similarly, those who see blindly will have difficulty in forming visual mental images. And it is indeed possible to see blindly. All of us probably have had the experience of walking right past a friend on the street without noticing him/her, because we were preoccupied by our thoughts. Another type of blind seeing occurs when we view an object solely with regard to a specific function and ignore all its other attributes. For example, when we are tired, we may regard a chair only as a place to rest and not notice anything else about it (Samuels & Samuels, 1975).

Samuels and Samuels (1975) suggest that the first step in developing the ability to see is becoming fully alert and aware as we look around, and, of course, this suggestion is applicable also to the cultivation of the other senses. A number of specific exercises toward that end have been proposed.

1. It is beneficial to focus upon the various traits of an object, one after the other. One should take note of the way the light strikes the object, the highlights and shadows, and the color variations it creates. One should focus on the texture of the object, its color, its perspective, and its many other properties (Samuels & Samuels, 1975).

2. It is very helpful to stare at an object and to attempt to experience it. This means trying not to react verbally or to label but rather to admit the object into one's consciousness (Samuels & Samuels, 1975).

3. The ability to perceive is improved by looking at an object from different physical perspectives and from different mental points of view. For instance, one could consider an apple from the viewpoint of an artist, a hungry man, a migrant worker picking the apple, etc. With each shift, different aspects of the object will come to the fore. Witnessing this rich procession of attributes helps one to become aware of the labels and associations which one unconsciously uses in ordinary seeing; and this awareness prompts one to break out of the habitual manner of viewing familiar things and to see them again with a degree of innocence (Samuels & Samuels, 1975).

4. Hooper believes that clarity of perception can be improved by sketching, photographing objects from various angles, attentively listening, smelling, tasting, and touching objects (Sommer, 1978).

5. Petitclere suggests that it is useful to describe an object that one can feel but not see (Sommer, 1978).

6. McKim (1980) uses puzzles and games to improve visual recognition. For instance, he may present five playing cards, of which four contain errors and one is correct. In order to find the minor errors, such as a spade which is upside down or a 10 written 01, the player must pay close attention to details. Analogous puzzles targeting the other senses could easily be devised. For example, a succession of tones could be played, and the player would be required to identify the one that was of a different pitch. Also, different fabrics or spices could be presented to a blindfolded person for identification.

7. Parmenter maintains that one can improve one's power of observation by pretending to be a reporter on a news assignment (Sommer, 1978).

Numerous other exercises designed to sharpen one's awareness of the world have been outlined, and the interested reader can find those elsewhere (Lazarus, 1977; McKim, 1980; Samuels & Samuels, 1975; Sommer, 1978).

## Practice in Imaging

Practice in imaging seems to yield improvement in imaging ability, and a number of apparently useful exercises have been devised for that purpose.

1. McKim (1980) proposes the following: A person closes his/her eyes and visualizes a wooden cube whose sides are painted red. Then he/she images two parallel vertical cuts through the cube, dividing it into thirds, and two more vertical cuts perpendicular to the first ones, dividing it into ninths. Next, he/she visualizes two parallel, horizontal cuts through the cube, dividing it into twenty-seven cubes. Now he/she tries to imagine how many cubes are red on three sides, on two sides, on one side, and how many cubes are unpainted on all sides.

2. McKim (1980) suggests the use of two-dimensional designs which can be folded together to make three-dimensional figures. The task consists of mentally folding a design and then indicating which one of several test figures has been created.

3. McKim (1980) recommends sketching to promote thinking schematically. The student starts with free doodling, then he/she progresses to disciplined doodling, then to realistic drawing, and finally to drawing his/her images. Later still, he/she draws things which are felt rather than seen, such as objects concealed in a bag. McKim's exercises focus on vision; however, they could be adapted without difficulty to involve the other senses. The guiding principle which runs through all these procedures is that practice promptly followed by feedback will improve performance.

4. Parameter, a reporter, found the search for similes to sharpen his powers of observation. He stumbled upon this technique during an airplane trip—as he discerned a certain feature in the landscape, he asked himself, "What does it recall?" And he attempted to answer in a different material, species, or modality every time.

For example, a winding road reminded him of a tortoise shell hairpin, and he compared a brook to worm tracks in wood (Sommer, 1978).

5. Lazarus (1977) has found the blackboard exercise to be effective. The student relaxes, closes his/her eyes, visualizes a blackboard, and imagines writing the letter "A" on it, followed by "B," and so forth. Throughout the process, the student tries to retain a clear image of all the letters on the board. Initially, most people find that, as they add more letters, the beginning ones tend to fade. But with practice, the clarity of the letters improves.

6. Lazarus (1977) also recommends the light bulb technique. The student closes his/her eyes and imagines a dim light bulb suspended in front of him/her. While focusing on the light, he/she attempts to make it grow brighter and brighter until it illuminates everything, and then dimmer and dimmer.

7. Another technique involves careful study of a common object. The student scrutinizes the object until he/she is familiar with it. Then he/she closes his/her eyes and pretends to still be studying the object. He/she tries to see it as clearly as possible and studies it as he/she did the real object. Next, he/she opens his/her eyes and re-examines the real object to compare the difference between it and its image. Then he/she closes his/her eyes again and repeats the exercise, taking care to add to the image those traits which were missed the first time (Lazarus, 1977).

8. Lazarus (1977) also claims to have used the seashore exercise with success. The student relaxes, closes his/her eyes, and imagines that he/she is strolling along a quiet beach on a balmy day. He/she is wearing a swim suit, and he/she feels the warm sun on the skin and the sand between the toes. He/she smells the fresh sea air and listens to the waves breaking on the sand. He/she summons other soothing images associated with a stroll on the beach and enjoys the serenity that accompanies them.

9. Samuels and Samuels (1975) recommend the following sequence for improving visualization ability: A) With the eyes closed, image a two-dimensional object, such as a geometrical shape. Then close the eyes and try to visualize it. B) Repeat Exercise A with a three-dimensional object. C) Visualize your childhood room. D) Imagine a large object, such as a house, and move around and through it. E ) Visualize a complicated, three-dimensional object from various angles. F) Return to the child-hood room of Exercise C, and imagine that you are doing several things in it, such as picking up items, switching the lights off, etc. G) Visualize a person. H) Imagine yourself as if you are looking in a mirror.

There is some evidence that hypnotic suggestions can lead to more vivid imagery; hence, many of the above exercises may be more effective when they are performed under hypnosis (Korn, 1983; Samuels & Samuels, 1975). Also, some clinicians claim that listening to concrete descriptions of scenes, either recorded ones or ones presented live by the therapist, can stimulate imagery.

Many other procedures have appeared in the popular literature. But "what is lacking for all these techniques is information on how they work. As parlor games, they are fun and harmless. However, before they are included in school curricula or mnemonics workshops, some efforts must be made to measure their effectiveness" (Sommer, 1978, p. 147).

## Multimodal Training

Related to the ideas discussed in the preceding section are Cautela and McCullough's (1978) suggestion concerning the involvement of all sense modalities:

> Vividness must not be equated with solely visual imagery, for the greatest effectiveness is obtained when the client reports a vividness in all sense modalities. For example, if a client had trouble imagining or visualizing an airplane, the sound of the plane would be described, the kinaesthetic feeling of the takeoff or the seatbelt, the physiological responses such as increased heartbeat or shortness of breath, and the appropriate affective state such as anxiety or exhilaration. It is emphasized that the client not simply imagine the scene, but try to feel that he is actually experiencing it. Recent research suggests that the largest and most consistent physiological responses occur in response to imagining somato-motor and visceral responses and to imagining "being there" rather than just imagining detailed descriptions without affective components. (p. 236)

## Convincing the Client

Imagining ability probably is universal; yet, some clients claim that they lack it. An important preliminary step with such individuals is convincing them of the contrary. Korn (1983) proposes a simple yet effective procedure: The client is directed to imagine that the therapist is a window washer contracting to clean the windows of the client's residence. In order to quote a price, the window washer must know how many windows are involved. The client is asked to furnish this information. In response to this request, the client's eyes will turn to the side opposite the nondominant hemisphere, which may indicate stimulation of the nondominant hemisphere, and if the client is questioned at this point, he/she will reveal that he/she actually was counting the windows. But

> how can one count the windows without visualizing them, even if the image is not clear and tends to be a mind's eye image? This will demonstrate to even the most recalcitrant of subjects that imagery is not only possible, but that he or she uses it every day for the solution of many of life's problems. (Korn, 1983, p. 62)

Shorr (1977) mentions another method of demonstrating to clients that they are capable of producing imagery: "When people tell me they never see images, I ask them to imagine sexual scenes. . . . So far this has resulted in no failures" (p. 157).

## Developmentally Determined Images

Images of past key events seem to be effective in rendering the individual aware of his/her images in general: even those individuals who do not have vivid imagery, with some encouragement and concentration, can visualize developmentally determined images from significant life situations in the past. These images tend to open up the general imagination and fantasy processes (Sheikh, 1978).

## Enhancing Right-Hemisphere Activity

Research on cerebral specialization has revealed that "the left hemisphere seems to be more concerned with the temporal analysis of incoming information which it labels verbally, for storage and for later retrieval and manipulation in recall or problem solving. The right hemisphere on the other hand, seems to deal with organizing incoming information on the basis of complex wholes, and acts as a synthesizer rather than analyzer" (Richardson, 1977, p. 112). Paivio (1971) proposes that verbal or mathematical processes, which involve sequential processing, occur in the left hemisphere; spatial or imaginal processes, which entail parallel processing, take place in the right hemisphere. Oyle (1979) expresses the differentiation of the hemispheres in this manner: "The self is hermaphroditic. Each one of us is two individuals, a male and a female. The former is rational, can speak and think thoughts. The female side makes the pictures, dreams, mental images, and empirical reality" (p. 99). Ley (1979) stresses that the right hemisphere "seems to predominate in a variety of states of consciousness, such as dreaming (day and night), hypnosis and meditation, as well as in religious and drug-induced states, in which emotional and imagery components are salient" (p. 42).

Since right-hemisphere functions are linked to imagery, enhancement of the former would be expected to produce amelioration of the latter. Thus, participation in activities which generally are regarded as right hemispheric, such as music, art, poetry, dancing, humor, and meditation, would be expected to lead to enhanced imagery production. Although some support for this contention can be found in the literature, there is an obvious need for further empirical validation.

Oyle (1979) suggests two general approaches to imagery enhancement which are relevant to this section:

> The left hemisphere can be put at rest by a variety of techniques. These have, by and large, been formalized as religious rituals, hypnotic suggestions, or sensory deprivation among others. Another way to shift the balance in favor of the image-making right brain is to overload the thinker in the left brain. (p. 87)

This may be accomplished by the use of Zen Buddhist koans, insoluble problems, like, "What is the sound of one hand clapping?" Oyle (1979) feels that "if the thinker is quiescent or overloaded to the point of exhaustion, energy flows from the right cerebral hemisphere to form an image" (p. 87).

## The Role of Somato-Affective States

Imagery has long been thought to have a direct relationship to emotions. Many psychologists have noted that images possess an amazing ability to effect extensive affective and physiological changes (Sheikh & Kunzendorf, 1984; Sheikh & Panagiotou, 1975). A recent memory image may elicit an emotional response and a physiological arousal whose intensity rivals and even surpasses that of the reaction to the actual event (Ellis, 1962; Horowitz, 1970). Bauer and Craighead (1979) state:

> A basic assumption underlying the use of imagery techniques in behavioral therapy has been that the patterns of physiological response to imagined and real stimuli are essentially isomorphic. For example, Wolpe (1958) suggested that the pattern of arousal elicited by visualization of fearful scenes in desensitization directly corresponded to that brought about by actual contact with an anxiety-eliciting stimulus. (p. 389)

Recently, attempts have been made to integrate three fundamental aspects of all human experience (Ahsen, 1968; Gendlin, 1980; Sheikh, 1983). These include: the image (I), the somatic response, including emotional arousal (S), and the meaning, including affective signification (M). It seems that all significant images are a triadic unity (ISM). Clinicians often work with the image component of this triangle. They ask the client to concentrate and to repeatedly project an image that originally had been weak or vague, until it becomes vivid, precise, detailed, and stable. Through the image, the individual attempts to recreate the original experience, that is to re-experience the affect and meaning and the accompanying bodily responses, which form the memory in its entirety. If the concept of the ISM is valid, then focusing on any aspect of this triangle, not only on the image, should bring the entire experience into relief. In other words, concentrating on the image's meaning or on the affect and bodily response it evokes, should render the whole event more real. For example, if the focus is on an aggressive image, the production of bodily responses involved in aggression may help to make the image more vivid.

Support for the ISM approach to the enhancement of imagery can be found in the research of several investigators. For instance, Ley (1979) considers imagery and emotions to be inseparable: "Given sufficient, affective potency, stimulus salience, and the vast and elusive differences in imaging ability and cognitive styles (i.e., 'picture' thinkers vs. 'word' thinkers), imagic and emotional stimulus components may be inextricable in practice" (p. 47). Perhaps these imagic and emotional components are inextricable because they are bound together by the meaning they convey. Gendlin (1980), who has developed a form of therapy called "focusing" which relies substantially on imagery, recommends emphasizing the somatic component to enhance imagery; for, he has observed that a by-product of doing so is increased *meaning* for the individual:

> In summary, I believe that whatever your method of working with imagery may be, you will find your method enhanced quite powerfully, if you employ focusing. . . . Imagery and body-sense are inherently related, but on different planes. It is more powerful if one not only works with the body and imagery, but devotes specific attention to the formation of something directly sensed in the body, yet implicitly meaningful. (Gendlin, p. 72)

Lang's (1977) bioinformational theory of emotional imagery is also relevant here. Lang conceives the image in the brain to be a "conceptual network, controlling specific somatovisceral patterns, in constituting a prototype for overt behavioral expression" (in Korn, 1983, p. 73). He believes that instructions to the client would be more effective if they consisted not only of the usual stimulus propositions but also of response propositions. Therefore, a statement such as, "The wooden walls of the small room surround you, closing you in . . ." would change to "You tense all your muscles of your forehead, squinting . . . your eyes . . . dart left and right to glimpse the exit" (in Korn, 1983, p. 73).

### Overcoming Resistances

In some cases, the inability to image or to image vividly may be a function of certain kinds of resistances on the part of the client. These resistances may affect imaging ability in specific areas, or they may inhibit the total imaging process. Such resistances need to be identified and understood before proper evolvement of imagery can take place. Shorr (1983) offers an explanation for these resistances: "It is inevitably the fears, anxieties, or frustrations inherent in people's internal conflicts, which lead to curtailment of an imaginary capacity, in order to shrink the boundaries of their self-hood to more manageable dimensions" (p. 15).

A detailed discussion of various types of resistances is beyond the scope of this chapter and the reader is referred to other sources (Ahsen, 1965; Bry, 1972; Korn, 1983; Sheikh, 1978; Shorr, 1978).

### Drugs

It has been known for centuries, for instance by participants in religious rituals, that certain psychoactive drugs stimulate mental imagery (McKellar, 1972). For example, the religious rites of the American Indians culminated in the ingestion of psychoactive drugs, such as peyote and psilocybin, which prompted intense religious experiences mediated by remarkably vivid imagery (Castaneda, 1968, 1972). In the 1960s, thousands of America's youths made the expansion of their mind and conscious awareness a top priority. The means they most commonly chose were LSD, marijuana, and cocaine, and their major shared experience was intensification of sensory awareness through hallucinations (Leary, Metzner, & Alpert, 1964).

Subject accounts indicate that drug experience often involves an attitudinal shift or change in level of awareness that fosters the production of imagery or the greater awareness of imagery. For example, ordinary awareness has been compared to spotlighting: this focused lighting is like our linear, logical thinking—specific and task oriented. Drug-induced awareness represents a shift toward floodlighting; it is more global, more panoramic (Tart, 1969). The analogy parallels comparisons of left- and right-brain functioning, which are different but complimentary types of perception (Bakan, 1980). Holt (1972), too, links the attitudinal changes which accompany drug-induced conditions, such as weakened defenses, to increased imagery.

The image-enhancing quality of certain drugs may be also due to their relaxing effect on the system. For instance, Segal (1971) found that subjects who were under the influence of tranquilizers displayed a stronger Perky effect than those who were not.

Obviously, drugs are not a recommended means of enhancing imagery. Nevertheless, it is possible that some subjects who have experienced vivid imagery by means of drugs will be more highly motivated to enhance their imagery, simply because they already have had a taste of the experience.

### Developmental Factors

Qualls and Sheehan (1983) believe that "the origins of imaginal skills and the readiness to spontaneously utilize imaginal capacities lie in the imaginative, make-believe play and fantasy experiences of childhood" and that "early childhood may represent a sensitive period for the development of imaginal abilities" (p. 91).

Investigators have identified a number of factors that seem to enhance make-believe play in children which in turn may lead to better imagery abilities later in life:

1. Positive interpersonal experiences early in life are beneficial (Tower, 1983).
2. Security of attachment is an important factor (Tower, 1983).
3. A parental model who enjoys artistic pursuits and verbal and other forms of inventiveness enriches the child's play activities (Tower, 1983).
4. Opportunities for space and time to be alone, accompanied by the approval of a parent figure, contribute to meaningful play (Tower, 1983).
5. The child should be encouraged to engage in role-taking activities and to *behave* toward an object as if it were something other than what it actually is (Saltz, Dixon, & Johnson, 1977).
6. Storytelling by parents and other significant individuals can be helpful (Hilgard, 1980).
7. Television viewing in moderate degrees also can be a useful catalyst for imaginative play. However, the presence of an adult to encourage the creative use of television rather than passive viewing is very important (Singer, 1977).
8. Both sociodramatic play, which involves themes and events within the realm of the child's everyday experience (e.g., playing school or pretending to go to the doctor), and thematic fantasy play, whose themes and events are remote from personal experience (e.g., fairy tales), are effective in stimulating the child's imaginal abilities (Qualls & Sheehan, 1983).

## DIRECT RESEARCH EVIDENCE

Although numerous techniques to enhance imagery have been proposed, research directly investigating their efficacy is extremely limited. However, the results of the few existing studies are encouraging.

Walsh, White, and Ashton (1978) found that imagery training can be beneficial and that marked improvements can take place in a relatively short time. They identified vivid and weak imagers by means of the Betts Test and then formed three groups, each consisting of six vivid and six weak imagers. Every group met for twenty minutes on four successive days. One group was not exposed to any imagery-related activities. Another group discussed the therapeutic uses of imagery but did not undergo any formal training. The experimental group practiced visual, kinesthetic, and auditory imaging on the first day, gustatory and olfactory on the next day, tactile and organic on the third day, and an exercise which involved all seven modalities on the last day. Also, they were assigned exercises to practice at home between sessions.

The posttest revealed no significant change in the first two groups. Of the third group, the vivid imagers revealed no change, but the weak imagers exhibited a very significant change. Not only did they rate their imagery as markedly more vivid, which may represent simply a response to the demand characteristics of the situation, but also, when they were asked to imagine their favorite food, they salivated as copiously as untrained vivid imagers.

Richardson and Patterson (1986) felt the need to extend and refine the study of Walsh et al., for a number of reasons. First, Walsh et al. had not separated the effects of sensory-awareness training from the effects ascribable to relaxation. Richardson and Patterson took care to do so. Second, the earlier study invited the question whether training in a single major modality (vision) would suffice to produce the reported amelioration in imagery vividness. Consequently, Richardson and Patterson exposed two groups to multimodal training, and they gave the other group practice solely in the visual modality. Third, Walsh et al. had conducted the evaluation only immediately after the training period. Richardson and Patterson added a follow-up test administered two months after the conclusion of training. That is, Richardson and Patterson evaluated the relative effectiveness of three training procedures: multimodal imagery training with relaxation (RMM), multimodal imagery training by itself (MM), and visual imagery training with relaxation (RV).

They found an increase in imagery vividness for the RMM and MM training groups both on experiential (Betts Questionnaire) and on physiological (salivation) measures. However, the posttest two months later did not reveal significant differences. It is possible that weak imagers need periodic refresher training sessions to maintain their gain in imagery vividness and to prevent the relapse to their habitual modes of thought (Richardson & Taylor, 1982).

There are several other recent studies which have implications for the enhancement of imagery which the reader may wish to consult (Crawford & McLeod-Morgan, 1986; Heil, 1982).

## THE ISSUE OF IMAGERY CONTROL

The success of imagery procedures is determined not only by the ability to form vivid images but also by the ability to control them. If the individual can produce vivid images but is unable to control them, the prospects for effective use of imagery techniques are dim. "In fact, the most difficult state in which to cause behavioral change is one in which the client experiences intensely vivid imagery but cannot control or maintain adaptive thoughts and continues to revert to maladaptive images" (Cautela & McCullough, 1978, p. 237). According to Richardson (1969), the combination of high vividness and high controllability correlates the most with behavioral change, while the combination of high vividness and low controllability correlates the least with behavioral changes.

Quite typically, an individual who lacks control over his/her images, will experience difficulty in focusing on beneficial images. He/she may begin by imagining a very positive situation but then find himself/herself constantly interrupted by aversive thoughts; for example, he/she may visualize himself/herself skiing downhill on a sunny day, only to fall. Cautela and McCullough (1978) propose a number of procedures that seem to aid in controlling and redirecting negative imagery:

1. The individual is reminded that the fantasy is his/hers, that he/she has created it and hence also can change it in any way. Then he/she is asked to describe the scene again but with a positive outcome (e.g., he/she skis downhill without a

mishap). Sometimes this exercise suffices, and the person is able to control his/her imagery.

2. If the above exercise is not effective, then undesirable images are modified gradually by shaping. For instance, the individual proceeds to imagine falling down while skiing, but the fall does not hurt. He/she visualizes the skiing scene repeatedly, and each time he/she images that he/she is able to maintain better balance or to stop before falling.

3. The person keeps a log of all the situations which cause tension, anxiety, or depression. After a week of recording these incidents, he/she learns to identify them quickly. He/she attempts to relax in the face of aversive thoughts and to interrupt them at the onset, when they are easier to control and stifle.

## CONCLUDING REMARKS

A survey of the literature relevant to the enhancement of imagery reveals that investigators share the persuasion that everyone possesses the potential for imaging. Furthermore, it appears that even if the imaging ability has whithered due to neglect, it can be revived. The literature contains a number of methods which have been used for stimulating mental imagery. Nevertheless, little research has been carried out to establish the efficacy of these various methods and also to determine their relative merit under different circumstances.

Furthermore, it appears that investigators have been disproportionately fascinated by visual imagery. Although visual images are the most common kind, they are not the only type or even the preferred one for some individuals. Undoubtedly, the other modalities deserve more of the investigators' attention than they have hitherto received.

Also, researchers seem preoccupied with the issue of vividness, and although they recognize the importance of control of imagery, they have made little attempt to explore this area. More sophisticated measures of control as well as scientifically developed procedures to improve control are sorely needed.

If the increase of interest over the last fifteen years in imagery-related topics can be used as an indicator, then it seems virtually certain that within the next ten years a host of pressing questions will be answered and clearer guidelines will be available to educators and clinicians.

## REFERENCES

Ahsen, A. (1965). *Eidetic psychotherapy: A short introduction.* Lahore: Nai Matbooat.
Ahsen, A. (1968). *Basic concepts in eidetic psychotherapy.* New York: Brandon House.
Bakan, P. (1980). Imagery, raw and cooked: A hemispheric recipe. In J. E. Shorr, G. E. Sobel, P. Robin, and J. A. Connella (Eds.), *Imagery: Its many dimensions and applications.* New York: Plenum.
Barber, T. X. (1984). Changing "unchangeable" bodily processes by (hypnotic) suggestions: A new look at hypnosis, cognitions, imagining, and the mid-body problem. In A. A. Sheikh (Ed.), *Imagination and healing.* New York: Baywood.

Bauer, R., & Craighead, E. (1979). Psychophysiological responses to the imagination of fearful and neutral situations: The effects of imagery instructions. *Behavior Therapy, 10,* 389-403.

Berdach, E., & Bakan, P. (1967). Body position and free recall of early memories. *Psychotherapy: Theory, Research, and Practice, 4,* 101-102.

Bry, A. (1972). *Visualization: Directing the movies of your mind.* New York: Barnes & Noble.

Castaneda, C. (1968). *The teachings of Don Juan: A Yaqui way of knowledge.* New York: Simon & Schuster.

Castaneda, C. (1972). *Journey to Ixtlan.* New York: Simon & Schuster.

Cautela, J. R., & McCullough, L. (1978). Covert conditioning. In J. L. Singer & K. S. Pope (Eds.), *The power of human imagination.* New York: Plenum.

Crawford, H. J., & McLeod-Morgan, C. (1986). Hypnotic investigations of imagery. In A. A. Sheikh (Ed.), *International review of mental imagery* (Vol. 2). New York: Human Sciences Press.

Ellis, A. (1962). *Reason and emotion in psychotherapy.* New York: Lyle Stuart.

Galton, F. (1883). *Inquiries into human faculty.* London: McMillan.

Gendlin, E. T. (1980). Imagery is more powerful with focusing. In J. E. Shorr, G. E. Sobel, P. Robin, & J. A. Connella (Eds.), *Imagery: Its many dimensions and applications.* New York: Plenum.

Gendlin, E. T. (1981). *Focusing.* New York: Bantam Books.

Goleman, D. (1977). *The varieties of the meditative experience.* New York: Dutton.

Heil, J. (1982). Visual imagery change during relaxation meditation training (Doctoral dissertation, Lehigh University, 1982). *Dissertation Abstracts International, 43,* 2338B.

Hilgard, J. (1980). *Personality and hypnosis: A study of imaginative involvement.* Chicago: University of Chicago Press.

Holt, R. R. (1972). On the nature and generality of mental imagery. In P. W. Sheehan (Ed.), *The function and nature of imagery.* New York: Academic Press.

Horowitz, M. J. (1970). *Image formation and cognition.* New York: Appleton Century Crofts.

Korn, E. R. (1983). *Visualization: Use of imagery in the health professions.* Homewood, IL: Dow Jones-Irwin.

Kroth, J. A. (1970). The analytic couch and response to free association. *Psychotherapy: Theory, Research, and Practice, 7,* 206-208.

Lang, P. J. (1977). Imagery in therapy: An information processing analysis of fear. *Behavior Therapy, 8,* 862-886.

Lazarus, A. (1977). *In the mind's eye.* New York: Rawson Associates.

Leary, T., Metzner, R., & Alpert, R. (1964). *The psychedelic experience.* New York: University Books.

Ley, R. G. (1979). Cerebral asymmetries, emotional experience, and imagery: Implications for psychotherapy. In A. A. Sheikh & J. T. Shaffer (Eds.), *The potential of fantasy and imagination.* New York: Brandon House.

Lichstein, K. L. (1988). *Clinical relaxation strategies.* New York: Wiley.

Marks, D. F. (1977). Imagery and consciousness. *Journal of Mental Imagery, 2,* 275-290.

McKellar, P. (1972). Imagery from the standpoint of the introspection. In P. W. Sheehan (Ed.), *The function and nature of imagery.* New York: Academic Press.

McKim, R. H. (1980). *Experiences in visual thinking.* Monterey, CA: Brooks/Cole.

Morgan, R., & Bakan, P. (1965). Sensory deprivation hallucinations and other sleep behavior as a function of position, method of report, and anxiety. *Perpetual and Motor Skills, 20,* 19-25.

Ostrander, S., Schroeder, L., & Ostrander, N. (1979). *Superlearning.* New York: Dell.

Oyle, I. (1979). *The American medicine show.* Millbrae, CA: Celestial Arts.

Paivio, A. (1971). *Imagery and verbal processes*. New York: Holt, Rinehart, Winston.

Pope, K. S. (1978). How gender, solitude and posture influence the stream of consciousness. In K. S. Pope & J. L. Singer (Eds.), *The stream of consciousness*. New York: Plenum.

Qualls, P. J., & Sheehan, P. W. (1983). Imaginative make-believe experiences and their role in the development of the child. In M. L. Fleming & D. W. Hutton (Eds.), *Mental imagery and learning*. Englewood Cliffs, NJ: Educational Technology Publication.

Richardson, A. (1969). *Mental imagery*. London: Routledge and Kegan Paul.

Richardson, A. (1977). Verbalizer-visualizer: A cognitive style dimension. *Journal of Mental Imagery, 1,* 109-126.

Richardson, A., & Patterson, Y. (1986). An evaluation of three procedures for increasing imagery vividness. In A. Sheikh (Ed.), *International review of mental imagery*. New York: Human Sciences Press.

Richardson, A., & Taylor, C. C. (1982). Vividness of mental imagery and self-induced mood change. *British Journal of Clinical Psychology, 21,* 111-117.

Rychlak, J. (1973). Time orientation in the positive and negative free phantasies of mildly abnormal versus normal high school males. *Journal of Consulting and Clinical Psychology, 41,* 175-190.

Saltz, E., Dixon, D., & Johnson, J. (1977). Training disadvantaged preschoolers on various fantasy activities: Effects on cognitive functioning and impulse control. *Child Development, 48,* 367-380.

Samuels, M., & Samuels, N. (1975). *Seeing with the mind's eye*. New York: Random House.

Segal, S. J. (Ed.) (1971). *Imagery: Current cognitive approaches*. New York: Academic Press.

Segal, S. J., & Glickman, M. (1967). Relaxation and the Perky effect: The influence of body position and judgements of imagery. *American Journal of Psychology, 60,* 257-262.

Shapiro, D. L. (1974). The significance of the visual image in psychotherapy. *Psychotherapy: Theory, Research, and Practice, 7,* 209-212.

Sheikh, A. A. (1978). Eidetic psychotherapy. In J. L. Singer & K. S. Pope (Eds.), *The power of human imagination*. New York: Plenum.

Sheikh, A. A. (Ed.) (1983). *Imagery: Current theory, research, and application*. New York: Wiley.

Sheikh, A. A. (Ed.) (1984). *Imagination and healing*. New York: Baywood.

Sheikh, A. A., & Kunzendorf, R. G. (1984). Imagery, physiology, and psychosomatic illness. In A. A. Sheikh (Ed.), *International review of mental imagery* (Vol. 1). New York: Human Sciences Press.

Sheikh, A. A., & Panagiotou, N. C. (1975). Use of mental imagery in psychotherapy: A critical review. *Perceptual and Motor Skills, 41,* 555-585.

Shorr, J. E. (1977). *Go see the movie in your head*. New York: Popular Library.

Shorr, J. E. (1978). Clinical uses of categories of therapeutic imagery. In J. L. Singer & K. S. Pope (Eds.), *The power of human imagination*. New York: Plenum.

Shorr, J. E. (1983). *Psychotherapy through imagery*. New York: Thieme-Stratton.

Singer, J. L. (1974). *Imagery and daydream methods in psychotherapy and behavior modification*. New York: Academic Press.

Singer, J. L. (1977). Imagination and make-believe play in early childhood: Some educational implications. *Journal of Mental Imagery, 1,* 127-144.

Singer, J. L. (1978). Experimental studies of daydreaming and the stream of consciousness. In K. S. Pope & J. L. Singer (Eds.), *The stream of consciousness*. New York: Plenum.

Sommer, R. (1978). *The mind's eye: Imagery in everyday life*. New York: Delacorte Press.

Tart, C. (Ed.) (1969). *Altered states of consciousness*. New York: Doubleday.

Tower, R. B. (1983). Imagery: Its role in development. In A. A. Sheikh (Ed.), *Imagery: Current theory, research, and application*. New York: Wiley.

Watkins, M. M. (1976). *Waking dreams*. New York: Harper & Row.

Walsh, F. J., White, K. D., & Ashton, R. (1978). *Imagery training: Development of a procedure and its evaluation*. Unpublished research report, University of Queensland.

Wilson, S. C., & Barber, T. X. (1983). The fantasy-prone personality: Implications for understanding imagery, hypnosis, and parapsychological phenomena. In A. A. Sheikh (Ed.), *Imagery: Current theory, research, and application*. New York: Wiley.

Wolpe, J. (1958). *Psychotherapy by reciprocal inhibition*. Stanford, CA: Standard University Press.

# Index